Diagnosis and Remediation Practices for Troubled School Children

Harold F. Burks

Rowman & Littlefield Education
Lanham, Maryland • Toronto • Plymouth, UK
2008

Published in the United States of America
by Rowman & Littlefield Education
A Division of Rowman & Littlefield Publishers, Inc.
A wholly owned subsidary of The Rowman & Littlefield Publishing Group, Inc.
4501 Forbes Boulevard, Suite 200, Lanham, Maryland 20706
www.rowmaneducation.com

Estover Road
Plymouth PL6 7PY
United Kingdom

British Library Cataloguing in Publication Information Available

Library of Congress Cataloging-in-Publication Data

Burks, Harold F.
   Diagnosis and remediation practices for troubled school children / Harold F. Burks.
          p. cm.
   Includes bibliographical references and index.
   ISBN-13: 978-1-57886-656-4 (hardcover : alk. paper)
   ISBN-13: 978-1-57886-706-6 (pbk. : alk. paper)
   ISBN-10: 1-57886-656-1 (hardcover : alk. paper)
   ISBN-10: 1-57886-706-1 (pbk. : alk. paper)
   1. Problem children—Education—Handbooks, manuals, etc. 2. Problem children—Diagnosis—Handbooks, manuals, etc.
3. Behavior disorders in children—Treatment—Handbooks, manuals, etc. I. Title.
LC4801.B874 2008
371.93—dc22
                                                                                                    2007042953

To my wife, Ann, who has strewn my life with roses,
and joy and happiness beyond all expectation.

Contents

CHAPTER 1

Introduction

According to a recent poll by Scripps Howard News (C. Susman, 2007), one out of every three American families has had to cope with a child who has a learning or a mental disability, and most health experts believe the occurrence of these problems is increasing in number.

EXTENT OF THE PROBLEM

In a national survey of 1,054 people (Lowy, 2007) the following facts emerged:

- Sixty-five percent said they believe learning disabilities are becoming more common.
- Seventy-two percent said mental health problems are becoming more common.
- Thirty percent of the respondents said they had a child under age 18 in the family—a brother or sister, son or daughter, niece or nephew, grandchild, or first cousin—who had been diagnosed as having a learning disability.
- Eight percent said they had more than one child diagnosed with a learning handicap.
- Twelve percent said they had had a child diagnosed with a mental illness, and 3% said they had more than one child so diagnosed.

Other studies (Burks, 1999) reveal the following facts:

- Boys are up to three to four times more likely to be diagnosed with autism than girls.
- Boys are up to seven times more likely to be diagnosed with learning and attention disorders than are girls.
- Many youngsters are diagnosed with multiple disorders.
- Approximately half of children with attention disorders have a learning disorder, and more than a third have an emotional disability like anxiety, depression, or a bipolar problem (characterized by mood swings).

No one knows for sure why an increase in the number of handicapped youngsters has been reported. What is certain is that learning disabilities, attention disorders, autism, and emotional disorders like anxiety and bipolar disease *appear* far more prevalent in children than was thought even a generation ago.

But do these differences actually exist? The conflicting opinions are as follows:

Pro arguments. Some scientists, public health advocates, and parents are convinced that environmental agents ranging from viruses to chemicals such as alcohol, PCBs, lead, pesticides, and mercury are interfering with brain development in children.

Con arguments. Other experts maintain there is no real increase in the prevalence of childhood disorders (except perhaps autism). Rather, they say, there has been a relabeling of children who are less intelligent, less industrious, or who appear more dangerous to society. Also, the increase in the use of prescription drugs (pushed by pharmaceutical companies) requires the possible treatment of new types of disorders. And, finally, parents seek ever more sophisticated learning disability diagnoses for their offspring in order to get extra help or consideration from school authorities.

CAUSAL FACTORS LINKED TO CHILDHOOD DISORDERS

Investigations of human behavior reveal that much of what is represented in later life has beginnings in childhood experiences and organic predispositions. Psychologists have examined early childhood development with great care, hoping to discover which factors assist in the formation of a healthy personality and which do not.

In spite of gains, many questions are not well answered. Parents and teachers struggle to understand and then change patterns of undesirable conduct in children. In a society skeptical of old values, parents are unsure of proper behavioral standards. In educational systems under attack for the irrelevancy of curriculum offerings, teachers find themselves sympathizing with bored and restless students while at the same time feeling chagrined at such behavior. All children exhibit negative behavior to some extent, but a few demonstrate it so severely and chronically that ordinary educational methods and control measures prove inadequate.

Why do some children show displeasing behavior? Does it stem from organic problems beyond the control of individuals? Is it the result of poor training procedures? Is it the product of physical or emotional deprivation? Above all, the question remains: What, from a moral and practical sense, should be done about unacceptable conduct? These inquiries represent some of the most important concerns facing parents.

And, of course, while diagnosis of a problem is important, that calculation, by itself, is not enough. Many experts emphasize the belief that diagnostic efforts must be followed by adequate educational and therapeutic programs that treat the evaluated disorders. This book was written as an effort to meet that challenge.

IDENTIFYING AN AUTHENTIC CHILDHOOD PROBLEM

I have found that most parents seeking counseling assistance for their children begin first interviews with me by saying, "I don't know if my child really has a problem." A litany of child-rearing difficulties follows. The parents look confused. Is the conduct normal, usual, or irregular?

In spite of the fact that it usually takes a significant amount of provocation from a youngster to get parents motivated enough to seek help, these same adults are doubtful about their ability to judge the significance of what they think is unusual behavior. Considering current debates surrounding the concept of normality in children's conduct, these parental perplexities must be considered legitimate and therefore need exploration.

What standards are used to decide what is normal and what is unacceptable behavior?

Criteria for Judging the Seriousness of Behavior Aberrations

Parents tend to rely on what they have read or heard about so-called "average" conduct (which is, of course, an imaginary concept). Therapists, who rely on their training and experience in psychopathology, may, early in their professional lives at least, tend to see more abnormality than actually exists. Finally, teachers, in their anxiety to create a calm and optimal school learning environment, often refer more children for special guidance assistance than is necessary or even helpful.

Where does all this lead? Well, two things are certain: (a) no child is completely free of problems, and (b) the problems are widespread in the population. A long-term study by the Berkeley Guidance Group identified the following behavioral manifestations (and their frequency at various age levels) as having been demonstrated by one-third or more of all normal children 21 months to 14 years of age:

- enuresis (bed-wetting most pronounced in very young children);
- soiling (declined with age);
- disturbing dreams (worse at 6 and 10 to 11 years);
- restless sleep (worse in very young children);
- insufficient appetite (peak frequency at about 6 years);
- food finickiest (most pronounced in infancy and early childhood);

- excessive modesty (evenly distributed across age spans);
- nail biting (worse in upper age levels but drops off at age 14);
- thumb sucking (worse in infancy);
- overactivity (pronounced in ages 3 to 9);
- speech problems (evenly distributed across age spans);
- lying (peaks in ages 3 to 7);
- destructiveness (evenly distributed across age spans);
- overdependence (evenly distributed across age spans);
- attention demanding (evenly distributed across age spans);
- oversensitivity (very pronounced in ages 3 to 14);
- physical timidity (greater frequency in ages 4 to 5);
- specific fears (very pronounced in all ages up to 12);
- mood swings (not seen in early and middle years but pronounced in ages 11 to 14);
- shyness (evenly distributed across age spans);
- somberness (more pronounced in ages 5 to 6);
- negativism (more pronounced in ages 3 to 5);
- irritability (evenly distributed across age spans);
- temper (very pronounced at all ages);
- jealousy (not seen in infants but pronounced at all upper age levels);
- excessive reserve (pronounced in ages 5 to 14).

This study also revealed some gender differences in relation to certain problems. The incidence of problems such as overactivity, temper tantrums, demand for attention, and lying proved significantly higher for boys. Difficulties for girls centered on shyness, excessive modesty, and specific fears. Of great interest to parents is the fact that the incidence of all of the above listed problems declined with age. Thus, it may be concluded that many so-called abnormal behaviors (such as being overactive or fearful) are displayed by large numbers of toddlers and may typically characterize normal development.

Further, adults must be careful about assigning delinquency labels to adolescents. Studies have shown that 50% or more of legally nondelinquent teens report skipping school, stealing small articles, buying liquor or drugs, and intentionally damaging property. Parents should look back at their own early years. Didn't they ever thumb their noses at authority by committing unlawful acts? Don't misunderstand: Chronic antisocial and destructive behavior cannot be overlooked if it is serious, but remember that most adults indulged in some form of antisocial conduct as juveniles that would not, in retrospect, be considered deviant.

Factors to Be Taken into Consideration

So what's normal and what's deviant childhood behavior? Although it may never be possible to arrive at absolute definitions of normalcy and deviancy, the following issues must be contemplated whenever a diagnostic evaluation is made.

Developmental level. What is considered typical at one age may well be thought abnormal at a later age—for instance, unrestrained aggressiveness or constant crying are common traits in toddlers but not ordinarily observed in 10-year-olds.

Gender. Behavioral expectations tend to be somewhat different for girls than for boys—for example, passive conduct is regarded as more socially normal for girls than it is for boys.

Social environment. Behavioral expectations can vary from one culture to another. I found the Mexican-American community, for example, to be more tolerant of child dependency behaviors.

Individual disparities. Each youngster is different, having been born with temperamental tendencies that make him or her unique.

Tolerance level of adults involved with the child. The judgment of normalcy or deviancy can be affected by the tolerable threshold levels of annoyance in adults having daily contact with the child.

CHARACTERISTICS OF SO-CALLED NORMAL CHILDREN

In truth, so-called normal behavior in youngsters is difficult to evaluate in view of the fact that conduct is highly influenced by cultural and inherited influences. In my opinion, normality is chiefly characterized by behavioral flexibility. Flexible individuals adapt to a variety of stressful situations, do not impose rigid performance patterns on others, and are less likely to create problems for themselves and those about them. Flexibility is based on the ability to concentrate and the capacity to repress, inhibit, or disguise stress responses.

Most children do pay attention and, obviously, do learn. Furthermore, most are able to internalize a considerable amount of discomfort without demonstrating unacceptable behavior symptoms. For example, in one investigation I conducted, four classrooms of seventh grade students rated their feelings about common classroom experiences. An important finding emerged. Nearly all said they experienced a considerable degree (and some said a large degree) of physical, emotional, and social distress. The teachers were largely unaware of these feelings of discomfort, probably indicating the students were successful in hiding negative emotions.

Why were the students able to keep these emotions hidden? I believe that this capability is possible in normally behaved children because they are able to draw upon sustaining inner resources. A child under stress who possesses a normally functioning nervous system and who is not burdened with unpleasant emotional impulses demanding overt expression can ordinarily retire to a comforting world of imagination, presenting him or her with attractive alternative responses to problems.

Why can't maladjusted children draw upon similar assets? They cannot because these resources do not exist for them. Children with an attention deficit disorder, for instance, have trouble sustaining inward imagery (Burks, 2001). It is hypothesized that because of organic cerebral dysfunctions (Burks, 1960), the ability of the brain to route, sort, and modify incoming stimuli is somehow impaired. For disturbed children without organic involvement, the picture is different. Like most children, they possess an active imagination, but because these youngsters often suffer from an impoverished family life (Burks, 1960, 1968b), much of this fantasy life contains unpleasant content offering no comfort in the face of nervous tension. Instead, disagreeable thoughts push for recognition, and active mental efforts are required to keep these thoughts out of consciousness. As a defense, they may console themselves by formulating daydreams not tied to reality. Whatever mechanism is employed, disturbed children are denied emotional outlets that are open to less disturbed individuals. Because these children lack such outlets, they are, by definition, less flexible and can appear socially, emotionally, or intellectually less able.

Importance of a Rich Fantasy Life

The importance of a rich, rewarding, and flexible inner fantasy life well related to and regulated by the outward life of the individual cannot be overestimated. A fantasy life of this nature provides the person with multifaceted ways to observe and resolve situational conflicts. Learning is facilitated and embedded better, selections can be made from a greater number of possible responses and creativity is expedited. It also supplies the person with an escape hatch to circumvent unpleasant and distracting aspects of reality. For instance, in one study I conducted, teachers reported poor attention to be the most annoying symptom shown by the greatest number of students. I hypothesized that students turn their thoughts inward to find comfort in their imaginations. If this is the case, drifting concentration cannot be considered an abnormal manifestation. Much basic curriculum is boring to children; since they cannot physically withdraw, they psychologically pull away. This inattention may help prevent the appearance of more disagreeable defense symptoms.

This brief discussion of "normal" behavior attempts to point out that there are behaviors that can hinder an individual regardless of the culture he or she inhabits or the time in which he or she lives. As far as I am aware, no culture esteems erratic attention in children, no society ignores individuals who chronically break rules, and no group (with rare exceptions) remains comfortable with people who are out of touch with reality. Anything that inhibits the development of abilities or the expression of constructive aspects of the personality may, in most instances, be considered a handicap.

CHILDHOOD SYMPTOMS DEMANDING ATTENTION

Many childhood problems show themselves to a small degree and for brief periods of time. Adults need not become too concerned about these difficulties. On the other hand, some youngsters demonstrate unusual and serious characteristics that need special treatment from adults. Who are the children who need help? In all probability they are the ones who show, over considerable time, one or more of the following characteristics:

- serious inability to function in school learning settings;
- clear inability to behave at a level commensurate with developmental status—that is, immaturity;
- unusual inability to get along with peers; lack of friends;
- inability to cope with authority; disregard for adult rules;
- unusual insecurity, anxiety, and fear;
- unusual aggressiveness or destructiveness;
- severe mood changes; inability to regulate emotions;
- severe unhappiness or depression;
- handicaps resulting from physical disabilities.

PURPOSE AND USE OF THIS BOOK

This volume is designed to be a guide for educators. As such, it hopefully provides innovative evaluation techniques and intervention strategies that have worked with many children experiencing school problems. Thus, it attempts to (a) clarify the understanding of observed, unwanted symptoms in children; (b) investigate, with parents and teachers—and sometimes children—the possible causal factors that antedate these behavior manifestations; and (c) create, in cooperation with parents and teachers, well-proved and sometimes inventive intervention techniques to help children learn accepted behavior patterns.

The methods outlined in each chapter are intended for teachers, school and clinical psychologists, and those in related professions, such as social workers, counselors, therapists, and psychiatrists. It is assumed that users possess some psychological skills (acquired in college courses and professional experience) in the areas of diagnostic methods, aberrant behaviors, personality theory, learning disorders, special education, and counseling and therapy techniques. In addition, the text is appropriate for use in graduate courses concerned with child exceptionality and psychopathology, diagnosis, therapy, remediation of school problems, and guidance practices.

Although laws target children with handicaps and demand they receive special education aid, concern should not center solely on children with obvious disabilities. Normally behaved youngsters can suffer unhappy episodes affecting school achievement and home tranquillity. In such instances, school personnel should (and often must) ask for parental assistance, which, hopefully, leads to better diagnosis and treatment. Given the opportunity, most parents cooperate willingly and gratefully with these educational requests.

CONTENT AND SCOPE OF THE BOOK

Nature and Purpose

The contents of this publication were, in large part, derived from the use of the Burks Behavior Rating Scales (BBRS) (Burks, 1977a, 2006a), instruments that have been employed for decades by teachers and parents to identify patterns of pathological behavior shown by children who have been referred to school or community counseling agencies because of conduct difficulties in classrooms or homes. While the BBRS were designed to be of assistance in the differential diagnosis of children already known to be in difficulty, it should be pointed out to the reader that the scales were not designed to assess how a child's inner world is experienced. That was done with other measuring devices, such as personality and educational tests.

The handbook is structured around the 19 behavior disorders originally identified by the Burks Behavior Rating Scales. The BBRS-2 form, published in 2006, is organized around seven major scales or domains of behavior disorders and related subcategories (the same 19 categories identified by the BBRS-1):

- excessive self-blame;
- excessive anxiety;
- excessive withdrawal;
- excessive dependency;
- poor motivational strength;
- poor physical strength;
- poor coordination;
- poor intellectual ability;
- poor academics;
- poor attention;
- poor impulse control;
- poor reality contact;
- poor social identification;
- excessive suffering;
- poor anger control;
- excessive sense of persecution;
- excessive aggressiveness;
- excessive resistance;
- poor social conformity.

For each specific subcategory, a description of symptoms, associated characteristics, and etiologic considerations is included. Treatment suggestions are provided both for direct intervention by educators in the school environment and, when appropriate, for interventions that can be implemented by parents in the home.

These behavior classifications are labeled in clear, operational terms. For example, "poor anger control" is defined as the chronic inability to control, repress, or inhibit outbursts of rage. In addition, conduct manifestations are commonly and reliably associated with various etiologic stimuli that adversely affect children. For example, a child showing symptoms of self-blame is assumed to have acquired the trait from authority figures who taught the youngster to be overly concerned about proper standards of deportment.

Each behavior disorder is dealt with in a separate chapter (chapters 3 to 21) in the same order listed above. Generally, this order represents a gradation from overcontrol of impulses and hostility turned inward (e.g., self-blame and withdrawal) to lack of control of impulses and anger turned outward (e.g., excessive resistance and poor social conformity).

The first five categories of behavior (excessive self-blame, excessive anxiety, excessive withdrawal, excessive dependency, and poor motivational strength) are thought to be largely learned defense mechanisms against outward stress. The individual inhibits or sublimates anger so that he or she does not bother or upset others. Unfortunately, the ability to overcontrol the expression of inward impulses probably means the child pays a heavy price of increased tension and feelings of alienation from others.

In the absence of complicating factors such as poor intellectual ability, poor academics, or excessive suffering, the prognosis for the presence of the first five categories of behavior remains fair since the individual has demonstrated the character strength to control and channel impulses. Mild neurotic character tendencies in the personality structure of any youngster are probably desirable because they are often accompanied by a well-developed conscience and a demonstrated wish to please others and to accomplish what is expected of him or her.

The next group of categories (poor physical strength, poor coordination, poor intellectual ability, and poor academics) is difficult to classify. Demonstrated problems in these areas probably have strong genetic roots. By themselves these traits do not constitute behavior pathology. Theoretically, the individual showing these symptoms learns at a slower rate than most children. Treatment consists largely of accepting exhibited limitations and modifying the school curriculum to fit a child's needs.

The prognosis for children showing slow motor, intellectual, and academic growth depends on whether other untoward symptoms are present. If additional manifestations (poor attention and poor impulse control) are present, the child possibly is suffering a form of neurological dysfunction. In the absence of severe hostility patterns (poor anger control, excessive sense of persecution, excessive aggressiveness, excessive resistance, and poor social conformity) in the child, teachers will usually accept the child's conduct while still recognizing the need for giving special academic assistance.

The classifications of poor attention and poor impulse control refer to conduct patterns that need not alarm educators unduly. Most students seem to outgrow these problems by early adolescence (Burks, 1960). However, nervousness and poor concentration may annoy peers and the youngster may endure social rejection. The prognosis for school adjustment then becomes less favorable.

Poor reality contact, poor social identification, and excessive suffering are behavioral traits exhibited by children unwilling to become involved with the environment in constructive ways. Hostility is implicated but is less channeled and focused than are behavior traits described in the final five BBRS categories. The outlook for youngsters exhibiting these symptoms is generally poor.

Poor anger control, excessive sense of persecution, excessive aggressiveness, excessive resistance, and poor social conformity are all categories describing conduct characterized by an outward expression of hostility, a basic unwillingness to go along with socially accepted standards of behavior and an extreme resistance to becoming dependent on the goodwill of others, particularly adults. Pupils showing these traits have proven difficult to treat.

In summary, my findings from previous investigations (Burks, 1960, 1964b, 1968b) lead to the following generalization: For any child, the greater the number of demonstrated negative behavior symptoms, the worse the prognosis. When granted help in special classes, children who show few high scores on the behavior categories tend to show improvement in academic achievement, in attitudes toward authority, and in reduction of conduct disorders. Those given many high ratings do not show significant improvement and continue to distress their teachers.

This abbreviated description of the BBRS provides some understanding of the conceptual basis that led me to match rated behaviors to treatment methods. The astute practitioner will comprehend the need for assessment that goes beyond these rating categories. For example, the categories do not measure the quality of the person's inner world. This evaluation must, and should, be done with other measuring devices such as personality and educational tests. A differential diagnosis is ordinarily strengthened when information is acquired from multiple sources.

Diagnostic Counseling

Although there is an increased recognition of the need for adequate treatment interventions to follow evaluation studies (Blanco, 1972; Reschly, 1981, 1982), these prescriptions often lack effectiveness because of the methods used by guidance personnel to communicate the treatment procedures to parents and teachers. For example, some practitioners simply recite diagnostic findings to the parents and suggest treatment steps without adequately explaining the ramifications of their statements. Lack of understanding or involvement in the diagnostic treatment process may cause parents and teachers to distrust evaluation instruments and their power to predict change. Behavioral assessment technology by itself, when not coupled with consultation skills, prevents psychologists from employing optimal means to assess and develop interventions in natural face-to-face settings. When the practitioner includes the parent and the teacher in the diagnostic treatment process, the outcome is more likely to be a success.

Diagnostic counseling, a term I coined, is an intermediary process between assessment and treatment; it can illuminate and improve the outcomes of both. The diagnostic counseling techniques suggested in this handbook involve teachers and parents directly in the interpretation of assessment devices. Data acquired from standardized psychological tests are supplemented with information from teachers and family members, which is obtained from a combination of clinical interviews, checklists, and questionnaires. In this process, the child's interpersonal skills, attitudes, and ability to use primary language can be considered. The method allows the respondent (ordinarily a parent) to express beliefs and feelings that give clues to family problems, customs, and aspirations. These expressions may elicit insights that can be woven into the treatment process.

Diagnostic counseling is facilitated by the use of checklists and structured interviews. These devices are used informally to stimulate discussion in home and school counseling sessions. The checklists in this handbook have not been standardized, the answers have not undergone statistical analysis, and no attempt has been made to evaluate reliability and validity assumptions. The answers to such checklists are not collected, kept, or tabulated by the psychologist or counselor. Rather, the value of these instruments lies in their ability to spark conversations in guidance interviews. Thus, they function as a resource aid for the counseling process.

I have used diagnostic counseling extensively for years, both in school sessions with parents and teachers and in a clinical setting. Based on the use of this technique, I have made the following observations:

1. Relevant material that prompts valuable insights is often recovered. For example, a mother who is worried about her child's inattentiveness completes a questionnaire and is suddenly made aware (through her own answers) that members of her family seldom finish tasks because they are often distracted by new ventures. For the first time, she understands that her child's flighty behavior may have roots in family habits.
2. The technique is interesting to most people. They like being involved in the assessment process because it actually is a process, not a static recital of evaluation content by a professional.
3. This approach promotes a more equitable relationship between the counselor and the client than that of expert versus listener. Thus, it may result in a closer and more meaningful counselor-client relationship.

Diagnostic counseling is an attempt (albeit one of many possible approaches) to implement the findings of diagnosis in a stimulating and constructive manner.

CONCLUSION

This handbook provides some innovative evaluation techniques along with intervention treatments that have worked with many children suffering school-related problems. By law and by popular demand, school guidance personnel must provide prescriptive diagnoses for students who have handicaps. Blanco (1972) maintained that school counselors have often abdicated this responsibility because they simply do not know how to conceptualize plans to effect changes in children. If educational psychologists do not meet the challenge, Blanco said, less well-trained individuals will make the required recommendations.

This book attempts to remedy that condition. It offers some novel assessment approaches to supplement and confirm the BBRS findings, and it presents a number of possible treatment procedures. The step from diagnosis to educational prescription is truly an exquisite exercise, one that can measure the true worth of a psychological practitioner. Because all overt symptoms have roots in multiple causations, it is up to the diagnostician to determine, as best he or she can, the principal reasons why negative symptoms are being demonstrated. With this knowledge, counselors can formulate treatment programs to help eliminate unacceptable behavior in children.

Note: I am well aware that in the field of human behavior many evolving, conflicting, and competing theories exist about the identification and treatment of unwanted conduct symptoms. That being the case, I cannot maintain that the writing in this book always represents the latest and/or most accepted psychological approaches.

CHAPTER 2

Putting Childhood Problem Behaviors in Perspective

Sensible talk about problems in children should deal not only with the question of what is and is not abnormal conduct but also with recent research that attempts to answer the following questions:

- How much do genetic factors contribute to the formation of human behavior?
- How much is the formation of human behavior due to gender differences?
- How much does birth order affect the formation of human behavior?
- How do parenting styles affect human behavior development?

GENETIC FACTORS

Since the late seventies, genetic research (J. R. Harris, 1999) has made inherited temperament a more acceptable topic. In that early period, the eminent psychologist Jerome Kagan, a Harvard developmental investigator, tended to believe environmental factors played the primary role in character formation, but now believes biological factors are also important. He stated, "I have been dragged, kicking and screaming, by my data to acknowledge that temperament is more powerful than I thought and wish to believe" (P. Sears, 1992, p. 32). Hans Eysenck, a biological researcher in London at the Institute of Psychiatry, made the point that studies in 36 countries have found the following three basic behavior types: fear, which helps people to avoid danger; aggression, which empowers people to fight fear; and sociability, which helps people to face fear with calmness (P. Sears, 1992). Fundamentally, human temperaments tend to be distinguished by characteristics of anxiety, irritability, and élan (Burns, 1999; Mc-Graw, 2001).

Philip Gold, a research scientist who is chief of the neuroendocrinology branch of the National Institute of Mental Health (NIMH), believed that such traits vary in individuals according to the following inherited temperaments (Penifold, 1994):

- Stable individuals described as uninhibited, bold, and relaxed. Stress responses aren't triggered by every little form of stress, they handle ambiguity well and tend to enjoy life.
- Those that react to the unfamiliar or threatening with excessive fear (flight or fight). Stress reactions spike often and excessively and ebb slowly. These individuals tend to get worn down easily because they are so reactive, and they often feel worthless or depressed. They avoid conflict, but that avoidance may worsen their situation because troubles do not tend to go away and may even intensify over time.
- Those who show traits like aggression, impulsivity, and irritability. Their feelings of potential defeat are so painfully intense that they cannot bear to be accountable for these emotions in depressed ways and, instead, blame these emotions on others and strike out at the world.

The three obvious qualities of genetic temperament, then, are boldness, fearfulness, and aggressiveness. Most individuals are not colored solely by any one of these emotional tones. It is interesting to note, however, that a small percentage of infants seem inherently shy, withdrawn, and anxious, and stay that way throughout their life span; a larger number are bolder and more sure of themselves; and another small percentage are chronically irritable and aggressive. Most people, rather than fitting these clear-cut profiles, are a mixture of traits, but no matter what the mix, all parents know that each baby is born with a characteristic mood and style of responding.

Two of these three types of inherited temperaments, fearfulness and aggressiveness, may hamper a child's social development. Some of the developmental characteristics shown by these two personality types are listed below:

Fearfulness

easily upset by stimulation (i.e., able to take little stress) as a baby
very anxious around strangers as a baby or toddler
anxious in strange surroundings at any age
unusually shy at any age
unusually hesitant to join in group activities at any age
covers up feelings when older
seldom speaks up when older

Aggressiveness

colicky as a baby
difficult to hold as a baby
irritable and cranky as a baby and toddler
easily made angry at any age
when frustrated, hits out at others at any age
difficult to discipline at any age
overactive

Inherited Characteristics and Life Outcomes

Do inherited temperamental attributes significantly affect life outcomes? They may, but more often probably do not. Much depends on surrounding social environments. If the setting is supportive and understanding, even a shy or irritable youngster has a good chance of overcoming these adverse hereditary traits. But if circumstances are rejecting, cold, or too judgmental, children may show unwanted genetic characteristics to an even greater degree.

Positive and Negative Aspects of Shy and Irritable Temperaments

Nathan Fox, a professor of psychology at the University of Maryland, reported some of the positive aspects of being unusually withdrawn and shy (Penifold, 1994). He found inhibited seven-year-olds tended to excel at contemplative intellectual functioning even though, because of sensitive natures, they had trouble putting personal theories into practice in rough-and-tumble childhood environments.

It's interesting to note that while investigators find the irritable temperament most difficult to define, it tends to be easiest to observe. Its characteristics may be seen in movie characters portrayed as jumpy, restless individuals prone to express intense, uninhibited, and unpredictable emotions. It should not be assumed that these strongly shown emotions are without merit—in some situations they get a point across swiftly and accurately (for instance, when an officer must galvanize forces being led to battle). Potentially, however, irritable tendencies tend to produce the most unwanted social consequences. Researchers have spent the least amount of time on the study of the irritable disposition, possibly because it tends to arouse negative feelings in those investigating it. Irritability—the tendency to be easily annoyed—is not the same as the trait of aggressiveness (which is thought to be a personality expression springing from learned experiences). However, the two behavioral characteristics are often linked in the personalities of irascible people, who, along with exhibited tetchiness, may attack others verbally or physically. This can be a problem when these reactions are serious in nature and occur outside the law.

No temperamental style is considered to be either good or evil. Even aggressiveness, for instance, can be socially helpful if it enables a person to raise a fist to demand justice.

GENDER DIFFERENCES

When I was first involved in the standardization of the Burks' Behavior Rating Scales (Burks, 1977a), it soon became apparent that in all areas of behavior dysfunction, more boys than girls were involved. Not only were numbers greater for males, but they were judged as more disturbed than females. In some areas, boys were seen as being significantly at risk by showing greater immaturity, as demonstrated by added acting-out aggressive propensities and showing more tendencies to give up easily.

To gain additional knowledge about gender disparity, it is interesting to note that research efforts indicate inherited temperament tendencies are altered to some extent by sex differences (Horn, Wagner, & Ialongo, 1989). According to Ruben C. Gur, director of the brain behavior laboratory at the University of Pennsylvania, "We have known that males and females behave differently in all sorts of ways and one of the most striking is the way men and women deal with emotions" (K. Kelly, 1994).

Apparently, the intense feelings that trigger the male to fight cause the female to react with words; these emotions are not merely learned behaviors—they also have a physical basis. Gur and his colleagues found that the brains of men and women are identical except in the region that deals with emotional processing.

William Calvin, a neurophysiologist at the University of Washington School of Medicine, goes a bit further when discussing the differences discovered in the structures of male and female brains. He maintains that the variations in neural organization affect everything from language development to how children organize play activities (Colter, 1995).

Boys and girls differ temperamentally, and this must be taken into consideration when devising ways to treat childhood problems. My early observations (Burks, 1960) convinced me that there are innate differences in the activity levels of boys versus girls. For every overactive girl there are about seven overactive boys. For that reason, people must be more tolerant in their judgment of young males' so-called overactivity. Boys simply cannot be expected to remain as quiet and controlled as most girls, because their nervous systems will not allow them to be passive. It is also important to recognize society's unfortunate tendency to see natural boyish misbehavior as pathological. This inclination may lead some adults to overemphasize the need for the stringent discipline of males.

Social Conditions That May Affect Boys Negatively

Some professionals believe society has set standards for boy behavior that are unrealistic. For instance, if a boy becomes a bit too active, he can find himself under the scrutiny of many adults—parents, teachers, school counselors, and therapists—all poised to catch the early signs of an undesirable medical condition (a particularly relevant concern given the current unease about the condition known as attention deficit hyperactivity disorder and the fact that many more boys than girls are on Ritalin or related medications).

The rising parental apprehension about the occurrence of aggressiveness and its relationship to boyish play has its genesis in the reports of violence among the nation's male children. Nancy Kenny, associate professor of psychology and women's studies at the University of Washington, believes many people are confused. She said, "You've got the ingrained tradition of what boys are like—strong and aggressive—and then you've got the fear of excessive aggression" (Walsh, 1994, p. 13).

It must be realized, though, that the normal roughhousing of boys has a healthy side to it—the element of cooperation that is instilled through male games of "good guy, bad guy" and team sports. These interactions serve a vital function in the formation of the male social personality. In light of the fact that boys often engage in rougher activities and that society is apprehensive about boyhood interests, counselors may want to suggest to parents that they take some of the following steps to encourage male children.

Tips for Parents Raising Sons

- Relax about boyish enthusiasm.
- Do not encourage aggressiveness beyond his natural tendencies.
- Help him understand others by encouraging him to talk to you about his feelings and by discussing with him the probable emotions of other individuals after he has had an argument or fight.
- Recognize his need for privacy by not pushing for overt signs of intimacy after puberty.
- Do not demand communication from your teen. Let him take the initiative in conversations.
- Provide male companionship, either from the boy's father or a male substitute.
- Offer help even when he does not solicit it (like helping him find a part-time job).
- Talk about your experiences when you were his age.
- Help him understand that social interdependence is often preferable to independence.
- Speak clearly and forcibly about what it is you want from him, but do it in a nonthreatening way.
- Talk to him about sexual matters when he is older.
- Make going to school a nonnegotiable matter. Encourage him to succeed academically.

Social Conditions That May Affect Girls Negatively

Most girls are temperamentally less aggressive than most boys; thus, acting-out tendencies do not form the basis for the majority of female referrals to guidance clinics. Instead, girls (particularly teens) are seen to be more disturbed than boys in the dysfunctional areas of depression, low self-esteem, and eating disorders.

Depression. Both older girls and older boys can experience depressive episodes, but the professional evidence (Blatt, 1995) suggests that depression is more common for girls and that this gender difference persists into adulthood. Males tend to distract themselves while sad; girls tend to ruminate on the condition, and this rumination usually makes the sadness worse. Also, most girls enter puberty earlier than boys, which leads to the supposition that girls face greater challenges concerning sexual identity. In addition, girls take the divorce of parents more seriously than do boys.

Depressive moods are related to other personality disorders. While depression and acting-out are commonly related among boys, depression and low self-esteem are more often associated with girls. Anxiety can accompany depression for both sexes (Ferguson, 1999; Maxym & York, 2001).

Low self-esteem. An extensive quantity of research has found girls tend to be more vulnerable to lack of social approval than boys. Females, unlike most males, are trained to be nurturing, and this proclivity to look after others makes them unusually sensitive to rejection by significant people. Some school experiences do not help. Girls may feel inferior to boys in sports and in some classroom experiences (as a group, males do better in math and the physical sciences, and they tend to be more adventuresome when completing classroom projects).

Eating disorders. Eating complaints, occurring with depressed mood, are more common among females than among males. Societal expectations probably play a significant part in this outcome. If girls do not perceive themselves as having what they think is a commonly expected body form, they may become upset, misuse food intake, and eventually become depressed.

Tips to Parents Raising Daughters

- Fathers should remember that an older daughter needs as many signs of affection as she did when a little girl.
- Mothers should be a reliable source of information to help a growing daughter cope with bodily changes and social challenges.
- Both parents should not overpraise a daughter for being a "good girl" when she already behaves herself (she may then overrepress appropriate assertive tendencies).
- For mothers, seek out information, with the daughter (in libraries, bookstores, and so on), that praises the accomplishments of women.
- For mothers, discuss sexual matters clearly when the daughter is older.
- Both parents should appreciate a daughter's femininity, commenting frequently and favorably on her appearance and comportment.
- Both parents should take a keen interest in a daughter's school studies and accomplishments.
- Both parents should encourage a daughter to seek out good female role models.
- For fathers, never belittle females to make males appear superior.

BIRTH ORDER

While the following tendencies may be difficult to verify in particular individuals, no one would suggest that birth order is irrelevant to human development. Other factors (e.g., temperament, environmental conditions, and parental handling) must, however, be included in any equation that attempts to resolve the riddles of personality development.

Firstborn

Compared to those born later, firstborn children tend to

- get more adult attention; feel special;
- feel more early pressure to conform;
- talk earlier;
- be better achievers, probably as a result of higher motivation;
- be somewhat more creative;
- hold more leadership positions;
- be somewhat more inhibited;
- hold more exalted career positions;
- be favored, along with the youngest child, by parents.

Middle

Compared to siblings, middle children tend to

- experience more relaxed parents;
- feel less worried about obtaining approval;
- feel squeezed out of the family constellation;
- gain attention by acting out (and are thus perceived to be more difficult);
- be more popular.

Youngest

Compared to siblings, youngest children tend to

- be easygoing;
- have high sociability ratings;
- be made the "baby" of the family;
- be less willing to take responsibility;
- feel picked on;
- lack skills at helping others (no younger siblings to help);
- be skilled at letting others do the work;
- be somewhat more aggressive (stand up for their rights).

Only

Compared to children with siblings, only children tend to

- talk sooner;
- be less comfortable in social relationships;
- be more responsible;
- develop faster;
- be more competitive;
- lack nurturing skills (no younger siblings to help raise).

Other Birth Factors

Families with more than one child may observe the following tendencies:

- Boys with an older sister may be less assertive.
- Girls with an older brother tend to be more dominant and aggressive.
- Two girls born close together tend to be very feminine.
- Two boys born close together tend to be very masculine.
- Older brothers of male siblings tend to get along well with males and may be leaders.
- Younger brothers of female siblings tend to get along well with girls.

Birth order has one other important implication—sibling rivalry. Sibling rivalry exists in every multiple-child family. This rivalry can be shown in mild or extreme forms. In all likelihood, its effects are never completely outgrown. It can surface in later years as competition with professional colleagues, a striving to be the center of attention, or an inability to share love and possessions. Sibling rivalry can be minimized if parents take the certain approaches.

Minimizing Sibling Rivalry

- Avoid making comparisons. The "good" child can influence a sibling to be the "bad" child of the family.
- Do not try to treat all offspring in the same ways. A young child given equal rights to an older sibling may cause him or her to be to be excessively competitive.
- Reinforce sibling differences in constructive ways. Children feel more worthwhile when personality variation is considered unique and special.

• As much as possible, remain apart from sibling arguments and altercations. Children tend to become more socially adept if allowed to work out compromises.

PARENTING STYLES

While hereditary, or inborn, characteristics can influence the way a person turns out in life, many studies show that the parenting style a person is exposed to has, by far, the greatest effect on development (Day, 2002).

Authoritative

According to many experts (Gottman, 1979; McCubbin, 1987; Samalin, 1992b), the parenting style that appears to be most effective is authoritative parenting. Authoritative parents tend to explain rules and be responsive to a child's changing needs.

Psychologist Laurence Steinberg, professor of psychology at Temple University and a leading authority on child raising, said to watch a rerun of *The Cosby Show* to gain insights into this kind of parenting. "Cosby is warm, affectionate and relatively strict, but it's a strictness that is reasoned and reasonable, based on the belief that what children need from their parents is guidance and training" (Porter, 1991, p. 42). Steinberg believes that one of the most important aspects of authoritative parenting is parental affection, which lays the basis for a child's positive self-esteem. When youngsters know they are treasured, this knowledge gives them a stable emotional foundation that enables them to approach life confidently. Because authoritative parents trust and respect children, they offer youngsters many opportunities to make choices. This opportunity for empowerment is critical if youngsters are to learn to make suitable decisions and solve problems, even if they make mistakes along the way.

Nancy Samalin (1992a), director of Parent Workshops in New York, advocated teaching children the nature of limits and why restrictions are given. She believes that, depending on the child's growth stage, the authoritative parent makes demands, sets boundaries, and follows through on mutually understood consequences.

Authoritarian

Parents using an authoritarian approach are convinced adults need to maintain power over children because youngsters are easily spoiled. Such parents are controlling and stern, are likely to have a large number of rules and have a propensity to spank and punish. This style is characterized by a "because-I-said-so" attitude.

Indulgent

The assumption of indulgent parents is that children are basically good and behave best if adults keep their hands off. Samalin (1992a) called this style "the happiness trap." When the child screams, "I hate you!" at the parent or even appears unhappy, the adults are devastated (in their eyes, the child must always demonstrate love toward them). Most often, it is the mother who makes this demand. To get an appearance of affection, she is very loving and warm toward the youngster but is also wishy-washy and also is either inconsistent in setting limits or sets no limits. Often the child is allowed to set his or her own behavioral boundaries (in ways often infuriating to other adults).

Disengaged

The disengaged parenting style is characterized by coldness and noninvolvement in the activities of offspring. While not ordinarily abusive, the approach tends to be neglectful. The adult, when faced with child-rearing problems, ordinarily abdicates and defers to other authority figures ("Well, if that's what the teacher wants . . ." or "I guess it's all right if Grandma says so . . ."), leading to the creation of an uneven patchwork of affection and limits. This type of parent may be a low-income individual with a latchkey child or a high-powered career individual who employs a long-term nanny to look after the youngster.

Outcomes of Parenting Styles

Parenting styles send messages that can affect children in significant ways, but a child's innate temperament must also be considered. A bold child, for instance, might resist and fight authoritarian parents, while a more shy youngster may fear them and become overanxious. An aggressive youngster could become a bully under the care of indulgent adults, while a less irritable child possibly will be more rule-abiding. Nevertheless, researchers have found that parental style does have a profound effect on the way a youngster turns out. Some of the following differences have been discovered.

Authoritative parents. Steinberg (Porter, 1991) believed that youngsters raised by authoritative parents tend to

* be self-starters;
* be creative problem solvers;
* be happy;
* reach their potential;
* excel in relationships.

Authoritarian parents. Doris Blazer (Porter, 1991), parent educator at Furman University in South Carolina, believed that children raised by authoritarian parents tend to

* know how to avoid punishment;
* follow orders, which is valuable in the early school years, but may later be less beneficial, when being a self-starter is essential;
* rarely reach their potential;
* be unhappy, moody, sulky, and fearful;
* be susceptible to unwanted peer pressure.

Indulgent parents. Samalin (Porter, 1991) believed that children brought up by indulgent parents tend to

* feel like winners in the short run because they get what they want, but end up feeling unsettled and insecure;
* be self-centered because they have too much control;
* have short-lived superficial friendships;
* disrespect authority and be disliked by adults;
* have many life problems.

Disengaged parents. Blazer (Porter, 1991) believed that the children of disengaged parents tend to

* experience low self-esteem, often leading to depression;
* think something is wrong with them because they feel unloved by their parents, this perception instilling the belief that nobody else will care either;
* endeavor to get attention by being obstreperous, manipulative, and rebellious;
* give up in school because of feelings of worthlessness;
* be susceptible to peer pressure that can lead to alcohol and drug dependency and trouble with the law.

PARENTING STYLES CHECKLIST

Harold F. Burks, Ph.D.

Read the items and place a check mark in the box next to any item that describes your usual behavior.

1. When your child says he or she is having trouble with other kids in the neighborhood, you say: "Well, that sounds like a tough problem but go ahead and work it out yourself. I'm too busy at the moment to do anything about it." ☐

2. When your child makes a mistake, you say, "I've told you over and over how to do it right. If you did it my way, everything would be OK!" ☐

3. When your child does something wrong, you tend to feel tired and disgusted and do nothing about the situation. ☐

4. When you see that your child is upset about a problem, you say, "Don't worry; I'll figure something out for you." ☐

5. When your youngster can't figure out how to spend his or her allowance, you say, "Let's sit down together and try to figure out what it is you really want." ☐

6. When your child makes a mistake, you say, "By now you know what the rules are and because you broke a rule I think you need a spanking." ☐

7. When your youngster disobeys, you say, "Oh dear, I was so hoping you wouldn't do that sort of thing because it makes me feel so bad. Why don't you try harder?" ☐

8. When your child disobeys, you say, "We have rules about that sort of thing and you know what happens when you break a rule. However, maybe there's something I don't know. Want to talk about it?" ☐

9. When your child disobeys, you say, "Can't you ever learn? Nothing I do seems to help. I'll have to leave this up to someone else to handle." ☐

10. When your child gets into trouble, you tend to ignore the situation. ☐

11. As your child grows up, you find yourself often exploring and explaining problem issues to your youngster. ☐

12. When your child cries, you tend to say, "Don't be a wimp," "Stop being a crybaby," or something similar. ☐

13. When your child comes sobbing to you, you say, "Tell me how I can take the hurt away." ☐

14. When your child becomes visibly upset, you say things like, "It's OK to feel bad (or angry) about what's bothering you." ☐

15. You tend to find yourself laying down many new rules to your child. ☐

16. You make rules but it doesn't take much coaxing from your child for you to make exceptions to the rules. ☐

ANSWER KEY			
1. Disengaged	5. Authoritative	9. Disengaged	13. Indulgent
2. Authoritarian	6. Authoritarian	10. Disengaged	14. Authoritative
3. Disengaged	7. Indulgent	11. Authoritative	15. Authoritarian
4. Indulgent	8. Authoritative	12. Authoritarian	16. Indulgent

Figure 2.1.

Many parents are unsure about which parenting style they employ. Even though most mix styles to some extent, they usually use one style more than others. The Parenting Styles checklist (see figure 2.1) can be used to help parents gain a clearer understanding of which parenting styles they use. School guidance personnel may instruct a parent to read the items and place a check mark in the box next to any item that describes his or her usual behavior when interacting with offspring.

After the quiz has been completed by the parent, the counselor should discuss with them the response styles that emerge (I have found it advantageous to allow parents to keep the discovered information to themselves—thus avoiding any possibilities the counseling relationship would be threatened by parental defensiveness). Actually, most parents recognize their dominant parenting style. For instance, they see the difference between a youngster who has been hammered into obedience by authoritarian parents and a child who has had everything done for him or her by indulgent adults.

During an interview I stress most parents operate along a continuum, using whichever style is appropriate for their child's age, stage of development, and immediate situation. It may not always be easy to see, but the prevailing style tends to emerge over the years, with related childhood behavioral differences showing up during the elementary school years and becoming more pronounced during adolescence.

Webster-Stratton and Herbert (1994) have studied and written about methods that can be employed to change family behavior styles. Along with other professionals, they do not believe that parenting style inflexibly determines life outcome for any child. Personality, temperament, economics, school experiences, parent-child matches, environmental conditions, peer group influences, and television viewing are all factors that can influence life patterns.

Nevertheless, I believe it is important for parents to be aware of the effectiveness of authoritative parenting. This parenting style gives youngsters a better start in life, and it is never too late for parents to change their approach to their children. The counselor may wish to offer parents reading materials that discuss child behavior problems.

Suggested Reading for Parents

In response to the many questions raised by parents regarding the care of their children, counselors may suggest appropriate reading from the following list.

How Does My Child's Behavior Influence the Way I Act?

Ambert, A.-M. (1992). *The effect of children on parents.* New York: Haworth Press.

What Are Some Family Behaviors That Are Self-Defeating?

Berglas, S., & Baumeister, R. F. (1993). *Your own worst enemy: Understanding the paradox of self-defeating behavior.* New York: Basic Books.

Which Children Are Particularly at Risk under Stress?

Crow, G. A. (1978). *Children at risk.* New York: Schocken Books.

How Do I Help My Child to Cope with Stress?

Brenner, A. (1984). *Helping children cope with stress.* Lexington, MA: D.C. Heath.

How Can My Spouse and I Reach an Agreement Regarding Our Parenting Style?

Duncan, B. L., & Rock, J. W. (1991). *Overcoming relationship impasses: Ways to initiate change when your partner won't help.* New York: Plenum Press.

How Can I Help My Child to Become Less Fearful?

Huffington, A. (2007). *On becoming fearless.* Boston: Little, Brown.

How Can I Help My Child Solve Sibling Problems?

Kluger, J. (2006, July 10). The new science of siblings. *Time, 168*(2), 46–55.

How Can I Help My Child to Be More Self-Disciplined?

Herbert, M. (1989). *Discipline: A positive guide for parents.* Oxford, England: Basil Blackwell.

How Can I Help My Child to Control Inner Impulses?

Hicks, E., & Hicks, J. (2005). *Ask and it is given.* Carlsbad, CA: Hay House.

Do I Misunderstand My Child?

Silver, L. B. (1992). *The misunderstood child.* Blue Ridge Summit, PA: Tab Books.

How Do I Answer the Questions My Child Asks About Sex?

Younger, F. (1992). *Five hundred questions kids ask about sex and some of the answers: Sex education for parents, teachers, and young people.* Springfield, IL: Charles C. Thomas.

How Can I Help My Child to be More Motivated?

Dyer, W. (2006). *The power of intention.* Carlsbad, CA: Hay House.

How Can I Recognize Unusual Shyness in My Child?

Marshall, J. R. (1994). *Social phobia: From shyness to stage fright.* New York: Basic Books.

How Can I Help My Child to Be Fiscally Responsible?

Kiyosaki, R. T. (2002). *Rich dad, poor dad.* London: Time Warner.

CHAPTER 3

Excessive Self-Blame

Self-blame, as defined in the Burks Behavior Rating Scales (Burks, 1977a, 2006a) is the exaggerated need to accept responsibility for real or imagined wrongdoing. Children with this neurotic behavior problem tend to

- become disturbed if they make an error;
- ask queries that point to unusual fears about the future;
- become excessively remorseful for wrongdoing;
- hold selves responsible if things go wrong;
- become troubled if events turn out less than perfect.

Children showing an excessive degree of the above symptoms tend to demonstrate other neurotic tendencies as well. For example, self-blame is often associated with another defense mechanism, anxiety. Impulse-ridden or aggressive youngsters, however, tend not to demonstrate guilt. Interestingly, self-blame may stand by itself as a conduct category. Apparently, the ability to turn aggression inward and show undue remorse helps the individual suppress or avoid the expression of other untoward symptoms.

THEORETICAL BACKGROUND

Effects of Guilt

Guilt feelings have positive as well as negative functions in the development of the personality structure. In any individual, a demonstrated sense of remorse is deemed appropriate when that person harms someone else. As a matter of fact, the absence of conscience may make a person a potential menace to society. Conversely, an overactive sense of self-blame can cause an individual to feel miserable. Oppressive feelings of guilt in the absence of demonstrable antisocial acts have their genesis in highly rigid parental training standards. Cronbach (1954) defined the following five stages of character development:

Amoral. Infants, who possess no concept of good or evil, are unaware that their actions affect others. Without further moral training, those who remain at this stage of development would become social monsters, demanding and insatiable. As a matter of fact, some borderline personalities (see poor reality contact, chapter 4) demonstrate many personality remnants from this early stage.

Self-centered. Self-centered people, like amoral individuals, are driven to satisfy immediate needs. However, at this stage there is some understanding that personal actions can cause others pleasure or discomfort. Even with this realization, self-centered people are not interested in the effects of their behavior on others. Most children behave egocentrically up to about age 4. Older impulsive and aggressive individuals can sometimes demonstrate self-centered traits.

Conventional. People in the conventional stage of development make ethical choices in line with the standards they perceive to be acceptable to a chosen group. Such people are driven to adopt the behavior thought to be most proper in the eyes of others, even when that conduct is potentially harmful to the group or individual (e.g., they may defend ideals that no longer serve any practical purpose).

Many individuals, particularly older elementary school–age children, remain at the conventional stage of development. As a matter of convenience, most daily adult activities are based on regulations established at this level. These rules are seen as realistic by most and are seldom questioned, even when they are contrary to reason and judgment. (For example, how many people speak up when given poor service at a restaurant?)

Irrational-conscientious. Irrational-conscientious people are more inflexible than conventional individuals, and they invest more emotion in ethical ideals and conflicts. People at this stage feel that they must meet certain standards of deportment, even when given permission to lower such unrealistic expectations of excellence.

For example, I once counseled a teenager who was trained to think that telling a lie was unforgivable. The teenager's parents expressed genuine anguish when he told a fib and punished him severely. Eventually, even the thought of telling a lie caused him to experience anxiety. The primary problem was no longer the question of whether the child would tell a lie (which might or might not have caused harm to others) but of the anxiety the youngster felt when he so much as contemplated a lie. The discomfort that accompanied the imagined transgression was great, but he thought it a proper price to pay for his "sinful" thoughts. Teachers, other adults, and even the parents conceded that the emotional cost was too high for the youngster to bear. Counseling helped the parents understand that white lies are sometimes necessary social catalysts that most people employ without undue stress. The parents relaxed their standards and the adolescent felt more at ease; many of his guilt symptoms disappeared.

Children suffering from self-blame adhere to irrational moral values that contribute to other neurotic symptoms, such as anxiety and self-deprecating behavior. Although self-blame may be the only problem behavior demonstrated by a child, most guilt-ridden children also have symptoms that indicate a poor ability to express aggression in normal ways (Burks, 1977a, 1977b).

Rational-conscientious. Cronbach believes this stage is desirable. Because all values conflict with one another at times, people who can reconcile these differences, and not feel too guilty if one rule is broken in favor of another, will tend to remain in synchrony with their environment. In short, rational-conscientious people are flexible and have an organized system of beliefs with established goals that are in harmony with their ethical priorities. Whereas an irrational-conscientious person might be plunged into anxiety for telling a white lie, the rational-conscientious individual perceives the falsehood as a necessary act to achieve a greater good and is not unduly upset by it.

The Role of Shame in Guilt Reactions

Many professionals (C. Goldberg, 1991) are not satisfied with the traditional view of guilt as a central issue in human suffering. They feel that shame, not guilt, is the emotion most likely to cause distress. Shame resembles self-blame but is often accompanied by withdrawal and depression. Shame is fundamental to the human condition because it reflects failure of the self. Compared to embarrassment, which can be mild and transient and which arises when a person becomes an object of unwanted attention, shame is always intense. The person hides from it, withdraws, and feels abandoned. Shame arises when a specific failure is perceived as what attribution (causal) theorists call a global attribution (a complete failure of the self). When people fail and think they have done some particular thing wrong, they may feel guilt, remorse, or even anger, but they then try to make a repair or consider how to do better next time. By contrast, shame arises when the focus is not on a specific action but on the whole self.

According to Harper and Hoopes (1990), shame is often a feeling of inferiority that may be manifest in one individual, a whole family, a subsystem, or a particular relationship. I once counseled a 14-year-old African American girl who had been referred for school counseling because of her negative attitude and because she had attacked a white female classmate. At the beginning of the first interview she sullenly refused to talk. When she saw that I did not press her to speak, she began to mutter to herself and then burst out, "Everybody thinks I am no damn good! And you know what? It's just because of the color of my skin! They make me feel I'm to blame for that!" She broke down and began to cry bitterly. Beyond sympathetic listening, I found myself unable to offer significant reassurance. This case illustrates the burden of shame thrust upon minority groups by the majority culture for attributes minority members are helpless to change. People with disabilities can also learn to resent their mental and physical challenges. They, too, may feel ashamed because they possess hindrances they think are socially unacceptable.

Mental health professionals can help parents and teachers counter feelings of shame in children by helping adults to meet the three most important needs of developing personalities (Harper & Hoopes, 1990):

- Dependency—the need of every child to trust that adult support is always available.
- Intimacy—the need of every child to confide in others.
- Affirmation—the need of every child to be told that he or she is loved and valued.

An emphasis must also be placed on the inadvisability of shaming children out of emotions or actions. Parents and teachers can demoralize children when they say things like "Why are you crying like a little baby?" or "Everybody is behaving. Why are you acting so stinky?" or "Johnny was brave—he dove off the diving board. What makes you such a scaredy-cat?" Statements such as these can make youngsters feel inferior, doubtful about themselves, and inadequate.

Another topic of interest regarding shame is the issue of gender differences. Females may be more prone to shame because of their early socialization and their greater tendency to blame themselves for so-called relationship failures (males are more likely to attribute blame to other, less personal factors).

DIAGNOSIS

Children who receive self-blame high scores on the Burks Behavior Rating Scales (Burks, 2006a) or other measurement devices may wish to examine specific guilt feelings and possible causes. Keith (1981) pointed out that guilt in children tends to center around the following family conflicts:

- sibling rivalry;
- sexual conflict (fear of sexual impulses; doubts about physical size, prowess, or attractiveness);
- inability to measure up to parental standards of achievement.

Sibling Rivalry

Even though the majority of parents experienced early jealousy toward siblings and felt some degree of guilt about those feelings, few tend to think their own children could be afflicted with the same emotions. When school personnel observe a child showing symptoms of undue guilt, possible sibling envy should be one of the items on the agenda of a family interview, even if the parents do not raise the issue. The role of sibling jealousy may be explored in more detail by asking the parents the following questions:

- Does the child have unusual difficulty getting along with one or more siblings?
- Does the child seem openly pleased when a sibling is punished for wrongdoing?
- Does the child express undue anger about one or more siblings?
- Does the child complain at length about the amount of attention parents give other siblings?
- Does the child steal possessions from another sibling?
- Does the child constantly interrupt conversations between parents and other siblings?
- Does the child misbehave seriously when parents try to attend to the needs of another sibling?
- Do parents tend to express preference for particular siblings (e.g., show a desire to do more things with another child)?

The parents can be told that guilt stemming from a child's anger toward siblings cannot be eliminated by exhorting the child's conscience (e.g., by saying, "You shouldn't feel that way toward your brother"). The youngster will only interpret such injunctions as further proof that the parents do not favor him or her. Devices that rely on criticism or reproach can only exacerbate guilt. On the other hand, expressions of affection and understanding tend to reassure the youngster, with a probable concomitant reduction in self-blame.

Sexual Conflict

Although the role of sexual conflict in the formation of neurosis is well known and documented (Kessler, 1966), the subject is not easily discussed with parents or children. Conversations about sexual attitudes and identity tend to arouse feelings of uneasiness, and school counselors who venture into these subjects may soon wish they had not. Under such circumstances, it may be advisable to refer the family to private counseling, where negative transferences can be more safely explored. To a certain extent, all aberrant behavior in children contains some elements of sexual conflict (Koenig et al., 2004; Schewe, 2002), but school guidance personnel may have cause for concern when a child demonstrates the following symptoms:

Hysterical behavior. Hysterical symptoms (e.g., tics) in younger children tend to be short-lived and represent transitory conflict, but it is not out of the ordinary to observe longer-lasting hysterical outbursts in teenagers. As with all neurotic syndromes, repression of forbidden impulses (often sexual) is the first defense mechanism employed by the hysteric. Sudden outbursts of emotion occur when ideas and emotions that are normally kept hidden come to conscious recognition and the individual flies into a panic, weeps, rages, and loses self-control. Such behavior can be accepted more readily in an adolescent than in an adult because of the unique conflicts faced by teenagers and the more fluid nature of ego defense systems present in adolescents.

Obsessive-compulsive behavior. Kessler (1966) pointed out that signs of obsessive-compulsive disorder (OCD) are present in the clinical picture of disturbed children, but that the symptoms do not fit the classical, rigid personality picture often demonstrated by compulsive adults. Instead, youngsters tend to show a single compulsion, which emerges and is identified by clinicians as a "habit disturbance" (e.g., nail biting) or as a pathological fear (e.g., fear of the dark, fear of dogs) clinical problem whose origins (perhaps sexual in nature) are uncertain and whose treatment remains questionable.

The haunting, repetitive, and nagging ideas that consume these subjects and the seemingly irrational actions that result form an association that seems to possess a life of its own. A number of theories have been advanced to explain why these particular mental and physical markers occur. The most plausible explanation assumes the symptoms are employed to conceal a basic problem—to hold off frightening anxieties that threaten to burst into consciousness.

Obsessive-compulsive disorders are thought to have origins in experiences making an individual feel afraid and helpless. Usually these emotions do not stem from single frightening occurrences but rather from long-term living conditions involving being put down, ridiculed, shamed, or made to feel guilty.

Signs of obsessions differ from those of compulsions. Obsessions are composed of thoughts and images difficult to stop. A child troubled by obsessive thoughts feels driven to concentrate on them as if magically the effort will prevent a horrible happening. Compulsions are composed of behaviors that the individual feels driven to do in an attempt to reduce inner anxiety. The repetitive actions serve to bind anxieties to contain fears and to focus worry on current threatening stimuli rather than attending to what is truly fearful (usually an abhorrent sexual or aggressive impulse that threatens to burst into awareness).

Symptoms may include the following anxiety-reducing traits:

* a need for perfection and excessive discipline (make everything predictable);
* a preoccupation with orderliness (messiness is equated with lack of control);

- a need to be inflexible (must maintain power at any cost);
- a lack of generosity (can't reward those who show inferior qualities);
- an agitated concentration on details and regulations (got to keep those worrisome thoughts out of mind);
- an excessive devotion to the job at hand.

Youngsters with the disorder are overly focused on orderliness and perfection. The requirement to do everything "right" can impede productivity because the individuals

- get caught up in details and tend to miss the bigger picture;
- set unreasonably high and unreachable standards for themselves;
- are critical of others that do not measure up to these principles;
- do not like to work in teams, believing partners are too careless and inept;
- avoid decisions for fear of making mistakes.

Obsessive-compulsive youngsters may talk to themselves in the following ways.

- "That spot on my desk is driving me crazy; I've got to clean it up."
- "Nobody knows how to run the classroom so I should take charge."
- "Working with others is a pain in the butt."
- "Perfection is my goal."
- "That kid not doing class work should straighten up and run his life better."

A lifetime may be consumed by an uncontrollable need to fulfill compulsive rituals. The person seeks total control over all aspects of life. Every possibility must be anticipated. Endless mental lists are required and composed. Every effort is made to arrange perfect outcomes. Uncertainty is hated. Because awful harm could result if he or she ever forgets these relentless requirements, the individual remains everlastingly tied to the obsession.

Recent figures indicate that 1–3% of the general population suffers episodes of OCD at some point in their lives (Goodman et al., 2000; Perry, 2002), making the disorder much more common than previously assumed. Of even more concern is the fact that OCD has typically been refractory to psychiatric and traditional psychotherapeutic interventions (De Silva & Rachman, 1992). Recent drug treatments have been only moderately successful. Further, most patients tend to relapse when they stop taking medications.

De Silva and Rachman (1992) stressed that behavioral treatments that emphasize (a) placing individuals in real-life situations that make them feel anxious and trigger their compulsive urges and (b) preventing patients from engaging in compulsive behaviors. These approaches may have to be modified for children. I believe most youngsters do not possess the conceptual capacity to tolerate anxieties generated by such direct approaches, although I have not had outstanding success in treating OCD in children. Instead, I have counseled parents to relax ethical standards and have used play therapy to encourage children to "mess up" without censure. Parents, however, must be cautioned to be patient when the child acts out formerly repressed impulses (that is, shows erratic and disordered conduct).

Counseling guilty or compulsive children and their parents can be difficult because the youngsters are often the picture of conformity and compliance—a personality structure much admired and applauded by adults. Such a child's attempt to suppress "bad" impulses may enable him or her to maintain the status of "perfect child." However, other children may regard the child as a goody-goody or self-centered prig. Slavish dependency on rules will rob a child's personality of spontaneity and creativity. A child with rigid self-control may grow up to be an adult who is unable to maintain warm, satisfying relationships and who, because of dependency on regulations, achieves only mediocrity.

INTERVENTION STRATEGIES

Techniques for School Personnel

1. Refrain from using rebukes to control the child. Guilt-ridden children tend to feel worthless and will accept any judgmental comments as true. They will show remorse and modify their behavior to fit the standards set by the teacher but will become even more guilt-ridden.
2. Talk to the child privately about things that bother him or her. Discontinue discussion attempts if the child is reluctant to talk and do not show disappointment if the youngster does not respond (to do so will only make the child feel more guilt).
3. Build the child's self-confidence. Children who turn aggression inward (e.g., fail in schoolwork, are self-destructive, or invite correction by misbehaving) can be assumed to have a negative self-image. Such children do not hold even their positive characteristics in esteem and tend to believe that others hold them in contempt. To help such a child change this downgraded self-image, take the following steps:

   • Tell the student that others have confidence in his or her skills.
   • Give a compliment when the student makes an effort.
   • Allow the child to do something special for the teacher.
   • Involve the student in class discussions and compliment him or her for contributions.
   • Give special assistance to make sure assignments are finished and done well.
   • Ignore self-destructive acts and reward positive behavior (particularly acts that bring the child pleasure).
   • Tell the parents about the child's positive effort and achievement.

4. Move the student to another educational setting if he or she demonstrates distress because of an inability to meet class standards.
5. Give special assistance to the student who shows embarrassment in physical education classes. Some children who are guilt-ridden do not know how to shoot a basket, perform tumbling exercises, and so on, but are afraid to ask for help, because they fear they will be scorned by their peers.
6. Institute a unit of study dealing with issues such as the importance of feelings, why people feel guilty, how guilt helps people, how guilt can be harmful, what to do about bothersome guilt, and how people can distinguish between useful and irrelevant guilt. Allow children ample time to discuss and explore these issues. Accept differences of opinion and, as much as possible, avoid predetermined, adult-oriented answers to these moral questions.
7. Encourage guilt-ridden students to become involved in classroom discussions of emotionally laden topics that affect modern society (crime, inflation, unemployment, etc.). Do not censor the feelings expressed.
8. Invite the school psychologist or counselor into the classroom for a talk on human ways to handle the problem of undue self-blame.
9. Plan classroom discussions of common temptations faced by children. Hoffman (1977) and Harrell (1979) pointed out that many students welcome these verbal exchanges. The discussions carry more meaning if sociodrama is also employed.
10. Use bibliotherapy, particularly for older students. A classroom can be supplied with books that discuss the well-recognized problems of children.

Techniques for Parents

Initially, it is important to explore with the parents their awareness of the child's excessive feelings of guilt. More often than not, adults fail to perceive that the child is showing any untoward symptoms. They may see the child as admirably well-behaved. The parents may need to be told about the "superkid syndrome," a condition character-ized by the loss of motivation, the absence of spontaneity, and the presence of unusual anxiety. Once parents are aware that a problem exists, it is important to explore the causes and nature of the child's guilt. Finally, advice can be provided to help parents change their behavior to modify unwanted traits in the child. In interviews with par-ents, counselors may want to address the following questions.

Are the parents asking their child to obey too many rules and regulations? Parents are often surprised that this is an issue that should be discussed; they may ask, "Don't all children need constructive direction?" Clinicians should recognize the anxiety underlying this question—that is, the parents' fear that their child will misbehave if not constantly controlled with directions and admonitions. Parents can be assured that their self-blaming, worried children already have a well-constructed conscience, that they are not learning to become delinquents, and that they can be trusted to explore their environment without constant supervision. Such assurances are more likely to be ef-fective if the parents perceive the counselor as a respected authority figure.

Are adults the child admires (relatives, teachers, friends) too uptight about ethical standards? This is an-other question that, at first, does not make sense to many parents. Most have never been challenged on this issue. Many adults assume that a child can always improve his or her comportment, even if the youngster is currently be-having appropriately. It may be something of a revelation for them that a child trained in this manner may feel chronically dissatisfied and guilty about his or her daily performance. Further, many parents have never been asked to conceptualize and articulate exactly what they want in the way of proper deportment from their children. When they do so, they are often surprised to see that their child is already meeting their standards.

Many parents of self-blaming children suffer the same guilt neuroses as their children. If a self-blaming child lives with an adult who sees constant guilt as natural and acceptable, it will be difficult for the school counselor to help the youngster. Such a parent cannot conceive that the child's guilt is harmful and will tend not to take reme-dial advice seriously. The family should be referred to an outside agency for long-term therapy.

Are the parents over-punishing the child for wrongdoing? Some parents have few realistic ideas of what con-stitutes a proper consequence for an act of disobedience. They may need to be told, for instance, that physical pun-ishment used too frequently and too early removes many suitable discipline options that are more effective and less likely to disrupt feelings of affection between child and parent. Fortunately, many parents who overdiscipline their children already suspect that their discipline methods are unsuitable (because the youngsters are reacting in un-pleasant ways) and are open to suggestions on ways to improve control procedures.

A word of caution is needed here. If a counselor or clinician perceives that the personality structure of the over-correcting parents contains strong sadistic tendencies, other counseling approaches should be considered. A parent who defends severe punishment, who relates with evident satisfaction a history of severe discipline meted out by his or her own parents, or who continues to administer severe punishment to a child even when advised not to, may be told that the mistreatment of the youngster is unacceptable to school authorities and that outside agencies (legal and otherwise) may be contacted to investigate such family discipline procedures if the parents do not modify them.

Are the parents overreacting to signs of aggression in the child? If grown-ups interpret pushiness, strong-mindedness, willfulness, and some forms of obstinacy in the child as manifestations of "bad" or "evil" conduct, the child will naturally go along with this evaluation, repressing aggressive impulses and feeling guilty when the im-pulses are inwardly experienced. The Christian ethic has long favored the notion that simply wishing to commit a forbidden act can be equated with actually doing the act (possibly originating from "As ye think, so ye are").

The overrepression of aggressive impulses can have at least two unfortunate consequences: (a) the attenuation of energy levels—because emotional forces are directed toward inhibitory processes—which causes the child to appear listless and tired; and (b) the loss of spontaneity and creativity because the child cannot express appropri-ate assertiveness and initiative.

Parents can be told that children are generally relieved to know that adults, too, experience malignant impulses, are able to acknowledge these urges and not act upon them, and are willing to discuss and accept these same ag-gressive impulses within children. Parents may also be interested to know that many overpunished children believe they have lost the affection of correcting adults. Actually, a vicious cycle can be set up. The child feels guilty for misdeeds; to expiate guilt feelings, he or she acts "bad" to provoke an aggressive reaction (punishment) from the parents. The child then feels better, but the misbehavior can only lead to more self-blame, more compulsive misdeeds, and so on. Long-term therapy may be needed to break this cycle of pathology. Even when involved adults understand the problem intellectually, the child may not. Children cannot conceptualize the dynamics of the dilemma.

Guilt can lead to unusual behavior that is debilitating to the child and alarming to adults—for example, unusual fear of being attacked or hurt, severe nightmares, worry that others do not love and respect the child, and an excessive desire to perform well. If such symptoms are shown to an unusual degree and have existed for an extended period, parents should be advised to seek professional assistance from sources outside the school.

Talking over problems with children is generally considered helpful, but it can be overdone. For instance, a youngster who cannot find ways to satisfy a demanding parent will become even more self-conscious and guilty if the parent insists on extended discussions about the child's shortcomings. Eventually, the youngster may defend against failure by adopting an I-am-stupid attitude, no longer trying to succeed. Adults, of course, are then frustrated in their efforts to convince the child that he or she is not worthless.

This unfortunate state of affairs is best addressed by convincing parents and other involved adults to be less critical. They should not argue when their child insists a task is too hard to complete, nor should they fall into the trap of doing assignments for the child. Instead, they should gently but firmly insist that the child do it on his or her own. When the child demonstrates initiative, the parents should offer praise for constructive conduct.

DIAGNOSTIC QUIZ FOR PARENTS OF GUILT-RIDDEN CHILDREN

The following questions for parents can stimulate parental insight into behavior that may cause a child to experience excessive guilt. These questions can be used as a guide in individual or group interviews. The related interpretations, advice, and illustrative examples can be presented by the counselor during the discussion.

Do you sprinkle a lot of "dos" and "don'ts" into your conversations with your child? Constant admonitions can come across as nagging. Constant concern about behavior can keep a child tense and anxious. Increased acceptance of the child's conduct will often result in the youngster's showing more initiative, a more adventuresome spirit, continued good behavior, and more affection toward adults.

Do you constantly try to shush your child if he or she does things somewhat differently than you would, argues with you, or expresses views different from your own? Children showing too much guilt tend to show a corresponding loss of aggression. They assume they must demonstrate a quiet, unassuming demeanor. A loss in the willingness to express aggression is worthy of concern if accompanied by a decline in achievement.

Do you constantly tell your child that mothers and fathers always know best? The child who grows up feeling that parental rules can never be questioned may spend too much energy in adult life trying to please authority figures. Rules should be firm, but children should be given a chance to express their needs. Family discussions can help children express themselves.

Do you suspect you are overpunishing your child for wrongdoing? Both the emotional and physical components of punishment must be considered. Some parents of guilt-ridden children react to their child's misbehavior by withdrawing affection, acting distraught (via tears, sadness, or worry), or talking about problems too much. This may cause youngsters to feel that their misconduct has somehow hurt their sorrowing parents. Overly repentant children then come to believe that anything but correct behavior will damage others.

Physical punishment can be overused. Isolating children for long periods of time and taking away privileges for weeks or months are punitive actions that can cause children to feel they have committed unacceptable crimes. For younger children, especially, punishment ought to be short and to the point, with parental forgiveness quickly available.

Do you overreact if your child fails to achieve? Guilt-ridden adults often relate that, as children, the only way they could get affection from their parents was to excel at something (do their chores well, practice faithfully on a musical instrument, bring home good grades, earn money, etc.). Without exceptional performance, warmth was difficult to acquire.

Tying self-worth to achievement is risky. Individuals who do so tend to feel empty when they are not working at a task; they can become compulsive strivers, endlessly seeking approval through work. To a certain extent, children must be loved for themselves—for what they are, not for what they do. Families can do this by having fun together. Appreciation of family members should be spontaneous and not necessarily tied to some achievement.

Do you constantly point out to your child that he or she must do better? Generally, it is futile to tell a child that his or her performance should be improved. Without specific directions and close support, entreaties to do better simply make the child feel more guilty and less able to act independently. If, on the other hand, parents help the child set goals that are reachable and then assist the youngster to gain these objectives, the child will feel a genuine sense of pride and accomplishment.

Do you encourage your child to use imagination and creativity in play and work? Children who blame themselves too much tend not to demonstrate aggressive self-confidence. In the minds of these children, aggression is equated with being bad. (To the parents, passivity is seen as good; assertiveness is "getting into trouble.") For some guilt-ridden youngsters, even thinking of doing something on their own brings unpleasant feelings, so spontaneous thought is stifled. Unfortunately, intellectual functions may also be suppressed. The child then becomes an underachiever. Fantasy, properly used, helps children become more productive. Inhibited students learn to become more aggressive when encouraged to engage in imaginative play activities.

Do you constantly discuss your child's problems with him or her? Children (particularly younger ones) cannot employ mental insight to a significant degree. Unlike adults, they are unable to stand back, examine, and understand inward motivations and impulses. Thus, it is useless to demand that a youngster explain why he or she committed an act. Cause-and-effect relationships are poorly understood. When a youngster answers "I don't know" to questions about reasons for acting in an unacceptable manner, it can be assumed the child is telling the truth (even though, to the adult, the reasons for the misconduct appear obvious). Many adults, however, place great faith in lectures. They are tempted to moralize because the child shows gratifying signs of remorse when they do. Unfortunately, lectures tend to make the child feel even more guilty and self-conscious and less self-worthy. When the youngster becomes discouraged and less productive, these same adults will try to cheer the child with assurances of his or her worth. Now the child feels even more inadequate and thinks, "I must really be a problem or else why would these people be so worried about me?" Discussions of the child's problems and attempts to reassure him or her simply reinforce guilt feelings and a sense of inadequacy.

Do you try to shame your child into acting better? Shame is guilt's close relative: Guilt results from the violation of the conscience (the internalized source of the rules we live by); shame ensues from not measuring up to the expectations of others (an external source). The shamed person feels small, unworthy, and embarrassed. That person can also feel defective and often fears that he or she will be found to be ridiculous and ineffective.

Do you put too much emphasis on rules and regulations? As discussed earlier, most parents of self-blaming children are surprised to hear this question, because they fear that their child will misbehave if not given many admonitions. Naturally, youngsters need directions, but child monitoring can be overdone. A tense and worried child is already demonstrating a well-organized conscience and will probably never be a delinquent. Such children need to explore their environment without constant supervision.

Are any admired adults (relatives, teachers, friends) imposing high standards on your child? Well-meaning grown-ups can sometimes influence your child adversely. Sometimes, for example, teenagers join religious organizations that impose unrealistically high standards of conduct that can cause youngsters to feel stressed and worried.

Do you have trouble accepting imperfections in yourself and others? Achieving perfection is a noble goal, but it is not part of the human condition. Not only is perfection unattainable, it is also not a requirement for joyful living. Children need to hear parental views on this matter. The following ideas may help them understand.

- Even parents can never be perfect, no matter how hard they try.
- People often have to take action without full knowledge of the consequences.
- It's futile to burden yourself with unrealistic demands.
- Don't expect to be free of anger in unpleasant situations.
- Don't punish yourself for thinking "bad" thoughts.

Has your child suffered some real or imaginary traumatic event that causes him or her to feel guilty? Adults must be alert to the possibility that children blame themselves for unfortunate happenings; the common occurrence of divorce can be used as an example. Guilt about the divorce of parents differs in degree according to the child's age. The most painful experiences occur for two- to five-year-olds (youngsters under the age of two show little awareness of what is happening). One mother of a four-year-old reported that when her husband left, their child clung to her leg and sobbed, "Make Daddy come back. If he comes back, I promise to be good." Another little girl took to beating her doll and yelling, "Bad doll, naughty doll. I'm going to leave you!"

Older youngsters may also feel blameworthy but are more likely to lash out in anger at their parents. Most suffer some degree of impaired self-esteem. I found it effective to have the custodial parent bring in the children for family group counseling where unspoken feelings could be aired and new understandings established. Naturally, the other parent was also offered counseling, but only on a one-to-one basis with the therapist.

Do you tend to compare the achievements of one child to the accomplishments of a brother or sister? Sibling rivalry occurs in all children who have brothers or sisters, but adults tend to ignore its capacity to make youngsters feel ashamed. Even though the majority of parents experienced jealousy in their own sibling relationships and felt some degree of guilt about these emotions, few tend to think their own children are (or should be) afflicted with similar feelings.

Are you encouraging your inordinately well-behaved child to be a so-called super kid? This is a well-known phenomenon for children of theologians (ministers or other clergy), who try to please their ethically demanding parents by being extra "good." Becoming a "perfect" kid, though, can be hard to accomplish. Many later succumb to depression for at least two reasons: (a) the requirement to maintain a high level of vigilance against the possible emergence of impulses to transgress rules and (b) the absence of emotionally satisfying activities that are open to those less concerned about violating high standards of conduct (Hendlin, 1992; Mallinger & De Wyze, 1992). Other types of environments can produce super kids. Some youngsters feel they are to blame for unstable home conditions and try desperately to stabilize the family situation by being extra well-behaved.

Parents of a super kid always admire the child's excessively correct conduct. The child is delightful to adults. Even though it is not easy to give up dreams of having such an unusual youngster, parents may wish to delve into the reasons for the unusual behavior and, eventually, to change child-raising practices to lighten the ethical burden that has been placed upon their youngster (Baumeister, 1993).

Even if your child is succeeding academically, do you push for even more excellence? The secret hope of some parents is that their child will someday turn out to be a truly outstanding individual. This wish cannot (in their eyes) be fulfilled if the youngster demonstrates only adequate motivation and accomplishment. The boy or girl must be urged, over and over, to "go for the gold." Some adults even resort to bribery to spur children on. If these same parents were to be asked what their feelings would be if they worked for a supervisor who expressed constant dissatisfaction with what they did and continually urged them to do better, they would say they might hate such a situation because of the guilt it would generate.

It is generally futile to tell a child that performance must be improved. In the absence of specific directions and close emotional support, such entreaties ordinarily make the child feel guilty and less able to act independently. If, on the other hand, parents help the boy or girl set reachable goals, gain those objectives, and praise their child's accomplishments, all family members are likely to experience a genuine sense of pride and mutual affection.

Do you often feel guilty? Guilt-ridden parents tend to produce children who are similarly laden with guilt. Parents who feel self-blame may want to consider the following questions.

- What areas of life give me the most guilt (marriage, sex, bringing up the children, work, relations with others)?
- Is my guilt justified (did I actually do something wrong) or is it unjustified (a response, perhaps, to past moralistic teachings)?
- How much is this guilt affecting me today (making me edgy, critical, accident-prone, less efficient, less attractive to others, less healthy, more depressed)?
- If my guilt feelings are justified, how can I right the wrongs I have caused?
- Am I trying to pay for my guilt by suffering (punishing myself, making myself unhappy, refusing to engage in pleasurable activities)?
- Can I forgive myself or are my moral standards too high?
- Before I can feel better, do I need forgiveness from someone else?
- Am I easily made to feel guilty by other people (both from the past and the present)?
- Do I run away from guilt feelings through the use of alcohol, drugs, overeating, frantic activity, sexual escapades, or any other escapist conduct?
- Do I refuse to communicate my feelings of self-blame to anyone else?
- Do I dump my confessions of guilt on others who don't want to hear about them?

Feeling guilty can become a habit. At its worst, it can paralyze a person with anxiety, worry, fear, and humiliation. Children cannot escape the effects of self-blame they observe in parents.

CHAPTER 4

Excessive Anxiety

Anxiousness is the outward expression of a particularly unpleasant or painful feeling, or affect, that causes a fight-or-flight reaction (Burks, 2006a, 2006b). Children possessing an unusual degree of worry tend to

- demonstrate numerous fears;
- appear uptight;
- be bothered excessively;
- flush easily under stress;
- seem edgy.

Youngsters showing these symptoms may also be withdrawn, self-blameful, bothered with many feelings of low self-esteem, and emotionally distressed (Tiedens & Leach, 2005). Children with impulse disorders, neurological handicaps, and aggressive tendencies tend not to show these characteristics (Burks, 2006a).

THEORETICAL BACKGROUND

Chronically anxious children are responding to imagined dangers. Some past event(s) caused physical and emotional pain, and they remain afraid that the trauma will be reexperienced. Suppose, for instance, that an infant is frightened by a noisy dog. The child cannot understand the logical nature of the experience and cannot predict when a similar event might recur. The child's anxiety about dogs may grow into a fear of other animals. If severe enough, anxiety can pervade the personality structure.

Anxiety as a Neurotic Trait

Anxiety is generally considered to be a neurotic symptom because it involves repressive mental mechanisms. Repressed emotions are hostile-aggressive in nature (Horney, 1939). The person using this personality defense remains concerned that the suppressed impulses will break forth at some vulnerable and unpredictable point. The child who feels uncomfortable about aggressive impulses may show unusual signs of low self-worth, apathy, regret, worry, shame, embarrassment, avoidance patterns, or guilt reactions. Persistent angry feelings, unacceptable to the child's conscious mind, create inner conflicts that drain physical and emotional resources. The youngster wants to express these angry feelings but the strictures of the conscience (learned rules and regulations) will not allow such expression.

In younger children, anxiety symptoms tend to dissipate quickly when treated properly. For them, worries tend to center around a home situation that could be changed by concerned adults. For example, suppose a youngster takes a cookie without permission and feels guilty about this act. Since the child still experiences the impulse to take sweets and feels this urge must be stifled, the child experiences anxiety. If, however, the parents take steps such as loosening controls and playing down the seriousness of minor infractions, the child's worries are likely to disappear. If the causes of anxiety are not treated soon after the events that initiated the worry, anxiety can become a more integral part of the personality picture and end up more difficult to treat in later years.

Causal Factors

Kessler (1966) reported five hazards of childhood that can leave individuals with unusual symptoms of anxiety. Most children overcome these dangers with relative ease, but others struggle with the residue of the following events for many years.

1. Fear of abandonment by a loved person. Bettelheim (1976) stressed the universality of this fear, which is intense during the first three years of life when children feel most helpless and dependent.
2. Fear of losing the love of a previously supporting individual. The threat of psychological, rather than physical, separation is of concern here. Again, the anxiety is most easily aroused during the first three years of life.
3. Fear that sexual-identity demands cannot be met adequately. The struggle for sexual identification continues through all stages of childhood development and, for some, continues to be an unresolved dilemma in adult life. Children face many threats to their emerging sexuality. For instance, between the ages of three and five years, little boys are afraid they cannot meet challenges from larger, stronger males (this is a time for fathers to be especially understanding). Little girls, too, are frightened by feelings of inadequacy.
4. Fear that societal demands cannot be met. The discussion of self-blame illustrates the problems faced by children who believe they have failed to meet ethical and achievement standards set by parents and educators.
5. Fear of losing emotional control. Strong emotional feelings that well up in a child—seemingly strange and uncontrollable—can make the youngster afraid that he or she will injure others if these impulses are expressed. The problem is exacerbated if surrounding adults are also fearful and instruct the child to suppress even legitimate signs of anger. These fears can generate anxiety because afflicted individuals are faced with conflicting demands; they wish to ventilate feelings that society says must not be expressed.

Jenkins (1973) reasoned that anxiety-arousing conflicts can produce depression, physical disability (e.g., ulcers, rashes, headaches, and a multitude of other organic disorders) and obsessive-compulsive reactions. All these pathological signs are defenses against anxiety. For example, people with elevated blood pressure may be suppressing feared anger, and people with obsessive hand-washing tendencies may be afraid to give up their compulsive behaviors because to do so would mean facing severe worries about personal cleanliness. Children who are aggressive and uninhibited, on the other hand, tend not to show symptoms of this nature. As Jenkins points out, youngsters who act out (that is, attack their environments) do not blame themselves for unfortunate events. Instead, they assume that a hurtful world wishes to frustrate them. Methods effective with neurotic children will not work as well with these hostile individuals.

Normal and Abnormal Anxiety

Most adults express some degree of confusion about what can be considered "normal" worry versus what is thought to be unusual anxiety. Various levels of anxiety, ranging from normal to abnormal, can be differentiated as follows (Kessler, 1966):

1. Is the feeling a vague worry or a full-fledged anxiety attack?
2. Does it last a few hours or many weeks or months?
3. Is it possible to reassure the individual that his or her worries are unrealistic? If not, the anxieties are assumed to be more entrenched in the personality structure.

4. Does the worry limit the individual's freedom of action? If so, the greater the limitation, the more severe the anxiety.

Relationship of Developmental Age to Anxiety

It is unclear whether the number of childhood fears and anxieties remains constant over time. It is known with some certainty that the focus and quality of childhood apprehensions change with age, as follows:

Young infants. Greatest fears are heights, loss of physical support, and sudden, unpredictable, and intense stimuli (like loud noises).

Children one to three years. Most common fears are strangers, loud noises, unusual stimuli, separation from caretakers, and toilet activities.

Preschoolers and first graders. Major fears focus around animals, darkness, separation or abandonment by parents, monsters and ghosts, and natural phenomena (e.g., thunder and lightning).

Older elementary school–age children. Continued fear of natural events like thunder and lightning, earthquakes, tornadoes and hurricanes, but most fears center around activities at home (parental conflicts and parental punishment) and at school (poor grades, taking tests, rejection by classmates, and school punishment). Health events (physical injury, illness, and medical procedures) are also noted.

Adolescents. Anxieties tend to center around school events, personal effectiveness, physical illness, economic status, and sexual matters.

While it is useful to consider the common worries shown at different age levels, it must also be noted that inner tensions are also expressed in ways peculiar to individuals.

Expressions of Distress in Children

Since children are not born understanding how to manage unwanted emotions, they often rely on unproductive strategies. For example, the technique most commonly employed by preschoolers is to act out current feelings in the often vain hope that surrounding people will interpret the emotional messages accurately and respond correctly. They do this because physical reactions have been their primary mode of communication since infancy—crying begot comfort, laughing prolonged pleasant interaction, and turning away brought the caretaker closer. In addition, children of this age do not have the vocabulary to describe their emotions or the intellectual maturity to know what their feelings represent. Sometimes, these infantile behaviors get the message across (the crying of a youngster who has bumped his or her head will bring an appropriate adult action), but at other times the cues are not easily understood. The child becomes frustrated—he or she jumps up and down to show excitement, but surrounding adults may think this is misbehavior. If the youngster lashes out in anger, adults may speculate that the child is hungry or feeling ignored, which may miss the mark entirely.

Some youngsters show emotions openly; others hide them. Feelings such as discouragement, frustration, anticipation, curiosity, guardedness, and suspicion are often not obvious to outsiders. The presence of mixed or conflicting emotions may cause a child to appear blank or confused. Many such subtle behavior cues tend to be ignored by adults. The lack of an appropriate adult response can mean a missed opportunity for a child to gain insight into his or her inappropriate conduct.

Younger children may exhibit undesirable behavior to show how they feel (e.g., they may dash around recklessly to show excitement or break toys to demonstrate disappointment). They behave this way because they have never been taught acceptable behavioral alternatives or because they are not old enough to figure out more effective avenues of expression. Immaturity can also be expressed in a tendency to recognize just one emotion at a time, often shown totally and with great intensity (e.g., the child may suddenly become affectionate shortly after being angry). Adults may see these dramatic actions as inappropriate.

Finally, young children have trouble recognizing the emotions felt by others. The problem can be made worse if the other individual is a peer who also lacks social skills.

Anxiety as a Common Disorder

Recent epidemiological studies have confirmed that anxiety disorders represent the most prevalent mental health problem in the United States (Barlow, 1988; Rapee & Barlow, 1991). Little doubt exists that children are showing more signs of tension than did their counterparts of even a few years ago. For example, a recent report (Olin, 1996) states that a survey of 4,000 Kansas kindergartners through third graders discovered that 42% experienced unwanted stress symptoms—including sleep disorders, fingernail biting, headaches, and irritable-temper outbursts. Although the causes of stress varied, investigators involved in the study agreed that the number-one source of child stress is the child's home environment.

Home-based stress was of significant concern to the survey experts because such tensions could turn youngsters into pencil-chewing bundles of nerves. Later, according to the researchers, many of these same children turned to drug use and sexual experimentation for emotional release. Some older individuals even attempted suicide.

DIAGNOSIS

Diagnosis of anxiousness in a child requires the use of formal diagnostic procedures, such as a standardized measure like the Burks Behavior Rating Scales (Burks, 2006a). Once such a diagnosis is made, diagnostic counseling can be employed to identify specific areas of concern. Diagnosis comes from analyzing the behavior picture seen by parents and teachers and from probing the inner feelings of the stressed child.

Warning Signs of Childhood Stress

Children who are highly stressed and anxious usually *look* distressed. Body posture may be slumped or rigid; behavior passive or "charged up"; breathing shallow; the voice shrill, explosive, or strained; speech may be accelerated; and the child's face may be haggard. Somatic complaints are common (Crow, 1978). The following symptoms (adapted from Kuczen, 1982) are common signs of childhood stress.

Somatic Complaints

  neck or back pains
  pounding heart
  stomach upset, queasiness, vomiting
  headaches
  teeth grinding (at times, during sleep)
  muscle spasms or tics

Involuntary Conduct

  bed-wetting
  soiling pants
  being easily startled
  explosive crying
  extreme nervousness
  frequent urination or diarrhea
  hyperactivity or excessive tension
  many falls and accidents
  inattentiveness

irritability
listlessness
nightmares or night frights
sleeping and eating poorly
stuttering

Affective Complaints

generalized anxiety (cannot identify source of fears)
sadness or depression
excessive worry
irritability
lack of enthusiasm
unusual loss of interest in activities
unusual anger

Ego Compensations

boastfulness
compulsive neatness
cruel behavior toward people or animals
defiance
perfectionism
excessive self-criticism
daydreaming and retreat from reality
lying
attention seeking
overeating
alcohol or drug use
stealing
thumb sucking
extreme shyness or jealousy
unusual sexual behavior

The preceding list of symptoms should be reviewed with adults who know the child well (e.g., parents, relatives, and teachers). Some symptoms may be transient. Those that have endured for a long period and to an excessive degree must be taken seriously.

Other aspects of childhood anxiety can be discussed with concerned adults. For example, when children have been exposed to intense pressure for prolonged periods, there is a marked reduction in their ability to attend to relevant stimuli (because demanding psychic energy is being directed inward to maintain psychological equilibrium) and to make decisions (because they cannot pay attention to incoming information).

Adults also need to know that disturbing amounts of stress call into play two different coping strategies: (a) facing the stressor and (b) adapting to it or avoiding it. When a child flees, he or she generally uses one of the following categories of evasive action (Brenner, 1984).

Denial. The child acts as though the stress does not exist. For example, when told that her father has died, a youngster goes on playing with toys. Another child, on hearing distressing news, talks to imaginary playmates. These children are using denial to alleviate pain.

Withdrawal. Children use physical or mental withdrawal to take themselves out of a stressful environment. They may concentrate on toys or pets or lose themselves in daydreaming.

Regression. By acting younger or engaging in conduct used at an earlier age, youngsters who are stressed are using regression, a defense mechanism used to elicit extra love and attention from adults. Often they become dependent and demanding.

Impulsive acting out. By acting impulsively and thoughtlessly children can avoid thinking about painful events. This rash behavior can make observers angry (possibly a consequence desired by impetuous youngsters for inwardly felt guilt).

All of the above defenses may work for a time to keep children in psychological equilibrium. When these strategies fail, however, youngsters may exhibit more severe symptoms, such as increased irritability, panic reactions, depression, agitation, feelings of dread, attention deficits, and nightmares. Even more serious traits can be shown by children showing severe stress, like temper tantrums, deliberately annoying others, defying authority, frequent stealing, and demonstrating inordinate or indiscriminate affection toward adults. Some children who are extremely disturbed claim they hear voices or see things that are not there; they may also have very unusual fears, or be preoccupied with death (Blauner, 2002). These children may refuse to respond to others.

Probing Inner Feelings

I constructed a diagnostic counseling technique that can be used to explore specific areas of concern about childhood anxiety. The Worry List (see figure 4.1) is a nonthreatening instrument that can be employed by concerned adults who wish to uncover a particular child's worries. For each statement on the Worry List, the child is asked to indicate whether it is something he or she does not worry about, sometimes worries about, or worries about a lot. A response of "I worry about this a lot" indicates a concern of significant proportions. "Sometimes I worry about this" should not be ignored (the item should be discussed with the child), but ordinarily it represents a less serious sign of anxiety. In nearly all cases, youngsters remember a response of "I worry about this a lot" when asked about it later and usually want to talk about such items at length (see table 4.1).

When discussing responses with a child, explore the child's feelings sympathetically. The child may find comfort in ventilating feelings about worries. Do not attempt to placate the child. Accept any show of emotion without comment. After the child has expressed his or her concerns, offer suggestions as to how threats may be removed or circumvented.

INTERVENTION STRATEGIES

Techniques for Counselors

Kazdin (1979), in recounting recent advances in child behavior therapy, reminded us that fears are common in childhood. Most pass with age and are not of clinical concern. However, if the fear is extremely intense, does not abate over a period of time, and obviously obstructs the child's everyday functioning, it should be treated therapeutically. Kazdin mentioned several types of fear that yield to clinical intervention, including fear of dogs, dental and medical treatment, the dark, social interactions, and separation from parents. Treatment includes:

Modeling. The child observes grown-ups or other children acting out approximations of the desired conduct.

Desensitization and graduated reinforcement. The child is exposed to small, graduated doses of the stimuli that provoke the anxiety.

Practicing competing responses. The child is asked to imagine pleasant events in place of the feared response. Kazdin reported that adult praise and attention have also proved helpful in reshaping avoidance behavior.

Another method of treating fears, used mostly with older children and some adults, is to ask clients to imagine a situation in which they feel upset, fearful, or worried. When they report an unusual fear or conflict, they are asked

THE WORRY LIST

Harold F. Burks, Ph.D.

Put a check mark in the column that tells about …

	I don't worry about this	Sometimes I worry about this	I worry about this a lot
the way you feel			
1. Getting mad	☐	☐	☐
2. Being nervous	☐	☐	☐
3. Feeling sad	☐	☐	☐
4. Daydreaming a lot	☐	☐	☐
5. Not being able to say what you want to say	☐	☐	☐
6. Thinking you don't do things right	☐	☐	☐
7. Being shy	☐	☐	☐
8. Being a worrier	☐	☐	☐
9. Being afraid	☐	☐	☐
10. Thinking about things you did wrong	☐	☐	☐
11. Getting mad but not being able to tell people about it	☐	☐	☐
the way you act			
1. Having nervous habits	☐	☐	☐
2. Telling fibs	☐	☐	☐
3. Taking things you shouldn't	☐	☐	☐
4. Making mistakes	☐	☐	☐
5. Saying bad words	☐	☐	☐
6. Being noisy	☐	☐	☐
7. Making excuses for yourself	☐	☐	☐
8. Not paying attention	☐	☐	☐
9. Not being neat	☐	☐	☐
10. Interrupting others	☐	☐	☐
11. Not sleeping well	☐	☐	☐
12. Not listening when you should	☐	☐	☐
13. Not obeying rules	☐	☐	☐
14. Not doing chores	☐	☐	☐

Figure 4.1a.

	I don't worry about this	Sometimes I worry about this	I worry about this a lot
your family			
1. Fighting with your brother or sister	☐	☐	☐
2. Not understanding your father	☐	☐	☐
3. Not understanding your mother	☐	☐	☐
4. Your father not understanding you	☐	☐	☐
5. Your mother not understanding you	☐	☐	☐
6. Your family expecting too much of you	☐	☐	☐
7. Your family not having enough fun	☐	☐	☐
8. Being punished	☐	☐	☐
9. Being teased	☐	☐	☐
10. Being bossed	☐	☐	☐
11. Not having enough freedom	☐	☐	☐
12. Not talking things over	☐	☐	☐
13. Being left alone	☐	☐	☐
14. Your family thinking you're never right	☐	☐	☐
15. Your family arguing	☐	☐	☐
16. Your family not leaving your things alone	☐	☐	☐
17. People in your family not helping each other out	☐	☐	☐
18. Your family not paying attention to what you want	☐	☐	☐
your health			
1. Chest pain	☐	☐	☐
2. Coughing	☐	☐	☐
3. Sore eyes	☐	☐	☐
4. Not seeing well	☐	☐	☐
5. Not hearing well	☐	☐	☐
6. Itching skin	☐	☐	☐
7. Dizziness	☐	☐	☐
8. Sore stomach	☐	☐	☐
9. Difficulty breathing	☐	☐	☐
10. Headaches	☐	☐	☐
11. Feeling tired	☐	☐	☐
12. Weighing too much	☐	☐	☐
13. Not weighing enough	☐	☐	☐
14. Being too short	☐	☐	☐
15. Being too tall	☐	☐	☐
16. Food not agreeing with you	☐	☐	☐
17. Going to the doctor	☐	☐	☐
18. Sore throats	☐	☐	☐
19. Not being strong	☐	☐	☐
20. Sore muscles	☐	☐	☐

Figure 4.1b.

other things that bother you	I don't worry about this	Sometimes I worry about this	I worry about this a lot
1. Loud noises	☐	☐	☐
2. Scary movies	☐	☐	☐
3. Ghosts	☐	☐	☐
4. Bullies	☐	☐	☐
5. Getting lost	☐	☐	☐
6. Dying	☐	☐	☐
7. Getting shots	☐	☐	☐
8. Animals	☐	☐	☐
9. Insects	☐	☐	☐
10. Riding in the car	☐	☐	☐
11. The dark	☐	☐	☐
12. Thunderstorms	☐	☐	☐
13. War	☐	☐	☐
14. Getting sick	☐	☐	☐
15. Strangers	☐	☐	☐
16. Fire	☐	☐	☐
17. Noises at night	☐	☐	☐
18. Getting hurt	☐	☐	☐
19. Going to strange places	☐	☐	☐
20. Eating	☐	☐	☐
21. Swimming	☐	☐	☐
22. Not going to sleep	☐	☐	☐
23. Nightmares	☐	☐	☐
24. Going to the doctor	☐	☐	☐
25. Falling	☐	☐	☐
26. How you look	☐	☐	☐
your friends			
1. Not having enough friends	☐	☐	☐
2. Not understanding your friends	☐	☐	☐
3. Your friends not understanding you	☐	☐	☐
4. Needing one good friend	☐	☐	☐
5. Not having enough time to play with your friends	☐	☐	☐
6. Not being as smart as your friends	☐	☐	☐
7. Your friends thinking you're too smart	☐	☐	☐
8. Not being as good in sports as your friends	☐	☐	☐
9. Some children not liking you	☐	☐	☐
10. Being afraid of some children	☐	☐	☐
11. Not being chosen as a leader by other children	☐	☐	☐
12. Your friends being too old	☐	☐	☐
13. Your friends being too young	☐	☐	☐
14. Being bossy with other children	☐	☐	☐
15. Fighting with your friends	☐	☐	☐

Figure 4.1c.

Treatment Suggestions for Excessive Anxiety

Trait	Treatment Suggestions
Unusual sensitivity or worry about a specific object or episode *Example:* The child is afraid of dogs.	1. Talk with the child about animals in general and their characteristics. 2. Gradually, begin to talk with the child about dogs in general and their characteristics. 3. Have the child play with small toy animals. 4. Introduce a small toy dog into play activity. 5. Have the parents go with the child to pick out a puppy. Emphasize the puppy's helplessness and explain how the child can take care of it. Work with the child to train the puppy.
Feelings of inferiority *Example:* The child feels that he or she does poorly at games and will not participate in sports.	1. Talk over any aspect of sports that may embarrass or upset the child (lack of coordination, fear of being hurt, shame about undressing in front of others, etc.). Do this only if the child is willing to communicate these feelings to you. 2. Allow the child to do a special sports-related job, such as keeping score, umpiring the game, or distributing equipment. 3. Practice with the child to enhance specific coordination skills necessary for sports. 4. Include the child in a group where competition is played down. 5. Do not permit group members to tease or ridicule the child. 6. Make winning or losing a relatively unimportant aspect of sports. 7. Praise the child for effort and achievement; ignore lack of success. 8. Arrange team selection for games by some means other than having team leaders choose members.
Sleep disturbances (can't sleep, walks in sleep, has frightening dreams, wakes up early, or is afraid to go to bed because of dreams) *Example:* The child has nightmares.	1. Allow the child to recount his or her nightmares to an adult. Children can find relief in retelling their dreams. 2. When a child identifies a threatening or scary figure in a dream, help him or her give it a comical name (e.g., "Old Joe"), and use that name thereafter. Naming a demon tends to demystify it and drain it of its fearsomeness. 3. Help the child fantasize about the frightening properties of dreams, then face those conditions in his or her imagination, and defeat them by creative reveries. Do this in a light-hearted way. 4. Explain that everybody has unpleasant dreams sometimes. 5. If nightmares are chronic and severe, ask the family to seek professional assistance.
Depression or discouragement *Example:* The child despairs of ever having friends.	1. Ask more mature students to be friendly toward the child. 2. Seat the child next to more mature students. 3. Have the child's parents encourage other children to visit their home. If the parents are financially able, suggest that they acquire equipment attractive to youngsters, such as a pool table, trampoline, ping-pong table, paddle tennis court, or even a swimming pool (although families should proceed carefully with such an investment—too many households have pools that are not used). A perfectionist parent who overvalues cleanliness and orderliness should be reminded of the extreme value of friends and that fun activities should not be restricted by too many rules and regulations. 4. Encourage the father or mother to come to school to show off a hobby or activity that the parent and the child both enjoy. Include the child in demonstration activities so that his or her value in the eyes of other children is enhanced. 5. Encourage the father or mother to enter Scouts or another similar group with the child. If the parent does not like group activities, suggest an activity that can be taken up alone with the child, such as bike riding or fishing, that will help the child develop skills that can be shared with other children. 6. Encourage the parents to invite other children to their home for a "sleep-over." 7. If a child demonstrates annoying habits with other youngsters, such as bossing them, fighting, or arguing with them, instruct the child how to act in the company of friends. Follow up on this instruction periodically.

Table 4.1a.

Trait	Treatment Suggestions

Daydreaming
 	
Example:
The child, lost in fantasy, cannot attend to chores or work.
	1. Determine the source of the child's ruminations.
	  • Is the child bored? This is often true of very bright children who lose interest in an easy curriculum.
	  • Is the child concentrating despite appearing inattentive? Some creative children are actually producing in areas other than those assigned.
	  • Is the child disturbed? Many anxious individuals must spend an unusual amount of time "processing" emotional problems.
	  • Is the child retarded? Some children are intellectually slow and simply give up.
	  • Can the child see and hear well? Attending to tasks may be too difficult if the child has a physical disability.
	2. Use special techniques to get the child's attention.
	  • Call the child by name.
	  • Touch the child gently on the shoulder.
	  • Stand near the child.
	  • Ask the child's opinion about a classroom problem.
	3. Channel the child's imagination into more constructive activities.
	  • Ask the child to make up stories that can be read to other children.
	  • Suggest the child draw pictures to accompany stories.
	  • Encourage the child to make up class plays that involve other children.
	4. Set time limits to complete assignments but make the tasks short (from 5 to 15 minutes). Check completed tasks immediately and reward the child if he or she has done the task properly. Reward younger children with prizes; for older children, use praise.
	5. Give the child engrossing assignments, such as completing puzzles and riddles, correcting tests, painting murals, arranging room decorations, or making special reports.
	6. Get the child involved with other children in group projects, but make sure he or she has a clearly defined role in these activities.
	7. Reward the child immediately with attention and praise if he or she initiates any activities.

Overconformity *Example:* The child follows rules to the letter and may become distressed if others break any rules.	1. Do not play upon the child's anxiety to please by emphasizing rules and regulations. 2. Present yourself to the child as a nonthreatening helper who rewards independent action. 3. Help the youngster engage in physical activities such as games and projects involving hammering, pounding, and other large-muscle activities where aggression can be released safely. 4. Ignore the child's efforts to become teacher's pet. These may include informing on other students, doing unasked-for extra jobs in the classroom, or behaving in exemplary ways. 5. Arrange for the child to be the bad guy in a class play. 6. Appoint the student to be the leader of an activity (e.g., team captain or chairperson of a group discussion). 7. Suggest to the child that he or she not always do things that please others. The child can be encouraged to do things that please himself or herself, not classmates. 8. Ask the parents to look at their child-raising practices. Are they too controlling? Are they modeling fear-producing attitudes (e.g., by exhibiting apprehension about the neighborhood or the school)? Are they too protective? Are they intervening in the child's social activities too much? Are they preventing the child from confronting others in altercations or arguments so that the youngster is not learning to assert himself or herself?

Table 4.1b.

to think of some figure—a friend, guardian angel, good fairy, or whatever—who will come in to support their efforts to overcome the imagined difficulty. Many report a sense of relief after identifying this figure (often a person they have not thought about for some time), and they report later that they were able to use this introjected image in a positive manner when needed.

Table 4.1 provides specific examples and treatment suggestions for children with unusual anxieties, feelings of inferiority, sleep disturbances, depression, daydreaming episodes, or overconformity. Although not all children showed all the traits reported, they were likely to demonstrate several of them.

When counseling tense and unhappy youngsters, I try to relate the worries they tell about to possible home conflicts. Sometimes the connection of tension to child symptoms is not easily perceived by parents. "After all," they say, "we're only trying to protect our child. How can my child be upset about that?" They may have a point. Who can blame a mother, for instance, for constantly warning her child to be wary of strangers? It probably never occurred to her that the message could turn to emotional overkill for a small youngster who, unlike herself, cannot discriminate who may or may not be dangerous and ends up classifying all adults as potentially threatening.

Children are at a disadvantage whenever they are asked to judge the meanings of outward events. Unlike adults, they do not possess mature reasoning powers. As the brain develops, children become better able to distinguish what is and is not friendly and to suppress alarm reactions. Grown-ups should be advised to exercise patience with youngsters, allow them to process fears slowly, and give them the opportunity to learn the nature and meanings of their emotional reactions.

The ability to handle stress varies from individual to individual. Some youngsters are easily made anxious and remain tense for long periods of time. Others are relatively immune to stress and disturbing events are quickly forgotten. Why some individuals remain disturbed for long periods while others recover quickly from trauma is uncertain, but inherited factors, developmental age, and environmental conditions all play a role.

In addition, the way people interpret a stressful event is often more important than the occurrence itself in determining the duration and intensity of emotional responses. Children closely observe adult behavior and do not become overly upset during a crisis if grown-ups remain calm.

Treatment approaches must be tailored to the particular needs of individuals. What works for some may not succeed for others. For example, relaxation techniques have proven helpful to some people but arouse even more anxiety (to the point of panic attacks) in others. The difference may be centered in the way people view the world. Those who become more tense tend to think events are unpredictable and beyond their control. To guard against potential danger, they must remain ever vigilant.

Most anxiety disorders are easily treated. More than 80% of those seeking help and given medications or counseling or both, show a significant reduction in the number of symptoms. The more closely treatment regimes follow anxiety-producing events, the greater the likelihood of improvement. In general, postponing therapy makes therapeutic efforts more difficult because tension has become entrenched in the personality structure.

Techniques for School Personnel

The problems of a child who is chronically worried and fearful are sometimes overlooked by teachers because the youngster often wants to please adults. However, this type of student can be under unusual pressure. A certain amount of tension is desirable—most children accomplish more if they are slightly or moderately concerned about the way others view academic accomplishment. However, too much anxiety may cause a child to be distractible. Further, if the student feels it is impossible to meet expected standards of performance, he or she can become a discouraged underachiever. Every effort should be made to diagnose the source of the child's difficulties and to give proper assistance to change unfortunate circumstances (if that is possible).

The following intervention strategies may aid teachers to assist pupils who are anxious.

1. Help fearful students understand the school environment. For example, make sure children know that they can ask the teacher for directions to the school office, to the bathrooms, or to the equipment room, and that it is permissible to call their parents when they are distressed at school.

   If a child does not know how to get help from the teacher, the teacher and child should meet after hours to discuss the child's fears. The meeting should be handled in an atmosphere of calmness and sympathy, and the student should be given every opportunity to make his or her fears known and to have all questions answered. Although the child's fears may appear groundless to the teacher, it must be assumed the child feels they are not. The student may interpret any attempt at quick reassurance as a brush-off. The adult must take time to listen to the complaints and to show the student that his or her fears are received seriously.

   Secret anxieties are characteristic of all young children but particularly those with disabilities that make them vulnerable to environmental threats. Several years ago, I conducted discussion group sessions with a class of students with orthopedic disabilities (many in wheelchairs, some wearing protective headgear, and others supported by braces of one type or another). According to the teachers, these students were generally well-behaved and gave little indication of inward worries. After only a few minutes of encouragement, however, they burst forth with an outpouring of feelings. One child told the class about his constant fear of being tipped over in his wheelchair. Others chimed in, expressing worries about going back to the hospital for more operations and of anxieties they experienced while riding the school bus. So it went, each child unburdening his or her pent-up feelings, until all finally fell silent. When asked if they would like to have further meetings where they could ventilate feelings, they shouted, "Yes!"

2. Reassure worried students that surrounding people do not harbor hostile feelings toward them. These verbal assurances, of course, should be accompanied by actions that communicate that the student is liked (e.g., ask the child to lead a group or assume a special assignment that is within the capacity of the pupil to accomplish).

3. Refrain from asking anxious children to do things they say they cannot accomplish. Agreeing with the youngster's assessment may sharply reduce anxiety (i.e., children are not made to feel guilty and/or defensive about failure to meet expectations). Of course, children should never be subjected to ridicule or sarcasm and reports to the teacher of uncomfortable feelings must be treated sympathetically.

4. Direct the student to another task if a present assignment produces anxiety.

5. Reward the child with immediate praise when correct behavior is observed. On the other hand, no adverse comments for incorrect conduct (unless too obvious).

6. Place the anxious student in a small group of friendly peers. De-emphasize competition and pressure. As much as possible, allow the child to choose his or her own activities.

7. After getting parental permission, send the child to the school counselor when fears appear to be out of the ordinary.

8. Help the child to overcome fear of testing by employing some of the following procedures:

   • Acknowledge the possibility that he or she may do poorly on exams.
   • Tell the student that test failure is not that big a deal.
   • Say little or nothing to the student when he or she receives poor grades.

9. Place the child in a low-stress classroom environment. Nongraded, primary classes are ideal for fearful, younger students. Unrealistic goals can be eliminated through appropriate grouping and individualized teaching.

10. Assist the child to acquire a more positive self-image by eliminating grades, marks, and other symbols of success and failure that maximize negative comparisons with peers.

11. Provide activities that allow expression of resentment in nonverbal ways (pounding nails, hitting clay, etc.). This is especially useful for students who do not express worries by complaining openly (Brophy & Good, 1970).

12. Provide highly structured schoolwork. Anxious children are more likely to succeed with a specific phonics reading approach than a whole-word method for example. Grimes and Allensmith (1961) discovered a relationship between anxiety and learning ability: The more anxious the child, the less likely he or she was to be adept at abstract (versus concrete) tasks.

13. Award tokens or points for each correct response, but give no demerits for incorrect answers. When a certain number of points or tokens have been collected, the child may be given a small reward (gum, candy, relaxation time, or a chance to sit near someone he or she likes).

14. Provide the child with special classroom jobs designed to enhance his or her status in the eyes of peers.

15. If the student possesses leadership abilities, place him or her in charge of a project.

16. Provide counseling and training sessions for students who demonstrate unusual anxiety about the ability to succeed in certain activities (such as art classes and physical education exercises). For example, the student who shows little artistic aptitude may be assured that creative drawing is not an ability essential for adult survival. The youngster may also be shown methods (e.g., painting by numbers) that produce satisfactory art results without dependency on originality or drawing skills.

Unlearning a Behavioral Disturbance

Anxiety is a central component of neurotic behavioral disturbance (Rhodes & Paul, 1978). Behavioral disturbances take two forms: (a) the anxiety response itself—with its visceral, skeletal, and central nervous system components—and (b) the conditioned response that is instrumental in avoiding the anxiety-producing stimuli. The conditioned response can originate from

- the punishing agent itself (e.g., the child is frightened by a dog and worries about dogs from then on);
- incidental environmental stimuli at a time of stress (e.g., the child is taken to a dreaded funeral service at a church; churches become a source of anxiety);
- personal conduct at a time of stress (e.g., the child breaks down in tears during his or her parents' divorce proceedings, is reprimanded, and is thereafter afraid of losing emotional control during a crisis).

Rhodes and Paul believe that individuals must unlearn both the anxiety response and the conditioned reaction, and they suggest the use of the following techniques. Each method is followed by an example of a solution to a common childhood problem encountered in classrooms.

1. Symbolically reenact the original trauma. Example: A kindergarten boy is told by his teacher to speak up because he "sounds like a little girl." The boy subsequently refuses to talk in class. Eventually he whispers to the counselor the facts surrounding the episode. After the counselor has formed a relationship with the youngster, the two meet with the teacher and the scene is reenacted, first by the counselor, who explains to the teacher the discomfort the original remark caused, and then by the child, who is now able to express his resentment (of course, the teacher has been prepared beforehand for this meeting.)

2. Reassure the child regarding environmental and interpersonal factors that promote anxiety in new situations. Example: A boy has been placed in a new foster home after being removed from several previous homes because his behavior alienated previous foster parents. The school complains that the boy cannot be contained in a regular classroom because of his disruptive behavior. The new, court-appointed foster parents have been told they must make arrangements to get him special help. Therapeutic consultations and diagnostic evaluation reveal the youngster is terrified that he will be given up by the newest set of parents. The foster mother and father are told to overlook most of the boy's minor misbehavior and to flood him with affection and attention. Finally, the parents and the child sign a paper pledging the youngster will never be removed from the home. After undertaking this program, the parents eventually report that the child has stopped acting out at home and at school (Burks, 2001).

3. Help the child interact with his or her teacher to solve interpersonal problems. Example: A withdrawn, tense third grade girl leaves a note on her teacher's desk that reads, "I love you and I wish you were my mother." Disturbed by the note, the teacher contacts the school psychologist for advice. The teacher does not think she can provide the emotional support the girl needs, but, at the same time, she does not want to make the child feel rejected by ignoring the note. The school psychologist makes a preliminary investigation of home conditions that reveals that the student's mother has been ill and hospitalized for a long time. The teacher is told this and is advised to offer the girl some special attention. No diagnostic evaluation is made, for fear the girl would feel rebuffed in her attempts to gain better communication with the teacher. In order to allay the teacher's anxieties about the meaning and possible consequences of this evolving symbiotic relationship, the psychologist promises to confer with the teacher once a week for a number of weeks. The increased teacher attention produces a happier demeanor in the child and a noticeable improvement in the quality of her work.

4. Show examples of the long-term consequences of undesirable conduct. Example: A teenage boy skips classes because he is worried about upcoming tests and is picked up by police for loitering and smoking marijuana. His parents seek family counseling. The boy remains obstinate (although upset) and maintains that he has done nothing wrong. He boasts to the therapist that "there is nothing at juvenile hall that can scare me." The psychologist receives court permission to tour the juvenile facilities with the student. The tour appears to be an emotional shock to the boy, who says several times, "I never knew it was like that!" The boy agrees to remain in school, and the psychologist arranges with the court referee to have him placed on probation.

5. Extinguish the fear of a necessary, but avoided, situation by having the child face it gradually while being given positive reinforcement. Example: A teenage boy with school phobia is brought to a psychologist by his mother, who asks for assistance in getting him to attend classes. For several sessions the psychologist does little but listen to the child sympathetically. No attempt is made to get him to go back to school. When the counselor judges that the boy has formed a strong enough therapeutic transference to the therapist and decides that the mother (who is also attending counseling sessions) can withstand the anxiety of the child's moving away from her, it is suggested to the teenager that he and the psychologist make gradual approaches to the school. The plan calls for the child to leave the therapist's car, walk toward the front door of the school and continue walking until he reaches his tolerance level for anxiety, stand at that point and count to ten, and then return to the car. The child continues this regime for eight days in a row, until he can stand in the school building without experiencing debilitating anxiety.

6. Teach skills that will give the individual control over feared conditions. Example: A shy, fearful, teenage girl, who is a Vietnamese refugee, shows unusual anxiety during physical education classes, and her teachers are concerned about her emotional well-being. The school nurse is asked to make a home visit. The nurse learns from the parents that the girl is afraid of the classes because she feels she does not know how to perform the exercises properly. Arrangements are made to give the youngster extra tutoring in performance skills, and the symptoms vanish.

7. Expose the individual to anxiety-producing conditions but arrange the situation to avoid unwanted behavior. Example: A shy, anxious boy in junior high school is afraid of the other boys, who tease him constantly. Arrangements are made for the student to attend a counseling group where, in a more supportive environment, he learns to stand up to other boys.

8. Reduce the intensity of conflicting motivations faced by the anxious person. Example: A teenage girl who is depressed wants to try out for a cheerleader position at school. However, she also wishes to please her mother, who demands she achieve high grades, which she cannot do if she becomes involved in extracurricular activities. The psychologist discusses the problem at length with the mother, who finally understands that she sees the student as the measuring rod for her own worth as a mother. The mother is willing to modify her stand, the girl feels less pressure from home, and teachers observe the teenager to be more relaxed and accepting of school roles.

9. Use negative reinforcement (deliberately overdo the unwanted behavior). Example: A fifth grade boy is referred to the guidance department of a school district because of disruptive behavior. A diagnostic analysis reveals that the child is anxious and fearful that he has no standing in the classroom which, in turn, leads him to strive to be the center of attention. Discussions with the student reveal that he has no perception or real understanding of the effects of his conduct on others. It is suggested to the teacher that she urge the child to jump to his feet and answer all questions regardless of whether others want to talk and regardless of whether he knows the answers. The employment of this technique in a classroom period (lasting about a half hour) has the child laughing in embarrassment; he asks the teacher if he can sit down. Thereafter, he does not jump out of his seat so readily. The teacher continues to use the method whenever needed, and the student remains less disruptive.

10. Reduce anxiety in a tension-provoking situation. Example: A teacher reports many students in her sixth grade class appear tense when asked to stand for recitation. The teacher is advised to reduce levels of anxiety by offering a candy token to anyone offering to recite and to cease making critical remarks about the recitations. She later reports a marked reduction in evidence of student anxiety.

Techniques for Helping Parents

The following questions for parents may be used by counselors to spark parental interest in the possible origins and treatment of anxiety in their children. The list of queries is not a test, and no attempt should be made to quantify responses. It is simply a guide that can be used in individual or group interviews.

Do you encourage your youngster to speak out about things that worry him or her? Many parents choose only to hear certain questions from their offspring, ignoring queries that raise embarrassing issues. For instance, a father may be glad to discuss sports activities but shies away from talking about sexual matters.

Do you assure your child that he or she has a right to feel fearful? The youngster who is denied permission to acknowledge worries will eventually learn to react with shame when facing fear. Fear becomes too humiliating to be acceptable. Some children deal with this problem by denying that they are small, weak, and helpless, pursuing fantasies of boundless personal strength (the Superman complex). However, under these conditions self-confidence is shaky and the child needs reassurance constantly. For instance, the mother who raises her son to take the place of an absent father may need a male figure around her who never expresses doubt about his abilities or self-worth. Her evident relief and gratification that the son plays a male adult role makes it difficult for him to express his inward concerns.

Do you encourage your child to experiment with household tools and other materials? Children learn to become constructively aggressive and more confident when allowed to construct materials. They tend to feel more in control of their worlds. Of course, the youngster must not be permitted to use potentially dangerous implements.

Do any members of the family try to control the child by using threats he or she will lose affection of adults (e.g., "Mother will not like you if you do that")? Loss of love is a universal childhood fear and threats to remove affection should never be employed as a discipline device.

Can you think of ways to cut down home conflicts where you criticize, argue with, scold, punish, or get angry with the child? One way is to eliminate some high parental expectations. For instance, it is possible that the child, no matter how hard he or she tries, will simply not be able to bring home top grades. Another way is to abandon severe punishment as a discipline procedure. Unusual punishment can result in unfortunate consequences (e.g., the child may end up disliking the parents, become more hostile, or learn to disregard punishment as a serious threat).

Is the child surrounded by familiar routines and rituals designed to make family life predictable? Children, being more helpless than adults, are likely to become anxious when they see future events as unpredictable. Young children especially have trouble evaluating temporal connections (the attempt to explain a later event on the basis of an earlier one); they cannot discriminate between chance circumstances and central causes. Hence, any departure from ordinary rituals is regarded with alarm.

Is the child warned ahead of time about impending family crises? If adults know an unfortunate family event is in the offing but withhold knowledge of it from a youngster, the child will not only feel tragic events are unpredictable but will, in addition, may experience a sense of betrayal.

Do you refrain from making achievement the principal reason for showing affection? In my experience, many adults who enter therapy reveal themselves as troubled because, as children, they found it difficult to receive signs of parental love unless they first pleased the parents with a demanded accomplishment. An early scenario between mother and child may have gone something like this: "Mary, if you help with drying the dishes I will think you are the dearest little girl in the world, but if you don't do them I will be very disappointed!" It doesn't take much imagination to see how this type of interchange gets extended to other activities: Mary could get strokes for bringing home good grades—she's not worth much if she doesn't. Training procedures of this nature can lay the foundation for the adult overachiever who becomes anxious whenever there is nothing to do and feels guilty about relaxing or taking a vacation.

It is proper to deliver compliments and affection when a child does something worthwhile, but it is emotionally hazardous to allow the youngster to think that accomplishment is the only way to gain approval. Love and acceptance must be communicated to an offspring even if he or she fails to produce. Emotional security is based on the certainty of receiving steadfast love.

Feelings of adequacy, on the other hand, are based on an individual's conviction that he or she can produce valued and worthwhile achievements. It is possible to feel secure but inadequate. Possibly the best example of this would be the person with a chronic disability who cannot work but feels love from surrounding individuals. It is also possible to feel insecure but adequate. One example might be a lonely, anxious overachiever who feels he or she receives little affection from others.

All people need to feel both secure and adequate, but the methods for gaining these qualities are not the same. To feel secure, a youngster must never lose his or her sense of being loved by others. To feel adequate, a child must receive many signs of interest and approval from others that what he or she achieves is important.

Do you tend to stop your child from showing anger even when he or she has a legitimate reason to be upset? Anger, both inwardly felt and outwardly expressed, is a difficult emotion for many individuals to handle; however, it is a legitimate and potentially healthy reaction to frustration. Obstacles to the fulfillment of desire are encountered constantly by everyone. When such frustration happens, aggression develops and gives individuals the impetus to overcome these stumbling blocks. In short, anger gets much of the world's work done!

Of course, parents should not tolerate destructive expressions of anger. Many researchers warn children should be taught to control most manifestations of hostility. Their premise is that a show of anger does not dissipate feelings of resentment; instead, it tends to fuel further angry feelings. These findings create a dilemma: How can children be helped to handle aggressive and angry emotions? Youngsters must be given other outlets for hostile feelings, including taking the following steps:

- Permit the child to feel anger even though he or she is not allowed to express it. Unfortunately, in this culture the feeling and the expression of anger have come to be equated. Acceptance of a strong inward emotion as a legitimate experience can help the angry person feel better; denial tends to intensify the feeling and make the person feel worse.

- Give the child the feeling that others are trying to understand the source, intensity, and meaning of his or her anger. Parents can do this by simply listening (without particular comment) to the expression of fears and by demonstrating consistent affection.

- Help the child gain a sense of control over his or her world by indicating that the child's anger (if properly directed) can change the environment or the conduct of others. The importance of this process is pointed out by researchers who suggest that individuals may acquire self-defeating habits when nothing they do causes their stress to abate and when their every move is met with inconsistent or otherwise controlling responses from others.

- Do not become overly concerned if the youngster loses his or her temper occasionally. Such a display is not an uncommon occurrence for individuals who oversuppress aggressive impulses. Treat it as a temporary symptom rather than as a personality characteristic.
- Set aside time for weekly family group discussions. Topics for these meetings can include how to accept criticism more gracefully, how to get things off one's chest, and how to listen to what others want.
- Avoid the use of sarcasm, teasing, or belittling remarks when communicating with the child. These approaches are often outlets for otherwise hidden hostility that could be expressed better in more open ways. In addition, they offer no adequate defense to the person receiving the jibe. Teasing, for instance, is usually conducted jokingly. If the person who is the butt of the joke objects to being tormented, he or she may be accused of being a poor sport. Sarcasm and belittling remarks can be equally hard to bear.

Are you concerned about how your child appears to others? Some children worry that they do not meet acceptable standards for physical appearance, performance, or sexual prowess. They imagine these deficiencies will cause them to lose friends (a prime concern of all youngsters). Such worries are not without foundation. Researchers have found that youngsters who are intellectually slower, overweight, physically disabled, physically unattractive, or slovenly are less likely to be chosen as friends than are those who fit peer concepts of beauty and performance. It is interesting to note that the standards of attractiveness held by youngsters of all ages and cultures fit the stereotypes promoted by the popular media. Children who look appealing are also assumed to be friendly, intelligent, and socially competent.

Concerned parents will make sure their child is dressed appropriately for the child's peer group (this may take some dress code research at school and in the neighborhood). The parent should also make certain the youngster is groomed satisfactorily.

My own research (Burks, 1972) uncovered problems faced by students demonstrating poor physical stamina and coordination. Among any group of average youngsters there exist a few individuals who appear weaker and more awkward and who face some degree of both short- and long-term discrimination from peers (Vicere & Fulmer, 1996), depending on the expectations of the group.

It does not take much imagination to see why lack of stamina and coordination can downgrade a child's self-image. For example, a boy who is physically inept may be rejected in sporting events. Unable to defend himself adequately, he gains little respect from other boys, feels unwanted, and finds it difficult to handle leadership roles. The consequences of poor stamina and coordination may be less severe for girls if they are physically attractive.

Parents whose children show unusual problems in coordination and physical strength may want to try the following:

- Consult medical sources for a proper diagnosis of the child's physical difficulties.
- Pay close attention to the child's daily nutrition, television viewing, and rest routines.
- Cooperate with the school to make sure the child feels comfortable in the classroom.

Youngsters who are physically weak and uncoordinated are often identified in preschool and kindergarten years but are less often noted in middle and upper school years. Withdrawal, anxiety, and dependency, associated with poor physical stamina in young children, tend to disappear in older youngsters but are sometimes replaced by unwanted aggressive characteristics—attention deficits, impulsivity, poor school achievement, poor social conformity, and rebelliousness. These traits are frequently shown by children who are neurologically impaired (for a discussion of children with attention deficits, see chapter 12).

Delayed puberty can be upsetting to both boys and girls. Unkind remarks from peers can result in a loss of self-esteem for late developers, who are eagerly awaiting physical signs of sexual maturity. On the other hand, sexual precociousness has deep emotional meaning for those who develop early. Youngsters whose sexual development is other than average can suffer distress; the cultural importance of being in step with peers may cause them to conceal feelings, for fear they will be ridiculed. Some adolescents welcome the opportunity to share thoughts about their developing sexuality with a counselor. Others will open up in teen-counseling groups. These groups are most effective when they include both sexes.

Do you tend to lecture your child on what is right and what is wrong? Naturally, all youngsters must learn what behavior is and is not acceptable. But some adults continue exhortations even when it is obvious that their youngsters have adopted the correct standards. No doubt parents do this to guard against future remissions. Beyond the fact that lectures tend to be tiresome, at best, is the possibility that the recipients of such preaching will end up thinking that nothing they do will ever be good enough. Even worse, they can develop chronic worries about making mistakes.

Children learn best from emulating admired adults—not from listening to sermons. Lectures should be kept to a minimum. Adults must not be too concerned if behavioral boundaries are occasionally overstepped. Treat mistakes as specific incidents rather than as evidence of permanent personality defects.

Do you place a lot of importance on assigning blame? Adults may feel constrained to place responsibility for mishaps on a particular family member. The intent is, of course, to prevent future mistakes; however, the consequences of this approach may not be as benign as parents might wish. Chronically blamed individuals can eventually react with anxiety, resentment, and anger.

Allocate blame with caution, even when the target for the denunciation is proved to be the cause of disputes. Remember that youngsters (like adults) commonly attempt actions with good intentions. Like adults, they cannot always divine ultimate outcomes. Boys and girls who grow up in environments that permit few, if any, mistakes can become overly cautious.

Do you tend to preach the value of competitiveness? American culture glorifies competition, but this avid pursuit of excellence can have a dark side. The most obvious problem lies in the fact that there are few winners and many losers, and many of those who are defeated end up feeling disappointed and anxious. Sometimes they feel they have let down the most important figures in their lives—their parents.

Competition should not be emphasized, particularly if a youngster shows signs of being discouraged by lack of success. A child will quickly gravitate to those activities at which he or she feels competent. There are many reasons why a child may not succeed. Immaturity, lack of interest, poorly developed skills, and so on may contribute to a lack of proficiency. Trying to overcome these deficiencies by prodding a youngster is ordinarily a vain effort at best. The safer approach may be to avoid comparisons with other children, gently praise improved performance, go easy on criticism, and assure the youngster of your continuing affection and support.

Even though your child is plainly worried about class work, do you avoid going to the school? When a child seems fearful of school, the parents should arrange an interview with the teacher and, if possible, with the principal. They should go, not as complainers (some school personnel react to complaints with defensiveness), but to become part of the educational team that is instructing their child. Parents should then follow up the conference with telephone calls and notes to the teacher.

ANXIETY-RELATED DISORDERS

Perfectionist Children

The perfectionist is a person that determines faultlessness in all efforts will win him or her success, acceptance, love, and fulfillment. Unfortunately, striving to be perfect can be an emotional two-edged sword—the compulsion can lead to severe disappointments (allied with anxiety) and the possible loss of desired goals.

Causal Factors

Perfectionist strivings in adults has psychological roots in parental demands of the following nature:

- made unrealistic demands for achievement;
- were never satisfied with any accomplishment;
- withdrew affection when the child didn't measure up academically.

Characteristics

Perfectionists, because they are basically insecure, tend to show the following anxieties:

- self-doubts;
- fears of disapproval, ridicule, and rejection;
- obsessive thoughts of achieving perfection;
- severe disappointments at not being "the best";
- critical self-appraisals;
- a desire to set up standards beyond reach or reason;
- a strong tendency to see mistakes as evidence of personal unworthiness.

Costs of Perfectionism

According to mental health experts, perfectionism can exact a great toll. Individuals suffering the trait tend to show the following characteristics:

- outbursts of anger;
- periods of acute frustration;
- incidences of impatience;
- intervals of loneliness;
- occasional suicidal thoughts;
- writer's block;
- interludes of social anxiety;
- frequent test anxiety;
- spells of depression.

Internal Dialogue

In all likelihood, the child perfectionist talks to the self in the following ways:

- "I can't take the driving test today; I need a lot more time to prepare."
- "Hardly anyone can measure up to my standards of behavior."
- "The way to be happy is to do everything just right."
- "I get terribly discouraged if I don't measure up to my principles."
- "Nobody understands the pressures I'm under."
- "I came second in the exam—that sure makes me mad."
- "To be accepted by others you have to be faultless."

Intervention Techniques

Some children show a generalized type of anxiety associated with compulsive desires to be perfect. The following suggestions for teachers and parents of such children address most of the common circumstances leading to generalized anxiety.

- Assure the child that he or she is not being censured by others.
- Refrain from pushing the youngster to achieve perfection.
- Go easy on punishment.

- Allow the child more freedom of action.
- Allow the youngster to make more mistakes without adult intervention and monitoring.
- Give more praise.
- Remove the child from the presence of anxious role models (this may not always be possible if the role models coexist in the home).

Children with Physical Illness or Disability

Education professionals need to develop a basic understanding of the philosophy and goals of the treatment of children who are physically ill or who have a physical disability because these youngsters ordinarily possess many anxieties (Hooper, Hynd, & Mattison, 1992; Kessler, 1966; and Livingston, Kom, & McAlees, 1982).

During periods of illness, children are often susceptible to worrisome fantasies related to sickness. For most, the images fade when health is regained, but a few children retain emotional sequelae that arouse anxiety. Some children are reluctant to put these fears into words because they think talking about them will make them come true (a typical fantasy of young children), and emotional problems may worsen.

What are the themes of these fears? Most center about the following worries:

1. Will the awful, out-of-control symptoms of the sickness (like diarrhea and throwing up) come back?
2. Will I be scolded if I show these symptoms? (This concern often occurs in very young children who have been reprimanded for making messes.)
3. Will the terrible pain come back? (This fear generally relates to pain inflicted by others—for example, doctors' injections.)
4. Will I be helpless again, where others do bad things to me and I can't do anything about it?
5. Will other people continue to worry about me because they are afraid I am not healthy or there is something wrong with me?
6. Will I be able to do things on my own as I did before I got sick?
7. Did I do something wrong that caused me to get sick? (This fear is more common among older youngsters, who tend to blame themselves for acts of disobedience, than among younger children, who tend to blame all-powerful parents for the sickness.)

Discussing these worries with youngsters who are ill or have a disability may eliminate concerns, but, unfortunately, it is seldom known with certainty what particular fears a child possesses. The Worry List (figure 4.1) may help in this respect. When adults can pinpoint the child's health worries, simple reassurances may suffice in most instances. Sometimes, however, the problems and solutions are more complex.

For example, children have a proclivity for blaming themselves for the onset of illness—they may be worried about forbidden hostile impulses and feel that sickness is a just punishment for such feelings. It may prove difficult to convince such children that they are not to blame for their ailment. Adults may assist most effectively by allowing youngsters to discuss these fears without remonstrance. It is helpful to tell the child that feelings have nothing to do with being sick.

Another important emotional aspect of childhood illness is the fantasy world of youngsters. For example, any bleeding may convince fearful children they will lose all their blood. A bruised arm or leg may suggest a broken limb. The fear of shots and associated pain may be embellished by a worry that the needle will break and remain stuck in the skin forever or make a hole that releases bodily fluids. The needle is often so large that it looks like a dangerous weapon, and youngsters may become frightened. What actually happens during an injection then becomes less important to the child than what might happen. Similarly, youngsters fantasize about the mysteriousness of germs—what they look like, where they come from, and so on. Since so much is made about the relationship of germs to dirt, fearful youngsters may, for a time, resort to excessive cleanliness. Thus, it is important to prepare children so that they know exactly what is going on during events associated with illness, to make sure they get plenty of physical and emotional support, and to guarantee that they have opportunities to vent anxieties.

A child's severe physical illness can bring serious emotional consequences. At times, parental anxiety is intense, medical care is complicated, and fears of possible long-lasting side effects are realistic. In addition, the following serious illnesses are characterized by unique features involving causation, possible or probable permanent physical effects, and treatment modes that can generate emotional complications.

Juvenile Diabetes

The many difficulties involving dietary restrictions and daily injections of insulin make juvenile diabetes a focal point of psychological concerns. The mother of a child with diabetes is at particular risk because she is usually the one who must withhold prohibited foods and administer shots. This role often promotes resentment in her youngster. If the medical regime falters or goes out of control (too much sugar or too much insulin), she feels guilty and inadequate.

Several years ago I counseled a 12-year-old diabetic boy and his parents. The youngster was chronically confused, angry, and guilty. He had only a hazy idea of the cause of his illness. He felt different from his peers because he had to avoid sweets and sometimes ate sugary foods just to avoid standing out from the crowd. He did not know and did not wish to fully understand the medical consequences of eating these forbidden foods. Over the years, he had gotten the idea that his desire for sweets was somehow "bad" and had to do with a kind of excessive greed (after all, his parents were always cautioning him about the evils of eating forbidden foods). Constant urine testing caused him to think something was wrong with his genitals.

After I formed a warm relationship with the boy, he was able to discuss some of the conceptions (mostly erroneous) he had about diabetes. Over time, he was able to discard many of his fancied exaggerations about its ill effects. When he and I met with his parents in family group therapy, he decided he would cooperate more intelligently with the prescribed medical program.

Rheumatic Fever

Many of the psychological aspects of rheumatic fever differ markedly from those associated with diabetes. In most instances, recovery is complete, but during the acute stages of the ailment there looms the possibility of permanent heart damage and this ominous possibility can cause children much worry. This anxiety can affect heart rhythm, thereby leading youngsters to think they actually have a heart injury.

Imagined fears can become more exaggerated if youngsters are forced to restrict activities ("My heart must really be bad if they won't let me move around!"). This has prompted many physicians to allow children with rheumatic fever and congenital heart difficulties more physical freedom up to the point where they become fatigued.

Physical Disability

Secret anxieties are characteristic of all children but particularly those with an orthopedic physical disability, because they are more vulnerable than most children to unexpected environmental threats. As related earlier, I once conducted group sessions with a class of generally well-behaved students who were orthopedically disabled. After introducing myself, I related that I had had polio as a small child and was left with throat difficulties after a period of hospitalization. In answer to their questions, I described some of the worries I had had about shots, being weak, and maybe dying. After only a few minutes of my personal story, the children burst forth with a torrent of pent-up feelings.

This story highlights the ability of children to hide anxieties and underscores their need to communicate their worries to sympathetic listeners.

Hospitalization

During the last few decades hospital personnel have become more concerned about the emotional well-being of hospitalized children. While most children recover quickly from the physical effects of surgery, about 20% continue to show adverse emotional signs (sleep disturbances, eating disorders, tics and other physical mannerisms, fears, regressive conduct such as wetting and soiling, and increased dependency). The more troubled a youngster is prior to hospitalization, the more likely it is that he or she will be adversely affected by hospitalization. Hospital anxiety centers around the following themes:

- separation from parents;
- exposure to strange and threatening hospital surroundings;
- apprehension about going to sleep;
- anticipation of the operation;
- fear of needles.

Beyond these more obvious fears, other anxieties may involve fear of abandonment, mutilation, and death.

Hospital-related fear and separation apprehensions are most intense in preschool children. Children 5 to 10 years old are most distressed about the operation itself, while early teenagers fear the effects of anesthesia the most (possibly because they are apprehensive about losing control).

Parents and hospital personnel can minimize the unpleasant emotional consequences of hospital stays and surgery as follows:

1. Prepare the youngster for what is likely to occur, using realistic, easily understood terms.
2. Refrain from painting a rosy picture of the hospital environment and staff in an effort to obtain more cooperation from the child. This dishonest assessment can lead the youngster to indulge in hopeful fantasies that will not be borne out postoperatively. Unexpected pain and discomfort can leave the little patient feeling disappointed and betrayed.
3. Arrange for the parents to stay with the child as much as possible before and after the operation.
4. Allow the youngster to bring a treasured belonging and dress in familiar clothing (boys tend to dislike hospital gowns, which seem to them to be made for girls).
5. Cooperate with all hospital personnel and discuss the need for sensitivity to the particular emotional needs of this boy or girl. Ask the following questions:

- Is there collaboration between psychiatric and pediatric personnel?
- Are pediatric nurses involved in this collaboration?
- Are special supervised play-therapy activities provided to help children cope with their pain and suffering?

Children Threatened with School Violence

The dramatic rise in juvenile crime in recent years has dismayed many because of its infiltration into schools (Peretti, 2001). Children are being victimized as never before. Arnold Goldstein, clinical psychologist at Syracuse University, warns that forms of aggression like bullying and sexual harassment (versus serious crime such as shootings) are particularly important because they are widespread and hidden from the view of most adults (Neuland, 1995). Bullying behavior such as name-calling, threats, physical attacks, rumor spreading, shunning, and racial slurs demand the attention of parents and teachers. Sexual harassment is also widespread and can have unfortunate emotional and academic consequences for both girls and boys. Neither the race nor the age of a student seems to affect the likelihood of victimization.

Perhaps no other person (outside of a lover) arouses more visceral feelings in all of us than the remembrance of a confrontation with a bully. I can recall with great clarity how I was terrified, as a seven-year-old, by a school tyrant who picked me out to be a victim. Fortunately, my father rescued me. He talked to the parents of the bully and I was no longer bothered.

Causal Factors

The bully may have experienced one or more of the following background factors:

- being born with an aggressive temperament;
- living in a family the abuses him or her;
- being exposed to adult models who browbeat others;
- living in a competitive family;
- having inherited a body that is larger and stronger than surrounding peers.

Internal Dialogue

In my clinical experience, students who browbeat peers tend to talk to themselves in the following ways:

- "Everybody else does it."
- "I gotta do it if I want to join the right crowd."
- "Well, it makes me feel stronger and smarter than the person I pick on."
- "It's the best way to keep from being bullied."

School Violence Intervention Techniques

Teachers and parents can use the following techniques to assist children who fear such persecution.

1. Demonstrate, through friendly and supportive behavior, their concern for the youngster's predicament.
2. Help the child come to some agreement about how the problem can be solved. Actively support any attempts by the child to overcome difficulties.
3. Discuss the child's problems with the school staff. Is the school environment safe for children? To discourage gun use, some schools are installing metal detectors, removing lockers, searching lockers and cars, requiring shared lockers (sometimes between students and faculty), placing lockers opposite the school office, and requiring students' book bags to be made of see-through materials. In some schools, attempts have been made to make classrooms safer by

   - bolting teachers' desks to the floor and arranging them to aid surveillance and provide avenues of escape;
   - using solid doors with unbreakable windows;
   - keeping supplies in a locked cabinet;
   - bolting student desks to the floor;
   - using windows made of Plexiglas or a polycarbon;
   - arranging classroom aisles so they are traffic friendly.

Under pressure from parents, schools have been making attempts to control the violent behavior of some students. However, the following approaches have not generally proved effective (Neuland, 1995):

1. Punishment. Punishing students for their misdeeds is currently the most common and most ineffective method for dealing with misbehavior. Corporal punishment, in particular, merely teaches the child that might makes right. In addition, because the behavior ceases for the moment, it rewards the punisher. Other punishment favorites are reprimands and suspension, which may work in the short term but fail to teach new ways of behaving.
2. Allowing emotional release. Catharsis—allowing the student to ventilate anger—does not lead to a reduction in violence; it simply teaches the person to become more aggressive.
3. Toleration of violence. Living with violence is both unproductive and unnecessary.

The following interventions appear to be more productive:

1. Customize solutions. Interventions should be based on specific environmental conditions and the needs of the individual.
2. Show children how to handle aggression. Teach students to overcome conflict through modeling, role playing, feedback (to let the child know how well he or she is acting), and homework centered on behavior habits.
3. Teach youngsters to overcome anger. In addition to the preceding methods to reduce the arousal of anger, direct instruction methods are also helpful. To strengthen the child's self-control, try to become aware of the circumstances in which the youngster gets angry. Then model correct behavior, making appropriate and positive statements (e.g., "First I think, then I act"; "This is not worth losing my cool"; "I'll count to 10 and stay calm").

Children with School Phobia

School phobia (fear of attending school) is more common among children than is generally realized. Most teachers of the early grades and some who teach the later grades have had to deal with this problem. The causes for this type of behavior are deep and complex. Kessler (1966), along with many others, treated it as a dependency problem between mother and child. Mothers of school-frightened youngsters typically

- fear leaving the child as much as the child fears leaving;
- teach the child (in largely unconscious ways) to fear school;
- tend to think of school as a cold, impersonal place and sympathize excessively with the child's complaints about school;
- teach the child that they would like him or her to stay home;
- are determined that the child shall suffer no physical or emotional deprivation and feel excessively guilty if the child is so deprived;
- provide adequately for the child when he or she is small but have difficulty when the youngster moves toward independence;
- are unable to express their own aggression adequately and teach the child to be afraid of showing anger.

Understanding the causes of school phobia may or may not be helpful because the pathology is not treatable from a commonsense point of view. Attempts to counsel the parents often result in their feeling threatened and resentful. Counselors should have concrete suggestions ready and should insist, calmly, that the parents follow through with the program.

Intervention Suggestions

I support the widely held view that primary school students who refuse to go to school are best treated by forcing them to attend classes, even though they put up a fuss. Once they are in the classroom, things invariably go smoothly. The main problem is getting the parents to act decisively. Older children (particularly teenagers) who are school phobic are a different matter. They seem unable to tolerate being in school—the very high anxiety they experience can be reduced only by fleeing the school. Long-term therapy is called for in these instances. Anxiety-reducing medication has also proved helpful for some fearful children (Clarizio & McCoy, 1976). The following suggestions for school personnel may be helpful when trying to keep the child in school:

1. If one parent's anxiety is affecting the child adversely, ask the other parent to bring the youngster to school each morning. Later, have the parents ask neighborhood children to walk with the child to the bus or to school.
2. Allow a parent to come to school and sit near the student. The parent should then gradually move away as the child gets involved in classwork and, as soon as possible, should leave the classroom.
3. Reward the student's attendance with special experiences (e.g., more time in the playhouse) or some other inducement. Gradually phase out rewards as the need for them diminishes.
4. For older students, institute a desensitization program. With the aid of a sympathetic adult from outside the home, have the child approach the school as closely as possible and stay in that proximity as long as possible. The next day, have the student get a little closer and stay a little longer. In some cases, phobic reactions can be worn down with this approach.
5. Permit the child to phone a parent if necessary. Acknowledge the child's physical complaints, but do so in a casual manner.
6. Encourage anxious parents to speak to their child's teacher and principal often so they can see that their fears about the school are unfounded. The parents need to feel the school is a more friendly place.
7. Permit the child to bring a beloved object to school (e.g., a toy or blanket).
8. Schedule high-interest activities at the beginning of the day.
9. Have all school personnel (bus driver, custodian, principal, other teachers) show an active interest in the child.
10. Recognize that illness often intensifies phobic reactions. Keep in touch with the child when the youngster is sick, and repeat many of the preceding strategies when the child returns to school.
11. When the child does not attend school, train the parents not to make home a happy haven. The child should do schoolwork while home, not watch television or indulge in other diversions.
12. If the child with school phobia is also a poor student, provide special academic assistance.
13. Provide a tutor until the child feels ready to return to school.
14. Help the parents realize that part-time school attendance is preferable to no attendance.
15. Help the parents understand that it is not the school program that keeps the child from attendance. As long as they think it is the child's curriculum, teacher, or peers that cause their child's fear, they will not realize that their own overprotectiveness and indulgence have led to the child's avoidance behavior.
16. Advise the parents to let the child do more things independently (e.g., dressing, eating, or going to the store).
17. Help the less protective parent see that the child must not rely so much on the overprotective parent. The less protective parent must become more involved in the child's activities. Realize, however, that the father of a child who is school phobic often overprotects his wife and is afraid to hurt her feelings.
18. Get permission from the family to talk to their physician. Warn the physician that he or she should not express undue concern about the child's or the parents' physical complaints. If the physician seems alarmed, the family is likely to become more anxious.
19. Tell parents not to bribe, reason, coax, plead, or threaten their child regarding school attendance; they must learn to depend on others to handle the situation. When parents leave the child at school, they should depart quickly without communicating their fears to the youngster about what might happen that day in class. If these things are not done, the child will continue to control the parents with his or her conduct.
20. Tell parents not to discuss the next day's potential for success or failure but to assume that their youngster will go to school.
21. Advise school personnel not to become upset or angry about the child's behavior. Such emotions simply make the situation worse. Remember, commonsense procedures do not work well with children who are school phobic.

Children Suffering Home Abuse

Many school youngsters suffer home abuse. Educators must be aware of the many concerns surrounding this anxiety producing issue because, even though school personnel cannot intervene to change home conditions, they must be able to recognize and report signs of child abuse to the proper authorities

Causal Factors

Most abusers are persons who

- are living empty and unfulfilled lives and possess poor self-worth;
- are themselves in need of love and acceptance and cannot tolerate demands children place upon them for affection;
- are quickly frustrated by stress and lose emotional control;
- are not trained to act as parent figures and have not had adequate parent role models to emulate;
- were abused as children.

Types of Child Abuse

Neglect is a form of abuse that can include

- physical abandonment (failure to provide adequate food or shelter or appropriate supervision);
- medical ignoring (failure to provide necessary medical or mental health treatment);
- educational overlook (failure to educate a child or have special educational needs met);
- emotional desertion (failure to attend to a child's emotional needs, failure to provide psychological care, or permitting the child to injure himself or herself with the use of addictive substances).

When describing a situation where a child is apparently neglected, you might want to keep in mind that sometimes cultural values, the standards of community care, and existing poverty can all be factors that contribute to the inability of a family to care for offspring adequately. If the family fails to use offered public resources, then child welfare intervention may become necessary.

Physical abuse pertains to bodily injury (ranging from minor bruises to severe fractures or death) as a result of someone punching, beating, kicking, biting, shaking, throwing, stabbing, choking, slapping, hitting with fist or stick, or burning a child. Any injury resulting from the above described actions is considered abuse whether or not a caretaker intended to hurt a child. Signs of physical abuse that cannot be explained include

- bruises;
- burns;
- fractures;
- abdominal or head injury.

Sexual abuse includes parental or caretaker activities like fondling a child's genitals, penetration, incest, rape, sodomy, indecent exposure, and exploitation through prostitution or the production of pornographic materials. Signs of sexual abuse include

- fearful behavior (nightmares, depression, unusual fears, attempts to run away);
- abdominal pain, bedwetting, urinary tract infection, genital pain or bleeding, sexually transmitted infections;
- extreme forms of sexual conduct inappropriate for child's age.

Emotional abuse is considered to be any pattern of adult behavior that impairs a child's emotional development or sense of self-worth (constant criticism, threats, rejection, and efforts to withhold affection). Emotional abuse is almost always present when other forms of abuse are observed. Signs of emotional abuse include

- sudden changes in self-confidence;
- headaches or stomachaches with no medical cause;
- abnormal fears, increased number of nightmares.

Abuser Motivations

An abuser may be motivated to mistreat a child because he or she is

- aggravated by a youngster who is too troublesome, too different, too stubborn, too ugly, too smart-alecky, too active, or too stupid;
- "at the end of his or her rope" trying to deal with a crying, demanding, or complaining child;
- unable to restrain sexual impulses to molest a child;
- unable to control sadistic impulses to hurt others.

Internal Dialogue of Abuser

The child abuser can make self-excusing statements (in order to justify his or her aggressive behavior) such as:

- "The kid is impossible and has to be disciplined."
- "Sure, I hurt the kid but it's for his (her) own good."
- "My old man knocked me around and it didn't screw me up."
- "The only way to make a man of the little punk is to bust him every now and then."
- "I'll teach the kid not to mouth off to me."
- "Yeah, I fool around with her but she enjoys the action as much as I do."
- "I've got to show these kids who is boss around here."

Children of Divorce

Approximately 50% of marriages in this country end in divorce court. Nobody in a family, it seems, forgets going through a divorce. Children probably suffer the most intense memories.

Residual Feelings of Children

Children of divorcing or divorced parents may suffer severe emotional anxiety whose effects spill over into classrooms and are an inevitable blow to the self-esteem that takes a long time to mend.

They can be affected by

- fears ("Who is going to look after us?");
- sadness ("I'll never see my daddy again");
- anger ("Why did Mommy send Daddy away?");
- grief ("We had to move away and I'll never see my friends again");
- panic ("Daddy's gone and maybe Mommy will soon be gone too");
- self-doubt ("Daddy left because I was a bad person");
- guilt ("I'm the one who made them stop being married").

The kind and degree of emotional upsets depends to some degree on why the parents split up.

Causal Factors Leading to Divorce

Common marital disputes include arguments about

- finances (a real worry to children if they have heard the parents quarrel about money);
- friends (positive and negative adult views of family friends can differ widely from those held by youngsters);
- incompatibly (a confliction predicament between mother and father that is mysterious and incomprehensible to most offspring);
- problems in communication (a state of affairs youngsters can't figure out);
- infidelity (something too horrible for children to contemplate);
- lack of shared interests (of vital interest to the parents but of little concern to offspring);
- differences in religious beliefs (something that can leave children with divided loyalties);
- problems with in-laws (again, a state of affairs that can affect children deeply, particularly if they have established firm interfamilial bonds).

Any of the above reasons can be used as sufficient cause for divorce but, obviously, they are not the only grounds that can be employed. Who knows why people fall out of love? Perhaps one spouse snores too loudly; another chews food with mouth open. Whatever the motivation, though, it's perhaps safe to assume the child spends his or her life wondering what went wrong in the adult relationship.

Father Involvement after Divorce

You may center your investigation around the father's involvement with a child after separation. Research studies indicate the following:

1. A father's active participation in the lives of his children is important to their emotional health and recovery from the trauma of divorce.
2. If the father is not emotionally disturbed, abusive, or alcoholic, then he, the mother, and the children benefit from his continued engagement.
3. The father's predivorce closeness to a child is not always an accurate predictor of his postdivorce involvement. Some become closer (having escaped marital discord); others unexpectedly deteriorate (often because former wives interfere with the attachments).
4. A visiting father is often afraid he will lose his child's love if he does not entertain them enough or buy them suitable presents. The child, in turn, wants to please so the father will come back. Each fears losing the other but this apprehension is usually not expressed—to keep things pleasant, painful issues are avoided.
5. Children who do not see their fathers tend to idealize them or reject them (much depends on how the mother presents his leaving. If she recalls his presence with fond regret, children romanticize him. If she is bitter about his absence, they remain loyal to her and shut the father out.

In my experience as a therapist, postdivorce quarrels center around three main issues:

1. nonpayment of support (leading ex-wives to bar fathers from seeing offspring);
2. rivalry for children's affections (youngsters are used as pawns in this parental struggle for self-esteem. To gain the loyalty of sons or daughters, one or both parents tell the children (explicitly or implicitly) to turn their backs on the other parent);
3. allotted time for visitation (there are many variations on this theme). Father is not given enough time to maintain a firm relationship; when he arrives to pick up the children they are not ready, are not feeling well, are not there because of an emergency, are not happy to see him; father does not return the children on time; one

parent has an adult friend who stays at the home and is seen by the ex-mate to be detrimental to the moral welfare of the youngsters; and the father does not make his visitation agenda clear to the mother and she worries whether the offspring are well supervised or cared for properly.

School Involvement

Counselors should recognize the uselessness of trying to resolve specific issues one by one when the parents angrily refuse to support each other's relationship with the children. Instead, the parents first must be persuaded to work out a mutually supportive parenting arrangement. Such an agreement can often come about when both see that cooperation means (a) support payments are more likely to arrive on time, (b) sharing the parenting burden gives the mother more time for herself and for new relationships, (c) the children are likely to be better adjusted and easier to handle, and (d) the children will benefit when they receive both male and female viewpoints during their developmental years.

Sometimes the guidance worker can best help divorced parents by acting as a sympathetic listener. This approach is advised when one or both parents have stored up so much anger that ordinary counseling cannot proceed until the hostility is vented. If the anger is known to have existed for a long time and does not subside in initial interviews, the parents should be advised to seek professional help.

CHAPTER 5

Excessive Withdrawal

Withdrawal is the unwillingness to respond emotionally to others (Burks, 1977a, 2006a). Children who are excessively withdrawn tend to

- appear shy;
- cover up their feelings;
- show little interest in the activities of others;
- seem standoffish;
- withdraw from group activities.

Withdrawal is a common defense used at one time or another by everyone (Marshall, 1994). As a childhood trait, it may not require attention from adults if the youngster shows no other conduct problems. If, however, a youngster shows many signs of being dependent or anxious or weak physically, the individual is probably exhibiting neurotic manifestations stemming from commonly accepted causes (high ethical standards held by the parents, too many restrictions placed upon the child and an inability to show suitable aggression). Depending upon the degree to which these symptoms are demonstrated, the child and his or her family may need professional assistance beyond what is offered by the school.

If symptoms of withdrawal are strongly associated with signs of poor reality contact, the individual is most likely experiencing a more serious personality disorder. If the youngster is also self-centered, consideration should be given to the possibility that the child is schizophrenic and may need special medical attention as well as therapeutic assistance.

Some children thought to have forms of organic brain dysfunction demonstrate withdrawal symptoms (Burks, 1968b). For such children, attempts to contact peers have ended in frustration; they have abandoned these social approaches and remain isolated.

THEORETICAL BACKGROUND

Behavioral Manifestations

A study by Zimbardo, Pilkonis, and Norwood (1975) indicated that shyness or withdrawal is a normal manifestation in the lives of most people. However, three-fourths of a sample of 800 respondents stated that they did not like being shy. For those whose withdrawal was chronic, 90% disliked the condition. The negative consequences of shyness, according to those experiencing the problem, include

- difficulties with social relationships (making friends, meeting people);
- negative personal feelings (loneliness, isolation, depression);
- problems with being assertive;

- confusion among other people about the shy person's actual assets;
- inability to project one's true feelings (others see the person as being snobbish, unfriendly, bored, ineffective);
- difficulty thinking clearly and communicating properly in the company of others;
- chronic self-consciousness and preoccupation with one's own reactions.

The majority of people reporting these conditions were sufficiently distressed to express a need for therapeutic assistance.

According to Zimbardo et al. (1975), the typical shy, withdrawn person

- is nearly always silent (particularly in the presence of strangers);
- frequently avoids eye contact;
- often tries to avoid meeting other people (takes refuge in reading or some other solitary pursuit);
- tends to avoid taking action;
- speaks quietly.

Although withdrawn people may appear emotionless on the outside, they frequently experience unwanted physiological symptoms, such as blushing, increased heart rate, profuse perspiring, and nervous stomach.

The principal difference between the self-evaluation of a shy and nonshy personality lies in what the person believes is the cause of shyness. The nonshy individual tends to suppose that external events lead to shyness, while the shy person thinks shyness is a negative element of the personality. Further, the outgoing individual sees withdrawal as something normal, impersonal, and not too serious. The withdrawn person, on the other hand, perceives the condition as being aberrant, personal, and painful (Swallow, 2003).

Zimbardo et al. (1975) believed that the extremely shy person suffers from a demanding conscience (superego). They liken the role of the conscience to that of a guard who constantly enforces unpleasant restrictions. The shy person is the prisoner who meekly follows the rigid orders, much to the contempt of the guard, who knows that the prisoner wants to engage in freer behavior, knows how to do so (i.e., has the ability to perform), but cannot bring himself or herself to act spontaneously.

Withdrawal as an Innate Trait

For many years, psychologists clung to the idea that the personalities of shy individuals were formed largely by the environment into which they were born. This notion has been challenged by the social scientist J. D. Kagan and his associates, who found that 15% of the population is born inheriting particular behavioral traits, such as extreme shyness, that remain consistent in their expression throughout life (Azar, 1995b). In short, the characteristics appear to be basic, inherited components of the temperament. Traits like dependence, aggression, dominance, and competitiveness do not remain consistent in their expression from early childhood to adulthood. However, one trait, which Kagan calls "behavioral inhibition," does remain unchanged in its expression over the years. Kagan found these youngsters to be more than usually tense and overresponsive to stress, even when the stress was mild.

Shy toddlers are quite common—they cling to their mothers and fathers and venture timidly into unfamiliar surroundings. When they encounter strangers, they tend to freeze, become silent, and stare. Until they have assessed a situation they seem visibly tense—almost overly alert. Parents of such youngsters invariably rationalize this type of behavior (e.g., "My child has always been like that" or "I guess it's just my child's way").

Kagan's studies delineate other aspects found in the life histories of chronically shy, withdrawn children. Because emotional circuits in the nervous systems of these youngsters are more easily aroused, they can be described as having a form of stage fright—when placed in an unfamiliar situation they become apprehensive and uncertain. They examine the environment with great care and usually take a long time before talking. Because they are so cautious, they also tend to do more poorly on some learning tasks, either leaning toward impulsivity—together with wrong answers—or taking too long a time to think over replies, which come too late to be effective.

Kagan and coworkers found that timid youngsters, as a group, tended to have been more colicky, constipated, and irritable as infants than were outgoing children. Many demonstrated allergies that continued into later childhood. Most of the uninhibited children he studied were allergy free. These findings reinforce the belief that withdrawn traits in shy youngsters have an inherited origin.

Kagan is careful to point out that there is nothing unchangeable about the early behavior patterns shown by socially inhibited toddlers. Just because nature happens to endow a newborn with a temperamental leaning does not mean that the environment cannot alter it profoundly. Supportive parenting can alter outcomes significantly. From interviews with parents who helped their children overcome shyness, Kagan found that most of these parents encouraged other children to come into their homes and encouraged their own children to cope with stressful situations. Kagan advises parents of very shy children to recognize the problem early in the lives of the youngsters, to protect them from as much stress as possible, and to help them learn social coping skills. Many people have overcome shy beginnings. Such famous performers as Barbara Walters, Johnny Carson, and Carol Burnett started life, by their own admission, as very shy people. All came up winners.

Withdrawal as a Learned Attribute

A child may be unable to communicate with others for one or more of the following reasons:

1. The child cannot derive love and affection from the home, the child feels a sense of rejection from outsiders. Withdrawal is a reflection of the child's lack of self-confidence.
2. The child has not had the opportunity to associate with other youngsters and so lacks social skills.
3. The child has not been allowed to show self-expression and take independent actions.
4. The child has not been allowed to meet and overcome ordinary frustrations that are dealt with by most children.
5. The child lives in an impoverished home or neighborhood and has developed feelings of inferiority.
6. The child has undergone an anxiety-producing, frightening experience, and rumination about this unpleasant event has left the child with little energy for socializing.

DIAGNOSIS

Like all defense mechanisms, withdrawal is a device to reduce anxiety. If testing results indicate a problem with isolation, the investigator should diagnose possible threats to the shy child's ego, remove these sources of fear as much as possible and help the child develop normally by providing opportunities to communicate with others. If there are many other negative behavior symptoms, the child and his or her family should be referred to a professional counseling agency.

Withdrawal, or the refusal to make emotional contact with others, may range from a normal manifestation to a pathological one. Two factors must be considered when judging the severity of a child's withdrawal: (a) the child's environment, and (b) the nature and severity of other negative traits shown by the youngster.

Outward Manifestations

The following questions are designed to help practitioners decide whether withdrawal symptoms should cause concern.

Is the child a member of a disadvantaged group? Many disadvantaged children characteristically show withdrawal because they feel inadequate. Mexican American children tend to show this defensive trait (Burks, 1977a);

so do other minority-group children. If a child's withdrawal matches that of peers, such tendencies may have little meaning, particularly if the child socializes well with other minority-group members and demonstrates few emotional problems.

Does the child have a language barrier? Children who cannot understand and express the language of the majority culture can be truly isolated. Because of this language barrier, many children appear more intellectually handicapped than they actually are. Adults often do not know how to help them. Withdrawal symptoms may not be serious, however, if the child demonstrates other signs of emotional health and socializes well with others in his or her language group.

Are the withdrawal symptoms temporary or long-term? Has a situational conflict arisen that might cause the youngster to isolate himself or herself? In general, isolation from others is a more serious problem if it has been shown to exist for a long period and if the child does not respond readily to positive changes in the environment (e.g., being given extra attention or help in schoolwork).

Has the child been separated from others because of sickness, a handicap, or another reason? The youngster who has been separated from playmates or classmates for an extended period has suffered an inevitable interruption in social development. Living skills acquired through interaction with peers are among the most important lessons of childhood. Children know this intuitively, and that is why friends are held in such high esteem and why the lack of friends becomes a matter of true despair for a child. The inability to share interests, feelings, possessions, and thoughts with age-mates may result in the child's feeling depressed, although the classic symptoms of depression as seen in adults are rarely observed in children. Children express their inwardly directed aggression in exaggerated but unwarranted feelings of inferiority: "Everybody hates me," "I'm stupid," and so on. Apparently, the child is reflecting views he or she feels others have of him or her. The sad child appears to be withdrawn. This type of child needs attention from adults.

Has the child suffered an upsetting or frightening experience? Many children have experienced their parents' divorce. Divorce is nearly always an emotionally frustrating experience for youngsters, inflicting anguish in ways not always well understood by adults. Adults' mature ego structures help them process the pain of separation more readily, but children's defense systems are inadequate to deal with the problem. Loyalty conflicts, feelings of loss (children may experience the absence of a parent as a death in the family), and guilt (more often than not, the child blames himself or herself for the parental breakup) can haunt the youngster for a long time. It is not uncommon for youngsters to become preoccupied, unhappy, and withdrawn during and after a divorce. Feeling unworthy, they isolate themselves from others. The death of a close family member can also be a frightening experience, causing some children to ruminate about the mysteries of life and death. Their worried conduct can make them seem withdrawn.

Does the withdrawn child demonstrate other unusual symptoms? A schizophrenic disorder may be indicated when the following traits are shown (Burks, 1977a; Remschmidt, 2001):

- a poor ability to relate to reality;
- unusual self-centeredness;
- bizarre perceptions;
- lack of interest in the environment;
- immature interests;
- excessive emotional response to opinions and actions of others;
- irritability when withdrawal is challenged;
- excessive fantasy life.

A neurotic complaint may be indicated when withdrawal is associated with:

- overdependence;
- poor self-esteem;

- unusual anxiety;
- evidence of suffering (possible depression, self-punishing conduct);
- self-blame.

An attention deficit disability may be indicated when withdrawal symptoms are accompanied by the following characteristics (Burks, 1977a, 1999, 2006a):

- short attention span;
- restlessness and over activity;
- poor judgment and impulsive action;
- low frustration tolerance and irritability;
- poor perceptual and conceptual abilities (reflected in serious academic difficulties);
- defective memory;
- poor muscular coordination.

A social disability may be indicated when interaction with others is judged inadequate. In American society, children are viewed as socially competent if they tend to have the characteristics listed in the column on the right side of table 5.1.

The parent or teacher who evaluates a child must take the child's age into consideration—that is, social actions should be compared to those of children of a similar age. For instance, most toddlers act impulsively, and this kind of behavior is accepted from them. Older children, however, are expected to be more self-controlled.

Inward Manifestations

It is often helpful to explore the inner world of withdrawn children in order to pinpoint attitudes that obstruct adequate social adjustment. I constructed the Child Shyness inventory (see figure 5.1) to help counselors uncover feelings of frustration in shy youngsters.

Most children don't mind filling out the Child Shyness inventory; however, a few do. If the child resists, don't push him or her to complete it. Other youngsters—those who are very anxious to please their parents—indicate no problems in any area. Accept their replies with no comment. Parents of withdrawn children may also benefit from completing the inventory for themselves; many shy youngsters have at least one parent who is also withdrawn.

Social Competency Scale

Not responsible	Somewhat responsible	Very responsible
Very suggestible	Somewhat suggestible	Very independent
Very unfriendly	Somewhat friendly	Very friendly
Very resistive	Somewhat cooperative	Very cooperative
Very aimless	Somewhat focused	Very focused
Very impulsive	Somewhat controlled	Very controlled
Very unhelpful	Somewhat helpful	Very helpful
Very silent	Somewhat talkative	Very talkative
Avoids playing games	Sometimes plays games	Enjoys playing games

Table 5.1.

CHILD SHYNESS INVENTORY

Harold F. Burks, Ph.D.

Put a check mark in the column that tells how you usually feel about the following statements.

	Not True	Sometimes True	Often True
1. I don't feel that I can get anybody to do what I want.	☐	☐	☐
2. I don't feel that I can change things that happen around me.	☐	☐	☐
3. I often think things will turn out bad.	☐	☐	☐
4. I often feel as if I have done some bad things.	☐	☐	☐
5. I think other people look better than I do.	☐	☐	☐
6. Most people are bigger and stronger than I am.	☐	☐	☐
7. Most other people are better at sports than I am.	☐	☐	☐
8. I often think other families have more money than mine does.	☐	☐	☐
9. I often think others are smarter than I am.	☐	☐	☐
10. I often think I am too old for my friends.	☐	☐	☐
11. I often think I am too young for my friends.	☐	☐	☐
12. I don't understand the words that people around me use.	☐	☐	☐
13. I feel terrible if I have to stand up and talk in front of others.	☐	☐	☐
14. When I try to talk to others, I seem to stumble around and can't say what I want to say.	☐	☐	☐
15. I feel I could do some things better than other people, but I can't seem to let others know how good I am so I lose out on good jobs.	☐	☐	☐
16. I think other people believe I am standoffish but that's because if I got too friendly they might find out what a dope I really am.	☐	☐	☐
17. Sex is a subject that makes me very uncomfortable.	☐	☐	☐
18. I worry because I am shy.	☐	☐	☐
19. I don't like myself because I am shy.	☐	☐	☐
20. I can only trust a few people so I guess that is why I have few friends.	☐	☐	☐
21. I would rather do things on my own—like read, paint, draw, listen to music, or just think—than do things with others.	☐	☐	☐
22. I think other people may be laughing at me or making fun of me.	☐	☐	☐
23. If I tried to be a leader, other people would think I was a joke.	☐	☐	☐
24. If I said something good about myself, people wouldn't pay any attention.	☐	☐	☐
25. Sometimes in situations I don't like I get sweaty hands, or a pounding heart, or my face blushes, or I feel panicky.	☐	☐	☐

Figure 5.1.

The Child Shyness inventory can be used to help identify timid youngsters who

- compare themselves unfavorably with others;
- suffer pangs of shame, anxiety, guilt, and pessimism;
- cannot muster enough ego strength to be assertive;
- possess poor social skills.

Child Self-Identification

The basic difficulty most shy people face is the notion that they are somehow deficient and that because of their supposed inadequacy, they do not measure up to most other people. Their fears tend to become self-fulfilling prophesies when they do try to face up to others—their demeanor is often timid and ineffective. As a result, others can be unresponsive. The shy individual then feels truly rejected.

Youngsters who feel inferior have to contend with the fact that they must continually compare themselves favorably or unfavorably through interactions with significant people—family members, teachers, and other children. Of course, such estimations may or may not be in tune with other people's actual perceptions of the child.

The Child Shyness inventory covers several areas of possible comparison. The answers to statements 5 (appearance), 6 (strength), 7 (sports ability), 8 (family financial status), 9 (mental ability), 10 and 11 (age), and 12 (understanding language) can all be used to gain some estimate of how children feel about themselves in these areas.

Home. Adults who want to discuss any of the following topics with a child should proceed carefully and uncritically and take plenty of time to listen to the youngster's comments.

1. Are you being compared unfavorably to your brothers and sisters?
2. Are you being treated differently from others in the family?
3. Do the other kids in the neighborhood like you?
4. Do the people in the neighborhood say anything bad about you?
5. Does your mother or father expect too much of you?
6. Does your mother or father get cross with you too much?
7. Do other family members put you down too much?
8. Do other family members listen to you when you want to say something?

Talking over the child's feelings is not enough. The youngster must feel, and learn from experience, that revealing confidences to an adult will result in some kind of positive action to remedy his or her problems. Such action can include:

- talking with individuals who make the youngster feel unworthy;
- rearranging the physical environment so the child feels less threatened;
- discussing the child's perceived differences and the possibility that they may not be accurate;
- following up the original interview with another talk to see how the child feels.

As a matter of fact, if the adult and the child take the Child Shyness inventory together and enjoy a successful experience, that alone is a positive contribution to the child's feelings of self-worth. One of the basic ways for adults to show concern for children is to demonstrate a desire to become involved in their activities and to have conversations with them. Interactive talk with a powerful adult authority figure who is warm and attentive and responds in meaningful ways conveys a significant message to children about their value. That message is even more powerful if the chosen topics are those that interest the youngsters most.

School. Since school experiences can play an important part in the life of a shy and withdrawn child, it behooves the clinician to investigate the educational environment. Visit the school. Explore the following questions with the youngster's teacher.

1. Is the child a newcomer to any groups?
2. Is the child older or younger than classmates?
3. Is the child able to keep up with others in classwork?
4. Is the child, in any way, being rejected by other students (in the classroom or on the playground)?
5. Is the child being bullied by others?
6. Do others listen to the child?
7. Would it be hard for the child to break into cliques of popular children?
8. Does the child have any mannerisms that cause others to avoid him or her?
9. If the child is doing something that offends, has he or she been taught to understand the effect of this behavior on others?
10. Has the child been instructed to understand the needs of others?
11. Is the child sitting apart from friends in classrooms?
12. Is help available to the child from more popular students?
13. Is the child dressed in a manner acceptable to peers?
14. Does the child understand the best ways to make friends?
15. Would it help the child to have a parent assist in the classroom?

If the child has had a long history of peer rejection, he or she has probably come to feel a profound sense of separateness from other students and, in all likelihood, this feeling cannot be changed for the better in the present situation. Instead, consideration should be given to placing the youngster in another school setting.

If the child is largely ignored, not rejected, the counselor and the teacher should discuss specific steps that might ensure the child more attention from others. For instance, the youngster might be encouraged to try out various seating placements in the classroom until a satisfactory one is found. The student may need some suggestions on the best ways to approach others to ask for assistance. Those children receiving no classroom help from other students may need more teacher support.

Identifying Children with Shame, Anxiety, Guilt, and Pessimism

The shy child who is afflicted with a negative self-image needs help to become more self-confident. This help cannot be provided by confronting the child, pleading with the youngster, or trying to bolster the child with praise. Such efforts are generally not effective for at least two reasons:

1. The parents have not made any real effort to change their own conduct, which produced the child's shyness in the first place.
2. Such approaches can seem artificial and demanding to the child, who is wary of overly critical adults who set unattainable high standards.

I have found that it is usually the mother who plays the pivotal role in the development of shyness in children. She tends to block normal manifestations of aggressiveness by keeping anger, resentment, and rebellion to a minimum. The mother, like her children, shows traits of withdrawal. Sometimes the father is shy, but his influence tends to be less significant.

The following parental approaches are crucial in the development of withdrawn behavior in children. They are employed by many parents of shy, withdrawn children—parents who sincerely believe that the techniques and the reasons for their use are valid in the eyes of most people. But these methods must be questioned if they produce socially inadequate youngsters.

Unusual rigidity in the establishment of rules. Parents tend to suppose that

- children should be strongly admonished for dereliction of duties;
- good children seldom, if ever, deviate from regulations;
- parents should act as perfect models who never make errors.

Excessive use of discipline. Parents tend to believe that

- they should spend much time explaining what is right and wrong to their children;
- they should be very vigilant in crushing signs of rebellion in children;
- unusual behavior in children (like sexual experimentation) is reprehensible and deserves harsh parental reaction;
- lack of discipline will spoil children, causing them to become weak adults.

Excessive use of dominating and critical approaches. Parents tend to have the opinion that

- children should never start activities without parental permission;
- they should hover over children so that nothing will go amiss;
- good children are quiet children;
- a good parent should always be aware of what children are thinking and doing.

Poor ability to demonstrate affection. Parents tend to believe that

- family members are better off if they keep strong feelings to themselves;
- playing with children too much will spoil them;
- work, not pleasure, should always be the number one priority;
- showing children affection might cause them to grow up with an unsuitable, soft personality;
- holding grudges or being unforgiving when children misbehave is a suitable discipline policy;
- children will know they are loved even in the absence of signs of affection.

Use of isolation. Parents tend to suppose that

- children should be isolated from the family group when they misbehave;
- adults should avoid other adults as much as possible;
- it's not necessary to stress the importance of school attendance;
- it's not important to have close, supporting relationships with other families;
- it's best not to invite other children to the home;
- it's okay if adult family members exclude themselves from most activities.

Overprotectiveness. Parents tend to believe that

- children really can't do well unless adults actively assist;
- children can avoid most misfortunes if parents closely supervise them;
- children should be taken by adults to social functions, even when most other youngsters of the same age go on their own;

- good parents should always sacrifice for the welfare of children even if the children can fend for themselves;
- children need constant praise;
- children will have everlasting gratitude for parents who always do unasked-for things for them.

Azar (1995a) pointed out that shy people see themselves as socially inept and are painfully self-conscious when interacting with others (probably as a result of early family training). Parents and children possess inaccurate self-concepts that must be changed: The parents (many of whom are withdrawn themselves) erroneously believe their child management procedures will produce independent individuals; the children believe they are helpless to control events and blame themselves for failure while crediting others for success.

Group therapy for adults has proved helpful, according to Azar (1995a), particularly role-playing. When group members act out independent and assertive roles, they are instructed to try their newly learned skills in real-life situations. Some older children also benefit from group therapy. It is important to choose a proper therapist for this kind of clinical work. A cool, distant, or overly directive clinician is likely to lose shy patients. A more suitable therapist may need to be exceptionally warm and supportive.

In my experience, many shy children change for the better when they are placed in classrooms with friendly and encouraging teachers. They also tend to improve when the parents employ more realistic child-raising procedures.

Identifying Children Who Need to Be More Assertive

Healthy assertion—the ability to take positive, purposeful, and goal-directed actions—serves the purpose of self-protection. Assertive children are able to (a) resist unreasonable demands ("No, I won't give you the crayons; I still need them"), (b) evaluate disagreements in logical ways ("Yes, you may be right; I'll think it over"), and (c) offer solutions to disagreements ("Okay, I'll use the crayons for a minute and then you can use them").

Research (Marshall, 1994; Rakos, 1991) has shown that grade school children who fail to adopt assertive behavior tend to be rejected by classmates and disliked by adults. The ability to express themselves and exert some control over others helps youngsters develop self-esteem.

Typically, the passive youngster will show the following characteristics:

1. Poor capacity to speak up for legitimate rights. For example, the child is unable to respond or stand up for himself or herself when teased.
2. Inability to establish a legitimate place in conversations and discussions. Others just ignore the child.
3. Poor ability to initiate beneficial conversations with others. For example, the child refuses to ask for needed help.
4. Inability to resist being drawn into unpleasant situations or to demand that they stop. For example, the child is told to take sides in a fight that is of no interest to the youngster.

The inability to be appropriately assertive can have both immediate and long-term effects: lost opportunities, unwanted and potentially harmful physical stress, self-doubt that can interfere with productive work, and resentment and anger that eventually may be expressed in unproductive ways (lonely withdrawal, substance abuse, or inappropriate emotional outbursts).

The following techniques are applicable to the treatment of shy, unassertive children:

- Illustrate the disadvantages of passive behavior in discussions with the child. Stress its fruitlessness—how it leaves the unassertive child feeling upset and gives others a poor image of the withdrawn person.
- Train the child to know what to say and do in specific situations (how to resist unwelcome suggestions, how to break into conversations, how to take the lead in discussion groups, and so on).
- Help the child deal with the anxiety that goes along with assertiveness. For instance, the adult might employ some behavior rehearsal like reading from a script. Role-playing that prepares the youngster for a coming event has proved useful. Review and replace counterproductive beliefs the child may hold about assertiveness.

- Provide the youngster with practice situations that require assertiveness. The child can employ (a) self-instruction ("I can do this. Everything will turn out okay. I know more about this than anyone else"), (b) rational thinking ("Nobody really cares if I don't do well"), (c) relaxation techniques ("I will take deep breaths"), and (d) reinforcement from others ("It's good that Mom can help me out").

INTERVENTION STRATEGIES

Zimbardo et al. (1975) believed that simple shyness and withdrawal can be treated successfully with therapies that combine (a) guidance procedures to help the person know that many others suffer with the same problem, (b) modeling procedures to put the individual in the company of those who are less shy, (c) practice in social skills, such as contrived group experiences, and (d) assertiveness training. It is their belief that shyness is not generally a personal problem but is essentially a social difficulty brought on by cultural norms that overemphasize competition, individual success, and the acceptance of personal responsibility for failure.

Some young children tend to fear novelty, and if the caretaker (parent, teacher) deals insensitively with the child's responses to novel situations, the child may become clingy, dependent, socially avoidant, and reluctant to separate from the caretaker (Schwarz, 1979). Adults should carefully evaluate the temperamental differences among these children. The skill and patience of the caretaker are the principal factors in determining whether such children will develop cooperative interaction with others. Schwarz was careful to point out that this cooperative interaction is the all-important goal. If the caretaker meets antagonism with antagonism, the youngster may withdraw or intensify his or her resistance toward cooperation (thereby increasing the likelihood of a future conduct disorder occurrence).

Thus, it can be seen that the response of caretakers (primarily the parents) to the socially avoidant behavior of a fearful young child may exacerbate this conduct, ameliorate it, or leave it unchanged. Predictable parental styles and gentle encouragement may build the youngster's tolerance of separation and novelty. On the other hand, the trauma of unexpected abandonment by parents in strange situations may intensify anxiety, and parental overindulgence may crystallize the child's avoidance patterns and lead to neurotic adjustment styles.

Generally, a secure, cooperative relationship with the adult caretaker is predictive of future peer adjustment but it is no guarantee of smooth sailing throughout childhood, since this harmony can be disturbed at any level of development. As Schwarz (1979) pointed out, unrelenting criticism, shame, and embarrassment will move the child in the direction of social avoidance, and unreasonable and painful punishment will move the child toward antagonism. The longer a child practices a negative behavioral style, the more difficult it will be to change the conduct.

Techniques for School Personnel

The following approaches may be used to assist withdrawn youngsters:

1. Arrange for a parent conference to determine whether the child's withdrawal is

   - situational (e.g., shown only at school) or pervasive;
   - temporary or long lasting;
   - characteristic of other family members;
   - a cause of concern for the family.

2. Encourage and reinforce even the smallest signs of extroverted behavior.
3. Praise any efforts by the child to communicate with others.
4. Refuse to allow the student to isolate himself or herself in the classroom.
5. Refrain from criticizing the child.

6. Reinforce any efforts the child makes to become involved in classroom activities, but do not push the child into these activities.

7. Allow the young child to bring favorite objects from home. If holding an object is comforting to the child, do not take it away.

8. Permit the child to express anxieties. Do not play down these worries.

9. Involve the student in small-group activities.

10. Encourage the child to participate in free discussions and creative play, but let the involvement emerge spontaneously.

11. In the classroom, allow the child to demonstrate skills that have been discovered through diagnosis.

12. Encourage the youngster to practice answers ahead of time. On schedule, ask him or her to state these answers in front of classmates. Do not ask the child unexpected questions.

13. Arrange to have the withdrawn student read a story to a classroom of younger children. To ensure success, give the child class time to practice.

14. With permission from the school office secretary, permit the student who can handle the job to help with lunchtime office duty (answering the phone, taking messages, collecting milk money, etc.). If needed, an older, more mature student can act as a teaching model.

15. Permit the child to sit next to a student he or she likes. Ask that student to be extra friendly to the shy youngster.

16. Encourage young, shy children to communicate with peers through the use of classroom telephones. At first, the withdrawn youngster may remain out of sight of classmates.

17. Arrange class time for puppet play, role-playing behind masks, and games that so engross the withdrawn child that he or she forgets to be self-conscious.

18. Include older withdrawn students in peer-group counseling sessions.

19. Encourage other students to praise the shy child. Place the youngster among friendly peers.

20. Assign a buddy to the withdrawn, recent-immigrant child. This friend must speak English fluently and be able to help the immigrant youngster learn local customs and the nature of school activities.

Techniques for Parents

According to Jenkins (1973), the most commonly seen withdrawn child is overinhibited and shy. Jenkins identified the following neurotic symptoms displayed by this type of individual:

- exclusiveness;
- underactivity (listlessness);
- anxiety or worry (sometimes);
- discouragement or depression;
- absence of close friendships;
- dependency;
- immaturity (particularly when young);
- sensitivity or timidity.

Jenkins pointed to the pivotal role of the mother in the development of this pathology. The mother blocks normal manifestations of aggression in the child. It follows then that any treatment of the child must include retraining of the mother regarding her attitudes toward child rearing.

Other family dynamics are commonly encountered in the clinical treatment of the withdrawn child and his or her parents. The mother typically demonstrates many or most of the traits mentioned in the preceding list. In unspoken ways, the mother's ego status is of paramount concern to other members of the family, who make constant efforts not to upset her. Manifestations of resentment, anger, or rebellion are kept to a minimum. The mother perceives her own emotional defenses to be fragile. She fears that clinical treatment might bring out unwanted disclosures. The role of the father tends to be a diminished one. As an unimportant figure, he cannot command the loyalty from his children that would allow him to wean them from dependence on their mother.

The family with these characteristics requires skillful and patient counseling. The mother, especially if she has had an inadequate and uneasy relationship with her own mother, cannot be adequately treated until she perceives the counselor to be trustworthy and nurturing (characteristics of a good parent). If she can transfer some of her loyalties to the counselor, then the father and children may feel free enough to express previously withheld needs and resentments and, eventually, to break away from their unhealthy dependence on her.

Occasionally, a parent may wish to investigate his or her own behavior in order to become a better role model. If the counselor has a good relationship with that parent, it may be helpful to administer the Parent Shyness inventory (see figure 5.2), which can be introduced as follows:

> Would you like to change your conduct in order to be a better role model for your child? Of course, it would be easy to urge you to be more open and gregarious, but that kind of change is difficult to attain when you've spent a lifetime hiding your gifts. Instead, why don't we look at specific behaviors often employed by shy people who are open to change? Rate yourself on this Parent Shyness inventory. It is composed of items describing adult behavior that, with thought and effort, can be modified.

It would be naive to think that any adult with long-standing social difficulties could take this inventory, agree with some of the items, and make fundamental personality changes overnight. That is not possible. Some individuals, however, can become more outgoing over time by (a) deciding they no longer want to put up with the misery of being in an emotional prison, (b) realizing that their inferiority complex, which was derived from the actions of others, has nothing to do with any actual personal deficiencies, and (c) deciding to reverse defeatist behavior patterns such as fleeing and hiding.

In my opinion, a more promising approach involves the shy parent working in association with a withdrawn son or daughter. The parent might go to the youngster and say, "Look, I have trouble getting along with others. Could you help me? Maybe we could do something together that would help both of us get more friends." The parent should not go to the child with the notion that the youngster is the only one with a difficulty.

Together, the parent and child can do the following:

1. List all the good qualities they see in themselves (being good listeners, being imaginative, being good artists, or whatever).
2. Discuss how these good qualities are seen (or not seen) by others.
3. If the child seems ready, they can ask other members of the family if they recognize the good qualities that each feels he or she has.
4. Discuss the personality traits that each would like to have (the list may be somewhat different for each; the parent should not press choices on the child). Talk about people who seem to have these traits and how such people influence others.
5. Practice being more assertive with one another. Start with a funny situation. For example, one puts on two different-colored socks. The other one has to be firm and insist the socks be changed. From there they go on to comment how each of them could improve their appearance by dressing better, and so on.
6. Talk about bothersome people. Discuss what is irritating about these individuals. One can pretend to be a provoking person, while the other practices standing up to that person. Make a game of this exercise.
7. Practice making eye contact. Stare at the other person for as long as possible. The winner is the one who can do it for the longest time.
8. If either dislikes talking to groups, that person should rehearse a speech and practice giving it.
9. If talking to strangers is a problem, rehearse things like saying hello, asking for directions, saying thank you, and so on.

PARENT SHYNESS INVENTORY

Harold F. Burks, Ph.D.

Put a check mark in the column that tells how you usually feel about the following statements.

	Not True	Sometimes True	Often True
1. I give up easily when things get difficult.	☐	☐	☐
2. In front of others, I often use phrases like, "What's the use?" "That's life," or "I really don't care."	☐	☐	☐
3. I could never tell my parents what I really wanted from them or talk about some of my unpleasant feelings.	☐	☐	☐
4. I seldom make eye contact with others.	☐	☐	☐
5. I usually ignore my true feelings and give in to others.	☐	☐	☐
6. I hardly ever meet the standards I set for myself.	☐	☐	☐
7. When I get frustrated, I become very emotional, even depressed.	☐	☐	☐
8. Criticism upsets me very much.	☐	☐	☐
9. I very seldom take risks.	☐	☐	☐
10. I usually run away from bad situations.	☐	☐	☐
11. I have great trouble fighting for my rights.	☐	☐	☐
12. I have a lot of trouble accepting compliments.	☐	☐	☐
13. I guess I really don't think very much of myself.	☐	☐	☐
14. Most people are more powerful than I am.	☐	☐	☐
15. In my imagination I keep thinking of things that will go wrong.	☐	☐	☐
16. I have real trouble initiating conversations.	☐	☐	☐
17. I hate being the center of attention.	☐	☐	☐

Figure 5.2.

10. Practice ways to remember names.

11. Practice giving and graciously accepting compliments from each other.

12. Practice keeping cool when put down or insulted. Rehearse and employ responses like, "I don't believe you are correct," or "Excuse me; I must leave now," or "I think what you said is just silly."

13. Review personal standards. Ask whether the standards are too high and whether either person is a perfectionist. Come to an agreement about what is acceptable to others as well as to each other.

14. Talk about getting mad at yourself for doing something dumb with other people. Examine ways each could have acted better.

15. Pick out a person he or she would like to impress. Decide what each needs to do to gain the person's attention (like becoming more knowledgeable about a topic, saying interesting things, becoming more complimentary, looking more attractive, or whatever).

16. Pretend one of you is very shy. The other has to practice concentrating on making the shy person feel at ease and overcome the shyness.

Most shy children enjoy getting personal help with social problems, apparently because their awkwardness causes them pain. I remember one little withdrawn girl who attended a number of counseling sessions with her mother. We discussed how the preceding exercises could be employed in the home with the girl and her mother (who was also timid). Both agreed the program sounded interesting. Over a period of weeks they practiced the suggestions and came to my office periodically to discuss their gratifying results. The most beneficial consequences for the mother were that she felt closer to and more at ease with her daughter.

CHAPTER 6

Excessive Dependency

Dependency is the exaggerated need to gain support from others. Children with high scores on measurements of dependency (Burks 1977a, 2006a) tend to

- want to be guided about;
- crave constant commendations;
- hang on grown-ups;
- demand help from others;
- be excessively dutiful.

Many children who are inhibited and show neurotic signs also tend to be dependent. They may demonstrate symptoms of poor self-esteem, withdrawal, anxiousness, and emotional distress. For many younger children, dependency has been associated with immature patterns (Burks, 1977a, 1977b). Teachers describe these unready youngsters as showing problems in attention deficits, poor coordination, academic difficulties, poor self-esteem, and poor physical stamina. Dependent older students, at the seventh and eighth grade levels, can show dependency traits associated with patterns of poor social conformity and rebelliousness. These older individuals often have guilt conflicts; they may be trying to break out of their dependency status by being rebellious.

Clarizio and McCoy (1976) and Bornstein (1993) cited the following signs of the overly dependent child:

- demands help and rarely shows initiative; typically turns to adults, not to other children, for assistance;
- demands attention from adults by insisting they observe and comment upon his or her activities;
- seeks physical contact with others by clinging to them;
- shows undue passivity; often sits alone and ignores classroom activities;
- seeks approval and appears overly sensitive to the attitudes of others;
- tends to be overly obedient;
- tends to become sad or downcast if left alone.

Other investigations of dependency in children (Baumrind, 1968; Burks, 2006b; Hartup & Smothergill, 1966) have shown that, compared to most other children, those who are not self-reliant tend to be more guilt-ridden, less able to resist temptation, more selfish and self-centered, and less able to suppress urges for immediate gratification.

THEORETICAL BACKGROUND

Etiology

Attachment to others, commonly referred to as dependency, is a necessary and important human trait. During the first year of life a dramatic change takes place in the baby—there is a great advance in the quality of human relationships. It occurs because of the bond between infant and mother, which serves as a prototype for later relationships. The youngster who develops a secure sense of trust can later deal effectively with personal anxiety (i.e., not fear the loss of others too much), develop a strong moral sense (i.e., wish to please others by conforming), and express aggression in acceptable ways (i.e., strive to achieve because the approval of others is believed to be gained by personal effort). The early, intense dependency of the infant on adults cannot be allowed to continue into later years; such continued dependency would eventually interfere with the individual's ability to function autonomously. For that reason, dependency in older individuals is thought to be an undesirable trait.

According to Wetzell (1978) and Garbarino (1992) unusual dependency stems from the negative effects of an early, unsustaining environment. Wetzell held that the unloved individual is left with a deep-seated need to seek reassurance from environmental sources. However, the theory does not seem to explain all forms of dependency. Parker and Liscombe (1980), for instance, described hypochondriasis as a form of adult dependency, which apparently arises from a parent's overconcern about illnesses that occur in the child's early life. Apparently, both the neglectful or rejecting parent and the oversolicitous parent can produce unwanted symptoms of dependency in their children. The common thread appears to be parental aggression: The neglectful-rejecting parent expresses hostility toward the child openly, the overcaring parent, in more hidden ways (Kessler, 1966).

Levy (1943) studied the relationship of dependency in children to maternal overprotectiveness. He identified two main patterns of maternal behavior that contribute to dependency:

1. Overprotective and overindulgent conduct. If the mother shows these character traits, the youngster tends to be selfish, tyrannical, and demanding and to seek constant attention, affection, and service. When frustrated, the child reacts with assault and rage.
2. Dominating and overprotective behavior. Children of mothers with these traits tend to react with anxiety, shyness, fear, and submissiveness. Levy found that fathers are rarely overprotective, but when they are, the overprotectiveness is generally directed at a daughter rather than a son.

An inconsistent parental response to a child's demands for help may also contribute to the formation of child dependency patterns. Sears, Maccoby, and Levin (1957) found that parents who irritably reject their children's requests for assistance, then eventually succumb to these demands, produce the most dependent children; the children must attend to the parents' reactions carefully because the responses are so unpredictable.

The counselor should explore the possibility that the dependent child has suffered a serious emotional loss—such as the death of a loved one—that may have left the youngster with unresolved fears.

Finally, the counselor should investigate the child's role in the family constellation. Is the child seen as the baby of the family, someone who must be protected, cuddled, and helped? Youngest children are most often chosen to play out this disabling function. Conley (1980) explored the relationship of the so-called youngest child syndrome to the later formation of an alcoholic personality. He believes that early infantilization patterns may also be associated with drug dependency.

Types of Dependency

There are two types of dependency:

1. task dependency—the inability to work independently;
2. emotional dependency—the inability to maintain healthy emotional independence.

An issue of frequent concern to parents and teachers is the tendency of some children to seek help from others rather than to find solutions on their own. I believe such students benefit most from management systems that encourage them to work independently whenever possible and to make their own decisions. They should be given a model to follow and should be assigned tasks that are within their ability to complete. Direct teaching methods, along with behavior modifying programs, work hand in hand to instill confidence and encourage independent performance. The gradual fading out of support systems is preferable to abrupt withdrawal.

Emotional dependency, on the other hand, is a disorder that often requires individual or group therapy treatment. It is a complex disability, sometimes accompanied by task-dependent behavior. Excessive emotional dependency will be discussed extensively later in this chapter.

Psychodynamic Theories of Dependency

The diagnostic significance of symptoms of dependency cannot be fully understood by observable manifestations alone. The symptom pattern must also fit some theoretical postulates of personality development to determine whether the behavior traits of the individual match known conditions that presume either normality or probable pathology.

Symbiosis. How can an interdependent relationship be evaluated to determine whether it is healthy or noxious? First, a determination must be made about the symbiotic nature of the dependency interaction. Woollams and Huige (1977) maintained that symbiotic relationships are always pathological because one or more of the developmental ego states (child, parent, or adult—as defined by transactional psychology theories) are discounted. In a normal dependency relationship (whether in infancy, childhood, or adolescence), each individual is allowed to grow and to leave the affiliation, whereas in symbiosis both parties want to maintain the relationship as it is.

For example, a boy was brought into therapy because his mother was told that he was doing poorly in school, and educational authorities believed that the slow progress was caused by emotional difficulties. In counseling sessions, both mother and child exhibited defensiveness about the family situation. After mentioning a recent divorce, the mother insisted all has gone well. The boy, according to her, had taken over the management of younger siblings and was exhibiting adultlike independence and responsibility. Diagnostic measures indicated that the son was resentful of the emotional and physical burdens placed upon him but was afraid to indicate this to his mother. When attempts were made to inform the mother about the boy's inner feelings, she expressed disbelief and insisted the child was relieved that the father was gone and liked his present role. She threatened to leave counseling but remained when the therapist told her the boy's problems would likely worsen if she departed. Long-term counseling, conducted primarily with the mother, resolved many family conflicts.

This case illustrates the pathological nature of symbiosis, particularly as it pertains to the demand of at least one person in the relationship that the other abstain from the use of an available ego state—in this case, the mother's insistence that the son refrain from using his child ego state. As a matter of fact, it is the child ego state that is probably most neglected in symbiotic affiliations, since one or both of the involved individuals are given injunctions to suspend the search for enjoyment. (Of the three ego states, only the child ego state is available for pleasure-seeking activities; the parent state administers rules and the adult state makes decisions.) Of course, the adult ego state, which has the power to make logical judgments, may also be stunted because it could allow the involved individuals to see the absurdity of their situation. In the example just cited, the mother has, in reality, commanded the child to play an exaggerated parental role in order to satisfy her own need to be protected by a strong, authoritative figure.

Summers and Walsh (1977) made a fine distinction between simple overprotectiveness and symbiosis. While overprotectiveness may be harmful to a child, the person who is solicitous tends not to show the following characteristics, which are exhibited by those desiring a symbiotic relationship:

1. Undifferentiation. The dependent person makes no distinction between his or her own needs and the needs of the other person involved in the relationship.
2. Dependency. The dependent person actively prevents the other person from being self-reliant.
3. Intervention. The dependent person, to gain signs of support, actively interferes with the activities of the other person.
4. Disapproval of other relationships. The dependent person fears and defends against the possibility that the depended-upon person might form a new relationship.

5. Separation difficulties. The dependent individual, fearing the loss of psychic fulfillment if the depended-upon person leaves, constantly clings to that person.
6. Injunctions. The depended-upon person is given commands (by either verbal directions or emotional reactions) to perform in prescribed, supporting ways.

Scapegoat Syndrome

Children are often caught up in symbiotic relationships over which they have no control. The so-called scapegoat syndrome is an example of this phenomenon. One individual in the family (generally a child, but sometimes an older person) is seen by the other family members to possess unwanted characteristics that they deny possessing themselves. In other words, a child is seen by the family to possess features like laziness, hostility, or irresponsibility; and that perception allows the other family members to appear less guilty of having similar characteristics. The poorly regarded youngster forms a poor self-concept and the other family members a more exalted self-perception.

The dimensions of this destructive arrangement are hidden to the family members because the original selection and subsequent management of family roles stem from largely unconscious motives. Meanings of the scapegoat mandate can be appreciated only when the dynamics of the arrangement are brought to a more conscious level in the participants' minds. Much discomfort may be evidenced in counseling sessions when the poorly esteemed member begins to show improvement. The child may begin to show signs of rebelliousness or other indications of misbehavior, and the clinician must convince the adults in the family not to leave counseling.

Often, it is not easy to determine the degree of seriousness of abnormal personality signs. As Hirschfeld (1977) pointed out, dependency status refers to a complex of thoughts, beliefs, feelings, and behaviors revolving around the need to associate with others. However, this same author found three components of dependent conduct to be indicative of pathology: (a) overreliance on another person, (b) an unusual lack of social self-confidence, and (c) the inability to assert autonomy.

Depression. Closely allied to the discussion of symbiosis are theories associating depression with dependency. Hirschfeld (1976) stated that excessive unmet dependency needs are present in many cases of depression. When dependency satisfaction is removed and ordinary methods to obtain esteem (e.g., by earning money, achieving something, etc.) are not effective, then self-esteem fails and depression ensues. Blatt (1982) also believed depression is associated with unmet dependency needs but contends that some people are too self-critical and become depressed if they do not measure up to the high standards of achievement they have set for themselves.

Depressive states are not as commonly observed in children as in adults (Kessler, 1966), but they do exist. They are manifested in periods of sadness, self-deprecatory remarks ("I am bad," "I am stupid," "I can't do anything right"), a loss of energy, and spells of disinterest. It is not uncommon to observe symptoms of depression in children, particularly adolescents, when supporting relationships are terminated. Educators must not underestimate the importance of peer friendships to children, and children's need for each other's support must not be considered unusual in any clinical sense (Burks, 1968b). The child who is separated from friends may experience a developmental crisis (social isolation in chapter 15). However, the child who bases all his or her self-esteem on the maintenance of positive social relationships and derives little or no satisfaction from the acquisition of good grades, the rewards of an after-school job, and so on, may need counseling (Marshall, 1994). Is the family placing too much emphasis on upward social mobility? Is the child receiving enough emotional support at home? These and other questions can be explored with the child and his or her family.

Dependency and Children with Disabilities

Pleas for help cannot be ignored when they originate from children who are disabled, but how much help should be offered? The question is not easily answered. Two factors must be considered: the child's attitude toward his or her dependency needs, and the educational philosophy of the person administering the aid.

The needs of the individual who has a disability can be strongly influenced by the nature of the disorder. For instance, Stores and Piran (1978) reported that people with epilepsy are more dependent upon physical contact with others than are most other people with disabilities (perhaps because individuals with epilepsy feel they have little control over their illness). Patients with asthma tend to exhibit one of two pathological signs: helpless dependency and anxiety, or excessive and inappropriate independence (Dirks, Schraa, Brown, & Kinsman, 1980).

The child with a disability can also be swayed by early and morbid family upbringing practices. Morrison (1977), for example, found that the person who accepted a disability (and presumably its limitations) exhibited more dependency symptoms than a person who did not.

A child with a disability is much influenced by the quality of recent experiences with friends and teachers. Segal and Moyles (1979) noted that children placed in highly structured, authoritarian environments tended to show more dependency reactions than those placed in a more laissez-faire milieu.

Those who help children with disabilities must periodically evaluate their own motives. The "helping parent" model, while sometimes necessary, can result in regressive dependency (Barton, Baltes, & Orzech, 1980). Helpers oriented toward fostering independence will not act disappointed if children turn down proffered assistance; in fact, they will ignore many pleas for help and reward any indications of independent conduct.

The Inconstancy of Dependency Traits

Dependency needs are not static. They vary over time and from one situation to another. Age, gender, and cultural factors all play a part in the formation and expression of dependent behavior.

Age factors. Especially among younger children, immaturity is associated with dependency. These students are rated by teachers as showing difficulties in the attention deficits, poor coordination, academic difficulties, poor reality contact, poor self-esteem, and poor physical stamina categories on the Burks Behavior Rating Scales (BBRS) (Burks, 1977a, 1977b, 2006a).

Other dependent primary- and elementary-age youngsters demonstrate neurotic symptoms. Teachers rate them higher on the BBRS categories of poor self-esteem, withdrawal, and poor physical stamina. For other children, anxiousness and emotional distress may be added as character components. For some older students (seventh- and eighth-grade level) the preceding neurotic symptoms are accompanied by higher ratings on the BBRS poor social conformity and pebelliousness categories. Interestingly, these rebellious attitudes are often associated with higher scores on the BBRS self-blame category.

Gender factors. Girls of all ages are rated by their teachers as showing more dependency traits than boys (Burks, 1977a, 1977b). This finding is not surprising. Saviola (1981) described practices that lead women to live lives of economic and emotional dependency. However, the learned dependency role can have positive aspects. Miller (1979) found female dependency to be strongly related to empathy and sharing, whereas a negative relationship was found between male dependency and sharing.

Cultural factors. Neki (1976) examined the cultural relativism of dependence and reported significant differences between the way Indian culture views dependency and the way Western societies see it. Western culture postulates a fundamental conflict between the wish to remain dependent and the push to become independent and advances the belief that this conflict is basic to proper personality development. Neki believes that theories of this nature have caused dependency to acquire pejorative connotations in the Western world. The derogatory attitude toward dependency causes parents and teachers to foster early independence in children. Conversely, dependency is not seen to be an undesirable trait in Indian societies. Children are taught to rely on mother figures for extended periods of time, in the belief that self-reliance will emerge as a personality characteristic in the continuum of long-term, structured interpersonal relations.

I agree that various cultures have different views of dependency traits (Burks, 1977a). I found that Mexican American children tend to be seen by their teachers as having many dependency characteristics. This observation was reported at both primary and intermediate grade levels. Lack of self-reliance, however, must be evaluated in the context of cultural expectations. Friedman (1973) pointed out that young children, especially young girls in Mexican American families, tend to be very close to and dependent upon their mothers; by dominant cultural standards, they seem overprotected. Both boys and girls in Mexican American families manifest shyness and withdrawal symptoms stemming from difficulties in separating from their parents.

INTERVENTION STRATEGIES

Summary of Intervention Studies

Studies of dependency in children (Baumrind, 1968; Cowan & Inskeep, 1978; Dowling, 1991; Hartup & Smothergill, 1966; Morrison, 1977; Segal & Moyles, 1979; Shamoo & Patros, 1992; Sinha & Pandey, 1975; Symor, 1977; Tjosvold & Fabrey, 1980; K. E. Wilson & Shantz, 1977) have produced the following findings:

1. The more adults punish children for clinging behavior and for resistance to being separated, the stronger the children's dependency responses.
2. Dependent children tend to develop a strict conscience. For this reason, adults must be careful not to overuse lectures with these youngsters; moralizing tends to make them even more cautious or withdrawn.
3. Children who resist temptation tend to be less dependent. Teachers can help the easily led child to be less impulsive by supplying the youngster with admired, independent models he or she can emulate.
4. Generous children show fewer dependency reactions than their more selfish contemporaries. Since being generous implies the capacity to suppress desires for immediate gratification and to hold impulses in check, it follows that generous children possess moral maturity that, in turn, stems from identification with satisfying and nurturing adult models.
5. Firm discipline does not produce dependency in children. On the contrary, parents of the most self-reliant and assertive children are rated high in firm control and assertion of their power.
6. When learning goals are unclear, lecturing and giving directions increases students' dependency on teachers and lowers achievement levels.
7. Overdependency on adults for affection is negatively correlated to three indexes of popularity for young students: sociometric scores, teacher judgment, and social acceptance. The student who is not self-reliant will want to cling to the teacher. This conduct must be discouraged gently but firmly because great dependency on the teacher is incompatible with peer acceptance (other children cannot get attention from the instructor). Seeking help from the teacher, however, is accepted by peers if not accompanied by undue demand for affection.
8. Popular children do not reject overtures from adults but do not seek approval either. Although dependent children need encouragement, teachers should not make too much fuss about their academic achievements.
9. Highly structured, authoritarian classrooms tend to produce more dependent students than do less structured, laissez-faire environments.
10. Highly dependent children respond more rapidly to efficient models (well-organized, independent children) than do less dependent individuals.
11. When efficient models are not available, dependent children will still respond well to rewards given for self-reliant conduct.
12. Dependent children tend to possess high role-taking abilities. Their need to have frequent contact with others helps them develop a capacity to view themselves as others see them. This role-taking ability can be used in group counseling sessions to provide useful insights.
13. By itself, insight therapy is not enough. To become fully and normally interdependent, the dependent child must move from an "I'm not okay/you're okay" position to a counterdependent phase "I'm not okay/you're not okay," to "I'm okay/you're not okay," and, finally, to "I'm okay/you're okay."

14. During this process, the dependent youngster will probably need some help from knowledgeable adults to deal with other children who may resent and challenge perceived changes taking place in the dependent individual. The dependent individual may be disinterested in taking another person's perspective because he or she feels socially powerless. However, a classroom that emphasizes interdependence (i.e., sharing responsibility) can help the dependent child develop interest in others.

15. Other children are more likely to help the dependent student when the time and effort expended to do so is minimal and when the satisfaction (appropriate positive feedback from the assisted student and from the teacher) is high.

16. The dependent child is more likely to become self-reliant when his or her problems (emotional, physical, mental, or social) are not taken too seriously by others. The lack of attention to such problems can help the child become more self-confident.

Techniques for School Personnel

Because overdependency stems mainly from inappropriate parent-child interactions, the disorder must be treated at the home level; however, the school can help to some degree. The main educational objectives are as follows:

1. Establish practical goals that the child can reach independently. Avoid objectives that the child can attain only by asking for assistance.
2. Structure goals in graduated increments that guarantee success.
3. Make activities realistic and intrinsic to the academic situation. Being a room monitor, for instance, requires arithmetic and verbal skills as much as it demands self-reliant conduct.
4. Help the child eventually establish success as its own reward, although supplementary awards (praise or tokens) may be supplied as intervening measures at first.

School procedures that have proved helpful to dependent children include the following:

1. Arrange a diagnostic study of the child to determine possible causes for the demonstrated poor self-reliance.
2. Seat the child near popular, efficient, and mature peer models.
3. Form discussion groups in which the student can talk about personal difficulties in a noncritical atmosphere. Ask the student to act out roles in these groups.
4. Advise the parents of a very young, dependent child to have him or her repeat a grade. This step should be taken only when the dependent behavior interferes with academic achievement and repeating a grade will not seriously damage the child's self-esteem.
5. Provide the child with special school counseling when the dependency is too severe to be handled by ordinary classroom procedures.
6. Ask the child or the parents about the child's interests and then include these interests in curriculum activities.
7. Delegate authority to the student to the extent that he or she is able to handle responsibility.
8. Include the child in social group dramas; ask him or her to play mature roles.
9. Gently encourage the student to participate in competitive activities (e.g., spelling bees, sports events).
10. Allow the child to demonstrate verbal and writing proficiency to classmates.
11. Gear assignments to the level of the child's abilities.
12. Provide frequent positive reinforcements for the child—many small successes tend to be more effective than one large success.
13. Ignore but do not reject pleas for attention and reward independent classroom work.
14. Refrain from overdirecting the child, even though he or she willingly follows suggestions from adults.

15. Give praise but don't overdo it. Praise is useful but can be interpreted by the child as another outward gauge of success or failure.

16. Refrain from making value judgments about the student's work assignments; instead, ask the child how he or she feels about the quality of the product.

17. Refuse to allow the child to retire to solitary reading activities (a chief interest of overprotected children) when he or she could profitably engage in more energetic tasks.

18. Encourage the child to cease making unusual efforts to please others. Instead, urge the youngster to engage in activities that genuinely interest him or her.

Techniques for Parents

Earlier in this chapter a distinction was made between task dependency (seeking help in doing things) and emotional dependency (seeking social responses from others). Certain parental practices promote task dependency, while others promote emotional dependency.

Parental Practices that Promote Task Dependency

Parents interfere too much, and do not allow the child to do things on his or her own initiative. One way to ensure that a child will continue to ask for parental direction is to play the heavy hand of "Mother (or Father) knows best." Long exposure to this adult role model behavior can undermine the child's faith in making and following through on personal choices.

A few years ago, David C. McClelland, a professor at Wesleyan University, pointed out that successful young people had mothers who expected them to be self-reliant at an early age—to make their way around in their neighborhoods, make their own friends, do well in sports, and so on (Burns, 1993). He was careful to point out that this training for self-reliance did not include caretaking activities, such as putting themselves to bed, preparing their own food, or earning their own spending money—needs that, if unmet, would suggest rejection by the parent. Instead, these mothers demonstrated a general but positive interest in their child's independence, growth, and development while meeting the child's basic needs. Outstandingly able children have been shown to possess a significant measure of independence before 8 years of age. The practice in their homes was to give rewards for accomplishment.

Remedial suggestions. Establish home goals that the child can achieve independently (for example, figuring out family games, doing chores, deciding where to go on outings) but avoid objectives that the child can attain only by asking for direction. Be satisfied when the youngster shows initiative—don't raise the ante by asking for more effort. Structure the goals in graduated steps so that successful completion of projects is guaranteed.

Parents communicate unusual anxiety about the child's whereabouts and activities. A parent who continually expresses a need to know the child's exact location and activities may cause that child to be unduly concerned about the emotional well-being of the parent. In the child's view, upsetting his or her parents brings guilt which can be worsened if the child also believes that he or she is upsetting the parents by failing to perform adequately at school. The child who is encouraged to think that disappointing a parent is a reprehensible act is likely to be tense and anxious about the possibility of committing errors and is apt to be overly dependent on parents for signs of approval (to safeguard against the pain felt for making mistakes).

Remedial suggestions. Obviously, the parent's anxiety must be treated first. That will take time. In the meantime, parental anxiety may be lessened if the child is allowed to join supervised activities (Scouts, Blue Birds, YMCA, and so on) where the child is seen by the parent to be safe. As time goes on, it is essential for parents to gradually increase opportunities for older children to go to parties, friends' homes, local stores, school functions, ball games, and so on. Parents must communicate approval when children act independently.

Parents constantly remind the child of the possibility of making mistakes. Remind such adults that their self-confidence would be affected if they had supervisors standing at their shoulders constantly, anxiously monitoring their performance. They would probably become tentative and angry and, at the same time, would feel that they needed constant guidance to avoid mistakes.

I interviewed one little girl who had trouble showing initiative. She said her parents gave her an adequate allowance, but she never spent any of the money. When asked why not, she said, "Well, every time I think of something I need, Dad and Mom ask me to think about it a lot, and they always tell me that there might be better things to buy. That makes me worried, and I just don't buy things because they might be the wrong things."

Remedial suggestions. To avoid making the child unsure about his or her own judgment, parents should refrain from offering opinions about a child's achievements (e.g., "Oh, honey, I really think you did better this time" or "Don't you think it would be better if the picture was a different color?"). Instead, just ask the child how he or she feels about the production. Accept replies without comment.

Parents don't give enough recognition or praise when their child acts independently. Children must receive parental approval for actions requiring initiative and independent behavior. This lays the emotional groundwork for the lifelong trait of personal independence. If one or both parents do not commonly commend their child for taking initiative, ask the following questions:

- Is it possible you fear that your youngster might become too independent?
- Do you tend to think your child doesn't need praise?
- Are you a quiet person who comments little on what goes on around you?
- Do you think you are copying the behavior of your own parents, who also said little about your achievements?
- Do you tend to think that praise might spoil your child?

Remedial suggestions. Praise is important, but quiet parents can offer commendation in other ways. They can supply positive rewards (e.g., tangible articles like refreshments and toys for very young children) for displaying independent conduct. The parent may want to construct a chart on which a check mark is made whenever the youngster does something on his or her own, such as initiating homework sessions. After a certain number of check marks are recorded, the child is eligible for a prize. When used wisely, commendation is useful, but if it is overdone, children sense it is false. Most youngsters know what deserves praise. If praised for unworthy efforts they may turn a deaf ear to future praise because they do not trust its validity.

Parents pay too much attention to actions that demonstrate a lack of initiative. Suppose a child dawdles, which upsets the parents. They make unpleasant remarks about the child's procrastination, in an effort to change his or her behavior. Although the parents believe the child feels punished, the child may actually feel rewarded. In the first place, the boy or girl gets more attention for noncompliance than for compliance. In the second place, the child may feel avenged for bad feelings resulting from parental pressure.

Remedial suggestions. When parents know the child is capable of solving a problem, they should calmly ignore dawdling and pleas for help. Responding in almost any other way (e.g., getting angry, lecturing, irritably giving in) simply signals to the youngster that he or she is able to get attention with little effort.

Some procrastinating youngsters learn to play a complicated dependence game with parents. The scenario goes like this: upset by a stalling child, the parents harp at the youngster to "get going." By carefully gauging parental tolerance for frustration, the boy or girl resists taking action until the parents reach the end of their patience and explode in anger; only then does the youngster start to move. These emotional maneuvers allow the child to exploit parental feelings. He or she becomes progressively less interested in taking independent action as more and more energy is invested in keeping the game going.

This futile cycle may be broken if the parents ignore the stalling tactics and allow the child to face the consequences (sometimes unpleasant) of inaction. I once counseled the parents of a procrastinating child named Jimmy. Jimmy refused to come to dinner when called. I suggested they call him once and then go on with dinner while allowing his food to become cold. If he did not come in by the time the family finished eating, his plate was to be removed and he had to go to bed hungry. The parents reported that it took only two times for Jimmy to learn they meant business. He stopped stalling. They went on to use the technique successfully in other instances where Jimmy procrastinated.

Parents are too eager to solve their child's problems. Parents may be doing a disservice to their child and to themselves when they constantly try to anticipate and smooth over difficulties faced by the child. Typically, the youngster becomes less able to solve problems, and the parents become more and more frustrated by the youngster's apparent passivity.

Remedial suggestions. To break this unfortunate cycle, parents should present the child with difficulties he or she must solve—of course, the problems must be within the youngster's problem-solving capacity. For instance, ask the child to buy some food at the market for a family trip, but don't specify what food is necessary. The youngster may also be asked to figure out what games the family will play on the trip.

Parents cannot substitute for the important social and emotional benefits of association with age-mates. That is why youngsters should be encouraged to join organizations such as Boy Scouts, Campfire Girls, or similar clubs. Very young children can learn valuable social skills at day-care centers.

Not only are parents who are too available likely to produce a dependent child, but, worse, they may encourage the youngster to become self-centered and unable to check impulsive behavior—actions are not thought through; gratification comes too easily.

Parents change their responses to the child's demands whimsically. Investigators have found that some of the most clinging children are produced by inconsistent parents. The child-parent scenario often goes like this: First the adults irritably reject their children's request for assistance, and then they succumb to the demands. The children must attend to parental reactions carefully because responses are unpredictable.

Remedial suggestions. The lesson here is obvious: Teach children that home rules are firm and predictable. Of course, both parents must agree on the regulations and on consequences if rules are broken.

Parents infantilize the child (make him or her the "baby of the family"). The youngest child is usually assigned this role. Along with the parents, siblings also see the youngest as the one who should be protected, helped, and cuddled. Researchers see the dependencies produced by this family pattern as potentially harmful because, as adults, some (but by no means all) of these babied children do not later assume responsibility for their actions. Some refuse to face stress. Others become underachievers.

Remedial suggestions. Parents who tend to baby their children can be given the following hints:

- Refrain from overdirecting your youngster, even when you know he or she will make mistakes, and even when the child actively and willingly accepts suggestions.
- Allow your child time to indulge in hobbies and interests. It is in these activities that initiative and independent behavior are most likely to occur.
- Don't allow the youngster to make a habit of solitary behavior such as reading (a chief interest of many overprotected and nonaggressive children) when more outgoing activities are available.
- Encourage signs of curiosity in the child—probably best done in the context of family activities. Each member may be given an assignment (for instance, to make a family-related video) that he or she is responsible for completing. Questions are received and answered and individual initiative is rewarded with praise.
- Help the youngster face competition—many nonproducing children dread failure and avoid initiating activities. To help the child face and overcome competitive stress, try gentle family games and sports. These activities allow parents to model competitive behavior, not the least of which is to teach ways to lose gracefully and with good humor. Teach the child that failure is a common and acceptable experience for everyone.
- Read about and observe same-age children to get a realistic picture of what society (primarily the school and neighborhood) expects of the youngster. Sometimes parents of overprotected, nonproducing children possess an incomplete or sometimes fanciful view of the world's expectations. They may think the child should be quiet most of the time and cause no trouble. Carried too far, this expectation could blunt the constructive aggression needed to achieve.

Parents worry and communicate their anxiety to the child. Tense and worried parents tend to have anxious children. Some of these youngsters are so preoccupied with their worries that they cannot achieve adequately.

Remedial suggestions. Parents of chronically fearful children who underachieve may be given the following hints:

- Sit down with your child and explore the fears he or she expresses.
- Leave an upsetting situation if you think you are contributing to your child's anxiety. If leaving is a problem, exit when the child is occupied.
- Be sympathetic but firm about requirements the child dislikes.
- Keep your child informed about family plans.
- Fully explain family misfortunes.
- Set a time and place to listen to the child's chronic complaints.
- Don't discuss your own fears with the child. Talk over anxieties with other adults.
- If your child is far behind in schoolwork, consider tutoring—but don't do the tutoring yourself! I have seldom seen a parent (particularly of older children) who is equipped to handle this chore. Most parents are too worried about their child's difficulties and simply communicate their concerns. The child then becomes less self-confident and less able to produce. Turn over tutoring to professionals who are skilled in academic remediation.

Parents overprotect the child who has a disability. Parents of a youngster with a mental, physical, or emotional disability can find themselves asking a perplexing question: How much extra help does my child actually need?

Remedial suggestions. Two factors must be considered: (a) the child's attitude toward his or her dependency and (b) the needs of the caregiver.

1. The child's attitude. As discussed earlier, a child's attitude can be influenced by the nature of his or her disorder. For instance, youngsters with epilepsy tend to be more dependent on physical support than are individuals with other disabilities because they feel they have little control over their disability. Children with mental disabilities tend to become shy and withdrawn because they have been socially rebuffed. Patients who have asthma can show either helpless dependency and anxiety or inappropriate independence. All people with disabilities tend to become more dependent if they accept their disabilities (and presumably the accompanying limitations) than if they deny being disabled and strive to act in normal ways.
2. The caregiver's needs. Adult caregivers of disabled children must periodically evaluate their motives. The helping role, while gratifying to the caregiver, can result in the child's overdependence. On the other hand, forcing the youngster with a disability to do things on his or her own, allowing the child to take personal initiative, and not acting disappointed when the youngster turns down proffered help can be important steps that enable the individual with a disability to form a more competent self-image.

Parental Practices that Promote Emotional Dependency

Task dependency problems in children are bothersome but generally not as difficult to treat as the problems demonstrated by children who show emotional dependency or person-oriented dependency (Clarizio & McCoy, 1976). Although they often show the characteristics of task-dependent youngsters, children who are emotionally dependent cannot seem to exist emotionally without excessive amounts of parental support, approval, and attention. Emotionally dependent children are more interested in gaining social approval than in obtaining help to complete a task (although some dependent youngsters are so insecure that they seek both kinds of assistance).

The child whose goal is social approval per se demands constant praise and attention (to bolster self-confidence); is very sensitive to criticism (which could heighten the child's doubts about his or her ability to stand alone); and demonstrates a wide variety of distressing symptoms including sadness, depression, anxiety, anger, and even aggression when ignored (as a result of fears of being emotionally abandoned). If the child does not show these emotionally intense signs when left alone, the dependent condition, while annoying, is probably tolerable.

Identifying Parental Behavior that Produces Emotionally Dependent Children

Any adult behavior that leaves children with emotionally "unfinished business" can produce emotional dependence. Youngsters who receive little encouragement from their parents for achievement are left with doubts about their self-worth. These uncertainties may linger into adult life, causing unusual sensitivity to and dependence upon the evaluations of others. Such anxiety may be exacerbated by parental practices that prevent children from developing social skills. For example, if a parent rushes in to solve most of a child's normal problems (infantilizing him or her), as the child grows, he or she will remain dependent on the help of others to an unusual degree.

To identify problematic behavior, ask parents to agree or disagree with the following statements regarding child-raising practices. To make the conduct categories more specific and meaningful, I have included descriptions of parental actions that could produce emotional dependency. These statements may prove productive in diagnostic counseling.

Overprotective parents. Children of overprotective parents do not learn social coping skills; they remain dependent on others to protect them.

- I check on my child's actions constantly.
- I rush in to solve any little problem presented by my child.
- I refuse to let my child face most stresses.
- I am very sympathetic when my child avoids solving problems.
- I am delighted to treat my child as the baby of the family.
- I protect my child from all controversy.

Overindulgent parents. Children of overindulgent parents do not learn to cope with adversity; they remain dependent on others to indulge them.

- I am very permissive and seldom discipline my child.
- I indulge my child's demands on most occasions.
- I take the child's side regardless of circumstances.
- I feel that my child is deprived and I give him or her many presents.
- I usually give in when the child is upset.
- I feel that other parents are too strict; I compensate by being sympathetic.

Overcontrolling parents. Children of overcontrolling parents remain passive and dependent on the wishes of others or become resentful and fight the control of others.

- I tend to stop my child from taking the initiative.
- I treat the child as being slow; I give directions over and over.
- I restrict the child from spending allowance money.
- I prevent the child from playing with other children.
- I insist that the child please others at any cost.
- I spend a lot of time lecturing the child on right and wrong.
- I constantly remind the child to do better.
- I set up goals that the child must meet.

- I constantly ask questions that the child resents.
- I constantly remind the child that parents know best.
- I will not allow my child to question or contest any adult demands.

Disapproving parents. Children of disapproving parents are unsure of how to get the affection of others.

- I seldom give my child praise for independent conduct.
- I show much disapproval when the child does not conform.
- I show much disapproval of clinging behavior.
- I accent the negative rather than the positive actions of the child.
- I am never satisfied with my child's achievements.
- I hold up standards of conduct the child cannot meet.
- I ask for decisions but generally disapprove of the child's choices.

Inconsistent parents. Children of inconsistent parents feel uncertain about the intentions of others. Investigations have found that parents who initially reject their children's requests for assistance (often irritably) and then eventually give in to those demands tend to produce the most dependent children. Apparently, the children must attend to the parents' reactions carefully because the parents' responses are so unpredictable.

- My discipline efforts tend to be inconsistent.
- My reactions to the child depend largely on my mood.
- I make it difficult for my child to know what I want.
- My goals for the child change whimsically.
- My behavioral standards for the child change whimsically.
- My unpredictable emotional changes keep the child tense.

Emotionally upset. Children of emotionally upset parents worry about their own and others' mental stability. Such children may tend to exaggerate the problems of others in later life.

- I become upset over even the small mistakes of my child.
- I ask the child to share in adult problems.
- I present a sad, worried, or depressed face to my child.
- I explode in anger; my child is not sure when this will happen.
- I keep the causes for family problems from my worried child.
- I blame my child for family problems.

The more statements a parent agrees with, the more likely it is that the child has an emotional dependency.

Certain combinations of the preceding behaviors are known to produce the following effects:

Overprotective and overindulgent. If the mother, in particular, shows these characteristics, the youngster tends to be selfish, tyrannical, and demanding and to seek constant attention, affection, and service. When frustrated, the child reacts with assault and rage.

Overcontrolling and overprotective. In these cases, the child tends to react with signs of anxiety, shyness, fear, and submissive conduct.

These parental behaviors are all amenable to change by parents who are anxious to help their children become more autonomous and show more initiative.

CHAPTER 7

Poor Motivational Strength

Poor motivation on the part of a pupil may lie in the fact that the youngster suffers a lack of self-confidence (Burks, 1977a, 2006a). These students tend to

- "put down" their own abilities;
- lack a feeling of self-assurance;
- sometimes act silly;
- stay away from competition;
- be easily gratified with inadequate performance;
- become easily frustrated.

ASSOCIATED CHARACTERISTICS

I have found that poor motivational intensity affects a great many children with a wide variety of complaints (Burks 1977a, 1977b). In one investigation of 175 students who were retarded in schoolwork and also demonstrated behavior problems, the item on the Burks Behavior Rating Scales (BBRS) "depreciates and distrusts own abilities" was seen by teachers to be the most common conduct manifestation of disturbed children. Apparently, loss of self-confidence is a frequent consequence when youngsters are put under pressure, when they are threatened with failure, or when they have suffered an unsettling experience linked to defeat.

THEORETICAL BACKGROUND

Unusual feelings of insecurity are learned characteristics acquired from developmental experiences (Berglas & Baumeister, 1993). A student may employ a variety of techniques to avoid comparing his or her achievements with those of other children.

Fruitful and satisfying interpersonal relationships facilitate the development of inner character strength. In one study I conducted (Burks, 1968c), it was discovered that pupils attached the greatest importance to peer relations. Second most important was getting along with teachers. Of least concern was the curriculum and the school environment.

It is not surprising to find that poor motivational strength manifests itself as classroom underachievement (Lippitt, Fox, & Schmuck, 1967). Lippitt et al. also reported that strong motivations in children were characterized by wide friendly relationships. It is interesting to note that Barnes (1980) found that travel, accompanied by fatigue, tends to reduce motivational impulses.

DIAGNOSIS

When the BBRS indicates inadequate achievement may be tied to poor self-esteem, efforts should be made to see if the youngster is isolated from peers. The youngster who is rejected by the majority of his or her classmates is in a psychologically precarious position. Thus, it is important that the teacher work toward a better understanding of the network of interpersonal relationships in the classroom. One way to achieve this is to use a simple peer-nominating method. For instance, the teacher may say to the class:

> For our unit on the settling of the West we are going to need committees to work on different parts of the project. I need to know who you would like to have on a committee with you. Please write your name at the top of the paper that I gave you. Under your name, write the names of the students you would like to have on your committee.

The teacher can review the results of this sociogram in pictorial form by drawing a number of circles, lettered to represent the students in the class. When a child selects another youngster, the teacher draws a line from the first child's circle to the circle representing the chosen student. It will immediately become apparent that some children are chosen by a large number of other students, some are chosen by only a few others, and some are ignored by all (these children are called isolates). Mutual friendships can also be noted.

At some slight risk to particular individuals (those who could discover that they are rejected by most students), the teacher can also ask the children to name those students they definitely would not want to have in their group. This method gives an even more complete picture of the group structure.

The teacher should analyze the sociogram results in terms of the following factors:

1. The nature of the clusters. In some classrooms, interpersonal acceptance and rejection are narrowly focused (i.e., a large number of students give high status to a small cluster of peers); while in other classrooms, acceptance and rejection are diffuse (i.e., acceptance is bestowed on a large number of classmates).
2. The number of fringers and isolates. In a classroom where there are many fringers (those not completely accepted by cliques) or isolates (those neglected entirely), class morale tends to be low and group planning and coordinated group action are more difficult (Thorndike & Hagen, 1961). On the other hand, classroom peer groups characterized by friendly relationships tend to have positive emotional climates conducive to the enhancement of ego structures among the students.

Sociometric choices describe the present flow of interactions among students; they do not indicate any permanent, strong emotional structuring of relationships. Periodically, the teacher may wish to repeat sociographic measurements. Further, sociograms frequently point up teacher errors in judgment about a child's social status. If a sociometric device illustrates that a particular child is rejected by most of his or her peers, educators should be alert to the child's potential relationship problems even if they think the child has friends.

The sociogram by itself tells only which children are liked or rejected, not the reasons for the acceptance or rejection. The teacher who is attempting to enhance a particular child's ego strength may do so by exploring the student's learning milieu and attitude.

Learning Milieu of the Rejected Student

The following questions may be helpful in the exploration of a rejected child's educational environment. The student's teacher is probably most qualified to answer these questions.

1. Is the child new to the group?
2. Is the child older or younger than classmates?

3. Is the child significantly less intelligent than classmates?
4. Does the child have a long history (i.e., reputation) of peer rejection?
5. Is the child presently ostracized or bullied by peers?
6. In your estimation, would it be very difficult for the child to break into the cliques that are influencing student activity most strongly?
7. Does the child meet rejection by peers in the classroom or on the playground?
8. Do other children listen to the child?
9. Does the child have personal habits that are unacceptable to peers (e.g., annoying mannerisms, or lack of personal cleanliness)?
10. Does the youngster understand the effect of his or her behavior on others?
11. Does the child understand the needs of other children?
12. Has the child been taught to seek out resources provided by more popular children?
13. Is the child sitting apart from friends in the classroom?
14. Does the child have a long history of poor school achievement?
15. Does the child live far away from classmates?
16. Is the child a member of a minority group unfamiliar to most classmates?
17. Is the child a member of a socioeconomic group unfamiliar to most classmates?

Many rejected students do not believe that emotional nurturance can be acquired from within the educational system. Teachers have either accepted and resigned themselves to these students and their slow academic achievement or are annoyed by them. Classmates are disinterested in such students because they present little social value.

The preceding questions may be used as a starting point to help the rejected student. For instance, the youngster who is new to the class will need help to understand classroom routines. If the child is out of place in the classroom because of age, size, or intelligence, consider placement in another educational setting where such differences are not so noticeable. The child with a long history of peer rejection has a deep sense of alienation and must not be expected to overcome this profound feeling of separateness from students who have always disliked him or her. Consider placing this student in another school. The alienated child should be allowed to try out various seating placements in the classroom until he or she finds a satisfactory one. Then the child may need specific suggestions on the best ways to approach peers and how to ask for assistance. The youngster, if bitter about felt teacher neglect, may also require help in understanding that classmates also need attention from the teacher. The child who receives no academic attention from age-mates may need additional teacher support. The instructor can insist that surrounding children give the youngster proper consideration during class time (no teasing, disparaging remarks, or overt signs of disinterest). The alienated student who exhibits unacceptable personal habits will need personal hygiene instruction from school staff members. The child's parents may also need caretaker directions along the same lines.

Attitude of the Rejected Student

Teachers of nonproductive, isolated children can be encouraged to use simple diagnostic tools that give a reasonably accurate picture of a student's feelings, attitudes, views of interpersonal relationships, and his or her perceptions of academic performance. I developed the following diagnostic measures to evaluate affective ego strength, cognitive ego strength, and social ego strength (i.e., classroom social relationships).

Affective ego strength. Questionnaires of various kinds can be used to acquire information about a student's emotional (affective) self-evaluation. For example, the following sentence completion inventory might be used to solicit valuable information about an individual's affective ego strength.

1. When the teacher calls on me for answers, I feel . . .
2. When I get my report card, I always . . .

3. When I'm doing my schoolwork, I feel . . .

4. I'm happy with myself when I . . .

5. I'm unhappy with myself when I . . .

6. When the teacher shows my work, I usually . . .

7. During recess, I . . .

8. The other boys and girls make me feel . . .

9. In the morning when I think about going to school, I feel . . .

10. In the classroom I mostly think about . . .

11. When I work with the other children, I . . .

12. If only school would . . .

13. The thing that would make me happiest in school is . . .

14. The thing that makes me feel the worst in school is . . .

15. I wish the teacher would . . .

16. The other boys and girls think I'm . . .

The above inventory presents material that makes other people more aware of the child's hopes, aspirations, worries, and concerns—all areas of affective functioning that are, to some extent, hidden from the viewer. Unfortunately, the answers represent evidence of personality functioning that must be accepted with caution. Well-functioning students sometimes express worries that at first appear serious but turn out, on further examination, to be insignificant. Poorly functioning students (particularly anxious children with neurotic symptoms) sometimes present a trouble-free protocol that later diagnostic efforts indicate is invalid (Burks, 1968e). Further, as Thorndike and Hagen (1961) pointed out, what people tell others about themselves is limited by their willingness to reveal the self, their self-understanding, and their understanding of the language in which the material is worded.

Cognitive ego strength. Generally, a student's level of academic achievement matches his or her intelligence as indicated on an IQ test, but not always. One way to assess the relationship between a child's classroom performance and his or her intelligence is to rank all students according to their academic performance and then rank them all in the order of their IQ scores (or some other estimate of intelligence). The difference between the given student's position on these two rankings should provide some indication of the utilization of his or her intellectual potential. If a youngster has obvious potential but is not using it, educators are under some obligation to investigate the reasons for this discrepancy. Perhaps the classroom atmosphere (peer pressure, worries about academic standards, or interpersonal relations with the teacher) should be examined. The My Feelings about Schoolwork checklist (see figure 7.1) can be useful in this regard.

Pay particular attention to responses of "often true," since this response has proved most indicative of student discomfort. Always discuss findings from the use of this checklist with the student. Such interviews enable the teacher or counselor to estimate more accurately the degree of discomfort felt by the child and helps to reassure the child that there is genuine concern about his or her welfare. Finally, counselors should be aware that some inhibited children with neurotic signs will indicate no discomfort on the checklist even though they demonstrate obvious classroom anxiety. In such cases, special help should be offered despite the checklist results.

Social ego strength. Lippitt et al. (1967) maintained that it is possible to identify and create a classroom atmosphere that enhances ego building in groups of children. Sociometric questions can provide the teacher with an estimate of the peer relationships among the students in a classroom; however, a sociometric device does not give insights into why some children feel free to approach others while some remain inhibited. I developed a checklist called How I Feel about Myself (see figure 7.2) to investigate children's feelings of social self-confidence, an attribute thought to be necessary for the adequate formation of supportive relationships.

Responses to this checklist provide a rough guide to the child's assumed motivational strength, based on his or her willingness to take aggressive action to solve problems, meet other individuals, and take leadership roles. The odd-numbered items are worded so that a response of "often true" indicates high social self-confidence; for the even-numbered items, a response of "often true" indicates low social self-confidence.

MY FEELINGS ABOUT SCHOOLWORK

Harold F. Burks, Ph.D.

Put a check mark in the column that tells how you usually feel about the following statements.

	Not true	Sometimes true	Often true
1. I worry about going on to the next grade.	☐	☐	☐
2. I worry about report cards.	☐	☐	☐
3. I'm not sure that I know what to do in the classroom.	☐	☐	☐
4. I can't read as well as most kids.	☐	☐	☐
5. Spelling tests make me so nervous I get words wrong.	☐	☐	☐
6. Even when I try to write clearly, my handwriting seems bad.	☐	☐	☐
7. I need more help than I'm getting in arithmetic.	☐	☐	☐
8. The teacher and the other kids think I'm a poor reader.	☐	☐	☐
9. It's hard for me to catch a ball.	☐	☐	☐
10. I get scared when we play games.	☐	☐	☐
11. I don't understand the rules of the games we play.	☐	☐	☐
12. I wish the teacher would take more time to help me.	☐	☐	☐
13. I wish I could talk to the teacher about things that bother me.	☐	☐	☐
14. I wish the teacher would give me more important jobs to do.	☐	☐	☐
15. I wish I could do some of the more important jobs in the room.	☐	☐	☐

Figure 7.1.

HOW I FEEL ABOUT MYSELF

Harold F. Burks, Ph.D.

Put a check mark in the column that tells how you usually feel about the following statements.

	Not True	Sometimes True	Often True
1. The other kids probably think I'm a pushy person.	☐	☐	☐
2. The other kids probably think I'm a shy person.	☐	☐	☐
3. When someone wants me to make a decision, I make up my mind quickly.	☐	☐	☐
4. When someone wants me to make a decision, I usually take a long time to make up my mind.	☐	☐	☐
5. When someone gives me a new job, I like to take complete responsibility for it.	☐	☐	☐
6. When someone gives me a new job, I usually ask several other people to help me figure out how to do it.	☐	☐	☐
7. If a stranger needs help, I usually offer my assistance right away.	☐	☐	☐
8. If I see someone I don't know, I'm not very likely to talk to that person first.	☐	☐	☐
9. I'm usually one of the first ones to volunteer to be the head of a committee.	☐	☐	☐
10. I usually take orders better than I give them.	☐	☐	☐
11. I usually don't like to ask others for advice.	☐	☐	☐
12. I would rather do one thing at a time than do many things at a time.	☐	☐	☐
13. I usually do a lot of talking in groups.	☐	☐	☐
14. I usually don't like to take risks in front of others.	☐	☐	☐
15. I usually feel that if I try hard enough there is a way to solve most problems.	☐	☐	☐
16. I usually feel better if someone else is in charge of things.	☐	☐	☐

Figure 7.2.

Unmotivated, unaggressive, underachieving children. Educators have become increasingly concerned about children who, despite apparently adequate intelligence, simply refuse to produce academically (Schaefer, 1977).

Based on the findings of a number of investigators (Atkinson, 1965; Burks, 1964b; Fink, 1962; D. S. Johnson, 1981; Kagan & Moss, 1962; McClelland, 1961; Ollendick, 1974; Uhlinger & Stephens, 1960), underachieving, unmotivated children

- do not like to and do not choose to take responsibility for their own actions;
- tend not to take academic risks;
- do not attempt to obtain knowledge from others concerning the results of their own efforts in the classroom;
- seem unable to delay gratification;
- seldom search for a more perfect solution to problem tasks;
- tend to believe failure is due to their lack of ability rather than their lack of effort;
- do not seem curious;
- prefer routine activities; seldom seek novelty or changes in their environment;
- seldom show a desire for complexity in learning tasks;
- do not seem ambitious;
- appear immature for their age;
- demonstrate poor work habits;
- are behind in their schoolwork;
- possess few childhood enthusiasms;
- have their feelings hurt easily;
- get discouraged easily.

Repeated classroom failure places many poor achievers in a psychological state called learned helplessness. They believe that nothing they do matters, and they no longer endeavor to succeed—even on assignments within their ability. They do not think that an expenditure of effort is responsible for success or that a lack of effort is related to failure. These youngsters risk little, curb their curiosity, and settle for safe, routine tasks. They curb their ambitions because, in their view, aiming too high ensures failure. Many are immature and show some characteristics of younger children (impulsivity, the inability to delay gratification of needs, and delayed motor skills). These traits tend to be rejected by peers and, to some extent at least, by most teachers.

In one study (Burks, 1964b) many underachievers who demonstrated poor self-esteem and were chronically unmotivated in academic areas were found to be secretly interested in a hobby or other activity. For these children, daydreaming appears common. They shy away from responsibility and depend on others. Instead of learning to reduce anxiety and find emotional comfort in the process of facing difficulties, they have been taught by experience that it is safer to call on others to solve problems. They often like to play with younger children or associate with adults. Apparently, such interactions present fewer chances for competitive encounters than do relationships with peers.

The same study also revealed that unmotivated students demonstrate a damaged self-concept ("I'm dumb," "I'm bad," "I'm lazy," etc.). They approach problems in a disorganized manner and have a low tolerance for frustration when the task appears difficult. Also, the unmotivated child sees a rejection of his or her behavior as a rejection of himself or herself.

Several characteristics identify these children's families. The parents tend to be ambitious. They present the child with a high level of aspiration, which the youngster dislikes and, after a period of time, habitually rejects. They become extremely threatened if the child does not succeed and often try to motivate the child verbally (e.g., "Why don't you try harder?" or "Look, you've failed again") and by depriving the child of affection. The child sees the parents as punitive, aggressive figures who give insufficient emotional support. Thus, seeing no profit in trying to succeed, the child gives up. The parents may or may not be dominating; in either case, they fail to show any permanent satisfaction with the child's efforts.

Certain children are likely to become school dropouts. In addition to those who physically leave school, usually during the early years of high school, there are those who pull away emotionally—they simply don't try. This re-action, of course, can occur at any age. Both types of youngsters tend to lack ego strength. They see school as an institution that presents challenges they are unwilling to face (Burks, 1977a).

Spivack and Swift (1977) maintained that high-risk children can be spotted in kindergarten and first grade by classroom behaviors that are predictive of poor achievement in the third grade. These behaviors include a lack of self-confidence in decision making, difficulties in taking action without specific adult support and guidance, the in-ability to attend to and utilize support and guidance when it is offered, and a lack of personal involvement and re-flectiveness while in the classroom.

The following symptoms, conditions, and events tend to occur in the background of this type of high-risk child (Howard & Anderson, 1978):

- family is rejected in the community;
- family occupies low socioeconomic status;
- parents' education level is low;
- siblings' education level is low;
- parents place little value on education;
- parents' occupational status is low;
- student is unambitious and unmotivated;
- student has few friends;
- student's mental or physical health is poor;
- child is overly interested in material possessions (e.g., a car);
- student's school and community participation is poor;
- child has failed in one or more grades;
- child shows poor reading or arithmetic progress;
- child has attended several schools;
- child shows irregular school attendance;
- teacher's expectations for student are low;
- teacher rates child as having personality problems.

Naturally, not all students who drop out of school early show all of the preceding conditions. They are likely, how-ever, to show many of them. This type of high-risk child needs attention and special help from educators. The par-ents must be counseled as well. Traditional educational programs tend to be inadequate for this kind of student.

INTERVENTION STRATEGIES

In treating the underachieving child whose motivational strength is poor, educators must realize that the difficulty is primarily a personality disorder; academic underachievement is just one aspect of a multifaceted problem. The underachieving student knows that he or she is a failure and, consequently, feels unworthy. Any program of reha-bilitation must start with a basic acceptance of the child as he or she is. Teachers must understand that improve-ment in school deportment will be slow because the disorder has existed for years and is well fixed in the child's personality structure. Adults must recognize that, even though this child seems to be a model of conformity, a rec-ognizable and serious problem may be present. Also, these children are classroom problems—just as aggressive, noisy youngsters are—they, too, have not learned the mature self-direction that will make their behavior satisfying to themselves and acceptable to others. These realizations provide the following philosophical basis for suggested intervention strategies.

Techniques for School Personnel

Taylor (1989) suggested the following approaches to help unmotivated children with learning disabilities.

1. Help the child comply with basic rules of conduct at home and at school. Noncompliance may take a number of forms. At home, these children may dawdle, not get ready for school on time, not come home at designated times, not wash their hands or brush their teeth, not do their homework or chores, and so on. At school, they may not stay in their seat, may ignore instructions to raise their hand before asking questions, or may not complete teacher-directed assignments. As time goes on, such children learn a pattern of direct avoidance of schoolwork. They learn to avoid the frustration of academic failure by ignoring instructions and do not learn the comprehension and organizational skills necessary for classroom achievement.

   If the noncompliant behavior is restricted to school settings, Taylor suggests the following:

   • Give clear, specific behavior rules, limits, and consequences for misconduct.
   • Use reward-oriented behavior contracts.
   • Employ time-out procedures and other restrictions for misconduct.
   • Accommodate the child's inherent limitations.

   Taylor makes the point that improvements in school behavior will not automatically transfer to home settings. Parents must also become participants and administer discipline when necessary. In my opinion, parents and teachers should jointly participate in management programs to avoid working at cross-purposes. Behavioral goals should be similar at home and at school. However, such ideal outcomes face certain realistic hazards:

   • Parents and teachers often have differing standards or concerns.
   • Any reward or punishment administered by parents for school conduct is unavoidably distanced from the target behavior.
   • Some teachers, by giving prime responsibility to parents, may abrogate responsibility to manage student conduct (threats by teachers to inform parents of misbehavior are seldom as effective as direct classroom action).
   • Good communication between home and school is often difficult to maintain.

   With these concerns in mind, it is probably advantageous for parents and teachers to establish some common goals and strategies but to focus on the behaviors over which each has independent control.

2. Help the child become actively involved in the learning process. Dweck (1986) suggests attribution retraining as a method to enhance motivation. Children are taught (through group or individual instruction) to attribute learning difficulties to insufficient effort rather than to a lack of ability, in order to instill the belief that effort and persistence pay off. To achieve this goal it is important that children be exposed to both achievement success and failure (to teach them the value of both constructive and unproductive efforts). Dweck further recommends that the emphasis of instruction be on the capacity to acquire new abilities, rather than on the capacity to meet objective performance standards. Failure to meet performance standards is likely to be interpreted as personal inability to achieve and children react by giving up easily. Some researchers (Licht & Kistner, 1986) recommend praise and rewards for academic improvement rather than attainment of a fixed, established performance level.

   Taylor (1989) advises other motivational tactics for children with a learning disability:

   • Involve them in planning their own programs.
   • Set short-term goals for work completion.

- Place them in cooperative work groups with peers who are not disabled.
- When possible, encourage them to show off strengths to peers.

3. Improve the learning environment. Teachers who are overly critical of a youngster with a learning disability can instill feelings of hopelessness. Brophy (1983) studied the distinct ways individual teachers respond to hard-to-teach children. Teachers who held to fixed standards tended to give less praise and more negative feedback to students with learning disabilities than they did to normal learners. More accommodating instructors administered positive feedback in accordance with individual standards of performance, rather than in relation to general grade or age standards. Some teachers reward the final product while others esteem effort (older students, in particular, are rarely credited for effort, for intent, or for products that have some merit but contain improper grammar or misspelling). When considering the proper placement of students who are learning disabled, teacher-related factors must be taken into account (Wang, 1987).

4. Help the child relate better to others. Schumaker and Hazel (1984) found that many children with learning disabilities were deficient in social skills. I suggest that such students be taught to compliment and praise others, to react appropriately to negative behavior by peers, to sustain and reciprocate social conversations, and to engage in sharing and helping activities.

   Schumaker and Hazel (1984) recommend that any social skills training program be supplemented by procedures to assure that students apply and practice what they have learned. For instance, the teacher can discuss possible applications of newly learned material with the student, reinforce any student-initiated application of such material, and involve other school personnel (the janitor, the bus driver, and so on) in the proceedings.

5. Discuss the problem with the child. If such a discussion cannot be done sympathetically, it should not be attempted. Children experiencing learned helplessness tend to construe any discussion of their behavior as a personal criticism.

6. Develop a close, warm, personal relationship with the child. How well a youngster does in school depends, in large measure, on how well he or she likes and respects the teacher. When the child is young, the strongest incentive to study comes from the desire to win the approval of admired grown-ups. If a child is to succeed in school, he or she has to identify with the teacher as if the teacher were a loving parent (Davidson & Lang, 1960; Hamachek, 1973).

7. Show an interest in the child's activities.

8. Never attack the child's ego. Reproofs must be clearly directed toward negative overt behavior and not toward assumed personality defects. Never threaten the child. This will only cause the youngster to feel insecure and anxious; worry interferes with the capacity to think clearly and objectively. Avoid expressions such as "Do this or else" or "Don't do that or you've had it" because the child's fantasy of what "or else" and "you've had it" mean could be seriously magnified.

9. Develop a curriculum in which the child can be successful.

- In the beginning, avoid activities in which the youngster has little interest.
- Allow the child to pick activities where his or her skills are best shown.
- Communicate the child's achievement and effort to the parents through notes or telephone calls.
- Encourage the child to play a leadership role in group activities, but only if you are sure he or she can accept the responsibility.
- Ignore failures and praise accomplishments.
- Encourage the child to do special jobs in the classroom or the school office.
- Do not allow other students to ridicule the child.

10. Have the child do low-pressure extracurricular activities (e.g., run errands, collect milk money, collect answer sheets).

11. Look for latent talents in the child through tests and observations, then help the youngster develop these abilities.

12. Help the child acquire peer group support. A teacher should watch for the child who is chosen last in a game, plays alone, or stands at the edge of the game and never mingles with the other children. This youngster requires special help. The student needs the teacher's adult experience as a model for behavior that is socially desirable. The child who attracts the teacher least is often the child who needs the teacher most (Schaefer, 1977).

13. Ask the child about hobbies he or she is involved with at home. Encourage the child to share such interests with classmates.

14. Arrange to have the child tutored. Ward and Trembley (1972) emphasized the need for one-on-one instruction. This therapeutic tutoring (Schaefer, 1977) seems essential for the majority of underachievers. Tutoring works because it ensures more on-task behavior by the student—a necessary step before better academic achievement can be expected (Bennett, 1976). The child not only increases his or her body of knowledge but also learns better work habits and skills. Initially, the tutor should present learning tasks that are just below the student's current level of functioning so that the child will immediately experience success. The program should continue to provide a sense of achievement (McClelland, 1961).

One important objective of tutoring (beyond the obvious one of imparting knowledge) is to improve the underachiever's self-confidence and self-esteem (Fink, 1962). Schaefer (1977) pointed out that many underachievers send themselves mental messages that undermine their confidence. The tutor should help the child construct more productive mental messages, as follows.

Self-Defeating Messages

- I must have instant success.
- I don't understand this. I'll just give up.
- Nobody cares what I do.
- Schoolwork is a bore.

Productive Messages

- If I work hard on this problem and check my work, I'll do okay.
- If I don't understand the assignment, I'll ask the teacher, rather than just quit.
- If I do my work, the teacher will tell the other kids how good I am.
- The teacher says that if we get our work done, we can play some games.

Techniques for Parents

Improving a child's ego strength requires that parents modify the family environment. The following insights and conditions will facilitate the needed changes.

1. Parents must be made aware of the underlying dynamics of the problem and be helped to form a supportive, accepting relationship with the child.

2. Parental pressure must be removed in areas of functioning where the child has developed patterns of rejection.

3. The child must be given standards and responsibilities within the limits of his or her growing abilities and, like any child, must be held accountable for meeting parental expectations.

4. The parent must give the child frequent opportunities to make his or her own decisions.

5. The parents must be helped to understand that their disapproval of the teacher handicaps the child, making the child feel that pleasing the teacher is a form of disloyalty to the parents.

6. The parents must be persuaded to allow the child to show curiosity, experiment with the environment, and question authority.

7. The parents must learn that their child needs to be more self-reliant. They can assist by providing the youngster opportunities for success. When a child discovers that academic performance gives satisfaction, he or she becomes more motivated.

Psychologists or counselors advising a family may wish to investigate the following questions to develop a more in-depth understanding of the situation.

Is a parent too involved with the success or failure of the child? Fathers are sometimes overly concerned about their child, but, in my experience, it is more often the mother who expresses anxiety. One scenario commonly seen in the offices of counselors is the covert power struggle between mother and child, with the child fighting back by not succeeding in school. According to Kessler (1966), this type of youngster

- performs close to expectancy on tests but does not perform in the classroom;
- flirts with academic failure but narrowly avoids total failure;
- exhibits unpredictable ups and downs in academic achievement, doing just enough to convince adults that he or she could perform adequately if he or she decided to do so;
- frustrates adults at home by refusing to complete chores or maintain good hygiene habits; constantly loses and misplaces objects and fights with siblings;
- manages to keep out of serious trouble even though he or she conveys a subtle threat to commit unacceptable deeds;
- characteristically acts silly and lighthearted even though he or she complains bitterly about being nagged constantly.

The mother often agrees with the teacher that the child is immature and irresponsible and will use this rationale for pushing the child. The mother may feel that if she doesn't keep after the child, he or she won't do anything. The parameters of the psychological game are well defined: The mother behaves as though she is responsible for the child's well-being, and the child also acts as though this were true. The child will even blame her for his or her academic misadventures ("You forgot to give me my drawings to show the class!").

As long as the mother accepts responsibility for the child's performance, she is also accepting the anxiety for the child's failure and will continue to assume that she can motivate him or her. This deprives the youngster of the capacity to feel tension about negative conduct and to learn how to correct unwanted actions. At least two fears motivate the mother to continue her behavior. First, she may be afraid that if she withdraws from the struggle, the school will blame her for indifference. This fear is justified; teachers often do look to parents for explanations of a child's unsatisfactory performance. Second, she may have an underlying (and probably unconscious) feeling that she is an inadequate parent who must prove her competency by prodding her child.

The problem and its solution are complex. Attempts by school personnel to alleviate the mother's anxieties only tend to make her more tense. She does not consider anyone in the educational system to be trustworthy enough and caring enough to warrant letting go of her defenses. A properly trained therapist, however, can help her establish a transference to a strong parent figure and allow her to examine the insecure child within her (a figure that she identifies as being like her child).

Do parents expect the child to fail? Grunebaum (1962) described a type of family whose dynamics contribute to a failure syndrome in sons. The families examined were middle class, and the involved children were reported to have no neurological or other physical impairments. Further, the homes were said to be without gross social dysfunctions.

Grunebaum found common characteristics in these families: The fathers regarded their own work achievements as being below standard. With helpless resignation, they accepted a self-derogatory role. They considered their wives to be superior to them, and the wives accepted and agreed with this analysis. The son in such a family, if he succeeds in a school situation, may be exposed to parental jealousy. He may have to face his oedipal guilt, or he may have to confront admiration or resentment from his mother (depending on the structure of her own neurosis).

As Grunebaum pointed out, the son's school performance is affected by the nature of his identification with his father. Since the mother is the model for success, femininity is equated in the boy's eyes with achievement, while masculinity is correlated with passivity. The life of an adult male is not seen by the boy as desirable; it is viewed as tedious, dull, and full of responsibility. Should the son emulate the weak, passive, so-called masculine role of the father, or should he copy the competitive, active characteristics of the mother? In this conflict, passivity is accepted as the easier choice. The mother's view that males are inadequate and the father's acceptance of his own incompetence permit both parents to believe the boy will fail in school. Again, this is a clinical dilemma best handled by counselors outside the school.

Do the parents expect too little of their child? In some cases, parents (usually the mother) infantilize a child by doing too much for the youngster. The child's initiative is blunted. When passive and compliant, the child elicits adult interest and sympathy. Teachers spare the student stress by offering special help, which strengthens dependency. This type of youngster (usually a boy) is required to deny feelings of hostility toward the parents and is taught to give in to them in order to receive approval. Often, the child is led to believe that some disaster could occur if he or she does not comply (e.g., the father's ulcer will get worse, or the mother will have to go to bed with a terrible headache).

Why does this type of youngster want to fail? Apparently, to get sympathy. Kindness is associated with being liked. The child has been taught to submit to any indignity for the sake of being accepted. Aggressiveness (necessary for the learning process) is avoided because it is equated with being rejected.

During clinical therapy, as the child becomes more aggressive and outgoing, the parents typically become distressed and anxious. At this point, the clinician will need to clarify significant issues. The counselor may also offer additional emotional support to the parents so that they will not leave the counseling situation prematurely.

Many disadvantaged families have unduly low expectations of their children. These problems and their treatment by school personnel are discussed in chapter 24.

Do the parents view the school as an unfriendly, unsupportive, or disinterested institution? The child will pick up any parental resentment toward the school. The youngster then feels that academic success is a form of disloyalty toward the mother and father. Astute teachers should recognize antagonistic behavior from the child. It may be manifested as indifference toward work assignments, covert or open defiance of school rules, listless or resistant behavior, or attempts to sabotage the teacher's efforts.

Symptoms of this nature must be talked over with parents. Sometimes, if the parents are allowed to express hostility, their resentment disappears. If the parents are too disgruntled, they may be advised to approach school administrators for discussions of educational procedures.

Are the parents aware of the child's scholastic limitations? Some parents have unrealistic estimates of the mental capacity of their children, or they are determined that their children will succeed where they failed. They believe that hard work and devotion will make stellar students of their children. When it becomes apparent that parents are pushing a child and their youngster's academic performance is disappointing them, educators must intervene to discuss realistic expectations. This may prove to be a difficult task. The parent who has invested a child with responsibility for proving him or her to be an adequate, successful human being will not, as a rule, easily accept a diagnosis of limited capacity in that youngster. If the teacher or counselor appears sympathetic and supportive, the parent may accept the evaluation after appropriate discussion and consideration of the problem.

Do the parents tend to nag the child about school accomplishments? If this question is answered in the affirmative, advise the parents to take any of the following steps, as appropriate:

- Refrain from asking the child how he or she is doing in school.
- Spend more time with the youngster on pleasant activities unrelated to school.

- Stop parent tutoring and hire a professional tutor.
- Limit parental supervision of the child's homework.
- Refrain from saying to the child, "That's good, but I know you can do better," because the youngster can interpret this message to mean there is no chance for ultimate success in any endeavor he or she undertakes.
- Learn to be better listeners so the child will be stimulated to talk about school experiences.
- Review the purpose of homework assignments. If homework is a source of conflict in the family, then its goals are being defeated. Consult with school personnel as to what steps can be taken to relieve family pressure surrounding homework.
- Limit help to specific teacher-requested assignments. Parents should not devise extra assignments that they think will help the child at school. They can review a spelling list, drill the child on numbers, or help the youngster read a story, for example, but they should not try to teach new curriculum.

Do the parents express unusual concern about their child's school progress? When school personnel encounter a family deeply distressed about their child's poor performance in school, it is good to review the emotional climate of the home. The school, of course, should not pry. It is not the prerogative of educators to investigate home conditions if the parents do not wish to talk about them. With some encouragement, however, many parents will show a willingness to discuss problems that may affect the child's school progress. The family should be instructed to seek therapeutic assistance if these difficulties appear to be chronic and severe.

Parents' Assessment of the Parent-Child Relationship

The extraordinary importance of the parent-child relationship in the formation of character makes it mandatory that parents be helped to look more closely at their behavior. School counselors should be especially concerned if the parents

- do not act as advocates for their children;
- do not collaborate with teachers;
- have low expectations of their children;
- attribute any successful endeavor by the child to luck or the efforts of others;
- deny the seriousness of their child's problems;
- are overly protective and cannot see problems objectively;
- make a scapegoat of the child in an effort to resolve other family problems;
- seek quick and unreasonable solutions to the child's problems;
- see the child's problems as insurmountable;
- take all the blame for the child's problems but are unable to change their own behavior patterns;
- have unrealistic expectations of the child.

I do not believe it is realistic to expect school personnel to change these deep-seated parental attitudes except in peripheral ways. For instance, some parents may be helped to see that their behavior contributes to poor self-esteem in their children.

The following questions for parents may spark their interest in their children's problems and provide specific behavior-changing information. In group sessions, the questions can be read to parents and then the implications of each question can be discussed. In individual or family conferences, tailor discussion to the needs of the listeners. The counselor should explore the motivations of the parents, investigate the ways they handle their youngsters, and discuss other methods that might work better.

1. Do you think your child sees you as giving up too easily when a task gets hard? The hallmark of a poor achiever is the habit of giving up easily under stress. Parents can set a good example for their children by carrying through on difficult tasks.

2. Do you think your child sees you as avoiding unpleasant things rather than dealing with them quickly? Most problems need to be faced and conquered. Running away from distressing situations only tends to make things worse.

3. In front of your child, do you tend to use phrases like, "What's the use?" "I really don't care," "That's life," "C'est la vie," and so on? Perhaps these statements are ways to demonstrate to a youngster that you are giving up easily in order to obey the dictates of fate, but adopting this apathetic attitude gives your boy or girl permission not to get involved in a problem and its solution.

4. Do you demonstrate disappointment to your child that you are not accomplishing things in life that you would like to achieve? Adult underachievers settle for less than they want, don't stick to tasks, give up easily, back away from criticism, complain they don't measure up to potential, and become emotional when frustrated. Breaking such habits is not easy but is well worth the effort for both parents and their children.

5. Do you think your child sees you as giving up easily during arguments? Underachievers are basically afraid to lose. Arguments present the possibility of failure (i.e., of losing the dispute), but adults need to show offspring that they can hold on to their convictions and be heard.

6. Do you communicate to your child the feeling that most people possess more power than you do? The person who constantly bows to authority adopts a doormat pattern of behavior—those perceived to have more knowledge and power. This childlike stance can be another way to cover up an inability to express initiative and assertion.

7. Were you able to tell your own parents what you wanted and to discuss your feelings with them, even if they did not like what you said? If you could not, then it is possible that you discourage discussions with your child. The ability of members to talk openly and frankly to each other is one of the hallmarks of a healthy family. Children gain feelings of power and self-confidence when they can express needs and free expression tends to head off spells of pent-up anger.

8. Do you become depressed quickly and retire from contention upon being frustrated? Individuals, when aggravated, should take positive action (e.g., fighting back when mistreated) instead of emotionally running away. Hang in there—demonstrate to your youngster that you can remain assertive under stress.

9. Do you find yourself discouraging your child from trying new activities because you hesitate to meet challenges presented by novel situations? Of course, all new contests present the possibility of failure. Don't pass on this breakdown of nerve to your youngster. Get out of his or her way—let the kid learn how to face disappointment (as well as gratification) when tackling assignments.

10. When you become embarrassed, do you tend to make an unpleasant fuss? At times, anyone can become mortified, but if a parent shows excessive chagrin, children may emulate the expressed feelings of inferiority and unworthiness.

11. Do you show your child that criticism upsets you excessively? Criticism implies that a person has not measured up. Many insecure children secretly believe they could do better if only they were more self-confident. That is why parents should not run from criticism. Instead, they should demonstrate a willingness to persevere even when exposed to derogatory remarks. The children will observe their parents' tough egos and emulate them.

12. Do you think your child sees you as acting foolish or silly if others become angry with you? Acting foolish is a way to avoid facing the displeasure of others. Further, the silly person need not show anger in direct ways. The child who observes a parent acting in this manner never learns to handle hostility in strong, forthright ways.

13. Does your child observe you as seldom fighting for your rights, even when it is obvious you are in the right? The person who thinks little of himself or herself is often afraid to stand up for what he or she thinks is right. However, this behavior can be a form of running away. Children may emulate this conduct.

14. Is it hard for you to be firm with your child? The doubtful adult shows indecision by waffling on family regulations. Parents cannot always be right, but children feel more secure if adults show confidence and resolution when setting rules.

15. Does your child see you as being unable to stick to your guns? Are you easily swayed by others? If you do back down quickly, try showing more backbone by standing up for yourself more often. After all, children cannot be expected to show more social courage than their parents exhibit.

CHAPTER 8

Poor Physical Strength

Poor physical stamina is the inability to maintain energy levels in ordinary activities or to participate in physical contact with others. Children rated on the Burks Behavior Rating Scales (BBRS) (Burks 1977a, 2006a) as showing poor stamina tend to

- avoid physical play activities;
- be easily injured during play activities;
- be lethargic;
- repudiate participation in physically challenging activities;
- fatigue quickly.

Preschool and kindergarten children who exhibit symptoms of poor physical stamina tend also to be withdrawn, poorly coordinated, sometimes anxious, noncompetitive, and dependent (Burks, 1977b). Among older children, the behavior picture becomes more confused: Poor physical stamina can be related to many or most symptoms described on other BBRS scales. The neurotic traits associated with lack of stamina in young children tend to disappear in older youngsters and be replaced by acting-out disorders (attention deficits, impulsivity, poor coordination, academic difficulties, poor social conformity, poor reality contact, and excessive resistance). The reasons for this change in behavior patterns from younger to older children are not clear. However, gross physical inadequacy accompanies many chronic and severe emotional difficulties among older children (Bakwin & Bakwin, 1954). It may be assumed that physical inadequacy is more emotionally devastating to older individuals than to younger children; for this reason, counseling given parents of older children may need to be more intensive than that offered to parents of younger children.

THEORETICAL BACKGROUND

Among any group of normal children, there are a few individuals who lack physical strength. Bakwin and Bakwin (1954) pointed out that the reasons for lack of stamina and strength are many and complex. Such conditions may be inherited or acquired through disease or accident.

The unfortunate psychological effects of inadequate physical development can be great and long-lasting. An inept boy, for instance, may find himself rejected in sports activities. Unable to defend himself in physical fighting, he gains no respect. Since he is generally unwanted, it is difficult for him to become a leader. The lack of physical strength can affect all his social relationships. For girls, the consequences of poor physical stamina may be less severe but are still important if they are in any way negatively involved with physical attractiveness.

INTERVENTION STRATEGIES

Techniques for School Personnel

Educators and counselors cannot, of course, directly treat the organic problems of physically weak students. They may ask parents to consult medical sources if the child is not already under pediatric treatment. They can urge the parents to attend more closely to the child's daily nutrition and rest routines. Finally, they can ensure the child's physical comfort in school as much as possible and suggest to parents that physical arrangements in the home be geared to the child.

All students can benefit from environmental conditions that ensure physical comfort. Children with physical disabilities, even more than their nondisabled counterparts, need to experience feelings of well-being and must not be overly distracted by negative external conditions and events. Emotional and physical discomfort can affect learning in adverse ways. Thus, educators are obliged to investigate signs of distress in children that could spring from conditions in their surroundings. Educators can help ensure that children feel comfortable by asking them how they feel about classroom conditions and by investigating their home conditions.

Are some students physically uncomfortable in classroom settings? If so, does that discomfort interfere with their capacity to learn? Most adults would turn down the heat, for example, if they felt too warm and would want to do the same for students, particularly if many students were suffering the same discomfort. Yet many teachers do not consider it important for students to express such feelings of discomfort.

I created the How I Feel about My Classroom checklist to assess physical student discomfort in the classroom (see figure 8.1). Long experience with the checklist (Burks, 1968e) shows clearly that when a child checks an item as "a big problem," the youngster is having real difficulties in that area. If the child checks "not a problem" for an item, it can ordinarily be assumed that the situation is truly not a problem. However, a few very inhibited students are afraid to say that they are dissatisfied with classroom conditions; they should be quizzed further to see if any areas described as "sometimes a problem" are of real concern to them.

As with any instrument that asks children to reveal their inner feelings, this device should be used constructively. The children have been asked to give something of themselves and, rightfully, should be given something in return. They may be concerned and curious about how their replies compare with other students' responses, how the replies affect the teacher, and how the responses will be used to implement changes in the classroom.

These concerns, of course, must be handled with finesse. The following suggestions may be of assistance.

1. Approach the students in a comfortable, relaxed manner.
2. Conduct a frank and open discussion before asking the questions.
3. Do not promise the students any specific changes. A child may wish to change his or her seat, for example, but it may prove impractical to do that.
4. Emphasize to the children that the procedure is a cooperative attempt to improve the quality of the classroom environment.

After administration, discuss the questions with individual students or with the group. Individual discussions should take place if the teacher is unusually concerned about a student's adjustment, if a child's responses indicate a significant amount of discomfort, or if a child's answers are unclear and further information is needed.

Sometimes the questions may be worthy of classroom discussion. For instance, one large group of normal children who completed the checklist indicated that they could not hear the teacher. Group discussion about this problem, revealed that the teacher not only talked too softly, she spoke too quickly for the students to understand her. The teacher quite properly thanked the students for telling her and said she would attempt to remedy the situation.

HOW I FEEL ABOUT MY CLASSROOM

Harold F. Burks, Ph.D.

Answer each question by putting a check mark in the column that tells how you feel.

	Not a problem	Sometimes a problem	A big problem
1. Do you think you sit too far away from the other children?	☐	☐	☐
2. Do you think you sit too close to the other children?	☐	☐	☐
3. Do you sit close enough to your friends?	☐	☐	☐
4. Do you think the tables and chairs could be arranged better?	☐	☐	☐
5. Would you like to sit somewhere else in the room?	☐	☐	☐
6. Would you like to move around in the room more?	☐	☐	☐
7. Do you have enough space in the room to do the things you want to do?	☐	☐	☐
8. Do other children move around the room too much?	☐	☐	☐
9. Is there too much noise in the classroom?	☐	☐	☐
10. Would you like to sit closer to the chalkboard?	☐	☐	☐
11. Would you like to sit further away from the chalkboard?	☐	☐	☐
12. Would it help if the teacher wrote larger letters on the chalkboard?	☐	☐	☐
13. Is it hard to read the teacher's handwriting?	☐	☐	☐
14. Do you get tired in the classroom?	☐	☐	☐
15. Would you like to have more rest periods?	☐	☐	☐
16. Does the light in the classroom bother you?	☐	☐	☐
17. Is it hard to hear what the teacher is saying?	☐	☐	☐
18. Do you think the teacher should talk louder?	☐	☐	☐
19. Do you think the teacher should talk more softly?	☐	☐	☐
20. Is it too hot in the classroom?	☐	☐	☐
21. Is it too cold in the classroom?	☐	☐	☐
22. Do you get hungry at school?	☐	☐	☐
23. Are you bothered by something at school that you can't tell anyone about?	☐	☐	☐
24. Do the other kids pick on you?	☐	☐	☐
25. Do you get to use the equipment in the classroom enough?	☐	☐	☐

Figure 8.1.

Techniques for Parents

The following list of questions can be used in parent conferences to spark discussion about environmental conditions that can enhance children's learning. Many of the issues raised by the questions are relevant to all children, but they present special problems for a student with poor physical stamina. It is not necessary for the discussion leader to see the parents' responses. In group conferences, questions can be read to the audience and then discussed. Individual or family conferences must be tailored as needed. Parents should be allowed to take the questionnaire home with them.

1. Does your child have a quiet place in which to study?
2. Is it a comfortable and appealing place—not a place to which the child is banished?
3. Did the child help plan and set up the study area?
4. Does this space belong to the child alone and not to anyone else in the family?
5. Is the study area shielded from excessive noise and visual distraction?
6. If a suitable study location for the child cannot be found in the home, is it possible to find a place elsewhere (a relative's home, a library, a friend's house)?
7. Does your child have a set time for home study?

   - Homework should not be allowed to take up the child's entire evening. Ordinarily, homework should not last for more than 20 to 60 minutes (depending on the child's age).
   - Parents should not try to help with their child's homework if the child objects. Most parents are not the best teachers for their own children.
   - Communications must be kept open between teachers and parents about the successes and difficulties of home study (too much or too little may be demanded by the school or home).

8. Has your child had a physical checkup recently?

   - If a child is chronically hyperactive, irritable, inattentive, or explosive, a medical examination may need to go beyond routine studies (e.g., to include a study of the nervous system or glandular system).
   - A child who has never experienced normal vision or hearing may not complain. Therefore, vision and hearing checks should be routine.
   - Medical findings should be made available to school personnel.
   - The child should be asked if he or she feels physically ill.
   - The child who tires easily in school should receive extra attention (special snacks, rest periods, lighter than usual exercise, etc.).

9. Are you satisfied with your child's eating habits?

   - A child's health is vitally dependent on blood-sugar levels. Some foods (e.g., starches and sugars) raise blood-sugar levels quickly, but the levels soon drop precipitously, leaving the child tired or irritable. Proteins tend to keep blood-sugar levels up longer.
   - Breakfast is usually the most important meal for children. Children require protein (e.g., eggs, cheese, meat, or nuts) as well as breads and cereals to see them through until lunch. Midmorning nervousness, tiredness, or inattention may indicate the need for a more nutritious breakfast (however, food should not be forced upon the child by school personnel).
   - Surveys (Burks, 1968e) have shown that some children's hunger pangs during the day may cause food fantasies that distract from schoolwork.
   - Some children need extra snacks during the day to keep up energy levels.

- Bland (1982) identified a junk food syndrome, in which children demonstrate symptoms of poor self-control, poor concentration, fatigue, muscle pains, stomach pains, constipation, and aggression. No one child is likely to show all these symptoms, but if several symptoms are shown and the child has not been diagnosed as hyperactive, the child's diet should be examined. The disorder has been traced to a diet high in empty-calorie foods—that is, foods with too many calories in relation to vitamins and minerals.
- Knapczyk (1979) described three major diet-related conditions that can lead to behavior disorders in school-age children: hypoglycemia (low blood-sugar level), vitamin or mineral deficiencies, and allergies to food substances or additives.

10. Does your child get enough sleep?

- Most children need 10 or more hours of sleep a night.
- Too little rest is reflected in symptoms such as rubbing the eyes, restlessness, irritability, inattention, and yawning.
- Children may be kept awake by noise or light.
- Some youngsters devise bedtime rituals that take hours to maintain. If the rituals are constructive and not manipulative, have the child start them earlier in the evening. Otherwise, parents should put a stop to these delaying tactics.
- Some children are genuinely afraid of being left alone and cannot go to sleep. Reasons for these fears should be explored.
- The child may be overstimulated by too much television viewing late in the evening.
- Dreams and nightmares can upset children. They may need to be reassured that dreams are not real (this is particularly true for younger children).

11. Is the time allotted for watching television under control in your home?

- Television is a mixed blessing: It can impart much information but may also keep children passive, physically and mentally. Time for viewing television should be controlled.
- Television can occupy much of a child's interests and take up time that could be spent on constructive activities.
- Television can keep the family from sharing experiences (storytelling, games, outings).
- The quality of television programs should be reviewed carefully. Exposure to unselected programs may complicate the process of helping a child distinguish between fantasy and reality (depending on the child's age).
- Blanco (1972) believed watching television can help distractible youngsters become more attentive if they are allowed to choose programs that interest them, watch those programs alone in a dimly lit room, and are encouraged to watch shows to the end without interruptions.

12. To protect your child from encountering trouble, do you usually know the whereabouts of your child, and do you know the nature of his or her out-of-school activities?

- Children who feel parental concern for their betterment tend to improve conduct because they internalize adult expectations.
- Parental concern helps keep a youngster out of danger. As the child grows older, of course, along with concern, more freedom should be allowed.

- Burks (1968e) stresses the emotional and physical benefits for children of healthy interaction with peers in play. Parents should promote activities with peers.

Counselors and teachers who use the preceding questions in parent counseling sessions should not assume that, because parents are well-educated they will necessarily understand the underlying principles of good nutrition, adequate rest, and proper environmental conditions for their youngsters. Some parents are content to let their children attend school after a sparse breakfast of dry cereal or a doughnut and milk. Some children, unfortunately, dictate to parents what they will or will not eat.

CHAPTER 9

Poor Coordination

Poor coordination is best described as the inability to use the voluntary muscles and sense organs properly in important activities. Children with high scores on the Burks Behavior Rating Scales (BBRS) (Burks 1977a, 2006a) poor coordination scale tend to

- be clumsy;
- be awkward at activities;
- show poor handwriting;
- produce messy drawings and paintings;
- run into and bump others.

Among primary school students, poor coordination is just one facet of a pattern of immature behavior that includes cognitive difficulties, academic difficulties, attention deficits, and dependency (Burks, 1977b).

Youngsters with a neurological disability often demonstrate problems in motor coordination. Their handwriting is commonly illegible, and they perform large-muscle activities (running, skipping, throwing a ball, etc.) awkwardly. In addition, such children tend to be impulsive, resistant, aggressive, and tend to have poor social skills (Burks, 1957a, 1960, 1968b). Schizophrenic children may also show coordination difficulties (Bakwin & Bakwin, 1954). These youngsters ordinarily do not relate well to reality (poor reality contact in chapter 4).

Coordination difficulties often seem to be associated with cognitive and emotional capabilities. Children who are withdrawn, less intelligent, or inactive and lethargic also seem less well coordinated. The problem, however, may be observed in students who otherwise behave normally.

THEORETICAL BACKGROUND

Poor coordination may result from slow maturation of the nervous system or from injury to the nervous system. It can be assessed only in the context of what is to be expected of most children at any particular age. Lanning and Robbins (1966) provided the following rough guidelines regarding age expectations:

Kindergarten. Muscular development is rapid and children find it difficult to be inactive. Most are able to feed and dress themselves. Many start to jump rope. They begin to develop a sense of rhythm—they can skip, alternating legs. Skills are gained through the use of simple tools. Visual functioning still tends to be immature, but some spatial relationships are recognized. Hand dominance is being established. Some hand movements requiring dexterity are employed. Most kindergartners are able to draw a person with related parts (head, body, limbs). Drawings should show recognizable shapes.

First grade. At this grade level, girls are about one year more mature than boys. Large-muscle activity is still preferred over small-muscle activity. Most basic skills (e.g., the ability to hold a pencil, ride a two-wheel bike, use tools, comb their own hair, help others with motor tasks) have been acquired. Rhythm is fairly well established. Children begin to judge distances more accurately. Writing is difficult for the average first grader, but by six to six-and-a-half years of age eye and hand muscles are well enough developed for reading and writing. By this age, children are able to draw a person with additional features (hands, fingers, face, etc.). Drawings show good shape and design.

Second grade. While large-muscle activity is still needed, muscular coordination is much improved. Second graders enjoy strenuous activity, play many ball games with skill, and like to use imaginative rhythms. These children can handle nearly all aspects of caring for themselves. Their eyes have matured enough to focus for long periods of time on pictures and writing. Eye-hand coordination is well established. The average second grader can sit still for considerable periods of time.

Third grade. By third grade, growth rates begin to slow, although the variation in growth between boys and girls is still considerable. The large muscles are still developing. Motor skills are rapidly improving. At this age, the game of tag is preferred to playing with toys. At this age, children are skillful at balancing, and they enjoy swimming, bicycling, and roller skating. Games requiring small-muscle control are sought out. The average third grader likes to draw. Writing is still difficult for many (particularly boys), but reading is enjoyed because eye muscles have strengthened.

Fourth grade. Growth is more slow and even. Children are is practicing skills gained at an earlier age, and they have good body control. Skills in sports activities are rapidly acquired. Stamina is improved. The ability to see and focus is good because eyes have reached adult size. In general, children at this age are alert, casual, relaxed, poised, and active (spurts of activity are noted). Compared with younger children, they may prefer less strenuous exercise.

Fifth grade and above. All aspects of coordination improve. Stamina becomes greater, attention span lengthens, and ocular skills are enhanced. By the sixth grade, reading ability may be equal to that of many adults. The child becomes more and more adept at games involving large and small muscles. Complex tools are employed with adeptness.

The preceding guide is a general index by which to judge the level of coordination development in individual children. If a youngster deviates too much from these standards, steps should be taken to diagnose and possibly treat conditions that might impede progress in the development of physical coordination.

DIAGNOSIS

I have observed and studied hundreds of children, both in and out of hospital settings, who were later diagnosed by medical personnel as experiencing some type of neurological disorder (Burks, 1955, 1957a, 1957b, 1960, 1968b). These children were ordinarily hyperactive and impulsive; in many cases, they displayed signs of learning disabilities and were socially and emotionally troubled, fitting the picture of the child with attention deficit hyperactivity disorder. Although neurological examinations rarely showed obvious signs of nervous system impairment (e.g., tremor, poor reflex development), these children were generally seen by others as being clumsy. This awkwardness was characteristically noted in motor exercises. The picture of uneven motor development was particularly noted in children less than eight or nine years of age.

A high score on the BBRS poor coordination scale should alert the counselor to a possible problem. During testing, give children the following coordination activities:

1. Stand on one foot with eyes closed: Normal children (even younger ones) are able to maintain balance for a considerable period of time; however, ADD children tend to find this difficult. Urge the child to keep the foot raised as long as possible. The test should then be repeated with the other foot raised. Ordinarily, right-handed children maintain balance on the left foot best, but this may not prove true for hyperactive children (possibly indicating pathology in the dominant hemisphere of the brain).
2. Close your eyes tightly and raise your arms so they are pointing straight out to the front: Very young, normal children will tend to screw up their faces and grimace. This may also hold true for older children (ages six to nine) who have a neurological handicap. A "windmill effect" is often noted; the hyperactive child cannot keep his or her arms from rotating slightly. Most normal children hold their arms on an even, steady plane.

3. Close your eyes and hold your arms straight out to the sides. Extend your index fingers, then touch the tip of your right index finger to the tip of your nose. Move your right arm back out to the side, then touch your left index finger to your nose in the same manner: It is usually wise to demonstrate this exercise to the child so he or she understands what is to be done. Most normal children (again, even younger ones) are able to complete this motor task quite easily. Hyperactive children tend to find it more difficult. They may miss the ends of their noses by a large margin.

4. Touch the tip of one thumb to the tip of the fingers on the same hand in sequence. Do this rapidly. Repeat the exercise with the other hand: Again, it is wise to demonstrate the exercise. Under pressure, many children with neurological dysfunction show problems with this task, while most normal children are able to do it quite easily.

5. Sit in a chair with hands placed palms down on your knees. Turn your hands over and back as quickly as possible: If the child does the task slowly or carefully, encourage him or her to speed up the operation. This exercise, easily done by most normal children, may prove difficult for the child who has a neurological disability. The hands do not move rhythmically; a "stuttering" effect is noted.

6. Skip across the room: By kindergarten age most normal children can skip quite well. Older children with brain dysfunction may not be able to skip properly, even at seven, eight, or nine years old.

7. Hop across the room on one foot and then hop back on the other: This task, simple for the majority of children, may prove difficult for many children who have an organic disturbance.

8. Catch a soft rubber ball (four or five inches in diameter): Hyperactive children may have great trouble judging the position of the ball in space and cannot catch it with dexterity.

9. Bounce the ball from hand to floor and back for a period of about 10 seconds: This is an easy task for the majority of children but not for those with an organic disturbance. Normal children can do this task fairly well even with their eyes closed, but this is a very difficult maneuver for the child who has a neurological handicap.

10. Watch the tip of a pencil while it is brought slowly to a point near the end of your nose: The child's eyes should converge evenly and maintain their position after the pencil point has stopped moving. The child with a neurological handicap often is unable to maintain this convergence even for a brief period of time.

Poor small-motor coordination is also a common problem for children with an attention deficit disorder. One of the best measurements for this skill (and for the ability to perceive and reproduce proper proportions) is the Goodenough-Draw-A-Man test (Goodenough, 1926). I have found (Burks, 1960) that many attention-deficit youngsters (eight years of age and above) could not meet the following qualitative standards for this test as well as normally behaved children could:

Proportion

- Head: Area of the head must not be more than one half or less than one-tenth that of the trunk. Judge rather leniently.
- Arms: Arms must be as long as the trunk or slightly longer, but in no case should they reach to the knees. Width of the arms must be less than the width of the trunk.
- Legs: The legs must be at least as long as the vertical measurement of the trunk, but must not be greater than twice that measurement. Legs must not be as wide as the trunk.
- Feet: The feet and legs must be distinctly different. The length of the foot must be greater than its height from sole to instep and not more than one-third or less than one-tenth the total length of the leg. In full-face drawings where the feet are shown in perspective, they must be distinct in some way from the legs.

Motor Coordination

- Lines: All lines must be reasonably firm, for the most part meeting each other cleanly at points of junction, without a marked tendency to cross or overlap, or to have gaps between the ends. All lines must be joined correctly. This is a more rigid interpretation of the preceding rule. Obviously this cannot be credited unless that standard has been met. Judgment should be strict.

- Head outline: Outline of head must be without obviously unintentional irregularities. The shape of the head must be developed beyond a crude circle or ellipse and must show conscious control of the movement of the hand. Judgment should be strict.
- Trunk outline: Same standards as for the head outline. A primitive circle or ellipse does not suffice.
- Arms and legs: Arms and legs must be without irregularities and without a tendency to narrow at the junction with the trunk. No arm or leg should be represented by a single line, and all must be attached to the torso.
- Features: Features must be symmetrical in all respects.

The preceding standards are an abbreviated version of the Goodenough scoring system. For the detailed scoring system, see *Measurement of Intelligence by Drawings* (Goodenough, 1926).

When small-muscle coordination is being judged, pay attention to handwriting. One of the hallmarks of an attention-deficit child is poor handwriting, described by most observers as "messy" or "scribbly."

INTERVENTION STRATEGIES

During curriculum research conducted with a class of elementary-age children with neurological handicaps (Burks, 1962), efforts were made to treat the problem of poor muscular coordination, which was a prominent symptom in most of the students. The following findings were reported:

1. Many of the activities most interesting to these children were those that would ordinarily be intriguing to younger children with normal neurological functions. For instance, 9- and 10-year-old students were willing to play with games and toys that would ordinarily interest younger children (e.g., pushing little cars around a sand pile or table). When the children found age-relevant materials too difficult to use, they simply put them aside.
2. Many of the physical activities these children were asked to do to develop coordination (e.g., building models, constructing kites, catching a ball) required many more preliminary instructions and much more practice than would be necessary for normally functioning children of the same age.
3. These students, perhaps more than others, seemed to need an admired model well versed in the physical skills commonly used in the classroom and on the playground. They were intrigued and motivated by the knowledge that the teacher was a former football player of note (often urging, for example, "Please, Mr. Smith, throw us the football!").

The problems of youngsters who are mentally retarded or physically handicapped (e.g., the child with cerebral palsy or the child with an orthopedic disability) are many and complex and cannot be treated adequately in a publication devoted to an overview of brief diagnostic and treatment approaches. However, school counselors and teachers, who may be asked to suggest curriculum materials or activities for children who are slow learners or who have physical disabilities, may find the following lists helpful. Of course, these supplies and classroom approaches can also be employed efficaciously with some normally functioning younger children.

Curriculum Materials

beads and string
paper for folding and cutting
scissors
blocks
Lincoln Logs
checkers

rings

marbles

yarn

jacks

pegboards

clay

beanbags

crayons and other coloring materials

balance boards

laces for tying

Play-Doh

zippers

Tinkertoys

balls

nuts and bolts

hoops

large rings

trampoline

Curriculum Activities

Laterality and directionality can be taught by using imitative movements, such as walking on stepping-stones made out of cardboard, playing "Simon says," practicing drawing from left to right, counting beads from left to right, tracing the left and right hands on paper, practicing jumping from the left leg to the right leg, touching the left and right parts of the body, and placing story pictures in sequence from left to right. Have the child lead in exercises of this nature. Instruct the parents to teach the child to shake hands with the proper hand and suggest that they talk about directions when traveling (e.g., help the child recognize which way the car is turning and explain the use of road maps).

Body awareness, necessary for a strong and integrated self-image, can be taught to young children by identifying body parts and their functions. Youngsters must also be taught how the body is located and positioned in relation to the environment. For children who react impulsively to stress, body relaxation techniques can help them become aware of tension. This awareness must precede the ability to control impulsive thoughts and muscular activity. Music is helpful in that it, rather than an adult, serves as an external control. Chosen musical pieces should be characterized by simplicity, clarity, and rhythmic qualities in order to provide a sense of predictability and consistency. Listening to music apparently enhances concentration and memory in students with emotional or learning problems.

The following activities, largely devised at New York University, have been used to determine the extent of long-muscle development in children. Children with normal muscle function should have no difficulty in completing any of the exercises. Getman (1957) found that many children with mental retardation actually benefited from these exercises.

Angels in the snow. Ask the child to lie flat on his or her back on the floor with arms at the sides and legs straight. First, the arms are moved in a full arc to a point above the head. Then they are moved back to the sides and held still as the youngster moves his or her legs apart as far as possible. These two actions are practiced independently of each other until the child can do them well; then the youngster is taught to do them in combination (i.e., as the child brings the arms up, he or she moves the legs apart). Getman believed that nearly every child, including those with cerebral palsy or spastic paralysis, can be taught to do this exercise (and gain flexibility) because the floor supports most of the body's weight.

Trunk lift. Ask the child to lie face down on the floor with the stomach on a pillow. With hands held behind the head, the child raises his or her trunk off the floor. If, in the beginning, the youngster has trouble raising the trunk, the teacher should place a hand on the child's heels as a counterweight. The purpose of this exercise is to develop strength, control, and flexibility in the upper back. Getman pointed out that children with cerebral palsy or spastic paralysis may need help to do this exercise. A sling can be placed under the chest for support. Many such youngsters have so little body control that they do not know which muscles to use for this activity. They can also learn the necessary direction of movement with the assistance of the sling.

Leg lift. The position is the same as required for the trunk lift, except that the hands are under the chin. The child is asked to raise his or her legs as high as possible. Some children will need to learn how to raise one leg at a time before they can lift both in the same motion. For some very poorly coordinated children, a sling placed under their ankles may be needed to start this exercise.

Straight-leg sit-ups. The child is asked to lie on his or her back with hands clasped behind the neck. While the teacher holds the feet down, the youngster tries to sit up. If the child demonstrates unusual weakness in the upper abdominal or flexor muscles, a sling placed in back of the neck should be used to help the child sit up.

Bent-knee sit-ups. As in the previous exercise, the child is asked to lie flat on his or her back, but now the knees are bent, with the feet almost touching the child's seat. The teacher holds the feet down while the youngster tries to sit up. If the child cannot do this exercise but can do the straight-leg sit-up, weakness is centered in the abdominal muscles. Again, a sling placed in back of the neck may be necessary until enough muscle strength has been gained.

Feet lift. The child is asked to lie flat on his or her back. A pillow is placed under the hips. The youngster is now asked to lift the legs straight to a distance of about 10 inches above the floor and to hold that position as long as possible. Nearly all children should be able to hold their legs aloft for at least 10 seconds. If they cannot, it may be assumed that they have weak hip-flexor muscles. A child may have to practice holding one leg up at a time until enough strength has been acquired to raise both.

Toe touch. Back and hamstring muscles can be strengthened by having the child stand with feet together, knees straight, and then bend at the hips to touch fingertips to toes. This position should be held for approximately three seconds. Children who cannot bend far enough to touch their toes should be asked to touch their knees, and later, as flexibility increases, to touch their ankles and then their toes. The teacher can help the child balance, if necessary, by placing his or her hands on the child's hips and holding the child as the child bends forward.

Accident Proneness

Despite all precautions, every school experiences events where children injure themselves. I remember well an incident in an elementary school where I had been asked to act as principal for a day. A child ran into the office and informed me that Jimmy (a fourth grade student) had fallen out of a tree and was lying on the asphalt. Sure enough, the boy was unconscious. Imagine my anxiety as I organized efforts to get medical services to the scene and at the same time phoned the parents to inform them of the accident. Jimmy recovered from his injuries; however, after a review of his school records with his teachers and parents, it became clear that he suffered many problems of poor coordination allied with a neurological dysfunction characterized by impulsive behavior and hyperactivity.

Youngsters with poor coordination are prone to accidents—they trip easily, run into objects and people more often than most children, and fall more frequently when climbing. School personnel must target such students for proper motor testing and must protect them from hazards where this is possible. On occasion, I have encountered children who are accident-prone but show no motor difficulties. When this occurs, school counselors should investigate possible unconscious self-destructive motives the child may have; it would be relevant to look for depressive symptoms.

Parents of accident-prone children should consider the following suggestions.

1. Protect the child's self-confidence by refusing to become angry about physical misadventures and by refraining from ridicule.
2. Abstain from efforts to overprotect the child by prohibiting participation in sports activities. Such responses may make the youngster feel even more incapable. Instead, instruct the child to be more cautious and provide protective devices (arm and leg supports, shin guards, knee protectors, and so forth).
3. Discuss any special problems with sport coaches.

CHAPTER 10

Poor Intellectual Ability

Intellectual difficulties describe behaviors indicating the presence of low mental capacity. Extensive research (Burks, 1977a, 2006a) confirms retarded children tend to demonstrate

- poor ability to follow directions;
- poor memory;
- poor imagination;
- poor ability to answer questions;
- inflexible responses;
- poor ability to ask questions;
- a limited vocabulary.

The presence of the above indicators can occur among children showing any kind of difficulty (Burks 1977a, 1977b, 2006a). However, slow-learning children with inherited deficiencies will not, in general, show the distracting, erratic, or impulse control problems demonstrated by children with accompanying neurological damage (Burks, 1955, 1977a). Among young retarded children, cognitive difficulties are often associated with test scores indicating problems in attention deficit, poor coordination, academic difficulties, dependency, and poor self-esteem. This pattern of symptoms implies slow developmental maturity. For some children, other negative characteristics (rebelliousness, distrustfulness, and aggressive tendencies) may be shown, possibly as a reaction to lack of success in school.

THEORETICAL BACKGROUND

The Nature of Intelligence

Possibly no psychological concept has engendered more controversy than intelligence, the definition of which continues to be a major source of debate. All cultures acknowledge differences in the degree to which people exhibit adaptive behavior (i.e., how they approach and solve problems); however, there is little agreement about the quality and demonstration of intelligence. Nevertheless, most would agree that intelligence has three facets: (a) practical problem-solving ability (reasoning logically, seeing all sides of a problem, and keeping an open mind); (b) verbal ability (being a good conversationalist and reading often and well); and (c) social intelligence (being sensitive to social cues, admitting mistakes, and displaying interest in the world at large).

Given the fact that commonly used IQ tests have only a moderate ability to predict school outcomes and a very low capacity (a validity coefficient of about .2) to predict real-world performance, the importance of implicit assumptions held by most people about the nature of intelligence may have been underestimated. Sternberg, Wagner, Williams, and Horvath (1995) decried academic intelligence tests, as opposed to practical intelligence measures, because they

- are formulated according to the biases of text developers;
- often have little or no intrinsic interest;

- often seek information that is outside the realm of ordinary experience for the person being tested;
- have only one correct answer;
- often have just one method for obtaining the correct solution.

None of these characteristics apply well to many of the problems faced by individuals in daily life. I believe it is important to assess practical intelligence when dealing with children thought to possess low mental capacity.

Low Mental Capacity: The Nature of Mental Retardation

Mental retardation is an arbitrarily defined diagnostic category that has changed frequently and substantively over the years (Landesman & Ramey, 1989). At the same time, the methods used to identify children with mental retardation vary dramatically.

Landesman and Ramey (1989) pointed out that in recent years major changes related to mental retardation have included the following:

- The concept of adaptive behavior has been incorporated into the definition of mental retardation.
- The IQ cutoff has been lowered so that a child must perform at least two standard deviations below the mean on a test of general intelligence, with concurrent deficits in adaptive behavior, to qualify for a diagnosis of mental retardation (thus eliminating from services those people with IQs between 70 and 85).
- The upper age limit for initial diagnosis has been extended (mostly to offer services to a large number of older adolescents and young adults who have undergone neurological impairment as a result of vehicle and sports injuries and drug abuse).
- Lifelong mental slowness as part of the concept has been dropped.

These changes ensued from an increased recognition that IQ scores, used in isolation, are not highly predictive of later adult functioning and from recent evidence that shows that targeted interventions and a supportive environment can facilitate remarkable developmental advances for individuals with even very low IQ scores. The real-world success of low-IQ people seems to be linked to practical intelligence, or common sense, frequently backed by a supportive environment and good social skills.

Extended research studies belie the notion that mental slowness is a permanent characteristic of any individual. Many children who are considered to have mild mental retardation during their school years are *not* so labeled, either by themselves or those around them, during their pre- and postschool years. Many lose the label of mental retardation in adulthood. Actually, labels of mental retardation have proved even less useful than IQ scores in predicting behavior in schools or in other settings.

For these reasons, school personnel must tread lightly when assigning labels to children who do not do well in school environments. Individuals who lack certain cognitive skills (much emphasized in commonly used IQ tests) can possess other kinds of intelligence (like spatial, musical, and interpersonal aptitude) not examined in paper-and-pencil tests of intelligence.

For example, years ago when I was a young man, I taught a class of junior high school children with mental retardation. One 14-year-old boy, Richard, was an indifferent student in the classroom. He seemed slow. At the end of each school day Richard would become agitated and insist that he had to leave just when the ending bell sounded. He refused to tell me the reason for his need to leave so quickly. Eventually, I made a home call. I expected to find Richard with his family (it being late afternoon) but he was not present. "Well, he has a job for two hours after school in a restaurant," his mother said. I asked what it was that Richard did in the restaurant. "He does things like cleaning and running errands and that sort of thing, I guess," she replied. Did he like the job? "Oh, he loves it and is always there on time!" What does he do with the money he earns? "He saves it and buys things that he needs." Did she know that Richard was underage for that kind of work? "My goodness, I never thought of that," she replied. "My husband and I thought it was a good experience for him. We think a lot of Richard. He is a good boy and works hard." I excused myself and drove to the restaurant.

The proprietor, a large genial man, was happy to talk about Richard. "He is one of my best workers," he said. "He's always on time and doesn't have to be told more than once how to do his jobs." What were these jobs? "He does things like washing dishes, cleaning floors, setting tables, and so on—just about anything I tell him to do." Could he handle money? "Yeah, he's good at that." I cautiously mentioned that Richard had some school difficulties. The owner looked puzzled. "Well, you could fool me," he said. I thanked the owner and left. Nothing was mentioned about the boy's being underage.

Outside of congratulating Richard on having such a good job, I did nothing about the legal ramifications of Richard's underage work status. Obviously, he was getting far more from his job than he was from being at school.

Causes of Mental Retardation

Causes of lowered intellectual capacity are numerous and complex. In general, investigators have classified these causes as follows:

- inherited factors;
- damage to the nervous system after birth;
- emotional problems that prevent the expression of abilities that would otherwise be available to the individual;
- lack of training or a nonstimulating environment.

Central nervous system damage can contribute to an apparent defect in intelligence by causing the student difficulties in paying attention and controlling impulses. It is not always easy to establish the validity of a diagnosis of cerebral dysfunction, but the problem may be inferred from sensitive medical and psychological examinations or from observations of daily behavior (generally, additional traits include hyperactivity, low frustration tolerance, irritability, defective memory, and poor muscular coordination). The association of learning difficulties with organic brain impairment (assigned the label of attention deficit disorders) has been extensively documented (Burks, 1955, 1957a, 1960, 1961, 1964a).

Because etiology can influence treatment approaches, the causes of retardation in any child should be determined. Symptoms of neurological and glandular deficiencies can be alleviated or eliminated by medical intervention, and the impact of noxious cultural factors can be lessened by educational and sociological remedial measures.

Characteristics of Mentally Retarded Children

Youngsters with mental retardation are socially incompetent to a marked degree. Unable to understand established rules of behavior and the complex subtleties of communication with classmates and teachers, these children compete or adapt much below the social level of their peers. They often prefer to play with younger children. They are labeled as immature by adults. They never lead a group, are never elected president of a club, and are not expected to execute complex roles or to understand social circumstances as well as their age-mates do. If these social limitations are not present, serious doubt must exist as to whether the child is truly intellectually retarded.

The problems of dull-normal children (IQ range about 80 to 95) are of great concern to most regular classroom teachers because these youngsters simply cannot meet many of the demands of a traditional academic program. Such students comprise about 15% of the general population (Blanco, 1972). In an ordinary classroom, five or six students will suffer some degree of mental slowness. The many and varied reasons for this retardation (inherited traits, impaired health, sensory defects, emotional difficulties, and minor neurological impairments) are difficult to diagnose; in a sense they are unmeasurable because investigators have not been able to estimate accurately what effect such conditions have on the learning process. Many of these students are unmotivated because they get little reinforcement from teachers and peers for the work they do in school. To compensate for this lack of appreciation, some resort to patterns of disruptive or withdrawn conduct.

DIAGNOSIS

For a child with suspected intellectual deficit based on BBRS results, the following procedures should be initiated:

1. Administer an individual intelligence test to determine the child's functional IQ.
2. Evaluate the child's adaptive behaviors in home, neighborhood, and school settings.
3. Examine the general environmental milieu in which the child resides.

Determining IQ

Although IQ tests are important, their results must be interpreted with caution. The fairness and appropriateness of conventional assessment procedures (and programs) for mental retardation have been the subject of intense debate (Reschly, 1982). The assessment of intelligence is difficult at any age but particularly for very young children for the following reasons (Burks, 1977a):

1. It is difficult to get and hold their attention.
2. It is hard to explain test directions because many young students have not yet established adequate verbal skills.
3. The child's maturational processes (organic and social) are proceeding at rapid and uneven rates.

I have long observed the instability of IQ scores in young children, especially during the preschool years. Even after this period, a child's IQ score does not necessarily remain constant with age. For this reason, test scores should be interpreted with care and educational plans should be based on data from other sources as well.

Evaluating Adaptive Behaviors

A proper diagnosis of retardation is especially necessary for students who are economically disadvantaged or part of a minority group. Although seen by teachers to be academic problems requiring special class placement (Tomlinson, Acker, Canter, & Lindborg, 1977), most of these children are not retarded but only appear to be. Reschly (1982) stressed the need to study cultural factors that artificially lower the performance of some children in deprived environments. Placing such youngsters in special classes where they are labeled as mentally deficient and where they associate with students who are genuinely retarded may condemn them to lowered intellectual functioning for long periods of time.

In the late 1960s, the so-called 6-hour retarded child was "discovered" (President's Committee on Mental Retardation, 1970). Such children were seen to be mentally deficient only within the public school context (thus the 6-hour appellation). In other settings, such as their home or neighborhood, these students were described as being exceptionally adaptive.

The concept of adaptive behavior has become an increasingly important issue in psychological assessment (Coulter & Morrow, 1978), and school guidance personnel cannot ignore this aspect of diagnostic assessment. A number of standardized instruments have been developed to assess adaptive behavior. In addition, I have developed an informal measure for assessing adaptive behavior, the Adaptive Behavior checklist (see figure 10.1), which can be used to probe children's everyday functioning in home and neighborhood settings. Using this checklist, parents can rate how well their child has done in various skill activities. Have the parents review their child's development, then ask, "How well has your child done in the following activities compared to other children the same age?" The checklist is only a rough index. It is important to expand on replies from parents or guardians with further questions that illuminate the degree of intelligence the child brings to common aspects of living.

ADAPTIVE BEHAVIOR CHECKLIST

Harold F. Burks, Ph.D.

For each of the following activities, place a check mark in the column
that best describes your child's ability compared to other children the same age.

	Not as well	About as well	Better than most
Self-Maintenance			
1. Feeding	☐	☐	☐
2. Dressing	☐	☐	☐
3. Washing and bathing	☐	☐	☐
4. Going to the toilet	☐	☐	☐
5. Keeping his or her own room in order	☐	☐	☐
6. Keeping busy around the house	☐	☐	☐
7. Handling family trips	☐	☐	☐
8. Behavior at restaurants	☐	☐	☐
Interpersonal and Communication Skills			
1. Talking with others	☐	☐	☐
2. Participating in family games and sports	☐	☐	☐
3. Acquiring neighborhood friends	☐	☐	☐
4. Playing with neighborhood children	☐	☐	☐
5. Communicating wishes to others	☐	☐	☐
6. Showing interest in others	☐	☐	☐
7. Telling funny stories	☐	☐	☐
8. Showing a sense of humor	☐	☐	☐
Social Responses			
1. Handling chores	☐	☐	☐
2. Understanding rules and regulations	☐	☐	☐
3. Accepting rules and regulations	☐	☐	☐
4. Managing money	☐	☐	☐
5. Carrying out errands	☐	☐	☐
6. Keeping promises	☐	☐	☐
7. Earning money	☐	☐	☐
8. Cooperating with parents	☐	☐	☐
Intellectual Abilities			
1. Working at hobbies	☐	☐	☐
2. Reading books	☐	☐	☐
3. Drawing pictures	☐	☐	☐
4. Solving puzzles	☐	☐	☐
5. Using tools	☐	☐	☐
6. Solving number problems	☐	☐	☐
7. Asking questions	☐	☐	☐
8. Using judgment	☐	☐	☐
9. Understanding the value of money	☐	☐	☐
10. Showing curiosity	☐	☐	☐
11. Understanding stories	☐	☐	☐
12. Showing adequate vocabulary	☐	☐	☐
13. Making himself or herself understood	☐	☐	☐
14. Showing memory	☐	☐	☐
15. Demonstrating attention	☐	☐	☐
16. Understanding cause-and-effect relationships	☐	☐	☐

Figure 10.1.

Examining Environmental Factors

School personnel should examine the general environmental milieu in which the child resides. Some mental retardation is thought to be the result of environmental factors that occur after birth. Sarason (1959) supported this belief, stating that intellectual deficiency may be associated with the following factors:

Cultural deprivation. Does the child reside in an economically destitute home? Does the child's neighborhood lack facilities common to middle-class communities? Are many of the individuals with whom the child comes into contact unemployed? Is the child isolated from other members of his or her ethnic or cultural group? Has the child resided in an economically deprived environment for most of his or her life?

Lack of stimulation. Does the child appear to be rejected by other members of the family? Does he or she seem to receive little warmth and affection from the family? Are there few material possessions in the home? Does the child have a room of his or her own? A place to study? Does the family have religious interests? Do they have a place of worship nearby? A public library? A public park? Does the family go on trips together? Does the child have neighborhood friends? Are there places in the neighborhood where the child can play with others? Is little or no English spoken in the child's home? Does the home lack pictures, books, and magazines? Are family members generally silent around the child? Do any family members have a speech or hearing handicap? Does anyone help the child with homework? Does anyone monitor the television programs the child watches?

Low expectations. Are most family members poorly educated? Are most individuals in the neighborhood poorly educated? Does anyone in the family show interest in the child's progress? Do any family members show up at school meetings? Is the child allowed to watch television for inordinate periods of time? Does the family ask the child to engage in activities that take the youngster away from studies? Does anyone in the family supervise the child's homework? Is the child asked to learn and do chores? Does anyone in the family take the responsibility to teach the child new skills? Does the mother or father contact the school to learn about the child's progress? Is the child a member of a group (Cub Scouts, Campfire Girls, etc.) where new skills are taught?

Deficient diet. Does the child complain of being hungry? Does he or she come to school without breakfast? Does the child eat a balanced lunch at school? Does the family spend enough money on food? Is the food they buy nutritious? Is the child underweight?

Absence of medical care. Does the child suffer many illnesses? Does he or she appear weak? Is the child underweight or overweight? Does the family have a family doctor? Do they attend a medical clinic? When did the child last see a doctor?

Neglect. Is the child unkempt? Do personal hygiene habits appear to need attention? Is the home run down? Does the family keep the child home when he or she is ill? Is anyone home when the child arrives from school? Is the child allowed to roam the streets unsupervised? Are the parents preoccupied with activities outside the home? Does the child associate with a group that is in trouble with the law?

The influence of these factors is difficult to assess, but undoubtedly they do contribute to developmental difficulties. The need for early intervention and remedial methods is obvious. Without such procedures, possibilities for normal adaptation are markedly lessened.

INTERVENTION STRATEGIES

Techniques for School Personnel

Some children acquire higher IQs as they grow older (Kagan, Sontag, Baker, & Nelson, 1958). These children exhibit the following personality attributes: (a) a high need for achievement, (b) competitiveness, (c) curiosity about their natural environment, and (d) a tendency to be active, not passive. Do children who show improvement in these characteristics also demonstrate increased intelligence? There are strong indications of such an association. Woodworth, Siegel, and Eustin (1958) found that withdrawal symptoms in children with mental retardation were replaced by increased aggression and activity when the children were given special treatment in a two-year program. It is not possible to know for sure that such personality traits can be enhanced in school settings, but it seems reasonable to hope they could be. Such attempts might include:

- providing a classroom environment that offers encouragement, recognition, and praise for accomplishments at all levels;
- avoiding loss of respect and frustration in children by eliminating high classroom standards of achievement for those who cannot meet such measures. Many slow learners are not really handicapped by a poor nervous system; they are simply frustrated by the failure of their environment to give them a sufficiently interesting and challenging curriculum to enable them to profit from school learning;
- facilitating curiosity about nature. Young children are particularly interested in birth, death, sexual anatomy, and other processes of the natural environment. The early school environment should include plants and animals that illustrate these processes. Frequent opportunity should be provided to discuss these natural events;
- encouraging passive or withdrawn students to express aggression in acceptable and constructive ways.

Educators may also wish to keep the following considerations in mind:

1. Do *not* place the child in classes for children with mental retardation. School districts around the country have been sued by parents of children who did not have mental retardation but who discovered that their youngsters were misdiagnosed and wrongly placed in special classes for very slow learners. Children who are inappropriately placed in special class for very slow learners will take on the characteristics of the students with mental retardation. Academically, they will behave no better than their slower classmates (Burks, 1999). Their intelligence will be consistently underestimated by teachers and they will be kept in slow groups. Socially, the brighter children will run the groups. Peers with lower IQs will be at the mercy of the higher IQ students, unable to outwit their maneuverings.
2. Evaluate the student's learning potential at an early age and periodically reevaluate his or her progress. If the child is required to repeat a grade, it should be at the kindergarten level; later retention tends to be ineffective. Worse, it may lower the student's self-esteem, with an associated depressed academic performance.
3. Place the child in a nongraded primary class where the rate of progress can be geared to the student's apparent mental capacity.
4. Place the child with a classroom teacher who can tolerate a lower rate of progress. Some teachers come to resent slower learners and do not relate positively to them (Burks, 1968b). Sometimes, when teachers can accept the fact that they do not always get along equally well with all students, they may be willing to trade students after the first two or three months of the school term. Children who feel liked by the teacher are more apt to produce for that person.
5. Whenever possible, provide special tutoring services. These services may be provided by a special class teacher, another regular class teacher, an aide, or an interested parent.
6. Recommend a summer school remedial academic program (but not if it appears that the student will resist or fail the program).
7. Give the child shorter classwork and homework assignments. However, as with other students, insist that the youngster complete assignments.
8. When presenting material, use as many visual cues and demonstration aids as possible.
9. Use short, dynamic instruction periods rather than long stretches of study that can tire the student.
10. Avoid meaningless memory drills. Instead, stress simpler comprehension exercises.
11. Make class assignments concrete and highly structured.
12. Have the child overlearn exercises, but employ interesting materials.
13. To reduce disruptive behavior, keep the child busy at tasks that are within his or her ability.
14. Start daily activities with known and familiar exercises so the child will believe that he or she can succeed.

15. Relate academic programs to practical activities (e.g., doing chores, making money, getting along with siblings).

Techniques for Parents

Parental understanding and cooperation is a prerequisite for the proper treatment of students with mild retardation. The following suggestions may be helpful.

1. Discuss the child's learning problems with the parents after the child has been evaluated in the classroom with proper diagnostic measures. Continuing discussions are advised if the youngster stands out in the classroom as a poor achiever (some dull-normal children, when placed in classes with many other students of like ability, do not appear conspicuous).
2. Advise the parents to take the child to a medical specialist for a complete physical checkup. (Do not suggest names of physicians; most school districts have regulations forbidding this practice.)
3. School personnel should stand behind their opinions about proper educational procedures for the student. They must not readily agree to parents' overly optimistic aspirations. If the parents disagree about the educational assessment, they can be urged to seek another source (private or public) for psychological diagnosis. If parents take this step, educators must be willing to accept the results of outside assessment even if those results differ from the school's assessment. Do not argue with parents about evaluation issues. Doing so simply hardens parents' convictions that their point of view is correct. If parents, contrary to the opinion of the school, insist the child is able to accomplish grade-level work, the teacher or counselor should simply say, "I really do not believe your youngster can keep up with others in the classroom, but I will do my best to help your child stay with the group." The parents will know that the educator, while not agreeing with the parental assessment, will still cooperate to the best of his or her ability. Records of all conversations and correspondence should be placed in school files and copies should be sent to the parents.
4. Give the parents concrete suggestions as to how they might assist their child. Complaints without specific suggestions can lead parents to suspect that the teacher does not like the child. School personnel can suggest that the parents seek extra tutoring assistance and provide more intellectual and educational stimulation at home.

Discussing the Relationship between IQ Scores and Achievement

Parents tend to be misinformed about the meaning of IQ scores and the relationship of scores to achievement. Educators who meet with groups of parents to discuss ways of helping slow-learning children may want to use the Facts and Myths about IQ Tests and Achievement checklist (see figure 10.2). After parents have completed the survey, discuss the answers for each item, as follows.

1. Partially true. IQ tests reflect potential in a rather narrow range of abilities (mostly verbal and reasoning). Important functions like long-term memory, creativity, motor skills, imagination, and social skills (to name a few) are neglected.
2. False. IQ tests are unreliable for young children. Many young children do not pay attention well, do not follow directions properly, do not understand how to take tests, and are too immature physically (e.g., do not know how to hold a pencil). These behaviors affect test performance. Thus, there is not much confidence in the predictive validity of intelligence test findings for very young children.
3. True. Even when the same test is given to the same person more than once, there are often differences from one administration to another. There is usually an even greater shift when a different test is given.

4. False. Experience tends to show that IQ test results cause parents to look at their children in distorted ways. If the parents feel the score is too low, they are disappointed; if the score is higher than they expected, they pressure the child to do more and better work. In any event, the youngster feels that he or she has somehow let them down.

5. True. Innate and acquired abilities interact with each other; it will probably never be possible to measure either one completely apart from the other.

6. False. Children are very sensitive about their status with friends and classmates. If they feel they are not as smart as their friends, they feel less acceptable. Further, research has shown that many children think that being dumb is like being bad.

7. False. Intelligence tests do not factor in illness, absence from school, lack of cooperation in the classroom, unrecognized physical deficits, or emotional problems—all of which can affect the way a child learns.

8. True. Although it is tempting to think there is a single cause for learning difficulties, it is hardly ever the case. For this reason, no single remedial approach to learning problems is valid for all students.

9. Partially true. The abilities necessary to perform well on commonly used IQ tests are much like those needed to learn school subject matter, but they are not exactly the same. For instance, some children with high scores on intelligence tests do not read well, and some lower-IQ children read at an above-average level.

10. True. IQ scores can be improved, but it is not clear whether *potential* can be. If a person is well rested, has had proper nutrition, is doing the best he or she can in a supportive environment, is relatively free from emotional tension, and is suitably motivated, the IQ score will more approximately reflect his or her true potential.

Parents' Self-Assessment

By understanding their own behavior, parents can help their child function more effectively in the family. The following questions and suggestions can be used with individual parents or in a group instruction session.

Do you put off your child's questions with simple answers because you assume he or she would not understand more complex replies? Parents may overprotect their slower child by talking down to him or her; however, inadequate explanations do not give the child enough information to comprehend common or unusual events. Devise ways to help the child comprehend some of the meanings of these phenomena. For example, create a special calendar to help the child understand the passage of time, or use a map that explains the measurement of distance.

Do you encourage your child to communicate his or her feelings? Unlike faster-learning children, slower youngsters are likely to hide emotions. This reluctance to talk occurs because slower children are more inclined to converse about the immediate environment rather than about past occurrences and because they sense the irritation of adults concerned about slow learners' inability to communicate fluently. Many retarded youngsters need help interpreting feelings. The parent might ask, "Does it make you feel sad [unhappy, mad, scared] when you don't understand what I say?" The following discussion (if and when it takes place) can help parents choose better ways to approach their youngster later on.

Do you encourage your child to ask questions? Sometimes parents do not push a slower child to ask questions because such inquiries might reveal the child's retardation. Instead, the parents ask simple obvious questions (e.g., "What color is your ball?") they are sure the child can answer. Unfortunately, this tends to stunt the youngster's curiosity about his or her world. Immature thinking is often prolonged, the child does not develop a proper cause-and-effect logic, and he or she continues to confuse fantasy with reality (typical of the magical thinking of young children). Parents should encourage children to ask questions even if the queries appear irrelevant or immature.

If your child does not answer a question, do you push him or her for a reply? When parents wait nervously for the "right" reply to a question (i.e., the answer that will prove the child has adequate intelligence), the youngster may withdraw and act stubborn (because the boy or girl realizes that he or she is being compelled to produce

FACTS AND MYTHS ABOUT IQ TESTS AND ACHIEVEMENT

Harold F. Burks, Ph.D.

Put a check mark in the appropriate column for each of the following statements.

	True	Partially True	False
1. IQ tests reflect a child's true potential.	☐	☐	☐
2. Results of IQ tests given when a child is very young are more likely to predict school performance than results of tests given when the child is older.	☐	☐	☐
3. Results may vary from test to test for the same child.	☐	☐	☐
4. It is a good idea to know the IQ scores of your own child.	☐	☐	☐
5. Hereditary factors cannot be distinguished from environmental factors in the development of intelligence.	☐	☐	☐
6. Children should be told how adults view their intelligence level.	☐	☐	☐
7. Children who do well on intelligence tests always do well in schoolwork.	☐	☐	☐
8. There is usually no single cause for a child's poor achievement in school.	☐	☐	☐
9. IQ scores are closely related to achievement—that is, a high IQ means a child will do well academically.	☐	☐	☐
10. IQ scores can be improved.	☐	☐	☐

Figure 10.2.

a reply that satisfies the parent rather than the child). Such a response makes it more difficult for the parent to work with the child in the future.

Do you have trouble tutoring your child? No parent should try to tutor a resistant youngster. Tutoring requires the adult to issue commands and instructions. If requests are not delivered in a manner acceptable to the student, noncompliance is a likely result. Most parents need careful instruction on how to structure tutoring sessions and how to perceive signs of child fatigue and irritation. (Chapter 11 discusses tutoring by parents in more detail.)

Do you take your child's fears seriously? Many slower-learning children do not understand cause-and-effect relationships well. That is why they can be frightened of things most children ignore. Their fears may appear irrational. Adults must realize that a five- or six-year-old slow-learning child retains many of the apprehensions of a two-year-old. The youngster cannot accurately estimate the dimensions of a threatening event. Further, such events may bring change and novelty—conditions the youngster feels he or she cannot meet successfully. The child resists the impending changes through inflexible, rigid, or stereotyped behavior and clings to safe and well-known routines. Fears must be taken seriously and discussed with the child. Adults can determine how bad a situation actually is and show the child practical ways to handle perceived threats.

Do you act gloomy around your child? Slow-learning children (particularly those who are young) tend to identify more easily than normal children with their parents' emotions. If a parent is cheerful and outgoing, the child becomes happier and more outgoing. If the parent is sad, the youngster becomes depressed and withdrawn.

Do you organize many or most home activities around the needs of your slower-learning child? Retarded children need extra attention; however, the needs of other family members should not be sacrificed more than is necessary to accommodate the exceptional youngster. For example, if a parent expects a faster-learning sibling to perform at a high level to make up for the deficiencies of a slow brother or sister, he or she may react with anger toward the adult or the slower sibling. The situation can be worsened if the parent reprimands the able child for exhibited hostility. Girls may be more affected by slower-learning siblings than boys are, perhaps because girls are more likely to be placed in a caretaker role by adults. The able child should not be put into the position of being an admired caretaker who is expected to demonstrate both unfailing devotion to the slower sibling and gratitude to adults for being given that assignment.

Do you give your child responsibilities around the house? A slow-learning child tends to be overprotected by family members. Parents with low opinions of a child's abilities may not give that youngster a proper share of duties and chores. The child then feels disrespected and alienated from family activities.

Do you allow your child to earn and spend his or her own money? The necessity of money is universally recognized and the slower child should be given the chance and the responsibility to earn and spend money.

Do you encourage your child to initiate some of his or her own activities? Slower children are often afraid to initiate actions. This fear of independent behavior is based on a number of conditions, including the following, that tend to inhibit the child and need to be addressed by adults.

- The low opinion of others toward the child: the parents can try to make people aware of the child's abilities and can discourage disparaging comments from onlookers.
- The child's fear that he or she could get into trouble: this apprehension is common among children who have been overcorrected for mistakes. Surrounding persons must be told to ignore the child's errors and should be encouraged to praise the youngster's accomplishments.
- The child's poor comprehension of his or her environment: parents must try to make other adults and children realize that the slow-learning youngster has trouble understanding his or her world. Further, it is important for others to realize that a patient approach assists the retarded youngster to become more self-confident.

Suggested Reading for Parents

Counselors may suggest the following reading material in response to questions raised by parents of slow-learning children.

How Can I Understand My Slow-Learning Child Better?

Farnham-Diggory, S. (1992). *The learning-disabled child.* Cambridge, MA: Harvard University Press.
Smith, R. (Ed.). (1993). *Children with mental retardation: A parents' guide.* Rockville, MD: Woodbine House.

How Do Family Practices Affect Learning in Children?

Friedman, R. (1973). *Family roots of school learning and behavior disorders.* Springfield, IL: Charles C. Thomas.
Snow, C. E., Barnes, W. S., Chandler, J., Goodman, I. F., & Hemphill, L. (1991). *Unfulfilled expectations: Home and school influences on literacy.* Cambridge, MA: Harvard University Press.

How Can I Learn to Live with My Slow-Learning Child Better?

Hayes, M. L. (1993). *You don't outgrow it: Living with learning disabilities.* Novato, CA: Academic Therapy.

What Kind of Intelligence Does My Child Possess?

Howe, M. J. A. (1990). *Sense and nonsense about hothouse children: A practical guide for parents and teachers.* Leicester, England: British Psychological Society.
Locorto, C. (1991). *Sense and nonsense about IQ: The case for uniqueness.* New York: Praeger.
Miller, L. (1993). *What we call smart: A new narrative for intelligence and learning.* San Diego, CA: Singular Publishing Group.

How Can I Gauge the Efficacy of Special School Programs?

Cutler, B. C. (1993). *You, your child, and "special education": A guide to making the system work.* Baltimore: Brookes.

What Can I Do at Home to Improve Learning Conditions?

Smith, R. (Ed.). (1993). *Children with mental retardation: A parents' guide.* Rockville, MD: Woodbine House.

What Can I Do to Improve My Slow Learner's Self-Image?

Jones, C. (1992). *Enhancing self-concepts and achievement of mildly handicapped students: Learning disabled, mild mentally retarded, and behavior disordered.* Springfield, IL: Charles C. Thomas.

When Does My Child Need to Be Tested?

Shore, M. F., Brice, P. J., & Love, B. G. (1992). *When your child needs testing: What parents, teachers, and other helpers need to know about psychological testing.* New York: Crossroad.

What Steps Can I Take to Motivate My Slow-Learning Child?

Licht, B. G., & Kistner, J. A. (1986). Motivational problems of learning-disabled children: Individual differences and their implications for treatment. In J. K. Torgesen & B. Y. L. Wong (Eds.), *Psychological and educational perspectives on learning disabilities.* New York: Academic Press.

How Does My Slow-Learning Child Affect His or Her Siblings?

Stoneman, Z., & Berman, P. W. (1993). *The effects of mental retardation, disability, and illness on sibling relationships: Research and challenges.* Baltimore: Brookes.

What Are Some of the Better Treatments for Slow-Learning Children?

Wang, M. C. (1987). Toward achieving educational excellence for all students: Program design and student outcomes. *Remedial and Special Education, 8,* 24–34.

CHAPTER 11

Poor Academics

The Burks Behavior Rating Scales (Burks, 1977a, 2006a) describe academic difficulties as the inability to succeed in basic school subjects. Children demonstrating poor learning progress tend to

- read inadequately;
- spell badly;
- misunderstand academic directions;
- write assignments unsuccessfully;
- neglect homework assignments.

Academic difficulties can occur among children showing any kind of handicap. However, slow-learning youngsters with inherited (endogenous) deficiencies will not, in general, show the distracting, erratic behavior or impulse-control problems demonstrated by students with postbirth (exogenous) brain dysfunctions. Students suffering only emotional problems will probably show such behaviors as anxiety, poor self-esteem, and withdrawal, but will not show complexities in areas affected by organic brain pathology (i.e., attention deficits, impulsivity, overactivity and poor coordination).

Among young children, academic difficulties are often associated with high scores on tests measuring attention deficits, poor coordination, dependency, and poor self-esteem. This pattern of symptoms implies slow maturation. Immaturity may be associated with habit disorders, character disorders, or handicapping conditions such as mental retardation. For other students, certain negative characteristics (rebelliousness, distrustfulness, and aggressive tendencies) may also be shown (perhaps as a reaction to lack of school success).

THEORETICAL BACKGROUND

Etiology

The causal factors leading to school learning disorders are many and complex; however, the following generalizations have been made by Pennington (1991) and Rabinovitch (1962):

1. low intelligence;
2. poor physical health;
3. emotional disturbance;
4. lack of motivation;
5. lack of opportunity for learning;
6. lack of developmental readiness.

Low intelligence. Poor academic achievement can be the result (but not in all cases) of lowered mental ability.

Poor physical health. Many studies over a long period of time have established that there is a strong relationship between good health and effective learning. Approximately 15% of school children show functionally important health problems, but this percentage may increase when medical services are poor or absent.

Health problems tend to vary with age. At the preschool level, the most common health problems are

- acute infectious diseases—respiratory infections account for 80% of reported problems;
- accidents—largely due to physical immaturity;
- emotional disorders centering around difficulties in adjustment to routines outside the home, speech problems, and bladder and bowel control;
- dental caries;
- speech, hearing, and other sensory defects;
- iron deficiency.

At the elementary school level, health problems affect attendance and classroom performance. Actually, these are among the healthiest years of life. A small percentage of children have hearing difficulties at this age (perhaps 3%), a larger percentage (25%) have visual problems, about 1% have a major speech disorder or epilepsy, and there is a scattering of other physical deficiencies such as malnutrition, obesity, poor posture, diseased tonsils, and flat feet.

At the junior high and high school levels, abrupt changes in body structure raise concerns about physical and social adjustment. Problems of menstruation, pregnancy, birth control, and venereal disease demand attention. Suicide is not uncommon. Among teenagers, obesity is a problem for 15% of females and 8% of males (most of whom become overweight adults). Skin diseases are a significant difficulty for many adolescents. In the final analysis, though, the most serious health problems for this age group center around the use of tobacco, alcohol, and drugs.

I have worked with many physicians both in and out of hospital settings and these associations have taught me that any child with a learning disability should undergo complete medical, psychological, and educational studies before plans are made for remedial instruction. The need for physical examination is important because some forms of organic disability can be mistaken for social or emotional disorders. For example, the majority of headaches have origins in environmental variations (e.g., atmospheric conditions or food allergies) or in personality conflicts, but it is not always clear whether a more serious physical problem underlies the symptom. For that reason, a sudden onset of headaches mandates a medical study.

Visual difficulties can also be overlooked. Most children who cannot see well do not spontaneously report vision problems because they do not realize that what they see is distorted. That is why all children should have periodic vision checks even though they do not complain of eyestrain.

The maintenance of proper hormonal levels is important for some children and especially for teens, because a hormonal imbalance is more likely to cause a loss of consciousness for them than for most adults. Any child demonstrating fainting spells should be given immediate medical attention. Spells of daytime sleeping or fainting do not necessarily point to a serious organic disorder, but a correctable neuroendocrine imbalance may exist. Passing out can have a variety of causes—undue stress, going to school without breakfast, dehydration, a low-grade seizure, rupture of a brain blood vessel, aftermath of a head blow, or anything that causes a drop in blood pressure.

Age-inappropriate clumsiness in a youngster may indicate the presence of an inherited congenital difficulty, a degenerative disease of the nervous system, or a minimal brain dysfunction (often accompanied by hyperactivity). Other physical problems among children can be associated with poor eating habits; exposure to heavy metals like lead, mercury, and manganese; and certain types of infections.

Emotional disturbance. Kuhlberg (1974) made the point that emotional disturbance does not, of itself, constitute cause for special education assistance, because many upset youngsters function quite well in the classroom. Actually, some types of emotional disturbance may facilitate school performance: perfectionist, compulsive, anxious students may be driven to accomplish. Kuhlberg further pointed out that good mental health is not always associated with academic achievement. Some children from unpressured backgrounds are serene but do not care to reach their academic potential. Among such students, improved self-image is not ordinarily associated with better performance. Although some children do not succeed because of emotional disturbance, Kuhlberg stated, others become disturbed because they are not achieving (a point the school diagnostician should investigate).

Parish, Ohlsen, and Parish (1978) confirmed that children who manifest an emotional disturbance are viewed adversely by students with no disabilities. When they asked 131 grade school children to state their attitudes toward three groups of students with disabilities and toward students without disabilities, the following order of social acceptance was established:

1. no disabilities;
2. physically handicapped;
3. learning disabled;
4. emotionally disturbed.

The lack of social acceptance experienced by children with handicaps has been chronicled by Bryan (1978), who reported that a significant number of children with learning disorders found it difficult to elicit positive responses from others and to establish social relationships. Bryan stated that the problem resides in the inability of these children to comprehend the nonverbal communications of other students or to become involved in expressive classroom language activities.

Cobb (1972) pointed out the tremendous importance of peer relationships in classroom learning. He found that the child who talks to peers while attending to classroom work is more likely to succeed than the student who attends to work without interacting. He also observed that even if a counselor improves a child's self-concept, little may be accomplished academically if the child is not also taught to relate better to peers. Kohn and Rosman (1974) helped explain why social interaction enhances classroom learning. They found that children who were interested in participating with others learned more from their environment. Curiosity and assertiveness were enhanced as personality traits. Cattell and Barton (1971) found that social empathy for others was a quality that predicted better achievement in all areas for sixth-grade students.

Some students become emotionally disturbed because they are mistreated by teachers (Enson, 1995). Diana Cordova, a psychologist from Yale University, relates the story of Jimmy, a sixth grader who was doing well in school and had many friends. One of six children, he came from a close-knit family. His demeanor was generally happy until one day he started to withdraw from social contacts. He stopped seeing friends, lost interest in soccer—his favorite sport—and complained to his parents about headaches, nightmares, and a chronic inability to sleep. The family physician found nothing physically wrong with this boy but recommended he undergo a psychological evaluation. The analysis revealed he was suffering a posttraumatic stress disorder triggered by a school incident.

During an art class, Jimmy was having difficulty drawing some required sketches. He requested help from the teacher. The instructor, irritated by what she perceived as Jimmy's constant whining, told him, "If you want to act like a baby, you can sit with the babies." The teacher then took him next door to a first grade class and made arrangements for him to sit there for the next three weeks until he finished the drawing assignment.

Unfortunately, these kinds of incidents are not rare. In my role as school psychologist, I was told about and observed a number of instructors and other school personnel who, because of lack of instruction or because of innate temperament, inflicted unneeded stress on students. Researchers have found that when students are belittled, humiliated, ridiculed, or mistreated, learning and interest decline dramatically and signs of maladjustment often appear. Even more alarming is the link between emotional maltreatment and the development of unacceptable aggression.

Lack of motivation. Children who apparently have adequate intelligence but refuse to produce academically have become all too familiar to educators (Baldoni, 2004; Phillips, 2001). Most learning experts see such youngsters as unmotivated, but another, unrecognized kind of influence may be at work here—the motivation to fail. These children are typically nonaggressive, irresponsible, incurious, and generally immature.

I have already described the behavior characteristics of unmotivated, nonaggressive, and underachieving children (see poor motivation in chapter 7), but it may be useful to consider some of the underlying reasons for these trait expressions. I am convinced that a significant number of otherwise able children are willing themselves (albeit unconsciously) to be failures. The root causes for this are many and varied, but they often include the following problems, which center on poorly developed goals and inadequate levels of parental interest and involvement in the child's learning activities.

Defeatist or Antagonistic Self-Concept

Students may think "I'm too stupid to do this" or "I'm not going to do what you want." Possible causes: Mandel and Marcus (1988) identified some parent-child interactions that can lead to poor attitudes toward learning. An otherwise normal youngster can be affected adversely by the following parental behaviors.

Parents push their children too hard. Children of mothers with extremely high expectations were less creative, had more academic test anxiety, and, in early grades, performed no better than students whose mothers felt that kids should just be kids. Mothers who want to see their children become school superstars can end up making these children feel more anxious, less creative, and less positive toward school. Adults should convey to children that they expect them to do well, without being overly demanding and chronically dissatisfied with their child's academic progress.

Parents become involved in a power struggle with their children. This kind of family conflict is ordinarily covert—that is, the involved parties do not consciously realize they are involved in a battle of wills. The youngsters (usually boys) engaged in this dominance game often have a history of irritating habits that concern parents (usually the mother). They lose possessions, dawdle, don't finish assignments and chores, bicker with their brothers and sisters, neglect to bathe and brush their teeth, eat messily, and generally don't do things unless forced to. However, they avoid serious trouble and tend to behave better when away from home. Most adults describe this type of youngster as immature and irresponsible (they say, "He has to be kept after constantly"). The child complains about being nagged but acts happy-go-lucky.

The parents (usually the mother) believe that such children require close supervision because of indolent and indifferent behavior; the children feel that since they are hounded for no good reason, they might as well up the ante and be punished for something worthwhile—for instance, evading responsibility. The parents continue to behave as though they alone are responsible for the child's successes and failures (even when told not to); of course, the child reacts to the parents' conduct rather than to the wordy behavior goals they parade before him or her.

This conflict is self-defeating. Both parents and children feel self-righteous and put-upon. The parents, whose intentions are admirable (i.e., they want the youngster to succeed), regard the child's resistance to learning as a personal defeat. The child, who sees adult demands as unreasonable, perceives giving in as a defeat.

Poorly Developed Sense of Curiosity

Statements that may be made by incurious students are "I don't care," "It's not exciting," "Let's just do what we've always done," or "I don't care how well I do." Possible causes: A significant lack of curiosity is an important characteristic of the young, able, but willful underachiever. Inquisitiveness is a natural attribute of infants and toddlers, so why does the trait disappear for some children in later years? Parents can stunt the natural curiosity of their children in the following ways.

Avoidance of potentially embarrassing topics and questions. All families suppress discussions of sensitive topics (often sexual) to some degree, but some families avoid consideration of most questions that preoccupy children. Early childhood interest in topics like boy-girl differences, how conception takes place, where babies come from, illness and death, and the significance of parental differences can be discouraged when adults ignore such questions. In fact, discouragement may be just one unfortunate outcome—children may also come to believe curiosity is a dangerous trait, and this feeling may affect the learning process in negative ways.

Maintenance of unspoken and mysterious "family secrets." Does Mother have secret migraines, Father a disguised drinking problem, Grandma a hidden heart weakness? Covert family difficulties can divert a child's emotional and intellectual energy from useful learning to unhealthy rumination.

Poorly Developed Ability to Express Constructive Aggression

Students who have difficulty expressing constructive aggression may say things like "Don't ask me to do anything scary," "I don't care about doing anything better," or "Whatever you say—I'll do it your way." Possible causes: Children cannot be merely passive or inert recipients of knowledge. Some underachievers seem to have inherited timid, fearful personality characteristics. Other nonaggressive slow learners have been taught to be passive by parents who apparently fear spontaneous impulses in children. These parents are apprehensive that the impulses will get out of control. I have also observed overcompliant children who learned to give in to adults as a way to gain approval ("You must never question your mother or father; they are always right!"). These youngsters can become so frightened of making mistakes that they avoid becoming involved in the learning process.

Do not blame the parents for this situation. The strict upbringing practices were initiated by the adults in good faith, grounded in the belief that aggression is harmful. Unfortunately, instructional overkill can stamp out beneficial assertion, a necessary attribute of constructive learning.

Reluctance to Grow Up

Children who seem reluctant to grow up may say things like "If I do this, you'll ask me to do something hard like the big kids do," "I like to play with the little kids," or "Don't ask me to be responsible for that—that's a job for the leaders." Possible causes: Some children are put off by the competitiveness inherent in American society. For that reason, and because some parents portray maturity as consisting of unpleasant responsibilities, many youngsters fear growing older. Achievement represents a progressive step toward an unwanted adulthood.

This condition is difficult to diagnose, particularly in younger children, who are not expected to show as many signs of maturity as teenagers are. By the time an individual reaches high school, however, adults recognize that the youngster is only a step away from having to leave home and be self-supportive. This tends to make adults anxious about teens who continue to parry all efforts to get them to be productive. Again, the focus here is on a pattern of failing grades or significant underachievement in an individual who otherwise demonstrates adequate ability and who has no medical disorders that could account for a learning lag.

Lack of Role Models Who Stress Motivation and Achievement

Students whose parents do not have high academic expectations may say, "What do you mean, 'do better'; I do just what Mom and Dad do." Possible causes: Authorities (Mandel & Marcus, 1988) have pointed out that many parents are not actively involved in their children's academic pursuits. Other parents hold low standards for their children; the children may actually try to fulfill their parents' low expectations by underachieving (Mukherjee, 1972).

Although most people have the potential to act as positive academic role models for children, certain individuals are more likely to be copied than others (Staub, 1978). Children tend to copy the actions of those who are

- supportive;
- friendly;
- good listeners;
- responsive;
- able to provide meaningful rewards and consequences.

Children tend not to pattern their lives after those who are

- critical;
- withdrawn;
- impatient;
- overdirective;
- punishing;
- powerless to give meaningful rewards and consequences.

Finally, parental modeling has its greatest impact when what adults say about education is congruent with what they, personally, do about acquiring knowledge (that is, when youngsters see their parents meaningfully and enthusiastically engaged in learning activities).

Lack of developmental readiness. The factors relating to a child's readiness to learn have been well established. According to Mills (1972), these factors are intelligence, physical condition, emotional stability, social adjustment, language development, and experiences the child has had. Wagner (1962) added interest, or the proper mind-set, to the list. Mills proposed that children should also be stimulated, challenged, and free of tension and fear. Hoggard (1957) suggested that if all of these criteria were met, all but 5% of school failures could be prevented.

Developmentally delayed children show symptoms characteristic of younger children. These delayed children are unable to meet the behavioral and emotional school requirements. This fact is of great concern to educators cognizant of the problems that incorrect placement can promote. The developmentally delayed child may develop a poor self-concept or negative attitudes toward teachers and school. Lack of readiness is particularly problematic in kindergarten and first grade, where a chronological age difference of 11 months represents a considerable percentage of a child's current life span. Boys, who mature at a slower pace than girls, are more vulnerable to problems of this nature.

If immature behavior cannot be traced to slow organic maturation, then the symptoms may be explained in terms of inadequate training procedures. Josselyn (1950) pointed out that parental overindulgence during infancy leads to a child's reluctance to relinquish dependency gratification for more mature satisfactions. Overindulgent training tends to be grossly inconsistent because the parent overidentifies with the child by keenly feeling the frustrations perceived to be experienced by the offspring, and hastens to rid the boy or girl of any frustrating restrictions so that the parent will not suffer. The adult, usually the mother, is herself so easily hurt and has so many needs to be gratified that she is seldom satisfied by the child's responses (generally thinking that they are indications of the youngster's needs). She also tends to make impulsive and unpredictable efforts to solve assumed difficulties.

The overindulgent parent may also be expressing masked feelings of ambivalence toward the child. The parent feels that anger at the child must be denied; every effort must be made to prove parental affection. Many youngsters with handicaps grow up in such an atmosphere. Parents resent the burdens put upon them by children who are disabled but feel guilty because they know the children cannot be held responsible for the situation. To make up for their resentment, they become overconsiderate. It is a rare child who does not try to exploit such a situation. The child can increase demands, wait for a parental blowup, and get what he or she wants without further effort. This pattern of never-ending resentment, remorse, and manipulation can absorb much of the family's emotional energy.

Kessler (1966), in discussing the etiology and remediation of character disorders in children, pointed out that the emotional development of children can be impeded when they are overindulged or spoiled and made the center of a family's attention. Children of this nature are characterized by a refusal to take responsibility for their behavior and by an inability to use self-correcting strategies. Behavioral strategies with greater than usual emphasis on negative intervention are considered the treatment of choice.

The parents' lifestyle can facilitate or impede a child's emotional growth. Kessler (1966) presented evidence that parents' delayed maturation or prolonged adolescence can lead them to treat offspring in neglectful and/or violent ways. If the children prove too disruptive and the parents refuse to cooperate with the authorities, the children may have to be placed in foster homes or other treatment facilities.

Children exhibiting immature behavior patterns may also exhibit habit disorders. These complaints, while not confined to the developmentally immature child, are often identified as problems because they represent age-inappropriate conduct (e.g., thumb sucking, enuresis, encopresis). Tics, refusal to eat certain foods, and the unwillingness to observe health practices may or may not depend on role or age expectations (Kazdin, 1979).

For relatively circumscribed habit disorders, simple incentive systems instituted and augmented by the parents in home settings have proved effective. The technique of combining several procedures has proved useful in developing specific skills. These procedures may involve instruction, practice, guided rehearsal, reinforcement, and even mild punishment (quite effective in developing appropriate toilet skills in normal and slow-learning children, according to Azrin and Foxx [1974]).

DIAGNOSIS

Organic Causes

Any child diagnosed as learning disabled should have medical, otologic, ophthalmologic, and neurologic examinations, along with a psychoeducational evaluation (Mason, Richmond, & Fleurant, 1976).

The following behavior symptoms (Mason et al., 1976) should alert teachers and parents to the possibility of organic pathology in children:

- loss of memory regarding recent events;
- loss of mental functioning;
- frequent headaches, vomiting, or nausea;
- clumsiness (dropping objects, falling, stumbling, etc.);
- loss of consciousness (passing out);
- evidence of visual difficulties;
- drastic changes in personality;
- convulsions or tremors;
- slurred speech or other speech problems;
- evidence of being out of touch with reality (confusion or fear);
- poor sleep patterns or nightmares;
- bizarre thoughts or conduct;
- lethargy or depression.

Teacher-Inflicted Stress

Irwin Hyman, director of the National Center for the Study of Corporal Punishment and Alternatives at Temple University, maintains that a lot of emotional maltreatment is going on in schools (Enson, 1995; Schewe, 2002). The following symptoms are commonly found in mistreated youngsters:

Personality change. A dramatic and sudden change in behavior is usually associated with extreme school stress. Some previously well-adjusted youngsters may withdraw, some become aggressive, and others develop mood swings or bodily symptoms like facial tics, nail biting, or stomachaches. Daily functioning may be affected in the following ways:

- avoidance (the child may avoid contact with the person responsible for the abuse or the place where the trauma occurred);
- academic deficiency (psychologically abused youngsters may suddenly stop functioning in class);
- sleep disturbances (extreme stress can result in bed-wetting, nightmares, or insomnia);

- somatic traits (abused students can develop stomachaches, headaches, fatigue, or bowel disturbances);
- unwanted memories (similar to war veterans or otherwise traumatized adults, abused children may develop flashbacks of the frightening incident when observing the offender, or someone resembling the perpetrator, or when revisiting the place where the abuse occurred).

Poor Motivation

Diagnostic implications for unmotivated, passive, and nonaggressive children differ somewhat according to age. Younger elementary-age students

- avoid taking responsibility for their own actions ("It's not my problem; you didn't tell me to do my home-work");
- won't take academic risks ("No, I don't want to be the leader of our study group");
- are incurious about the results of own efforts;
- have trouble postponing gratification ("I want what I want right now!");
- hardly ever look for a better solution to a problem ("Never mind, that's good enough");
- usually think failure is due to their poor abilities rather than a lack of effort ("Even if I try hard, I can't do it because I'm dumb");
- show a lack of curiosity about the world;
- like routine; dislike change or novelty;
- like things to be kept simple; shy away from complex activities requiring effort;
- seldom seem ambitious ("What I have is okay; I don't need anything more");
- appear developmentally immature;
- show poor work habits (find it hard to get going; are slow to finish);
- seldom get enthusiastic about anything;
- give up easily ("It's too hard; I don't want to do it anymore");
- if criticized, are easily hurt ("You don't like what I'm doing, so you must be mad at me").

There are many causes for these symptoms, but most seem to center around poorly developed personality goals and inadequate levels of parental interest and involvement.

Older passive-dependent underachievers emerge after about age 10. These academic underachievers are typically and consistently described by teachers, parents, counselors, and even themselves as lazy, unmotivated procrastinators, who could do better "if only they would try harder." These youngsters (usually boys) appear to lack a sense of purpose in life and seem to "float" or "cruise" through each day while constantly promising or reassuring adults that things will be better in the future (which never turns out to be true). These individuals

- consistently put off doing home chores;
- consistently put off doing school assignments;
- underachieve in school even though they may have done better in previous years;
- make promises but do not follow through on commitments;
- show a loss of interest in most future areas of commitment (school, home, hobbies, work);
- give up easily when things get tough;
- possess selective memory: they forget responsibilities but remember pleasurable activities;
- are easily distracted while doing chores or school assignments;
- give many excuses for their inability to perform;
- show no unusual personality problems (such as fear, sadness, depression, or moodiness);
- show little real concern about their poor achievement except, possibly, during school evaluations;

- usually get along with family and friends;
- evade talking about themselves or their inner motivations;
- seldom, if ever, get into serious trouble with authority figures (school or police, etc.);
- tend to cruise easily through life;
- show no evidence of mental slowness or neurological disorders;
- do not perform better even when heavily rewarded or punished;
- tend to think things are better (schoolwork, grades, and so on) than they actually are;
- agree amicably with others that they should try harder but do nothing about the situation;
- follow, but do not lead;
- tend to drift from day to day, tinkering with a variety of amusements (toys, cars, gadgets).

This disorder, while not difficult to diagnose, is unusually resistant to therapeutic efforts. Mandel and Marcus (1988) hypothesized that these children are subtly hostile to authority figures but can show this anger only by not producing the academic outcomes desired by grown-ups. The problem is treatable but not by traditional means.

The Developmentally Delayed Child

Bentzen (1963) described some of the traits of children who lack developmental readiness. Many of these traits are included in the following list, which is applicable to elementary school students, not older students.

- uses baby talk;
- cannot follow directions;
- has poor attention span;
- seems shy;
- tires easily;
- is frequently absent from class;
- has trouble cutting and coloring;
- cannot work alone;
- is constantly on the move;
- gives up easily and cries;
- is easily frightened and stays close to the teacher;
- cannot finish work;
- chews on objects;
- is easily distracted by other students.

Bentzen (1963) found that the great majority of children with the preceding traits were boys. She believed that the reason for this difference was the physiological retardation of boys compared to girls. Further, she believed that the social system should recognize the wide developmental differences between the genders in the early years, and she proposed the formulation of curricula that would better meet the needs of boys.

These symptoms represent a conglomerate of motor, mental, and emotional problems (Kessler, 1966). Developmentally delayed children demonstrate low frustration tolerance, unusual dependency, and an absence of self-control and direction. They feel little sense of responsibility for completing work, tell their teachers that classwork is not fun, and if forced to complete assignments, believe the teacher does not like them. When praised, they are delighted and sometimes demonstrate to the teacher that they are able to complete their work. As soon as the compliments cease, however, they may drift away from the assignment and the group. Without rewards, these students show little pride in achieving. According to Kessler, this may indicate a poorly developed superego or conscience. Such students still need the gratification that motivates much younger children.

Assessing Academic Readiness

Children who have trouble completing formal curriculum tasks at the first grade level often demonstrate low cognitive abilities on intelligence tests, suffer health problems, or exhibit motor, perceptual, motivational, and social deficits. Teachers often provide the best evaluation of these disabilities.

The validity of teachers' assessments. Starr (1965) reported that the studies of Ilg and Ames (1965) yielded an 83% agreement between the results of developmental examinations and teachers' estimates at the kindergarten level. Interestingly, the greatest agreement was reached regarding students considered "fully ready" or "fully unready." Kermoian (1962) found essentially the same results. He stated that 85.3% of teachers' judgments fell within one rank of his test ratings. The length of a teacher's experience was not found to be significantly correlated with results. Further, he stated that teachers' assessments are valid and highly significant, and that it is better for educators to spend time on nontesting techniques.

One should not conclude from this that reading tests and intelligence scales do not play an important part in the assessment of children. Correlations between teachers' judgment and readiness tests have revealed, however, that teachers are doing an excellent job of assessing children. Their judgment can be relied upon.

The literature pertaining to young children's aptitude for formal learning is too extensive to cover here. In general, however, researchers agree that children should show sufficient ability in the following areas:

- motor;
- perceptual-motor;
- cognitive;
- motivation and interest;
- social adjustment.

The Academic Readiness Profile. I developed the Academic Readiness Profile (see figure 11.1) to evaluate children suspected of being unready to face the challenges of a first grade curriculum, and to attempt to estimate development in each of these areas. It can also be used to single out advanced students who may need a more challenging curriculum in the first grade. The profile should be administered at the end of the kindergarten year or the beginning of the first grade year.

In general, a child whose profile is mostly on the left is likely to be unready for a standard first grade curriculum. A child whose profile is mostly on the right, however, is probably bright or even gifted.

The motor category attempts to gauge the child's physiological readiness.

The perceptual-motor category is divided into two parts. The first measures the ability to draw the human figure, an ability that has long been recognized as a measure of intelligence in younger children (Goodenough, 1926). The second measures the overall quality of drawings, which can be of even greater value in judging eye-hand coordination, because teachers have the opportunity to observe such drawing over an extended period. Kephart (1965) found drawing forms to be more closely related to school achievement than standard IQ or intelligence tests. Starr (1965) came to the same conclusion regarding a child's perceptual functioning as a means of diagnosing academic readiness.

Cognitive ability is measured by several categories: memory, number recognition, counting, word recognition, and vocabulary. Obviously, a child must possess memory skills to succeed academically. Attwell, Orpet, and Meyers (1967) found that a kindergartner's ability to remember the proper sequence of beads in bead stringing was significantly related to the child's fifth grade reading comprehension scores on the California Achievement Test (Tiegs & Clark, 1972). Vocabulary skills have long been recognized as related to reading readiness (J. A. Wilson & Robeck, 1965). Parsons (1957) stated that readiness is enhanced by building the child's vocabulary based on needs and interests that sensitize the child to his or her culture. Rice (1962) felt that children must be able to draw upon general language at their own level to help provide a bridge between the spoken and printed word. The cognitive ability categories tap a variety of intellectual skills (perceptual and recall) that are necessary for later reading success.

ACADEMIC READINESS PROFILE
Harold F. Burks, Ph.D.

Child _____   Gender: ☐ Male ☐ Female

Age _____ Grade _____ School _____

Teacher _____ Counselor _____

For each category on the left, put a check mark in the box on the right that corresponds to the best description of the child. When you have marked all the categories, draw a line to connect the check marks.

	☐	☐	☐	☐	☐
Motor *Predictive value:* Moderate	Needs help with most motor tasks	Can do simple tasks, but needs some help with eating, dressing, using toilet, and resting	Can eat, use toilet, and rest independently	Can tie shoes, use scissors, button clothes, skip, and catch a ball	Holds pencil properly; can ride a bicycle, use tools, and comb hair; helps others do motor tasks
Perceptual-Motor 1 *Predictive value:* Moderate	Cannot draw a recognizably human figure; scribbles	Can draw a crude but recognizably human figure	Can draw a person with a head, body, and limbs	Can draw a person with hands, fingers, and a face	Can draw a person with good proportions, clothing, and other details
Perceptual-Motor 2 *Predictive value:* High	Drawings are scribbled	Drawings are very crude	Drawings show recognizable shapes	Drawings have above-average shape and design	Drawings have very good shape, design, and detail
Persistence *Predictive value:* High	Seldom finishes tasks	Occasionally finishes tasks if pressured	Finishes tasks fairly often; sometimes has to be reminded	Usually finishes tasks with little reminding	Finishes difficult projects independently
Memory *Predictive value:* High	Very poor memory for instructions; forgets daily routine	Below-average memory; must be reminded frequently of routine	Remembers instructions fairly often	Usually remembers and understands instructions	Unusually good memory; recalls at abstract level
Attention *Predictive value:* High	Difficult to get and hold attention	Easily distracted	Can concentrate in some situations	Shows above-average concentration	Not bothered by outside stimuli
Number Recognition *Predictive value:* High	Cannot recognize any numbers	Recognizes numbers 1 and 2	Recognizes numbers 1–5	Recognizes numbers 1–10	Recognizes numbers beyond 10

Figure 11.1a.

Counting	Cannot count	Can count to 5	Can count to 10	Can count to 20	Can count to 100
Predictive value: High	☐	☐	☐	☐	☐

Word Recognition	Cannot recognize any letters	Knows some letters	Recognizes first name	Recognizes full name	Recognizes several words
Predictive value: High	☐	☐	☐	☐	☐

Vocabulary	Speaks very little	Is somewhat nonverbal	Speaks in short sentences; can be understood	Uses above-average amount of language	Initiates conversations; has high-level vocabulary
Predictive value: Moderate	☐	☐	☐	☐	☐

Interest in Curriculum	Is disinterested in pictures, games	Shows slight interest in pictures, games, and books	Shows fair interest in pictures, games, and books	Enjoys story time; contributes to show-and-tell; explores books; plays games	Can repeat stories; contributes more than required to show-and-tell; wins games
Predictive value: High	☐	☐	☐	☐	☐

Social	Plays alone	Plays with others occasionally	Plays with others fairly often	Enjoys and contributes to social activities	Initiates and enjoys activities that others enjoy
Predictive value: Moderate	☐	☐	☐	☐	☐

Humor	Essentially humorless	Seldom sees the point of a funny story	Sees humor in funny stories fairly often	Often laughs at humorous situations	Keen sense of humor; tells jokes
Predictive value: Moderate	☐	☐	☐	☐	☐

Emotions	Gets upset very easily	Is frustrated by difficult tasks	Can handle some stress	Above-average ability to handle stress	High tolerance for stress
Predictive value: Moderate	☐	☐	☐	☐	☐

Figure 11.1b.

Motivation and interest were also measured by several categories: persistence, attention, and interest in curriculum. Persistence (the ability to finish tasks) and attention (the ability to concentrate) may be tapping a common personality factor. The ability to persist and pay attention must be rooted in both physiological and environmental factors. I have long noted the inability of children with neurological handicaps to concentrate well (Burks, 1960). Delacato (cited in Ross, 1963) said that most reading problems stem from inadequate neurological organization from birth on. However, research with children who are disadvantaged (National Conference on Education of Disadvantaged, 1966) has also pointed out the importance of a stimulating environment that trains children to concentrate and follow through on tasks. The interest in curriculum category attempts to gauge the motivation a child brings to the learning situation.

Hoggard (1957) said that fear and tension can produce language deficiency. Others (Miller, 1957; Parsons, 1957) emphasized the importance of emotional maturity as it relates to academic readiness. Heffernan (1965) cautioned that children must not engage in the learning process with fear or anxiety but with self-confidence. The social, emotional, and humor categories attempt to assess the child's social adjustment. Children who are rated low in these categories may need further testing and evaluation to uncover the sources of their difficulties. The Burks Behavior Rating Scales (Burks 1977a, 2006a) have proved to be a definitive and complete instrument for that purpose.

Psychometric properties. Preliminary studies of the reliability of the Academic Readiness Profile involved teacher ratings of 110 kindergarten children, followed by a second rating of these same children within a 10-day period. Correlation coefficients, t values, and levels of significance were calculated. No significant shifts in the means of any of the scale categories were noted. Correlation coefficients for the categories were moderate to high, ranging from .64 to .83. Thus, the preliminary teacher's rating for a child on any of the scale classifications was quite similar to the teacher's rating for the child a short time later.

Evidence of the validity of the Academic Readiness Profile rests on data derived from several sources. The instrument was originally constructed and used successfully in a school district in 1961. Since then, it has undergone a number of refinements. Changes stemmed from (a) the content evaluations performed by 18 kindergarten teachers who reviewed the instrument on several occasions, (b) a review of the literature pertaining to the attributes in young children that have led to successful school performance, and (c) a statistical analysis to determine the ability of each category to predict first grade success as measured by a first grade reading test and a first grade teacher rating scale.

In May 1967, five teachers completed ratings on 190 kindergarten children. The students in the study were from a small school district in Los Angeles County, California. In May 1968, the same children, then in first grade, were administered the reading test in the Stanford Achievement Test (SAT) (Madden, Gardner, Rudman, & Kelley, 1964) under the supervision of the district school psychologist. A total of 152 scores on both instruments were available for comparison.

Because each category on the Academic Readiness Profile contains five levels of scoring, raw scores on the SAT (reading) were also divided into five groups to facilitate comparisons between the two instruments. A significant positive relationship was found between all Academic Readiness Profile categories and the SAT reading scores. Twelve of the 14 categories (86%) correlated at the .01 level of significance. The correlations ranged from .19 to .48. The total Academic Readiness Profile score, with a correlation of .48, was the single best predictor of reading success.

In another district, a study was conducted using 277 children, who were rated one year later on a first grade Academic Progress Scale (Burks, 1968a). Ratings in two categories of the Academic Progress Scale—word recognition and reading comprehension—were compared with certain categories on the Academic Readiness Profile. All the correlations were significant at the .05 level or better. The four ratings having the highest correlations with word recognition and reading comprehension, respectively, were counting (r = .45 and .40), number recognition (.47 and .44), memory (.45 and .46), and persistence (.40 and .42).

The predictive value of each of the categories is shown on the Academic Readiness Profile. Categories that correlate with all the criterion measures of first grade success at the .01 level or better are designated as highly predictive. Those categories that did not meet this standard for all criteria are designated as moderately predictive. The criteria include the relationships between the category and (a) success on the SAT reading test in first grade, (b) success on the word recognition category of the Academic Progress Scale as rated by the first grade teacher, (c) success on the reading comprehension category of the Academic Progress Scale as rated by the first grade teacher, and (d) the total score derived from teacher ratings on the first grade Academic Progress Scale.

The following list shows the categories ranked from those showing the greatest relationship with the criteria (most highly predictive) to those showing the least relationship (least predictive). The first eight categories were found to be highly predictive, and the remaining are moderately predictive.

1. memory;
2. number recognition;
3. persistence;
4. counting;
5. interest in curriculum;
6. attention;
7. perceptual-motor 2;
8. word recognition;
9. vocabulary;
10. humor;
11. motor;
12. emotions;
13. perceptual-motor 1;
14. social.

As noted earlier, Attwell et al. (1967) found that the ability of kindergartners to string beads was significantly related to fifth grade reading comprehension scores on the California Achievement Test. It can be hypothesized that the capacity to string beads entails the ability to count, recognize total numbers or quantify, remember a sequence, and finish what is started. This finding corresponds to Academic Readiness Profile results.

Factor analysis. A factor analysis was performed on the validation sample data (152 original teacher rating scales). The rotated factor matrices identified four factors, which are almost identical for both boys and girls. These factors, and the category cluster for each factor (significant rotated factor value of .5 or above), follow. Categories in parentheses are those with factor loadings very close to the arbitrary cutoff of .5.

Memory/Concentration

memory
persistence
attention
(emotions)

Academic Skills

counting
number recognition
(word recognition)

Perceptual-Motor

perceptual-motor 1
perceptual-motor 2

Social/Intellectual

> interest in curriculum
> vocabulary
> social
> humor

The Academic Readiness Profile apparently taps four aspects of personality and skill-centered activities. Factor 1 contains categories showing some of the highest predictive correlations with indexes of first grade success. Furthermore, these categories primarily estimate inhibitory control. I found the ability to pay attention to be an essential factor differentiating normal children from those showing evidence of organic brain dysfunction (Burks, 1960). Memory probably appears to the observer as another form of sustained attention. The development of a normal personality depends on inhibitory processes. In the classroom, the ability to inhibit responses to distracting stimuli is a necessary prerequisite for learning.

Factor 2 also contains categories showing a high correlation with first grade success. The ability to count, recognize numbers, and recognize some words obviously foretells later academic success in arithmetic and reading. In short, a child who shows these skills has demonstrated perceptual and memory abilities much like those needed in formal first grade curricula.

Factor 3 taps perceptual-motor abilities, which have been related to reading ability by a number of researchers. Bender (1956) stated that studies of sensory aphasia indicate that the visual-motor gestalt function is fundamentally associated with language expression. Frierson and Barbe (1967) described disturbances in auditory, visual, and kinesthetic perceptual abilities as a frequent and underlying cause of learning difficulties. Harris (1964) described perceptual-motor functions as being related to reading achievement in a normal second grade population.

Factor 4 singles out categories involving verbal ability, interest in the curriculum, social skill, and a sense of humor. These elements may reflect the degree of the child's perceived involvement with the classroom environment. Active participation in activities suggests that the child derives satisfaction from his or her endeavors and is ready to meet school challenges.

Gender and socioeconomic differences in ratings. During early childhood, girls tend to be more mature than boys. According to Lee and Lee (1958), girls are, on the average, one year more physically mature than boys at the beginning of first grade. Although educational researchers appear to agree that girls have an edge over boys in academic readiness, it is not clear in just what areas the superiority is expressed. Thus, gender differences in Academic Readiness Profile ratings were studied along with socioeconomic differences.

The profile was originally administered in two school districts in Los Angeles County. One district (mostly white) consisted of families with an average yearly income significantly higher than that of the other district (70% Mexican American), according to Bank of America (Burks, 1968a).

In the higher socioeconomic district, the girls were rated higher than boys in all 14 categories, and these differences were significant ($p < .05$) in 12 of the categories. In the lower socioeconomic district, girls were rated higher than the boys in 11 of the 14 categories but scored significantly higher in only the two perceptual-motor categories.

Reasons for the differences between the two socioeconomic populations are not well understood. Girls were given higher ratings in most classifications in both districts, but results show a real difference in levels of achievement for the higher versus the lower socioeconomic district. Comparisons of the results for these two districts indicate that the high-socioeconomic students had significantly higher scores in 9 of the 14 categories. These included both of the perceptual-motor categories, counting, number recognition, interest in curriculum, vocabulary, social, humor, and memory.

Results of this study indicate that different districts have different means. However, the profile was not constructed to measure the average progress of large numbers of children in any school district but rather to locate the child who is a potential slow learner in first grade (regardless of the socioeconomic status of the district). Any child in any district whose Academic Readiness Profile falls sharply to the left is likely to be at risk for slow progress in first grade. On the other hand, any child in any district whose profile falls sharply to the right is probably bright or gifted.

Despite the general trend, it is not reasonable to provide cutoff scores for students at risk. Such arbitrary points cannot supplant judgment based on the careful evaluation of results obtained from the Academic Readiness Profile and other instruments.

Poor attitude and reading achievement. Kennedy and Halinsky (1975) believe that most underachievers possess a poor attitude toward the reading process; such attitudes cannot be observed directly, of course, but must be inferred from verbal and nonverbal behavior. Further, they believe that the development of a positive attitude precedes the development of interest. For the classroom teacher, then, students must have a positive attitude toward reading before the goal of making them lifetime readers can be achieved.

Because the ability to read is a prerequisite to achievement in nearly all other subjects, it is important to investigate the attitudes of underachievers toward the reading process. I developed the My Feelings about Reading checklist (see figure 11.2) for older students who exhibit reading disabilities.

I have used this checklist with many poor readers, and not surprisingly, the worse a student's reading problem, the greater the number of items answered "very true." In fact, those who see themselves as having problems in most of the described areas have simply given up hope of ever learning to read.

Other observations based on the clinical use of this checklist include:

- Students with emotional difficulties tend to answer "very true" to items 5, 8, 10, 24, 26, and 30.
- Students with physical problems (usually eye dysfunction) tend to answer "very true" to items 5, 6, 9, 22, and 28.
- Children who have not learned the mechanics of reading tend to answer "very true" to items 1, 2, 15, 20, 29, 30, and 32.
- Students with a low self-concept tend to answer "very true" to items 8, 21, 29, and 30.
- Children with a loss of interest in reading tend to answer "very true" to items 3, 11, 12, 13, 14, 16, 17, 18, 19, 23, 25, 26, 27, 32, and 33. Most children experiencing reading difficulties indicate a loss of interest in reading.

These observations are not based on any empirical evidence. However, they may alert the educator to areas that need further investigation.

INTERVENTION STRATEGIES

Techniques for School Personnel

Whatever factors cause poor academic performance, a number of techniques and placement options are available in the school to improve a child's performance. It is essential that students experiencing academic difficulties receive assistance as early as possible. The following intervention strategies begin with teaching methods that can be used in the regular classroom. In addition, placement options such as retention and special education should be considered if modifications to the regular program do not substantially improve the student's academic performance.

Teacher Behavior that Enhances Learning

Studies by Veldman and Brophy (1974) illustrate conclusively that the behavior of teachers can affect student learning to a degree that is both statistically and practically significant. The following teacher suggestions may improve the performance of underachieving students:

1. Do not assign the student a disparaging label (e.g., "poor worker," "lazy," "dull," etc.). Disapproving tags are likely to lower the expectations of other adults working with the child (Brandt & Hayden, 1974).
2. Give the disorganized student attention when he or she demonstrates good study habits, but ignore nonstudy conduct (Hall, Lund, & Jackson, 1968).

MY FEELINGS ABOUT READING

Harold F. Burks, Ph.D.

Read the following items and put a check mark in the column that best describes how you feel.

	Not true	Somewhat true	Very true
1. I am a slow reader.	☐	☐	☐
2. I find reading hard because of the big words.	☐	☐	☐
3. I am not interested in the things we read at school.	☐	☐	☐
4. I am not interested in the things I read at home.	☐	☐	☐
5. Reading makes me nervous.	☐	☐	☐
6. Reading gives me a headache.	☐	☐	☐
7. When I read, I daydream a lot.	☐	☐	☐
8. If someone tells me I have to read something, I don't want to read it.	☐	☐	☐
9. Reading makes my eyes sore.	☐	☐	☐
10. I feel bad if I have to read out loud to someone.	☐	☐	☐
11. It is hard for me to get the point of a story.	☐	☐	☐
12. Most stories are a waste of time to read.	☐	☐	☐
13. Reading bores me.	☐	☐	☐
14. When I read, I am usually thinking of something else.	☐	☐	☐
15. I seldom finish what I read.	☐	☐	☐
16. I don't get many new ideas when I read.	☐	☐	☐
17. I only read when I have to.	☐	☐	☐
18. I never read newspapers.	☐	☐	☐
19. I only read things that interest me.	☐	☐	☐
20. When I read, I lose track of what I am reading.	☐	☐	☐
21. I don't think I will ever be a good reader.	☐	☐	☐
22. It's hard for me to sit still when I read.	☐	☐	☐
23. The school doesn't have books about things that interest me.	☐	☐	☐
24. Most of the time I'm not in the mood to read.	☐	☐	☐
25. During my free time, I usually don't read.	☐	☐	☐
26. I don't understand what the characters are doing in stories.	☐	☐	☐
27. Most books are not interesting.	☐	☐	☐
28. I tend to get tired when I read.	☐	☐	☐
29. Most stories are too long.	☐	☐	☐
30. I hate taking reading tests.	☐	☐	☐
31. Most of my poor marks in school are caused by my poor reading.	☐	☐	☐
32. I'm not interested in learning new words.	☐	☐	☐
33. I don't talk to others about things I read.	☐	☐	☐

Figure 11.2.

3. Meet the following prerequisites before assigning work to a nonlearning child.

   - Teach the child to pay attention.
   - Help the child learn to control impulses.
   - Help the child to acquire a trust of adults.
   - Train the child to deal effectively with symbolic materials (Hill, 1978).

4. Group the class for optimum learning conditions. I found that, although students with learning disorders tend to accept students without learning disorders, the reverse is not true (Burks, 1965). Further, girls with learning disorders are more rejecting of other failing girls than poor-achieving boys are of other failing boys. Because of these acceptance problems, it is unwise to include too many underachievers in a regular classroom (Burks, 1964b). Cassidy and Vukelich (1977) found that small groups were a better learning situation for young children than large groups.

5. Stress classroom exercises that require cooperation for girls with learning problems. Emphasize a curriculum that demands competitiveness for underachieving boys (Ahlgren & Johnson, 1979).

6. Provide token reinforcements (candy, check marks, pats on the back, etc.) for underachieving students. Studies have shown that positive results are almost invariably obtained with this technique (Axelrod, 1971).

7. Arrange to have classroom aides. Loos, Williams, and Bailey (1977) found that aide-assisted classrooms produce better academic results than rooms without aides.

8. Provide adolescent problem students with a daily progress report card. When poor marks on the report card are allied with home consequences (e.g., loss of privileges), improvement in behavior tends to be significant (Shumaker, Hovell, & Sherman, 1977).

9. Assign the young underachieving child to a nongraded primary classroom (Pevan, 1973). Compared with students in graded classrooms, poor learners doing nongraded work achieve more, show greater improvement in self-concept, and demonstrate a better attitude toward school.

10. Establish a transitional first grade for young, immature students.

11. Keep the parents informed of progress and allow them to observe classroom programs.

12. Lower classroom expectations. Reduce negative consequences and increase positive ones.

13. Allow the child to attend a part-time tutoring class.

14. Use the child's interests to get him or her involved in classroom assignments.

15. Institute rest breaks to reduce fatigue (best for young children).

16. Do not try to motivate the child by saying, "I know you can do it, so why don't you?" Instead, discuss the child's feelings about work.

17. Use behavior modification whenever it appears to succeed. Start with concrete rewards (e.g., candy or prizes) and graduate to verbal praise.

18. Allow extra time to complete classwork.

19. Recognize improved work by putting it on a bulletin board or sending it to the principal, school nurse, or anyone else who will show an enthusiastic response.

20. Use a contract. Plan assignments with the child and agree upon appropriate rewards and sanctions. The child then has the security of knowing what will happen.

21. Be friendly. Tell the child that completed work is for the teacher alone and not for the parents.

22. Suggest ways to improve appearance, speech, social interaction, and so on. These themes are likely to be more important to the youngster than strictly academic subjects, and the child will be motivated to participate.

23. Set up a special time when the child can ask for assistance.

24. Offer a special place in the school where the child can study (especially if the student is from a disadvantaged home where there is no place to work on assignments).

25. Consider placing the child in another classroom with another teacher if performance drops during the school year.

26. Help poor writers by allowing them to dictate stories to a tutor or tape recorder, then have the stories typed up by an adult.

27. Enroll the child in a summer school program (not recommended for the child motivated to fail in that special situation).

Activities that Enhance Social Participation

As discussed previously, peer relations and social interaction have been found to be related to academic performance. Consequently, activities that enhance social participation are valuable intervention strategies for students demonstrating academic difficulties. The following intervention techniques may prove useful.

1. Establish a play activity program. Bower (1960) pointed out that some emotionally disturbed children find it difficult to play because they are either unable to express feelings or are unable to control their activity. In group play settings, however, young children are given an opportunity to learn how to release pent-up tension. As Bower explained, energy within a child bound by emotional conflict, self-doubt, and anxiety can be freely and realistically expended in a play situation. Many roles can be adopted and acted out. Play helps youngsters define themselves and the world around them—through play they explore frightening feelings and practice innovative responses to negative emotions.

   Bower further believes that play activity programs may be the only school pursuit that can help some impulse-ridden and frightened children. Play programs should be scheduled at the end of the school day somewhere on the school grounds. Selection and training of teachers requires careful attention, and mental health consultation should be available to the play leader. Finally, care must be taken to place children properly; they should be tried out in the group for a period before obtaining a permanent assignment.

   I experimented with one example of such a program. Nonachieving and disturbed sixth grade boys were asked to come to meetings in the school cafeteria before classes started in the morning. Breakfast was provided. The program consisted of free play and talk sessions. No child was forced to attend, no child was urged to eat, and no child was prevented from leaving. After initially testing the frustration tolerance of attending adults, the children settled down and most remained in the program. Teachers were so impressed with changes in classroom behavior that they voluntarily contributed money for refreshments.

   Another such play group was established for children who were emotionally disturbed and children with neurological handicaps. All were underachievers with poor work habits. Working closely with the teacher, I set up a program of play activities (games, hobbies, painting, construction, etc.) that engaged the children's interest for the first two or three months of the class session. I believed that the children would eventually weary of the play activities and ask for curriculum assignments. This hypothesis was confirmed; the children, individually and in small groups, did finally request and use curriculum materials (Burks, 1962).

2. Use guidance games. Educational bookstores carry many games designed to explore feelings and attitudes. As a matter of fact, I constructed such a game (Burks, 1994, 2001). This colorful printed game presents the child with easily read question cards that pertain to common fairy-tale situations (e.g., "What do you think you should do if the talking tree asks for help?") or relate to philosophical pursuits (e.g., "What do you think would make the princess happy?"). The youngster gains question cards by throwing dice and landing on game board spaces. Children (and adults) find the game intriguing. It promotes communication. It is noncompetitive and can go on indefinitely. It tends to end when participants tire. When it and other guidance games are employed, a supervising adult should be present.

3. Involve the child with peers. The following activities may increase a child's social interaction:

   • Have the child participate in small-group activities. Assign particular tasks with the understanding that other children cannot appropriate these duties.

- Plan to have an older student (perhaps a junior high or high school student) tutor the child before or after school. Ideally, the older individual will become an admired model.
- Permit the underachieving student to tutor younger (perhaps primary school–age) children who need extra help. The helper and the receiver, both in need of academic assistance, will tend to identify with each other (Price & Dequine, 1982), a mutually beneficial process.
- Allow the student to choose his or her classroom seat. However, it is not a good idea to let the child sit next to high achievers who might inhibit the child's verbal expression.
- Group underachievers together so they can discuss mutual problems and disappointments with a counselor. If warranted, the teacher can be asked to attend a meeting with the students and the counselor.
- Ask other students to be social reinforcers. Teach them to listen to and praise the efforts of the slower-achieving student. A more mature youngster can be chosen to act as a buddy to the underachiever.

Motivation

The role of motivation in the learning process is a complicated one. A summary of my research efforts (Burks, 1977a) points to the validity of the following principles:

1. A combination of verbal reward and punishment is the most effective learning reinforcement.
2. A period of isolation from social activities (about 20 minutes) arouses a social drive among children (especially those who are highly independent), pushing them to participate in learning activities).
3. When paired with verbal criticism, the teacher's silence is construed as approval.
4. When paired with verbal praise, the teacher's silence is construed as disapproval.
5. For young children, material rewards (gold stars, candy, etc.) are most effective. For older students, social rewards (as well as material rewards) are attractive.
6. Children identify with, and emulate, people in their environment who have the power to reward them. Warm and rewarding role models are imitated. I found that young children receiving high reading readiness scores had more verbal and physically demonstrative maternal models than those with low reading readiness scores.

Teachers can help young, unaggressive, nonachieving children to become more motivated by

- being firm about academic requirements;
- making sure the child understands the curriculum;
- interrupting isolating techniques initiated by other students;
- pairing the child with more able students;
- de-emphasizing competition in the classroom;
- praising every observable incident of academic progress;
- working closely with parents on behavior goals.

Mandel and Marcus (1988) provide the most insightful analysis of older, passive, nonachieving children that I have found. I will attempt to summarize their findings here, but I recommend reading their book for a detailed understanding of this most difficult youngster. They believe that these older students have made an unconscious but highly motivated choice to fail academically. Attempts to motivate such children to succeed based on rewards, punishment, heightened interest, or feelings of shame will all be defeated in the face of the child's desire to flunk.

Why are these older youngsters so resistive to treatment? According to Mandel and Marcus (1988), a closer look at underlying personality dynamics reveals that these students tend to be antagonistic—particularly toward authority figures that show no satisfaction with any efforts the student makes. This hostility is expressed in hidden ways, best described as a passive-aggressive style. Most resentment is directed at parents. The animosity remains hidden because from an early age these children

- were taught to suppress the expression of emotions;
- were rewarded for maintaining a pleasant demeanor under stress;
- were given unrealistic goals by parents who seldom expressed pleasure at what their child accomplished (hence the child's aversion to the influence of authority and unwillingness to gratify the wishes of adults);
- learned from their parents that adults accept all responsibility for the child's performance (hence the child's attitude that events are beyond his or her control).

This training produces youngsters who are afraid of aggressive impulses, fearful of showing enthusiasm or emotional involvement, reluctant to go along with the wishes of authority figures, and basically unwilling to participate in the adult world because they see no way to fulfill its requirements.

Mandel and Marcus (1988) pointed out that it is difficult to change family conduct patterns. Parents do not like to be told that their efforts to raise their child effectively may be futile. In the case of the nonassertive, passive underachiever, the plot may go like this: The child comes to depend on the disapproval of authority figures to relieve guilt for not being productive but still finds it gratifying to frustrate adults. The parents, who feel guilty because they have not produced a functioning child (it being their responsibility to do so, of course) become increasingly frustrated and more and more determined to make the child perform. They cling to the notion that outward incentives and the satisfaction the child would experience for achieving will get him or her to respond enthusiastically. This scenario is a blueprint for disaster.

Given these circumstances, counselors who try to treat these children must be aware of the following:

1. The child's underachievement is not due to poor motivation, nor to an unrewarding environment. It is due to a strong impulse to fail based on the perceived perils of accepting adult responsibilities.
2. Passive underachievers convince themselves (and try to convince everyone else) that their inability to perform is beyond their control and understanding and that their grades are poor because of unfortunate circumstances. Rationalizations and excuses proliferate as these "victims" of their surroundings attempt to convince others of this.
3. The real motivation not to achieve is kept from the underachiever's awareness because knowing would force the individual to accept the unpleasant fact that he or she wants to remain infantile and dependent.

The first step, and probably the most important one in the rehabilitation of this kind of youngster, is for the parents to stop futile attempts to change the child's behavior with traditional, seemingly commonsense approaches (exhortations, appeals, rewards, punishment, displays of parental disappointment, and parental self-blame).

Mandel and Marcus (1988) suggested that counselors ask parents to:

1. Stop asking the child how he or she is doing at school. If the parents quiz the child, they will be told that all is well. The parents thereby signal that they accept the burden of anxiety, not the child. Instead, parents can be instructed to check with school authorities periodically to find out about the child's progress.
2. Stop showing distress about low grades and elation when the child succeeds academically. The child wants others to accept the emotional burden for his or her failure and interprets their joy as an external contrivance designed to elicit even more achievement.
3. Stop paying serious attention to the child's endless excuses for nonperformance. The child simply becomes more and more adept at inventing reasons for failure. The parents must show that they do not believe outside forces cause the child's poor achievement and that a professed lack of interest is not a valid excuse. After all, everyone gets bored but they must still finish work.
4. Stop making excuses for the youngster's failures. Invented reasons for the child's failure—such as not having a good place to study, poor teachers, family discord, not having enough special help, being an only child, an uninteresting curriculum, not having the right friends, and so on—are simply evasive tactics employed by parents to explain a phenomenon engendered by an entirely different cause: the child's unwillingness to grow up.
5. Work closely with school authorities to establish the following course of action.

Establish agreed-upon goals. These objectives must be accepted by the parents, by the school representative (usually the teacher), and, most important, by the student. The student will acquiesce because, as usual, he or she will agree (based on the impulse to keep everyone happy and nonprobing) that getting good grades is important. The student's acceptance of and agreement to meet established goals is pivotal. It is the most necessary step in the recovery program because it shifts the prime responsibility for change from parents and teachers to the student. All future moves will be linked to these objectives.

Document what is expected of the student. List current courses, find out what requirements have and have not been met, and what difficulties are perceived by school personnel (in terms of classroom deportment, amount of studying, how the child prepares for tests, and any other behavior that affects performance adversely). Document all of this without evaluative comments. This information is an important gauge that can be used to measure future improvement. This step is very important even though it is a troublesome task that requires patience and persistence.

Work closely with the school (preferably with a counselor or teachers) to focus on specific learning difficulties and to pinpoint excuses given by the child for each problem. Ask the youngster to identify obstacles that stand in the way of achievement in a given subject. This should be no problem for the child, who will have many excuses at hand. It is up to the counselor to review the details of the difficulties presented.

Suppose, for example, the student says the teacher is hard to understand and that is why the student misinterprets instructions and consequently cannot complete assignments. The counselor remarks that a misunderstanding could account for the student's poor grades in social studies. The student agrees, saying that he or she can't figure out what the teacher wants. The counselor pursues this by asking if the teacher tells the class what they are supposed to do and whether the other kids get the message and complete their homework. The student has to admit that the others do the work but then comes up with another excuse, such as that the teacher gives too many directions—the student cannot remember all of them. The counselor asks the student why he or she does not write down the directions. The student may admit that he or she sometimes does but then says that the instructions often get lost. At this point, the counselor sums up the conversation by saying that the student apparently knows what the teacher wants but either does not write down the instructions or loses them.

It is important to understand that this conversation starts out with a surface generality that sounds reasonable, logical, and even convincing (like many familiar idiomatic expressions such as, "Gee, things sure are tough"). This generality is not, however, a sound basis for remediation attempts.

At this point, the counselor is not really trying to get an account of what occurred, but rather to acquire a more complete picture of the student's perception of the problem. The objective is not to change the student's conduct but to understand how the child perceives the difficulty. The child could have given a variety of excuses for not completing assignments. He or she could have said the teacher mumbled, talked too fast, skipped over material, neglected to hand out appropriate papers, or was intimidating. Instead, it became clear that it was the student who caused the problem by either not writing down directions or losing them. The counselor could have pursued the matter further by inquiring what steps the student took to keep track of written directions: Where were they kept in the classroom? How were they carried home? What happened to them at home? No matter what problems arise during this interview, the counselor should limit inquiries to one area of difficulty.

Link the child's excuses to consequences. Although most youngsters understand that the amount of preparation and work one puts into a task is related to the quality of its outcome, it cannot be assumed that passive underachievers comprehend this association. Such children are masters at avoiding this logical conclusion because accepting the link would mean they would have to admit that it is not unpredictable outside forces that cause their poor achievement but their personal unwillingness to produce. Random excuses would no longer suffice.

Continuing with the preceding example, the counselor might ask the student if it is true that he or she either doesn't take notes or loses them. The student is forced to admit that the accusations are true. Then the counselor reminds the student that he or she wanted to do better by taking and keeping notes. Again the youngster has to agree. Next, the counselor reminds the child that he or she is not doing these things and asks how the student expects to get good grades under these circumstances. The child has to agree that he or she cannot. The counselor asks if that is what the student wants. The child says no. When asked what action the youngster should take, he or she is forced to agree to try to do better.

This apparently simpleminded linkage of cause and effect is a crucial step because it impresses upon the child that what he or she does in the present influences what occurs in the future.

Ask the underachiever to imagine ways to overcome the academic obstacles discussed. At this point, the student has expressed his or her perception of what causes the poor achievement, has detailed what he or she thinks obstructs production, has focused on specific areas of difficulty, has isolated excuses, and has linked failed current behavior to future consequences. Now the child is asked to suggest specific ways to solve the problems.

The temptation for adults is to pepper the student with commonsense, practical, and logical solutions—but that won't work. The student has long evaded such reasonable suggestions and will not likely acknowledge them now. Instead, the counselor should innocently ask the child to think up solutions. Usually the student will come up with an effective solution. When that occurs, the adult should discuss the suggestion in greater detail, examine how practical it is, speculate on possible reasons it could succeed or fail, and refine the details. If the student cannot think of a solution, the adult may offer one, but it must be discussed as a mutual problem that both the interviewer and the child will attempt to put in perspective. All efforts must now focus on placing the underachiever in a position where he or she must accept personal responsibility.

In the ongoing conversation between counselor and student, the counselor states the obvious: It is hard for the student to take notes and get them home and probably difficult for the student to see what can be done about that. The counselor might suggest taping the notes to the student's school locker or desk or to the television set at the child's home. The student will say that that is a ridiculous idea. The counselor will remind the student that getting good grades is the most important objective and that he or she should use whatever method works.

The student is now forced to accept responsibility for improving his or her school performance. As Mandel and Marcus (1988) pointed out, the student may show some discomfort as he or she begins to be more aware of inner conflicts that have led to poor achievement.

Once all of the preceding steps have been completed, take action. The action must not be based on adult expectations, however, but on the crucial question, "What do you think you should do now?", and this question must be addressed to the student. The adult should interrogate the student further about specifics: How does the teen expect to accomplish this goal? How often are attempts to be made? When should they be made?

Adult interrogators face a common but crucial trap at this point: The student has been brought to the point of being asked to formulate his or her own solution to academic difficulties, but the student cannot be counted on to follow through on these intentions. Concerned adults must be prepared for and accept the fact that passive, apparently unconcerned poor achievers are likely to complete only a small portion of the agreed-upon goals. The fear of maturity still exists in these youngsters, and change is not likely to be apparent after only a few adult-child discussions.

It is at this juncture that adults are most likely to show anger and disappointment at the student's apparent lack of progress. After all, elaborate efforts have been made to make the student understand the role of excuses, how excuses stall achievement, and how excuses may be circumvented; and still the child evades responsibility!

Behavior is not changed quickly. Adults have to admit that, because they can't change their own conduct readily, even when they recognize the necessity for doing so. (Consider, for example, the adult who must try to act cheerful when asked to give up leisure activities so that home chores can be completed.) As far as the underachieving child is concerned, the intention is not necessarily to try to get the student to accomplish more. Instead, the aim is to try to help the student to shrink the gap between his or her intentions (promises) and actual production—the "crap gap," according to Mandel and Marcus (1988). The youngster must develop a realistic acceptance of his or her personal role in the achievement process. Faced with this recognition and acceptance of reality, the student can choose one of three alternatives:

1. The student can decide that he or she really has no desire to succeed and just wants to do something besides go to school.

2. The student can continue to fail and come up with excuses.
3. The student can start to achieve to a small extent, perhaps in one area of endeavor.

The first alternative is rarely chosen because it would mean dropping out of school, and that would mean the student would have to assume the dreaded responsibility for his or her own future. The second or third alternative is more likely to be chosen. The important thing to remember is that interrupting the child's use of just one excuse is not likely to lead to an academic transformation.

Determine whether the student has followed through on the agreed-upon assignment (that is, has successfully overcome the impediments put in place by a former excuse). The study difficulties remain but it soon becomes apparent that a new excuse will be given: "I remembered to write down what it was I was supposed to do, but I couldn't read my writing!" The student must discard the former excuse because using it would be tantamount to acknowledging that he or she deliberately decided to fail—and that decision must be kept out of conscious awareness.

Deal with new excuses. When the student stops using an excuse (because it is no longer a useful defense against being responsible), the adult should address another, then another, and so on. Focus on specifics, not generalities.

As more and more excuses are made unusable, the student edges ever closer to the realization that he or she is really in control of what occurs. This process can take a considerable period of time, and involved adults must be patient. As the fund of excuses is exhausted, a variety of personality symptoms may become evident—including unusual worries, panic, anger, confusion, sadness, extensive periods of looking inward, and even changes in relationships with friends.

As personality changes occur in the student, the adult advisor must change the orientation of counseling. Become a friendly and supportive listener, rather than a confrontational investigator. Explore the many and intense questions the youngster brings up about his or her future. If these character changes take place, there may be a significant and positive new direction in the child's academic orientation.

Methods to Improve Reading

The My Feelings about Reading checklist (see figure 11.2) can be used as a first step to improve a student's attitude toward reading. Most children like to discuss their reading problems with sympathetic adult listeners. The completed checklist should be reviewed with the student; no other person should be present. Listen carefully to the youngster and take notes about individual items. At the end of the interview, promise to think about what the child has said. Further, make an appointment with the student to talk over what might be done to alleviate his or her reading difficulties. Naturally, this appointment must be honored. Venting feelings and receiving adult interest and support are valuable therapeutic experiences for children with special problems.

The majority of children support adult efforts to improve classroom conditions and procedures, even when the efforts do not satisfy them completely. If the teacher says, for example, "I've noticed that you become very nervous when you're waiting to be called on to read. Instead of reading an assignment, how about just reading the page numbers of the arithmetic assignment to the class?", the child recognizes a compromise and will most likely cooperate. As time goes on, other curriculum modifications can be made to help the child become less nervous and more willing to read to others.

Some children are bored with classroom reading materials. If a student is not interested in assigned books or articles, ask the youngster what subject matter might be exciting to read. No matter how the child responds to this question, treat the answer with respect and make an effort to acquire reading matter in the child's field of interest. Of course, the child must not be given literature too advanced for his or her reading level.

If a child is chronically tired, bored, or distracted, a change in classroom routine may be indicated. Perhaps too much time is being devoted to reading exercises. Perhaps the reading period should take place earlier in the day. Perhaps the child needs more rest breaks.

Many poor readers dread assessment measures that gauge reading ability. They do not need the humiliation of being told over and over that they are not performing well. If a child is worried about test procedures, make arrangements to give that child high marks for any efforts to improve reading and stress the progress achieved rather than the distance the child must traverse to reach the academic level of most students.

Be sure to report checklist results to the parents and inform them of steps the school will take to help the student. Ask for parent support and outline ways mothers and fathers can augment classroom remedial approaches.

Grade Retention

Teachers at the preschool and kindergarten levels sometimes identify students as immature and unready for advancement in school on the basis of infantile habits and inappropriate behavior, but this conduct alone is not sufficient to warrant retention. Studies of very young children (Burks, 1968a, 1977b) indicate that the term "readiness" must be reserved for those students who have the ability to succeed in formal curricular tasks (particularly reading) at the first grade level. Symptoms of social and emotional immaturity often accompany signs of slow-developing intellectuality, but these symptoms are not reliable predictors of future cognitive performance.

It is generally recognized that grade retention is a poor remedy for most children (Chansky, 1964). If it must occur, it should probably take place at the kindergarten level, before the individual faces a formal curriculum and undergoes the experience of failing it. Many feel that ungraded classrooms are a better answer (Beggs & Buffie, 1967). Few school districts, however, have gone so far as to underwrite and institute this concept. Other districts have experimented with a junior first grade, where students can be given readiness materials for a longer time than normal and still feel they have been promoted.

According to Cotter (1967), several procedures could help reduce failures in the first grade. First, children should be given complete physical and psychological evaluations in the preschool years. Second, instruction should be individualized, using programmed reading materials. Finally, Cotter recommends that special classes be devoted to children who are at risk of potentially failing first grade.

Grade retention almost never benefits the student. Without going into a detailed review of the literature on the subject, the following statements can be made:

1. In the United States, grade retention has had an aura of revenge and condemnation.
2. The argument that repeating a grade helps weaker students has largely been nullified by experience. Nearly one-half of these students do no better than the previous year; the others do worse.
3. Failing is an emotional blow the student never forgets.
4. Weak students do not do well when retained, but they also do not do well when advanced to the next grade. No matter how students are shifted around, there remains a wide range of readiness among these learners.

Does grade retention ever do any good? It may benefit a child who receives total remediation of the problems that led to failure, or a very young child (kindergarten or first grade) who is obviously unready for the next grade and whose parents are aware of his or her needs.

If grade retention is to be considered, it probably should occur after an evaluation of the child's progress in kindergarten and before he or she is placed in a first grade class. If the student has severe learning problems, special classes are another possibility.

The Student Placement checklist (see figure 11.3) has proved helpful in the evaluation of very poorly achieving students. Along with many other measures (IQ tests, achievement tests, and instruments documenting behavior and events in early infancy), it can be used by educators when making the decision to retain a student or place the student in a special class.

The following responses to the Student Placement checklist indicate a need for grade retention or placement in special classes.

STUDENT PLACEMENT CHECKLIST

Harold F. Burks, Ph.D.

Put a check mark in the appropriate column for each of the following statements.

Questions for Teachers

	Yes	No
1. Does the Academic Readiness Profile indicate retardation in most areas?	☐	☐
2. Is the child younger than most classmates?	☐	☐
3. Is the child older than most classmates?	☐	☐
4. Is the child smaller than most classmates?	☐	☐
5. Is the child larger than most classmates?	☐	☐
6. Has the child established hand dominance?	☐	☐
7. Does the child appear to be in good health?	☐	☐
8. Has the child missed much schooling?	☐	☐
9. Does the child have any observable physical handicaps?	☐	☐
10. Have the parents shown continuing interest in the progress of their child?	☐	☐
11. Has the child received a low score on an IQ test?	☐	☐

Questions for Parents

	Yes	No
1. Does the child have any disabilities or chronic illnesses?	☐	☐
2. Does the family feel that the child could meet the standards of first grade?	☐	☐
3. Would grade retention affect the status of the child among siblings?	☐	☐
4. Does the family see the child as a slow developer?	☐	☐
5. Would the child feel very upset if separated from classmates?	☐	☐
6. Would the family accept grade retention or special placement for the child?	☐	☐

7. *Estimate of physical readiness:*
   Has the child acquired most of the following skills? ☐ ☐

- Using toilet without help
- Washing hands and face without help
- Dressing without help
- Running, walking, and skipping without awkwardness
- Playing simple table games
- Holding a pencil correctly
- Using simple tools
- Building structures with blocks
- Drawing recognizable pictures

8. *Estimate of intellectual readiness:*
   Does the child possess most of the following skills? ☐ ☐

- Concentrates fairly well
- Understands the value of money
- Prints some letters
- Remembers instructions fairly well
- Is interested in picture books
- Can count to 10
- Makes self understood
- Recognizes own first name in print
- Listens attentively to stories
- Recognizes colors by name
- Sings words to some songs
- Acts out some stories
- Tells simple stories
- Has an imagination
- Remembers details of stories
- Finishes what he or she starts

9. *Estimate of social and emotional readiness:*
   Does the child demonstrate most of the following skills? ☐ ☐

- Can be trusted to play with others in the neighborhood
- Goes to school alone
- Completes simple chores
- Takes responsibility for belongings
- Amuses self if necessary
- Shares and takes turns
- Listens and responds to instructions
- Responds well to discipline

Figure 11.3.

Questions for Teachers

1. yes
2. yes
3. no
4. yes
5. no
6. no
7. no
8. yes
9. yes
10. yes
11. yes

Questions for Parents

1. yes
2. no
3. no
4. yes
5. no
6. yes
7. no
8. no
9. no

Special education services. A small number of children are severely slow learners who will need special education services. The Academic Readiness Profile may help in the preliminary identification of such students. A proper diagnosis requires the administration of intelligence tests, the acquisition of developmental histories, medical examinations, and, above all, the proper education of the parents regarding the needs of these children.

I have found that many children suspected of having mental retardation benefit from spending two years in kindergarten. This is more desirable than placing them in a class for the mentally retarded after the first year of kindergarten. Most parents of young children are unready to admit they have a child who is mentally retarded. Further observation of the child and conferences with educators can, over a period of time, help parents understand the problem more clearly. Also, intelligence tests are not as reliable for younger children as for older children. Personality variables and differences in rates of maturation make some kindergarten students appear retarded when they are not. It is a grave mistake to place these children in special classes, where they speedily take on the characteristics of retarded peers and later may not be considered for regular class placement. Removing a child from regular classes is a serious matter that affects relationships with family members and peer groups and has a negative influence on the child's self-concept.

Mordock (1979) suggested that much of the behavioral disturbance and immaturity displayed by children with disabilities is a function of their inability to move successfully through the early stages of development rather than a consequence of parental mismanagement. Mordock suggested that intervention programs that ignore these early developmental stages may actually interfere with, rather than enhance, personality development. Mordock also suggested that many program modifications can be understood only in relation to the meaning of attachment and of the separation and individualization processes.

Kazdin (1979) stressed the use of operant techniques with mentally retarded students who also have learning disabilities. The training focus varies with the severity of retardation or other disability, the age of the child, and the academic setting. For very slow-learning children, the emphasis has been on developing fundamental skills, such as independently eating, grooming, dressing, and using the toilet. Bizarre self-stimulation (e.g., rocking, ritualistic hand-arm gestures, head banging, and some forms of aggression) can be eliminated through the use of operant conditioning procedures.

Behavior modification techniques appear to be especially useful for individuals who are retarded or disabled. For academically disabled children, focus on skills to improve performance in traditional subject areas. For moderately retarded youngsters, focus on everyday skills, such as counting change when making purchases, using the telephone, using public transportation, obeying traffic signals, and so on.

The treatment of a poorly trained child must involve parents and older siblings. In family group therapy, member interactions can be observed and analyzed. Individual counseling sessions with immature children have generally proved ineffective because the child exploits the therapist's need to maintain a child-counselor rapport. Under the conditions of this unspoken blackmail, instead of learning to handle frustration in the counseling environment, the child is encouraged to avoid it.

To some extent, family group sessions can be endangered when the child observes the therapist giving the parents advice that is designed to frustrate the child's dependency needs. When this happens, the child withdraws his or her trust from the counselor. To avoid the loss of this therapeutic alliance, the therapist simply tries to teach the parents (in interviews where the child is not present) techniques they can use in the home to help the child become more independent.

TECHNIQUES FOR PARENTS

Encouraging Learning at Home

Many slow-learning children come from families and communities where education is not highly valued or fostered. The importance of a good learning climate was emphasized by Coleman (1979) in a study of lower- and middle-class achieving students. The following questions for parents are designed to suggest ways to foster a good learning atmosphere in the home.

1. Do you encourage your child to develop hobbies?
2. Do you praise your child in front of friends and relatives for his or her accomplishments?
3. Do you keep track of your child and know what he or she is doing outside of school?
4. Do you refrain from criticizing your child about schoolwork in front of other people?
5. Do you encourage your child to make high grades in school?
6. Do you praise your child when he or she makes good grades?
7. Do you refrain from pushing your child to make even higher marks when he or she comes home with a good grade?
8. Do you have interesting books, magazines, and newspapers around the house for your child to read?
9. Do you encourage and listen to your child when he or she talks about school?
10. Do you encourage your child to keep scrapbooks about trips?
11. Do you encourage (not push) your child to get a good education?
12. Do you encourage (not push) your child to think about getting a good job when he or she grows up?
13. Do you encourage family discussions?
14. Do you accept your child's views even if they do not agree with your own?
15. Do you try to help your child when he or she is not doing well in school?

Coleman (1979) found that families who demonstrate supportive concern, place a high value on education, emphasize intellectual accomplishment and verbal exchange, and provide supplemental materials at home tend to have children who succeed in school.

Helping a Teacher-Mistreated Child

If a parent believes that his or her child has been abused by school personnel and is showing stress symptoms (see teacher-inflicted stress in the diagnosis section of this chapter), that parent should be encouraged to take the following steps:

1. Consult with other parents who have children in the same classroom.
2. Ask permission from school authorities to sit in the child's classroom for several sessions.
3. With the principal in attendance, arrange an interview with the teacher.
4. If problems remain unresolved, talk to the school superintendent.
5. If the child remains disturbed about classroom conditions, insist the child be placed with another instructor.

Tutoring by Parents

Some parents, quite rightfully, wish to tutor their child. They may believe the youngster is lagging behind classmates, or they may want to help a child who is already succeeding in school to do even better. Parental tutoring may or may not be a good idea. Unfortunately, educators may find it difficult to convince parents to refrain from attempting home instruction, even when it apparently is not a good choice. Should a parent try to instruct his or her own child at home? This important question is not easy to answer.

A parent-child tutoring mismatch can, and usually does, have unfortunate consequences. Parents come to dread the nightly teaching sessions, and the child resents the restrictions placed on him or her. The situation worsens if both the parent and the child feel they are not profiting from home instruction. Some parents do find that they can work with their children in relaxed, pleasant ways. Under these conditions, parental assistance is valuable.

Parents who are thinking about tutoring their own child should consider the following questions:

Are you sure your child needs to be tutored? Can your child really benefit from extra assistance? Generally, parents want to tutor either to help an underachieving child or to help a child who is already doing well do even better in school. Your child may actually be achieving as much as can be expected. If the child is working at expected levels, he or she will feel pushed if asked to do more. The extra pressure will make the child resist parental efforts. If you have questions about your child's abilities, check with the classroom teacher. If you find that your child is doing well enough in class, be cautious about giving extra homework. Your child may be satisfied with his or her progress and your efforts may signal to the child that you are not satisfied. (Even though you protest that you are pleased, the child will be more swayed by your actions than by your words.) When you do help, keep the sessions as lighthearted as you can.

Is your child 12 years of age or under? Older children usually do not take well to tutoring from parents. The early and middle years of adolescence are traditionally marked by rebellion against authority, and the parent who thinks pressure will make the child cooperate will nearly always be disappointed. If an older child needs tutoring assistance, get someone else to do it.

In general, do you and your child like to do things together? If you and your child get along reasonably well in most situations, you are likely to have a constructive relationship in tutoring activities. If your child tends to be rebellious or resistant, do not expect him or her to become a willing participant in a venture that is largely shaped by you.

Are you generally relaxed when you teach your child? If you answer no to this question, ask yourself whether your youngster feels comfortable with you in the tutoring situation. If both you and your child are tense, nervous, or uneasy, little constructive learning will take place. An outsider can often give the child more reassurance than you can, because that individual tends to be less anxious about your child's school difficulties.

. If your child is very dependent, don't try to tutor him or her. A dependent child places parents in a bind. If they try to help, the child relies on their help even more; if they can't assist, the child doesn't produce. Again, it is easier for an outside, less-involved person to work with the child.

Do you and your spouse agree on how to help your child academically? Basic disagreements between parents about how a child should be taught probably reflect different learned lifestyles. For example, one parent may believe in an easygoing approach, letting the child find his or her own way, while the other is convinced the child should be told what to do. Because lifestyles are rooted in long-standing mind-sets, conflicts about learning approaches are not easily resolved. Find someone both parents trust and let that person assist the child.

Do you know specific teaching techniques? This is an important question. Many parents do not know about techniques, methods, and materials they can use in child instruction, nor do they have proper teaching materials at their fingertips. This material is often available, but it must be sought and the directions learned by the parents. Educational bookstores are excellent places to start gathering information. The personnel in these stores will be glad to help you. School personnel are eager to serve, too.

Have you talked to the teacher about your child's need for special help? Parental visits to the school are a must, for the following reasons:

- to find out whether, in the opinion of the teacher and educational consultants, your child really needs tutoring;
- to discover, if your child does need extra help, the specific areas of concern;
- to plan, with the aid of the school, how best to assist your child. This involves learning how and when to use teaching materials effectively, which requires further close contact with the school.

Would tutoring this child in any way harm his or her relationship with brothers and sisters? A child's status in the family is of great concern to him or her. Parental tutoring may, in the child's eyes, threaten the delicate equilibrium established with siblings. It can mean to the child that he or she is somehow deficient, and there is the possibility the youngster will lose face in the family. To protect against this reaction, take the following steps:

- Talk over the proposed tutoring with your child in a factual but sympathetic manner. The child must be reassured that school difficulties in no way detract from the affection other family members feel for him or her.
- Include siblings in the tutoring. They can receive a less specific and concentrated learning program. Including brothers and sisters will assure the tutored child that he or she is not different in ways that could lower self-esteem.
- Keep the tutoring low-key. Other members of the family should not see the parent-child interaction as a power struggle characterized by confrontation and emotional upset.

Do you have a suitable place at home where you can tutor your child, and do you have the time for this assistance? Even with the best intentions, tutoring is not likely to succeed without proper facilities or when it takes too much time away from other home activities. A quiet place is needed where you can give your child undivided attention. The time chosen for tutoring is important. Tutoring should not take place late in the day when the child is likely to be tired and distracted, nor should it occur when the child is preoccupied with other things (like getting ready to go to school, playing with friends, etc.).

Does your child have a severe reading problem or a diagnosed disability? If your child has a severe reading problem, do not try to teach him or her to read. Severe reading difficulties do not respond to usual teaching methods. The child's difficulties need to be diagnosed properly and remedial action needs to be instituted by trained individuals. If you try to instruct the child, you will probably become frustrated and the child will become upset. If your child has been designated a slow learner by the school, do not try to instruct him or her unless school authorities ask you to do so—which is not likely, since school systems have qualified personnel and facilities set aside for this purpose. You can, however, join your child in everyday activities that help him or her acquire practical skills (shopping at the market, helping around the house with chores, sharing kitchen duties, playing games to increase motor dexterity, etc.).

If your child has a diagnosed disability (speech problem, organic brain dysfunction, hearing or sight loss), do not try to tutor him or her unless you have been specifically trained to do so. Ordinarily, educational specialists can do a better job of educating the youngster than you can.

CHAPTER 12

Poor Attention

Attention deficit, as a disability, can best be described as showing the incapacity to bring stimuli into mental consciousness and retaining it for an appropriate period of time. Children demonstrating the problem

- seldom finish one task before jumping to something else;
- have a short attention span;
- become easily distracted;
- do not increase their attention span when given rewards or punishment;
- show erratic and flighty behavior.

Teachers view attention deficit as the most common and perhaps most annoying trait shown by children of all ages (Burks, 1977a, 1977b, 2006a). The prevalence of this behavior may be explained by the fact that any stimulus, internal or external, can intrude upon consciousness and detract from concentration.

Inattention can be more or less serious, depending on the presence of other behavior problem symptoms. By itself, the attribute of poor attention is not necessarily a serious manifestation. The problem is of increasing concern, however, when it occurs in conjunction with many indications of impulsivity, poor coordination, hyperactivity, and learning difficulties. It is even more grave if the child also shows many signs of aggression, poor social conformity, rebellion, and poor anger management. If a child shows many of these latter signs, the prognosis for improvement is poor; most teachers do not seem to be able to help this type of acting-out youngster.

Attention deficits are commonly seen in young, immature students and are often allied with poor academic achievement. It is typically shown by those with a neurological handicap (see chapter 22, with its discourse on attention deficit disorder). Although some older aggressive and hostile students are seen by teachers as demonstrating poor attention, most of these students are organically sound. They simply refuse to pay attention even though able to do so.

Inattention is often shown by children who are schizophrenic. If a child demonstrates many symptoms of poor reality contact along with attention deficits, a diagnosis of psychosis can be made with more surety.

THEORETICAL BACKGROUND

Do attention deficits exist apart from hyperactive disorders or other pathologies such as mental retardation and schizophrenia? Lahey, Green, and Forehand (1980) believe it does. In an investigation, these authors compared teacher ratings with (a) observations of time on task, (b) frequency of teacher interaction, (c) positive and negative peer interactions, (d) peer ratings of acceptance, rejection, and dislike, and (e) three measures of academic performance. They found that a factor resembling attention deficit disorder without hyperactivity was found to account for a substantial portion of independent variance in the multiple regression analyses. This separate rating factor was described by the authors as inattentive-passive.

Maurer and Stewart (1980) also reported on the presence of attention deficits in the absence of hyperactivity. In a study of 297 children (ages 7 to 14 years), they found 51 children with poor concentration; of these 51, however, 40 had psychiatric disorders (most demonstrating socialized conduct disorders and aggression). The participants with no psychiatric disorders tended either to have learning disabilities or to be unmotivated. Of course, most students with attention deficits but no outstanding behavioral problems are not likely to be referred to mental health clinics. It may be assumed that a substantial number of such students exist in the school population (Burks, 2001).

Undesirable conditions commonly associated with exhibited classroom attention deficits include

- an immature or unstable nervous system;
- an emotional disability;
- a conduct or psychotic disorder;
- an unstimulating environment;
- a distracting environment.

Unready or Unstable Nervous System

Immaturity. Many young, immature students demonstrate attention deficits along with poor school achievement. These youngsters seem to be unable to control their distractibility. This is less true of older aggressive and hostile students, who are often able to regulate impulsivity but choose not to.

Physical health. Physical illness can affect a child's ability to concentrate. Obviously, a student who does not feel well cannot attend properly to classroom exercises. More subtle organic disorders can also affect concentration. For example, M. Irwin, Belendiuk, McClosky, and Freedman (1981) investigated tryptophan metabolism in children with attention deficits and found that plasma total and protein-bound tryptophan levels were significantly lower in these children than in children with adequate attention abilities.

Mental retardation. In an extensive study by Finkelstein, Gallagher, and Farran (1980), it was discovered that attention was a key factor in identifying children with mental retardation and in understanding their developmental needs. High-risk participants had a lower attention span for complex or demanding auditory and visual stimuli (identifiable as early as 3 years of age). Investigators found few differences within the high-risk group between those who attended an intervention day-care program and those who did not.

Krupski (1979) also investigated distractibility in children with and without retardation. She discovered that attention-related behavior tends to be task-oriented. During academic periods, children with retardation were less attentive than those without retardation. In addition, the children with retardation spent less time on task, more time out of their seats, and more time looking busy but not working. In nonacademic tasks, the differences were not pronounced.

Porges and Humphrey (1977) found that children without mental retardation suppressed respiratory and heart-rate variability during attention-demanding tasks, while children with retardation exhibited increases in respiratory and heart-rate variability (which paralleled their poor performance on the tasks). These qualitative differences in physiological and behavioral responses, observed during sustained attention, may be viewed as a manifestation of a defective nervous system in children with mental retardation.

Finally, however, Landesman and Ramey (1989) challenged the existence of any permanent personality characteristic through longitudinal and ethnographic research. They found that, while an individual may, for example, show attention deficits in early years, the symptoms may not be apparent in later life.

Learning disabilities. Do students with learning disabilities show evidence of neurological dysfunction or developmental immaturity? Investigative efforts have been made to establish the connection between organ dysfunction and poor learning. Pelham (1981) discussed attention deficits within the framework of three aspects: (a) the ability to maintain alertness or sustained attention, (b) the power to select, and (c) the competency to sustain processing capacity. According to Pelham, children with learning disabilities, as opposed to normal children, appear to have deficits in their capacity to pay attention (poor vigilance) that interfere with performance on cognitive tasks. Hyperactive children, in addition to being unable to sustain attention, had a constitutional inability to respond in situations that required focused, directed, and organized effort.

Anderson, Halcomb, and Doyle (1973) found a strong relationship between attention deficits and learning disabilities. Using a system of visual signals (patterns of flashing lights), they found that students with learning disabilities were less able to concentrate upon and differentiate evoked signals than were normal students.

Samuels and Turnure (1974) reported the relationship of attentiveness to reading achievement in first, fourth, and sixth grade children. Girls were found to be significantly more attentive than boys and achieved higher word recognition scores. Further, word recognition was found to be significantly related to attentiveness for the group as a whole.

Some poor readers demonstrated attention difficulties that may have accounted for their generally low performance on verbal tasks (Hebben, 1981). Further, this attention deficit was associated with the degree of semantic or syntactic difficulty of the prose material the children were reading.

Attention deficit disorder (with and without hyperactivity). Although attention difficulties are one of the hallmark characteristics (Burks, 1960) of youngsters with attention deficit disorder (ADD), I discuss the diagnosis and treatment of children with ADD in a separate chapter (see chapter 22). Concentration problems are tied to a complex web of other symptoms and the ADD child often commands more attention from parents and teachers (because he or she is more disruptive) than do youngsters with other types of disorders.

Affective disability. The effects of anxiety on the ability to pay attention and the capacity to achieve are well known (Wolman & Stricker, 1994). Deffenbacher (1978) investigated the sources of interference in highly test-anxious individuals performing under test stress. Compared to a high-anxiety/low-stress group or a low-anxiety/high-stress group, those in a high-anxiety/high-stress group

- reported more anxiety during testing;
- rated themselves, their abilities, and the task more negatively;
- solved fewer test tasks;
- estimated spending less time on tasks;
- experienced more interference from anxiety;
- reported a relationship of distraction to heightened autonomic arousal (emotionality), worrisome thoughts, and task-produced competing responses (task-generated interference).

According to this study, highly anxious children achieve better if task stress is kept to a minimum.

Doyal and Forsyth (1972) reported that boys and girls showed opposite performance patterns in response to increased anxiety. Girls with low anxiety outperformed very anxious girls, while extremely anxious boys did better than relaxed boys.

Conduct disorder behavior. The etiology and treatment of conduct-disordered children are topics discussed extensively in the following chapters of this book, which are devoted to the aggressive dysfunctions: poor anger control (chapter 17), rebelliousness (chapter 20), and poor social conformity (chapter 21). Treatment methods using behavioral conditioning tactics have proved effective for changing patterns of inattentive conduct in these children (Ross, 1981).

Unstimulating environment. Kagan and Moss (1962) touched on the importance of attention involvement in the learning process. They pointed out that human beings are pleasure seekers and that a change in stimulation is a source of pleasure. They believe that when learners can predict perfectly what will happen, they form a schema. This schema then fails to hold the learner's attention as well as it first did because it can be predicted. Kagan and Moss believe that some discrepancy should exist—in short, variety is the spice of life.

Young children, in particular, need a great deal of stimulation from varied sources. The young brain is maturing very rapidly and needs an enormous input of sensory stimuli. Learning acquired during this period forms an essential undergirding for future acquisition of percepts and concepts. What passes for distractibility or misconduct may simply be behavioral manifestations of boredom. Research by Williams (1973) found that many apparently normal individuals required much self-stimulation (nail biting, nonnutritive sucking, thumb twiddling, various forms of self-scratching, and general restlessness) while solving thought problems.

Distracting environment. Commercial advertisers have discovered that viewers report better recognition and recall in an environment with limited exposure to stimuli (Barnard, Loomis, & Cross, 1980). Webb (1979) found that an individual's attention to and comprehension of a television commercial was affected by the structure of the environment (amount of clutter). High clutter tended to negate the value of the message. Finally, television clutter consisting of commercial breaks, promotional messages, and public service announcements negatively affected the viewers' attention, recall, and cognitive responses (Webb & Ray, 1979).

The results of these discoveries by commercial advertisers have direct implications for distraction in the classroom environment. Students should not be exposed to too many stimuli at one time. In any setting, they need an opportunity to absorb the meaning of a few objects or concepts. The physical environment of the classroom should be studied to ensure that background stimuli (lighted windows, pictures, student movement) do not interfere with classroom presentations. Also, ongoing activities in the classroom should be evaluated periodically to determine whether they are annoying; if so, unnecessary tasks should be postponed or modified whenever possible.

INTERVENTION STRATEGIES

Techniques for School Personnel

Physical health problems. Obviously, any student demonstrating symptoms such as irritability, apathy, restlessness, and outbursts of crying or rage, may require medical study. A preliminary examination by the school nurse may lead to a request that the parents take the youngster to a physician for a thorough study. The school can cooperate with the home by modifying the curriculum for any chronically ill child.

Children in poor health may be undernourished (Lozoff, 1989). Protein deficiency seems to limit human potential. While most poor nutrition occurs in underdeveloped countries, a substantial number of disadvantaged children in the United States are also affected. According to Lozoff, the long-term effects of protein deficiency include deficits in cognitive and behavioral functions. In one study, children who were undernourished in infancy showed a fourfold increase in symptoms of attention deficit disorder—that is, impaired attention, poor school performance, poor memory, and easy distractibility. Most of these symptoms, along with high school dropout rates, persisted into the late teens. School personnel should investigate the eating habits of any student showing these erratic behaviors. In conjunction with a cooperating principal, I once conducted an experiment in a lower economic school district to see if the acting-out conduct of fourth grade boys would improve if they were provided a school breakfast (it had been determined that they were not provided an adequate breakfast at home). All were reported by teachers to be quieter and better controlled in classrooms after receiving this extra nutrition.

Mental retardation. The following strategies may be useful when dealing with children showing slow mental abilities:

1. Decide whether the child would be better off in special classes or integrated into the mainstream educational setting. Studies investigating student placement issues found that segregated education appears to yield better scores on self-concept measures, while integrated programs tend to yield higher academic achievement scores. Variables within the setting (e.g., teacher attitudes, classroom climate) far outweigh administrative arrangements in importance (Haywood, Meyers, & Switzky, 1982).

2. Determine a proper curriculum by assessing the child's mental and physical capabilities and surroundings (where he or she lives and works, what support systems are available, and what skills may be needed for future employment).

3. Investigate the attitudes of peers toward the retarded student. Too often, the teacher's assessment of a child's conduct does not reflect the perceptions held by age-mates. These perceptions should be taken into consideration when proper placement considerations are being made (Mainville & Friedman, 1976). For instance, if a youngster is not accepted by peers, he or she should probably be moved to another classroom.

4. Use behavioral approaches that include (a) programming the course of studies to meet the retarded individual's problems (e.g., if necessary, teach survivor skills rather than formal subjects), (b) eliminating inappropriate behavior (like wandering around restlessly) that competes with classroom learning, and (c) using direct training strategies to enhance attention, memory, and problem solving (Mash & Barkley, 1989).

Learning disabilities. The attention difficulties of students with learning disabilities may call for the following techniques:

1. One-to-one instruction and alternative curricula (DeLoach, 1981).

2. Self-monitoring approaches that record on-task and off-task behavior (for instance, let the child record times when he or she is working and not working). These result in consistent increases in on-task behavior and some improvement in academic performance (Kneedler & Hallahan, 1981). Reinforcement is not needed to maintain performance and the child need not be accurate in recording on-task conduct. The self-recording procedure appears to be most effective with students whose primary problem is attention deficit. Hallahan, Marshall, and Lloyd (1981) found self-monitoring to be an effective device for students involved in small-group oral reading exercises.

3. Direct behavior instruction to help students acquire attending behavior. The teacher must show the student the exact attending conduct desired (Argulewicz, Elliot, & Spencer, 1982).

4. Specific self-instruction methods. Teach the child how to teach himself or herself new curriculum material or how to review previously learned lessons.

Affective disability. Use the following techniques to reduce anxiety in a child with an emotional disability:

1. Attention training procedures. Ribordy, Tracy, and Bernotas (1981) employed rewards for successful inhibition of irrelevant responses and correct attending behaviors on tasks. They found that highly test-anxious children performed as well as those with low test anxiety when this technique was employed. The method worked better for younger students than for older students.

2. Creative avenues of expression. For example, playing certain types of guidance games requiring imagination can assist the ventilation of hidden and repressed feelings in anxious children (Burks, 1994, 2001; Musick, 1980).

3. Psychodrama. Irwin (1977) reported the benefits of psychodrama for disturbed, anxious children, including progression from passivity to activity, separation of fantasy and reality, fusion with an idealized or hated parent, and mastery of conflict.

4. Psychological techniques tied to behavior modification procedures (Mash & Barkley, 1989), such as

   • teaching how to control feared situations (for instance, a child is rewarded for not showing fear to a dog—an object formerly dreaded);

   • reducing the intensity of one of the conflicting motivations (e.g., the child wants to do well on a test but is put under no stress to perform);

   • using negative practice—that is, deliberately practicing the undesirable behavior;

   • employing symbolic stimuli (such as using hand puppets to reinstate an original trauma and then learning a more acceptable response).

Conduct disorder or psychotic behavior. Children with severe thought disturbances are generally not placed in regular school classrooms. If, however, a teacher must accommodate a distractible youngster showing symptoms of bizarre behavior, unusual daydreaming, or emotional withdrawal, some of the following strategies may prove useful (Blanco, 1972):

1. Give the child small, specific assignments.
2. Set a time limit for the completion of these work units.
3. When one assignment is finished, immediately give the next assignment.
4. Explain changes in daily routine to the child well ahead of time, and make sure the child thoroughly understands the nature of the proposed changes and how he or she is expected to act.
5. If a full schedule appears to be too heavy a burden, allow the child to attend school for only part of the day. The student might initially attend classes that are particularly enjoyable. As the child develops motivational strength (Phillips, 2001), he or she can be urged to participate in other classes.
6. Place the youngster in a special, small instructional class of near-age emotionally disturbed children.
7. Advise the parents to make a residential placement if the child's behavior is too bizarre.

Unstimulating environment. Classroom boredom may be relieved by employing some of the following procedures:

1. Pay close personal attention to some distractible students. Russell and Low (1977) analyzed a teacher's responses to the appropriate and inappropriate behavior of students who exhibited unacceptable conduct. If the instructor paid attention to poor behavior, the students' conduct worsened. If, on the other hand, attention was paid to appropriate behavior, the conduct became better. (No evidence was found, however, to indicate that teacher attention can maintain high rates of appropriate behavior.)
2. Employ meditative-relaxation procedures. Redfering and Bowman (1981) found that relaxation techniques used 20 minutes a day for five days were effective in reducing nonattending behavior among disturbed students. They reported a significant improvement for treated children over untreated children.
3. Institute extra rest periods and additional nutrition breaks for distracted students who appear to tire easily (Burks, 1968e).
4. Avoid long drill periods. Make drills short, frequent, and highly motivating. Drill sessions will be more interesting if visual aids are employed, if the material is at the child's level of competence, and if the work is entertaining (e.g., if the assignment is a game).
5. Give the child an opportunity to release tension between work periods—to stretch, walk around, go to the restroom, talk to another student, and so on. I found, however, that vigorous playground games tended to overstimulate children who have a short attention span; they could not calm down as fast as nondistractible students (Burks, 1968e).
6. Allow the student to become involved in activities that absorb his or her interest.

Distracting environment. Blanco (1972) outlined some classroom techniques that can be used to help inattentive children:

1. Give clear and explicit directions.
2. Employ highly structured materials and routines.
3. Break up routine assignments into clearly understood components.
4. Assign small units of work that are within the child's ability.
5. Cut down visual and auditory stimuli, for example:

- Provide an isolation booth, and call it an office. Make it attractive. Do not use it as a punishment device.
- Cut a narrow, horizontal opening in a piece of cardboard and have the child use it as a window to view academic materials.
- Allow the child to work in areas of the room where distractions are limited. Do not seat the student near windows with attractive views, near doors that are frequently opened, near bulletin boards frequently visited by other children, or near any areas where students tend to congregate for work or relaxation.
- Permit the student, as a privilege, to isolate himself or herself in another part of the school to complete a specific assignment.
- Place the child's desk directly in front of the teacher's desk.
- Allow the student to take tests in another part of the school (e.g., the nurse's office or the library) if the student complains of being distracted by other children.

Suggestions for Parents

Many parents complain about the inattentive behavior of their children but do not realize that they themselves demonstrate poor patterns of concentration. It may be helpful to point out to these parents that children observe family practices and copy their parents' habits and mannerisms. Use the following questions to highlight parental conduct that can lead to distractible behavior:

1. Do you tune out others as they are talking to you? If parents do not listen to their children, the children will not listen to them. Further, the children may give up trying to communicate with them.
2. Do you interrupt others? Refraining from interrupting others is just good manners. Children often have trouble saying what they want to say and parents may become impatient with a child's fumbling speech. Parents break in on their thoughts or supply missing words too quickly. The child feels rushed and reacts in a distracted way. Give the youngster time to express himself or herself.
3. Do you often change the subject when talking with others? The hallmark of good concentration is to follow through on tasks. If children observe parents not allowing others the opportunity to bring a conversation to a satisfactory conclusion, they will assume it is OK for them to switch topics.
4. Do you interrupt projects and activities you are working on so much it becomes difficult to get them finished? Some parents complain that their youngsters do not finish assignments. They do not realize that they themselves tend not to complete projects or activities. Perhaps they intend to finish these tasks at some future time, but children do not construe time the same way adults do—to them, a delay can seem endless and they lose faith anything will be done.
5. Do you find it difficult to concentrate on anything? Often parents are unaware of some of the traits they demonstrate. If their attention wanders, their children will assume it is all right for them to be dreamy or distractible.
6. Do you lose interest in things quickly? If parents lose interest in activities and show they are easily bored, their children will tend to show similar attributes.
7. Do you encourage family members to finish projects? Do you respond happily when projects are concluded? Everyone needs to feel it is worthwhile to finish an assignment. The child expects, and should receive, signals of satisfaction from adults when he or she completes a project.
8. Do you promise to do things and then not do them? Children see unfulfilled promises as acts that discourage trying. After all, how do adults react if someone does not follow through on a pledge to them? Ordinarily, they give up trying to work with that person.
9. Are you absentminded? Do you tend to lose track of what you are doing? Absentminded parents may train their children to be dreamers. Many adults do not see themselves as inattentive, simply because they are concentrating on other things. Those around them, however, see the adults as being tuned out.

10. Do you neglect to set up good study conditions for your child? A youngster trying to do homework can be distracted by many household activities. Parents should try the following techniques:

- Provide the child with a study desk facing a blank wall.
- Restrict the hours the child spends watching television and listening to the radio, particularly during study time.
- Encourage the youngster to concentrate on one subject at a time.
- Deny privileges when work is not done.
- Offer rewards for completed assignments.

CHAPTER 13

Poor Impulse Control

Impulsivity, as a symptom, is best described as the inability to delay responses in an appropriate manner. Children with high scores on the poor impulse control category of the Burks Behavior Rating Scales (Burks, 1977a, 2006a) tend to

- be unable to control their actions;
- act without thought;
- be unpredictable;
- get overexcited easily;
- be hyperactive and restless.

According to teacher ratings, impulsivity is an independent trait that is not necessarily associated with aggressive tendencies, poor anger control, and poor social conformity scales (Burks, 1977a, 2006a). Analysis of student protocols revealed, however, that children with the following problems also tend to demonstrate impulsive conduct:

Severe anxiety. For children expressing severe anxiety, internal conflicts demand so much attention that to outside observers these children appear distracted and overactive. Traits of impulsivity, however, tend to disappear when worries vanish.

Antisocial inclinations. Teachers view these children as aggressive and often delinquent. Many such children fight authority figures, show little desire to please others (except like-minded peers), and are difficult to control. Even though able to, they will not exercise self-control.

Poor contact with reality. In addition to having impulsivity, children with this problem (some of whom may be labeled schizophrenic) have a wide variety of other negative traits.

Attention deficit disorder (ADD). Impulsivity is one of the cardinal symptoms demonstrated by children with ADD pathology (Burks, 1968b, 1968c, 1968d, 2006b). In addition to impulsivity, these disorganized children tend to show signs of poor school progress and sometimes aggressive behavior.

THEORETICAL BACKGROUND

As Doob (1990) points out, nearly all human behavior of any interest involves a delay between a stimulus and a resulting response. That delay, however, is neither shown constantly across individuals exposed to the same stimulus nor interpreted similarly by observers.

The reason for the delay between stimulus and response is not as important as the fact that it exists, because without it individuals could not consider and answer the following critical questions (see Doob, 1990):

1. What will I do? (An inquiry into personal motives)
2. What can I do? (A survey of potentials)

3. What must I do? (An analysis of rules and duty)
4. What might be the consequences? (A judgment of possible outcomes)
5. What ought I to do? (An examination of internal imperatives)
6. What shall I do? (A contemplation of possible actions to take)
7. What did I do? (A review of past history)

These questions reveal the complex interplay of causal factors that result in a particular delay between stimulus and response. Clearly, the seemingly simple notion of hesitation is not so uncomplicated after all. Like the factor of attention span, impulsivity is multidimensional (Mash & Barkley, 1989), and it is not clear which aspects of impulsivity (temperament, organic, learned behavior, or environmental factors) are at fault. Some researchers, however, have found impulsivity to be associated with other personality traits.

S. B. Eysenck and Eysenck (1977) isolated an impulse factor on the Eysenck Personality Inventory (H. J. Eysenck & Eysenck, 1969). This general factor was subdivided into four traits:

1. a "narrow" impulse factor (positively correlated with neurotic and psychotic tendencies);
2. a risk-taking factor (thought by some to be correlated with tendencies toward delinquency);
3. a no-planning factor (perhaps involved in poor learning capacity);
4. a "liveliness" or sociability factor.

All these subfactors correlated positively with the extraversion factor on the inventory. B. D. Smith, Rypma, and Wilson (1981) corroborated the finding that extraversion and impulsivity are related, and Gudjonsson (1980) discovered evidence that impulsivity, extraversion, and sociability are all interrelated (at least for males). These findings have implications for how children learn and how they control their behavior.

Impulse Control and Learning

The following themes are found repeatedly in the literature on impulsivity and its effect on learning:

1. Impulsivity, as compared to a more reflective personality style, is strongly linked to poorer learning ability (Adams, 1990; Epstein, Cullinan, & Sternberg, 1977; Hollander and Stein, 2005; Lesiak, 1978; Paulsen, 1978; Quay & Weld, 1980; Readence & Bean, 1978; Roberts, 1979; J. E. Shapiro, 1976; E. S. Shapiro, 1989).
2. Impulsivity is apparently more debilitating for younger than for older children—at least the achievement differences between reflective learners and impulsive learners tend to become less evident for older students (Lesiak, 1978; Quay & Weld, 1980). However, even college students who are reflective do better on tests and think of themselves as more successful than do impulsive problem solvers. Thus, the trait of impulsivity seems to encumber adult learners as well as children. In support of this notion, Loo (1979) found impulsivity to be the chief determinant separating safe drivers from unsafe (impulsive) drivers.
3. The more learning disabled a child is, the more likely he or she is to show an impulse disorder (Burks, 1965).
4. The more reflective (versus impulsive) a child is, the more likely the youngster is to show creative tendencies (Doob, 1990; Fuqua, Bartsch, & Phye, 1975).
5. Compared to reflective children, impulsive children do poorly on psychological tests. Ikegami (1979) discovered that reflective participants produced more whole responses on the Rorschach, were more able to regulate subjective and emotional responses, and showed more tendencies toward introversion. Brannigan, Barone, and Margolis (1978) established a significant relationship between errors on the Bender Gestalt Test (Bender, 1946) and impulsivity in children.

Impulse Control and Behavior Disorders

Impulsivity apparently plays a central role in many serious behavior disorders. S. B. Eysenck and Eysenck (1977) found impulsivity to be a factor in the test protocols of individuals demonstrating neurotic and psychotic tendencies. I found evidence that attention deficit hyperactive children tend also to be impulsive (Burks, 1977a, 2006a). Curtiss, Feczko, and Marohn (1979) established that delinquent adolescents differ from normal adolescents along the dimension of impulsivity, a finding relevant to psychodynamic theories of delinquency as it relates to serious ego deficits (inabilities to maintain motivations and effort).

Educators, however, should not assume that all children exhibiting impulse problems will turn out to be antisocial or mentally ill. The prognosis for this type of youngster depends very much on support systems in the family, the school, and the community. Frosch (1977) warned educators to distinguish between acting-out behavior disorders and impulse dysfunctions, even though both may encompass impulsivity. Delinquent children can differ from non-acting-out impulsive children by demonstrating stronger extraversion tendencies, more nervousness, aggressiveness, depression, excitability, openness, and emotional instability (Hormuth, 1977). People exhibiting these traits have a poorer prognosis than those without such symptoms (Getsinger & Leon, 1979). Diagnosticians should evaluate the child's ability to plan his or her actions. Impulsive delinquent individuals, compared to those who plan crimes, show a greater incidence of violent and nonviolent offenses (Erez, 1980).

Impulsivity, even when not allied with more dangerous signals of personality disorder, generally should cause teachers to be on the alert. It can affect learning adversely and can disrupt social-emotional relationships.

INTERVENTION STRATEGIES

Most researchers rely on behavior modification techniques to reduce impulsivity and increase learning capacity. For example:

1. Serbin, Geller, and Geller (1977) investigated the effects of social reinforcement (attention feedback) on disadvantaged preschoolers. They were able to reinforce attending behavior for auditory recall, but the same improvement was not noted for visual recall.
2. Brent and Routh (1978) investigated the effects of token reinforcement on response latency (time spent on reflectivity before giving a response) and the number of errors produced. Thirty children in the fourth grade were given word recognition lists under one of three experimental conditions: control, positive reinforcement (1 nickel for each word read correctly), and response cost (1 of 40 nickels taken back for each word read incorrectly). Relative to the control condition, positive reinforcement led to a significant increase in response latency but no change in errors, while response cost led to both a significant increase in latency and a significant decrease in errors. The decrease in errors supports the hypothesis that impulsive children evidence low concern about errors on academic tasks. It would be logical to suppose that raising the children's level of concern would make them less mistake-prone.
3. The effects of cognitive behavioral treatment strategies appear inconclusive. Kendall and Finch (1979) reported no significant effects for several specific verbal codes (e.g., task-related questions and thinking aloud); however, impulsive, emotionally disturbed individuals who received treatment evidenced a significant increase in total on-task verbal behavior. Eastman and Rasbury (1981) found no significant increase in on-task behaviors or academic performance after cognitive self-instruction training.
4. Margolis, Brannigan, and Penner (1978) attempted to modify the visual discrimination performances of primary grade, conceptually impulsive school children. By altering the directions and administration procedures of a visual discrimination match-to-sample test, Margolis et al. were able to slow down the impulsive conceptual tempo of students and improve visual discrimination capabilities, and demonstrate that

the visual discriminating powers of young, impulsive children can be underestimated. Lee and Cottreau (1979) were not able to replicate these kinds of results for mentally retarded adolescents, although they believe beneficial results can be achieved by making the training on conceptual tempo very task-specific.

5. Gupta and Nagpal (1978) discovered that highly impulsive individuals responded more to rewarding modes of reinforcement, while less impulsive individuals responded more to punishing modes of reinforcement.

6. Token reinforcement has proven useful (Mash & Barkley, 1989). Carter and Reynolds (1976) investigated the efficacy of poker chip reinforcers to control unwanted overactive behavior. When that did not work, they instituted a program of verbal cues followed by tokens to reinforce correct imitation of behavior. This regime produced dramatic improvement sustained for long periods.

7. Compared to normal children, behaviorally disturbed children typically ask more guessing and fewer constraint-type questions. This behavior tends to occur because many of these children, who are more anxious and impulsive, see themselves as having little control over their world (Ollendick, Finch, & Nelson, 1976). Efforts can be made to prevent them from postulating wild questions or giving wild answers.

8. Bugental, Collins, Collins, and Chaney (1978) experimented with two types of behavior management interventions to control the overactivity of impulsive boys: One focused on self-control and the other employed contingent social reinforcement. Of the two manipulations, self-control methods produced significantly stronger long-term benefits in terms of participants' increased perception of personal control over academic outcomes. Social reinforcement, on the other hand, produced significantly stronger long-term benefits in terms of hyperactivity or impulsivity.

9. Some impulsive, disturbed adolescents act out repressed emotions. These very anxious individuals may be helped by allowing them to talk out their feelings, which may seem to them to be unspeakable utterances (Hoffer, Goettsche, & Linden, 1980).

10. Behavior modification techniques may bring about short-term positive results with adolescents, but long-term benefits are more difficult to illustrate (McCombs, Filipczak, Friedman, & Wodarski, 1978).

11. Klein and Deffenbacher (1977) report beneficial results using progressive relaxation and exercise techniques with active and impulsive third grade boys. These tempo-slowing methods also reflected positively on cognitive measures.

Techniques for School Personnel

The following strategies can be used in the classroom to help impulse-ridden children.

1. Obtain the child's cooperation in efforts to get him or her to be more controlled. The child who senses that he or she is liked by the teacher responds better to firmness because the youngster wants to please the teacher. Requests for better behavior need not always be in words—some can be communicated better with actions, such as a raised-hand signal.

2. Lower expectations and achievement goals. The impulsive child tends to have a low tolerance threshold, and lowering standards may help the child become less anxious.

3. Follow through on all stated consequences for impulsive actions; otherwise, the student will disregard requests for control and attention. Each time the child feels that rules can be ignored safely, he or she is actually being trained to be disobedient.

4. Do not allow the child to play one adult against another. Those who instruct the student should get together with the parents to set up common goals and disciplinary patterns, which, at times, can be outlined to the child in the presence of teachers and parents.

5. Refuse to discuss the child's personality with the child or other students. Discussions of this nature tend to backfire—the reactions can reinforce unwanted conduct.

6. Provide an isolation booth for the child, to reduce visual and auditory distractions. Do not make time spent there feel like punishment for misbehavior.
7. Provide the child with small units of work and frequent short drill periods.
8. Let the child release physical tension with light activity.
9. Give much positive reinforcement for any small success in the child's self-control.
10. Have the child look at study materials through a narrow opening (perhaps a slit in a piece of cardboard) to reduce environmental stimuli to a minimum (but do not overuse this technique).
11. Use proximity control. Touching a child's shoulder, tapping on the desk, or softly speaking the child's name is generally more effective than lecturing, which many children have learned to ignore.
12. Limit environmental distractions.
13. Allow the child some time to concentrate on things he or she likes to do.
14. Set firm limits.
15. Present focused and structured activities, such as copying patterns on a pegboard, writing in clay with a stylus, sawing along lines, etc.
16. Discourage wild guesses.
17. The benefits of structured over unstructured classrooms were chronicled by Susman, Huston-Stein, and Friedrich-Cofer (1980). In less-structured rooms, very young impulsive students were less assertive, less likely to show understanding of others, and less likely to engage in social behavior (cooperation, helping, and sharing) than were reflective peers.
18. An experienced, reflective teacher, as compared to a more impulsive teacher, is better able to help impulsive children increase response time (Yando & Kagan, 1968). This effect was more pronounced for boys than for girls.
19. According to Margolis, Brannigan, and Poston (1977), research findings demonstrate that impulsivity can be modified in the classroom by (a) peer models who act reflectively, (b) student self-instruction and covert rehearsal of learning strategies, (c) increasing student concern about being correct, and (d) teaching students scanning strategies for visual discrimination (supplying the pupil with hints that improve the ability to spot differences).
20. Poorly controlled students who talk too much in class or talk out loud at inappropriate times can be controlled with behavior modification techniques. Bryan and Dickie (1976) described the use of a changing reinforcement criterion to control such episodes. The changing criterion allows behavior to be shaped gradually. The student who talks too much in class can be helped by the following methods (Blanco, 1972):

- Take the student aside and tell him or her privately that talking must be controlled.
- Get the child more involved in classroom activities.
- Set firm limits and consistently hold the student to those limits.
- Call the child's name to get his or her attention.
- Allow the student to relate interesting experiences to the teacher and to the class.
- Assign the child special, interesting projects that require attention and application.
- Demonstrate interest in the child's class assignments (not in his or her empty talk).
- Investigate the child's concerns. Is he or she being ignored by adults?
- Counsel the parents about home discipline procedures.

Techniques for Parents

I devised the following questions for parents to be used in parent conferences to spark interest in the impulse control problems of their children. In group conferences, the questions can be read to the audience, and the leader can discuss the implications of each question. Individual or family conferences must be tailored to the needs of participants.

Most behavior patterns, including impulsivity, can be learned by children by observing the behavior of adults. Many parents, however, are unaware that they themselves may act in hasty, impulsive ways. To help parents become aware of their behavior, encourage them to respond to the following questions and then discuss their answers in a group session or with the teacher.

Participants can answer yes, no, or perhaps. No scoring is necessary—a general impression of the answers will suffice. Encourage each parent to compare their replies with the other parent, if both are present at the meeting.

1. When you undertake projects at home, do you plan each step carefully?
2. When you ask members of your family to answer questions, do you discourage them from making wild guesses? Making wild guesses is a form of impulsivity. People who speak illogically may have trouble inhibiting impulses. Parents can help their child stop and think before giving responses.
3. Do you set firm limits on behavior? Before internal controls can be acquired, external restraints are necessary. Children need discipline; they cannot learn to inhibit impulses until someone first controls them.
4. Do you tend to get out of control when you become angry? Self-control is generally considered to be a mature response to environmental stress. The parent who shows excessive anger after a slight provocation is demonstrating poor self-discipline, and that person's children will likely also exhibit poor self-control.
5. Do you tend to think things through logically? We all tend to think logically when events are not stressful. When pressures build up, however, we operate more emotionally. Youngsters need to observe adults acting calmly and logically even under pressure.
6. Is your house arranged so that people who are studying can have peace and quiet? Some individuals have a low tolerance for distractions. An otherwise calm child can become nervous and distractible if bothered by too much noise and light.
7. Do you have a set of rules that your child understands and obeys? Parents sometimes set rules that are vague or stated so unclearly that children simply do not understand regulations. Some misbehavior may be the result of poor parent/child communication. Periodically, parents should review regulations and quiz their children to see if they understand the rules.
8. Do you tend to do things on the spur of the moment, much to the surprise of other family members? The inability to postpone gratification can have harmful effects. It may, for instance, teach children to act without thinking—a form of impulsivity.
9. Do rules and regulations tend to make you impatient? Some mothers and fathers expect their children to obey rules but subtly signify to them that rules are really "for somebody else" by demonstrating personal irritation at being constricted.
10. Do you think your parents were too strict with you and that you would like to be easier on your own children (thereby allowing them to flout rules)? Not a good idea if you want your boy or girl to act less impulsive.
11. Do you allow others to distract you easily from the task at hand? Adults who are easily distracted may teach their children to be flighty.
12. When you set a course of action, do you follow through on it? Parents who set a course of action and follow through on objectives can teach their children to be less impulsive.

CHAPTER 14

Poor Reality Contact

Poor reality contact, as a personality construct, is best described as the severely impaired capacity to correctly assess the events and requirements of everyday living and to act upon them appropriately (Burks, 2006b). Children with this disability tend to

- relate stories that are not believable;
- demonstrate poor awareness of surroundings;
- show bizarre emotional reactions;
- rotate and rock body parts;
- secretly talk to themselves;
- draw weird pictures;
- demonstrate tics and grimace;
- fantasize excessively.

Dissociated conduct is not commonly seen in children attending school. When it is observed, it may be confused with other diagnostic categories (e.g., attention disabilities or severe anxiety). Causal factors leading to poor reality contact probably are rooted in complex organic and social components not well understood at this time.

For a young child, extreme social maladjustment of this nature is serious. Very young children with poor reality contact often also demonstrate poor coordination, attention deficits, the inability to form close relationships, and aggressive tendencies.

Few older children show poor reality contact symptoms. When they do, they also tend to demonstrate poor social conformity, impulsivity, a poor ability to relate to others, emotional distress, poor anger control, and rebellion. These indications suggest the student is unwilling to conform to and cooperate with others in school and home environments. Symptoms tend to worsen as the child ages.

THEORETICAL BACKGROUND

Although clinicians agree that childhood psychosis exists, they do not concur on where to draw its limits. Some diagnosticians avoid using the term, and others see the problem in every severely disturbed youngster.

Kessler (1966) stressed that it is easier to say what childhood psychosis is not rather than what it is, because dissociated conduct in children is often confused with other diagnostic categories, such as anxiety and minimal brain dysfunction. In Kessler's judgment, the single most important diagnostic sign of childhood psychosis is a severely disturbed relationship with others. This circumstance may be evidenced by a lack of interest in or awareness of people, or by an inability to separate from another person satisfactorily (e.g., the child cannot see himself or herself as a personality distinct from his or her mother). The distorted nature of these social connections leads to or is associated with communication difficulties, an inability to imitate others, difficulties in engaging in play activities, an abnormal fascination with inanimate objects, and clinging to a reutilized, mechanical, repetitiously compulsive manner of living.

Deciding whether a child is relating well to his or her environment is difficult at any age but is particularly so for very young children. Normal 3-, 4-, and 5-year-olds in many respects live in a magical world and show responses to stress that would be considered abnormal in later years. A diagnosis of childhood psychosis must be made with great caution.

Autism. Mash and Barkley (1989) point out that autistic children are relatively rare and present an unusual constellation of severe problems. The outstanding complaint is that they cannot socialize: they show little interest in other humans and can remain immobile for long periods of time. They demonstrate no motivation to seek out play or affection or any interaction with peers, siblings, and parents. Another prime symptom is language deficiency. Many children with autism do not use gestures or attempt to speak, but some can demonstrate primitive communicative acts such as taking an adult by the hand to a door to have it opened, and some are able to throw tantrums to force adults to stop making demands. Others use meaningful words but will often merely echo the words or phrases without understanding them.

Autistic children present clinical challenges. The rigid behavioral repertoire dominated by self-stimulatory and stereotyped conduct along with disruptive, aggressive, and self-injurious behavior can daunt even experienced therapists. I well remember attempting to treat a 5-year-old boy who acted out the role of being a washing machine. His ritualized actions drove the parents to distraction. Fortunately, this child, unlike most autistic counterparts, was able to make some eye contact, could cuddle to some extent when held, could smile responsively to his mother, and was aware when the mother left the room. As this child grew older he achieved some normalcy in language and social development. Sadly, most autistic children (perhaps 90%) cannot match these beneficial outcomes.

Autistic children are occasionally seen in early school settings. They

- have a history of being aloof from earliest infancy;
- seem bright because of alert, thoughtful expression;
- show normal motor coordination;
- avoid eye contact and give no auditory response (seem blind and deaf to others);
- show no social smiling or evidence of pleasure in the presence of the mother;
- do not reach out to others;
- show no particular reaction to strangers;
- as babies, made few demands (were content to be left alone);
- as babies, made no imitation of gestures or sounds and were uninterested in social games;
- have largely absent speech (may echo "yes" or "no");
- are interested in toys because of their form or color (e.g., toys that spin or reflect lights or shadows) and not because the toys relate to anything else or because they were gifts from loved ones.

The complex problems of autistic children and the extreme difficulties encountered in treatment are explained in specialized publications (see A. O. Ross, 1981, for a bibliography on this subject).

Asperger's syndrome. Asperger's syndrome (Day, 2002) is considered to be a developmental disorder (as is autism) in which individuals show difficulties comprehending how people socially interact. Persons with this syndrome demonstrate some autistic traits (weak social skills, a preference for routine and sameness). Unlike autistics, however, Asperger children begin talking around two years of age (the normal time at which speech starts). In addition, they usually demonstrate normal to above-normal intelligence.

Tourette's syndrome. Tics are the trademark of Tourette's syndrome. A tic is a sudden, brief movement or a sudden production of sound. The movements may include excessive blinking, grimacing, shoulder-shrugging, head-jerking, or more elaborate movements like kicking, jumping, or gesturing. Sounds can include throat-clearing or the repetition of a word or sound. Tension builds within a child suffering this ailment and is not released until the tic is expressed. The syndrome usually begins between the ages of 2 and 15 (most often at age 6). Fifty percent of subjects continue the symptoms into adulthood at a diminished frequency. Causations are thought to lie in genes and the defective processing of the brain chemical dopamine. Parents can be informed that medical treatment is available. They can also be advised to join the Tourette Syndrome Association (the phone number is 888–4 TOURET and the Web site is www.tsa-usa.org).

Childhood schizophrenia. According to various writers (Bottoms, 2001; Tiedens & Leach, 2005; Torrey, 2001), childhood schizophrenia is a rare disease often misdiagnosed. Many onlookers confuse its symptoms with those shows by autistic children, but parents and educators should realize that the pathology is distinguished from autism by the presence of hallucinations and delusions appearing at age 7 or later (autistic characteristics, on the other hand, usually surface by age 3) and lasting for a period of at least six months. Further, childhood schizophrenia creates disabilities that pervade a youngster's life. The symptoms do not arise only in certain stressful situations and are not cyclical in nature, as is true of bipolar disease. Finally, any indications of interest by a child to form friendships (even if those efforts fail) rules heavily against a diagnosis of childhood schizophrenia.

In spite of the evident heterogeneity of behavior traits, a basic core disability exists—namely, the child's poor contact with reality—that profoundly affects the proper development of the youngster's inner and outer worlds.

The following list includes some of the major secondary characteristics often seen in childhood schizophrenia (Kaufman, Herrick, Willer, Frank, & Heims, 1959):

- unusual or bizarre body movements ("robot" walking; twirling, graceful gyrations);
- inappropriate emotional response (from explosiveness to flatness);
- stereotyped, repetitive movements (arm flapping, twirling objects);
- adoption of a nonhuman identity by sound, movement, or posture (e.g., barking, swaying, or calling oneself a washing machine);
- distorted use of body parts (e.g., an arm becomes the total body or vice versa);
- distorted time orientation (child may relate past events as if they were occurring in the present);
- inability to recognize the humanness of those nearby (e.g., uses others as stepladders, etc.);
- disturbances in speech patterns (e.g., employs fragments of sentences, parrots others, confuses identities by misusing personal pronouns, fails to make proper association of emotional affect to spoken words);
- special interest in or knowledge of a particular topic related to the child's pathology (e.g., the child who is phobic about dogs may know much about dogs).

It is important to realize that many of the features described in the list are observed developmentally in normally behaved children and that no single feature can, by itself, be considered enough evidence to warrant the assumption that psychosis exists.

Clarizio and McCoy (1976) emphasized that four characteristics—language disturbances, impaired interpersonal relationships, inappropriate affect, and slow educational progress—often appear in childhood schizophrenia.

Language disturbances. Although a distorted language process probably reflects disorganized thought patterns, it may also serve a child's need to become detached from others. Kanner (1944) contended that metaphorical language is designed to safeguard personal seclusion (when others do not understand the child's language, they do not understand the child).

In addition to problems in interpersonal communication, many childhood schizophrenics exhibit speech disorders. Goldfarb, Braunstein, and Lorgo (1956) noted symptoms such as an absence of inflections (giving the voice a wooden, or dull, quality), high-pitched speech, nasality, breathiness, throatiness, and glottalization.

Many of the speech disorders apparently spring from disturbed family interactions. For instance, Goldfarb, Goldfarb, and Scholl (1966) found that mothers of schizophrenic children, as sources of reinforcement and as objects for emulation, constituted a strong factor in the formation of aberrant communication patterns. This finding adds emphasis to the recommendations of Kint (1978) that other family members be treated along with the child.

Impaired interpersonal relationships. Impaired interpersonal relationships are significantly associated with the presence of schizophrenia in children. This dysfunction may express itself in various forms—empty, symbiotic clinging or estranged withdrawal, for example. Poor eye contact (probably an expression of the child's social discomfort) is often noted. These same investigators found that some children, while aloof most of the time, will react positively to certain surroundings.

Inappropriate affect. The emotional moods of schizophrenic children are often seen to be unpredictable—they may be withdrawn or acquiescent at times and out of control and dangerously aggressive at other instances. What seems to others to be a trifling change in the child's routine or surroundings can cause the child to express severe rage or anxiety. The psychotic child's distorted emotional responses make it difficult for others to understand the child's inner world.

Slow educational progress. The psychotic child typically has learning difficulties. According to Spring, Nuechterlein, Sugarman, and Matthysse (1977) and MacCrimmon, Cleghorn, Asarnow, and Steffy (1980), attention deficits continue to be a central aspect of schizophrenic psychopathology. As Clarizio and McCoy (1976) pointed out, such characteristics as unusual withdrawal, distorted speech patterns, and social inaccessibility make it particularly difficult for the individual to succeed in tasks requiring motivation, aggressiveness, and concentration.

On occasion, adults may underestimate the intellectual abilities of a schizophrenic child because they wrongly assume that the child is disinterested in his or her surroundings. Standardized achievement tests will sometimes reveal that the child has acquired skills not demonstrated in classroom exercises. Sometimes performances on tests or academic tasks are erratic; the child may complete one complex assignment, then fail a simpler work unit. Occasionally, a psychotic child is found to be mentally precocious.

Symbiotic psychosis. Clarizio and McCoy (1976) listed this type of individual as another subcategory of childhood psychosis, differentiated from other psychoses. Symbiotic psychosis demonstrates a later onset than autistic disorders (symbiotic psychosis appears between the ages of 2.5 and 5 years), and these children tend to appear less strange to observers than do autistic youngsters. Children with symbiotic psychosis often show traits diagnosed as borderline between neurotic and psychotic pathologies. Sometimes they show a normal developmental pattern until the onset of a traumatic event. This event usually occurs about the time most toddlers give up a normal dependency on the mother. Whereas the normal youngster can separate himself or herself from the mother figure, the symbiotic child cannot differentiate the self from the mother; the child is living on a borrowed ego. The symbiotic alliance with the mother is so strong that any attempt to break the tie is met with intense anxiety or rage, or both. Because an uninterrupted state of symbiotic harmony is impossible to maintain, the child defends against the devastating separation anxiety by becoming psychotic.

Mahler, Furer, and Settlage (1959) list the following primary symptoms of the disorder:

- panic and rage;
- unpredictable displays of destructiveness and aggressiveness, alternating with outbursts of excitement and pleasure;
- confusion of outer and inner reality (the child cannot distinguish between his or her own ego and that of another person);
- incapacity to distinguish between what is alive and what is inanimate (the child feels he or she has magical control over objects that may represent humans);
- a clinging attachment to adults that appears emotionally meaningless to others;
- the presence of inappropriate thinking, feeling, and acting.

After a period of time, the symbiotic child often becomes indistinguishable from the autistic youngster because the symptoms are so similar.

Adolescent borderline personality disorder. The borderline personality has received much attention in the literature (Alford & Norcross, 1991; Beck & Freeman, 1990; Burks, 1999; George, 1978; Linehan, 1993; Yoemans, Selzer, & Clarkin, 1992), but it is a term that is misused and poorly understood. To most researchers, a borderline personality disorder (BPD) is neither a neurotic nor psychotic state, nor is it a stable, chronic functioning on a borderline level between the two. Rather, BPD is a lifelong, chronic character organization. While the traits resemble symptoms of neurosis and character pathology, BPD is a more serious disorder and may actually be schizophrenic. Psychotic symptomatology tends to be shown when the individual is under stress or is taking drugs or alcohol. BPD is characterized by poor ego organization.

Mahler (1975) pinpointed the genesis of BPD as being in the early stages of infant personality development. Mahler believed that at around 16 to 18 months of age, during the time the child is trying to leave the symbiotic phase of development, he or she is in a very vulnerable position. The delusion of power (gained in the symbiotic phase because of feelings of fusion with the mother) is beginning to fade, and esteem is easily deflated. Fear of loss of love is very strong. Two defenses are available to the toddler: coercion of the object (making the object satisfy the child's wishes) and object splitting (seeing the object as either all good or all bad). These primary defenses can account for many, if not most, BPD symptoms.

Kernberg (1975) listed the following symptoms, which are characteristic of BPD:

- free-floating anxiety that cannot be understood or structured;
- multiple phobias (with paranoid tendencies);
- chronic, preoccupying hypochondriasis;
- obsessive-compulsive symptoms;
- conversion symptoms;
- disorders of consciousness (fugues, amnesias, twilight states);
- primitive, polymorphous, perverse sexual fantasies;
- impulse-ridden neuroses;
- addictions;
- psychogenic obesity;
- sexual identity confusion;
- lack of anxiety tolerance.

A presumptive diagnosis of BPD assumes the presence of two or three of these symptoms. According to Masterson (1972), adolescents with BPD experience three basic ego defects: (a) fluid ego boundaries leading to poor reality testing, (b) impulsivity, and (c) low frustration tolerance. Self-identity is shaky, affectional relationships are faulty, and affect (except for anger and depression due to feelings of loneliness) is largely absent (Collum, 1971).

Adolescents with BPD tend to have a confusing array of symptoms that can be seen as neurotic, psychotic, or characterological. Developmental histories and analyses of trait signs are helpful in assessment. George (1978) believed that, in the final analysis, the diagnosis is most likely to be confirmed through the therapeutic process. However, the therapeutic process is fraught with perils.

As Linehan (1993) pointed out, probably no other single disorder evokes as many feelings of bewilderment, inadequacy, and downright fear in practicing therapists as BPD. My own experience confirms this pessimistic view. Some years ago I acquired an 18-year-old male patient named Bill. His presenting symptoms included impulsivity, free-floating anxiety, obsessive compulsions, poor socialization skills, poorly disguised suicidal fantasies, and sexual-identity confusion. In the beginning stages of counseling, I struggled to establish a therapeutic transference with Bill—not much luck there. His self-destructive tendencies finally pushed me to try to establish a contract with him—if he felt suicidal he was to contact me. This arrangement did not succeed well either. He was after me constantly to refer him to a sex-change clinic (he wanted to become female). The request was never granted—I felt that his ego defenses were too fragile for such a serious step.

Social difficulties presented themselves at every turn. His emotional denseness was daunting, as evidenced by the following dialogue:

Therapist: Here, Bill, I know you like candy. I got you a candy bar. (Bill takes the candy and starts chomping on it.) Is the candy bar good?
Bill: (Grunts and nods head.)
Therapist: What do people usually say when somebody gives them something?
Bill: Huh? (Tries to bring the therapist into focus.)
Therapist: They say thank you.
Bill: Uh, yeah.

In an attempt to improve his social skills, I placed Bill in a group of adult patients, none of whom presented the extreme difficulties seen in Bill. Over a period of months his social indifference defeated them but they tolerated his presence (mostly out of loyalty to me).

It was predictable, in retrospect, that Bill would ignore the contract he and I made concerning his self-destructive impulses (he was to call me when overcome with thoughts of self-mutilation). One night I received a call from Bill's parents—he was in a hospital. He had tried to cut off his penis (an action related to his hatred of being male and the wish to be female).

The dialogue between Bill and me, at the hospital, went like this:

Therapist: Hi, Bill. How do you feel?
Bill: Okay. (Continues to stare out the window.)
Therapist: Bill, who am I?
Bill: (Tries to focus on his visitor.) Uh, you're Dr. Burks.
Therapist: That's right. It's your old friend, Dr. Burks. The one who has been trying to help you for the past year. The one who asked you to call him when you felt sad. How come you didn't call?
Bill: Uh, I dunno. (Goes back to staring out the window.)

Enough. This experience illustrates the inherent problems involved with this type of patient. Fortunately, I was able to confer regularly with a psychiatrist who trained me and who continued to act as a professional consultant. (Both of us agreed that no therapist should have more than one BPD case at a time.)

Bill continued as my patient for another year. At that time, the parents moved out of the area and took Bill with them. In view of our slow therapeutic progress, I continued to feel clinically inadequate.

INTERVENTION STRATEGIES

Techniques for Counselors

Mahler, Furer, and Settlage (1959) identified specific therapeutic goals for autistic youngsters. These therapeutic goals include helping the child to establish greater body integrity and a sense of identity, develop object relationships, and restore distorted or missing maturational and developmental ego functions. Mahler et al. believe that these goals can be at least partially realized by guiding the youngster through missing stages of development. Theoretically, the therapist supplies a substitute ego, thus helping the child progress through autistic, symbiotic, and separation-individualization phases. The child is protected from unpleasant realities until such time as he or she can face them. At the same time, the counselor provides the child with an understanding of some realities (social relationships, the meanings and purposes of bodily functions, and so on). The child is not allowed to use destructive behavior.

Mahler et al. (1959) believed autistic children should be treated in individual sessions. Symbiotic afflicted youngsters benefit from educational therapy in a residential treatment school (where many substitute "mothers" can take the place of one clung-to mother).

Group therapy has its advocates (Lifton & Smolen, 1966; Speers & Lansing, 1964). In one experiment by Lifton and Smolen, preschool autistic children and their parents were counseled together. Although some confusion and panic existed in the beginning, structured play activities became possible in time, the children communicated better, and they learned to follow directions. In another experiment by Lifton and Smolen, schizophrenic children were placed in a group. The therapist's role involved explaining the children's behavior to them, preventing self-destructive conduct and behavior harmful to others, providing praise for improvements in social behavior, and giving warmth and personal support when needed.

Lifton and Smolen (1966) found that group therapy resulted in higher levels of ego integration, reduced isolation tendencies, decreased bizarre behavior, and fewer irrational thought patterns. They pointed out, however, that those whose egos were most intact prior to treatment achieved the greatest conduct changes (a finding consistent with results obtained in other studies of psychotic children).

Some therapists insist on the involvement of parents in counseling sessions; others do not. Mahler (1965) endeavored to treat the mother and child simultaneously. Bettelheim (1950) claimed little luck in dealing with parents of psychotic children and believed that most such children should be separated from the home situation. However, if the child is left in the home, it is probably wise to train parents to play a therapeutic role in the child's rehabilitation (Risely & Wolf, 1964; Webster-Stratton & Herbert, 1994). Many investigators (Duke & Epstein, 1975; Hintgen, Sanders, & DeMyer, 1963; Lovaas, Freitag, Gold, & Kassorla, 1963; Mash & Barkley, 1989; A. O. Ross, 1981; Remschmidt 2001; Webster-Stratton & Herbert, 1994) have advocated the use of behavior reinforcement procedures. Autistic children can be taught to be more calm, to be less self-injurious, and to interact more with their environment through the use of reinforcement methods.

Whatever beneficial affects behavior modification can have with schizophrenic children, Leff (1968) stresses that this type of treatment has not yet transformed psychotic children into normally behaved minors.

A severely disturbed child from a harshly critical home should be considered a candidate for institutional placement, particularly when counseling attempts with the parents have proved unsuccessful. Before a child is placed in a facility outside the home, parents and educational authorities should carefully investigate the services offered by the institution. A residential center should emphasize treatment programs in which children are placed after a close and careful analysis of psychological, social, familial, cultural, financial, and medical factors. In this type of residential treatment center, no two children should ever be treated exactly alike because no two ever have exactly the same needs. Programs and goals should be modified to meet the changing requirements of inpatients, and parents should be given every opportunity to become informed about the progress of their child.

Children with BPD are difficult to treat. They do not respond to the usual therapeutic approaches. The therapist cannot assume that a BPD adolescent has made or will ever be able to make a meaningful emotional attachment to the therapist. Personality traits such as severe characterological defects, compulsions, and thinking disorders make the teenager's behavior unpredictable. This type of child must be supervised closely by adults who have been taught to understand the nature and development of the illness.

Many clinicians now favor the use of antipsychotic drugs in the treatment of schizophrenic children (Davis, 1976; Kozial & Stout, 1994; Torrey, 2001). These drugs fall into two basic classifications: tranquilizers and antidepressants. Unfortunately, there appear to have been few well-controlled investigations evaluating the effectiveness of these substances. Gellene (2007), for instance, reports that antidepressants may not help bipolar disorder. Actually, it remains difficult to predict the outcome of drug use with individual patients. When they do work, their efficacy seems to depend on the child, the attitude of the therapist who dispenses the substances, and the child's environment (Shaw & Lucas, 1970). Davis (1976) emphasized that antipsychotic drugs help alleviate symptoms in some, but not all, patients; the drugs must be continued indefinitely and must be monitored closely for interactive effects with other drugs.

Techniques for School Personnel

Regular classroom teachers are seldom in contact with psychotic children. Occasionally a psychotic child is seen at the kindergarten or first grade level. A good diagnosis of the child's problems is always necessary. Tests that tap the youngster's awareness of external reality can be most helpful. Is the child reacting to an untenable situation, or has the child genuinely lost contact with his or her world?

If the child's behavior is too bizarre, it is probably not a wise investment of professional skill for a teacher to attempt instruction in the regular classroom. A severely disturbed schizophrenic child needs a one-to-one relationship with a supporting adult and the help of clinical experts.

A less disturbed youngster can be maintained in a regular class setting. Invite the child to participate in classroom activities and encourage the child's peers to show interest in him or her. Keep a running anecdote of the child's behavior to assist in future planning.

The child's preoccupation with inner fantasy indicates attempts should be made to establish better communications with him or her. Many disturbed children will talk to adults who do not show fear of their symptoms. Many can be helped (not cured) to survive the childhood years. Others need expert assistance.

Some children who are withdrawn can be seduced out of their lonely world by a more rewarding environment. Punitive methods should be avoided. These children must be provided with feelings of security and personal worth. Major threats to their self-esteem should be removed. To prevent symptoms from worsening, the home, school, and community should cooperate when establishing rehabilitation programs.

School personnel can help parents by (a) asking them to make an appointment, for diagnosis and assistance, at the nearest agency where medical and psychotherapeutic services are available; (b) sending the agency a report of school findings and asking for a report in return; (c) working closely with any facility that can offer help to the child; (d) encouraging the parents to remain in therapy with the child for a long period of time; and (e) helping them cope with guilt about their interactions with the child.

CHAPTER 15

Poor Social Identification

Poor social identification can be described as the demonstrated desire to separate the self from peers. This type of child tends to

- show antagonism toward others;
- join with similar nonconformists;
- dress in radical clothing;
- act in oddball ways;
- reject standard forms of conduct.

These characteristics are evaluated by the Burks Behavior Rating Scales (BBRS) (Burks, 1977a, 2006a); the above behavior signs are shown by many antisocial, hostile, and aggressive students. The need to be a nonconformist appears to be highly correlated with behavior symptoms seen in the BBRS for poor social conformity, impulsivity, distrustfulness, poor anger control, aggressive tendencies, and rebelliousness.

For some children, another pattern of behavior emerges, in which social isolation symptoms are associated with other signs seen in scales that measure attention deficits, distrustfulness, excessive suffering, and self-blame. This constellation of indicators may characterize a masochistic withdrawal—the child sulkily refuses to participate in group activities.

THEORETICAL BACKGROUND

Children who are isolated because of the need to be a nonconformist can be in real social danger (Rufus, 2003). How children evaluate themselves and how they are perceived by their peers are important aspects of personality development that cannot be overlooked (Asher & Cole, 1990; Bolvin & Begin, 1989; Parke & Ladd, 1992). Asher and Cole speculated that there are two distinct paths to peer rejection. For some, rejection follows a history of antisocial behavior; for others, it stems from a primary disorder of anxiety and withdrawal. These paths lead to different outcomes that are best treated differently. Social behavior is, however, also strongly influenced by the social context in which it is embedded. In this respect, problems of alienation can spring from several sources:

1. The child may be frightened.
2. The child may not want to do something the group wishes to accomplish and therefore rejects the group.
3. The child may be a member of a minority group that is repudiated by the majority faction.
4. The child may feel unloved, unworthy, or unacceptable to others because of a devastated self-concept.

Kagan and Moss (1962) suggested that a child who rejects associates sometimes may not be able to understand peer social behavior. The child misinterprets the meaning of actions such as smiling, laughing, or friendly teasing, misreading them as indications of rejection instead of signs of acceptance. The rejection, of course, exists in the child's mind and is not based on reality.

Loners should not always be viewed with alarm. Independent thought and action can require courage. For that reason, children should be encouraged to undertake projects on their own. To accomplish something without the help of others can also develop motivational strength. However, despite these exceptions, all children need normal social contacts. To be a "minority of one" most of the time can place an individual in a precarious psychological position—the child may ultimately be rejected by others.

Social skills acquired through interaction with peers are among the most important lessons of childhood. Children seem to know this fact intuitively; that is why friends are held in such high esteem and why the lack of friends becomes a matter of true despair. Peer relationships are of crucial importance to children. Adults tend to underestimate the degree of concern children feel about the formation and maintenance of friendships.

The acquisition of social skills assumes such significance because people become human and remain human by sending countless messages to others, who then send back responses that confirm or deny the validity of those messages. There is substantial evidence to indicate that certain social skills can be learned only at particular stages of childhood and, further, that the best teachers of such skills are children about the same age as the learner.

Adults, who tend to forget the subtle social learning that took place in childhood, often fail to recognize the critical importance of children's peer relationships. Adults still need social contact, but they do not tend to hunger for it as much as children do.

It is important for teachers to remember that a child's peer group, in its decisions to accept membership, mostly excludes adults, even teachers. Teachers cannot, except in limited ways, influence how students achieve status and acceptance among peers. Teachers can, however, determine how a child perceives his or her own position among peers.

DIAGNOSIS

Some students seem isolated in the classroom but do not feel lonely; others apparently interact with peers but do not feel accepted; still others are spurned and recognize this rejection. It is often difficult for outsiders to gauge the nature and meaning of the social interaction that takes place among groups of children. Teachers are often surprised to learn that children do not experience peer relationships the way the teachers think they do.

I developed the How I Feel about the Other Kids checklist (see figure 15.1) to help teachers discern the differences that might exist between what is apparent and what is actually valid in the quality of children's social relationships. Items in the checklist are designed to gauge

- social isolation (items 1–14);
- active rejection (items 15–26);
- academic isolation (items 27–34);
- communication isolation (items 35–41).

Because children put so much emotional energy into interactions with peers, they tend to respond enthusiastically to any investigation of these relationships. If the examiner has established rapport with the child, there should be no difficulty getting the youngster to cooperate.

Most children check "not true" and "sometimes true" for most items. It is not surprising that a rather large proportion of children mark the "sometimes true" category, because at one time or another most youngsters experience many of the reactions mentioned. Many children also check "often true," indicating their concern about an item.

The checklist can be used as a vehicle to help children express negative feelings they may have about peer relationships. A skilled examiner, using a sympathetic and accepting manner and adept questioning, can help youngsters learn that their emotions are natural and are shared by many of their classmates.

HOW I FEEL ABOUT THE OTHER KIDS

Harold F. Burks, Ph.D.

Read each statement and put a check mark in the column that tells how you feel.

	Not true	Sometimes true	Often true
1. I have a hard time making friends.	☐	☐	☐
2. I don't even have one good friend.	☐	☐	☐
3. None of the other kids want to help me.	☐	☐	☐
4. The other kids don't play with me enough.	☐	☐	☐
5. The other kids are not interested in the things I share.	☐	☐	☐
6. When we work in groups, the other kids don't pay attention to me.	☐	☐	☐
7. I'm not interested in the things other kids share.	☐	☐	☐
8. I'm afraid I'll lose my friends.	☐	☐	☐
9. I feel bad because the other kids have more money than I do.	☐	☐	☐
10. I never get to be a leader.	☐	☐	☐
11. The other kids don't understand the problems I have.	☐	☐	☐
12. I can't count on the other kids to do what I want.	☐	☐	☐
13. The other kids think I'm not good-looking.	☐	☐	☐
14. I don't have fun with the other kids.	☐	☐	☐
15. The other kids are too bossy.	☐	☐	☐
16. The other kids don't play fair.	☐	☐	☐
17. I'd like to get even with the other kids.	☐	☐	☐
18. The other kids bother me.	☐	☐	☐
19. I'm afraid of some of the other kids.	☐	☐	☐
20. I don't get chosen to play games.	☐	☐	☐
21. The kids make fun of what I wear.	☐	☐	☐
22. Some kids tease me.	☐	☐	☐
23. Some kids don't like me.	☐	☐	☐
24. Some kids make me mad.	☐	☐	☐
25. Some kids make fun of what I do.	☐	☐	☐
26. The other kids take my things.	☐	☐	☐
27. I'm not interested in the things the other kids do.	☐	☐	☐
28. When the kids talk about schoolwork, I don't understand them.	☐	☐	☐
29. The other kids aren't interested in what I do at school.	☐	☐	☐
30. The other kids don't care about the things I want to share at school.	☐	☐	☐
31. The other kids bore me.	☐	☐	☐
32. The other kids think I can't play games well.	☐	☐	☐
33. The other kids make fun of my schoolwork.	☐	☐	☐
34. Even if I was chosen to be a leader, I wouldn't know what to do.	☐	☐	☐
35. I don't talk much to the other kids.	☐	☐	☐
36. The other kids don't talk much to me.	☐	☐	☐
37. The other kids don't think I talk very well.	☐	☐	☐
38. Sometimes I don't know what to say to the other kids.	☐	☐	☐
39. I can't seem to explain what I want to the other kids.	☐	☐	☐
40. The other kids argue with me too much.	☐	☐	☐
41. I'm afraid to say what I want to the other kids.	☐	☐	☐

Figure 15.1.

Children who check "often true" for many of the first 14 items may feel socially isolated. A sociogram (see diagnosis section of chapter 7) can help determine whether these children are as isolated as they think they are. The amount of interaction with the teacher may also be of concern. For children who lack social skills, special training may be of assistance. Students with disabilities may be unattractive to other students and may require additional assistance to become integrated with peers.

Children who indicate that items 15 through 26 are "often true" may feel actively rejected by classmates. Examine the student's history of rejection and his or her age in comparison to classmates. Modifications in the student's school or class placement may be indicated. Some students who indicate feelings of active rejection may fear for their physical safety. This possibility warrants investigation as well. The fearful child may react aggressively toward others.

Children who check "often true" for items 27 through 34 may feel academically isolated when they are intellectually superior or inferior to the group. Some children may be academically isolated because they are poorly prepared for the curriculum. Further investigation to determine the cause of feelings of isolation can assist in the development of a modified program for the child.

Finally, the child who feels communicatively isolated will select "often true" for many of the remaining items (items 35–41). This child may have a speech handicap, a language deficiency, or a nonverbal background. Students with articulation difficulties will benefit from speech therapy. Students who lack English skills or who never learned to communicate well will benefit from efforts to encourage active classroom communication.

INTERVENTION STRATEGIES

Techniques for School Personnel

Many factors may contribute to a child's feeling of isolation. To determine what is affecting a given student, school counselors may want to ask the following questions of parents and teachers:

Does the child seem to understand the curriculum? What are his or her worst and best subjects? What can the child contribute to subjects? What specific help is needed by the child?

Is the child too old or too young for the group? What are the reasons for the child's placement? What can be done to rectify poor placement?

Has the child been isolated from peers for a long period of time? Should the child be placed in another classroom or school?

Is the child too aggressive? What brings on the aggressiveness? What can be done to control it? Does aggressiveness contribute to the child's isolation? Does the child's aggression appear to be a natural personality manifestation or is it caused by environmental factors?

Is the child too shy and withdrawn? What brings on the shyness? What can be done to help the child? Does shyness contribute to the child's isolation? Does the shyness appear to be a natural personality manifestation or is it caused by environmental factors?

Does the child appear to be picked on by peers? What conditions bring on such persecution? What does the child do to provoke criticism? What can the child do to ward it off?

Are there cliques in the classroom that reject the child? Should such cliques be disbanded? Does the child have any chance of being accepted by these cliques?

Is the child being isolated on the playground? Is the isolation due to the child's lack of physical skills? Is it due to a poor understanding of game rules?

Is the child being ignored in the classroom? Does the child's social behavior turn others off?

Is the child's isolation due to his or her appearance or habits? If so, is there congruence or agreement between the family and school personnel on these matters?

Does the child understand the effects of his or her behavior on others? What cultural or family training methods might contribute to a lack of understanding? Is the child's social reputation so poor that placement in another school is indicated?

Does the child understand the social skills that are necessary to attract peers? What possibilities exist to teach the child social competence?

Does the child sit close to friendly classroom peers? Where would the child like to sit?

Do the child's parents welcome other children into the home? To what degree does the family feel it is accepted or rejected by other families? To what degree can the family change its social habits? As Asher and Cole (1990) have pointed out, children respond to rejection and isolation in different ways based on parental social styles.

Techniques for Counselors

Each following description of behavior causing social isolation from peers is followed by ways in which a school counselor can assist the child to make changes that will invite greater peer acceptance.

Gender-inappropriate behavior. Children who exhibit gender-inappropriate conduct (i.e., who do not act in stereotypical ways) are often rejected by peers (Jordan & Goldberg, 2001). This is particularly true for boys (tomboys are apparently better accepted by both genders than are boys with effeminate characteristics). According to Ross (1981), the problem is best treated with behavior therapy. Rekers, Lovaas, and Low (1974) used behavior intervention with a boy who employed a full repertoire of so-called feminine behavior. The aim of the therapy was to supplant the feminine conduct with behavior that society associates with masculinity. Before embarking on treatment, the investigators pinpointed specific behaviors (e.g., gait and speech) as targets for change. The therapist in charge of the case was able to make significant changes in verbal expression simply by showing interest when the child's statements had masculine or neutral content and withdrawing attention when references were made to feminine topics.

The boy's mother was taught a modification program based on token reinforcement. The youngster was told he could earn tokens whenever he engaged in masculine play with his brother. These tokens could be traded for rewards such as candy and television-viewing privileges. After two weeks, the boy was told that if he used feminine gestures he would be given a new type of token that would cancel out one of the original tokens.

An analysis of data revealed a decrease in feminine behavior by the boy and an increase in masculine play. However, the early emergence of masculine characteristics did not generalize from the home to the school or vice versa, and it was not until treatment was extended over a period of 15 months that generalized, permanent gender conduct changes were noted.

Through clinical experience with a number of boys showing gender-role confusion, I have made the following observations:

1. All participants were apparently unaware of the sexual implications of their conduct. They were simply not cognizant of the fact that they were using hand gestures, voice inflections, and bodily postures characteristic of the opposite sex.
2. Some refused to believe they were demonstrating such traits until convinced by members of a therapy group, by a studied and guided reflection of themselves in a mirror, or by a review of a videotaped social situation in which they were involved.
3. Some boys who have acquired a reputation for behavior labeled by peers as "sissy" or "queer" should be transferred to other schools. Even the best treatment procedures cannot overcome deeply rooted biases of schoolmates who feel threatened by gender-inappropriate behavior.
4. If treatment is instituted, parents must be involved and told that therapy will extend over a long period of time (because the conduct to be changed is thought to be deeply rooted).
5. Boys with cross-gender problems should be treated by male therapists; girls, by female therapists. These children have had poor same-sex models. The therapist must exhibit deportment the child admires and wishes to copy.

Lothstein (1980) studied 27 adolescent gender-identity patients (10 girls and 17 boys; average age about 16 years) who presented with transsexual wishes for sex reassignment surgery. Four major stressors correlated with the request for sex reassignment: (a) a recent loss or change in a relationship that reactivated separation anxiety, (b) physical maturation that threatened self-esteem, (c) stigmatized homosexuality, and (d) a flight from masturbatory activity. The family of an adolescent wishing sex reassignment should be referred to agencies specializing in problems of this nature; school personnel should not attempt to go beyond the initial stages of investigatory counseling.

Unpopular, underachieving children. Unpopular, underachieving youngsters may not receive enough educational attention. Of overriding concern is the poor social acceptance by achieving students.

The following strategies may improve the social desirability of such students:

1. Lilly (1971) reported an investigation in which low-acceptance students worked for 5 weeks with popular peers to produce a movie later presented to the class. This approach produced significant gains in social acceptance; however, the shared gains did not endure over a six-week follow-up period—indicating, perhaps, that unpopular children need continual and long-lasting involvement with accepted peers.
2. The physical and social distancing in teacher-student relationships was investigated by Schwebel and Cherlin (1972). Students who had been assigned seats in the front, middle, and back rows of grade-school classrooms were observed by investigators. An analysis of adult observations and teacher and student questionnaires found that teachers strove to assign seats in ways that minimize classroom disruption. Children assigned to the front row are more attentive to classroom activities than classmates in the middle and back rows. Occupancy of seats in the front, as opposed to those in the middle or back, has a positive effect on the way in which students are perceived by their teacher and peers and the way in which students evaluate themselves. Although teachers indicated they shared a common demand for equal classroom control, they apparently assigned seats according to the perceived status of the observed individuals. For instance, in one inner-city school, not one of the 10 white students was assigned a seat farther back than the second row. The implications of this study are obvious. Students near the teacher receive more attention and feedback. They are perceived by peers to have more social value. The low-achieving, unpopular child can sometimes be made to appear more desirable simply by being moved closer to the teacher.
3. Bruininks (1978) found that students with learning disabilities are not only significantly less socially accepted than their regular class peers but are, in addition, less accurate than peers in assessing their own status in the group. These inaccurate social assessments raise questions about classroom social planning. For one thing, an individual who misunderstands the feelings of others may participate in unwise social ventures. This type of child needs personalized help in acquiring and keeping friends. In the second place, the teacher must seek activities that the child can complete successfully so the child's success will earn peer respect.
4. In a study by Bruininks (1978), teachers gave more positive feedback for work produced than for ideas or personal and social behavior in the classroom. The high emphasis on achievement puts the poor student in a most untenable position. Even if the youngster has other attributes that will later be valued by society, he or she cannot receive current credit for them. The fact that personality influences job satisfaction and success in adult life as much as job skills do seems to carry little value in the educational system. The obvious solution is to continue to promote the acquisition of basic skills in the classroom but at the same time honor and promote other types of accomplishments and personality attributes in students who show little aptitude for traditional school subject matter.

Adolescent acne. Acne is a skin disease that affects more than 85% of youth at puberty, but only about 10% seek help for the condition (Emerson & Strauss, 1972). Since adolescence is a time of great self-consciousness and undue worries about peer reactions, persistent facial eruptions can be a source of major embarrassment. School counselors should encourage teenagers to discuss the problem in private interviews or in health classes and should recognize that acne can cause adolescents to feel they are unliked. In addition, Schroeder, Schroeder, and Devine (1977) outlined the following information about acne:

1. Only severe and untreated acne leads to permanent scarring.
2. Emotional stress may increase acne because of increased sweating.
3. Acne may be aggravated by moisturizing creams, hair tonics, sweatbands, oil and grease encountered in certain occupations, the ingestion of kelp tablets containing iodine, and certain hormones and drugs.
4. There is no known cure for acne, but most individuals show excellent control and improvement of the condition with medical treatment. Benzoyl peroxide and retinoic acid are two topical agents that have proved successful in the treatment of acne. Improvement may not be noted for four to six weeks, however, and irritation and redness of the face may occur. It is important for the teenager to know what to expect in the course of treatment (such information is readily accepted by most individuals and greatly increases cooperation and compliance with treatment).
5. Contrary to popular belief, diet appears to have little effect on the severity and course of acne infection.
6. Acne is not the result of unhygienic cleansing. Further, the individual with acne is advised to avoid abrasive soap and vigorous rubbing of the skin, which can make the condition worse and harm the skin.

Children demonstrating adult-like behavior. Occasionally, a student is considered a curiosity by peers because he or she demonstrates behavior that is not age-appropriate. The student has adopted conduct (seen to be valuable by parents) more suitable for adults than for children.

For example, I once observed a first grader who was not accepted by classmates. Jay was described by the teacher as an excessively polite boy who used pedantic language. The other children did not like his tone of voice, nor, apparently, did they understand him. When I asked Jay to step outside the classroom for a conversation, Jay said, "Why, thank you. I should be most happy to do so." He opened the door for me and then carefully closed it. Outside the room he held out his hand to be shaken and said, "How do you do, sir? My name is Jay. What is your name?" Throughout the interview, formalities of this type occurred. While technically appropriate, these incidents were truly child-inappropriate.

I hypothesized that Jay's parents would be correct, conforming, and possibly tense. This was indeed the case. After calling the parents, I was invited to the home for a conference. Upon arriving, I found that the parents had prepared an elaborate, formally served lunch, which I was asked to attend as an honored guest. Table manners were impeccable, conversation was kept light and amusing, and no mention was made of possible reasons for my presence.

After the meal, everyone "retired to the drawing room." I then thanked the parents for the delightful lunch but asked if they thought it appropriate to provide a school psychologist with such a reception when all I had requested was a simple home visit. The question apparently came as a great surprise to the mother and father. No, they did not think it inappropriate to have made such an effort. At this point, I asked them to speculate on why I was there and why Jay could be having problems in the classroom. The ensuing conversation made it clear that the parents were satisfied with Jay's behavior but felt he did not have enough friends.

The way was now open to draw an analogy between the parents' inappropriate behavior during the home visit and Jay's unsuitable conduct with other children. After the initial discomfort, the parents expressed keen interest in the problem and promised to reevaluate some of their training procedures. They met with the teacher a number of times. Their expectations for the child were lowered, and his behavior gradually became more childlike.

Unassertive children. The inability to be assertive can distance the child from others. Interpersonal problems may include

- reduced capacity to speak up for legitimate rights (e.g., the child may be belittled by others but feel no basis for defending himself or herself);
- inability to establish a rightful place in discussions and conversations (the child feels that to state his or her point of view represents inappropriate aggression);
- inability to initiate interchanges with others that would benefit the child (e.g., the child refuses to ask for needed help);

• inadequate resolve not to be pulled into unpleasant circumstances or to demand they stop (e.g., the youngster, asked to take a stand in an argument, does so even though he or she has no interest in the outcome).

The immediate and long-term effects of unassertiveness include loss of opportunities, unwanted and potentially harmful physical responses (stress), mental involvement with negative fantasies (ruminations about low self-image), and resentment and anger that can eventually be expressed in unproductive ways (social withdrawal, substance abuse, or emotional outbursts).

Some withdrawn, unassertive children may be helped by the following strategies:

1. Illustrate the disadvantages of being unassertive, perhaps through classroom discussions. Stress the counter-productive nature of the problem, the negative emotional consequences, and the poor image it gives others (Wolpe, 1973).
2. Help the child know what to say and do in particular situations (Goldfried & Davison, 1976).
3. Help the child deal with the anxiety that accompanies assertiveness. The following techniques may be useful:

   • behavior rehearsal (reading from a script);
   • modeling (role-playing);
   • symbolic desensitization ("walking through" the situation several times);
   • reviewing and replacing counterproductive beliefs about assertiveness.

4. Provide the child with practice situations that require assertiveness. The youngster can use techniques such as self-instruction, relaxation techniques, and covert modeling along with coaching, feedback, and reinforcement from others.

Techniques for School Personnel

Withdrawn children. Mash and Barkley (1989) studied ways to enhance the frequency of target behavior (smiling, sharing, positive physical contact, verbal compliments, initiation of interaction with peers, and extension of such interaction) in groups of socially withdrawn children with learning disabilities. They found that praise (either token reinforcement or verbal praise) was effective in increasing specific prosocial behavior.

Several procedures have been developed to enhance the effects of such techniques. Greater improvements have been noted when peers are involved, when group contingencies are used to reinforce the prosocial behavior of a specific child, and when gradually decreased adult reinforcement and booster training sessions are instituted. The long-term beneficial effects of prosocial training efforts, however, have proved difficult to assess (improvements, over time, tend to disappear).

Considerable evidence indicates that the most successful interventions have been those in which the rejected child and the peer group are both targeted for treatment. The child learns new social skills and the group is coached to respond positively to the child's improvements. Many rejected children have an attitude of hopelessness. They think nothing they do will improve their status in the eyes of others. Many have parents who hold exalted standards of behavior for children and tend to give negative feedback and little praise to offspring.

Some of these parents can be taught that their youngsters are likely to do better socially if the parents are supportive, collaborate with teachers and other professionals, and employ effective child management strategies. Parents can also be told that children are at a disadvantage if parents

• have low expectations of their child (Smith, 1983);
• attribute poor achievement to bad luck or intervention by others (Pearl & Bryan, 1982);
• deny the seriousness of their child's problems;

- become overly protective of the child;
- fail to resolve family conflicts that affect the child adversely.

A prime objective in working with parents is to clear up any misunderstandings associated with the child's abilities, current needs, and future possibilities. Parents must also be urged to deal with their child's problems one step at a time and not to count on a quick cure.

Antagonistic children. Children who alienate themselves from others are in need of immediate attention from educators. Diagnosis is important to pinpoint sources of anxiety, which can then be removed, circumvented, or made more palatable to the child. The following treatment suggestions may be appropriate:

1. Ignore the child's antagonism except when it is physically harmful to others.
2. Reinforce nonantagonistic conduct with concrete rewards, then gradually replace such rewards with social reinforcement like praise and recognition.
3. Move the child to another classroom if antagonism is directed at the teacher but not at peers.
4. Rearrange seating if the child shows irritation directed at specific, neighboring students.
5. Place the child in a position of responsibility and leadership, but do so gradually so as not to antagonize peers.
6. Refuse to allow the child to place the teacher in the position of being an antagonist. The teacher must remain firm when administering discipline but abstain from showing anger at the youngster.

Techniques for Parents

The roots of childhood misbehavior lie in the home. Ask parents the following questions to stimulate discussions about practices within the home that tend to foster disagreeable child conduct. The questions are useful as a device to spark parents' interest in their offspring's problems and to provide specific information that can help parents change their child's behavior. For group conferences, read the questions to the group, then discuss the implications of each query. Individual or family conferences should be tailored to the needs of those involved. Parents should not be required to divulge their responses.

Do you tend to have firm rules for your child? Overindulgent parents may train their children to think that rules are only for others or that children will be forgiven quickly for infractions. Worse, such children never learn to properly control the expression of impulses.

Do you supervise your child's play activities and intervene if he or she shows bossy behavior? Children who develop the notion that others will naturally obey their whims tend to be domineering. This behavior can be modified if parents explain to the child how to get along with others better and if they use proper punishment when the child tries to control others.

Do you have ways to separate your children from each other when they are fighting? Sibling rivalry exists in every home, but in some, the competition is extreme and steps must be taken to lessen the problem. One way is to isolate the warring parties so they have a chance to cool down (i.e., each child goes to a designated place in the home for a specified period of time).

When you discipline your child, do you abstain from the use of sarcasm and criticism? Sarcasm should probably never be employed as a controlling device, and criticism should seldom be used. Both devices cause recipients to feel resentful and occasionally vengeful. Children may bring these negative feelings to school. Children who are fearful of disparagement overreact to any perceived belittling action. Such angry reactions are interpreted by others as antagonistic.

Does anyone else in the family tend to be touchy or irritable? Children emulate their parents. It would be unrealistic to expect a child to act passively around an antagonistic parent. Irritable family members may need to become more aware of how their behavior is perceived by other people and to learn to instigate more pleasant social interchanges.

When your child becomes upset, do you give him or her extra time and attention? Most children are not willfully naughty; they are simply expressing a protest against conditions that seem unfair. In most instances, parents will find it profitable to arrange time alone with the youngster (e.g., playing or working together) where difficulties can be talked out and where the youngster feels the parent is in the child's corner.

Do you have rules in your home that protect your child from feeling ashamed or humiliated? Some families promote teasing in the belief that all participants find such mockery enjoyable. That is usually not the case. Those who promote teasing may experience pleasure, but the recipients ordinarily do not (particularly when there is no acceptable way to respond to put-downs). The best plan is to draw up a regulation against family teasing. Is there someone associated with the child (a relative, friend, or acquaintance) who consistently evaluates the youngster negatively? Take the person aside, insist that such criticism not be heard by the child, and keep the child away from the individual if the behavior continues.

Do you arrange pleasurable peer activities for your child? Any youngster's social value is enhanced if his or her home is seen by other children as an enjoyable place to visit. They will congregate there to share toys and unique games (e.g., a trampoline), and the child will be courted at school.

Do you include other families in your home and community activities? Inviting other families to share in the parents' interests can also help a child. As a rule of thumb, parents should enlist the social support of at least four or five other families. The association with these families will give the child many friends he or she would not ordinarily make.

Do you protect your child from overly competitive experiences with peers? Some children simply cannot succeed at competitive activities (especially sports), and because they cannot perform, they feel unworthy. This low self-esteem causes them to withdraw from others or to show antagonism toward them. When in doubt about the benefits a child is receiving from competitive sports, parents should take the child out of the activities until he or she expresses an interest to return. Parents can discourage relationships with children who belittle the child with an exhibition of superior skills and encourage their child to play with less threatening peers.

CHAPTER 16

Excessive Suffering

Excessive suffering is the outward expression of an inward desire to fail or to injure the self (Burks, 1977a, 2006a, 2006b). Children experiencing sorrow or inner torment tend to

- be self-pitying;
- seem depressed;
- have their feelings hurt easily;
- sulk;
- seek punishment;
- arrange to be scolded;
- seem unhappy.

Children with masochistic (self-punishing) symptoms are also likely to have high scores on the Burks Behavior Rating Scales (BBRS) in the excessive sense of persecution , poor anger control, excessive resistance, and excessive aggressiveness scales. All such traits indicate unresolved hostility toward the world. Emotional distress is often associated, however, with other aberrant behavioral manifestations. Older neurotic children, for instance, tend to show signs of suffering (this is consistent with the psychological literature that has tended to classify masochism as a neurotic disorder grouped with the anxiety states).

THEORETICAL BACKGROUND

Masochism

Suffering (masochism) is a personality topic avoided by most psychology researchers. First, it is difficult to define, mixed as it is with conduct characteristic of depressive and anxiety states. Second, treatment is hard to plot because the disorder is resistant to change.

Everyone feels sad or dejected at times because of loss or disappointment, but deportment of this nature does not qualify as being masochistic; it is of short duration and is responsive to commonsense approaches (everyday logic and offers of comfort). There is, on the other hand, a general kind of suffering that is not responsive to rational treatment. People who show this type of suffering find innumerable opportunities to feel disappointed, frustrated, humiliated, treated unfairly, and so forth. All these symptoms spring from a complicated matrix of suppressed anger, unconscious guilt, and rigid defense systems.

This unhealthy mix of symptoms was well illustrated by Watzlawick (1993). He found that the following tendencies are among the many paths to unhappiness:

- persistent low self-esteem ("I must always try to be better");
- belief that failure is the most likely outcome ("I'm sure this will turn out badly");

- inflation of trivialities ("That glance was evil!");
- avoidance of anticipated problems ("I can't go to the party; something bad will happen");
- negative self-fulfilling prophecies ("My mother always said the family was cursed, and what just happened proves it!");
- overconcern about being loved ("I have to keep concentrating on my faults").

I have studied the role of aggression in chronic suffering disorders (Burks, 1977a, 2006a) and found that excessive suffering in children was associated with feelings of persecution, anger, aggression, and resistance.

The angry reactions of small children who are forced to do something they do not like are familiar to most. What is not so commonly recognized is the anger that is frequently expressed through the manifestation of suffering. Take, for example, the case of a 3-, 4-, or 5-year-old whose parents are insisting that he or she eat spinach: The child refuses the spoonful of vegetable; the parent steadfastly fills the child's mouth; the child refuses to swallow the food, gags, holds his or her breath, and turns blue; the parent becomes frightened and angry and gives up the feeding attempt. Thus, the dynamics of sadomasochistic behavior are set up in the child. The child resents the intrusive parental efforts and gets back at the parents by expressing distress that forces the parents to discontinue their course of action. Many factors operate to reinforce the continuance of this drama. If, however, the parents teach themselves not to show discomfort when the child exhibits misery, a key element in the establishment of suffering conduct is missing; that is, the child observes no satisfactory response for manufactured signs of pain.

This observation should provide some therapeutic direction. Teachers and parents must not overreact to the suffering of a chronically upset child. When adults remain relatively impassive, some children respond favorably—they discontinue their expressions of distress. This outcome may not, however, always be realized. One example from my own experience involved a counseling effort with an unhappy, friendless boy in junior high school who complained he was picked on by peers. This child was a talented chess player, and he readily entered therapy when it was made known to him that he could play chess (as well as talk) with me. It was his expectation that he would always be the winner. Usually he was, but when on one occasion he did lose, his reactions were interesting. His eyes clouded up, he complained bitterly about my strategies, and he refused to finish the game.

Operating on the thesis that such behavior would diminish in frequency if it was ignored, I paid little attention to the tantrums. However, the expressions of suffering did not disappear; instead, the boy expressed the feeling that I "did not care." His conduct became increasingly perverse and erratic. Upon observing these reactions, I decided to treat the parents in company with the adolescent. In family therapy, the masochistic actions of each member could be examined and discussed more safely (i.e., the therapeutic transference was in less danger of being disrupted). The family group approach worked more successfully, but only over a long period of time, accompanied by many regressive actions on the part of the participants.

Much of the hostility expressed in sadomasochistic behavior is, of course, subconscious. The unrecognized aggressiveness can emerge in ways that are rationalized as being helpful to others. For instance, a parent may explain the severe punishment of a child as being necessary to control negative behavior. The provocative, aggressive child may be seen as an uncontrollable individual who insists on torturing the helpless parents. Sometimes, a passive, victim-prone parent, whose aggressive impulses have been completely submerged, will complain bitterly of domination by a child. In this case, the parent plays the masochistic, blameless role while the child is portrayed as being provocative and sadistic.

The role of guilt in masochism was originally discussed by Freud (Arlow & Brenner, 1964). He extended the masochistic concept to include a kind of irrational martyrdom, which he labeled "moral masochism." The moral masochist actively seeks to suffer as a way to expiate a subconscious sense of guilt. Sometimes the intensity of such guilt can be reduced only through punishment. For some criminals, punishment is obtained via antisocial behavior. This approach is less common for the ordinary sufferer, whose behavior is exemplary. Because the noncriminal sufferer believes his or her behavior is beyond reproach, there is only one perceived reason for the suffering: punishment by unfair circumstances or people.

Above and beyond the need for punishment, there are secondary dividends associated with self-pity, depression, sensitivity, and general unhappiness:

1. A person may feel that he or she is obtaining power by being passive (taking) but not giving. This sense of power helps protect the individual from a dangerous world.
2. The individual gains gratifying attention from others by being an object of concern.
3. The male cannot be demasculinized if he has already castrated himself psychologically by not being aggressive.
4. By being helpless, the person can appeal to, and gain the mercy of, a threatening person.
5. By seeing himself or herself as sinful, the individual can keep his or her own hostile impulses out of consciousness. The person is, in effect, saying, "I am helpless, weak, no good, and must be protected and looked after." The unlikable part of the individual, then, does not have to be confronted.

Suffering behavior in young children is instilled from watching the actions of others. Parents may model masochism. A mother, for instance, can demonstrate suffering behavior by being dissatisfied with everything the child does, being depressed, constantly complaining about her life, and claiming she is unjustly treated by others.

Glasbourg and Aboud (1981) pointed out that certain cognitive and character structures are prerequisites for adult reactions to painful life events. For instance, the self-denigrating adult may be acting out a discrepancy between self-representation and the ideal self. In a child, these structures may not be stable enough to withstand critical self-appraisal and the child has to express distress in other-than-adult ways.

Depression

The last two decades have seen an explosion of interest in childhood depression (Bottoms, 2001; Dowling, 1991; Wodasrski, et al., 2003). Notwithstanding the shortcomings of available diagnostic criteria, studies of patient populations do converge in finding that child depressive disorders are more pervasive than hitherto thought, can be reliably identified, and are more impairing than previously believed.

Social interaction in the family can play a significant role in the development of childhood depression. Mothers who are depressed show higher dysphoric affect and lower rates of happy affect in their relationships with family members and are less likely to be supportive of their children. Depression in children is promoted when parents show resentment and rejection of their children or when they are emotionally detached, unaffectionate, or uninvolved.

Depression is often associated with social-skill deficits. Children seen by peers as depressed seem more isolated and less effective in social interactions. Compared with nonsymptomatic children, they also exhibit difficulties in proper self-monitoring (self-control), expect to perform poorly on tasks, set higher standards for personal success, evaluate their own performance unfavorably, and receive less positive peer reinforcement.

Depression can ensue from the reduction or loss of environmental reinforcement. The socially inept person's conduct does not produce enough encouragement from others, and the individual becomes passive and socially withdrawn. Punishing and aversive consequences from others make depressive reactions even more likely.

Symptoms of depression may be expressed because of inward feelings of helplessness (Sacco & Hokanson, 1978). Seligman (1973) postulated that people learn to feel helpless if they believe that their efforts have nothing to do with how the world reacts to them. Seligman speculated that people who are very resistant to depression have had extensive experience in controlling and manipulating the sources of reinforcement in their lives and thus see the future optimistically. Adults who lost parents when they were children are unusually susceptible to depression and suicide.

DIAGNOSIS

Assessing Depression

Causal factors. Depression in children can have a locus in absent, inadequate, or poor mothering. The disorder can also ensue from harmful current conditions (loss of a loved one, being abused, or suffering failure). Allergies, certain diseases and medications, and inherited tendencies (depression tends to run in families) are factors that may contribute to the complaint.

Symptoms. The frank clinical picture of adult depression (apathy, sadness, and self-hate) is seldom seen in children (Blumberg, 1978). When childhood depression does occur, it appears in disguised forms. Brumbach and Weinberg (1977) presented 10 criteria that characterized the disorder:

1. sad mood;
2. self-deprecation ("I'm no good");
3. spells of agitation (unusual activity for no apparent reason);
4. loss of energy; appears tired;
5. reduced interest in socializing with others;
6. decreased school performance;
7. increasingly poor attitude toward school;
8. sleep disturbance;
9. appetite disturbance;
10. complaints of bodily pain (persisting for at least a month).

Studies of depression in adults indicate it is more prevalent in women than in men. This difference is not seen in children. Gender differences have been found in depressed children, however, that are found in adults—including an association between depression and other characteristics (e.g., nonverbal behavior, unpopularity, somatic complaints) that appears to be higher and more consistent among girls (Mash & Barkley, 1989). Also, some of the serious symptoms of depression are clearly less evident in children. For instance, suicide in children below the age of 12 is extremely rare. The child clinician should, however, be aware that suicidal ideation, threats, and attempts at suicide in this age group are not rare.

Manifestations of the depressive disorder are not identical for children and adolescents. When characterizing depression among adolescents, it is important to distinguish depression as a symptom from depression as a syndrome disorder. As a symptom, depression is a common occurrence. A depressive syndrome, on the other hand, is a group of symptoms that are tied together (i.e., sadness associated with a larger group of problems such as a loss of interest in everyday activities, a feeling of worthlessness, an inability to sleep, a loss of appetite, and so on). While there are many identified mood disorders, the severity, duration, and precipitants of the symptoms are major determinants of the defined disorder.

Depression as a symptom. As previously mentioned, periods of unhappiness or sadness are common to everyone. In adolescents, these moods may occur in response to many situations, such as failure on a school test or loss of a significant relationship. A mood may last for a brief or an extended period of time. Adolescents experiencing such a mood may have no other emotional difficulties. A sad or depressed mood is often accompanied by other negative feelings such as fear, anger, guilt, disgust or self-loathing, anxiety, and withdrawal. It is interesting to note that depressed mood has been found to be the single most powerful trait in differentiating clinically referred and nonreferred youth.

Depression as a syndrome. Achenbach (1991), in his studies of clinically depressed children, identified a syndrome that includes both depression and anxiety, as well as the following traits:

- cries easily;
- feels isolated;
- fears doing unacceptable things;
- feels the need to be perfect;
- feels unloved;
- thinks others are out to get him or her;
- feels worthless;
- is nervous;

- feels guilty;
- feels self-conscious;
- feels suspicious;
- experiences sadness;
- worries.

This syndrome is highly associated with eight other syndromes:

1. withdrawal;
2. somatic complaints;
3. social problems;
4. thought problems;
5. attention difficulties;
6. delinquent behavior;
7. self-destructiveness;
8. aggressive behavior.

Adolescent clinical depression. The American Psychiatric Association (1994) has developed guidelines for the diagnosis of adolescent depression based on the preceding syndromes. These guidelines require a review of the presence, duration, and severity of sets of symptoms. A correct diagnosis assumes that these symptoms are associated with significant levels of current distress or disability and with increased risk for impairment of the individual's functioning.

To meet the criteria for major depressive disorder, an adolescent must experience five or more of the following symptoms for at least a two-week period at a level that differs from previous functioning:

- depressed mood or irritable mood most of the day;
- decreased interest in pleasurable activities;
- change in weight or perhaps failure to make necessary adolescent weight gains;
- sleep problems;
- psychomotor agitation or retardation;
- fatigue or loss of energy;
- feelings of worthlessness or abnormal amounts of guilt;
- reduced concentration and decision-making ability;
- repeated suicidal ideation, attempts, or plans.

INTERVENTION STRATEGIES

Suffering behavior is relatively inaccessible to ordinary manipulation or control. Commonsense approaches do not unravel the dynamics underlying this pattern of conduct. Teachers and parents should not be encouraged to try to treat the suffering child. The best approach is to direct the parents to a therapeutic setting where they and the child can receive counseling. If parents are reluctant to take this step, it is permissible to point out the possibility of eventual significant self-harm: The severely masochistic child can become a depressed adolescent or a suicidal adult.

Pharmacotherapy

Several varieties of psychoactive medication have been evaluated as treatments for teen depression; however, so far, no study has totally supported the efficacy of pharmaceutical drugs for adolescents. Given the efficacy of these agents in the treatment of adult depression, researchers can only speculate on the lack of good results for teenagers. Perhaps adolescents have different biological substrata, or perhaps a depressive disorder is more serious for younger people because of earlier onset. Nevertheless, there are medications that, for certain children, do produce positive effects (Mash & Barkley, 1989). Most children who do show improvement also need psychosocial intervention because medication does not affect significant areas of social functioning.

Techniques for School Personnel

Students who are depressed are not likely to perform well in the classroom. School personnel can take the following steps to help students control more areas of their life and to manipulate conditions to their benefit.

1. Give the child jobs in the classroom so that he or she is too involved to brood about problems.
2. Seat the student near the teacher's desk so that the student can get needed instructor responses quickly.
3. Reinforce all spontaneous physical movement made by the student, whether in play, discussions, or work projects, and do this often enough and emphatically enough so the child begins to feel he or she has control over the environment. Token reinforcements are permissible if nothing else works.
4. Do not reward passivity or immobile behavior.
5. Interrupt the child's daydreaming with instructions, demands, and work assignments. If the student becomes defiant, irritable, or resentful, the prognosis is more hopeful. Seligman (1973) described a technique called the "antidepression room," in which the depressed patient is deliberately frustrated. Whenever the person does something he or she is told to do, the therapist berates the individual for doing it wrong. The abuse continues until the depressed patient becomes angry. At that point, apologies are offered and the patient is led out of the room. The two actions—the outburst of anger and the reaction by the person perpetrating the abuse— tend to break up the depression. The patient is able to use an emotion (anger) that traditionally is used to control the actions of others, and the patient sees that the outbreak actually did influence someone's conduct. When a depressed child shows strong emotion after being frustrated, it is important for the child to see that his or her expressed feelings have some effect on others.
6. Give the child challenging work (but work well within his or her capability), make sure the task is completed, and praise the youngster's efforts liberally.
7. Some adolescents do well in group therapy sessions (initiated by school counselors) where participants discuss self-control skills, examine attitude distortions and faulty beliefs, receive self-reinforcement ideas, and learn ways to evaluate themselves (Reynolds & Coats, 1986).

Techniques for Parents

Counseling with family members should focus on the reasons for the depression and on resources that may be of assistance. Explore with the family possible reasons for the onset of the depressive reaction. Was it related to a death in the family, the loss of an important family member, a bitter disappointment, unexpressed anger, or unreasonable pressure to perform?

Suggest that the parents take the child to the family physician to seek the source of any physical complaints. In addition, the doctor may prescribe medication (mood elevators) to alleviate symptoms of depression. In addition, ask the family to take the child to a local mental health clinic for evaluation and possible treatment.

Kessler (1966) discussed some of the unspoken psychological "contracts" that exist in excessively suffering families. I formulated the following questions for counselors based on Kessler's treatment of contract issues:

1. Do the parents complain endlessly about the child's behavior but seem unable to do anything about it? If this psychological arrangement has continued for a long time, it may be safe to assume that it somehow serves

the suffering needs of the parents, who, in order to be proper victims, must have a (child) persecutor. This contract is easier to recognize than to treat.

2. How does the mother (usually it is the mother who most influences the child) react to her child's small successes? Practical experience indicates that if the mother is grateful for the child's accomplishments, she can be helped. If she continues to act disappointed, she will prove difficult to assist.

3. How does the mother react to the counselor as a person and to the proffered assistance? Sometimes a mother may appear masochistic but in reality is simply convinced of her incompetence and feels she cannot do anything worthwhile. This kind of person may be helped through an alliance with a supporting authority figure who teaches her how to achieve success and do things on her own.

SUMMARY

In therapeutic conversations with depressed children I found many have internal conversations of the following nature:

- "I feel so lousy that I wish everyone would let me alone."
- "School is so bad I don't want anything to do with it."
- "I'm no good."
- "I'm a bad person."
- "I'm so tired that all I want to do is sleep."
- "What's the use of trying, it doesn't do any good."
- "I feel sad all the time."

As a therapist, I worked with many teens. I found periods of unhappiness or sadness to be common. The moods could occur in response to unhappy situations, such as failure on a school test or the loss of a significant relationship. The dejected spells might last for a brief or extended period of time. However, when a sad mood was accompanied by other negative feelings such as fear, guilt, disgust or self-loathing, anxiety, or extreme withdrawal, an adolescent sometimes entertained thoughts of suicide. When that possibility occurred, it became extremely important to get at the reasons for the wish to self-destruct. In my experience, they tended to center around

- worries about sexual identity ("Am I a real man?" "Am I a real woman?");
- concerns about being perfect ("I'm failing my parents' expectations");
- problems in the family ("I'm to blame for my folks breaking up");
- mortification felt about personal inadequacies (e.g., "I'm so ugly, no one likes me").

CHAPTER 17

Poor Anger Control

Poor anger control is a trait described as being the chronic inability to control, repress, or inhibit outbursts of rage. Children with high scores on the poor anger control category of the Burks Behavior Rating Scales (1977a, 2006a) tend to

- become get incensed quickly;
- explode at others;
- be offended by requirements from others;
- fly into a rage under pressure;
- quickly abandon emotional management.

As might be expected, the Burks Behavior Rating Scales (Burks, 2006a) establish the poor anger control scale as being closely associated with the behavioral traits evaluated by the impulsivity scale (see chapter 13). However, the rage that accompanies poor anger control indicates the addition of hostility to the clinical picture. This hostility is difficult for teachers to handle (Burks, 1968a). High scores on the rebelliousness, poor social conformity, social isolation, and aggressive tendencies scales often accompany the traits of poor anger control.

THEORETICAL BACKGROUND

Some aggressive children are frankly angry, and they express hostile impulses with displays of temper in the classroom or on the playground (Munday, 1999). Educators become concerned because an angry child can disrupt learning programs and threaten established systems of rules and regulations (Greene, 2001; Jordan & Goldberg, 2001).

The inability to control outbursts of anger can stem from a variety of influences. Some causal factors are understood by the angry person, some are beyond conscious comprehension and are classified as repressed material, and some spring from internal or external stimuli whose significance may or may not be recognized by the angry person (Johnson & O'Neill, 1999; Verdick & Lisoviskis, 2003; Wyer & Srull, 1993).

The Nature of Anger

Anger is a natural reaction occurring in all people and is present in a wide range of human experiences (Goldberg, 1993). The naturalness of angry feelings belies a commonly accepted attitude that individuals are born either good or bad and that showing hostility is sinful. In truth, neurologists have discovered that people are born with brain centers that impel them to express anger (witness the outrage of frustrated infants), and it is assumed that these groups of brain cells are placed there to help people survive. It is therefore unrealistic to think angry reactions can be eliminated in any individual, and, further, it would be unwise to make such an attempt. Legitimate anger is a powerful motivation to right the wrongs of the world, and it plays a role in spurring individuals to greater achievement.

Factors Promoting Anger

Poor anger control may result from or be aggravated by organic factors, negative environmental conditions, and psychotic disorders. Organic factors include hunger, fatigue, illness, and so on. Such conditions can lower an individual's ability to withstand stress and cause the person to show signs of irritation and anger. Allergies (e.g., to food, pollen, or dust) can cause some children to be fretful or even depressed. ADD children (see chapter 22) are often unable to inhibit the expression of negative emotions (Burks, 1957a, 1960, 1964a, 1968b, 1968c, 1968d, 1977a). Speech-deficient youngsters experience frustration that can be expressed in outbursts of anger.

Negative environmental conditions include excessive smog, heightened barometric pressure, excessive noise, crowded classroom conditions, and anxieties stemming from racial tension. All these negative environmental factors can cause children to feel irritable and make them less work efficient.

Poor anger control may be associated with psychotic disorders. Schizophrenic youngsters are often so anxious that a slight provocation can release intense rage (Clarizio & McCoy, 1976).

The complexity of anger must be understood. A child's demonstrations of hostility can cover up insecurities and anxieties. Further, adults must learn to accept their own hostile feelings toward expressions of child anger along with the fact that they often cannot work effectively with an enraged youngster (Verdick & Lisoviskis, 2003).

Anger and Poor Parental Training Practices

Poor parental training practices emphasize either the suppression or repressive distortion of hostile impulses or encourage forms of overt, socially unacceptable expressions of rage. Various authors have outlined the following unhealthy ways children can be trained to control or express anger (Day, 2002; Revenson, et al., 2005; Veldman & Worchel, 1961).

Repression. "If you get fussy, I'll be very upset." "Don't you dare get mad at me. If you do, you'll get spanked." "I know you're miserable but you'd better put on a happy face." If all expressions of hostile behavior are met with severe parental counteraggression, the child is taught to repress feelings. To maintain an acceptable self-image, the child is compelled to deny any hostility. In short, a facade of self-acceptance is maintained by keeping the self-image congruent with an ideal image that does not express anger. This congruence is affirmed at the psychological expense of continued repression and a posture of high defensiveness (after all, hostile impulses could break out at any time, upsetting the precarious equilibrium between self-image and ideal image). Compared to children trained by other methods, severely repressed children present a socialized appearance and demonstrate the least amount of hostility to the world. However, the psychic energy required to maintain such a neurotic facade can be great. At best, the afflicted child may appear tired and distracted; at worst, psychosomatic illnesses can stem from these internal conflicts.

The psychic energy required to hold negative feelings in check can cause a repressed child to

- appear tired;
- be distracted by internal thoughts;
- have nightmares;
- complain about physical symptoms (aches and pains);
- refuse to fight back when provoked;
- deny feeling angry even when he or she should be upset;
- have trouble sleeping;
- be upset when others show hostility;
- worry;
- cling to high moral standards;
- be sad or depressed.

Highly repressed individuals sometimes erupt in rage. I once counseled a young man who related that he had never talked back to his controlling and demanding mother. Over a period of several weeks he discussed some of his difficulties with her. I received an unusual call from him asking for an emergency appointment; he then came into the office to relate an upsetting event. The previous evening, his mother had burst into his apartment, unannounced, and asked him to drop what he was doing and set the time on a new watch she had just bought. This trivial demand caused him to see red. He screamed at her in rage and finally ordered her to leave. The hidden anger he felt about this controlling parent had suddenly surfaced. He remained shaken, and I could only surmise his mother's state of mind.

So-called perfect children can also suddenly erupt in rage (Chelinsky, 2005; Flett & Hewitt, 2002). I have talked to dismayed parents who had no idea that so much anger resided in their children. When this occurs, symptoms of childhood depression tend to disappear.

These explosions, however, can be used in positive ways. They reveal to involved parties that something is wrong. Feelings of guilt and rage need to be examined, so that new ways of interacting with the angry individual can be explored.

Treatment of the repressed child must proceed in the context of family counseling. The child and his or her parents should be taught to accept the presence of normal aggression in all people and should be instructed that aggressive impulses can and should be expressed in healthy ways (Munday, 1999; J. Johnson and O'Neill, 1999).

Anxiety. "Always smile, even when you're upset. That's what other people want to see." "Don't be a loser. Always try to do better than others. That's a good girl. We're proud of you." "Your uncle never said a bad word to anyone. He just did his best. Why don't you try to be like him? We would like you very much if you did." Children who have been taught to be anxious are likely to see authority figures as threatening (Barlow, 1998). Retaliation cannot be taken against these powerful figures because of an excessive fear of punishment. The self-image and the ideal image are highly incongruent. These children see themselves as weak, bad, and inefficient, while the ideal role held by their parents is seen to be strong, good, and effective. Continued failure to meet ideal standards contributes to an escalation of anxiety, tension, and self-deprecation. However, since anxious children accept their poor self-image, they are not defensive. Hostility is commonly displaced to scapegoat figures perceived to be worthy of scorn.

Anxious children who disguise feelings tend to

- seem fearful;
- be tense and jumpy;
- blush easily;
- be unable to tolerate uncertainty;
- be apprehensive about coming events;
- talk constantly about problems;
- cry often;
- seem sad;
- worry about taking risks;
- have many nervous habits;
- demand help constantly;
- whine constantly;
- be hypersensitive;
- be indecisive and cautious;
- daydream excessively;
- have nervous laughter;
- have tantrums when under stress;
- be mute or have a strained voice under stress.

The worried child comes from an anxious family. The youngster is sometimes made a scapegoat by parents in order to displace their own aggressive feelings. Therapeutic treatment of the anxious family requires time, tact, and professional expertise. School settings (as opposed to some kind of mental health placement) may not offer enough emotional protection for a family suffering neurotic problems of this nature.

Distortion. "Everything is beautiful—all the time!" "Our ancestors were extraordinary." "Our family is the smartest and the best around!" "You are my child, and I can see that you are just about perfect. I know and expect that you will be able to do anything you set your mind to." The child who has been taught to distort reality defends himself or herself against anxiety and tension by rationalizing and distorting. The child maintains a facade of adjustment by asserting, "I'm doing as well as others." As a result, the individual feels above reproach and, therefore, maintains an attitude that is accepted by the child as being congruent with an ideal image. However, this facade is maintained at the expense of high defensiveness. Aggression is occasionally displaced by scapegoating. Those chosen to be scapegoated are regarded as deficient, deviant, or unworthy in order to justify the hostility directed toward them.

Children who distort reality tend to

- be unable to take criticism;
- be tense;
- maintain that everything is okay when that is obviously untrue;
- have rigid deportment;
- act superior;
- employ many excuses;
- blame others;
- deny unpleasant feelings.

Families that employ distortion as a prominent psychological adjustment technique are difficult to treat in therapy because they do not see themselves or their assumptions to be out of the ordinary. School personnel should avoid confrontations with this type of family. Other authorities can be utilized to control its socially unacceptable behavior (e.g., the police can be called in if a family refuses to let a child attend school because of religious or other convictions).

Rebellion. "You never do what we expect you to do. You're a bad boy [girl] and always will be!" "You're going to come to a bad end, Jimmy, just like your father." "Mary, you're the bad seed of the family. That's why you're not getting anything from us!" "Listen, kid, I can keep this fight up longer than you can."

Rebellious children tend to

- be stubborn;
- be sullen;
- refuse to accept discipline;
- deny responsibility for their own actions;
- insist on having their own way;
- refuse to take suggestions;
- be excessively negative;
- reject adult standards;
- react angrily to criticism.

The rebellious child comes from a family offering little nurturance and affection. The family tries to contain the child's impulses with numerous rules, along with rejection when the child does not respond properly to these regulations. Because there is no apparent payoff for behaving properly, the child rebels against those who try to control him or her. To the child, this rebellion seems justified, since the self-image and ideal image appear congruent (at least, insofar as the expression of hostility is concerned). The youngster, therefore, shows no defensiveness about his or her angry posture.

The imperious "prince" or "princess." "Well, all right; I'll give in just this one time. You can have the candy. But remember, next time you make a fuss you will be punished." "I've asked you over and over to be nice. Why won't you be pleasant to me?" "I'm very sorry that I've upset you, but you did do wrong. Don't you see that?" "Well, I tried; God knows I tried, but I guess I'm just not able to control you!"

Royal personalities tend to

- be impatient with the views expressed by others;
- get enraged when crossed;
- throw a tantrum if they can't get their own way;
- have an imperious attitude toward others;
- always demand to be the leader;
- treat others as if they are inferior;
- refuse to take orders;
- demand special favors.

The prince or princess personality may develop when parents are not emotionally strong enough to enforce disciplinary demands. The child can develop an overbearing personality, often showing temper outbursts when his or her requests are denied. The anger is a result of the child's perceived lack of parental caring; the youngster interprets the absence of proper early discipline as evidence that the parents are not interested in his or her welfare and safety. The child may possess an unconscious fear that giving in to others is dangerous; unlike most children, he or she has not been taught that submitting to regulations enforced by an angry person (in this case, a parent) can be a safe avenue. Finally, the child's anger may result from an inability to understand how individuals should act when forced to conform; the child has not been given the opportunity to learn proper submission coping skills.

The dynamics of an imperious personality structure require

- defensiveness (people around the child may not tolerate being treated like "subjects"; they may rebel and cause the child distress);
- a facade of self-acceptance (i.e., "I am the proper person to dispense authority");
- a congruent self-image and ideal image (i.e., "I do not show anger except when crossed and then my anger is justified");
- the notion that other authority figures are dangerous (i.e., "They may make me submit").

Interestingly, many imperious children who enter therapy in adulthood are surprised to realize that they were not well disciplined as children. Initially, they complain bitterly about parents who overcontrolled them, but such overcontrol can mean that the parents expected them to perform but were disappointed in their achievement. The parents' distress, however, was not accompanied by firm disciplinary measures. This lack of discipline left unconscious fears about submission and uncomfortable feelings about perceived parental disappointments. All of which, of course, represent unfinished psychological business that can hamper an individual's ability to mature.

When delineating the imperious person, it can be pointed out he or she is vulnerable to taunts and ridicule from those tired of the arrogant conduct. It's also worth noting that lordly individuals seldom become criminals (they are too afraid of being controlled). Because their parents lavished early attention upon them they are capable of showing affection.

Overbearing children and their parents generally prove amenable to counseling. The parents are genuinely interested in their child's progress and will respond to school requests with alacrity. Also, the love (distorted as it might be) that the parents have lavished upon the child tends to provide the youngster with considerable ego security. This beneficial self-regard allows the youngster to withstand disappointment when attempts are made to correct the imperious conduct.

Ventilation. "Don't anyone interrupt me when I get mad!" "Who says I can't get mad whenever I want?" "Shut up. When I'm pissed off, everybody better get out of the way!" Children who ventilate express anger openly and frequently, along with a lack of concern for the effect this hostility has on others, tend to come from families who believe in the beneficial effects of airing aggressive feelings.

Children who express anger openly and frequently, with no concern for the feelings of others, tend to

- be verbally aggressive;
- speak in a harsh, abrupt manner;
- seem angry at everything and everybody;
- be openly critical of others;
- lose control when they get angry;
- be impatient with the mistakes of others;
- enjoy expressing negative emotions;
- get very frustrated if told to be quiet.

Although some inhibited, neurotic youngsters benefit from release of angry feelings, Berkowitz (1973) presented evidence that ventilating violent emotions simply strengthens the tendency to behave fiercely, weakens whatever inhibitions the individual does possess, and reinforces acting-out behavior. If teachers and/or parents allow or encourage a child to reduce tension by expressing hostility quickly, they are simply rewarding the expression of rage. Further, they allow the youngster to experience the pleasure of injuring his or her "enemies," which simply strengthens the desire to injure others in the future. The child is not purged of hostile impulses; instead, he or she becomes even more aggressive. Berkowitz further believes that aggressive fantasies (prompted by television, stories, and pictures) encourage a greater degree of aggression. Finally, the individual who is allowed to ventilate feelings of hostility whenever he or she likes ends up acting on aggressive impulses without proper fear and anxiety. Anxiety and guilt, when in conjunction with hostility, are favorable signs in a child. Acting-out youngsters need stronger, not weaker, controls.

Manipulation. "I know you got a good grade in reading but you could do better. What if I gave you a prize for getting an A next time?" "Why don't you go tell your father what it was that made me so mad?" "I forgot to get a babysitter, so would you mind, just this one time, staying home from your scout meeting to look after your little brother?" Manipulation of others is a device to get what is wanted by avoiding more direct but feared confrontation.

Children who manipulate others tend to

- have trouble cooperating with authority;
- procrastinate;
- be suspicious of others' motivations;
- be passive;
- argue when given orders;
- be resentful of the wishes of others;
- pretend to be cooperative but often are not.

As usual, parents are the model for the controlling child; manipulative mothers and fathers often produce a scheming child. I once counseled a mother whose usual response to stress was to become overly emotional, a reaction she probably hoped would force others either to look after her or leave her alone. She had come into counseling because her son, Bill, was constantly throwing tantrums and delivering tirades in order to get his way. At first, she saw no connection between her conduct and his. The goal of counseling was to help her to realize Bill could not change until she changed.

Parental manipulation can be both benign and harmful to children. In the early years of child development, mothers and fathers must employ techniques that maneuver children into adopting socially acceptable behavior. As children grow older, however, they can be expected to handle daily affairs with less and less direction from adults. For older children, the following parental behavior would be considered unhealthy manipulation:

- The parents insist that the child play a role that denies the youngster opportunities to develop his or her personality fully. For example, a mother, in the absence of a spouse and because of her dependency needs, may demand that a growing son act as her parent, thereby depriving him of chances to act in age-normal ways. She might accomplish this by approving all of her son's conduct that seems strong and authoritative and by disapproving all of his childlike behavior.
- The parents demand that the child fulfill unmet needs of the parents. These requirements, of course, can be endless. The adults in question may feel that they never accomplished enough in school, or never got the social approbation they felt they deserved, or never received the affection due them, or never reaped economic rewards like friends, or whatever. These inadequacies rankle. Now that they have a smart (in their eyes) child, they can get that youngster to compensate for their perceived insufficiencies. They will show love when the child acts in a desirable manner and demonstrate rejection when the behavior is seen as unhealthy. Of course, the child comes to feel he or she is in a precarious position: "I get love if I accomplish; I lose affection when I don't measure up." The usual outcome is a frustrated parent and an insecure and angry child.
- The parents force upon the child all the unwanted characteristics of the family. The untoward effects of this kind of maneuver are generally unrecognized by other family members because it seems to them to be appropriate—the chosen individual deserves disapproval. What is not acknowledged, of course, is that the person has come to act just as he or she is expected to ("You're a rotten person—look, you're acting stinky right now!").

Most chronic displays of child anger are rooted in family practices. An astute diagnostician will particularly note the mother's behavior: How permissive is she about her child's aggressive practices? Does she allow the child to direct anger at her freely, or does she suppress it quickly? How does she administer punishment for hostile, lasting rage in the child?

Both anxious and acting-out children express anger in inappropriate ways. Fortunately, most youngsters are taught acceptable ways to adjust. The child with a more wholesome adaptation (a) has a relatively congruent self-image and ideal image, (b) tends not to be defensive, (c) accepts hostility as a normal occurrence, and (d) does not see authority figures as threatening. Families producing adjusted children tend to possess the emotional freedom to express proper restraint when needed and to show anger when appropriate.

DIAGNOSIS

Environmental Factors Leading to Anger

Just as for adults, a great number of things make children angry. These can include

- being teased;
- being disliked;
- not being able to do the work at school;
- not being listened to;
- being called a sissy;
- being chosen last in games;
- being cheated;

- being ordered around too much;
- being unable to express feelings;
- being bullied;
- having no friends;
- not getting attention;
- not getting to play enough;
- not having enough toys;
- fighting with brothers and sisters;
- hearing too many arguments around the house;
- going to the doctor;
- getting shots;
- being alone in the dark;
- being interrupted;
- not getting to see your favorite television programs;
- not getting enough parental attention;
- having too many rules and regulations;
- not having enough time to play with friends;
- having too many chores;
- always being told that you could do better than you are doing;
- not understanding what is expected of you;
- not being understood;
- people thinking you don't know anything;
- not having enough fun;
- being punished too much;
- brothers and sisters not leaving your things alone.

When interviewing angry children, counselors may find the preceding list helpful (but are urged to expect constructive outcomes only from children who wish to cooperate).

Additional diagnostic assistance may be derived from the Child Anger questionnaire (see figure 17.1), which I constructed for counselors' use when interviewing children. The questionnaire does not, of course, cover all causes for childhood anger. Clinicians should explore other leads revealed during postinterview discussions.

I limited the questionnaire to those areas of emotional pain that could most often cause a child to feel resentful or enraged, inferior, vulnerable, humiliated, or overcontrolled.

It is hoped that discussing the child's responses to the questionnaire (and any other issues that may arise during the conversation) will result in a lessening of tension, but that positive consequence is not, in itself, enough; attempts must be made to change undesirable circumstances mentioned by the child. The counselor may not be able to realize this objective, but the youngster must see that an attempt is made to accomplish alterations.

Other Factors Associated with Anger

We may assume that angry children (as well as adults, of course) sometimes experience difficulties in attaining desired goals and in being able to escape or avoid unpleasant situations. Consequently, youngsters may typically verbalize some of the following statements (among many that could be imagined) to themselves:

- "Nobody let's me do what I want."
- "I'm always afraid the teacher will call on me to read aloud."
- "I need friends but the kids don't like me."
- "Mom and Dad make me obey too many rules."

CHILD ANGER QUESTIONNAIRE

Harold F. Burks, Ph.D.

Read the following questions and put a check mark in the column that best describes how you feel.

Feeling Inferior or Vulnerable

	Never	Sometimes	Often
1. Do you think you are doing well with your classwork?	☐	☐	☐
2. Do you think your teacher likes you?	☐	☐	☐
3. Are you ever chosen to be a leader in the classroom?	☐	☐	☐
4. Do you think the classwork is too hard?	☐	☐	☐
5. Do you think the other kids are interested in what you do?	☐	☐	☐
6. Are the other kids interested in your hobbies?	☐	☐	☐
7. Do you think your mom and dad are interested in what you do?	☐	☐	☐
8. Do the other kids think you play games well?	☐	☐	☐
9. Do the other kids talk to you enough?	☐	☐	☐
10. Do you think the other kids have more money than you do?	☐	☐	☐
11. Do you think you have more problems than most other people?	☐	☐	☐
12. Do you have friends?	☐	☐	☐
13. Do you think the other kids like you?	☐	☐	☐
14. Do the other kids want to help you?	☐	☐	☐
15. Is there anybody in your house that makes you feel bad?	☐	☐	☐
16. Do you think you get enough attention at home?	☐	☐	☐
17. Do you think you are as big and strong as the rest of the kids?	☐	☐	☐
18. Are you ever unhappy about what you wear?	☐	☐	☐

Feeling Humiliated

19. Does the teacher ever say things to you that make you feel bad?	☐	☐	☐
20. Does anybody bully you at school or at home?	☐	☐	☐
21. Are you sometimes afraid of the other kids?	☐	☐	☐
22. Do the other kids ever take your things?	☐	☐	☐
23. Are the kids at school too bossy?	☐	☐	☐
24. Do the other kids make fun of you?	☐	☐	☐
25. Do the other kids tease you?	☐	☐	☐
26. Do the other kids play fair?	☐	☐	☐
27. Has anybody made you feel mad because of the way you look?	☐	☐	☐
28. Do you ever feel bad because you are not chosen to play games?	☐	☐	☐
29. Does anybody make you feel bad because of the way you talk?	☐	☐	☐
30. Does anybody tease you because of the way you do things?	☐	☐	☐
31. Is it easy for you to make friends?	☐	☐	☐
32. Do you ever get to be a leader at school or in the neighborhood?	☐	☐	☐
33. Is there anything that happens at home that makes you mad?	☐	☐	☐

Feeling Overcontrolled

34. Do you think your mom bosses you too much?	☐	☐	☐
35. Do you think your dad bosses you too much?	☐	☐	☐
36. Does anybody else at home boss you too much?	☐	☐	☐
37. Do you think the kids at school are too bossy?	☐	☐	☐
38. Do you think the teacher is too bossy?	☐	☐	☐
39. Do you think there are too many rules at home?	☐	☐	☐
40. Do you think there are too many rules at school?	☐	☐	☐
41. Do you think the punishments at home for breaking rules are too hard?	☐	☐	☐
42. Do you think the punishments at school for breaking rules are too hard?	☐	☐	☐
43. Do you think you hardly ever get to do what you want?	☐	☐	☐

Figure 17.1.

- "There are a lot of scary bullies in my school and they make me afraid."
- "People keep expecting me to do things I can't do."
- "When I try to tell people how I feel, they don't listen."

Early adolescents (12 to 14 years of age) show temporary rebellious traits. They are trying to assert autonomy by resisting adult authority. This is an insecure time in life—youngsters are still dependent but they increasingly want personal freedom. Parents can wait out this rebellious period by being patient and understanding. Family conflicts ordinarily tend to be resolved rapidly and are not associated with chronic and pervasive dissatisfaction with family relationships. Most of the time, a more compatible parent-child relationship eventually evolves.

Severe parent-child conflicts, on the other hand, usually last a considerable period of time and are often characterized by

- verbal disagreements—often ugly and repetitious;
- unworkable attempts at agreement—arguments that fail to produce satisfactory outcomes; continuing disputes over the same things;
- lasting anger—combatants remain bitter about difficult issues;
- chronic dissatisfaction—family members are chronically upset about family difficulties, relationships, and the conduct of others.

INTERVENTION STRATEGIES

Techniques for School Personnel

The following methods can be used successfully in the classroom to help students control anger:

1. Anticipate and avoid situations that tend to arouse anger.
2. Designate a time-out room as a place where an angry child can simmer down. Do not reward children placed there with pleasurable experiences; they should feel somewhat isolated. Explain that when children have angry outbursts, they will be placed in the isolation room. The teacher should try not to behave angrily. Once the time-out procedure has been established, it is important to follow through consistently. A child should not be left standing in a hallway or other public place to cool off—contact with passersby will provide too much positive reinforcement to the angry child.
3. Enlist the aid of the parents when necessary, and explain to them what you are trying to do for the child. If possible, however, the problem should be handled in the classroom.
4. Reward the child when he or she copes without anger, but make sure such rewards do not set the angry child apart from the other children.
5. Explain situations to a student who is easily frustrated by the unknown.
6. Do not give an angry child special consideration as the result of a tantrum—to do so reinforces hostile behavior. In the beginning, deal with angry outbursts by measures less severe than expulsion from the classroom. Exclusion should be a final step.
7. Separate fighting children quickly to try to prevent more serious antagonism.
8. Provide a highly structured environment for students who are easily irritated by contact with others.
9. Avoid harsh punishment, particularly physical punishment. The teacher is a model, and his or her aggressive behavior will be emulated by the child. Physical restraint of a child may be necessary at times, but it is best done out of sight of the other children.
10. Do not force the child to complete a task he or she is poorly equipped to do. Some small children, in particular, are easily frustrated by challenging motor and intellectual tasks. If possible, place the child in situations where there is sufficient time to complete easier assignments and where adults are patient.

11. Seat the angry child next to a more friendly and stable peer.
12. Allow the child to ventilate anger on objects (e.g., hammering nails, pounding clay) rather than other people.
13. Use a modified school program (e.g., a shortened day) for students who tire quickly.
14. Investigate the student's physiological status. A child who has angry outbursts may do so because of poor nutrition, a slow-maturing nervous system, or a physical ailment.
15. Assign special jobs you know the child is good at and can complete successfully.
16. Employ vocabulary well understood by the child and speak softly.
17. Offer the child a way out of an aggravating situation.
18. Do not allow the child to play with materials he or she can use to hurt others.
19. Place the child in small groups.
20. Avoid physical-contact games.

Techniques for Parents

Dealing with illogical beliefs. Because adolescents have neither the inclination nor the power to reconstruct af-filiations, parents must initiate efforts to improve family relationships. Unfortunately, many parents of angry ado-lescents cling to rigid, perhaps unrealistic and illogical, child-raising beliefs that run contrary to what is known about human nature (Scott, 2002). Counselors who work with parents of teens should be aware that some belief systems are difficult to penetrate because people believe them so deeply—everybody grew up with people who knew the "right" ways to do things. Consider the following illogical parental beliefs and suggested responses:

My teenager is required to do everything I ask. If my orders are not followed, the child faces ruination. Looking back, did you do everything your parents asked of you? Did any acts of disobedience on your part have terrible outcomes? Are you demanding total obedience from your child because you are perhaps unsure of your own authority? Do you think that if you don't get complete adherence to rules you will lose the respect of your youngster?

Everything is my fault. Any mistakes my child makes are the result of my ignorance. Oh, if only I had been smarter! Are you the only one who has influenced your child? Must you accept full responsibility for every action taken? At this point in time, can you be anything but a guide or an adviser?

Our teenager is out to get us and wants to make us irritated or mad—just for revenge! Are you giving your child too much credit? Teens ordinarily don't plan in advance to misbehave. In addition, they seldom think much about the needs of adults.

By this time, my teenager should be mature and use good judgment and behave correctly. Even adults make errors in judgment, and your youngster is not an adult yet. Like everybody else, teenagers stumble occasionally and then learn from their mistakes.

My kid was born bad—it runs in my spouse's side of the family, and that causes the kid to misbehave. This can be a dangerous line of thinking. It gets you off the hook (you're certainly not to blame for your spouse's bad genes) while, at the same time, it leaves your child swinging in the wind (believing in some kind of inherited de-fect beyond his or her control).

Teenagers can also cling to unrealistic beliefs:

It's just plain unfair. My parents have no right to make me obey rules. Suggested answer: Since you are un-derage, your parents are legally responsible for what you do. Anyway, life is never totally fair.

I'm old enough to run my own life. I know what I'm doing and should have the liberty to do whatever I want. Suggested answer: No person, young or old, has total freedom to act in any way he or she desires. Do you give your parents freedom like that or do you sometimes demand they help you with time and money? Is it possi-ble they know some things you do not, and isn't it their desire as well as their duty to guide you in positive ways?

If I do what my parents want, the other kids will laugh at me. Their house rules will ruin my life because they'll stop me from seeing my friends and from acting like other kids. I'll never have a good time. Suggested answer: Hold everything! Can you think of a time when a parental rule cost you friends or prevented you from acting like the other kids? Is your life really miserable because of home regulations (or would you just like to get out of some chores)?

It's just terrible that I upset my parents. My behavior should be perfect! Suggested answer: You're too hard on yourself—nobody's perfect.

Investigating Parental Behavior

Counselors may use the following questions and suggested responses to investigate parental behavior that leads to poorly controlled conduct in children. The questions were designed for use in parent conferences to spark parents' interest in the problems of their angry youngsters and to give parents specific information to assist them in changing their own behavior. Counselors might explore the parents' motivation, investigate the ways they handle their children, and discuss at length other methods that could have a better chance of success (Englander, 2001).

Do you set unrealistically high standards for your child? Children who constantly feel they fail to meet their parents' expectations can become withdrawn, ashamed, or angry. Anger (as opposed to depression) is perhaps the healthiest reaction to pressure; it indicates that the youngster has not given up and is fighting back at perceived as persecutors. Long-lasting anger, however, is not conducive to healthy parent-child relationships. If a child reacts in chronically negative ways then it may be a good idea to lower home standards.

Do you surround your child with many rules and regulations? Home laws are necessary, but if a child is reacting to restrictions in a hostile manner, perhaps the restrictions should be loosened.

Do you react consistently to your child's infractions? Assuming that disciplinary demands are reasonable, children who are given consistent consequences for rule violations tend to be calmer than those who are treated inconsistently. If a child's misbehavior results in harsh discipline on one occasion and no response another time, the child is left in a state of ongoing tension and irritation. The youngster never knows what consequences to expect, resulting in anxious dependency on the parent (i.e., the child must try to read the adult's mood).

Do you teach your child to respect the rights of others (e.g., to wait his or her turn, to abide by the rules of games, to show respect for adults, and so on)? Suggested answer: Unless trained to think otherwise, children do not understand that it is impermissible to express strong emotions in the presence of others whenever an impulse strikes.

Do you demonstrate you can lose gracefully? Children who observe adults that can accept defeat without undue irritation tend not to be too upset when they experience a loss.

Do you respond calmly to your child's temper outbursts? Parents who lose their temper and strike their child will soon see offspring hitting smaller youngsters; adult yelling will elicit child yelling, and so on.

Do you express anger openly and frequently, with no concern for its effect on others? Carrying on in front of children presents them with an unsatisfactory role model. They will, in turn, assume it is permissible to throw tantrums. If parents get something they want by a temper outburst, their children, in turn, will endeavor to control others by showing anger.

Does it make you furious if someone disagrees with you? Strong emotion tends to disrupt intelligent communication. The furious person cannot use or listen to reasonable facts or logic. Teach your child to accept criticism calmly.

Do you think it is a bad idea to hold in angry feelings? Some emotions should be expressed; others held in. Disturbing feelings can be vented later, under suitable conditions. It is important to teach children to use good judgment regarding the display of feelings.

Do you become enraged when someone tries to control you? Many who were not well disciplined as children grow up intolerant of controls. It has been found that they were raised by vacillating and unsure parents. Be firm with your kids but also show them you can back down and change your behavior when you're in the wrong.

Do you have good ways to let your anger out (like engaging in sports or talking things over with friends)? Legitimate avenues for letting out emotional feelings are important. Encourage your child not only to acknowledge strong emotions but to express them in acceptable ways.

Do you think the way to get what you want is to show anger? Parents may not realize they may control others with anger. Anger can take the form of tantrums, sulking, refusing to cooperate, physical aggression, and so on. Both open and more subtle forms of hostility are then copied by offspring.

Do you use sarcasm, swearing, or teasing around your child? These verbal practices are all forms of displaced anger, used when people cannot safely demonstrate physical hostility. Teasing is especially difficult for a child to handle, especially when it is presented as "just good fun."

Do you show impatience with others' shortcomings? Children must be taught that expressed anger sometimes alienates others. Further, they must recognize they possess deficiencies others must tolerate.

When you become angry, do you sulk, isolate yourself, or refuse to speak to others? These are forms of temper tantrums observed and emulated by children. Pouting is a way of punishing others for alleged crimes, leaving the room can be a way of running away from problems, and silence is a difficult defense to penetrate—it inflicts suffering on others. These immature methods of handling anger can be replaced with better techniques. For instance, hostile feelings can be talked over with others at an agreed-upon time (usually when passions have cooled).

Do you often criticize your child's conduct? Exposing a child to criticism is not recommended. Angry children often possess poor self-images made worse when others point out shortcomings.

Do you hold grudges? Cherished resentments are devices used to extract revenge upon others who supposedly caused physical or emotional injury. The designated guilty party may or may not know what it is he or she did (often revenge is sweeter when the guilty party is at a loss to understand causes). Grudges can be destructive. They create unequal relationships. The injured party, by definition, is a victim who is entitled to payment from the supposed aggressor. Grudge-carrying adults quickly teach their children the power ploys involved in this social arrangement. Of course, when all is said and done, both the alleged tormentor and the injured party often end up feeling like resentful victims.

When confronting your child, do you do all the talking? Few people enjoy sitting in the company of someone who pontificates; listeners tend to get angry and mentally shut the speaker out. A one-way speech is not a dialogue. Doing all the talking may make the speaker feel better but the message can easily become lost. Try listening—you might learn something!

When confronting your child, do you tend to use grandiose, abstract terminology (e.g., "There is no doubt about it, you do not honor the rights of others and, consequently, others feel resentment . . .")? Keep directions simple, clear, and direct—for example, "I don't like it when you ignore me." Most young children do not comprehend complicated adult concepts. Further, such abstractions often fail to convey the emotional impact needed to get the message across to a child. A statement like "Your present conduct is unacceptable in civilized societies, and it is our urgent intent to persuade you to act differently" does not impress like "Knock it off; I don't like what you're doing."

Do you tend to make crises appear catastrophic (e.g., "If you go on as you're doing, this family will be ruined!")? Try saying something like "Sometimes, when you don't do your chores, other family members get upset." Overstating feelings is a bit like the boy who cried wolf. After awhile others may discount the messages because the events giving rise to the outbursts do not seem to match the resulting distress. At worst, cries of pain simply annoy and irritate others.

Do you tend to "put down" your youngster's ideas (e.g., "Get a maid to do all the odd jobs? That's the dumbest thing I've ever heard!")? Try a less offensive approach—for example, "Sorry, we can't afford a maid." Ignoring or scoffing at a child's thoughts can have two unfortunate consequences:

1. It can make the youngster resentful.
2. It can lower the child's self-respect.

Listen to the child. Treat offered thoughts kindly even though they appear inconsequential. Much is at stake here. Treating a child respectfully causes both the child and the adult to feel more esteemed.

Does your body language indicate impatience? The following behaviors are irritating at best; at worst, they can make a child angry.

- moving about restlessly;
- avoiding direct eye contact;
- answering too quickly (reflect on your response);
- towering over the youngster (lower yourself to his or her level);
- jumping from one topic to another;
- indicating that you have another agenda that is more important;
- gazing away as if you are losing concentration;
- interrupting;
- failing to pay attention as the child speaks;
- neglecting to thank the child for his or her contributions.

Do you often imply that you can read your child's mind? If you want to irritate somebody, try implying that you are omnipotent enough to read their thoughts. For example, "Wait. Don't tell me. I know by your crude remarks that you're really just trying to spoil my day." It would be less offensive to say, "Are you trying to upset me on purpose?" Do not claim the ability to divine the thoughts of others. Simply state your feelings and ask the youngster why he or she is acting unacceptably.

Do you dwell on your child's past mistakes? Nobody likes to be reminded of past poor performance. To do so brings shame to the listener. Concentrate on present activities. Bring in the future when it is important to point out the consequences of current behavior, but make these predictions realistic.

Do you belabor your case when admonishing your child (e.g., "Two days ago you didn't do your chores. Yesterday I caught you lying. Today you look a mess. I don't know what to do with you . . .")? It would be more effective to say, "Let's explore together why we can't communicate." Overstating your position turns people off and your main message gets lost. Good intentions (the desire to help your child) do not excuse such behavior. If an adult has something to say to a child, it should be said simply and clearly.

Do you belittle your child (e.g., "You never seem to do anything right! There must be something wrong with you! Why can't you behave?")? Most such accusations are difficult to refute. A better approach might be to say, "I get upset when you don't do your chores." Comparing a child's behavior to some idealized standard of conduct can leave the youngster feeling downgraded, guilty, and helpless to do anything positive about the situation. Worse, the child may experience resentment at being forced to concentrate on inadequate measures rather than on ways to improve behavior.

Tips for Good Communication

After reviewing the preceding questions, counselors should remind parents that good communication and the willingness to cooperate are key goals in parent-child interactions. The Community Boards of San Francisco (Olin, 1996) offer the following 10 suggestions for managing potential family conflicts:

1. Be direct. Direct conversation is much more effective than general complaints, angry remarks, pleas, and so on.
2. Choose a good time to talk. Try to talk in a quiet place where both of you can be comfortable and undisturbed for as long as the discussion takes. Don't engage the other person just as he or she is leaving or after a terrible day.
3. Plan ahead. Think out what it is you want to say ahead of time. State the problem clearly and explain how it affects you.
4. Don't blame or name-call. Avoid antagonizing the other person.
5. Give information. Don't interpret or judge the other person's behavior. Instead, give information about your own situation and feelings and how the other person's behavior affects you.
6. Listen. Allow the other person time to tell his or her side of the story. Relax; try to learn how the other person feels.

7. Demonstrate that you are listening. Even though you may not agree with what is being discussed, tell the other person that you hear him or her and are glad that you are talking the problem over together.

8. Talk problems all the way through. Get all the issues and feelings into the open. Don't leave out parts that seem too difficult to discuss.

9. Work on joint solutions. Two or more people cooperating are much more effective than one person instructing another to change. Be specific. "I will do my homework before watching television" is better than "I will try to do better at homework."

10. Follow through. Agree to check with each other to make sure the arrangements discussed are working.

Helping the Unusually Conflicted Family

Counseling sessions with parents and children who are unusually hostile toward one another often are difficult. The parents will assume that the counselor, in an effort to control the child's willful conduct, will side with them against the youngster. The counselor, who wants to help the parents regain disciplinary control, may be tempted to acquiesce. It is a therapeutic mistake, however, to allow the child to see the counselor as an ally of the parents. The child (usually a teenager who is large enough and strong enough to challenge the parents) is often too angry, too cynical, and too hopeless about the home situation to allow himself or herself to give in to authority figures. In fact, the counselor may be perceived as an enemy who must be frustrated at all costs. Since the youngster and the parents are skilled at knowing how to frustrate each other, neither side will back down gracefully. Some parents do not understand how to control an angry child. Many act that way themselves.

To assist the family, school personnel can suggest the parents (a) attend school-sponsored group meetings where anger-control problems are discussed under the tutelage of a professional, (b) seek out a therapist skilled in family counseling practices, or (c) consider sending the child to a special school away from home. The therapist might ask the parents to abstain from adult-child confrontations for a specific period of time (e.g., two months) to allow the counselor an opportunity to make a friendly alliance with the youngster. This course of action is feasible only when the parents have trust and confidence in the therapist's abilities. If a determination is made that a solution of the parent-child problems is not possible within the context of the family, the therapist may suggest that the child be allowed to live with a relative for a period of time.

CHAPTER 18

Excessive Sense of Persecution

Distrustfulness is best described as the outward expression of an unusual feeling of being mistreated. Children with high scores on the persecution scale of the Burks Behavior Rating Scales (BBRS) (Burks, 1977a, 2006a) tend to

- claim others pick on them;
- complain that they never get a fair share of things;
- hold grudges;
- accuse others of things they did not do;
- complain that others dislike them;
- have high, even unrealistic aspirations;
- hypersensitivity to criticisms;
- a craving for recognition;
- have little sense of humor;
- have an aloof manner.

Studies of large groups of students (Burks, 1977a, 2006a) indicate a wide variety of children show persecution symptoms. One group of children with high scores on the BBRS poor social conformity and rebelliousness scales also tended to feel picked on. Many of them also had high scores on the poor anger control and aggressive tendencies scales. Teachers said these youngsters tended not to have symptoms measured by the dependency, anxiousness, poor motivation, or withdrawal scales. Generally, youngsters with high scores on the persecution scale are antisocial and lack the ability to blame themselves for disruptive behavior. In short, they will not accept responsibility for their misconduct, tending instead to put the blame on someone else.

Another group of children who demonstrated persecutory feelings were described by teachers as showing symptoms measured by the academic difficulties, attention deficits, poor coordination, impulsivity, and poor motivation and intellectual scales. Apparently, such students are demonstrating slow physical and mental maturation.

Some children with neurological handicaps (Burks, 1968b, 1968c, 1968d) seem unable to relate well to other students and their unpleasant social experiences have made them afraid of others. This fear is translated into the attitude that someone is out to get them.

THEORETICAL BACKGROUND

To define distrustfulness as a pattern of behavior is not easy (Munro, 1999; Keen, 1996). Behind feelings of persecution lie other negative emotions—poor self-concept, aggression, and anxiety. Children who feel persecuted tend to be distressed, angry, and fearful. Experience has taught them to feel this way (Tiedens & Leach, 2005; Webster-Stratton & Herbert, 1994).

Rotter (1980) has chronicled some characteristics of individuals with differing levels of trust. Compared to people with low levels of trust, those who are very trusting are less likely to lie and probably less likely to cheat or steal. They are less inclined to be unhappy, conflicted, or maladjusted. They are more likely to give others a second chance, respect the rights of others, and be sought out as friends. Trusting people are also not more gullible than those who are not.

Suspicious or fearful children may find that friends are hard to acquire. Worse, their behavior may turn others against them. Social outcasts become more distrustful, and feelings of inferiority worsen. If the student is doing poorly at school, he or she will tend to defend against accepting responsibility for failure by blaming others and twisting reality to suit his or her needs. This type of child needs teacher assistance.

Occasionally, an adolescent with feelings of persecution may demonstrate classical signs of paranoia. J. C. Coleman (1979) listed the following symptoms:

* high, even unrealistic, aspirations;
* hypersensitivity to censure;
* craving for applause and recognition;
* overly critical of others;
* aloof behavior toward others;
* strict and formal adherence to socially approved conduct;
* lack of a sense of humor.

Such youngsters must be handled with care. The brittle nature of their defense system warns of a deeper pathology. One may expect such a child to demonstrate, under sufficient stress, a break with reality. The following account of a teenage boy, brought to counseling by his parents because he lacked friends, illustrates this possibility.

Al, the 17-year-old son of a ranking military officer, entered therapy readily. Al's ambition was to become an Army parachutist when he turned 18 and then quickly become a hero, outdoing his father. Early therapy sessions consisted of the counselor's listening to this youngster's well-organized but rather unrealistic plans.

After a therapeutic alliance had been established, it was suggested that Al join an adolescent counseling group. The boy agreed. Although the other participants accepted Al, they never ceased being suspicious of his motives, actions, and goals. He contributed to discussions but often at an esoteric level. He never formed a close relationship with another group member. In fact, he held them off with his aloof and hypercritical manner. When they questioned his plans to go into the service, he reacted without humor. This pedantic demeanor soon taught the other members not to challenge him—they just shrugged and smiled as if to say, "There goes Al again!"

Al valued the group, however, and when he left after a year's attendance, he bid them farewell with a little speech in which he said he "would never forget them." After graduating from high school, Al joined a parachute unit but could not take the pressures of the program. When he showed signs of suffering a psychotic break, he was placed in a military hospital and was eventually given a medical discharge. Later, he reentered therapy and also received continuing medical treatment.

This case is recounted in some detail because it parallels others seen by school counselors—cases in which youngsters with fragile, paranoid personalities have difficulty making it into adulthood. Typically, their parents expect them to snap out of it and continue to have high aspirations for their child. When it becomes apparent the youngster has serious problems, the parents usually want to treat the difficulties within home confines. This action should be discouraged. The parents are too much a part of the child's problems; they cannot be expected to maintain an objective viewpoint and their own defenses will be overwhelmed by the child's needs.

INTERVENTION STRATEGIES

Techniques for School Personnel

Educators may take the following steps to help children with expressed feelings of persecution:

1. Make a diagnosis to determine the sources of the child's fears and suspicions. If other children frighten him or her, remove the youngster from their presence.
2. Avoid confrontations with this type of child, even when the youngster makes statements that are obviously untrue. Accept the allegations and later, when things have become calmer, point out to the child, in private, the realities of the situation.
3. Determine whether the student thinks he or she is persecuted by a teacher. If this turns out to be the case, ask what other teacher he or she would prefer—then move the child to that classroom.
4. Structure the student's work carefully and watch for negative reactions. If the child builds resentments, take him or her aside quietly and try to find out what is wrong. Endeavor to convince the child you are on his or her side. Do not become angry; this kind of child is used to dealing with angry people and can defeat them.
5. Attempt to become an ally. If the student can trust one person deeply, he or she may trust others.
6. Arrange situations where the student knows what is expected of him or her. Do not pressure the child if resentments build. Divert the child to another task.
7. Remove the student from the classroom if his or her antagonism upsets other youngsters. Always inform the parents about these actions.
8. Discuss problems with the student in a friendly manner. Find out whether the child realizes that he or she constantly accuses others. Explain how others react to these accusations.
9. Role-play a typical school situation that arouses objections from the child. Let the accusing youngster play the part of a student he or she dislikes.
10. Follow up on child complaints. Sometimes a grievance is justified. Some children, for instance, are picked on by other students for one reason or another. If these injustices are discussed with the student, it is important that the teacher do something about them.
11. Praise the child more often for work well done.

Techniques for Parents

School personnel should confer with parents of children who feel persecuted. If the parents show a willingness to cooperate, discuss methods of making the child feel more adequate, of how they deal with the child's complaints, and of how they apply discipline. Consider the possibility that another child in the home or in the neighborhood is tormenting the youngster. Also, investigate the parents' attitudes toward the child—they may be oversympathetic. Do they feel persecuted by the school or the community? If they do, the prognosis for helping the child becomes less favorable. If they say the child not only complains of being persecuted but also seeks out situations where others punish him or her, the seriousness of the case and the need for professional assistance becomes more certain. If there is evidence the child is being abused or mistreated in the home, further investigative efforts must be made by the school or another agency.

CHAPTER 19

Excessive Aggressiveness

Aggressive tendencies describe the desire to inflict undue injury on others through words or actions. Children with high scores on the aggressive scale of the Burks Behavior Rating Scales (BBRS) (Burks, 1977a, 2006a) tend to

- tease others;
- laugh at others' problems;
- hit others;
- make fun of others;
- boss others;
- play tricks on others.

Many children with high aggressive scores also demonstrate a large number of other pathological signs, indicated by high scores on the poor motivation, excessive sense of persecution, poor reality contact, and poor social conformity scales. Typically, children with these symptoms do not score high on withdrawal, self-blame, dependency, excessive anxiety, poor self-esteem, or social isolation BBRS scales, but any or all of these defensive traits can be shown to some extent in conjunction with evidence of unusual aggression.

THEORETICAL BACKGROUND

Overly aggressive conduct in children concerns parents and teachers. When a child is referred to a behavior specialist for assistance, the most likely complaint is that the child inappropriately acts out impulses. Parents may report that the child will not obey rules; teachers say that the student upsets classroom routines; brothers, sisters, and classmates say they are afraid of the child (Berkowitz, 1993a; Tate, Reppucci, & Mulvey, 1995; Webster-Stratton & Herbert, 1994).

The initial reaction of most individuals is to strike back at the aggressive youngster, but retaliation is an extremely limited behavior-changing technique. It may be effective temporarily but it tends not to have long-lasting effects. Adults should seek to understand the reasons for the child's offensive conduct, channel aggression into more harmless areas, and find more efficient ways to control, contain, and diminish its impact.

The appearance of uncontrolled aggression in most very young children is not entirely unexpected. The youngster has not yet learned how to contain impulses. In older children, the inability to control and inhibit aggression suggests that they are socially immature and cannot handle frustration in acceptable ways (Osofsky, 1995; Rakos, 1991).

Aggressive behavior is a direct consequence of frustration. It is probably the most fundamental reaction to conflict. Since all persons experience discord, all are frustrated at times. Some thwarting is desirable because it raises energy levels and produces better achievement. From this point of view, a moderate amount of aggression is normal and desirable. In fact, aggression is expected in our society and desired in some areas of accomplishment (e.g., sports and other forms of physical prowess). Excessive passivity is of more concern than undue aggression because of the extraordinary difficulty of getting a passive child to be productive. It is only when a child's aggression exceeds cultural norms that adults seek to limit its expression.

An article by Eron (1980) reviewed the philosophical ramifications and research findings on childhood aggression over several decades. Defined as an act that injures another person, aggression has elements of interpersonal hostility that are expressed through direct or indirect physical and/or verbal channels. Eron contended that aggression is a learned constellation of behaviors, although genetic predisposition or other physiological components may contribute to its development.

This contention received support from Tieger (1980). The literature pertaining to cross-cultural studies of children's behavior, the behavior of nonhuman primates, and sex hormones and aggression indicate no biological predisposition toward aggression in human males. Furthermore, according to Tieger, the evidence suggests that the gender-dimorphic nature of aggression is readily observable in children's spontaneous behavior only after the age of five years, making it difficult to suggest a biological basis for aggression.

The possibility, however, that some children can be made aggressive more easily than others cannot be ruled out. Camp (1977) postulated a defective genetic system that makes it more difficult for some young aggressive boys to develop an effective linguistic control system (impulses are translated into immediate actions rather than being delayed and processed through verbal mediation processes). In support of this postulate, Krynicki (1978) found repetitively assaulting and aggressive adolescents to show brain wave abnormalities and other dysfunctional signs.

Children suffering attention deficit disorder (ADD) symptoms often demonstrate unusual aggression. This type of youngster often cannot interpret properly nor understand the world about him or her and simply attacks it (Burks, 1968b, 1968c, 1968d). Aggression and fear apparently are two sides of the same coin: The aggressive child is usually fearful but if he or she shows sadistic behavior, it is probably part of an effort to dominate others and gain power. If the child succeeds in this objective, he or she will repeat the conduct. If the child finds the situation too dangerous to overcome, he or she will remain aggressive but will have to repress hostile impulses. Placing aggression in the unconscious conceals its meaning from the individual. Aggressive acts will be committed on the sly and camouflaged as sarcasm, profanity, or wit (safer substitutes for hostile feelings).

Because aggression is a learned trait, it can be unlearned, but the unlearning process is not likely to be easy and the task may not be a realistic aspiration for educators working in an ordinary school environment. Bankart and Anderson (1979) reported that exposure to prosocial television (*Sesame Street*) had a strong short-term effect in reducing certain types of aggressive behavior. The exposure, however, did not increase prosocial conduct or result in more obedience.

If a child's aggressive behavior is cyclical or transitory, it is probably being augmented by temporary frustrations arising in the immediate environment. Locating and removing the source of stress will ordinarily eliminate signs of hostility.

Some youngsters, however, are habitually aggressive regardless of the situation. These chronically hostile children express aggression in a wide variety of overt and hidden forms. Chronically hostile children tend to

- be hypercritical of others;
- put others down (disparage or belittle others);
- nag others;
- hold grudges;
- hold stubborn prejudices;
- be cynical;
- be suspicious of others;
- intimidate others;
- fight rather than talk out differences;
- exploit others;
- see others as enemies;
- must have their own way;
- be sarcastic;
- play tricks on others;
- yell at others.

Children demonstrating many of the preceding behaviors to a severe degree may need psychological assistance of a degree and quality beyond the range of what most schools can offer and should be referred to community agencies that specialize in the treatment of aggressive disorders.

Belligerent behavior generalizes across situations and time (see below):

- Children who are aggressive at home are aggressive at school and in the larger social environment.
- Children who are physically aggressive are also verbally and indirectly aggressive.
- Aggression, as a trait, is predictable over at least a 10-year period (i.e., primary school–age aggressive children are very likely to be aggressive teenagers).

A. Harris (1979) sought to determine the degree of consistency in boys' aggressive behavior. He found that, in the classroom, aggressive boys were significantly more belligerent than normal boys. Normal boys, however, showed about the same level of aggression on the playground as in the classroom, while aggressive boys were significantly more forceful on the playground than in the classroom. Thus, Eron's (1980) contention that aggression generalizes across situations is at least partially substantiated but situational specificity exists for some subjects.

On the other hand, Olweus (1979) claimed that, over time, a high degree of stability exists in an individual's belligerence. Olweus contended that marked individual differences in habitual aggression levels manifest themselves as early as three years of age.

Belligerence is learned early in life and learned very well. The establishment of early aggression in the personality structure suggests the trait will be difficult to change in later years. It substantiates the notion that aggressive impulses might be controlled but not changed. Because assertive conduct has many positive attributes, aggressive conduct should be directed into constructive channels where achievement can be counted upon as a favorable outcome (Mash & Barkley, 1989; Webster-Stratton & Herbert, 1994).

A child's aggressiveness at school is thought to be associated with certain home conditions. The more aggressive the child is in school, (a) the less nurturing and accepting the parents are toward the child at home, (b) the less the child identifies favorably with the parents, and (c) the more likely it is that the child comes from a lower social class (Eron, 1980).

In general, Olweus (1979) agreed with Eron on the familial determinants of aggressive behavior, but he added one more factor—the child's innate temperament. He also believed that negativism and permissiveness on the part of the mother are the factors having the greatest causal impact. Bandura and Huston (1961), however, maintained that the mere observation of aggressive role models, regardless of the quality of the parent-child relationship, is a sufficient condition for producing imitative aggression in children.

Many studies have chronicled the association of parental belligerence with childhood aggression. For example, Reidy (1977) investigated the aggressive characteristics of abused and neglected children and found both groups demonstrated significantly more aggression in school settings than did normal children. Reidy linked physical punishment in the home with hyperaggressiveness in children. Ray (1980) and Raden (1980) conducted studies that substantiated findings from previous investigations that authoritarian parents tend to be hostile toward others and to produce aggressive reactions from others.

Children rated as belligerent by peers tend to rate themselves as aggressive, rate others as aggressive, and see the world about them as an aggressive place. In one study (Ohbuchi & Oku, 1980), hostile and nonhostile participants gave shock stimuli to opponents in a competitive reaction task. Nonhostile participants' shock choice was governed by the norm of reciprocity, but hostile participants did not reduce the intensity of their shocks under decreased attack, presumably due to the hostile individuals' tendency to attribute a malicious intent to opponents and to an inner need to prolong aggression.

Children who are rated as aggressive at eight years of age are three times more likely to have police records by the time they are 19 years old than are those not so rated (Eron, 1980). This finding should be tempered with research findings that indicate it is the nature of the early aggression that puts the child at risk for later court appearances. For example, Moore, Chamberlain, and Mukal (1979) studied children who either showed aggression in the home or demonstrated stealing problems. They found that 77% of those with stealing problems had court-recorded offenses later, a much higher incidence than that recorded for the aggressive individuals (whose rate did not differ from a normative sample).

Children who at age eight years had parents strongly oriented toward upward social mobility are more aggressive 10 years later than are those who had less-striving parents (Eron, 1980). Worchel, Arnold, and Harrison (1978) made a strong case for linking aggression to the need to gain or restore power. Their studies confirm that a person who has his or her influence reduced will demonstrate more aggression. Upwardly striving parents may possess a need to move from a less powerful to a more commanding position, and the aggressive efforts they make to achieve this goal are perhaps copied by their children.

Children who gave indications at age eight of refusing to internalize society's standards of proper behavior are more aggressive 10 years later than are those who gave signs of accepting the standards (Eron, 1980). Youngsters who exhibit guilt, confess wrongdoing, and attempt to rectify mistakes give signs of possessing a well-developed conscience. This conscience (or superego) will prevent them from committing injurious acts toward others. On the other hand, children who break societal rules without regret may continue to commit aggressive acts toward others in later years.

Children exposed to aggressive role models at age eight tend to be more aggressive in later years than those not exposed to such models. Further, those who accepted television violence as reality at eight years of age are more aggressive at age 19 than those who saw the violence as fantasy. Girls, with few aggressive female models to copy from television, do not become as aggressive as boys. Girls also see television programs more clearly as fantasy shows. In effect, most girls are apparently trained to be nonaggressive (Eron, 1980).

The major predictors of aggression for boys are viewing television violence, showing a preference for traditional masculine activities, and having aggressive fantasies (e.g., beating up others). The major predictors of aggression for girls are viewing television violence, having a perception of television violence as real, having a lack of interest in traditional feminine activities, and having fantasies about action (involving heroes and heroines, winning games, and accomplishing achievement) (Eron, 1980).

Feshbach (1976) supported the thesis that a reality set in television viewing can stimulate aggressive responses, while a fantasy set reduces it. Further, television violence tends to desensitize the emotional response sensitivity of children to real-life aggression (i.e., youngsters become indifferent to victims of real-life dramas).

Fantasy does not have a cathartic effect in reducing aggressive hostility. Children who fantasize about aggressive acts tend to act aggressively. The more a person mentally rehearses an aggressive act, the more apt he or she is to remember the aggression and to use it in problem solving. Berkowitz (1973, 1993b) maintains that ventilation through fantasy simply rewards aggression—it extends hostile-aggressive tendencies across a wide spectrum of activities. Instead of rehearsing aggression through mental processes, Berkowitz is in favor of more control over aggressive impulses (in order to stem violence) and of giving cognitive feedback to the aggressive individual. He or she can be taught to talk about and interpret feelings and to describe emotional reactions without attacking others physically or verbally, directly or in fantasy.

Most mothers inhibit aggression in their children. One study of mothers (Sears et al., 1957) showed differences in their tolerance of aggression and the amount of punishment they administered for belligerent behavior. Results generally showed that permissive mothers produced more aggressive children. However, allied with this fact was the finding that the greater the amount of punishment administered, the more the child showed aggression. In short, mothers who were most permissive and gave the most punishment had the most aggressive children. (These mothers both tolerated initial aggression and then provided the children with an aggressive role model.) The way to produce a nonaggressive youngster, then, is to frown on initial aggression and then not punish the child. Mothers using this approach did not shape as much aggression as did mothers employing opposite methods.

Other patterns of parental control play a major part in the production of aggression in children. Several approaches that parents use to regulate children's behavior can, instead, result in unruly, negative, or combative conduct. These behaviors are grouped below according to parental type.

The competitive parent. This type of parent feels that his or her uncontested will should be imposed upon offspring (the parent has to be boss). Some children reject this approach; clashes between parents and these youngsters tend to be frequent and vigorous. As parent and child become more adept at frustrating each other, the confrontations become lengthy and contentious. Parents complain that every conversation turns into an argument. Along with defiant behavior, the children may instigate whining tantrums. Some youngsters eventually refuse to communicate with parents.

The helpless parent. This type of parent cannot withstand child pressure. Often, a feeble token attempt is made to constrain unwelcome activities, but when the child offers resistance, the parent becomes confused and resentful. An ineffectual and pained adult response allows the youngster to control home events and to exact an emotional toll on the parent (which the child often enjoys).

This type of behavior may carry to the school. Teachers complain these students disregard rules and enjoy being disruptive. The student's parents, in response to school complaints, adopt a resigned demeanor and say that the child is uncontrollable. They may also complain the child heeds demands only to the point where the youngster can organize a better attack on authority figures.

The inconsistent parent. Many parents are more inconsistent about discipline methods than they realize. Children from loving, supportive homes may forgive parental inconsistencies, even though they prefer more reliable behavior. If parental inconsistency masks neglect or rejection, however, or if the parents have no deeply rooted sense of right and wrong, the children may react in aggressive or even hostile ways.

The unpredictable parent may admit that he or she institutes disciplinary methods based on moment to moment adult moods—if the parent feels good, the misbehavior is overlooked; if the parent feels irritable, a negative consequence ensues. Further, the inconsistent parent may state that he or she is not sure what standards of conduct should apply in a given situation or, for that matter, what controls should be used at any given time. In general, this type of parent is dissatisfied with the child and is easily influenced to change discipline methods after reading an article on child control or upon hearing about a new regulatory technique.

Children brought up by inconsistent parents tend to be apprehensive; they do not know what to expect. Some become angry and harbor lifelong resentments toward parents. Those who enter therapy as adults tend to say they do not think their parents cared enough about their emotional or physical safety to be predictable.

The explosive parent. Some parents overreact to child misbehavior. They may be overconcerned about what currently is considered proper conduct and may put into effect inflexible child-rearing standards. When infractions occur, these parents may become so upset they initiate immediate and intense emotional outbursts. Of course, an apprehensive child then complains about these reactions, protesting that he or she does not understand why the parents act that way. Some fearful children continue to try to please the parents; others make demands for parental approval by misbehaving; still others emulate parents by staging outbursts of their own in the hope they can irritate the adults.

DIAGNOSIS

The Four Types of Aggression

Parental actions can spur the appearance of childhood aggression, but other factors must be considered. Children act belligerent for a variety of reasons—influenced by maturity levels and environmental conditions, issues sometimes beyond adult control. If these circumstances remain unknown, misunderstood, or mishandled, childhood aggression may be aggravated.

There are four types of childhood aggression:

1. accidental;
2. expressive;
3. instrumental;
4. hostile.

AGGRESSION CHECKLIST

Harold F. Burks, Ph.D.

Put a check mark next to any trait that is chronic and shown to a fairly large degree.

Accidental
- [ ] 1. Falls over things
- [ ] 2. Runs into objects or people
- [ ] 3. Is easily confused; moves in unexpected directions
- [ ] 4. Has trouble recognizing environmental dangers
- [ ] 5. Is overactive; dashes here and there
- [ ] 6. Is surprised when he or she causes damage or injury
- [ ] 7. Blurts out unexpected, offensive comments
- [ ] 8. Accidentally hurts pets
- [ ] 9. Accidentally hurts others in play

Expressive
- [ ] 1. Takes pleasure in rough play
- [ ] 2. Playfully hits, slaps, or pushes others but overdoes it
- [ ] 3. Uses toys as aggressive tools or weapons
- [ ] 4. Pokes fun at others but is indiscriminate
- [ ] 5. Enjoys teasing others
- [ ] 6. Is easily bored; needs to be active as a source of stimulation
- [ ] 7. Takes joy in scattering objects or pushing things over
- [ ] 8. Has a lot of nervous energy; bangs on things

Instrumental
- [ ] 1. Jumps ahead of others in line
- [ ] 2. Tends to lash out at others when frustrated
- [ ] 3. Aggressively takes more than his or her share of things
- [ ] 4. When frustrated, yells at others
- [ ] 5. Gets upset in obvious ways when ordered to obey rules
- [ ] 6. Tends to be opportunistic; grabs for what he or she wants
- [ ] 7. Uses force to achieve his or her desires
- [ ] 8. Is easily irritated; flares up
- [ ] 9. Aggression that occurs in interaction with others is not planned

Hostile

Primary and Elementary School Ages
- [ ] 1. Disregards authority
- [ ] 2. Bullies others
- [ ] 3. Takes things without permission
- [ ] 4. Tells falsehoods
- [ ] 5. Is irresponsible
- [ ] 6. Deliberately gets into scrapes
- [ ] 7. Disregards the rights of others
- [ ] 8. Deliberately breaks rules
- [ ] 9. Is destructive of others' property
- [ ] 10. Is truant
- [ ] 11. Uses profanity
- [ ] 12. Is very stubborn
- [ ] 13. Blames others
- [ ] 14. Threatens others
- [ ] 15. Shows little or no remorse for wrongdoing

Junior and Senior High School Ages
- [ ] 1. Is disobedient
- [ ] 2. Puts blame on others
- [ ] 3. Brags
- [ ] 4. Shows off
- [ ] 5. Is easily angered; fights
- [ ] 6. Threatens others loudly
- [ ] 7. Has temper tantrums
- [ ] 8. Is jealous, sulky, argumentative, moody
- [ ] 9. Is impulsive
- [ ] 10. Scoffs at others
- [ ] 11. Has poor relations with friends
- [ ] 12. Is stubborn and negative
- [ ] 13. Lies
- [ ] 14. Is destructive
- [ ] 15. Steals
- [ ] 16. Runs with a gang or undesirable companions
- [ ] 17. Is truant
- [ ] 18. Abuses alcohol or drugs
- [ ] 19. Shows little or no remorse for wrongdoing

Figure 19.1.

These kinds of aggression can be identified by behavioral characteristics. Parents and teachers can scan the Aggression checklist (see figure 19.1) for symptoms that are characteristic of each of these types of aggression. Have respondents put a check mark next to a trait only if the behavior described is chronic and shown to a fairly large degree.

Accidental aggression. While playing, children can hurt others unintentionally. Running into others, stepping on someone's foot while climbing, or hitting another child while swinging a bat are all actions classified as accidental aggression. No conflict is present in such behavior; it occurs because of chance contact. For example:

- Danny, who has a strong arm, loves to throw a baseball. On one occasion, he throws it too far and breaks a window.
- Mary, who has a quick wit, innocently insults her best friend by calling her a crybaby.
- Jack, who is active, loves to tumble with his pet dog but sometimes overdoes it, causing the dog to yelp in pain.

Seen mostly in small children, accidental aggression is not characterized by malicious intent. For that reason, it seems unwise to rebuke or punish youngsters for what is, for them, age-appropriate conduct (even if the actions cause discomfort to others). Less punitive control methods are needed so that a rambunctious child will not feel guilt about normal behavior.

Expressive aggression. The perpetrator of expressive aggression does not actively look to destroy something or to inflict injury upon a victim. Instead, the aggressor seeks a pleasurable sensory experience by engaging in actions that inadvertently upset or injure others or obstruct their rights. While doing these things, the aggressor shows no angry or hostile behavior.

This category includes many traits similar to those of accidental aggression, but another personality aspect must be considered when dealing with expressive outbursts—that is, the need for boisterous verbal and physical contact.

To handle this type of energetic behavior, adults ought to avoid punitive measures such as spanking, berating, and physical restraint, because youngsters can be led to believe that their behavior is unwholesome and that being active is somehow bad. The child may then establish the inner conviction that he or she is not a good person—a conviction often difficult to alter in later life.

Instrumental aggression. Children, like adults, engage in goal-oriented aggressive behavior. A student may try to get attention from a teacher by waving an arm whenever the teacher asks a question. Another may force his or her way to the head of the line to get to the playground or lunchroom first. In spite of these forceful actions (waving, pushing, or hitting) the purpose of the behavior is not to injure someone else but simply to obtain something. The spontaneous physical engagements that result from arguments over privileges, rights, or possessions are simply spin-offs of actions designed to gain an objective. As with expressive aggression, instrumental aggression is characterized by a lack of premeditation and purposefulness. No attempt is made by the aggressor to demean or hurt others.

Hostile aggression. The wish of the hostile aggressor to experience pleasure, based on some other person's emotional or physical pain, distinguishes this type of aggression. The hurtful actions may be attempts to obtain revenge for perceived insults or injuries or be a way to manipulate people. The belligerence can be verbal or physical. Kicking, teasing, threatening, pinching, breaking, grabbing, shaming, biting, attacking, spitting, slapping, gossiping, degrading, reviling, and destroying are examples of hurtful actions. Hostile aggression is the most serious type of aggression. Consequences for the antagonistic perpetrator and for the victim are more unpleasant than are outcomes from accidental, expressive, or instrumental aggression.

Hostile behavior is characterized by a tendency to be overly assertive, to attack others, and to dominate them. While expected in very young children, these attributes suggest immaturity in older individuals. In extreme forms, these behaviors are considered intolerable (particularly in school settings where they disrupt classrooms, confuse and intimidate fellow students, and frustrate teachers).

Causes of hostile-aggressive behavior, as one would expect, are numerous. Belligerent conduct may stem from poorly controlled anger, from exposure to indulgent or repressive parents, from copying the antagonistic behavior of adults or peers, from attempts to compensate for poor achievement or low self-esteem or lack of sexual prowess, from the replication of disruptive behavior seen on television, from loneliness, from generalized anxieties, or from a need to plead for help (just to mention a few possibilities).

Symptoms of hostile aggressiveness are, in many ways, similar for both younger and older children, but older individuals tend to express anger in more varied ways. Teens, for instance, rarely kick and hit others (unlike primary- and elementary-age youngsters). Being more mature, they release their feelings in more sophisticated ways (e.g., stealing, cheating, truancy, lying, drug use, and inappropriate sexual behavior).

Because the two age groups express antagonism in different manners, the hostile characteristics of primary and elementary school–age children are listed separately from those of disruptive junior and senior high school students in figure 19.1.

Hostile aggression, at any age, is not well accepted. Its expression can vary from situation to situation. A youngster may suppress acting-out conduct in the home but show it at school (or vice versa). Some parents report they were astounded to learn their child was involved in an unacceptable episode (like vandalism), claiming the son or daughter would never do such a thing. Further investigation may reveal that the youngster does not demonstrate anger in the home (possibly because such behavior would be punished severely) but does so in situations where possible unpleasant consequences from parents are absent.

In my opinion, the aggressive acting-out behavior of younger children tends to center around the following causal factors:

1. The child is afraid of particular adults or peers.
2. The child feels incompetent (usually in school).
3. The child feels he or she cannot meet social standards. For example, a boy may feel he is not masculine enough, so he tries to act tough.
4. The child is responding to undue pressure (sometimes from the school but more often from the home).
5. The child is hyperactive (shows poor frustration tolerance).
6. The child is emulating the behavior of others (sometimes peers, but more often adults).
7. The child is being teased by someone (sometimes a peer, sometimes a family member).
8. The child is in poor health.
9. The child feels shame and may act aggressively in order to be punished.
10. The child has been overindulged and cannot tolerate frustration.

Interpreting hostile conduct is not easy because any behavior can be serious. Suppose, for example, that a youngster is stealing but demonstrates no other aggressive characteristic. The stealing cannot be ignored; something must be done about it. The same holds true for other hostile traits, such as destructiveness, drug abuse, and fighting. In my clinical experience, if the youngster demonstrates a number of hostile-aggressive symptoms, the outlook worsens (actually, it appears, the greater the number of hostile-aggressive signs, the more serious the problem).

Parental Approaches

Before a counselor can provide proper treatment for inappropriate parenting approaches, he or she must determine which approach a particular parent is using. The Parental Rules and Regulations checklist (see figure 19.2) provides a rough guide to such patterns of symptomatology.

The items on the checklist evaluate adult attitudes and child conduct as they relate to four parental approaches:

1. competitive: items 6, 13, 20, 24, 25, 34, 39, 41, 42, and 43;
2. helpless: items 1, 2, 10, 14, 19, 28, 31, and 36;
3. inconsistent: items 5, 9, 12, 15, 23, 27, 33, 35, and 38;
4. explosive: items 3, 8, 11, 17, 21, 26, 30, 40, and 45.

PARENTAL RULES AND REGULATIONS

Harold F. Burks, Ph.D.

For each statement, put a check mark in the appropriate column.

	Not true	Sometimes true	Often true
1. My child must learn to take rules from me instead of giving me rules.	☐	☐	☐
2. I tend to give up easily when my child puts pressure on me.	☐	☐	☐
3. When my child disobeys me, I tend to get upset and show everybody how upset I am.	☐	☐	☐
4. I make it very clear to my child which behavior will and won't be tolerated.	☐	☐	☐
5. It seems strange, but my child's misbehavior sometimes bothers me and sometimes does not.	☐	☐	☐
6. I'm determined to show my child who's the boss in this family.	☐	☐	☐
7. I make extra efforts to show my child how to behave in particular circumstances.	☐	☐	☐
8. When I get upset, my child looks pretty scared.	☐	☐	☐
9. I'm more likely to scold my child for disobeying when I feel bad than when I feel good.	☐	☐	☐
10. My child doesn't pay much attention to my rules.	☐	☐	☐
11. My child keeps telling me that I shouldn't get so upset about things that he or she does wrong.	☐	☐	☐
12. Whenever I hear about a new way to discipline my child, I try it.	☐	☐	☐
13. My child seems defiant no matter what rules I lay down.	☐	☐	☐
14. Even when I appear upset or hurt, my child goes ahead and does what he or she wants.	☐	☐	☐
15. I'm never sure when I should spank my child, so sometimes I do and sometimes I don't.	☐	☐	☐
16. When my child misbehaves, I just say "stop it" and he or she usually does.	☐	☐	☐
17. Sometimes my child seems almost afraid of me.	☐	☐	☐
18. When my child is called in from play to eat a meal, I don't permit the youngster to stall or disobey me.	☐	☐	☐
19. When my child disobeys me, I throw my hands up in despair.	☐	☐	☐
20. My child and I have long and unpleasant arguments where nobody seems to back down.	☐	☐	☐
21. When I get upset about something my child is doing, he or she becomes concerned and tries hard to please me.	☐	☐	☐
22. When my child gets too rambunctious, I try to give him or her something of interest to do.	☐	☐	☐

Figure 19.2a.

	Not true	Sometimes true	Often true
23. When my child is quiet, I know how to handle him or her; but when the child gets pushy, I have trouble.	☐	☐	☐
24. I have frequent clashes with my child when he or she disobeys.	☐	☐	☐
25. My child seems negative and cries noisily when frustrated.	☐	☐	☐
26. My child seems worried about what I will do.	☐	☐	☐
27. My child complains that I am always spoiling his or her fun.	☐	☐	☐
28. My child doesn't care about what I want.	☐	☐	☐
29. If I see that my child is going to get involved in an activity that could lead to trouble, I quickly stop him or her.	☐	☐	☐
30. I think my child disobeys just to get my attention.	☐	☐	☐
31. My child never seems to understand the reasons for the discipline I give him or her.	☐	☐	☐
32. My child and I seem to be pretty good friends even when we disagree.	☐	☐	☐
33. I am not sure that I know what standards of conduct I should apply to my child.	☐	☐	☐
34. My child and I seem to do a lot of screaming at each other.	☐	☐	☐
35. I never seem to be satisfied about the way my child behaves.	☐	☐	☐
36. My child seems to enjoy upsetting me.	☐	☐	☐
37. I can talk things over with my child and we both seem to understand what the other wants.	☐	☐	☐
38. I'm always eager to try new methods of discipline.	☐	☐	☐
39. My child has many long, whiney tantrums.	☐	☐	☐
40. I think my child is trying to upset me by disobeying me.	☐	☐	☐
41. My child refuses to communicate with me.	☐	☐	☐
42. My child obeys me just long enough to figure out how to get back at me.	☐	☐	☐
43. Every conversation with my child seems to turn into an argument.	☐	☐	☐
44. When I get angry with my child, I don't stay mad very long.	☐	☐	☐
45. Whenever I try to correct my child, he or she seems to explode.	☐	☐	☐

Figure 19.2b.

In addition, nine items on the checklist (items 4, 7, 16, 18, 22, 29, 32, 37, and 44) indicate positive interaction—that is, positive attitudes or adjustments in the family. Responses of "often true" on these items enable the examiner to commend some parents—even those with problems in other areas—for taking constructive action. The items also provide examples of parental conduct that should prove useful in the upbringing of most children. If a parent indicates that he or she is not using these techniques, the interviewer can suggest they be employed.

For the other 36 items, when a parent responds "not true," he or she is indicating that significant problems do not exist. Within a given category, if the average of the responses is below the "sometimes true" level, it means that the family does not suffer significant problems in that category. A higher average is indicative of possible parenting problems and warrants further investigation by the counselor.

Some categories overlap when a particular parent rates items on the inventory. For example, item 10 ("my child doesn't pay much attention to my rules") describes an aspect of child behavior that could be observed by the inconsistent parent, the competitive parent, or the helpless parent. This does not mean the item should be thrown out; it elicits a piece of information about family interactions that could be useful in a school-home conference.

Although few parents are likely to fit into a single category perfectly, the examiner will probably find diagnostically valuable tendencies. For example, the explosive parent may also be inconsistent or even helpless at times, and all these aspects of parental conduct may have to be discussed with the parent. If parents indicate problems across several categories, the likelihood of family pathology may be greater.

Responses to the checklist can assist parents to understand some of the negative dynamics of the child-raising techniques they may employ (and possibly might change).

INTERVENTION STRATEGIES

Techniques for Parents

The following treatment suggestions for the four types of child aggression may prove helpful for parents.

Accidental Aggression

1. Remove objects in the home that might contribute to accidental aggression (such as a lamp that might easily be tipped over).
2. Gently remove the youngster when he or she becomes involved in rough play.
3. Ignore accidental aggression and reward calmer conduct. For example, whenever your child becomes involved in satisfactory activities, reinforce those actions with praise, an affectionate touch, or just by being present and involved.
4. Discourage the presence of children who overexcite the child.
5. If adults are acting uncontrolled, don't encourage the youngster to become involved in their rough play.
6. Divert the youngster's attention if he or she becomes too exuberant.
7. Avoid corporal punishment—striking a child teaches him or her to hit others.

Expressive Aggression

1. Anticipate and prevent situations where the youngster is likely to offend others.
2. Try time-out procedures (for example, have a milk-and-cookie break when rough play gets out of hand).
3. When shifting to a new activity, allow time for the child to prepare for the change. High-energy children find it difficult to change direction.

4. Provide objects like punching bags, tether balls, clay, balls, finger paints, and crayons that help to use up excess energy.
5. Praise behavior that conforms to expected standards; divert the child's attention to a new activity when aggressive behavior occurs.
6. Remove objects that might inadvertently be used in aggressive behavior that could harm others.
7. Divert the youngster from rough play by teaching sports like fishing, handball, archery, or golf; do not encourage contact sports like football, wrestling, and boxing, which increase the desire to interact aggressively.

Instrumental Aggression

1. Try to anticipate and prevent the occurrence of situations that promote rough play.
2. Establish firm limits and teach the youngster to abide by these controls. Establish consequences for infractions, and enforce rules consistently. Make sure rules are specific and easily understood. Reward obedience; remove rewards when a rule is disobeyed.
3. Supervise play activities when it looks as though the child is getting into trouble. Often, the mere presence of an adult can have a quieting effect.
4. Structure a young child's day so that there is little opportunity for him or her to blunder into frustrating situations.
5. If a youngster complains that his or her rights are being ignored, show concern but point out that other individuals also have rights that must be observed.
6. Keep rival siblings separated when possible.
7. Stress the fact that possessions owned by other family members must not be touched except by permission of the owners.
8. Try a monetary reward system for approved social behavior. For example, give the child $3.00 to start, and promise to pay more money for every day that he or she abstains from fighting or abusive conduct—but make it clear that you will also fine the child for each altercation. Make sure the child knows exactly what behavior is not tolerated. It's best to have the youngster work toward acquiring a specific gift or other objective.
9. Aggressive children often learn to associate pleasure and thrills with rough play. To counteract this tendency, help the youngster to relate happy experiences to friendly activities. Take the child, with peers, to the circus, movies, parties, and so on.
10. When possible, avoid confrontations. Face-to-face arguments can bring the worst out in both parents and offspring—possibly even reinforcing aggressive qualities in the youngster.
11. Do not boast about the child's physical prowess to others. Such bragging reinforces the child's idea that physical aggression is a valuable asset.

Hostile Aggression

1. Keep rival brothers and sisters separated as much as possible.
2. Supervise the youngster carefully. If problems exist at school, contact the teacher for permission to observe the child in the classroom and on the playground. Cooperate with suggestions from school personnel.
3. Try spending more time with the child. Show affection and spend less time admonishing.
4. Stay calm. Talk things over with the child.
5. If the child gets angry, have him or her cool off in a quiet part of the home.
6. Examine rules and regulations. Are they too rigid or unpredictable (i.e., do they change whenever it suits the parent)? Are there too many, and are they not enforced consistently?
7. Help the child develop a more positive self-image. Encourage membership in the Boy Scouts or Girl Scouts, the Y, a gymnastic team, an active church group, or a competitive sports group (under competent guidance, of course).

8. Both parents should make it clear that they do not condone fighting (but make sure that the child is not being picked on by older or stronger youngsters or being targeted for gang retaliation).

9. Discuss alternative ways to handle aggressive situations—for example, teach the child to return home if neighborhood peers become threatening.

10. Involve fathers. Children need the presence and attention of dads. Boys need him as a model demonstrating patience, humor, and deftness in social relations. Girls need him as someone who can accept and treasure their femininity.

11. If the child is verbally aggressive (teases, shouts insults, uses sarcasm, and so on), examine the dynamics of family and peer interactions.

12. Give the child simple, nonnegotiable, clearly stated consequences for misbehavior. For example, if the youngster chooses not to do chores, he or she will not be allowed to watch a favorite television show.

13. Avoid making threats (threats can force both the parent and the child into unproductive and antagonistic situations).

14. Ignore infantile or negative behavior. The child, employing these tactics, may feel gratified by increased adult attention.

15. Support the child's efforts to act acceptably. Younger children respond to tangible rewards like M&Ms, tokens that can be traded for goodies, or even gold stars. Older youngsters respond to verbal praise.

16. Make sure the child knows what he or she is doing wrong. Without instruction, some children assume their behavior is okay.

17. Do not take the youngster's antagonistic conduct as a personal affront. To do so may reward aggression because the youngster feels avenged.

18. Do not try to correct all difficulties at once. Select one unwanted behavior and concentrate on it.

Treatment Suggestions

The following intervention techniques are suggested for the four parenting approaches described under the diagnosis section of this chapter.

The competitive parent. Short-term treatment efforts for competitive parents generally prove to be of little lasting value. This may occur because the competitive parent communicates rejection of the child—unrecognized by the parent but keenly felt by the youngster.

One or two school counseling interviews may help parents become aware of the dynamics occurring in their interactions with the child. They may, for instance, be shown they are often as contentious as their boy or girl. The child is copying their behavior—this will probably come as a surprise. At first, they may well reject this observation, preferring instead to argue its validity. The counselor may then point out to the parents how argumentative they are being and suggest they relate this adult stubbornness to home difficulties. Some parents—those with sufficient insight (and perhaps a sense of humor)—will benefit from this clinical revelation while others will not.

To avoid confrontations with their child, parents can be told to walk away from arguments, eliminate conditions that promote clashes, and modify rules and regulations.

Some families of aggressive children should be referred to agencies offering long-term therapeutic services if it becomes obvious the parents deeply resent the child's activities, have no apparent means to change the immediate situation, and have engaged in a long-standing and chronic battles with the child.

The helpless parent. The practitioner examining the dynamics of a family headed by helpless parents may want to try the following:

1. Estimate how much power remains with the parents. Does the child back down when an adult demonstrates firmness?

2. Gauge the balance of power between the two parents. Is one frustrating the other's ability to demonstrate authority over the child? For example, if the mother allies herself with a child against the father, the father's stature decreases in the eyes of the child and emboldens the youngster to violate regulations.

3. Evaluate the parents' disciplinary procedures. In all likelihood, they need instruction on applying proper control techniques. It might be suggested, for example, that they institute a system of inflexible negative consequences for disruptive conduct. The parents must be told specifically what behaviors require punishment and what the ensuing consequences should be.

The helpless parent (most often the mother) may be giving emotional distress signals to her child. A "hurt" response to misbehavior can be one manifestation of this tendency. She may also offer covert resistance to suggestions that she take positive steps to control a youngster. The school practitioner should not become too involved in this suffering syndrome, which is impossible to treat at a superficial level. The family should be referred to professional agencies for long-term help.

The inconsistent parent. Inconsistent parents seldom realize how unpredictable they are. They must be made aware of this fact. Depending on the judgment of the interviewer, the parent may further be told that inconsistency is often a behavioral device employed to control the actions of others. For example, by keeping a child apprehensive and anxious about adult decisions, the parent places the youngster in an unusually dependent position. Explain that parental inconsistency may force a child to use his or her own preferences as a guide for conduct. However, it also must be pointed out that an immature youngster probably does not possess a developed conceptual system necessary to execute choices properly.

In nearly all instances, the unpredictable parent suffered inconsistent treatment in childhood. For this reason, the counselor may have to adopt an authoritative role in early parent interviews, giving a mother or father a set of rules to apply to their child's misbehavior along with specific and appropriate consequences for each infraction (which must be followed to the letter).

If the parents refuse to change their conduct and the inconsistency continues to produce unwanted child behavior, the family should be referred to agencies offering extensive therapeutic services.

The explosive parent. Practitioners who analyze and treat explosive parents must be concerned about the genesis of such emotionality. Although it may appear that a specific pathological behavior is fixed and dominant in the personality structure of the parent, this may not be the case.

The diagnosis is always suspect if the parent reacts tempestuously to the conduct of one child and quietly to the antics of another. When this phenomenon is observed, the counselor should explore the following questions:

1. What is the child's natural temperament? Perhaps a passive child is accepted by the parent while a more rambunctious youngster is not, or perhaps the active child is admired and the quiet one rejected.
2. Does the child represent someone from the parent's past? Ask the parent to name someone from his or her own childhood that reminds the parent of the child. Nearly always, the parent will give a start and say, for example, "Oh, my goodness, he acts just like my youngest brother!" Further questioning may reveal that the parent had unusual difficulties with that sibling. For some parents, this sort of revelation changes some aspects of the way they view their child.

The tempestuous patterns of behavior in some households can be modified by helping parents find ways to avoid unneeded confrontations and by explaining to them that behavioral expectations for their child may be unrealistic.

Teacher Assessment

Efforts to help the aggressive student may have to start with an analysis of teacher behavior. A teacher's behavior or method of instruction may inadvertently promote aggressive behavior from students. The following areas of concern should be investigated:

1. Is the teacher generally treating the students politely, fairly, and courteously?
2. Is the classroom environment conducive to good student behavior?

- Should seats be rearranged?
- Are the students required to sit too long at a time?
- Is the work too difficult or too tedious?
- Are the students tired or hungry?

3. Is the teacher applying his or her values to an educational setting that demands different standards? Students from lower socioeconomic levels, for instance, may feel mistreated when asked to behave in ways that conflict with their upbringing.

4. Does the teacher approach aggressive students on a realistic, factual basis when discussing behavior problems with them? Discussions of this nature should be done in private, not in front of the class.

5. Does the teacher ever ask a disruptive student whether the teacher behavior is making the youngster angry? Although this procedure must be handled with care, aggressive children can sometimes be asked to share their complaints with the teacher or with someone outside the classroom (e.g., the vice principal or a counselor).

6. Does the teacher tell disruptive students how their behavior makes him or her feel? A statement of feelings, which involves the risk of openness and presumes a reasonably good teacher-student relationship, may result in a redefinition of a difficulty. For example, the student may say, "I talk back to you because you're sarcastic with me" or "I don't care about your feelings." In either case the problem shifts from the student's rudeness to a newly defined problem—that is, the relationship between student and teacher. The teacher must take responsibility for his or her portion of the problem. New attempts can then be made to alleviate the difficulty, and the student may react more positively to the teacher's changed behavior.

7. Has the teacher made a serious attempt to promote good student-teacher relationships? If not, the teacher should not be asked to undertake this endeavor without professional assistance. Outside help is needed; the teacher cannot be expected to understand how he or she is coming across to students.

Teacher Self-Assessment

The following questions for teachers suggest techniques for managing different types of disruptive students.

Those Who Generally Demonstrate Adequate Self-Control

1. Have you tried ignoring the misbehavior to see if it will disappear? Attention from the teacher can be positive reinforcement for some types of aggression—the unwanted behavior may stop when the attention is removed. This technique is most effective when used in conjunction with reinforcement measures that encourage appropriate behavior.

2. When the child misbehaves, have you tried quietly mentioning the child's name, giving the youngster a cool stare, pointing a finger at the child, or tapping a pencil? Signal interference is often a suitable technique for interrupting minor behavior deviations.

3. Have you tried conveying special interest in the child's work? This technique helps to draw the student's attention back to the task at hand. Of course, it is based on the assumption that the child is able to complete the assignment.

4. Have you tried using humor? Children tend to react favorably to friendly humor from adults.

5. Have you tried distracting the child from his or her aggressive pursuits? The diversion method is especially useful when it directs the student's attention to desirable activities.

Those Who Are Easily Frustrated or Distracted

1. Have you tried giving the child extra assistance? Added help can be a useful remedial technique for students who are chronically hard to handle when faced with new and difficult tasks. Instead of focusing on their misbehavior (generally a nonproductive approach), the teacher simply offers special tutoring.

2. Have you tried restructuring class routines? A change in routine is called for when students seem bored and irritable. Some children pick fights to relieve classroom dullness.

3. Have you tried establishing a more consistent routine in the classroom? A certain amount of regimentation is necessary in every classroom. Structure helps students feel more secure; they know what to expect, and the routine offers guidelines for their actions. If everyday occurrences (sharpening pencils, going to the restroom, paying milk money, etc.) are routinized, the aggressive child will be denied opportunities to distract the class.

4. Have you tried removing distracting objects from the room? Intriguing objects like athletic gear, shop tools, science equipment, and valuables of various kinds can distract children's attention away from classroom tasks. These objects can be so interesting that no amount of rule-setting will stop some students from investigating and handling them.

Those with Poor Impulse Control and Antagonistic Behavior

1. Have you tried removing the child from the room when he or she blows up? Some teachers have discovered the benefits of "antiseptic bouncing" when an aggressive child poses a danger to himself or herself or to others. The teacher should have a prearranged location to which the child can be sent. It should be a supervised area where the child can be given work to do. The child should not be able to bother other students (the opportunity to distract others can be a positive reinforcement for misbehavior). For this reason, students should not be required to stand in the hallway outside the classroom. If possible, someone should be available (summoned, perhaps, by buzzer or telephone) to take the child to the prearranged location.

2. Have you tried sending the child on an errand when he or she becomes unruly? This is another way to remove the child from a disruptive situation. The errand may be nothing more than giving the student a sealed note that explains the situation to the receiving adult (e.g., the nurse, counselor, or vice principal).

3. Have you tried asking the child what is bothering him or her? Student dissatisfaction tends to center around the following areas:

   Incongruity between student needs and educational approaches. If assignments are too easy or too hard, students become bored or frustrated—conditions that can lay groundwork for classroom unrest.

   Poor peer relationships. Is the youngster afraid of other students? Is he or she being rejected or ignored? Does the child feel academically inferior?

   Poor relationships with the teacher. If the student does not get along with the teacher, it cannot be assumed that the student is at fault. Certain teachers (unconsciously, perhaps) create a climate in the classroom that alienates students. If the teacher stimulates too much competition, makes students feel too guilty when regulations are violated, or sets unrealistically high academic standards, some children react negatively. However, resistance to such conditions may be a sign of a healthy personality.

   Poor classroom organization. A teacher adept at teaching subject matter may not be proficient at establishing good group organization. When a child does not get along with committee members or respect group leaders, he or she may feel tense or anxious. Aggressive reactions sometimes ensue. Some classrooms have distractions (noise, movement, unexpected changes in routines, etc.) that upset children.

4. Have you given the child a chance to discuss worries? Ventilation provides a chance for the child to reestablish feelings of personal power. This technique is particularly effective if the child sees changes in the classroom environment as a result of discussion. Shy youngsters may benefit more from private discussions, while outgoing children tend to like classroom forums.

   Researchers postulate that both learning and behavior problems in aggressive boys may be symptomatic of an ineffective linguistic control system. They believe that aggressive young boys often fail to use verbal mediation when it would be appropriate. When these children do attempt verbal mediation, it is faulty (because of poor vocabulary, impulsive reactions, immature and irrelevant private speech, or inhibition errors) and fails to control their behavior. I have long noted the poorly developed fantasy life of aggressive children with ADD symptoms. Without an ideational buffer (i.e., thinking matters over carefully), these impulsive children leap from impulse to immediate action.

Some overreacting, impulsive, and aggressive youngsters can be taught to use verbal mediation as a buffer between impulse and action, but others cannot. If the child becomes depressed as well as distressed when prevented from acting out inappropriate impulses, the prognosis tends to be favorable. If the child becomes angry and explosive after being frustrated, the outlook is less positive. At any rate, most children benefit to some extent from discussing their problems.

5. Have you tried setting clear, easily understood limits on the amount of misbehavior you will tolerate? Some children simply do not know what is expected of them. Teachers, who make up the rules and understand them perfectly, sometimes have difficulty comprehending that children may not hear the instructions, may not understand the concepts employed, may confuse one set of rules with another, or may simply forget what they are told. Children recall regulations better under the following conditions:

- The rules are very explicit.
- The rules are related to the student's behavior (e.g., "The rule is that everyone must hand in a paper, and you have all done that").
- The rules are carefully taught—for example, by listing them in a conspicuous place in the classroom, keeping distractions to a minimum while teaching the rules, encouraging children to explain in their own words what the rules mean, and keeping rules short and to the point.

6. Have you tried to determine whether the aggressive child is motivated to obey rules? If a disruptive student gains more pleasure from breaking rules than from obeying them, naturally he or she has little desire to honor conventional regulations. The following steps can help change this condition:

Make the penalty for disobedience more painful. This approach must be handled carefully. Some children are so habituated to the consequences of punishment that they disregard the possibility of increased suffering. Children who have become hardened to discomfort in their home environment may be difficult to impress with threats of more distress. Punishment has other disadvantages: It tends to slow unwanted responses rather than eliminate them, it fails to demonstrate correct behavior, it can result in the development of avoidance behaviors (e.g., cheating, lying, inappropriate silence, truancy) that may be more harmful to character development than the original conduct the teacher wishes to eliminate, and it can inhibit the development of socially desirable behavior because the child is afraid to be spontaneous. Also, punishment procedures tend to be copied by the recipient.

If punishment is used, it should be appropriate to the situation; that is, the child suffers a consequence for breaking an existing rule. It should not be employed to right past wrongs nor to establish the adult's power over the child. Punishment should be used in a rational manner. The adult who expresses indignation about a broken regulation confounds the message the child should receive. Instead of concentrating on the infraction, the adult is telling the child to be concerned about the adult's feelings of betrayal.

The child should understand ahead of time what the rules are, what constitutes breaking a rule, and exactly what will happen if an infraction occurs. If a rule has been violated, the stated consequences must be carried out. If the child's excuses and promises are accepted, the regulatory structure can be weakened. For some children, a warning (the nature of which has been explained to them) should precede the administration of punishment. A warning often eliminates the need for further action.

Initially, punishment should be mild; subsequent infractions can lead to more severe penalties. Harsh punishment, given too soon, leaves the authority figure with few disciplinary options. Because many children possess a poor sense of time (a week without privileges can seem like an eternity to them), extended periods of punishment should be avoided. Punishment should be accompanied by rewards for good behavior.

Finally, a child should be allowed the opportunity to end his or her own punishment by behaving more acceptably. This choice enables the child to develop better self-direction.

Make the consequences

Make the consequences for acting properly more rewarding. Rewarding correct conduct is, without a doubt, the most powerful behavior-changing tool at a teacher's disposal. A word of encouragement, a pat on the back, a display of the student's work, or a positive note to the parents about the student's progress are signs of teacher approval all children need periodically. Researchers point out that the greater the frequency and amount of the rewards, the faster the learning process. Disturbed children, in particular, need a great deal of reinforcement from the teacher. An aggressive youngster should be rewarded every time he or she responds nonaggressively, and positive reinforcements should continue until the desired behaviors have been learned. Even then, rewards should be given occasionally as insurance against the child's forgetting the improved behavior.

Timing of rewards is important. If they are granted before they have been earned, students have little incentive to comply with demands. Children who act out, have a short attention span, or are easily disappointed tend to need immediate and tangible rewards. As behavioral control is acquired, the interval between act and reward can be lengthened.

The nature of the reward can be significant. Younger aggressive students tend to respond better to tangible tokens; older students express satisfaction with more abstract compensation. The following rewards can be used to motivate students.

Tokens. Candy, play money that can be turned in for popular objects or activities, stars or points, comic books, football and baseball cards, tickets to events, trinkets of various kinds, or any agreed-upon object that appeals to the child can be given as a reward.

Teacher approval. Verbal praise, standing or sitting near the child, showing interest in the student's work, writing a note of approval that the parents can sign, giving the child a smile or wink, allowing the child to pick the teacher as a special helper or playmate, giving the child a membership in the "helpers club," or giving the youngster a special classroom job are approval-based rewards.

Classroom activities. Allowing the child to have a special rest period, permitting the student to tutor another child, assigning the student a special job (such as collecting milk money, acting as a timekeeper or hall monitor, reading a story to the class, or cleaning the chalkboards), giving the child the opportunity to read favorite stories, giving the child extra recreation time, or letting the child make special exhibits, complete a crossword puzzle, or make drawings for special projects are activities that can reward the child.

7. Have you tried working closely with the parents of the aggressive child? If the child is chronically antagonistic and aggressive, educators must make every effort to include parents in counseling procedures aimed at changing the youngster's behavior. Without parental involvement, many children will not alter their conduct. Established patterns of behavior in the home are ordinarily not flexible enough to accommodate trait modifications occurring when the child receives counseling apart from the family. Involving the parents also helps them maintain an interest in their child's problems and helps them to accept responsibility for the part they play in the formation and maintenance of the youngster's difficulties. In effect, the family acquires common knowledge that can help all members communicate and interact better.

The teacher should interview the parents first without the child present. At this meeting, the child's problem can be reviewed and possible approaches to a solution discussed. The teacher should have a well-thought-out program to present. This plan must make sense and must not be too difficult to implement. During this initial interview, the teacher should establish himself or herself as the person in charge of the program and should keep the participants focused on the central concerns of the meeting. Finally, the teacher should encourage the parents to get involved in school affairs.

8. Have you tried assessing the quality of your own relationship to misbehaving students? While most educators subscribe to the belief that helping children relate to teachers is a prime educational objective, many are reluctant to investigate this interaction. Perhaps the reason for this reluctance is that teachers (and those who observe and evaluate teachers) prefer to believe that any deficiencies in the quality of the adult-child relationship spring from a social defect in the child. This belief, which protects the adult's ego, assumes that the child should conform to all adult idiosyncrasies. It allows teachers to escape responsibility for evaluating and changing their own questionable habits.

How can teachers assess their interactions with children? One way is to observe the students' reactions to the teacher in the classroom. The following four danger signals should prompt the teacher to examine his or her own conduct: (a) chronic discontent, (b) chronic lack of cooperation, (c) disregard for classroom rules, and (d) a great deal of fighting among the children. If the children are displaying these tendencies, they may be telling the teacher that they are not interested in trying to please him or her and may actually be rebelling against conditions the teacher has set up. The teacher should not try to analyze his or her own behavior. Instead, a friend or a supporting supervisor should help with the task.

The How I Get Along with My Teacher Checklist

This measurement (see figure 19.3) can be used to evaluate a student's attitude about how the teacher relates to him or her. This checklist, usually administered by a counselor, should not be used lightly. Some children are reluctant to express dissatisfaction with a teacher for fear the teacher will dislike them. The checklist should be administered to a group only after rapport has been established with a considerable number of students in the group. The purpose of the checklist should be explained, and the students should be told that they are not required to share their responses with the teacher unless they wish to do so. If the children choose not to show their answers to the teacher, the counselor can suggest that they use the checklist as a reference for a later, private interview. All children should be interviewed about their answers.

For each item on the checklist, the child checks whether it is "not a problem," "sometimes a problem," or "often a problem." Items checked "often a problem" are indicative of serious concerns, especially if the child has many social problems. Items marked "sometimes a problem" are not to be taken too seriously for most children; however, they should be given more consideration if the child is withdrawn, tense, and anxious. Such a child tends to find it difficult to express aggression. For this type of child, an answer indicating even moderate concern deserves close attention.

This checklist can be an excellent aid in interviews with individual students. The give-and-take atmosphere of such meetings offers children an opportunity to express their feelings about teachers. Later, if the child has no objection, the counselor can communicate the findings to teachers, who are usually interested in the results. Some are surprised by the answers and indicate that they had no idea how the students felt.

Methods to Control Aggressiveness

A number of studies have investigated the efficacy of various intervention strategies designed to control aggressive behavior. The results of these studies are summarized as follows.

1. According to Bongiovanni and Hyman (1978), corporal punishment is contraindicated in the control of conduct disorders because it is generally ineffective and may actually reinforce undesirable behavior.
2. After-school programs that teach athletics, crafts, or other special interests can help some students achieve a sense of mastery over their environment and can enhance their social relationships (Alwon, 1979).
3. Boys with behavior problems showed improvement after being exposed to a seven-week filmmaking workshop. The children made up stories with different outcomes that allowed them to see how behavior other than aggressiveness produced social rewards (Arnott & Gushin, 1976).
4. Firm limitations on aggressive behavior are suggested for children who wish to control others sadistically, but not for children whose aggressive behavior reflects an effort to achieve a sense of order in an inconsistent external environment and/or a potentially chaotic internal personality environment (Frankel, 1977).
5. Some children can learn to control aggressive impulses by being trained to talk to themselves—first overtly, then covertly (Coats, 1979).

HOW I GET ALONG WITH MY TEACHER

Harold F. Burks, Ph.D.

For each statement, put a check mark in the column that tells how you feel.

	Not a problem	Sometimes a problem	Often a problem
1. I wish I could tell the teacher about some things that bother me.	☐	☐	☐
2. I don't think the teacher has enough time to help me.	☐	☐	☐
3. Maybe the teacher thinks I can't do things very well.	☐	☐	☐
4. I feel nervous about asking the teacher for help.	☐	☐	☐
5. I worry about the teacher asking me for answers.	☐	☐	☐
6. I don't understand why the teacher gets upset.	☐	☐	☐
7. I have some good ideas but I can't tell the teacher about them.	☐	☐	☐
8. I wish the teacher would let me help around the room more.	☐	☐	☐
9. The teacher gives some of the other kids too many special favors.	☐	☐	☐
10. I wish the teacher had more time to explain the lessons.	☐	☐	☐
11. The teacher doesn't understand the problems I have with reading.	☐	☐	☐
12. The teacher doesn't understand the problems I have with spelling.	☐	☐	☐
13. The teacher doesn't understand the problems I have with writing.	☐	☐	☐
14. The teacher doesn't understand the problems I have with arithmetic.	☐	☐	☐
15. The teacher doesn't understand the problems I have in playing games.	☐	☐	☐
16. The teacher doesn't know the problems I have with homework.	☐	☐	☐
17. I wish the teacher understood some of the problems I have with other kids.	☐	☐	☐
18. I wish the teacher knew that some of the kids pick on me.	☐	☐	☐
19. I wish the teacher would let me help some of the other kids.	☐	☐	☐
20. I wish I had a chance to tell the class about some things that are interesting to me.	☐	☐	☐

Figure 19.3.

6. Aggressive children who are compelled to select and observe a peer and then to model their behavior after that individual are reported to show a rapid and almost complete elimination of peer aggressiveness (Hayduk, 1978).

7. Consultations between counselors and teachers of disruptive students may effect behavioral changes in the children. If such meetings do not result in modifications, the psychologist or counselor may wish to intervene directly with the child as a "personal behavior manager." In addition to providing the teacher with methods for altering undesirable behavior, intervention permits school psychologists and counselors to increase their credibility with teachers and to train teachers in behavioral intervention techniques (Langhorne, Paternite, & Loney, 1979).

8. Boys with conduct problems who were placed in a contingency-managed classroom (in which children are allowed to engage in preferred activities contingent on their behavior) for 10 weeks before reentering regular classrooms were reported by their regular classroom teachers to be significantly more attentive (Elliot, Barrish, Hale, & Wessman, 1977).

9. Aggressive children who assumed roles in acting out stories did not become less aggressive or more empathic with others after training in role-playing and role-switching. However, altruism was significantly increased in six-year-olds and a significant improvement in role-playing was noted (Iannotti, 1978).

10. Self-recording (e.g., monitoring the number of correctly solved multiplication problems) coupled with teacher praise is a powerful technique for changing behavior and academic achievement (Dickie & Finegan, 1977).

11. Classroom token systems designed to reduce disruptive behavior are sometimes more effective when teacher visits to the home are introduced as an additional measure, contingent upon appropriate conduct (Diaddigo & Dickie, 1978).

12. Vicarious aggressive activity, such as hammering or pounding objects, will reduce subsequent aggressive behavior if the participant is emotionally aroused at the time he or she engages in this activity. If anger has not been aroused before the activity, however, the activity results in an increase in subsequent aggressiveness (Feshbach, 1961).

13. Resource rooms (as opposed to self-contained special classes) for behaviorally disordered children may be a mixed blessing (Glavin, Quay, Annesley, & Werry, 1971). Any intervention that removes the basic responsibility for the student from the control of the regular class teacher serves to make reintegration into the regular class more difficult. While conduct improvements are generally noted in the resource room, the improved behavior tends not to generalize to the regular classroom. Techniques found to be advantageous in the resource room may not work in regular classrooms, where teachers may be too busy to implement the procedures or may lack training in the specific techniques.

14. Aggressive, retarded individuals who are placed in a special class setting may respond better to structured interventions (Floyd & Hughes, 1980). These can consist of

   - self-charting of behavior;
   - token systems;
   - differential reinforcement of incompatible behavior;
   - verbal and physical prompts;
   - restraints;
   - time out from reinforcement;
   - seclusion;
   - varied teaching alternatives.

15. Aggressive behavior decreased and positive behavior increased in very young children when teachers explained to them that aggression can bring harm (Zehavi & Asher, 1978).

16. Application of some intervention techniques to difficulties in the home can improve the child's behavior at home and have a positive influence on school behavior. For example, Levi, Buskila, and Gerzi (1977) found that parental noninterference tended to decrease sibling fighting. Also, adaptation of the "beat the buzzer" technique to the home environment can help regulate morning schedules for elementary school–age children, thereby reducing the frustration of parents and children alike. Parents set a buzzer or timer to go off at a certain time each morning, by which time a habitually late child must have completed a posted list of duties. The granting of nighttime television viewing privileges (within reason) can be used as a reinforcement procedure (Drabman & Creedon, 1979).

CHAPTER 20

Excessive Resistance

Rebelliousness as a personality trait can be described as an unwillingness on the part of a child to cooperate with the wishes of others. Children with high scores in the excessive resistance (rebellious) category of the Burks Behavior Rating Scales (BBRS) (Burks, 1977a, 2006a) tend to

- refuse to take suggestions;
- insist on having their way;
- deny responsibility for their actions;
- be stubborn;
- be rebellious if disciplined.

Teachers indicate that there are a large number of these children in regular classrooms. Like the BBRS aggressive tendencies scale, the resistance scale is associated with other scales that measure antisocial behavior (i.e., poor social conformity, poor motivation, and poor anger control). It seldom correlates heavily with the self-blame scale.

THEORETICAL BACKGROUND

The refusal to cooperate with the wishes of others is an antisocial behavioral trait (M. D. Jordan, 2005). Some children express anger through nonconformity, physical force, or destruction of property. Stubborn, oppositional children, on the other hand, may show rebelliousness as covert disobedience. Unfortunately, they are often unaware of unproductive and self-defeating consequences (Webster-Stratton & Herbert, 1994).

Origins of resistance usually stem from unsatisfactory parent-child relationships (Bryant & Harvey, 2000). Negativism is common among children in the early years but tends to disappear in later years. If it continues in an extreme form, it may be due to nagging and bossy parents who are critical and fussy about rules and regulations. Some older overprotected children rebel against a home environment that does not allow them greater freedom. During adolescence, opposition is seen as a way to emancipate the self from emotional and physical dependence on adults.

Resistance, as a behavioral technique, is obviously learned. Secondary gains obtained from its use tend to fix it in as a character trait. The individual is able to ignore the presence of a problem by being stubborn or defiant. As the center of attention, the person gains power. Finally, the resistant, hostile individual can feel gratified when the technique inflicts psychic injury on others.

The passive-aggressive individual expects his or her nonresponsive actions to upset others (proving the youngster wields special influence). The best way to handle this type of conduct is to fail to respond or make a fuss about the passivity. The lack of response will create anxiety in the youngster (he or she loses power). Adults should wait out the unwilling child and should not fall into the trap of doing everything to please him or her.

INTERVENTION STRATEGIES

Techniques for Counselors

Counselors frequently encounter older children and adolescents who resist help. Treatment sessions bog down in long silences, repetitive or stereotyped conversation, or an outright refusal to attend. Many counselors are stymied by these maneuvers. Understanding a resisting youngster's need to preserve character defenses leads to an exploration of counseling methods that have some chance of success.

The following practices (Sherman, 1966) may be called "joining techniques" because the counselor sides with the resistant child to form a therapeutic alliance. These approaches share an acceptance and preservation of the child's personality defenses, particularly those that are paranoid or symbiotic in nature, until the child has gained enough insight and ego strength to replace these maladaptive traits with more effective behaviors. The choice of methods depends in part on the counselor's judgment of what the child or adolescent will tolerate and in part on the counselor's counter-transference feelings (anger, anxiety, resistance).

Joining techniques show individuals that the counselor honors emotional defenses. Neurotic defenses are basic and necessary for survival and have creative and protective characteristics as well as stifling functions. However, the very resistant individual has erected defenses that pervade the personality structure while symptoms of anxiety and remorse tend to be absent. The resistant person's symptoms of passivity, dependence, hostility, detachment, and passive-aggressiveness are difficult to treat. Many parents of resistant youngsters subtly reinforce such behavior by deriding their children, coercing them, and remaining dissatisfied with any efforts at improvement. Under such conditions, it is not surprising that the children decide to remain aloof and uninvolved. With joining techniques, the child is at first startled and puzzled but soon becomes relaxed and relieved to find an adult who, unlike his or her parents, values the child's personality integrity.

Joining techniques are best employed with late latency or teenage youngsters who possess some ability to analyze their behavior. Younger children (except some obsessive-compulsive children) lack the ability to externalize and objectify feelings. Individuals may be chosen who show no obvious signs of anxiety but who demonstrate prominent symptoms of denial, passivity, and projection—in short, those narcissistic disorders that have proved resistant to traditional inward-looking counseling methods.

Parents should be warned ahead of time that joining techniques will be used; otherwise, the child may present parents a bizarre interpretation of what goes on in the sessions, or the parents may become resentful or even angry when they see the counselor take the child's side. Sherman (1966) stressed that joining techniques are not an end in themselves; they are simply a means to establish treatment processes for difficult children. Joining techniques include the following strategies.

Ignoring. The counselor pays no attention to the resistance—this works particularly well in groups of teenagers when one or more refuse to become involved. The counselor can remain silent (drink a cup of coffee, eat candy, read a book) while paying no heed to the passive members, talk about himself or herself, or tell stories while remaining uninvolved. Passive-aggressive individuals have difficulty handling this kind of behavior, apparently because they have learned that their own passivity arouses anger and stress in others, which gives them a sense of power. All but the most resistant youngster will soon turn to the counselor in anger, inquiring, "Aren't we supposed to be doing something here?" At this point the counselor can apologize for his or her behavior and ask politely what it is the participant would like to say.

The counselor must not react in anger to attacks by the youngster, because to do so would be duplicating the behavior of the child's exasperated parents. The child is running the show at home, and the parents feel helpless and frustrated. The youngster cannot be allowed to manipulate the counselor, but at the same time, the child must feel the support and affection of this surrogate parent.

High-valuing. The counselor praises the child's ability to remain detached from others. The therapist may say, "I think it's really great that you can be so calm when everybody else is upset!" The therapist might go on to inquire about other detachment methods the child uses.

Countermanding. The therapist helps the child deal with unwanted parental demands during therapy. For example, a parent may insist that a youngster relate a recent episode of bad behavior to the counselor. As a counter-measure, the therapist instructs the child to relate only pleasant events, in the hope that the youngster will lose his or her fear of the counseling sessions and identify with the therapist more strongly.

This method can help subvert the game of resistance and counter-resistance that is played out in some families. If not interrupted, these games can be used by parents to defeat gains made in therapy. Some parents are unconsciously angry with their youngster and seek to inflict revenge on the child. If the countermanding method is to be employed, it is mandatory to counsel the parents in advance to explore any negative feelings (subconscious as well as conscious) they may have about their child—along with ways to handle such emotions. Otherwise, the technique will surely alienate them and cause them to abandon counseling.

Use-abuse. This method can be effective with underachievers who appear to want to achieve, appear to have genuine remorse about their failures, and who seem anxious to keep the goodwill of the counselor, despite the fact that they continue to fail. The core of the therapeutic dilemma is the problem of getting at underlying resentment. Treatment starts with the counselor making reasonable requests of the child which the child predictably ignores. Then, increasingly outrageous demands are made (e.g., asking the child to explain why he or she has so few friends, why he or she is doing so poorly at school), much like those the youngster perceives his or her parents make. Coercive extortion will bring hostile feelings to the surface, where they can be dealt with in counseling sessions.

Because rage is elicited, this technique has to be handled with care or it will interrupt the therapeutic transference. The young person must retain affection and respect for the counselor and not become alienated. Trust, once lost, is not likely to be regained. The method may be best employed with older teenagers who have demonstrated some ability to stand back and evaluate their own conduct and who possess a sense of humor. It goes without saying that the counselor must continue to convey a feeling of affection to the adolescent.

Teach the counselor. The youngster is asked to "tutor" the counselor to be as offensive as the child is. It can be a useful ploy to counteract attacks upon the counselor by the child. The assaults, passive in some cases ("I don't know," "I don't care") and aggressive in others ("You don't know anything"), are attempts to cover up fear and anxiety. The counselor must be sensitive to—and willing to handle—negative emotions.

To begin with, many of these children do not think anyone could understand or care about their problems. In addition, they are afraid of being put down by adults. Finally, they do not understand the futility of their resistant behavior. Such understanding must come before they can engage in more constructive conduct. "Teaching the counselor" can help the child see the counselor as a trusted, supportive figure. This method, along with most other joining techniques, should be conducted with humor and with the counselor verbally identifying with the problems the youngster faces. An excerpt from an interview with a passive-aggressive, early adolescent girl illustrates the use of this method:

Therapist: I talked with your mother yesterday.

Judy: Yeah.

Therapist: What a worry wart! "How's Judy doing? How's Judy doing?" Is she always that pushy?

Judy: I guess so. (Shows guarded interest.)

Therapist: You know what I did? I did the same thing you do, I guess. I said, "I don't know, I don't know, I don't know." Is that what I should have done?

Judy: Yeah. (Laughs slightly.)

Therapist: Is there a better way? Should I shrug like this? (Makes an exaggerated motion of throwing hands in the air.)

Judy: Yeah, that's better! (Laughing.) But you should also roll your eyes back, like this. (Demonstrates.)

The more the automatic (rather than voluntary) nature of the passive-aggressive conduct is revealed to the teenager, the more difficult it is to maintain defensive facades.

Mirroring. The counselor plays the role of a helpless, inadequate person who needs assistance from the child. As the young person becomes a helper, he or she, in theory, will become more aggressive and less resistant. The therapist can express frustration about, for example, the young person's parents or peers in the counseling group. This approach is most effective when the child knows the individuals about whom the therapist complains and the counselor mimics conduct used by the youngster (e.g., whining, negativism, being demanding). The externalization of behavior traits enables the child to deal with them more effectively.

This technique gives the child an immediate sense of power. In the beginning, he or she may come to the counseling session with deep underlying fears of parental rejection or abandonment. The child's reaction to these anxieties is to act overly independent and uninvolved. Now, the counselor says, in effect, "Please give me help; I need assistance from you."

I have used a variation on this theme. The therapist asks youngsters to help him or her become a better chess (checkers, pool, Ping-Pong, or backgammon) player. Most youngsters feel they are experts at some game and are enthusiastic about assisting an older individual. In addition, games are invaluable therapeutic devices in that they allow the counselor and the young person to become lost in a friendly interaction where much communication, both verbal and nonverbal, can take place. The child feels freer to talk about matters that concern him or her than if asked to discuss personal problems.

Insistent ordering. The counselor deliberately demands that the young person exercise resistant behavior. "I don't want you to participate in this conversation," the therapist may say, in a kind but insistent way. "I think I know everything there is to know about the problem, so you don't have to say anything." This technique is best employed in a group situation. After placing restrictions on the participant, the counselor goes on to converse with another group member. Under these circumstances, the child who is told to be quiet tends to feel less rejected than he or she might in an individual conference. Most children perceive the demand to be quiet as an unreasonable infraction of their rights and will eventually speak up, at which point the counselor drops the request for silence and listens respectfully to the youngster.

Child advocate. The counselor speaks for the child in groups that include educators or parents and the youngster. The child identifies the counselor as a supporting and sympathetic friend who goes to bat for him or her. This allegiance (or transference) is an invaluable commodity in the counseling process. It is wise for the counselor to sit next to the child so that the two of them face the others at the meeting (another form of togetherness).

Unless this technique is explained to them ahead of time, parents and teachers may be resistant when they observe the child being given support of this nature. This is not surprising since, in nearly all cases, the interview is being held because the youngster has "failed" in some behavioral or academic aspect. If the meeting is skillfully conducted, however, many insights can be gained by group participants.

One such meeting involved the parents, the teacher, a counselor, and a 12-year-old boy who had difficulty getting along with fellow students. The counselor said, "I think Bill gets mad and fights with the other kids because they make him nervous. Isn't that true, Bill? (Bill nodded vigorously.) I also think Bill would like to talk to the teacher and his mother and father about his worries. (Bill nodded again.)" These insights had been acquired in an interview between the counselor and the child and were based on the assumption that any child who fights with peers is likely to be covertly afraid of them. While the child's parents and teacher could have been informed of these facts in another manner, seeing the youngster agree to the spoken diagnosis made it more meaningful and perhaps helped them become more sympathetic to his plight.

Playing consultant. The child is encouraged to discuss the diagnosis and treatment of another person. Many young people will talk willingly about someone in their everyday world (e.g., a friend, parent, or sibling). They often believe they know what problems that individual faces and what the person should do about those difficulties. Such a discussion will reveal much about the child. These insights need not be pointed out to the child, however, since doing so may put the youngster off. The conversation itself is therapeutically beneficial in that it provides ventilation of suppressed feelings and helps the child feel closer to an adult figure.

Techniques for School Personnel

Teachers describe resistance as a major problem in children. Because the resistance is often toward learning tasks, extreme opposition cannot be ignored. In addition, resistance can adversely affect social relationships.

Teachers must realize that they are not responsible for severe resistance in students (although they may cause some children to be temporarily negative), and they should not feel guilty about it—even when parents try to make them feel responsible. Many stubborn children are not achieving in school because they are not motivated (Light, 2005). Teachers can take some effective action, including (a) keeping the parents informed of the child's actions, successes, and failures; (b) providing academic exercises that meet the student's ability level so that he or she has no real excuse for not trying; (c) encouraging the parents (through proper school resources) to seek therapeutic services for the child and themselves; (d) calmly refusing to accept the parents' complaint that the school is failing to "challenge the child's mind"; and (e) reinforcing in material ways all the student's positive efforts.

In school situations, the resisting child is probably best treated in a group. The teacher should not try to control the child with direct verbal commands. The resisting child can be gently encouraged to join in student activities, but the appeal should be made to the group. Direct confrontations between child and teacher should be carefully avoided because they can only result in one or the other losing. Physical punishment should be avoided.

Giving the child a set of options, in the hope that he or she will make the proper choice, has also proved successful. If this method is used, it must be accompanied by clear instructions about the consequences (both pleasant and unpleasant) that accompany any choice.

The preceding suggestions may be applicable to the home situation as well, but home conditions often make success less likely. Some parents may be able to modify their overanxious, nagging, authoritarian behavior; others may not.

Techniques for Parents

The school should work with the parents of a severely resistant child, but as with other types of disruptive children, this is no easy undertaking.

Sherman (1966) pointed out that when one individual in a family shows resistance, other family members evidence a similar quality. This resistance is based on the members' inability to communicate meaningfully with one another. Often there is a pretense that conflicts do not exist. This communication barrier extends to agencies outside the home. Efforts are made by family members to keep the family neurosis intact. For example, if the school helps an adolescent boy become more independent, his mother may become severely anguished and complain that her son's behavior has become worse.

Many parents of stubborn children have no wish to participate in counseling sessions designed to explore family behavior. For these families, the school is well-advised to do little more than conduct a mandatory conference with the parents, outlining what is expected of their children and suggesting to the parents that if they cannot meet these requirements, they should seek expert help elsewhere. Parental arguments should not be humored at this meeting.

For those showing more interest in the program, the school may set up a series of individual or group conferences designed to help parents manage their children better. Group meetings are most valuable because many parents, particularly those of resistant youngsters, do not care to confront an authority figure on a one-to-one basis, where they feel defenses might be broached more easily.

The main thrust of the meetings should be to change parental behavior, not parental motivation. The exploration of the inner dynamics of motivations can be a proper exercise for therapists who see patients over long periods of time, but counselors in school settings should restrict efforts to behavior-changing instructions, in the hope that the beneficial results of these conduct modifications will eventually alter parental attitudes.

The following questions address specific parental behavior that can be observed, examined, discussed, and possibly changed. These questions are intended to spark parental interest in the oppositional conduct of their children, as well as to provide specific information about behavior-changing techniques.

1. Do you tend to nag your child? Children who respond to a request with "Just a minute" or "Get off my back; I'll do it"—and then do nothing to comply—invite nagging. Parents should choose a few important things they want their child to do, tell the youngster what is expected of him or her, and then follow through on orders. Parents should not pay attention to child resistance. Oppositional behavior is often merely a surface phenomenon and the youngster will give in quickly if an adult insists (quietly) that he or she get started.

2. Do you "know it all"? If parents appear to their child to have all the answers, at least two unfortunate things can result: (a) the child may act as though he or she is submitting to the parents' authority but actually resists by not performing as requested; and (b) using the parents as a model, the child may come to believe that mistakes are reprehensible. In order not to make mistakes, the youngster avoids tasks that hint of failure. The child cannot mature fully if he or she sees the parents as infallible. The youngster is kept dependent and unable to make more adult decisions. The parents need to be more comfortable with themselves and to show the child that they, too, have understandable and forgivable foibles.

3. Do you avoid talking openly with your child? If the parents are uncommunicative, the child may emulate their silence. Others may interpret this unwillingness to talk as resistance (actually, the youngster may regard the parents' behavior as a way of resisting him or her). The parents should talk more with the child and discuss mutual problems. Their openness may encourage the child to be open with others.

4. Do you think your performance standards are too high? Most children would like to please by producing what parents ask of them. However, if children cannot meet expected goals, they can become resentful. If they are not allowed to voice this distress, they must express protests by refusing to work (adult workers do the same thing—when management turns a deaf ear to complaints, the employees slow down production, using the only avenue of protest left open).

   The parents might try lowering demands if their high expectations are the problem. The youngster may quickly respond. Additionally, they should try acting more pleased when the child does meet a goal.

5. When your child says no, do you react in extreme ways? Why not try ignoring the negative replies? The youngster who can upset his or her parents with negative answers is receiving a gratifying response: The child gets attention, demonstrates power over the parents, and is often able to get out of doing an unpleasant task. The parents should calmly ignore objections and insist that the youngster do what is expected of him or her.

6. Do you pay attention to your youngster only when he or she refuses to cooperate? Some children are trained to be negative by parents who pay attention only when the youngsters refuse to cooperate. When these same children behave in acceptable ways, the parents ignore them. It is obvious what must be done here—rewards must be given for correct conduct, not for resistant behavior.

7. Do you bribe your child into cooperating? Attempts to bribe (e.g., "You can have a cookie if you clean up your room") can soon backfire. The offered reward can further strengthen exhibited negativism. The youngster comes to expect a payoff for balky behavior.

8. If your child resists doing chores and homework, do you insist he or she do these things unassisted? This can be a doomed procedure. The youngster either does nothing or "messes up." The parents become upset and start pushing again. Parents might try helping more. They can teach the child to finish jobs in a more efficient and speedy manner by working in close proximity.

9. Do you make it easy for your child to argue with you? Skillful debaters are made, not born. When a child learns it is safe to argue with adults, he or she can grow up with the conviction that authority can be overcome. Parents

need to act like parents. They should insist on obedience for things the child cannot be allowed to challenge (e.g., eating on time, going to bed on schedule, arriving at school at the proper hour).

10. Do you explain to your child the consequences of resisting and then follow through with consequences when appropriate? It is not fair to punish a child for resisting if he or she does not understand what the parents want. Once the youngster knows what is expected, the parents make clear what will happen if a command is disobeyed. They can also point out the profitable consequences of heeding the directive. When a child is given the choice of behaving (with pleasant consequences) or not behaving (with painful consequences), he or she is likely to choose the correct path.

11. Do you give your child enough independence? Parents may think their child cannot handle freedom, but as a child grows older, he or she must be given opportunities to make decisions and manage events. Otherwise, the youngster remains dependent and possibly angry and resistant.

CHAPTER 21

Poor Social Conformity

Poor social conformity as a personality trait is described as the inability to control personal and social behavior in an ethically approved manner. Children with high scores on the poor social conformity category of the Burks Behavior Rating Scales (BBRS) (Burks, 1977a, 2006a) tend to

- be truant;
- be chronic liars;
- get involved in escapades;
- show little respect for authority;
- display a "don't care" attitude;
- take things that do not belong to them;
- be irresponsible;
- be tardy;
- tell falsehoods.

Delinquent children with character defects (those who demonstrate an inability to show remorse) often get high scores on this rebellious scale. If antisocial pathology is serious and diffuse in the character structure, if little insight into these deficiencies is demonstrated and if the child's harmful or negative social behavior causes him or her little or no personal suffering or remorse, the probability of helping the child is minimal. Associated BBRS high ratings are commonly seen on the poor motivation, excessive resistance, and excessive aggressiveness tendencies scales.

THEORETICAL BACKGROUND

Children who act out unethical and socially unacceptable impulses are usually seen by parents and teachers as a severe discipline problem (Englander, 2001). If a youngster lacks a sense of remorse for misdeeds, the outlook for changing unwanted behavior is not hopeful. The antisocial child with neurotic disorders, on the other hand, experiences inward tension about misbehavior and some may welcome help.

Etiology

The factors that lead to poor social conformity can be divided into three categories: psychogenic, genetic, and sociogenic (Didato, 1969).

Psychogenic. Influences leading to intrapsychic conflict can be considered under this heading. The most powerful contributions, as expected, come from disturbed family relationships. Snyder (1977) has pointed out that problem families provide more aversive and fewer positive consequences for prosocial behavior than do nonproblem families. In general, problem family members are less responsive to consequences than are nonproblem members (Fowles, Sutker, & Goodman, 1994).

Distorted and frustrating family relationships can have a number of disturbing effects (Brown, 2001). The child may develop powerful inner feelings of hostility, expressed through displays of rebellion against social controls. The child may develop low self-esteem. To enhance a self-concept, the youngster may attempt acts of daring to prove he or she can overcome authority. The child may feel inadequate in gender-role abilities. To compensate for feelings of inadequacy, a youngster may attempt to obtain admiration from delinquent peers.

Genetic. Investigators (Fowles et al., 1994; Mednick & Christiansen, 1977; Tate et al., 1995) have stressed the genetic components underlying the development of the antisocial personality. A study by Gleuck and Gleuck (1952), which lists characteristics such as impulsivity, restlessness, energetic activity, and extroversion as being typical of many delinquents, reflects an early interest in the possible association between inherited traits and antisocial behavior. I believe that these qualities, if genetically determined, are not in themselves entirely responsible for delinquent behavior but could make an individual more susceptible to negative environmental influences.

Sociogenic. Sociogenic factors reflect negative social forces impinging on the adolescent. The delinquent, perhaps not inwardly disturbed, still has subclinical needs that are not being met within the family constellation. A lack of parental nurturance and affection can result in an impoverished ego, leading the child to (a) seek out substitute family groups (such as gangs) where he or she may achieve a more clearly defined social position and receive recognition and acceptance, (b) attempt to introject (establish a guiding inner figure) a substantial father or big-brother model, and (c) develop a strong need for autonomy as a protest against perceived unjust familial controls.

THE TWO TYPES OF ANTISOCIAL PERSONALITIES

The Neurotic Delinquent

High poor social conformity scores on the BBRS may be obtained by children who are unconsciously driven to misbehavior by neurotic (irrational) forces. These youngsters have commonly received overly harsh training during early development. They often show a related high score on the BBRS anxiety scale. Fortunately, even though primary instruction was severe, the youngster was taught and retains the ability to feel guilt for wrongdoing. This type of individual merits further discussion.

Adolescence is a unique life stage. The personality is in dramatic flux. Bodily changes, emerging sexual urges, pressures from peers, parents, and teachers, anxieties about fulfilling looming adult responsibilities, and the struggles to find an identity all contribute to overwhelming strains for some individuals.

Causal Factors

Three categories of causation can be discussed:

1. Contributions of emotional distress: For whatever reason (sexual confusion, physical trauma, divorce in the family, personal failings, or whatever) a child can exhibit symptoms of fearfulness, social withdrawal, depression, low self-esteem, anxiety, low frustration tolerance, lack of self-confidence, poor social skills, or poor school performance. Complaints include statements that no one likes him or her. Periods of crying and upset behavior may be observed.
2. Contributions of factors leading to rebellious behavior: Family conflicts, poor parental cooperation, feeling manipulated by caregivers, and poor parental communication skills are all home factors that can inspire youngsters to hate rules and regulations, to form relationships with gang members, and to get into fights. The normal desire of the youngster to assert his or her autonomy takes on a distorted and antagonistic forms which can also include being chronically angry, manipulating others for short-term gains, feeling above the law, taking no responsibility, being selfish and self-centered, and taking risks.

3. The contribution of drugs or alcohol: Problems discussed above are complicated by the destructive effects of substance abuse. These addictions must be addressed first by counselors or therapists before attempts are made to deal with other problems.

Characteristics

The neurotic delinquent will often be noted for

- spending large amounts of time alone, in isolation from family and friends;
- suddenly doing poorly in school;
- exhibiting dramatic mood swings or changes in behavior;
- demonstrating changes in peer group affiliations or separation from long-time friends;
- showing a sudden lack of interest in hobbies or social and recreational activities.

Internal Dialogue

We may assume the troubled teen will talk to the self in the following ways:

- "The only kids I can trust are the guys in the gang I belong to."
- "The thing that bothers me the most is that I might be queer."
- "Everything makes me mad."
- "If I jump off a high roof the other kids will think I'm cool."
- "The whole world is against me."

The neurotic troubled teen can commit a crime while unaware of consequences. A girl can become pregnant due to ignorance of birth control methods. Either sex can become involved in a car wreck while racing. These actions can lead to tragic results (Ferguson, 1999; Maxym & York, 2001).

Sometimes the nature of the offense (e.g., setting fires, running away, engaging in sexual escapades) gives clues to the presence of neurotic forces. Kessler suggested that unconscious material plays a major role in the determination of expressed delinquent symptoms. Kessler also believes a particular youngster may exhibit certain signs because he or she is following a mandate from the parent's unconscious or is being led by impulses of aggression, guilt, or fantasy from the child's own internalized neurosis (similar to a classical neurosis). The following are possible scenarios for each of these types of neurotic delinquency.

Mandates from the parent's unconscious. Defects in the child's superego correspond to similar defects in the parent's superego. The parent finds displaced pleasure and gratification in the child's antisocial conduct and unconsciously sanctions the behavior. For example:

- The parent warns the child over and over what will happen if he or she disobeys orders. The parent constantly checks to see if the orders have been carried out. Message: "I expect you to get into trouble. See! You are in trouble and I'm proved right!" Result: The child senses the parent's need to have the child create trouble and follows the parent's unspoken orders.
- The parent may outwardly deplore the child's misbehavior but reveals his or her true motivation by a barely repressed smile or amazed tone of voice. Message: "I really admire what you're doing but I have to pretend that I don't." Result: The child senses approval for misconduct and continues to misbehave.
- The parent accepts a transparent lie as an excuse for misconduct. Message: "Oh, I see. John gave you that new bicycle. How nice!" Result: The child internalizes the parent's defect in moral judgment.
- The parent borrows something from the child, promises to return it, but does not. Message: It's not important to return what you take from others. Result: The child "borrows" (steals) from others and does not think it is important to return things.

- The parent teaches the child to lie by asking the child to confess to a delinquent act about which the parent already knows exists. Message: "I'm pretending (lying to you) that I don't know what you did." Result: The child comes to believe it is legitimate to lie.
- The parent teaches the child to be the black sheep of the family by acting unconsciously gratified when the child does something wrong and acting pleased when the child is punished. Message: "I'm glad you did that because I, too, would like to do it, but it's a bad impulse and I'm glad you're being punished." Result: The child senses the parent's pleasure at the child's wrongdoing, senses the parent's disapproval of the act, and accepts the need to be "bad" and to be punished for sinful deeds.

Kessler points out the neurotic equilibrium acted out between parents and children fulfills so many needs of the parents that it is generally a difficult interaction to treat in counseling. Many neurotic delinquents must be separated from the parents before treatment can be successful.

Mandates from the child's unconscious. Friedlander (1947) gave a detailed description of the neurotic delinquent who is driven to misbehave because of unconscious needs (e.g., stealing objects from an ungiving parent as a symbolic way to gain affection). The child often arranges to be caught (to satisfy the superego's demand for punishment). Kessler (1966) pointed out that the neurotic delinquent usually functions alone, is poorly rooted in reality, is not well aware of what he or she is doing, and feels more guilty when presented with evidence of misbehavior than a delinquent who runs with a gang or other associates.

The character delinquent. The term psychopathic personality was coined by early mental health workers who believed that certain individuals have constitutional (genetic) dispositions that prevent them from forming an adequate, functioning conscience during the early years of development. An increased understanding of the toxic effects of early infantile deprivation (which led to the postulate that psychopathy develops in the first two years of life) caused professionals to employ such labels as "unsocialized aggressive" and "antisocial character disorder" (Day, 2002).

I believe that this type of delinquent, whether genetically predisposed or socially conditioned (or both), suffers a severe character disorder that remains largely untouched by the usual counseling methods. The following list of characteristics (Burks 1977a, 2006a, 2006b) typical of delinquents is based on long experience with delinquents in jail, in school systems, and in counseling situations.

The delinquent child

- is unreliable;
- shows poor judgment;
- appears irresponsible;
- is impulsive;
- sets unrealistic goals;
- cannot delay gratification;
- is unable to give or receive affection;
- exploits others;
- shows little guilt;
- promises to perform but does not;
- disappoints others;
- shows little anxiety;
- lacks a sense of ethics;
- is easily bored;
- is apathetic to challenges;
- seeks constant excitement;
- is impatient;
- shows little interest in schoolwork;

- cannot accept rules;
- cannot accept competition;
- cannot resist temptation.

Myths and Facts in Relation to Poor Social Conformity

The antisocial juvenile can, but does not always, represent a severe problem to social institutions. The degree of threat rests in how a misbehaving act is defined. According to Haney and Gold (1973), delinquent conduct is measured against an individual's motives as well as a community's norms. A delinquent act, according to them, is one that is illegal and one that the person knows is illegal when he or she commits it.

Myths and half-truths abound in the field of juvenile delinquency, according to Haney and Gold. In an effort to place the topic on a more sure footing, they investigated the theories, practices, and policies of the public and the judicial system as they pertain to the management of misbehaving youth.

Socioeconomic status. Haney and Gold (1973) concluded that the stereotype of the juvenile delinquent—neglected, slum-spawned, and gang-associated—is largely a myth. According to these authors, everyone has assumed that *detected* delinquency accurately reflects *undetected* delinquent behavior. The assumption is largely wrong because official records are highly misleading. Delinquency is not confined to lower-class blacks or lower-class white males. Middle-class youngsters commit misdeeds, but officials tend to overlook their conduct (or the parents buy them out of trouble).

Further, only 3% of all delinquent acts are ever discovered by law enforcement personnel (Haney & Gold, 1973). In addition, getting caught and having a report filed in official records apparently make adolescents more likely to commit other delinquent acts.

Without doubt, educators and police officials tend to believe that the actions of lower-class children are more suspect than those of middle-class youngsters. I have represented many middle-class families in court hearings. Most of the young people involved in those hearings were put on probation (instead of, for example, being put into a youth detention program) and returned to their families. Court officials invariably were reassured by the presence of a mental health authority figure who stated that he or she was working with the family. This kind of service is not available to most lower-class families, and I suspect that many youngsters from such families are given harsher sentences.

One must not assume, of course, that socioeconomic status has no effect on child-rearing practices (Englander, 2001; Webster-Stratton & Herbert, 1994). Suh and Carlson (1977) claimed that an unsocialized aggressive reaction, related to hostile-permissive child-rearing methods, is more common among lower-class families. Aronfreed (1961) pointed out that lower-class parents are more likely to use aggressive methods in child discipline, particularly physical punishment, than are middle-class parents. The latter are more apt to use techniques described as "love-oriented" or "psychological," consisting primarily of withdrawal of love, isolation, ignoring the child, reasoning, and explanation.

Single-parent versus intact homes. Haney and Gold (1973) also concluded that single-parent homes do not always produce more delinquent youngsters than do intact homes. For example:

1. It is not true, as many court officials believe (Susman, 2007), that a stepfather is better for a child than no father at all. On the contrary, boys and girls who were raised by a stepfather and a natural mother were involved in more frequent and serious delinquent acts than were children brought up in single-parent households.
2. Boys raised solely by mothers were among the least delinquent of all studied samples.
3. Boys who had delinquent friends and poor grades were usually highly delinquent, whether their homes were intact or broken (Mandel & Marcus, 1988).

The ambiguous role of the stepfather has not received the professional attention it deserves. The role of the stepfather is fraught with hazards, particularly if the stepchildren are age 10 or older. While some children may accept the new parent, many feel that demonstrating affection would be tantamount to disloyalty to a departed natural father. Others experience jealousy—the perceived intruder captures the attention and love of the natural mother, properties the children feel belong to them exclusively.

When children misbehave in order to express distress about a stepfather, family adults must be counseled to understand what is occurring. Punitive methods employed in the absence of insight generally prove useless. The children will subvert established rules to get back at offending parent figures. Family group counseling has proved useful (Mash & Barkley, 1989).

Academic status. Boys are more seriously and frequently delinquent if their grades are poor, but no evidence has been found that academic status has any effect on delinquency among girls. Haney and Gold (1973) speculated that poor grades foster delinquent behavior in boys because, in American society, consequences for poor academic performance are more serious for boys than for girls, and male adolescents may turn to misbehaving friends and unwholesome pursuits for self-affirmation and comfort.

The supposition that a strong interplay exists between academic performance and choice of friends was supported by Kelly (1977), who reported that delinquency emerges as the strongest correlate of (a) negative student perceptions of school, teachers, and classmates; (b) poor academic performance; and (c) school misbehavior.

The relationship between poor academic performance and misbehavior may be influenced by motivational factors. Holt and Hobbs (1979) actually raised the IQ test scores of delinquent boys significantly by employing token reinforcements. (Students earned tokens for correct answers and forfeited tokens for incorrect responses.) Kumchy and Sayer (1980) found juvenile delinquents to be less achievement-motivated and to possess an attitude that outside forces largely controlled their lives (versus a perception of an inward locus of control). Achieving students, on the other hand, felt they could usually control their own lives.

Chapman (1978) maintained that schools lack adequate male models and tend to represent a feminized society, producing behavior-problem boys who are striving to establish masculine independence. These schools may appear lifeless to delinquents; disruption of classes, vandalism, and school violence may in part be attempts by adolescents to obtain some enjoyment in an otherwise spiritless environment (Csikszentmihalyi & Larson, 1978). The "dead" world of the school presents these children with no attainable challenges or clearly defined goals, gives them no reasonable avenue for self-expression, and denies them opportunities for positive and unambiguous emotional feedback.

Factors influencing type of chosen crime and recidivism. Although Haney and Gold (1973) thought that certain serious crimes (e.g., stealing car parts or armed robbery) are committed largely by boys, it has become clear that girls are increasingly likely to be involved in such offenses. Most other offenses, such as striking a parent or running away from home, are committed in equal proportions by boys and girls.

The question of who will commit serious or violent crimes remains an important one to parents, educators, and police officials. Some childhood precursors of criminality were reported by Mitchell and Rosa (1981). Over a 15-year period, they studied 642 boys whose behavior deviated from that typical of other boys the same age. Qualitatively, parental reports of antisocial behavior (e.g., stealing, lying, destructiveness, wandering from home) were shown to carry the worst prognosis for subsequent court convictions, particularly when teacher reports supported those of the parents.

McGurk, Bolton, and Smith (1978) studied delinquent boys at a detention center and found that those who were reconvicted within two years of their release had lower scores on reading and arithmetic tests, showed a greater degree of extrapunitive hostility, and had higher scores on tests of social nonconformity. The recidivists also began their criminal careers at an earlier age than nonrecidivists and had committed significantly more previous offenses. The prognosis for an individual showing these negative characteristics cannot be considered hopeful, but much of the acting-out behavior of even hard-core delinquents can be controlled.

Counseling delinquents and their families. Washburn (1963) emphasized the difficulties of treating the antisocial delinquent with ordinary counseling methods. The defense mechanisms of delinquents contain three protective attitudes that distinguish their value systems from those of most other people: (a) externalization (the exaggeration of threats from the environment), (b) denial (refusal to accept and face potentially threatening interpersonal problems), and (c) vindication (the attempt to avoid blame while maintaining the appearance of conforming to the norms of groups with which there is identification).

Few parents who are informed of their youngsters' misdeeds do much to help their children. Haney and Gold (1973) found that in 40% of the instances in which parents might have reacted, the children said that absolutely nothing was done; and the youngsters received the impression that the parents did not care what happened. In an equal number of instances, the parents' response was to scold or punish. In only five percent of the instances did the parents discuss the matter calmly with the teenagers.

As previously discussed (Snyder, 1977), problem family members are less responsive to consequences of deviant behavior than are nonproblem family members, but the extent of the nonresponses and the negative reactions reported by Haney and Gold (1973) is truly surprising. Aldrich (1971) maintained that many parents receive vicarious satisfaction from their children's delinquent acts and have no real wish to stop the misdeeds. School practitioners must involve significant adults "to identify the good in a child and make the child aware of it" (Taylor & Hoedt, 1974, p. 35). Much evidence exists to substantiate the belief that it is better to counsel parents and teachers than to counsel the delinquent child, even though that may do some good (Bernal, Klinnert, & Schultz, 1980).

Summary. Haney and Gold (1973) stated that traditional methods for identifying and treating juvenile delinquency are misdirected and are operating too far from reality to touch the right lives in the right ways. They reported the following findings:

1. Delinquent behavior is not a predominantly lower-class phenomenon.
2. Higher-status white males commit somewhat more serious delinquent acts than do their lower-status peers.
3. Delinquents do not expect to be caught. The reaction of most delinquents who are apprehended is resentment and surprise.
4. Getting caught encourages rather than deters further delinquency.
5. The least delinquent adolescents commit a large proportion of misdeeds with frequent companions, rather than alone.
6. Children of white-collar workers more often engage in delinquent behavior with friends than do children of blue-collar workers.
7. Girls are more likely to have a constant companion in delinquency than are boys.
8. Boys who have delinquent friends and who also have poor grades are usually highly delinquent, whether they come from broken or intact homes. The same is true for girls except that grades are not an important factor for them.
9. Delinquents do not see themselves as being the toughest, meanest, or most rebellious teenagers. To them, the classic delinquent is someone else, unknown to them, who fits the commonly accepted stereotype of a hoodlum.

The mythical delinquent casts a dark shadow over what may be called the delinquency-prevention industry (made up of courts, detention centers, juvenile officers, rehabilitation agencies, and so on). Traditional expectations, based on stereotypes of who delinquents are and of how these individuals should be controlled, obscure many realities, the most important of which may be the need of most delinquents to obtain outlets of intimacy with significant, worthy adults (Anchor, Sandler, & Cherones, 1977).

INTERVENTION STRATEGIES

Classroom Behavior Modification Techniques

Behavior modification remains the treatment of choice for misbehaving children. The vast literature on this topic attests to the positive effects that can be attained through the use of reinforcing consequences. Difficulties arise, however, in implementing and maintaining modification programs (Kazdin, 1979). For those who wish to try behavior reinforcement techniques, the following suggestions, summarized from a number of studies (Burks, 1999; Clements, 1978; Dougherty & Dougherty, 1977; N. Hobbs, 1982; S. A. Hobbs & Lahey, 1977; Kazdin, 1986; Main & Munro, 1977; Mash & Barkley, 1989; Webster-Stratton & Herbert, 1994), may prove helpful:

1. Pinpoint the exact behavior to be changed, the specifics of which are agreed upon and understood by all concerned.
2. Make the contractual agreement between teacher and child or parent and child simple to manage (a yes-no graph often serves best).
3. Reward *only* specified behavior; do not confuse the child with unexpected rewards.
4. Make feedback uncomplicated (vague, hard-to-understand verbal reinforcement, for instance, is not as helpful as check marks, stars, candy, etc.).
5. Give feedback frequently. Reinforcements that are spaced out over time fall on disinterested ears.
6. Make rewards appropriate for the child's age, gender, and interests.
7. Allow users of the reinforcement program to set up their own procedures (e.g., do not ask parents to implement a program that is largely meaningless to students).
8. Pick behaviors that can be changed quickly (e.g., a habit the child has recently acquired). Do not attempt to modify long-standing character traits (e.g., compulsions, overactivity, or temperament).
9. Choose a behavior that, when changed, is likely to be resistant to extinction. For example, a child may be trained to resist eating candy, but if relatives keep bringing the child sweets, the effort to modify the conduct is wasted.

Behavior modification techniques do not eliminate negative actions in all cases. This is particularly true if the aggressive conduct has been learned and practiced with success over a long period of time. Since classroom disruption mandates a degree of negative reinforcement, steps must be taken to control the child. In some instances, a quiet reprimand may be sufficient; in other cases, it may not. Critical and loud requests from the teacher may bring a student what he or she wants: the social and sympathetic recognition of peers. Consequences of this nature may increase the incidence of undesirable behavior. This type of teacher-student interaction can be broken by isolating the youngster so that he or she no longer receives classmates' attention. However, isolation also prevents the child from earning positive reinforcements (e.g., success in academic work). With this in mind, teachers should consider isolation a last resort.

Techniques for School Personnel

The antisocial child often demonstrates problems with authority figures. Teachers are perceived to be parent symbols, and the misbehaving youngster may enter into a struggle with them. Because the student is frequently skilled at baiting tactics, the teacher may feel just as helpless as the child feels at the hands of his or her parents. The method used to handle such a student is crucial. Teachers must not demonstrate behavior that permits the student to feel that he or she has gained an advantage over the instructor. Ordinarily, this entails showing the child that disruptive conduct will not be allowed to upset the teaching staff.

The antisocial child has learned that misbehavior gains attention. If teachers ignore this misconduct, classmates will tend to disregard it also. Of course, some children are so provocative that they cannot be ignored. The lack of affection and attention at home can cause them to react bitterly to any perceived rejection in school settings. Teachers are caught in an unenviable bind: Should they give an unusual amount of attention to the negative student, which might encourage the youngster to persist in provocative conduct, or should they ignore the child and risk the possibility that the student will become enraged and act out in more obvious ways? There is no easy solution. The teacher might arrange to have the child sit close to him or her to receive more personal attention. If the child is not calmed by this arrangement and continues to demand unusual attention, the school staff may decide to refer the family to an outside agency better equipped to handle difficulties of this nature.

The following techniques for managing antisocial children may be helpful:

1. Refuse to use physical force, which demeans both the teacher and the child, and do not explode at provocative conduct. Instead, deal with provocative conduct on a verbal level. Interpret the child's behavior with statements such as, "You feel bad, and maybe you're trying to make me angry" or "You want me to fight with you because you're unhappy, but I don't want to fight with you." The verbal reflection of the child's feelings may give the youngster some insight into his or her hostile actions.
2. Make jokes about silly comments and make light of profane language.
3. Provide the misbehaving student with a time-out period. If the child appears to be out of control, remove him or her from the room. Assign the child to duties outside the room when his or her conduct interrupts the teaching of other students. Removal also helps cool off a student who is in a conflict with another child (Hobbs & Forehand, 1977).
4. Challenge the child in every circumstance where he or she violates rules, but be sure the youngster understands established regulations and what constitutes breaking the rules. At this point, I would like to explain a discipline technique, developed by my son Tom Burks (a teacher in a middle school comprising mostly poor-achieving disadvantaged pupils) that has produced surprising results. Briefly, if a student misbehaves, he or she is immediately asked to accompany a school adult to the nearest institution phone to call a parent and explain why he or she acted incorrectly. My own observations verify that pupils dread this kind of confrontation and, in most cases, avoid further misbehavior.
5. Do not allow the child to develop a special teacher-student relationship that allows the student to think that rules apply only to others.
6. Remove temptations that invite the student to act antisocially (e.g., if money is left lying about the classroom, the student may not be able to resist taking it).
7. Remove pressures that might lead the child to cheat. Young students, in particular, should not be forced to face excessive competition.
8. Seat the child among students who are well-behaved.
9. Do not ask the child to indict himself or herself (e.g., "Everyone place their heads on the desk and whoever took the money will put it back"). Never force a confession.
10. Do not accuse a student of being dishonest unless there are sufficient circumstances to prove it.
11. Help the disruptive child acquire more status in the eyes of peers. A child may lie to impress classmates because the youngster perceives that he or she has little value in their eyes. Allow the child to do special classroom jobs and show off hobbies or talents, and praise the youngster for accomplishments.
12. Teach the child correct ways to act. Many young children do not understand the implications of their antisocial actions.
13. Avoid sermonizing. Many children do not understand the concepts employed in lectures.
14. Place the child in another classroom if there is a personality clash between the teacher and the child.

Techniques for Parents

Counselors who wish to help the parents of antisocial children change their child-raising practices should make the objectives of behavior change as specific as possible (generalized goals, e.g., "love your child more," are difficult for most individuals to implement).

Rather than trying to discuss and treat all forms of hostile expression (an impractical task) I will confine my remarks to the following, more serious childhood transgressions:

- undisciplined behavior;
- lying;

- truancy;
- stealing and kleptomania;
- substance abuse.

Undisciplined behavior. Parents of seriously misbehaving students do not, of course, deliberately teach their children to misbehave. Some educators presume that parents consciously teach their children poor habits, but that is not true. Parental intentions are mostly laudatory, but what parents say and do can lead to unexpected results. Even the most well-meaning parent can unwittingly teach a child to misbehave.

Educators should investigate parental discipline procedures, but it is just as important to explore the attitudes that predispose the parents of antisocial youngsters to choose the discipline techniques they employ. Without a change in these attitudes, much of what school personnel tell the parents will seem unnatural and even unreasonable. The following beliefs need particular attention:

1. Punishment is the most effective way to motivate children. (It is ordinarily the least effective.)
2. One reinforcement is enough to change a behavior pattern. (It ordinarily takes many rewards to modify conduct.)
3. Good behavior can be taken for granted; that is, it need not be reinforced with rewards. (Not true, accepted conduct should be rewarded.)
4. A child can suddenly make the leap from misbehaving to being a "good" child. (Most complicated social behavior must be broken down into small steps, and change will occur only after careful teaching and many reinforcements.)

Family practices that might contribute to misbehavior are the focus of the following questions. Both parents should answer the questions. Topics for discussion follow each question to generate further thought about home management methods.

1. Are disagreements between you and your spouse upsetting your child? Perhaps arguments, angry silences, or fights are making the youngster tense and upset, causing school disturbances. He or she may blame himself or herself for troubles at home and misbehaves in order to be punished for perceived misdeeds. Extended marital problems can be difficult to resolve. A professional adviser (perhaps a marriage counselor), may be needed.
2. Do you and your spouse disagree about how your child should behave? Contradictory or inconsistent standards in the home are confusing to children, causing them to act erratically at home and/or at school. To prevent a child from acting bewildered when he or she is asked to conform, parents must present a united front.
3. Does your child fight constantly with brothers and/or sisters? A child may secretly be afraid of an older brother or sister who teases or physically mistreats him or her. The youngster does not know how to defend himself or herself and is afraid to complain to parents because of possible retaliation from the sibling. The mistreated child then takes out his or her frustration on classmates or neighborhood children. The child may bully them—just as he or she feels bullied at home.

   Helping the child will take patience. First, parents should take time to observe interactions between offspring. Are patterns repeating themselves? Then they should note their usual responses to complaints and arguments. Are they locked into particular ways of seeing and handling these difficulties? For example, they may be convinced the younger child is just being a baby when, in fact, the youngster is trying to tell them that he or she cannot cope with a home problem. They may try really listening to the younger child. A series of family conferences may help. Sometimes a serious talk with the older child is necessary.
4. Do family members have trouble telling one another what is wrong or what it is they want? Members of families with communication problems may

- resort to silence when troubled;
- use emotional reactions (crying, outbursts of anger, sulking, etc.) to communicate instead of employing direct, give-and-take discussions;
- use indirect methods to express their needs (i.e., talk around the subject instead of getting to the point, or pretend they don't want something when they really do);
- use each other to get information across (e.g., tell one family member a secret in the hope the person will carry the message to another);
- talk to each other but leave out emotionally troubling topics.

These family communication difficulties are often so deeply ingrained that it is not reasonable to expect members to understand the problems easily. Professional assistance may be needed.

5. Is there a parental problem about who is in charge? Parents may engage each other in a silent (or not so silent) power struggle over who makes basic home decisions. This struggle can take various forms: One parent may always argue with the other about decisions affecting the family, causing a spouse to feel uncertain; one parent may simply not go along with a verdict laid down by the spouse; the parents may go their own ways; or one parent may keep emotional control of the family by complaining about decisions even though he or she goes along with them. At times, the child may run things by being unruly and becoming the focus of all attention. At other times, a relative may call the shots. An apparently weak member of the family may actually be the most powerful influence in some instances (e.g., an invalid aunt who has everyone running around doing her bidding).

If the parents can talk openly to each other, they may want to discuss the question of who is in charge. They may choose to divide responsibilities, each allowing the other to give directions to the family in areas where that parent is best qualified. They may decide to take power away from a particular family member (usually a child) who is not qualified to exercise authority.

6. Do you say (or imply) to your child that he or she is right and the teacher is wrong? Many people have had unfortunate experiences in school. They remember the "bad" teachers they suffered under when they were young. When their child complains about a teacher, the parents identify with that misery. In fact, they may say, "I can remember having trouble with teachers, just like you do." How do children feel when their parents say that? They might experience some relief with the identification but other messages might be picked up. They might feel justified in defying the teacher or evading school rules. Not only are they encouraged to do as they like, they may think mom and dad take pride in their rule flouting.

Parents may stop being so eager to sympathize with the child's school problems. First, it is possible that the child is bringing difficulties upon himself or herself. Second, they can go to the school and find out what is going on. It is often best to include the upset child in teacher conferences. When a joint conference is held, one party cannot play off the other.

7. Do you give in because it is easier than fighting with your youngster? When parents become overpermissive because of a child's demanding or bullying behavior, several things can happen:

- The child may not develop good inner controls.
- The child may not learn to tolerate frustration.
- The child may think that he or she can control others (including teachers) with overbearing conduct.
- The child may come to believe that he or she can demand constant attention from others.

Discipline is one of the great gifts parents can bestow upon children. Youngsters actually want to be controlled because it gives them an increased sense of security when someone cares enough to say "Stop!" Much childhood misbehavior is really an attempt to get someone to set limits. Children intuitively understand that external controls can keep them out of trouble.

To establish proper authority parents can coordinate actions with school personnel. First steps may include informing the child ahead of time what will happen if he or she breaks rules. Then, if the child decides to misbehave, stated consequences will occur. Parents should not hesitate to acquire professional help if the problems appear too chronic or severe for them and/or the school to handle.

8. Do you find yourself saying no to everything your child wants? If the family environment is too strict, the youngster may harbor bitter feelings unexpressed at home but acted out at school, where limits are less restrictive. Overcontrolling parents may feel that if they let down barriers, the child will abuse privileges. This may indeed be the case if the child is resentful and feels that he or she can get something only by outwitting the parents. For this reason, gaining better feelings in the family is a prime objective. Counseling may help family members to learn to compromise, to gain a deeper understanding of each other's motives, and to talk to each other more effectively.

9. Do you constantly punish your child for misdeeds? This question and its implications are closely allied to the preceding question. Again, the youngster may see the parents as too harsh and punitive. He or she may develop a hostile attitude toward authority figures and may engage in a power struggle with teachers by misbehaving. In this kind of confrontation, no one wins on a permanent basis. The answer lies in improved family relations.

10. Do you tell your child to stand up for his or her rights when he or she has problems with teachers? If overdone, this admonition has unfortunate consequences. The youngster may believe any means should be used to defeat misguided authority. Of course, school personnel see the child's actions as rebellious in nature.

    Parents and teachers must work together on this problem. Sometimes, school personnel are being too strict with the child. At other times, the child must be told by adults that he or she is not always right and must obey the same rules as other students. And, at still other times, parents must stop encouraging their child to rebel.

11. Do you tell your misbehaving child to do what the teacher wants, but then never contact the school to find out what the teacher really wants? If the answer is yes, the parent may be telling the child, "Do as I tell you, but don't bother me about going to the school, because I'm not interested enough to find out what is really taking place." Under this unspoken (but very real) mandate, the youngster may (quite naturally) believe that the teacher's desires are not important. The solution to this dilemma is obvious: The parent goes to the school with the youngster to find out what the teacher wants and keep doing so until behavior changes are evident.

12. Do you constantly disagree with your child? Chronic discord can produce an angry youngster. Enraged feelings cause the child to choose a school adult to defy (hoping, perhaps, to find someone less threatening than a parent). Sometimes family conferences can bring these difficulties to the surface.

13. Is your child the only family member getting into trouble? If the answer is yes, perhaps the youngster has been chosen by the rest of the family to be the bad guy. Possibly the youngster, because of bad experiences, has decided that he or she is indeed a "bad" character. Feeling unworthy, the child acts out this poor self-image.

    The bad-guy role is an unhappy one. The child grows up feeling like an outcast, and the family remains confused and uncertain about how to treat him or her. This situation calls for professional assistance. Parents should not try to treat the difficulty within the family circle; all members are locked in to reactions they do not understand.

14. Do you dislike your child's school? If you don't, your youngster is not likely to feel good about it either. When the child disobeys classroom regulations, he or she may think that getting back at the school is a gift to parents. That situation cannot continue. Parents should either settle their differences with the school or move the youngster to another educational setting.

Lying

Parents of older children often complain that their youngsters lie (G. R. Miller & Stiff, 1993), but how serious is a child's lying? All individuals lie, given particular circumstances, and children lie even if parents insist the absolute truth be told. Unless lying is severe and chronic, however, it should not be taken too seriously.

Children lie for many reasons, some more compelling than others. These may include:

1. A desire to avoid consequences of wrongdoing. This is a serious form of lying if the falsehoods are given over a long period of time and are associated with other kinds of misbehavior.
2. Revenge ("Jimmy doesn't like me; that's why I said he took the money"). This form of lying is serious if the child refuses to consider less vindictive alternatives.
3. The need to feel more important ("I'm the best player on the team"). Ordinarily, this is not a serious form of lying but the individual can suffer if others learn to distrust such statements and discount the character of the individual telling the lie.
4. A need to shield others who have misbehaved. Motives for this type of lying may vary from altruism (e.g., protecting a loved sibling from perceived harm) to loyalty to a gang whose members may have committed a crime. The seriousness of this form of lying can be judged only in relation to the degree of harm it causes.
5. A desire to manipulate others for personal gain. A child may tell a parent that he or she has eaten the main course of dinner (not true) in order to get dessert. A teenager may try to convince his or her parents that school grades are adequate (when they are not) in order to be released from probation. If conning others is a long-standing habit and if the individual is older, the problem must be considered serious—particularly if it is allied with conduct like stealing and truancy.
6. The need to create an inner world of enjoyable fantasy. Imaginative young children often let thoughts run rampant with made-up stories of danger and heroism whose content does not match reality. Fortunately, most outgrow this habit as they develop a capacity to distinguish between truth and fiction.

Researchers (Mash & Barkley, 1989; Reid, Hinojosa Rivera, & Lorber, 1980; Stouthamer-Loeber & Loeber, 1986) have discovered the following facts about lying:

1. Until about the age of four, small children operate on the principle of pleasing their parents. Whatever gratifies adults is good; whatever upsets them is not good. If Susie spills her mother's face powder, Mommy will be upset. Since it is bad to make Mommy unhappy, the obvious solution for Susie is to say she didn't spill the powder.
2. Several years must pass before young children can learn to distinguish between fact and fiction. Twenty percent of six-year-olds still cannot do this well. By the age of nine nearly all youngsters have mastered the ability.
3. By age seven, most youngsters are mature enough to experience guilt about lying even if the falsehood goes undetected. At this stage children tend to be anxious about misbehaving and whether "God will punish" them for acting wrong. This changes at about 12 years of age when youngsters look at truth telling from a new point of view—that is, that society is based on mutual trust. This stage of moral development is only a step removed from the idealism of adolescence.
4. Most falsehoods are lies of convenience (the frequency of this type of lying is about the same for adults as it is for children). Children learn to lie by observing the actions of people around them. Parents teach offspring in overt and subtle ways to suppress natural honesty (parents often believe youngsters are too blunt in the ways they assess others and express opinions). Directly and indirectly, mothers and fathers slowly teach youngsters that this kind of brusque telling ("Hey, Mommy, look at the funny fat woman") is not socially welcome. In short, children learn to lie to be discreet.
5. Chronic lying is highly associated with stealing, especially in teenagers (Atwood, 2002).
6. As a matter of convenience, children deceive themselves, as well as others. A youngster may tell a parent that he or she has finished homework assignments when, in actuality, the child has merely glanced through an assigned article or a math worksheet.
7. Children need to distinguish between white lies (falsehoods that serve as a lubricant in untidy social situations) and lies that cause the lying individual, and perhaps others, genuine distress. The nature and the meaning of both types of evasion should be made clear to children.

While a white lie is usually told to alleviate hurt feelings in others (saying, e.g., "I think your dress is quite beautiful" when that is not an actual belief), it still must be considered a falsehood. This fact can be made clear to a child. At the same time, the youngster can be helped to understand that perceptions of objects (in this case the dress) vary from person to person and it is important to consider the feelings of others. Since no apparent constructive outcome is likely to result from a derogatory remark about the dress, it is permissible to cover up true feelings. It must be pointed out, however, that one is not allowed to falsify a statement that could result in a dangerous action. For example, flattering an individual by saying that he or she has the physical ability to swim across a dangerous body of water, when the person actually does not have the capacity to complete the task, would be unacceptable.

When is lying considered to be a serious offense? Parents may legitimately consider lying to be a serious offense if it

- persists over a long period of time;
- is chronically compulsive and persists even when the truth would serve better.

Children who compulsively tell falsehoods may have a need to impress others (that is, appear more grandiose by telling tall stories), avoid disapproval or punishment by reassuring parents that all is well when it is not, or acquire something he or she could not get by being truthful. Some teenagers lie to insure privacy from adult supervision.

Serious untruths must not be ignored. Whenever possible, parents should use the lies of children as opportunities to teach the value of truth telling. A parent can, for instance, point out that lies about doing homework will be found out eventually and will result in the loss of privileges and more restrictive limits; the parent should also illustrate the rewards that can be expected for being truthful about the completion of homework. Of course, if a youngster is to be convinced that honesty is less stressful than dishonesty, parents must demonstrate that by their own actions. A parent's uproar in response to an unpleasant truth will not convince the youngster that honesty is the best policy.

Finally, some family practices contribute to childhood lying. These include:

Fear of consequences. Some family members chronically avoid confrontations. They find it easier to ignore untruths than to confront them (Miller & Stiff, 1993).

Family secrets. Family secrets can be an insidious form of lying. The father who drinks secretly (but actually fools no one) has issued tacit orders to the family that his problem must not be discussed. Family secrets involve sensitive and sometimes explosive issues. When these are uncovered and examined, the family group may undergo a rough period of readjustment. Family systems, like other complex organizations, do not change smoothly. When old patterns of behavior no longer work, new options and possibilities must emerge and be tested. Two family characteristics determine how well a family survives such a disturbance:

- the amount of emotional support family members can provide one another;
- the degree of social adaptability in the family.

Should an individual in a family group attempt to resolve the problems surrounding a family secret? In most cases, the answer is no. Individual and group resistance is usually so well organized that positive results seldom occur. Sometimes the situation is made worse, damaging group unity beyond repair. The person initiating changes is often condemned or ostracized by other family members. The family should seek the guidance of a dispassionate and trained professional who can safely orchestrate efforts to unearth and examine difficulties surrounding family secrets.

Poor instructions. Sometimes children are not provided with more desirable alternatives to lying. Young children often are not aware that a perplexing situation can be handled in ways other than fibbing. Here are some instructions and substitute behaviors that parents can teach their children.

- Tell children that lies are usually detected and often cause trouble for the person telling them. Point out that even if a fib is not discovered, the person who tries to fool others may feel ashamed.
- Explain that owning up to a fib will cause others to like them better and trust them more.

- Help children to be assertive, rather than vengeful, when they are angered by others. For example, suggest that they tell the offender to stop the unwanted behavior (rather than seeking devious revenge and then lying about it). If that doesn't work, instruct them to avoid such individuals.
- Remind children that they do not have to tell lies to feel important—they have genuine attributes that make them significant.

Truancy

Although a few cases of truancy are reported at the junior high school level, willful absence from classes occurs mainly in high schools. Chronic truancy is usually just one of many problems displayed by students with behavior difficulties. For instance, a youngster involved in drug abuse may skip classes to obtain drugs. He or she then must acquire funds to pay for such addictive substances and may do so by becoming involved in minor crime, which also requires absence from school. As time goes on, the adolescent may lose interest in school because of his or her addiction.

But drugs are not the only reason for cutting classes. I have counseled teens who simply cannot abide the dreariness of schoolwork. Many of these individuals have never done well academically, and a significant proportion do not have the skills to prosper in formal learning situations. Unfortunately, most school districts lack the resources to formulate programs that would suit their needs. In addition, there are youngsters from impoverished families who need the funds they earn from part-time work to help their families maintain minimal living standards (besides, these young people need pocket money).

In the final analysis, there are many unacceptable and a few legitimate reasons for truancy. However, the law insists that all minors up to a certain age must go to school.

Parents of truant students can try the following steps:

1. Keep in contact with the school attendance office. If necessary, ask for a daily report. Do not accept assurances from the child that he or she is attending classes.
2. Face the child. Insist on an explanation for the truancy, and do not accept evasive answers. Have the attendance records on hand. Further insist that the youngster explain where he or she was during the absences, what the child was doing, and with what companions. Explain the legal and educational consequences of poor school attendance. Even if the child professes no interest in his or her economic future, it is up to the parent to outline negative outcomes of truancy.
3. Arrange a school conference with appropriate school officials (principal, counselor, or teachers) and both a parent and the child. I have arranged and attended many such parent-school meetings. When the teen attends, long-term results are better achieved because the adolescent does not receive conference conclusions secondhand from parents (the teen may discount the information or think there are still ways he or she can maneuver around regulations).
4. Give the child as much support as possible at the conference. Help the child explain the truancy. Do not use the conference as a springboard to vent anger toward the youngster. When venting occurs, the focus of the meeting tends to center around parental feelings rather than on constructive ways to eliminate the truancy problem. Consider the possibility that the adolescent may believe there are legitimate reasons for the absences— for example, feelings of shame about lack of friends, poor appearance, having no money, or the inability to complete assignments—and these reasons must receive a sympathetic response (particularly when it is evident they cause the youngster distress). On the other hand, if the truancy occurred because the teen simply sought pleasure outside of school, penalties must be enforced.

To help the truant teen, the counselor may suggest that parents ask school personnel

- to continue sending reports of attendance to the home about remedial steps available to help the youngster catch up with studies;

- to evaluate whether the child can be placed in athletic or club activities where others depend on his or her presence;
- to consider making concessions in the teen's daily schedule so the student can engage in activities of his or her own interest and choosing;
- to consider giving the teenager daily contact with a counselor, preferably at the start of the school day;
- to consider arranging a work/school schedule if the child needs a part-time job, while making sure the youngster can continue to earn credits toward a diploma.

Stealing

Stealing is a relatively common act among conduct-disordered youngsters (Mash & Barkley, 1989; Williamson, 1990). Not surprisingly, the parents of such children experience more personal, interparental, and extrafamilial distress than do parents of normally behaved youngsters. These parents need direction and an explanation of the dynamics of stealing (Westlake, 2004).

Why do children steal? Youngsters commit thefts for a variety of reasons, including

- feelings of deprivation—the belief that others have more rights or possessions unfairly;
- revenge—the need to get back at someone who the child believes has hurt him or her;
- the thrill of a dangerous activity;
- a deficient sense of right and wrong—the belief that there is nothing improper about taking things that belong to others;
- peer pressure—you're not one of the gang unless you steal;
- helplessness—stealing gives a sense of control (for example, a youngster who feels inadequate in the classroom may take objects from the teacher to steal his or her power);
- membership in a social group that sees stealing as a natural act, done by everyone;
- temptation—the inability to resist taking attractive articles left carelessly about the premises by other individuals (for example, a parent leaves money out in the open, unguarded).

Kleptomania

The outstanding characteristic of kleptomaniac is the compelling need to steal. The disorder should be distinguished from shoplifting, an action usually well-planned and motivated by the wish or need for monetary gain.

To counsel kleptomaniac teens, be aware of the following facts:

- the thefts have nothing to do with material need;
- the individual steals to satisfy inner emotional demands;
- the person often experiences the impulse to steal as an alien, unwanted intrusion into their mental state;
- very often the items stolen are not worth much and are unneeded.

Causal factors. Theories of causation include the following motivations:

- a need to "steal" affection to counteract feelings of worthlessness instilled by parents who weren't loving or indulgent enough;
- a need to repay the self for imagined or real hurts and denials inflicted by others;
- evidence linking kleptomania to brain abnormalities.

Age and duration. For whatever reason, most person suffering the disorder are women, with an average age of 35. The duration of the illness is roughly 16 years. Some report an onset of kleptomania as early as age 5.

Emotional concomitants. Investigators have documented that

- just before a theft, the person experiences increased tension;
- at the time of the theft, the individual feels gratification, pleasure, or relief;
- thefts are *not* committed out of anger or revenge;
- thefts are *not* committed as a response to delusions or hallucinations.

Theories of motivation. The emotional payoff for kleptomania can include

- the pleasurable experience of conquering risk, danger, and suspense;
- the thrill of not getting caught (giving the act a dramatic, intense, game-like quality);
- the excitement of abandonment—throwing the self onto fate and asking destiny to inform the person whether he or she will be favored or punished.

Internal dialogue. In my clinical experience teen kleptomaniacs often offer to themselves the following rationales for stealing:

- "Store prices are too high."
- "Profit margins are excessive."
- "Store losses are always covered by insurance."
- "No one will miss the article."
- "The store has already made enough money off my former purchases."
- "Because I don't have as much as my friends, I deserve to own the stolen goods."

Why is it important to find out why a child steals? Since each youngster commits thefts according to individual needs, it becomes imperative to investigate the causes so programs can be tailored to fit each case. The search can be conducted in two ways:

1. By confronting the child for an explanation. This should not be done in anger. Adult outrage must not become the focus of attention. Calmly acknowledge the child's feelings and reasons for the thefts and later explain some constructive ways to deal with the problem.
2. By investigating the scene of the crime. This usually involves talking to neighbors, shopkeepers, or friends of the child. Again, do this sleuthing in a relaxed manner. Emphasize the fact that you are doing it in order to help your child, not to gather evidence to indict.

How should stealing be treated in very young children? Young children are not always aware that they have committed a misdeed when they take another person's belongings. Little tots are self-centered and regard everything in the immediate vicinity as somehow belonging to them (ownership goes beyond what is theirs to what they want). Many parents have been chagrined to find a strange doll or toy car in a little one's pocket after the child has come home from visiting a friend. As with any other desirable behavior pattern, parents must teach small children the meaning of ownership and honesty.

Start by explaining how items in the home were bought. Remind the youngster how adults go to the market, put articles in the cart, and then go to the checkout counter to pay for purchases. If the child is old enough to receive an allowance or earn money by doing special jobs, help the youngster understand that what he or she buys with that money belongs to no one else. Likewise, what other people purchase belongs to them. Extend this lesson by having the child go through the home to identify what belongs to him or her and what is owned by other family members. If the child becomes interested enough, play the label game—label items the youngster owns and what others possess. Point out that everybody must respect ownership by not taking other people's things without permission. The boy or girl can also be taught the social rules of borrowing and returning articles.

Role-playing is one way to explore feelings surrounding stealing. The parent can pretend to be another child who has taken something from the son or daughter. The child is asked how he or she feels about this "theft." The parent explores what can be done to rectify the situation. Remember that small children have difficulty identifying the emotional responses of others. For example, they often do not understand why others become angry with them.

If a child has stolen something from a store, the parent should take the youngster back to the store and have him or her pay for it from allowance money or return it if it is undamaged. Parents should not force the boy or girl to make a verbal apology because most youngsters in such a situation are so embarrassed they are speechless. Adults should not allow the owner or manager to reward the youngster for returning the item by giving it to the child.

Unless the theft occurred under unusual circumstances or appears to be a single event not congruent with the general conduct of the child, the parent should inform the youngster that there will be a loss of privileges if the problem occurs again.

How should parents treat older children who steal? Regardless of extenuating circumstances, if a teen is taking the possessions of others, he or she must be made aware that stealing is not socially approved. Although parents should avoid sermons, drama, and name-calling, they must tell the youngster that any stolen object cannot be brought home. Further, the article must be returned to its owner at once. Avoid arguments and try not to affix blame. Just say calmly, "You took it; now return it immediately." Consequences for stealing can include loss of privileges for the day and weekend restrictions.

Substance abuse. The currently reported extensive use of alcohol and drugs by children is a truly sad phenomenon. Most therapists confront this problem over and over (Allen, Nicholas, D'Amanda, & D'Amanda, 1992; Baugh, 1990; Dennison, 1993; Jaynes & Rugg, 1988; Kane & Lieberman, 1992; O'Brien & Jaffe, 1992; Stimmel, 1993).

In the past, LSD, PCP, and mescaline were the drugs of choice—along with marijuana, which is still used extensively today. Now other drugs have taken their place. Along with the widespread use of alcohol, there is a more potent selection of chemicals. Heroin and cocaine are injected and youngsters smoke cocaine and crack. Since crack is relatively cheap and easily obtained, it ranks high on the list of preferred substances. Sometimes children drink crack and cocaine. If no money is available, they inhale the fumes of gasoline or glue.

The easiest substances to obtain are capsules and pills from pharmacies, issued via sometimes forged prescriptions. Many chemicals, such as sedatives, amphetamines, tranquilizers, and barbiturates are already in home medicine cabinets.

Then there is nicotine, a drug often dismissed by adults as not belonging on the list of dangerous chemicals. Nicotine, however, is a very harmful substance—more addictive than cocaine or most of the other powerful drugs. Minors spend over $3 billion a year on cigarettes. The teenage segment of the population is the only group that did not show a decline in smoking rates from 1988 to 1998—despite antismoking campaigns conducted in all school grades. Some students experiment with cigarettes in the early elementary grades.

Finally, alcohol has been so widely used by all segments of society over such a long period of time that adults do not think of this substance as a drug. It is, of course. The harmful effects of both short- and long-term alcohol abuse are only now being appreciated (Baugh, 1990). Drug use among minors has declined, but the use of alcohol has risen dramatically, as reflected in the number of children attending Alcoholics Anonymous meetings. The easy availability of alcohol—the fact that most youngsters find liquor in their own homes or can obtain it in stores by having someone older purchase it for them—explains, in part, its current extensive use. In addition, most mothers and fathers express less apprehension about a child drinking alcohol than about a youngster ingesting other chemical substances—in spite of the knowledge that minors abuse alcohol more often than any other drug (Jaynes & Rugg, 1988).

Why do teenagers take drugs? This is a difficult question to answer. Nearly all adolescents want that top-of-the-world feeling that cocaine and other substances produce. There are some who equate a drugless existence with no fun. Many see "no more drugs" as being equivalent to no more friends and no more excitement. And there are those who just seem empty, and need something to fill their inner emotional void.

In my experience, teens minimize the amount of drugs they take. A typical response to questions about drug-taking is: "Hey, it's no big thing; don't worry about it." This is said in the face of facts like being suspended from school or arrested for substance abuse. This kind of denial merely emphasizes the fact that teenagers don't see drugs in the serious light that adults do. In addition, they do not see alcohol abuse as a problem. Only cocaine is considered to be a substance that causes difficulties. To many young people, drugs and alcohol are lighthearted avenues to fun and games; to adults, they are the road to ruin.

Adults must assume some responsibility for the unconcerned attitudes of teens. American society is drug oriented. Adults take pills and nostrums for every conceivable ailment—in fact, most feel cheated if doctors don't prescribe some kind of chemical cure in response to their complaints. This attitude toward drugs goes beyond medicine, however. Until recently, cocaine fit nicely with the values of the times—it was a trendy drug that began its rise to popularity by carrying a false promise of being nonaddictive.

What are the chief factors leading to drug abuse? Knowing the causes of drug abuse may be of some assistance, but only if the discovered factors involve conditions that can be changed or eliminated with a minimum of complications. For instance, while it is interesting to learn that genetics play a part in addiction (some children seem to be born with a predisposition to certain chemicals), most parents cannot do much about that kind of knowledge when their children become drug habituated. Similarly, the realization that adverse living conditions can expose minors to drug abuse is not much help to families caught up in poverty.

Other kinds of information, though, can prove helpful (Daley, 1991). It has been shown, for instance, that vitamin deficiencies sometimes contribute to the overuse of alcohol. It may also be useful to know that children from divorced homes experience unusual stress that, in some cases, makes them vulnerable to substance abuse. These youngsters obviously need additional kinds of emotional support. Parents should be on the alert for signs of stress such as being unusually shy, insecure, anxious, or aggressive. It is also a well-known fact that children who have drug-involved parents are more likely to abuse substances (Mash & Barkley, 1989). Adults must also be aware that drugs command media attention. Their use and abuse is portrayed on television programs, and peers discuss them at length. Like it or not, the mystique surrounding drugs and drug taking excites the curiosity of children.

All children are curious—if they were not, they would not learn much about their world and how to survive in it. But the shapes, feelings, sights, and sounds of a child's world are perceived without the knowledge and experience available to adults. Most grown-ups know drugs can be dangerous and do not wish to experiment with them. That is not so true for minors. Just as a child tries out new clothes and hair styles, he or she wants to experiment with drugs—a puff on a tobacco or marijuana cigarette, a taste of alcohol, or a sniff of glue. These are experiences shared with friends but not with parents. Unfortunately, perhaps, adults have forgotten the excitement they experienced in childhood when they dabbled in offbeat exercises frowned on by the establishment. That is precisely why adults have difficulty understanding some of the antics of teenagers. Better comprehension by adults might make them more tolerant of teen needs.

What are some of the signs that children are involved with drugs? Bruno (1993) and Polson and Newton (1984) outlined the following symptoms of childhood drug use:

Poor general appearance. Hallucinogens, narcotics, or deliriants can cause the face to appear flushed. Some stimulants and narcotics can lead to weight loss or even emaciation (due to a suppression of appetite). Some chemicals can lead to an attitude of carelessness and lack of concern for hygiene and personal appearance. Marijuana, sedatives, and narcotics are associated with sleepiness and tremors and shakiness can accompany the use of stimulants as well as the withdrawal stages of narcotic or sedative consumption. Unusual hunger may be related to marijuana abuse. Abscesses or needle marks may be visible when stimulants and narcotics are injected.

Eye abnormalities. Chronic marijuana use can cause reddening of the eyes and frequent episodes of conjunctivitis. Hallucinogens, deliriants, and marijuana can be associated with dilated pupils. Narcotic abuse, on the other hand, may cause contracted pupils. Deliriants can lead to temporary blindness.

Cardiovascular effects. Hallucinogens and marijuana tend to increase heart rate while narcotic ingestion slows heart rate. Stimulant abuse is associated with increased blood pressure and heart dysrhythmia (especially evident in those who use "speed," a form of methamphetamine).

Acute intoxication. The chronic use of sedatives and deliriants may produce intoxication signs such as slurred speech, confusion, unstable gait (ataxia), impaired general coordination, irritability, and impaired capacity to correctly determine time and place. Narcotics and marijuana may also produce these signs but to a lesser extent.

Other physical signs. Constant marijuana use can cause bouts of coughing and bronchitis. Stimulant overuse, sedative withdrawal, and, very occasionally, hallucinogens can result in convulsions. Stimulant abuse is associated with itching, tension, and muscular pains. A dry mouth and throat can ensue from the use of marijuana, stimulants, and deliriants; ringing in the ears is associated with the use of deliriants.

Early involvement with substances is seldom indicated by obvious signs. Aside from drowsiness, overactivity, or a hint of alcohol on a child's breath, parents are not likely to become alarmed even when they note a decrease in the level of liquid in liquor bottles in the home or the absence of pills from the medicine cabinet.

The physical and emotional manifestations of drug abuse naturally become more apparent as the problem progresses. Children move from the recreational use of drugs to habitual sessions of drinking, smoking, or popping pills with friends—much as adults drink alcohol at lunch, sip wine at dinner time, or celebrate with a can of beer at a ball game. Lies may become frequent and are often used to cover up actions disapproved by parents. Schoolwork can suffer. Money may disappear from the home and drug paraphernalia may be found hidden in the teen's bedroom.

When drug use becomes the focal center of the child's life, symptoms become more blatant. No longer are chemicals employed for socializing alone; the drugs are necessary now to get the child through stressful situations such as appointments, dates, tests, and work. Drugs are taken when the youngster is alone and may progress from drinking, pill popping, and sniffing to the injection of drugs. Money becomes a preoccupation; the constant need for funds to buy alcohol or other drugs causes the child to neglect friends and work.

Behavioral indications of the heavily drug-involved child can be alarming. Schoolwork is ignored. Truancy increases and, when forced to attend classes, the child is uncooperative. Parents note unusual mood swings, angry flare-ups, sullenness, coughing, bloodshot eyes, and unusual signs of fatigue. The teen may become involved in criminal activities.

At this stage of chemical dependence, parents feel helpless. Pleas, exhortations, and threats prove ineffective. The minor has become totally dependent on drugs. Unlike the previous stages of drug experimentation where the child was in control, he or she is now a slave to the substances. Day or night, the child's body demands the chemicals. That does not mean the youngster likes this dependency—as a matter of fact, he or she usually resents it deeply. The compelling need for drugs can cause panic stemming from fears that money or the drugs will not be available for release from pain. The lies and thefts the youngster is forced to commit bring guilt, self-loathing, and severe frustration because there is no apparent way out of the dilemma.

At this point, most parents feel they have lost their child. One mother told me, "My son is gone from me. I don't think I will ever get him back." This heartbreaking statement was true; her child had slipped away from the family into a world best described as an egocentric nightmare where friends, family, play, school, and work no longer mattered. Physically, he was around, but there was no recognizable being inside.

How can the parents of drug-addicted children be helped? In my experience, therapeutic attempts with the parents of drug-addicted youngsters often proved more difficult than counseling the children. How could this be? Even though the parents sought help, they did so only after they had been told by school or community authorities (often the court) that the youngster would be placed in an institution under the jurisdiction of juvenile authorities if the family did not get professional help.

Consider the shame and embarrassment parents of drug-addicted children feel when pushed, or forced, to have an intimate dialogue with a complete stranger about family failures. It is no wonder therapists encounter resistance from parents. After a period of time, I decided that individual sessions were not as effective as they should be. In their place I instituted parent groups for adults and teen groups for minors. This arrangement worked better. Participants in both groups seemed to feel less pressured than they did when sitting alone with a therapist. In addition, they tended to be more receptive to messages about substance control when the messages came from other group members. They also felt they received more emotional support from the group than they did from the therapist in one-on-one sessions. If the parents resist treatment, it is highly unlikely that their addicted children will improve significantly. As a matter of fact, when some of these youngsters are removed from the home environment, their outlook for improvement becomes brighter. Parents of drug-addicted children tend to employ some common psychological defenses: denial, fear of confrontation, and enabling.

Denial. The most common and most difficult parental defense to penetrate is denial—the refusal to admit that drug abuse is occurring even though evidence of it surrounds the child (e.g., the smell of alcohol, an obvious loss of initiative, conflicts at school, new and unsavory friends, defiance of rules, secretive conduct, withdrawal, staying out late, changes in personal hygiene, unaccountable mood changes, isolation, money missing from parents or siblings, changes in sleep patterns, disappearance of prescription drugs, or excessive weight loss).

I have witnessed parents crying out in anguish, "If only I had known! I just can't believe it!" Upon questioning, though, they admitted that signs of drug dependence were all about them. But the refusal to acknowledge the obvious made them accomplices to the crime—they allowed their child to develop the habit.

In adult group sessions, parents admitted that they used phrases around the home similar to the following:

- "Thank God our family would never do anything like that!"
- "Stop talking about how neat drugs are! I don't want to hear such rubbish!"
- "I don't care what anyone says about what is happening to you. I just know things are going to get better."
- "No matter what your teacher says, I know you are in the right!"
- "Even though my children have been criticized for wrongdoing, I know their intentions are always good."
- "You only took one puff of marijuana? And you say you didn't like it and won't do it anymore? That's good; I believe you."

Parents want to believe their children. They shrink from recognizing their children's faults. But too much denial, in the face of what is going on in schools and neighborhoods, is foolish—worse, it is dangerous.

During the experimental stage of drug use, when children satisfy their curiosity by taking a puff of marijuana or a sip of liquor, parents can do at least two things:

1. Have a serious talk with the child. Begin by saying, "I understand why you want to try this drug, but let's talk about what might happen if you keep using it." The child should be taught what the substance can do to his or her body, social standing, and security in the family and community.
2. Investigate and supervise the child's environment more closely. Are chemicals in the home medicine cabinet out of the youngster's reach? Are supplies of alcohol locked up? Is money in the home accounted for? Are the child's friends known to the parents? Are the homes of friends supervised? Are there gathering places for child activities that are unknown to neighborhood parents? If discovered, are these areas safe? Are parents and children interacting in community events or are youngsters largely left to their own devices?

Fear of confrontation. If a youngster has a severe drug problem, parents must confront the child in a no-nonsense manner, saying, "We're not listening to old excuses anymore. You are no longer able to control your actions. You have a serious sickness, just as though you had pneumonia or a broken arm, and we must all work together to get you well." After this conversation, the parents must go on demonstrating love and support while emphasizing that the problem can be licked only when the parents and the child work together. In all probability, the child has been feeling alienated. He or she must be assured of the family's affection.

Many family members simply cannot endure the stress of face-to-face confrontations. In my early years of counseling, I naively assumed that individuals, when told they needed to challenge others, would do so. This confrontation seldom occurred. It became apparent that most people had to be taught how to confront others.

Before assertive behavior can be taught, however, individuals who are afraid of confrontations must gain a clearer picture of how they act in challenging situations. Many people believe they behave more firmly than they actually do.

I constructed the following statements for adults to read aloud to others in group sessions.

1. When discussing the drug problem with your spouse, both of you tend to postpone confronting your child about his or her addiction because you are sure things will get better.
2. When you see family members engaged in a quarrel, you quickly leave the room.
3. When you contemplate a face-to-face showdown with another person, you become so anxious you avoid that person.
4. You constantly give in to others rather than speaking up for your rights.
5. When you do get into a confrontation, you get so ill you have to withdraw.
6. You see yourself as the family appeaser.
7. Deep down, you are afraid that if you have a confrontation with someone, they will no longer like you.

Parents who avoid confrontations should be asked to look at the situation from their child's point of view. Children want directions and limits. When a parent acts hesitantly or is ambiguous about enforcing discipline, they may become confused or angry. Sometimes they are put in the position of making their own rules and setting their own limits but most adults reject behavior parameters set up by minors, leaving the children even more bewildered.

No-backbone conduct is not easily changed; unassertive behavior is deep-seated and habitual. Counseling can sometimes help. However, I prefer not to engage adults in long-term therapy aimed at efforts to change their character structures. Things move more quickly when they learn practical communication skills that can be used on short-term notice.

Enabling. Alcoholics Anonymous (AA) coined the term "enabler" to describe a person who is dedicated to helping an addicted individual but who is actually contributing to that person's alcohol dependency.

What are the motivations of the enabler? The enabler sees himself or herself as a kind of nurse—someone who understands the needs of the victim, is going to make up for deprivations the victim suffered in the past, and who by giving the victim one more chance, will finally achieve the cure that the victim says he or she wants. To illustrate, here are the words of an older brother of an alcoholic:

> You know, for years I felt sorry for my brother. He had a lousy childhood, didn't have a father around, and I guess he felt rejected. I always felt I had to look after him. Later, when he began to get in trouble with drink I always felt kind of guilty because I didn't do enough for him. He would go off on binges and when he got sober he would swear he was going to get sober for good and then I would give him money to help him get back on his feet. That never seemed to do any good—he always got drunk again! Seems like I was addicted to giving him help and he was addicted to booze! Then I met this guy when I was playing golf one day and I told him the story of my brother. He just laughed and said I was helping my brother remain a drunk. I said that can't be because all I was trying to do was help him. Then he said he had been in AA for almost 9 years and that he had heard my story many times before. Seems like the alcoholic drinks to feel better, then feels very guilty about getting drunk, then beats himself about the head and shoulders in front of someone—like me, I guess—until he feels better, and, if he can get the dough, he goes off and gets drunk again! You know, that was the first time I had ever got an idea of what I was really doing with my brother. I stopped giving him money and told him I couldn't help him—he had to do it on his own. He got mad and stormed off, but eventually he ended up in AA and hasn't taken a drink in years.

The preceding speech was given to a group of mothers and fathers all interested in helping their children cope with addictive substances. After he finished, many of the adults looked at each other knowingly. There are many enablers. Mothers, in particular, play out this role protesting that if they ever stopped helping the troubled child, he or she would be ruined.

Enabling parents of drug-addicted children often have little or no idea that they are contributing to the delinquency of their child. This is not surprising. They are driven by the noblest of intentions ("When I pay off my son's debts for the money he used to buy drugs, I'm giving him the opportunity to get a new start in life") and by the wish to spare their child from unpleasant emotions (such as embarrassment and guilt and resentment) which, if experienced, could lower the child's self-esteem (leading to rack and ruin) and, worse, cause the child to lose affection for the family (woe to the unhappy parents!).

In view of the fact that the dynamics of enabling work heavily against insight, I constructed the following statements for parents of drug-addicted children to read aloud to other group participants. They should be asked to discuss and defend their position on each statement.

1. You often defend your child's actions as not particularly serious.
2. You often defend your child by accusing your spouse of being too tough on the youngster.
3. You give money to your child even though you suspect it might be used for wrong purposes.
4. Your great love for your child often makes you an easy target for your child's stories and pleadings.
5. You often feel guilty because you think of yourself as being one of the prime reasons for your child's problems; therefore, you should forgive the youngster for wrongdoing and try even harder to help.
6. You keep thinking that if you could only find the right helping formula your youngster would be cured of his or her bad habit.
7. You believe that love conquers all when it comes to your child's difficulties.

Parental denial, fear of confrontation, and enabling are all defense mechanisms that contribute to drug abuse in children. They are not the only factors, of course. Some boys and girls are angry with their parents and take drugs as a form of revenge. Some children are lonely and find comfort in alcohol or drugs. Some have turned anger inward as a form of self-punishment and try to overcome depression with chemicals. Some are merely imitating the drug abuse of parents. Finally, drug abuse is just one of many forms of social nonconformity demonstrated by hostile and delinquent minors.

What should parents do once their child is in a treatment program? The following suggestions may be helpful:

1. In the beginning stages of treatment, the youngster tends to think of counselors as being present only to be supportive of the parents. Take this attitude in stride—it will pass.
2. Take an active role in helping the treatment center identify which aspect of addiction is of greatest concern to the child. Is it fear of being thrown out of school, being involved in gang activities, anxiety about acquiring AIDS, being rejected by friends, concern about sexual identity?
3. When the center sets up a treatment program, find out what the routine is; the parents and the child must adhere to the instructions.
4. Do not trust the teen (or the teen's peers) to monitor the collection of urine samples. A parent or a clinic staff member should do that.
5. Do not lead the youngster to believe that the recovery program is designed to help the parents. A successful treatment regime must be presented to the child as something to assist him or her.
6. Acknowledge the child's power to sabotage or support the program. Since many youngsters fight drug programs, parents must say, "You are the one in control. Only you can put the drugs in your veins or mouth."
7. Try not to be angry with the child during treatment. Behave as if the child had been physically hurt in an accident.
8. Join a support group where anger and frustration can be released in a safe setting with other parents who have gone through similar experiences.
9. Listen sympathetically to fears expressed by the child about the treatment program. Remember, the youngster is probably not enamored of the prospect of going straight and may think he or she is being forced into an unwanted regime. Many have developed an erroneous but understandable fear of treatment. Some are terrified of the possibility of undergoing a lobotomy or some other dreaded medical procedure. They need to be assured that these things will not happen.
10. Remember that, in all likelihood, the youngster has experimented with a variety of drugs but probably thinks only one (e.g., cocaine) is a real problem. The child must be disabused of this notion. Make it very clear that addiction to any substance is dangerous.

11. Refuse to be taken in by the child's assurance that his or her drug use is minimal (in my experience, all kids make this assertion).

12. Be prepared for, and accept, that the youngster will not be ready for the fatigue, irritability, and inability to sleep that occur after drug abstinence. Remain calm, and suggest practical ways to cope (e.g., by exercising, working on hobbies, avoiding caffeine, and talking with friends).

13. Realize that the child will have to return to school and can't immediately join a new group of peers who don't indulge in drugs. Straight students may refuse to associate with the child. Since loneliness is like a death sentence to a teenager, the youngster should be encouraged to get a part-time job or join a discussion group (perhaps patterned after AA).

14. Help the teen to be honest with friends who were around when he or she took drugs. The youngster must tell them that he or she has to remain drug free because of constant urine testing and dire consequences (like going to jail or losing his or her driver's license) if drugs are ingested.

15. Be prepared for emotional reactions during recovery that can tempt the youngster to seek out drugs again. Teens feel emotionally naked after giving up cocaine and its accompanying highs. Urge the youngster to tough it out. Provide access to new avenues of stimulation, (e.g., specially ordered videotapes or lessons in some area of interest to the child) to help relieve boredom or sadness.

16. Realize that the teenager, in a treatment program, often expects instant renewal of trust from the family and the same level of confidence that he or she enjoyed before becoming hooked on drugs. The teenager must be told that this expectation is unrealistic. Explain that it took a long time to break down the family's trust and that it will take at least as long to restore the lost faith.

17. If a teenager owes money to a drug dealer, he or she may be in danger—old debts are not tolerated well in the drug world and pushers are unpleasant people. If the youngster is in a treatment program, parents may wish to help the adolescent obtain monetary assistance to resolve this dilemma.

18. Parents should know that during the time the teen was involved in drug abuse, health problems may have emerged. While taking drugs, some adolescents engage in sexual practices they would have avoided if sober. Some teens are afraid they have been exposed to the HIV virus (and sometimes they are right). Parents can assist by getting the adolescent medical diagnosis and treatment. Also, some drug-dependent teenagers become run down physically and need food supplements.

19. Recovering adolescents invariably slip and try drugs again. Expect the relapse and do not become too upset when it occurs. Teenagers constantly test treatment providers—and themselves, for that matter—and will readily admit they tried drugs after treatment despite warnings of serious consequences. Yet nearly all are able to quit again. Most simply like to prove adults wrong. Nevertheless, parents and counselors can take only a limited amount of testing—if relapses occur too often, the involved adults must say, "I'm sorry; we can't work with you any longer. You can leave now." In my experience, most teens back off from further experimentation.

20. If the teen fights the program from the start and continues to resist, consider taking him or her out of the program. Risk of treatment failure is greater with uncooperative participants, and the discouragement associated with flunking the treatment plan may erase the teenager's only chance of eventually breaking the drug habit.

21. Even though it seems like an invasion of privacy, parents may have to search their child's room for the presence of drugs. If drugs are discovered, parents must not permit the youngster to put them off with protestations such as, "Somebody else put them there," or "They're just left over from when I took drugs." Assume the child is taking drugs and take the following steps if the youngster steadfastly resists acknowledging drug involvement. Use Drug Alert, a litmus test for drug residue, or take the youngster for a blood or urine test. Make sure the teen understands well ahead of time exactly what will occur if evidence of drug use is discovered in the home. For further information on these courses of action, get in touch with a medical laboratory or hospital or contact American Drug Screens (Box 3068, Dallas, TX 75221).

22. Do not quit a program just because there are no immediate results. Remember how hard it is for adults to lose weight or give up nicotine. Youngsters need parental patience and understanding over a lengthy period of treatment.

23. Teens sometimes tell disturbing stories to counselors in treatment centers—stories of being angry with parents, of being unable to share feelings with others, of urges to run from responsibilities, and, primarily, of difficulties in admitting to drug problems. Parents, naturally, don't like to hear these tales and may protest that the stories are not true. Although the related experiences may not be correctly perceived by the teen, the teenager's feelings about himself or herself are revealed by the stories and they must be accepted as part of the healing process. Later, when parents and teens are brought together in group sessions, many familial differences can be resolved.

Where can parents turn for help? They can look in the phone book for drug abuse centers and their state alcohol and drug abuse agency. The local chapter of Alcoholics Anonymous can provide useful information and may be able to supply speakers and videotapes. In addition, the following organizations can advise parents: National Self-Help Clearinghouse (New York, NY), National Clearinghouse for Alcohol Information (Rockville, MD), Mothers Against Drunk Driving (Hurst, TX), National Federation of Parents for Drug-Free Youth (Silver Spring, MD), National Parents Resource Institute for Drug Education (Atlanta, GA), National Congress of Parents and Teachers (Chicago, IL), Alcohol Education Project (Geneva, NY).

Finally, public libraries have many books and pamphlets on the subject of drug addiction. Allen et al. (1992) have written on the long-term effects of drugs. Bean and Bennett (1993) discussed ways teens can solve life problems. Guided steps for recovering from addiction are enumerated by Baugh (1990), and ideas for working with teens with addiction are presented by Jaynes and Rugg (1988). Other related problems are discussed by Peretti (2000).

CHAPTER 22

Attention Deficit Disorder

A great deal of controversy (Bloomingdale, 1984; Busch, 1993) has surrounded attempts to understand, delineate, and label the variety of symptoms categorized as attention deficit disorder (ADD). This broad term encompasses the concept that there are underlying central nervous system abnormalities that correspond to behavioral traits and that, when exhibited to an unusual degree, constitute a clinical syndrome. At this point, the concept does not commit itself to a particular etiology. Of course, it does not preclude the likelihood that psychological difficulties (other than those related to organic problems) can exist in afflicted individuals and must be treated (Bloomingdale, 1984; Busch, 1993; Burks, 1960, 1977a, 2006a, 2006b; Resnick & McEvoy, 1994).

During the 1950s and 1960s, research suggested that minimal brain dysfunction was one of the causes of attention deficits, overactivity, and impulsivity. However, many youngsters showing these difficulties lacked a definitive history and signs of brain injury.

As time went by, the behavior disorder was found to include a common symptom, attention deficits. I first postulated this as a prime trait (Burks, 1960). Currently—although there is still confusion about how to classify a large number of children with a mixture of problems related to attention deficits, overactivity, and learning, emotional, and social disabilities—this jumbled bag of symptoms is labeled ADD (Burks, 2001, 2006b).

ADD SUBTYPES

Over the last few decades much effort has been expended (see Goodyear & Hynd, 1992) to delineate areas of behavior that are common to various ADD subtypes.

How successful have these investigations been? Total success seems to have eluded everyone. Apparently, no universal or even sectional ADD profile exists. Each child has a unique profile, shaped by inherent assets and deficits. It is, therefore, important to tailor therapeutic approaches to fit the individual rather than a hypothetical clinical group. Even though no two children have the same clinical profile, intensive investigation has resulted in findings that show some symptom interrelationship to a greater or lesser extent among groups demonstrating particular pathologies than those shown by other population clusters.

Researchers now believe that ADD children can generally be separated into two large groups: those who have ADD with hyperactivity (attention deficit hyperactivity disorder; ADHD) and those who have ADD without hyperactivity. A third group, the ADD residual type (ADD-RT), includes individuals who presumably had childhood ADD and must now contend with residual emotional and social difficulties in adulthood.

Attention Deficit Hyperactivity Disorder (ADHD)

The ADHD category includes the most restless, aggressive, and acting-out children designated as suffering with ADD. Their conduct makes them among the most worrisome and vexing of all behavior-problem children. Environmentally based theories that attempt to explain their patterns of behavior have largely failed to do so. Child-raising practices successful with most children have not worked. Common discipline methods, useful in controlling normal youngsters, often prove useless. Parents are reduced to taking desperate measures, teachers dread the presence of these children in classrooms, and physicians are often at a loss to know how to treat them.

The following symptoms are commonly found in ADHD children (Burks, 1960):

- short attention span;
- restlessness and overactivity;
- poor judgment and impulsivity;
- low frustration tolerance and irritability;
- poor perceptual and conceptual abilities (reflected in serious academic deficiencies);
- defective memory;
- poor muscular coordination.

If these symptoms are demonstrated to too great a degree for too long a period of time (particularly during the formative years), a child's character structure can be damaged beyond repair (Burks, 1960, 1973). It is essential, therefore, to get medical and therapeutic treatment as early as possible.

One of the difficulties facing physicians and other professionals is the proper categorization of problem children. When a child is brought in for consultation, the parents often present a confused picture of behavior disturbance. It is important to distinguish between the child who is primarily functionally disturbed and the child who has an organic impairment (even though the latter child may also have acquired emotional problems); this differentiation will determine the direction and duration of therapy.

Children who are organically healthy but functionally disturbed retain conduct flexibility that is not available to neurologically handicapped children. In short, emotionally troubled children are restricted by their disturbance to a smaller number of behavioral choices than would be available to normal children; however, this restriction is by choice, not because they are denied these opportunities as a consequence of organic deficiencies. Emotionally upset individuals with sound nervous systems can learn and execute defensive maneuvers adeptly and can, in the absence of mental retardation, perform adequately (even though they may choose not to) in cognitive and motor aspects of learning. They are able to channel incoming stimuli, integrate these messages meaningfully in sustained thought patterns, and translate these cerebral designs into functional motor activity. These processes may be denied to organically disturbed children.

And I emphatically believe ADD children suffer neurological dysfunctions—extensive research conducted by the author (Burks, 1955, 1957a, 1957b, 1960, 1961, 1964a) establishes the fact that the majority of ADD subjects acquire abnormal brain wave (EEG) readings and other signs of organic disabilities.

Functionally (environmentally) disturbed children tend to act out their problems. Neurologically handicapped children, on the other hand, may be said to act up. There are observable differences between acting-out and acting-up behavior (see table 22.1). Not all problem children have all of these symptoms, and some symptoms may overlap the two groups.

Typically, teachers complain that ADHD students have emotional outbursts, especially of an aggressive or even antisocial nature, as well as extreme hyperactivity, restlessness, and impulsivity. While academic difficulties are somewhat common, the incidence of learning problems is not as great for this group as it is for children who have ADD without hyperactivity. Small and large muscle coordination among ADHD children is generally poor. In contrast to ADD children without hyperactivity, ADHD children exhibit more daydreaming (alternating with hyperactivity), more stubborn behavior, and more explosive and unpredictable conduct. In addition, they tell bizarre stories, and do not benefit from ordinary discipline procedures.

Attention Deficit Disorder without Hyperactivity

Children who have ADD without hyperactivity may be difficult to recognize. Although they may annoy teachers and parents, they are much less often referred for guidance assistance than are ADHD youngsters. The relative

Acting-Out Versus Acting-Up Behavior

Acting Out (Functionally Disturbed Children)	Acting Up (Organically Disturbed Children)
Compulsive behavior patterns.	Impulsive behavior patterns.
Is able to sustain a pattern of behavior over time (i.e., can hold a grudge; can plan ahead).	Is unable to sustain a pattern of behavior over time (i.e., becomes angry but anger passes quickly; does not plan actions well).
Chronically unhappy; withholds affection.	Usually affectionate; may appear happy even when in trouble.
Can come up with a reason for misbehavior, even if it is obviously not true.	Is unable to explain his or her misbehavior; goes blank when questioned.
Mood is fairly consistent.	Moods fluctuate widely.
Teachers tend to find child's behavior predictable.	Teachers are nonplussed by child's conduct and become extremely frustrated.
Can be made to understand limits and inhibit behavior even though he or she may not want to.	Difficult to make child understand boundaries and inhibit behavior.
Academic picture may be unaffected; usually consistent. If the child is a poor student, it is apparently because he or she *won't* be a good one.	Academic picture is erratic, messy, and inconsistent. The child is a poor student apparently because he or she *can't* be a good one.
Relieves tension through symbolic behavior (i.e., gets back at parents by fighting with the teacher).	Relieves tension by direct motor action on the immediate frustrating situation.
Good attention span.	Poor attention span.
Environmental factors involved.	Organic and environmental factors involved.
Physical examination seldom reveals problems.	Physical examination reveals glandular, metabolic, or neural difficulties.
Parents are often problematic.	Parents may or may not be problematic, but they do need help with their child.
Intelligence is within normal distribution curve.	Intelligence is usually in dull-normal or average range.

Table 22.1.

absence of hyperactivity is apparently the main reason for this phenomenon; however, they also tend to be less impulsive and less aggressive and so are not as disruptive.

Although these children are less active than ADHD children, they still get high scores on the Burks Behavior Rating Scales (BBRS) attention deficits, academic difficulties, and poor coordination scales and often are rated high on the BBRS categories reflecting emotional and social difficulties.

According to Lahey and Carlson (1991), children who have ADD without hyperactivity are characterized by inattention and disorganization (often accompanied by depression, anxiety, and shyness) while ADHD children are noted for motor hyperactivity and impulsive behavior (often related to serious conduct problems). Beiderman, Newcorn, and Sprich (1991) supported this position. They also pointed out that these two groups of children might be differentiated on the basis of the disorder's association with other personality difficulties. ADHD children tend to be oppositional, defiant, and antisocial, with unusual mood swings, while ADD children without hyperactivity tend to have anxiety and learning problems. While both ADD classifications have depression and poor self-concept as common traits, these affective disorders often have differing causes (e.g., abnormalities in the brain). Children who have ADD without hyperactivity may be described as sluggish, drowsy, distractible, unable to remember directions, immature, somewhat impulsive, socially withdrawn, self-conscious, learning disordered, sloppy, disorganized, worried, downcast, daydreamers, unmotivated, moderately unpopular, and poor in sports—characteristics common to other childhood maladies.

Because ADD encompasses behavior that closely resembles the many problems exhibited by immature, unmotivated children (Burks, 1977a, 1985) many people question the validity of judgments that place children with such symptoms in an organically disturbed classification. For a long time, I did not think this type of child was an ADD candidate, but I was forced to change my mind when investigators (Safer & Krager, 1989) found that children who were inattentive but not hyperactive improved as much as hyperactive children did when treated with stimulants (usually Ritalin).

ADD Residual Type (ADD-RT)

A third type of ADD is now recognized within the professional community—ADD residual type (ADD-RT). In general, ADD-RT includes individuals who had untreated childhood ADD and who must now deal with the social and emotional sequelae of the disorder. The ramifications of the existence of this category should be well understood, because when a counselor approaches the parents of an ADD child, he or she may want to ask them about the possibility that other family members have ADD traits. ADD is believed to be inheritable (Hechtman, 1989).

Woods (1986) discussed the criteria and treatment for ADD-RT. The clinical manifestations are similar to ADD symptoms in children. He emphasized that a diagnosis must be prefaced by a history of early ADD. Symptoms include

- poor attention (inability to remain focused on an activity such as reading);
- motor abnormalities (usually coordination difficulties);
- impulsivity (e.g., making decisions with little reflection; abruptly beginning and ending relationships; being reckless);
- mood lability (happy one moment and angry the next);
- short temper or irritability (e.g., difficulty with waiting; extreme irritation when stuck in traffic);
- poor organization and poor task completion (may switch haphazardly from one task to another; cannot manage time);
- low stress tolerance with overactivity (easily overwhelmed by ordinary hassles).

As with many ADD children, ADD adults have a poor self-image and may be fidgety, restless, forgetful, absentminded, and clumsy, with a poor sense of direction.

Hales and Hales (1996) say ADHD isn't strictly kid stuff anymore; at least five million adults in the United States are afflicted. They believe that the characteristics of attention disorder are abundant in our culture and are noted everywhere. Although some individuals appear to have pseudo-ADHD, true ADHD in adults is entirely different—it is a neurological syndrome that always starts in childhood, usually before age seven.

According to Woods (1986), treatment for ADD-RT is basically the same as for a child with ADD—it includes both drug therapy and psychotherapy. He believes that psychotherapy without drug management is of little use.

DIAGNOSIS

Diagnosticians are rightly concerned about distinguishing between children who are organically unfit and those who are emotionally disturbed. The dilemma cannot be easily resolved. Most organically disturbed children also have emotional problems. At any rate, no one, at this point, is sure of all the ways that brain dysfunction can be expressed.

There are other problems in the diagnosis of neural involvement. The relationship of organic dysfunction to behavior must often be assumed; that assumption gains validity in relation to the number of clinical signs or events in the individual's immediate and long-term history. A multiplicity of occurrences strengthens the diagnosis of organic brain dysfunction.

Diagnosing ADHD

Symptoms. ADHD is a transactional disorder of the interface between a child and his or her social world. Youngsters with ADHD can be identified through the use of the Burks Behavior Rating Scales, which are designed to gauge this interface. Both teachers and parents should fill out the BBRS forms. High scores on the following scales can help establish the existence of the disorder.

Primary Characteristics

- attention deficits
- impulsivity (including high levels of hyperactivity)
- poor coordination

Secondary Characteristics

- poor self-esteem
- academic difficulties
- poor reality contact
- social isolation
- aggressive tendencies

There may also be high scores on other BBRS scales. Many ADHD youngsters are seriously disturbed; they have encountered unusual amounts of criticism and disapproval in their lives. The clinician should observe the child in the classroom and ask the teacher the following questions:

1. Does the child need more supervision than most?
2. Does the child seldom finish his or her work?
3. Does the child often lose things like work, books, and so on?

4. Is the child disliked by peers?
5. Does the child engage in more risk-taking behavior than most?
6. Does the child talk excessively?
7. Does the child intrude into the conversations of others?
8. Is the child unusually disruptive in the classroom?

Parents, of course, can also provide information about their hyperactive youngsters. After the parents have completed the BBRS, ask them the following questions:

1. Have others suggested that your child is overactive?
2. Have teachers suggested your child be held back a grade?
3. Does your child tend to get into trouble in the neighborhood?
4. Does your child have trouble making and keeping friends?
5. Does your child have any sleep difficulties?
6. Does your youngster tend to roam the house at night?
7. Does your child seem accident-prone?
8. Does your child seem clumsy to you?
9. Does your child have difficulty figuring out why he or she gets into trouble?
10. Even when rewarded or punished, does your child find it hard to concentrate?
11. Does your child often blurt out unwanted comments?
12. Does your child have a lot of trouble following rules?
13. Does your child have trouble waiting for his or her turn?
14. Does your child seem overaggressive to you?
15. Does your child have many mood swings?
16. Does your child seem to ignore the rights of others?
17. Do you think your child has learning problems?
18. Do you think your child is physically immature for his or her age?

The preceding questions for teachers and parents describe behavior typically seen in ADHD children (Burks, 1960). A diagnosis of ADHD may be strengthened or weakened by parents' responses to the following questions:

1. Have the symptoms of overactivity, impulsivity, and attention deficits been apparent from birth? (If they have, a diagnosis of ADHD is bolstered.)
2. Have the symptoms of overactivity, impulsivity, and attention deficits existed from the time the child experienced an illness or a head injury? (A "yes" answer strongly suggests trauma to the central nervous system.)
3. Are the symptoms of overactivity, impulsivity, and attention deficits evident at all times and in all places or only at home, at school, or in association with some special circumstance? (ADHD children show the symptoms regardless of time, place, or condition.)
4. Did the symptoms of overactivity, impulsivity, and attention deficits become apparent after a family crisis like a divorce, the loss of a loved one, a death, or some other unsettling event? (A "yes" answer contraindicates the presence of ADHD.)

Behavioral symptoms are the most important clues. Etiology may be a relatively unimportant issue; it is of interest only if it points out the direction for treatment. For example, during the course of diagnosis it may be determined that a child is suffering epileptic brain seizures in a form not easily recognized because obvious motor symptoms are absent. In such a case, seizures can ordinarily be medically controlled. The clinical origins for most ADHD children are not so easily seen and the relationship of the individual's history to his or her treatment may remain obscure. The hyperactive child must be treated—medically, educationally, and socially—in pragmatic ways. Whatever works for the betterment of the child is ordinarily acceptable as a treatment measure.

Conduct disturbances are the most reliable and consistent indication of minimal brain impairment. The exhibition of behavior disorders does not guarantee the presence of organic dysfunction, but it is the conduct disorders that drive parents to seek professional assistance. If the child does not show behavior patterns typically thought to be associated with brain dysfunction, medication is not likely to do much good.

Medical history. ADHD youngsters tend to show many adverse medical events in early childhood, but so do many normally behaving children (Burks, 1957a, 1960, 1977a, 2006a). Further, it is difficult to establish the association of early trauma to later conduct. Finally, pathological etiological events seldom suggest the direction of later therapies.

Nevertheless, the following questions may prove helpful when the following medical events occurred.

Was the birth abnormal?

- Extensive use of forceps?
- Blue baby?
- Birth weight under four-and-a-half pounds?
- Cord around the baby's neck?
- Premature?
- Unnatural delivery?

Has there been a history of unusual illnesses?

- High fevers?
- Convulsions?
- Seizures?
- Periods of unconsciousness?
- Severe headaches?
- Fainting spells?
- Unusual head injuries (perhaps with coma)?

Any of the preceding medical occurrences are more significant if ADHD symptoms (overactivity, impulsivity, and attention deficits) ensued after the traumatic event.

Medical examination. Any child suspected of having ADD symptoms should be examined by a physician, who will probably employ the usual clinical tests given any youngster entering his or her practice. Parents should determine what credentials the medical specialist possesses in the field of child behavior disorders. Having worked with many physicians, I have found some who did not wish to become involved in this specialty area and would say so if asked. If a parent receives this kind of answer, he or she should ask for a referral to a suitable colleague.

Finding the proper physician is an important first step. The study of ADHD youngsters is complicated (Burks, 1961, 1962). Most children with ADHD experience some degree of emotional and social difficulties (best treated by psychological means), and all endure attention and overactive symptoms (usually best handled by medication). The astute medical practitioner will not try to simplify treatment by just prescribing drugs while neglecting to investigate home and school conditions.

In some instances (particularly when the physician suspects the presence of a seizure disorder), an electroencephalogram (EEG) test may be necessary to help establish the existence of a neurological disorder (Burks, 1968c). Parents can be told not to be apprehensive about the brain wave exam; no electrical energy is put into the brain. It is simply a measure of cortex wave activity much like the forms emanating from the measure of heart rhythms. Children tend to dislike the examination so they need to be reassured that it is not a painful procedure.

I discovered that ADHD children received fewer abnormal EEG tracings than did ADD youngsters without hyperactivity (Burks, 1957a, 1960, 1964a, 1968b, 1985). Since the EEG apparatus cannot measure deep brain abnormalities, but does register unusual activity in the cortex, it was hypothesized that children in the ADHD group were expressing powerful impulses originating in the lower regions of the brain (perhaps toward emotional control centers), which impel certain individuals to action without thought of consequences. Anyone who has watched very hyperactive children in a state of drivenness can appreciate the lack of controls over these intense reactions.

Conversely, the ADD children with lower levels of hyperactivity and a greater incidence of learning difficulties showed a distinct tendency to acquire abnormal brain wave tracings. Surface brain (cortex) difficulties seemingly interrupted classroom learning, but emotional centers (deep in the brain) were not as much affected as they were for ADHD students.

Coordination tests. For reasons not well known, physical awkwardness is a characteristic sign associated with many ADHD children below age nine. While poor large and small muscle coordination cannot be considered a prime symptom of ADD, it remains a common associated sign and for that reason lends itself to the diagnosis of the disturbance. See the diagnosis section of chapter 9 for coordination exercises useful in the diagnosis of ADHD.

Psychological and academic tests. Educators need to know the mental strengths and weaknesses of the hyperactive student. ADHD students tend to have more difficulty with abstract reasoning, memory, and verbal tasks than with concrete tasks (Burks, 1960).

The relationship of poor academic achievement to the ADHD diagnostic classification is not entirely clear, but the fact that so many youngsters with poor concentration and overactivity also possess erratic learning skills creates the suspicion that a nervous system dysfunction somehow affects the ability to acquire and retain school subject matter. Whatever the relationship, retardation in reading, spelling, and arithmetic is *not* a primary sign in the diagnosis of the disorder. Many youngsters are slow learners, but they do not show the attention and motor activity problems characteristic of ADHD.

Summary of ADHD diagnostic signs. After investigating the characteristics of hundreds of ADHD children, I believe the following signs point to the disorder (Burks, 1957a, 1957b, 1960, 1961, 1964a, 1968b, 1968d, 1973, 1977a, 2001, 2006b). The list is ranked from the most important indications to the least important:

1. chronic and long-lasting conduct characterized mainly by hyperactivity, short attention span, impulsivity, explosiveness, and poor social adjustment;
2. a history of early physical trauma; long, difficult labor during the child's birth is the most commonly reported finding;
3. a record of uneven physical development (often reported as poor coordination);
4. an abnormal electroencephalogram;
5. "scattering" on test scores, indicating perceptual and conceptual difficulties;
6. a report that the child is the only member of the family who tends to show these signs;
7. chronic academic retardation (particularly in reading, spelling, and writing).

When investigating the origins of hyperactivity, do not underestimate the importance of environmental circumstances. At times it is difficult to separate the contribution of organic factors from environmental conditions, but it is important to do so to avoid improper treatment. Professional diagnosticians are concerned about the differences between children who are neurologically afflicted and those who are emotionally upset. For the following reasons the dilemma cannot easily be resolved:

1. Most neurologically handicapped children experience emotional difficulties to some degree.
2. Many emotionally disturbed youngsters have conduct problems (hostility, destructiveness, and so on) that may also be demonstrated by ADHD children.
3. No one, at this point, is sure of all the ways that brain dysfunction can be expressed.

In spite of these difficulties, many professionals tend to see the diagnosis as an either-or proposition, which can have tragic consequences for children and parents. I have conferred with many parents who reported that their children were diagnosed as brain-impaired and who then searched in vain for medical answers. Their quest may have continued for a considerable period of time, even for years. During this time, the children continued to show unusual emotional, social, and academic difficulties. Some were worse off than when the parents began their search for help. The problems of any disturbed child are too complex to be explained and solved simply. The multiple needs of a hyperactive child must be met intelligently and from a number of sources. Parents, ordinarily, must place their trust in the professionals who are asked to guide them. Unfortunately, these professionals do not always agree with one another, and parents may eventually find themselves bewildered by a confusing mass of contradictory and seldom useful information. Some professionals do not have a wide knowledge of organic processes as they relate to behavior and do not comprehend what therapies work best. I believe one individual should be in charge of directing the family, thereby saving time and money. This should be someone who has specialized in the diagnosis and treatment of ADHD children. In some cases, that will be someone other than a physician.

Briefly, the understanding of the ADHD symptoms should take the following into consideration:

1. ADHD refers to a wide variety of conduct disturbances—with inattention, hyperactivity, and impulsivity as prime traits.
2. No two overactive youngsters ever show the same range of symptoms nor demonstrate the symptoms to the same degree.
3. Causes for the disorder remain speculative and do not significantly affect treatment.
4. ADHD children often grow up to be overactive adults with attention defects that can disrupt home and business relationships.
5. ADHD children cannot be evaluated and treated as if they belong to a distinctly defined class by themselves. They have certain behaviors common to all children—but to a greater extent.

Diagnosing ADD without Hyperactivity

The Burks Behavior Rating Scales can help identify children who have ADD without hyperactivity. Teachers and parents should fill out the BBRS forms. Examiners should pay close attention to high scores on the following scales:

Primary Characteristics

- attention deficits
- academic difficulties
- poor coordination

Secondary Characteristics

- anxiousness
- withdrawal
- poor self-esteem
- poor physical stamina
- cognitive difficulties
- emotional distress
- social isolation

Like ADHD children, these youngsters can also have higher scores on almost any other scale. Much depends on the learning experiences of the individual. If home and school environments offer little encouragement, a child can develop unhealthy defenses.

The examiner should ask the teacher the same questions asked about the ADHD student. In addition, ask the teacher about the following behavior:

1. Is the child unusually disorganized?
2. Is the child's handwriting unusually poor (scratchy and uneven)?
3. Does the child take an unusually long time to finish assignments?
4. Does the child seem unhappy and frustrated or even depressed?
5. Does the child seem meek and defenseless?
6. Does the child try hard but still accomplish little?

These questions can also be posed to the parents.

The diagnosis of ADHD and ADD without hyperactivity can be more complicated if the child being examined is very anxious. Plizka (1990) demonstrated that some ADD children may have a primary problem with anxiety that causes a secondary symptom of inattentiveness. The examiner who notes an overriding anxiety syndrome should, perhaps, treat the anxiety before attempting to resolve other ADD difficulties.

INTERVENTION STRATEGIES

Techniques for School Personnel

Children who have the ADHD syndrome need firm discipline. I once studied 72 hyperactive-distractible children (84% boys) who had been placed in special classes (Burks, 1968d). The nine teachers of these classes rated discipline methods found most useful in controlling the children. The following methods were considered beneficial for the majority of students:

- a prompt approach to work (getting started on time);
- rigid routine;
- special individual attention;
- lack of interruptions;
- consistent approach;
- kindness;
- careful instructions on class standards;
- letting the hyperactive child shine in an activity;
- direct praise;
- direct commands.

In general, the control procedures thought to be most beneficial were characterized by methods that were consistent, prompt, reutilized, individualized, kind, commendatory, well understood by the children, and characterized by a close temporal relationship between command and response.

In addition, classroom experience with ADD students suggests the following:

1. Not all ADHD children can be in regular classrooms. Special education services and self-contained placement may be necessary to meet student needs.
2. The ultimate aim of special classes is to restore the child to a regular class setting. This is particularly true for older individuals, who badly need normal peer relationships.

3. ADD children have difficulty relating parts to the whole. They make mistakes because they often do not understand cause-and-effect relationships. They must be helped to make these connections. Many or most demonstrate significant difficulties in estimating the length of time periods (i.e., unlike most youngsters, they grossly under- or overestimate how long or how short one minute or five minutes is).

4. Good classroom management requires careful preparation. Special lesson plans are essential. Time should be allotted for the teacher to observe and evaluate ADD students in other rooms.

5. Teachers should be aware of and know how to treat the principal conflicts faced by hyperactive students. Psychological services should be made available when needed.

6. If classroom discipline breaks down, standby personnel (other teachers or administrators) should be available. They can remove the child, work with him or her, and return the child when he or she is ready.

7. If, as sometimes happens, a child and teacher dislike each other and this mutual dislike continues over a period of time, arrangements should be made to transfer the child to another classroom.

8. The teacher must create an atmosphere of respect for others. The teacher's rights and needs must be honored by the students.

9. Teachers should be aware of the ripple effect. Very deviant behavior demonstrated by one child can spread to other children. It is, therefore, important to control disruptive behavior in the early stages. Dealing with one disruptive student is obviously easier than dealing with several.

10. Disturbed children are notoriously unimproved by force or punishment. Outrage by educators is not a suitable response to disruptive student behavior. Adult demands must be kept to a minimum. All children have off days. Each day should start with a clean slate. Lingering resentment serves no useful purpose.

11. Have the student move to the teacher, not vice versa. When the student walks to the teacher's desk, he or she symbolically takes an active and aggressive attitude toward learning and independence.

12. Incipient strife can often be avoided by asking quiet questions about classwork or by instigating a new activity. Avoid asking the child about the causes of conflicts. If possible, let conflicts resolve themselves (actually, if the teacher intervenes predictably, students learn to count on being saved from the bad consequences of fights; thus, they feel free to start conflicts). Sometimes instructor intervention worsens situations.

13. If a student has a bad day and the parents, as per previous agreement, are asked to take the student home, they *must* come when telephoned and they *must* be willing to follow directives. The excuse that both parents work and are unable to come cannot be accepted. The parents and the child must understand that the child is to be taken home for the day, not as a punishing action but as a method to help the child learn self-restraint. Remind parents that other class members have rights, too.

14. Routine is important to the ADD child. An even flow of the day's activities provides a sequence that will not require the child to make frequent adjustments.

15. Play down competition with other children. Encourage the child to better his or her own record.

16. ADHD children need frequent changes of activity and opportunities to move about. They are conspicuous for their high energy.

17. Rewards for learning and proper behavior should be prompt, visible, and often tangible.

18. Whether a student replies correctly or incorrectly to a question, the teacher should respond in a neutral manner. Comments like "That's right!" or "That's wrong!" carry connotations of good or bad, love or rejection. The ego strength of some disturbed children is too weak to withstand failure. When a student says, "I don't know," the teacher should cheerfully accept this reply. The child, then, feels accepted even when he or she does not comprehend the answer. If possible, do not let the child give a wrong answer in front of other students. Keep giving hints until the child gives the correct response.

19. Provide an isolation booth the child can use when he or she wants to. Do not use it as punishment.

20. Provide a shortened day if the child becomes fatigued or more hyperactive as the day goes on. Gradually increase the length of the school day as the child demonstrates increased self-control.

Techniques for Parents

Budd (1990), Burks (1960, 1972, 2006b), Fadely and Hosler (1992), Goldstein and Goldstein (1992), Gordon (1991), Kirby and Grimley (1986), and R. N. Parker (1992) have all stressed the necessity of the involvement of parents of ADD children in counseling and treatment sessions.

Conduct problems of these children are poorly understood by most parents. They need help in comprehending the possible origins of such behavior, perceiving the emotional deprivations brought about as a consequence of social isolation, and discerning proper methods of establishing discipline and control. Failure of parents to acquire this wisdom can thwart the efforts of others to help.

Parental counseling ideally should occur when the active child is young. Unfortunately, many of the symptoms are not apparent until the child is in school. A single professional should coordinate therapeutic efforts. This individual, who may be the family physician, a psychologist, or a social worker, must command the respect of fellow professionals by knowing diagnostic and treatment procedures.

The parents should be advised to take the youngster for proper medical evaluation. Medical diagnosis and drug therapy may suffice for a few overactive children. For others, psychological therapy is also indicated. Parental understanding and the implementation of good training and discipline procedures are a must. Parents should understand the necessity of setting firm and consistent limits for child misbehavior.

The following suggestions have proved helpful to many parents:

1. The ADHD child should not be allowed to become overtired (this tends to exaggerate symptoms).
2. Because stress and tension are handled poorly by such youngsters, environmental stimulation should be kept to a minimum. If possible, the child should have his or her own room, far from home activities. Daily routines should be kept simple, organized, and consistently maintained.
3. Excessive reactions on the part of the child (e.g., temper tantrums or aggressiveness) should be met with prompt but quiet, gentle, and firm adult responses. Placing the child in seclusion in another part of the home is sometimes effective.
4. Many reasons for disciplinary action are best not discussed with the child. Too often the child learns to manipulate the dialogue to his or her advantage and the confrontation prolongs the duration of undesirable behavior.
5. The physical environment ought to be organized so the child has little opportunity to injure the self or others. Breakable objects can be removed from reach. This precaution assumes particular importance for the young child whose lack of coordination, strength, and judgment make him or her unusually vulnerable to accidents. Certain rooms of the home may be put off-limits.
6. It is best to establish and maintain household routines (chores, bedtime, eating times, homework times, and so on). Routines are kept simple, organized, and consistently maintained even under special circumstances (e.g., having visitors).
7. Do not force a tired ADD youngster to do late evening homework. Stress felt at this time of day can interfere with achievement ability.
8. Help family members recognize how the hyperactive child is different. They need to understand that the youngster is often unable to control impulsive, forgetful, clumsy, or loud behavior. Spend significant time helping siblings on these matters because their lack of patience is particularly galling to an ADD child.
9. When seeking professional help, it is helpful if both parents are in agreement about treatment objectives. I have found it nearly impossible to assist ADD children (or any other types of disturbed children for that matter) when parental disagreements become therapeutic hurdles.
10. Promote activities that help the child slow down, get organized, and improve coordination.

The following techniques may also prove beneficial:

Adult modeling (to counter overactivity and inattention). With the primary school–age child watching, demonstrate how a task is to be performed. Do it slowly, methodically, and accurately. Repeat the directions until the youngster does it satisfactorily.

Adult modeling with self-instruction (to counter impulsivity and reinforce attention). Model the behavior but, in addition, describe out loud how the task is performed. Have the boy or girl repeat the actions while also talking out loud.

Muscle relaxation (to counter overactivity). Encourage small children to relax while lying on a carpet or mat. Lie down with the child, speak in a soft voice, and, when appropriate, play soothing music.

Elimination of distractions (to assist concentration). Place the young child away from windows or open doors that provide distracting stimuli. It might be better to have the youngster face a blank wall while working. Adults need to refrain from needless talking.

Separation from peers who overstimulate (to promote quieter activity). Surround the child with calmer friends who can model desired behavior.

Carefully programmed home activities (to aid attention). Do not ask a young child to sit quietly for more than 20 minutes. Allow short activity periods where the youngster can release pent-up energy. After such an activity, allow time for the youngster to calm down before going on to a new assignment.

Imagining exercises (to promote attention and logical thinking). Ask the young child to imagine a task that requires total attention to complete. Then ask the youngster to think of a reward he or she would like to receive for doing the imagined job. Whenever possible, allow the child to actually do the task and receive the reward.

Self-direction (to promote logical thinking). Make up two cue cards—one that says STOP and one that says THINK. Teach the child to use these cards to monitor work assignments. For example, use the cards when the student is beginning homework activities or as a game with a friend of the child.

Clear and consistent rules (to promote self-regulation). This is a valuable technique for youngsters of any age. Formulate easily understood regulations, and make sure all family members comprehend and follow these rules. Post the rules in a well-traveled part of the home.

Routine home activities (to reduce frustration and distractions). Plan each day's activities. Make sure the overactive child understands what these plans are. ADD youngsters tend to become anxious when presented with unpredictable situations.

Time limits (to reduce impulsive and distractible conduct). Get a kitchen timer and show your child how it works. Pick a situation in which the youngster rarely sits still (such as at meal times). Set the timer to go off in, say, five minutes. Ask the child to sit still for that period of time. If he or she manages to do that, give praise or a small reward (such as an extra dessert). If the child becomes distracted during the waiting period, praise someone else at the table for waiting quietly. Do not censure failure, merely reset the timer and try again. If the technique (best used with young children) proves successful, employ it in other situations that require waiting.

"Quiet" games (to reduce overactivity and assist concentration).

- Quiet as a Statue: Parent and young child sit in chairs facing each other. Both place hands on knees. Each takes a turn playing "statue"—that is, staying as still as a statue, not moving even a finger or allowing the nose to twitch. In the beginning, do not expect the small child to manage more than a minute of no movement, but, with practice, this time period can be extended. Give plenty of praise for success and ignore failures.

- Erase the Sad Faces: If the parent wants the child to remain quiet during a 10-minute ride to the market, this game may help to achieve that objective. With a pencil, draw a row of sad faces on a piece of paper. Tell the child that for each minute spent sitting still, he or she can erase one of the faces. When all of the faces are gone, the child has won the game.

- Swap the Minutes: Tell the young overactive child that by obeying specific instructions to be quiet and sit still, time will be swapped. For each minute of desired behavior, he or she can receive a credit of one minute to do what the child wants. Praise the child for successful performance. Expand this game by adding minutes to a chore for minutes of observed overactivity.

- The Seatbelt Sign Is On: Here is a game that can be played almost anywhere. Ask the child to pretend that he or she is sitting in an airplane seat. The parent pretends to be the captain, who can turn the seatbelt sign on.

When the sign is turned on, the youngster must sit down and stay there. When the sign is turned off, the child can get up and move about. It may be more fun to mock up a sign. As the child matures, extend the "on" period of the seatbelt signal.

- I'm Glued to the Seat: When the child is brought to a gathering where calm behavior is required, pretend to coat the young child's chair seat with crazy glue (let the youngster pretend to put on the glue). The child is then allowed to sit down and be "glued" to the chair. The child may be entertained further by being instructed to look about and notice other people or things that seem to be glued in place.

- Zapping: Tell the child who has trouble completing assignments because of distractions to "zap" any extraneous stimulus with an imaginary finger gun. If the child learns to ignore distractions using this technique, reward that accomplishment.

- Deliberate Distraction and Rewards: While the child works at an assignment (such as homework), the parent goes about the room doing distracting things—like humming.

When the youngster ignores the distraction and finishes the assignment, he or she is given rewards of the following nature:

Self-awards (to promote concentration). Permit the child to reward himself or herself for setting up a program of self-regulation. The child may announce, "I will work for 10 minutes on my lessons without paying attention to anything else." If that objective is accomplished, the child may award himself or herself with a concrete, prearranged prize (e.g., a star or a cookie).

Free time for concentration on activities of interest (to promote greater attention span). Don't overdo attempts to get the child to be quiet and attentive. Allow some free time for the youngster to concentrate on activities he or she enjoys. Chances are the child will be less distractible than when working on parent-contrived tasks.

Discouragement of wild guessing (to counter impulsivity). Overactive children sometimes indulge in illogical guessing in response to questions, either because they were not paying attention or are unaware of ongoing events. Parents can help by supplying correct responses ahead of time or by teaching the youngster to say nothing if an answer is not known. Use this technique at any age.

Family activities (to enhance self-esteem). Play a wide variety of games and sports with the entire family, particularly those activities that require concentration. Such activities can teach cooperation skills and how to follow regulations (e.g., learning to wait for your turn) and can improve eye-hand coordination. Finally, family play brings family members closer and facilitates communication.

Memory exercises (to enhance recall). Poor memory is characteristic of many ADD youngsters. To improve a child's memory and concentration, try the following exercise. Put three objects on a tray. Have the youngster look at the objects for 30 seconds, then talk or write about what was on the tray. Gradually increase the number of objects in subsequent sessions and make the directions more complex. Use with younger children.

Constructive television viewing (to enhance concentration and reduce overactivity). The overactive and impulsive child should be encouraged to watch television alone and in a fairly dim room. The aim here is to promote attention span and quiet behavior. Selection of programs is, of course, important. They must have high intrinsic interest (many of the shows produced for children are excellent for nearly all ages, but have the child watch only those that hold his or her attention). Let the youngster select the programs (but only from a list of parent-approved choices).

Proximity control (to promote self-regulation and increase concentration). To gain a young child's attention, use prearranged signals that help the child focus (e.g., a tap on the table, a touch on the shoulder, or saying the child's name).

Eye contact (to reduce impulsivity). Many ADHD children have trouble maintaining eye contact with someone who is trying to exert control. They are impelled to look away by an apparently faulty nervous system and many cannot tolerate being forced to stop and look at someone else. If at any age, a child has this symptom, force him or her to focus on the speaker and repeat what is being said. Do not continue attempts to communicate until the child's attention is gained. Ignore crying and tantrums.

Teaching socially acceptable behavior (to reduce impulsivity). Many ADD youngsters pay little attention to social interaction, contributing to their inability to get along with others. For example, a seven-year-old boy bursts into a room where people are talking and, completely ignoring who is speaking at the moment, starts jabbering at everyone in general. Instead of lecturing the boy, his parents might try the "Binocular Game." Have the boy use binoculars (imaginary or real) to zoom in on whoever is talking and remain locked on that individual until he or she stops talking. This game can be extended to mealtime. Ask the child to watch and listen to whoever is talking in order to earn points on a chart. The point system can also be used when the youngster pays attention to parental instructions in other places and at other times.

Praise for being patient (to counter impulsivity). Research indicates that impulsive children of all ages eventually become more patient and are able to delay gratification better when they hear themselves described by adults as being patient (apparently they try to live up to an incorporated image of being self-controlled).

Self-instruction techniques (to promote concentration and to counter impulsivity). Thoughtless behavior can disappear when young children are taught to instruct themselves. For example, youngsters directed to say, "It's good that I'm waiting" find it easier to hold back than when they say nothing. They may also be asked to repeat rules to themselves, such as, "I shouldn't touch the CD player." Further, children are less impulsive when they talk to themselves about an immediate task rather than when they are asked to concentrate on a future reward for good behavior. That is, it is more effective to teach them to say, "I'm putting away my crayons" than to say, "When I'm finished, I'll get to go outside and play."

Well-explained rules (to promote logical thinking). Impetuous children may find it convenient to ignore home rules. Adults can minimize the problem by carefully explaining why the rules exist. Further, children who have a say about a code of conduct are more apt to adopt and obey the rules. Youngsters of all ages like discussion groups that deal with the purpose of regulations and why rules should be obeyed. When they are allowed to make up some of their own behavior guides, they quickly come to understand the value of and need for established standards.

SUGGESTED READINGS

The following books address questions often brought up by parents of ADD youngsters:

Why Does My Child Have so Much Trouble Paying Attention?

Goldstein, S., & Goldstein, M. (1992). *Hyperactivity: Why won't my child pay attention?* New York: Wiley & Sons.

What Are the Common Treatments for ADD?

Kirby, E. A., & Grimley, L. K. (1986). *Understanding and treating attention deficit disorder.* New York: Pergamon Press.

How Can I Recognize Adult ADD?

Hales, D., & Hales, R. E. (1996, January 7). Finally, I know what's wrong. *Parade Magazine,* 10–11.

What Are the Treatments for Adult ADD? What Are the Effects of Psychotropic Drugs?

Kane, J. M., & Lieberman, J. A. (Eds.). (1992). *Adverse effects of psychotropic drugs.* New York: Guilford Press.

What Are the Specific Effects of Ritalin?

Greenhill, L. L., & Osman, B. B. (1991). *Ritalin: Theory and patient management.* New York: Mary Ann Liebert.

Is There Reading Material about ADD that Is Suitable for Children?

Gordon, M. (1992). *My brother's a world class pain: A sibling's guide to ADHD/hyperactivity.* DeWitt, NY: GSI Publications.

Jones, C. (1991). *Sourcebook for children with attention deficit disorder in early childhood.* Tucson, AZ: Communication Skill Builder.

Moss, D. M. (1989). *Shelly the hyperactive turtle.* Kensington, MD: Woodbine House.

Neuville, M. B. (1991). *Sometimes I get all scribbly: Living with attention deficit/hyperactivity disorder.* La Crosse, WI: Crystal Press.

Quinn, P. O., & Stern, J. M. (1991). *Putting on the brakes: Young people's guide to understanding attention deficit hyperactivity disorder.* New York: Imagination Press.

CHEMOTHERAPY

Evidence accumulated over 35 years of drug research clearly indicates that some children are more quickly and efficiently treated by chemotherapy than by other therapeutic methods (Burks, 1964a; Gladwell, 1999; Greenhill & Osman, 1991; Pelham, 1993). In fact, the behavior of some individuals apparently cannot be influenced in a positive direction until they receive medication. Wender (1971) based his diagnosis of minimal brain dysfunction syndrome (MBD) in children on their reaction to stimulant drugs. He stated emphatically that the proper treatment of MBD (or as it is known today, as ADD) is ordinarily "brief, specific, and highly effective" (p. 87). Wender stated he was impatient with professionals who misdiagnose such cases. He further emphasized that current knowledge about drug therapy makes inadequate treatment unforgivable.

Numerous studies point to the efficacy of certain medications in ameliorating the symptoms shown by hyperactive children. Humphries, Kinsbourne, and Swanson (1978), in a study of social interactions between hyperactive children and their mothers, found stimulants to have a positive effect on the mother-child relationships. Yellin, Spring, and Greenberg (1978) found both parents and teachers sensitive to the fact that many hyperactive students improved on medication (although teachers were much more aware of the fact). I studied students' conduct before and after receiving amphetamine medication (Burks, 1964a); significant behavioral improvement was noted after the application of the drug. Treegood and Walker (1976) also stressed the use of stimulants in the total treatment of the hyperactive child.

Many researchers indicate that medication benefits attention span and concentration as well as overactivity. Some allege that, in addition, it can aid memory and have a direct effect on the learning process (Conners, 1969, 1970, 1971). Carpenter (1972) suggested that medication could aid hyperactive children by

- decreasing distractibility and fidgetiness;
- improving small and large motor coordination;
- improving speech patterns by diminishing or eradicating stuttering or "cluttering";
- aiding pronunciation;
- modifying temper tantrums;
- increasing feelings of adequacy and security;
- reducing variability in mood swings;
- reducing the severity of or eliminating headaches or stomachaches;
- eliminating or reducing the occurrence of enuresis (bedwetting);
- controlling sleep difficulties (problems of getting to sleep, uneasy sleep, bad dreams, walking while asleep, and irritability upon awakening).

Conners (1969) reported that children who received medication had improved classroom behavior, group participation, and attitudes toward authority. Later investigations noted helpful effects such as motivational changes in children (Werry & Aman, 1993). Sprague, Barnes, and Werry (1970) found that the drug Ritalin significantly helped most disturbed underachieving boys respond more appropriately in the classroom and also decreased their reaction time and hyperactive behavior. These boys showed better concentration and cooperation at school. This investigation deserves attention because it was well controlled and used laboratory as well as clinical methodology.

The subjective nature of judgments of improvement (or lack of improvement) by those who are asked to assess a child's behavior makes it difficult to assess how medications work. However, teachers and parents who are close to the child and see him or her over long periods of time are ordinarily sensitive to changes in conduct (Burks, 1961). Changes in behavior must of necessity be unique, because every individual is organically different.

Parents of ADD children are, naturally, apprehensive about stimulant medications. In my experience, they ask the following questions:

1. What are medication's side effects? Studies of psychostimulants (e.g., Ritalin, Dexedrine, and Cylert—all used in the treatment of ADD) have determined that the primary side effects include insomnia, loss of appetite, weight loss, and irritability. All of these symptoms were temporary and disappeared with a reduction in dosage. In some cases, however, it may be necessary to tolerate side effects to gain hoped-for therapeutic results. Possible long-term ill effects are not known at this time. In the final analysis, individual responses to any of these drugs cannot be known in advance.

2. What are the addictive qualities of psychostimulants? It is out of the question for a correctly diagnosed hyperactive patient suffering neurological deficits to become addicted at any time to a stimulant when the drug produces a physiological low and concomitantly does not elicit a psychological high. The fact that many, if not most, teenagers who are on medication want to stop taking the drugs seems excellent proof that these substances are not addictive. However, it should be pointed out that certain emotionally deprived adolescents apparently can develop a psychological (but not a physical) reliance on amphetamines (also used to treat hyperactivity and other common ADD symptoms).

3. What are some of the reactions of children taking psychostimulants? Younger children usually take medication without question, but teens may not be as willing. Reasons for this resistance may include:

- Teens may be reluctant to admit that there is anything wrong with them. They do not want to be different; for teenagers, feeling apart from friends is almost intolerable.
- Teens may dislike feeling that adults are trying to impose controls. Teens are trying to emancipate themselves from authority figures and they feel threatened when asked to take drugs that "will make them behave better." Many are simply not interested in conforming to standards of conduct imposed by grown-ups. I counseled an 18-year-old girl who decided she would no longer take medication, even though she had been taking it for over 10 years and knew it made her calmer and less impulsive. She maintained she was tired of being "treated like a little kid." The results of her decision to discontinue medication were not desirable. Her behavior became more erratic and uncontrollable, and I advised her parents that little could be done for her until she sought help for herself.
- Teens often resent drug-induced changes. Teens become anxious because the alterations they experience are beyond their control. On the other side of the coin, a significant number of youngsters are grateful for the changes they experience. A number of years ago, I was instrumental in persuading the California State Department of Education to grant money to a school district to establish a class for ADD-type youngsters. (The class, the first of its kind in California, continued for 5 years and became a model for similar classes elsewhere in California.) The students in this class showed a variety of behavior difficulties, but nearly all were hyperactive. One 10-year-old boy, Robert, who was put on amphetamine medication, showed a dramatic improvement in deportment. He began to complete his work and started to gain friends. After about six weeks, some of the old signs of hyperactivity and impulsiveness returned. The puzzled teacher finally made a home call to see if an already unstable home situation had worsened. The child was living with his maternal grandmother, and she appeared nonplussed as to why he was again behaving badly. Before he left the home, the teacher thought to ask whether Robert was taking his medicine regularly. To his astonishment,

the grandmother replied offhandedly, "Oh, that. He was doing so well I took him off those drugs about two weeks ago." The grandmother was told Robert could not return to the special class unless he was given the prescribed dosages regularly. This was done and Robert again became calmer. After a few days, Robert asked the teacher to allow him to say something to the other pupils in the room. The teacher let him address the class. With some effort, Robert said, "I would like to apologize for the way I was acting before, but I couldn't help it." Then he burst into tears.

4. Who will benefit from medication? Sixty to 70% of overactive children react favorably to psychostimulant drugs; however most researchers do not believe that there are absolute or reliable means to predict who will show symptomatic improvement. On the other hand, investigators have come up with a short list of factors associated with probable improvement:

- The younger the child (particularly those under 10 years of age), the greater the likelihood of beneficial reactions.
- The greater the degree of motor restlessness and attention deficits, the greater the likelihood of beneficial results.

Even when these factors are present, some youngsters show no improvement.

5. How long should children take psychostimulants? Hyperactive children should continue to take the drugs as long as they prove beneficial. There is a common belief (among professionals and others) that overactive children will outgrow their behavioral and academic difficulties after a period of time. This is not true for some hyperactive children and only partially true for others. Some individuals retain the hyperactive syndrome all their lives. Commonly, and with effort, they may be able to disguise the outward expression of the disorder, but inward discomfort remains, with the attendant attrition of sustained effort and achievement. Medication should be continued as long as it is beneficial—years if necessary.

In my experience, many or most hyperactive children overcome their hyperactive symptoms around the time of puberty. This may happen because of nervous system maturation. At any rate, a significant number of children can be taken off medication at about 12 to 13 years of age without ill effects. Discontinuation of medication must be done with the full understanding by parents that it is for trial purposes only. If adverse reactions appear, the drug is to be readministered. Off-drug behavior should be judged by several sources (i.e., teachers, parents, and other knowledgeable adults).

Breaks from drug therapy are sometimes advisable. Reasons for breaks include

- preventing the development of tolerance to the drug;
- decreasing the chances of toxic reactions;
- determining whether or not a child has outgrown the need for medication.

If a drug is discontinued during a low-stress period (like a vacation), unwanted symptoms may not appear. When the child returns to school, however, the symptoms may return.

6. How should psychostimulants be administered? Parents should not discontinue a medication on their own (such discontinuation is the most common cause of poor results). For instance, if a mother administers a drug to her child for several weeks without benefit, she may stop its administration without consulting the physician. Instead, she should call her doctor to report the lack of benefits. The physician can then increase the dosage or change the medication. Parents must not ask the child's teacher to administer medication during school hours because it may be illegal for school personnel to administer drugs.

7. How many medications should be tried? The efficacy of any drug depends on how an individual responds to it, and that cannot be known until the medication is administered. If results prove unsatisfactory over a period of time at different dosages, other medications can be tried. One-third to one-half of all patients achieve

satisfactory results with the first or second choice. For the rest, the physician must try other kinds of medication and vary the dosages. At times, combinations of drugs are required. Sometimes a drug loses its effectiveness and a change becomes necessary. Parents should not become discouraged if a particular substance fails to work. In some cases, a dozen or more medications have been tried before an acceptable drug or combination of drugs was found.

8. How can a child be encouraged to accept medication? It is important that a parent feel knowledgeable and reassured about the possible effects of stimulant drugs. If a parent is skeptical and anxious, the child will likely react in the same manner. If the parent is calm, the child will take the medication without trepidation. Unfortunately, fears picked up by children can undo beneficial drug outcomes.

9. Do medicated children need additional assistance? If the degree and amount of disturbance shown by the child is severe enough, the family may need appropriate professional help. The following factors may help determine what assistance is needed:

- If a child's undesirable conduct is limited to attention deficits, impulsivity, and overactivity but the child otherwise appears well-adjusted, counseling may be restricted to advice about the proper ways to administer medication along with suggestions as to how to help the child handle environmental stimulation better. For example, parents may be told to reduce distractions to improve the child's concentration.

- If the youngster is a discipline problem at home or at school, parents may want to seek advice about behavioral control. I believe permissive child-rearing practices have generally proved disastrous. A highly structured environment offers advantages for controlling undisciplined youngsters. In this stricter atmosphere, parents set firm limits and consistently deliver preset consequences when children misbehave. Children will eventually internalize these standards and channel impulses more sensibly.

- If the hyperactive disorder is characterized by learning difficulties, the picture can be further complicated. Both the parents and the child are likely to be disturbed about the academic losses. Medication may help because it increases the capacity to concentrate. Realistically, though, a large percentage of ADHD children need special school assistance.

- Finally, if, in addition to hyperactivity, discipline problems, and learning difficulties, the youngster presents unusual emotional reactions to stress (e.g., frequent and inappropriate crying, stubbornness, unhappiness, destructiveness, bossiness, and troubled social relationships), the diagnostic and treatment picture is even more complex. These displays of emotional instability may be the most unfortunate complaint among all other observed ADHD maladies. Most appear to be learned patterns of conduct. Unfortunately, because these irritating behavior symptoms are acquired during early, formative years, they often become an integral part of the character structure and remain as personality features into adult years long after other ADD signs, such as overactivity, impulsivity, and poor concentration, have faded.

Because people tend to reject ADHD youngsters with aggravating emotional symptoms, parents of such a child may need to seek professional counseling in order to learn child-rearing techniques that influence their youngster to act more maturely and to acquire an improved sense of self-esteem.

CHAPTER 23

Children with Behavior Problems

This chapter presents information that can be given by guidance workers to teachers dealing with behavior problem children. In this case, a behavior problem child is defined as one who is referred for special help or who shows a severe degree of difficulty in any category of the Burks Behavior Rating Scales (1977a, 2006a) or in any combination of categories. Because a maladjusted child is more vulnerable than the average child to negative classroom conditions, the first part of the chapter presents information to help teachers assess the suitability of their classrooms for learning. Dealing with classroom behavior problems is then discussed. Finally, discipline issues of interest to parents are presented in a question-and-answer format that can be used to stimulate discussion in parent conferences or meetings.

ASSESSING THE CLASSROOM ENVIRONMENT

Several years ago I was asked to speak to the teaching staff of a school district. My speech focused on the role of the teacher in the creation of a good classroom learning environment. Members of the audience asked me to make my aims and objectives more specific: Could I tell the staff what characteristics delineate a successful classroom versus a poor one? Would teachers show different traits in the two situations, and would children respond differently?

No single teacher personality appears to be more associated with desirable classroom results than any other (Nicholson, 2003). Good teachers are cast from many molds; it is futile to think otherwise. A more promising avenue of evaluation is one that measures student functioning in areas thought to be affected by teacher behavior or conditions set up and controlled by teachers. For example, both a permissive and a directive teacher might instill enthusiasm in students; a buoyant young teacher and a staid, older teacher might both establish a purposeful work atmosphere. The issue is not the teacher's personality but the *effects* of their teaching. Cronbach (1954) mentioned six highly desirable effects of teaching:

1. an orderly classroom;
2. a comfortable classroom;
3. interested students;
4. self-assured students;
5. self-controlled students;
6. responsible students.

I would add friendly students, achieving students, helpful students, respectful students, and creative students.

Are these conditions and attributes established by teacher actions? If so, to what extent is teacher behavior related to their presence or absence? For the majority of students in regular classrooms, this relationship is very close. Further, teacher conduct may be the major factor leading to the establishment of these effects.

For behavior-problem children, however, the picture can be somewhat (but certainly not totally) different. Behavior-problem children, depending on the nature of their problem, are a more refractory group. They do not respond as well to teacher approaches, because much of their energy is absorbed by inner psychic demands and by their defenses against an unaccepting, even hostile, world.

About 50% of the students referred to guidance departments by teachers fall into the hyperactive-distractible symptomatic classification (Burks, 1977a, 2006a; Snyder, 1984). These students tend to be most resistant to ordinary treatment. Most will exhibit organic symptoms in any designated classroom, regardless of teacher influences.

About 20% of referred students can be included in the aggressive-hostile classification. Some are so angry that even the best teachers fail to reach them; others prove more approachable.

The remaining referred students (about 30%) can be divided into the anxious, shy-withdrawn, and immature classifications. Many or most of these students respond well to teacher efforts.

Clearly, the behavior-problem label covers a wide variety of children with many types of symptoms. Although these children may respond to healthy teacher influences as well as normally behaved students do, they are affected negatively by unwholesome class conditions much more than others. For this reason, teachers with behavior-problem children in their classrooms need to make sure they are providing a supportive class environment. I developed the Teacher Self-Rating inventory (see figure 23.1) to help teachers determine what kind of classroom environment they are providing.

This rating inventory has been used for many years in school districts across the nation. It would be difficult to standardize, and even if it were subjected to the usual statistical analyses, standardized results might not even prove helpful. Completion of the inventory is essentially a subjective endeavor, and whatever it reveals to the rater is used subjectively. It is divided into the following classifications:

- student-student relationships;
- teacher-student relationships;
- student enthusiasm;
- teaching techniques;
- personal characteristics;
- classroom environment;
- teacher-parent relationships;
- student records and evaluations;
- staff relationships.

The inventory assesses a number of behaviors related to each of these important aspects of professional competence. This assessment may encourage reflection on the part of the teacher, and if the ratings indicate undesirable conditions, an attempt to change them.

The Teacher Self-Rating inventory was designed so that a teacher can evaluate his or her performance relative to a large number of educational characteristics and procedures as they are reflected by student behavior and teacher work habits. If desired, a supervisor or colleague can rate the teacher on the same attributes.

The inventory is simply a guide. It can be the basis for a discussion of ways to improve teaching performance. It must never be used as an administrative device to judge teacher competency.

DISCIPLINING MALADJUSTED CHILDREN

Problem children, more than normally behaved children, require discipline as well as sympathetic concern (McGraw, 2001). The following suggestions may help—none can hurt. This approach is based on the belief that desirable behavior is more likely to be repeated if it is reinforced by a positive response. Teachers should use direct rather than indirect discipline methods and demonstrate acceptable behavior to ensure the success of a discipline program. Discipline techniques should be tailored to the needs of individual students.

TEACHER SELF-RATING INVENTORY

Harold F. Burks, Ph.D.

Evaluate your teaching performance relative to the following characteristics or procedures by putting a check mark in the first box above the one statement in each row that best describes your classroom situation. You can also have a supervisor or colleague rate your performance by checking the second box. Agreement or disagreement between the two assessments can be the basis for a discussion of ways to improve your teaching skills.

Name of Teacher _____ Date _____

Name of Other Rater (Optional) _____ Date _____

Student-Student Relationships

Relationships with peers are of greatest concern to children of all ages.

	☐ ☐	☐ ☐	☐ ☐	☐ ☐
❶	Students show many signs of poor sportsmanship	Students show some signs of poor sportsmanship	Students can win or lose with grace	Unsure about this
❷	Extreme competition seems to make many students unhappy	Competition seems to make a number of students unhappy	Most students seem to be able to handle competition	Unsure about this
❸	There are many squabbles during group activities	Cooperation during group projects is unpredictable	Group activities seem generally harmonious	Unsure about this
❹	Many students try to be the teacher's pet	A number of students try to be the teacher's pet	Students show little interest in being the teacher's pet	Unsure about this
❺	Students tend to pick on certain classmates unmercifully	There is some scapegoating in the classroom	Students show little interest in scapegoating	Unsure about this
Overall Assessment	Needs more attention	Needs a little more attention	Is in pretty good shape	Unsure

Figure 23.1a.

Teacher-Student Relationships

Students rank their relationship with the teacher as their second highest concern.

❶ ☐ ☐ | ☐ ☐ | ☐ ☐ | ☐ ☐

| Students pay little attention to directives | Students pay a moderate amount of attention to directives | Students stop and pay attention to directives | Unsure about this |

❷ ☐ ☐ | ☐ ☐ | ☐ ☐ | ☐ ☐

| Students argue with commands | Students bicker somewhat about commands | Students respect commands | Unsure about this |

❸ ☐ ☐ | ☐ ☐ | ☐ ☐ | ☐ ☐

| Classroom controls seem to make students sullen or edgy | Classroom controls seem to make students somewhat edgy or sullen | Classroom controls are accepted with fairly good humor | Unsure about this |

❹ ☐ ☐ | ☐ ☐ | ☐ ☐ | ☐ ☐

| Much time is spent controlling students | Considerable time is spent controlling students | A reasonable amount of time is spent on class control | Unsure about this |

❺ ☐ ☐ | ☐ ☐ | ☐ ☐ | ☐ ☐

| Students seem controlled in the classroom but cause trouble elsewhere in school | Students seem controlled in the classroom but may occasionally cause trouble elsewhere in school | Students seem OK in and out of the classroom | Unsure about this |

❻ ☐ ☐ | ☐ ☐ | ☐ ☐ | ☐ ☐

| Students seem disinterested in the teacher as a person | Students are somewhat interested in the teacher as a person | Students express lively and friendly interest in the teacher | Unsure about this |

Overall Assessment ☐ ☐ | ☐ ☐ | ☐ ☐ | ☐ ☐

| Needs more attention | Needs a little more attention | Is in pretty good shape | Unsure |

Figure 23.1b.

Student Enthusiasm

Motivation is essential for learning.

❶

| Students have a lot of difficulty concentrating on their work | Students have erratic concentration | Students seem generally absorbed in their work | Unsure about this |

❷

| Students make few comments about class work | Students make some comments about class work | Students make many comments about class work | Unsure about this |

❸

| Students seldom bring contributions to class from outside school | Students sometimes bring contributions from outside school | Students often bring contributions from outside school | Unsure about this |

❹

| Few students volunteer answers in class | Some students volunteer answers in class | Many students are anxious to volunteer answers in class | Unsure about this |

❺

| Students show little humor in class | Students show some humor in class | Students tend to smile and laugh easily | Unsure about this |

Overall Assessment

| Needs more attention | Needs a little more attention | Is in pretty good shape | Unsure |

Figure 23.1c.

Teaching Techniques
Are classroom lessons being learned?

❶

☐ ☐	☐ ☐	☐ ☐	☐ ☐
Students do not seem to retain what they learn in class	Students retain what they learn in class to some extent	Students retain what they learn in class well	Unsure about this

❷

☐ ☐	☐ ☐	☐ ☐	☐ ☐
Homework is not done or is poorly done	Homework is done fairly well	Homework is usually done well	Unsure about this

❸

☐ ☐	☐ ☐	☐ ☐	☐ ☐
Students show little interest in the teacher's evaluation of their work	Students show some interest in the teacher's evaluation of their work	Students show real interest in the teacher's assessment of their work	Unsure about this

❹

☐ ☐	☐ ☐	☐ ☐	☐ ☐
Students tend to view class materials as the "same old stuff"	Students are somewhat interested in class materials	Students share class materials eagerly	Unsure about this

❺

☐ ☐	☐ ☐	☐ ☐	☐ ☐
Class assignments require a lot of explaining	Class assignments require some explaining	Class assignments require a minimum of explaining	Unsure about this

❻

☐ ☐	☐ ☐	☐ ☐	☐ ☐
Class work tends to be done very sloppily	Class work is somewhat sloppy	Class work is usually done carefully	Unsure about this

❼

☐ ☐	☐ ☐	☐ ☐	☐ ☐
Students are not interested in class decor (e.g., bulletin boards, pictures, exhibits)	Students are somewhat interested in class decor	Students are quite interested in class decor	Unsure about this

❽

☐ ☐	☐ ☐	☐ ☐	☐ ☐
Students are very worried about their grades or marks	Students are concerned about their grades or marks	Students are interested in, but not worried about, their grades or marks	Unsure about this

❾

☐ ☐	☐ ☐	☐ ☐	☐ ☐
Students show little originality	Students show some originality	Students show a lot of creativity	Unsure about this

Overall Assessment

☐ ☐	☐ ☐	☐ ☐	☐ ☐
Needs more attention	Needs a little more attention	Is in pretty good shape	Unsure

Figure 23.1d.

Classroom Environment
A comfortable environment helps students learn.

❶

☐ ☐	☐ ☐	☐ ☐	☐ ☐
Students shield or rub their eyes and complain about classroom lighting	Students show some signs of eyestrain	Students show few signs of eyestrain	Unsure about this

❷

☐ ☐	☐ ☐	☐ ☐	☐ ☐
Students seem tired and restless at their desks	Students sometimes seem tired and restless at their desks	Students usually seem relaxed and rested at their desks	Unsure about this

❸

☐ ☐	☐ ☐	☐ ☐	☐ ☐
Students complain a lot about the temperature in the classroom	Students sometimes complain about room temperature	Students seldom complain about room temperature	Unsure about this

❹

☐ ☐	☐ ☐	☐ ☐	☐ ☐
Students complain a lot about feeling hungry	Students complain to some extent about feeling hungry	Students rarely complain about feeling hungry	Unsure about this

❺

☐ ☐	☐ ☐	☐ ☐	☐ ☐
Students have a lot of trouble copying from blackboard	Students have some trouble copying from blackboard	Students seem to have no trouble copying from blackboard	Unsure about this

❻

☐ ☐	☐ ☐	☐ ☐	☐ ☐
Students are very irritable with those near them	Students are somewhat irritable with those near them	Students are relaxed with those near them	Unsure about this

❼

☐ ☐	☐ ☐	☐ ☐	☐ ☐
The noise level in the classroom seems very high	The noise level in the classroom is fairly high	The noise level in the classroom seems reasonable	Unsure about this

Overall Assessment

☐ ☐	☐ ☐	☐ ☐	☐ ☐
Needs more attention	Needs a little more attention	Is in pretty good shape	Unsure

Figure 23.1e.

Personal Characteristics
Students need good adult role models.

❶

Students seldom express pleasure at the teacher's appearance (clothes, etc.)	Students sometimes express pleasure at the teacher's appearance	Students often express pleasure at the teacher's appearance	Unsure about this

❷

Students tend to be very restless as the teacher talks	Students tend to be somewhat restless as the teacher talks	Students tend to be quiet and attentive as the teacher talks	Unsure about this

❸

Students' reaction to the teacher seems tense, worried	Students' reaction to the teacher is somewhat irritable	Students' reaction to the teacher is somewhat relaxed, friendly	Unsure about this

❹

Students seem to strain to hear the teacher (they ask to have instructions repeated)	Students seem to hear fairly well	Students seem to have no difficulty hearing	Unsure about this

Overall Assessment

Needs more attention	Needs a little more attention	Is in pretty good shape	Unsure

Staff Relationships
Teachers need each other.

❶

Teacher rarely interacts with other staff members	Teacher interacts with other staff members some of the time	Teacher actively interacts with other staff members	Unsure about this

❷

Teacher takes little interest in staff problems	Teacher takes some interest in staff problems	Teacher takes an active interest in staff problems	Unsure about this

❸

Teacher is not active in professional activities (committees, etc.)	Teacher is somewhat active in professional activities	Teacher is quite active in professional activities	Unsure about this

Overall Assessment

Needs more attention	Needs a little more attention	Is in pretty good shape	Unsure

Figure 23.1f.

Teacher-Parent Relationships

Parents should be the teacher's strongest allies.

❶

There are many calls from parents questioning teaching practices	There are a fairly large number of calls from parents	There are a few calls from parents questioning teaching practices	Unsure about this
☐ ☐	☐ ☐	☐ ☐	☐ ☐

❷

Parents do not respond well to requests for help	Parents sometimes do not respond well to requests for help	Parents usually respond well to requests for help	Unsure about this
☐ ☐	☐ ☐	☐ ☐	☐ ☐

❸

There is very poor attendance at PTA meetings, open house, and so on	There is fair attendance at PTA meetings, open house, and so on	There is good attendance at PTA meetings, open house, and so on	Unsure about this
☐ ☐	☐ ☐	☐ ☐	☐ ☐

❹

Parents show little interest in parent conferences	Parents show some interest in parent conferences	Parents show a great deal of interest in parent conferences	Unsure about this
☐ ☐	☐ ☐	☐ ☐	☐ ☐

Overall Assessment

Needs more attention	Needs a little more attention	Is in pretty good shape	Unsure
☐ ☐	☐ ☐	☐ ☐	☐ ☐

Student Records and Evaluations

Good student records help determine teaching goals.

❶

Student records seem hard to find	Student records are fairly hard to find	Student records are easy to find	Unsure about this
☐ ☐	☐ ☐	☐ ☐	☐ ☐

❷

Student records seem incomplete or inaccurate	Student records seem fairly complete and accurate	Student records are complete and accurate	Unsure about this
☐ ☐	☐ ☐	☐ ☐	☐ ☐

❸

The ability or achievement level of many students is unknown	The ability or achievement level of some students is unknown	The ability or achievement level of most students is known	Unsure about this
☐ ☐	☐ ☐	☐ ☐	☐ ☐

Overall Assessment

Needs more attention	Needs a little more attention	Is in pretty good shape	Unsure
☐ ☐	☐ ☐	☐ ☐	☐ ☐

Figure 23.1g.

Help the child acquire a sense of power. Most, if not all, problem children have feelings of helplessness. Some compensate by overreacting to correction. Others sink into despair or lethargy. Give these youngsters psychological power by helping them feel accepted. When an individual experiences affection or love from others, he or she feels more secure. The misbehavior of some students may actually be disguised attempts to prove that other people care. Teachers may use some of the following methods:

- Initiate a friendly talk with the youngster.
- Place a "good citizen" tag on the child's desk for a period of time.
- Give physical approval—a hug or a pat on the back.
- Reward the child with verbal praise.
- Smile at the student occasionally.
- Use humor when applicable.
- Be sympathetically available when the child asks for help.
- Accept offers of assistance from the youngster with gratitude.
- Show signs of interest in the child's family.
- Allow the child to be your special helper.

Achieving academically gives children psychological power by helping them feel more adequate. Those not succeeding tend to feel empty and isolated. The following techniques may also help:

- Give the child special tasks such as cleaning the blackboard, arranging exhibits, changing flowers in vases, cleaning the aquarium, replacing books, working on a bulletin board, being a monitor or messenger, or passing out papers.
- Allow the child to work on a special project, such as preparing a skit or redecorating the classroom.
- Permit the student to visit another classroom and report on what was observed.
- Encourage the child to help the teacher, the school secretary, or another student (if success is guaranteed).
- Permit the youngster to work on an individual assignment of his or her choice.
- Allow the child to read the spelling words to the class.
- Have the child lead the morning pledge (or any other daily ritual).
- Set up numerous opportunities for small academic successes and acknowledge these accomplishments. Pay as little attention as possible to failures.

Avoid teacher-induced misconduct. Teachers may inspire student misbehavior by their own actions. Even the best instructors sometimes play out classroom dramas that can lead to student boredom, unrest, or even rebellion. The following suggestions may prevent unwanted conduct:

- Avoid subliminal games fostered by ambiguous rules ("Let's see who can figure out what I actually want"); encouragement of copycat behavior (recognizable when students copy teacher virtues, not so easily recognizable when they copy unwanted behavior); blaming students for poor performance (when assignments are too difficult for them to finish); and blaming parents for lack of cooperation or support (when the parents actually have not been contacted).
- Treat the misbehaving child in a more relaxed way. A problem is only a problem if it is so defined. Many children will stop misbehaving if they get no reaction from adults.
- Fit the punishment to the crime. Do not have a standard restriction like, "You will lose your privileges no matter what you do."
- Avoid acting as though you expect trouble from the child. If you do, the youngster will certainly not disappoint you.
- Avoid selecting a punishment to reflect your level of anger (the least useful type of punishment).

- If criticism is necessary, censure the act, not the person.
- Refrain from demeaning a student publicly.
- Do not argue with the child. The youngster who is allowed to argue with an adult acquires power he or she should not possess.
- Treat the child as a dignified human being. An offended youngster thirsts for revenge.
- Refrain from using threats to enforce discipline. The child may call your bluff.
- Eschew physical strong-arm methods. At best, the child will resent you; at worst, he or she may fight back.
- Avoid inflaming an already upset child. Let him or her cool off before attempting further control.
- Avoid making major offenses out of trivial actions. The child is bound to commit mistakes—don't make too much of them.
- Invite a neutral observer (a fellow teacher or a supervisor) to sit in your classroom for a short time. Ask that person to analyze the interactions between you and a problem student.
- Refuse to be a "nice guy" all the time.
- Keep your cool so students can't blackmail you emotionally.
- Do not punish the group for the misdeeds of one.
- Do not put a child in the hall as punishment.
- Do not embarrass a child as a form of punishment.
- Refrain from walking around the classroom too much.
- Abstain from talking too much; it only distracts the students.
- Do not use sarcasm or verbal abuse as a control method.
- Do not carry a grudge against a child.
- Allow a misbehaving child to save face; give the youngster a way out of his or her dilemma.
- Refuse to have confrontations with a misbehaving student in front of other students.

Avoid actions that increase the child's feeling of anxiety. Worried youngsters cannot always attend to established regulations. They are distracted by inward ruminations. Good instructors learn to recognize signs of anxiety. Some of the following steps may help disruptive youngsters who are anxious.

- Speak slowly, simply, and pleasantly so that the child can hear and understand your instructions.
- Create a calm atmosphere so students will feel relaxed.
- Help the misbehaving student acquire positive recognition. Misconduct may seem to the child to be the only avenue to prestige, regardless of how negative the method may seem to adults.
- Shun labels like "lazy," "selfish," "unthinking," and so on, which tend to isolate the child emotionally and lower his or her self-respect.
- Be patient; the child will not change negative behaviors quickly.
- Remove the child from a conflicting situation by handing him or her a written request to run an errand or complete a task elsewhere.
- Do not add to the child's anxiety by informing the youngster that he or she is to perform in front of the class at some unspecified time.
- Find out if the child is afraid of someone or something at school. Some misbehavior has origins in counterphobic reactions (the student is acting aggressively to keep fears at bay).
- Whenever possible, avoid removing the student from the group; if he or she has to be removed, make the absence short.

Set up a discipline program. Some of the following suggestions may help maintain classroom order.

- Establish as few rules as possible and make them easy to understand.
- Make home calls to discuss the problems of a misbehaving student with his or her parents.

- Consult with your school's principal about unusual discipline problems.
- Refer a stubborn and severe discipline problem to the guidance department.
- Eliminate unnecessary distractions in the classroom.
- Ask whether the student understands what is expected of him or her.
- Keep the parents well-informed of the student's progress.
- Allow the student to explain unwanted conduct (but keep the explanations short).
- Separate chronic troublemakers.
- When misconduct occurs, suggest that the student write a paragraph describing what went wrong.
- Have the student give a progress report to his or her parents and have the parents call the school.
- Do not assign homework as punishment.
- Occasionally, allow the misbehaving student to set the consequences for his or her own poor conduct.
- Refuse to allow a student to talk while someone else is talking.
- Give the child as much routine as possible.
- Seat the child close to more well-behaved students.
- Establish clear limits and stick to them.

DISCUSSING CHILD DISCIPLINE WITH PARENTS

The following questions for parents focus on (a) why children misbehave, on (b) methods of discipline, on (c) children's need for discipline, and on (d) their reactions to various types of discipline. The questions can provide a stimulus for individual and group discussions. Parents may select the questions of greatest interest to them at the beginning of a meeting.

Should adults ever frustrate children? Life is a long series of frustrations—which all people must learn to tolerate. Children raised without restrictions grow up to be uncontrolled adults. Of course, children cannot be made to feel too restricted, or they may give up.

How important is it for children to feel guilt for misdeeds? If there is no remorse, there is little hope for change. Everybody needs to be taught to feel shame for hurting others or impinging on their rights. Uncontrolled behavior is not tolerated in a civilized society (nor should it be).

How does discipline help children feel more secure? Children often cannot accurately judge the limits between acceptable and unacceptable conduct. They learn that a caring adult will stop them from injuring themselves when they overstep boundaries.

Can physical punishment have a poor outcome? If used to excess, it can. Severe physical punishment can quickly eliminate better alternative disciplinary measures, and, further, the child may learn to tolerate physical pain and not be threatened by its use. Worse, punitive actions can encourage a child to show aggression toward those trying to control him or her.

Should all aggression be suppressed? No, aggression has positive results. It can impel a child to achieve and to strive toward independence. However, children sometimes need help to channel aggressive impulses in legitimate ways.

Is all discipline formally taught? No, much self-controlling behavior is copied from observing the conduct of admired adults and peers.

Do children ever deliberately misbehave? Yes, antisocial behavior is sometimes used by children to control adults. If this is the case, adults must analyze and change their reactions to manipulative conduct.

Is misconduct ever a cover-up for feelings of insecurity? It can be. For instance, a child who acts very sure of himself or herself may actually have little self-confidence, and may feel that it is unsafe to rely on others. Underachievers can cover feelings of low self-esteem by acting brash and cocky.

Do underachievers sometimes misbehave for other reasons? Yes, some are angered by the fact that classroom peers do better with less work. They express frustration by misbehaving.

Will a child who feels weak or helpless sometimes misbehave? Yes, some antisocial children feel that the only way they can get anything from their environment is to attack it and demand rewards.

How can discipline be made emotionally acceptable to a child? The child must be reassured that it is the behavior that is being disapproved, not the person. If given adequate reassurance of affection and concern, the child will accept restraints without undue resentment.

Can lack of discipline ever make a child resentful? Yes, the child may feel that his or her emerging impulses are out of control. Children need external restraints before they can learn to internalize self-control.

Why is withdrawal of affection while disciplining a child unwise? Withdrawal of affection is not only unwise, it is also unfair because it exploits and possibly damages desired relationships. Actually, maintenance of good feelings is one of the major goals of control procedures.

Do children expect their parents to exert order? Yes, even though children resist authority, they expect their parents to curb their unruly activities. The parents' failure to do so can lead to confusion and unhappiness.

Is praise for good behavior sufficient for disciplinary purposes? Praise for correct behavior is a better training procedure than disapproval for bad conduct, but both are sometimes necessary.

Are material rewards for good behavior desirable? Promising a material reward for good behavior, unfortunately, gives a child the choice of not behaving. Material rewards are generally better for younger than for older children.

Is it enough to explain to a child that he or she is doing wrong? Sometimes it may not be. Explaining to a child that he or she behaved badly but not doing anything about it has the effect of shaming the child and then leaving him or her with a sense of guilt that cannot be expiated in acceptable ways.

Will children behave properly just because they fear punishment? No, that kind of simplistic thinking may be appropriate for very young children, but it is necessary for older children to want to behave for their own sake.

Should punishment vary according to the transgression? Yes. When important and unimportant transgressions are treated with equal severity, the child becomes confused and discouraged and may give up trying to figure out proper ways to act.

Are words more effective than actions? Often they are not. Lectures are ignored because the child can tune out. Actions are more effective (tell the child what is expected and then follow through with consequences).

Should discipline be given publicly or privately? Usually it should be given privately. Public reprimands can be personally humiliating to the child.

Why is it important to discuss pupil misbehavior with the child? Much behavior (bad and good) is misunderstood by observers. A little insight can lead to changes that affect conduct in significant ways. For instance, a child may be anxious because he or she sits close to someone who is threatening, but the child does not know how to complain. When adults understand the situation, they can take steps to remove the threat.

CHAPTER 24

Disadvantaged Children

The term disadvantaged loosely describes children from lower socioeconomic groups, from groups for whom English is a second language, or from home situations that supply little emotional or intellectual stimulation.

The disadvantaged student who is referred for special school assistance does not tend to have behavioral symptoms that denote severe mental disturbance. On occasion, a clinical maladjustment (e.g., neurosis, acting-out disorder) may be observed, but more often, such students demonstrate a pattern of academic difficulties along with signs of social inadequacy (e.g., social isolation) and poor self-esteem (Burks, 1999).

Disadvantaged children are surrounded by forces that can contribute to limited educational growth—for example, an impoverished student may encounter poor school facilities, limited curricula, and rapid turnover among teachers. In addition, job discrimination, limited access to higher-paying jobs and professions, and social isolation are realities that foster parental resentment toward those who are viewed as trying to maintain the economic status quo.

Disadvantaged boys and girls can pick up feelings of distrust, anger, and resentment at home, which they may demonstrate at school. In the past, it was commonly believed that families in deprived circumstances did not value education and the benefits derived from it. This stereotype is surely no longer prevalent. Most parents in lower-class and minority ethnic neighborhoods are very concerned about their children's educational welfare and repeatedly demonstrate this concern by calling for better schools, more integration, and less discrimination. It is becoming clear that negative attitudes among minority groups toward the educational establishment are caused primarily by the unwillingness or inability of the educational establishment to provide relevant, quality instruction for students from so-called disadvantaged areas.

Furthermore, minority-group members and economically deprived individuals are increasingly resentful of cultural attitudes that work against disadvantaged children. Attitudes of this nature can be self-fulfilling prophecies as children learn to live up to (or down to) expectations.

CHARACTERISTICS

A survey of the literature on disadvantaged children reveals the following characteristics:

1. Many students are frustrated by their failure to achieve and tend to see authority figures as blocks to success (Janeksela & Deming, 1976; Mash & Barkley, 1989; Webster-Stratton & Herbert, 1994).
2. Contrary to myth, students who aspire to sports careers score higher on achievement tests than do those who aspire to low-prestige jobs (McElroy, 1981).
3. Disadvantaged children show a higher incidence of impulsivity than do middle-class children (Juliano, 1977).
4. Compared to the general population, disadvantaged children show a greater need for health services (Swire & Kavaler, 1978).
5. Children from disadvantaged groups make up a disproportionately high percentage of students in special classes (Tonn, 1974). They are often placed there, it is theorized, because of home deprivation or because of

the middle-class bias of IQ tests (which favors middle-class students over lower-class pupils) rather than because of actual intellectual deprivation. Many of these children probably would do better if placed in tutoring groups (while attending regular classes).

6. Parents of disadvantaged children tend to drop out of therapy before treatment is completed.

7. Parents of disadvantaged children tend to be both authoritarian and submissive (versus independent). Accompanying the submissiveness is a tendency toward orderliness, precision, and an avoidance of assertiveness.

In a study using the Burks Behavior Rating Scales (BBRS), I investigated the behavior characteristics of children of Mexican American descent (Burks, 1977a). These children tended to obtain high scores on the following BBRS scales: academic difficulties, poor self-esteem, attention deficits, poor coordination, intellectual difficulties, dependency, withdrawal, and impulsivity.

These high scores were seen at both primary and intermediate grade levels. Further investigation showed that for the academic difficulties and poor motivation scales, older students were rated as having more difficulties than younger students. Upper grade children, in short, were seen by teachers as less bright and less confident than were primary school–age children. These minority-group children tend to act like behavior-problem students, who also show a steady decline in self-esteem from grades 3 to 11. The main difficulty for these disadvantaged children, however, is academic achievement.

ASSESSMENT

Because both normal and disadvantaged groups are extremely heterogeneous, it is difficult to demonstrate real differences between the two (Heil, Barclay, & Endres, 1978). However, many investigators maintain that significant numbers of disadvantaged youngsters are discouraged and expect to fail in school (Liddle, Rockwell, & Sacadet, 1967).

Low expectations for success can affect the way disadvantaged children approach tests. According to Chavez and Gonzales-Singh (1980), psychological instruments are misused in schools in three ways: (a) inappropriate test selection, (b) poor test administration, and (c) misinterpretation of test results. Reschly (1981) contended that such tests are adequate for the measurement of disadvantaged children but the results are misapplied and often lead to discrimination. DeFilippis and Derby (1980) maintained that the poor performance of low-income and minority-group students resulted from the students' unfamiliarity with the testing situation and from their low level of motivation.

Many authors (Freund, Bradley, & Caldwell, 1979; Olmeda, 1981) have made a strong case for taking into account diverse social, political, and economic factors in assessment procedures. Freund et al. (1979) proposed that preschool screening techniques be supplemented with a review of the home environment. Scott (1981) suggested that the FM measure on the Rorschach test can predict the level of abstract thinking in young children and advocated the use of this test because it is less affected by cultural factors than are other tests.

INTERVENTION STRATEGIES

Techniques for School Personnel

Improving academic achievement. When a disadvantaged student is given help by another student, the helper should be of the same social class (Gordon & Grantham, 1979). Disadvantaged children, while showing a slight preference for a helper of the same gender, age, and race, demonstrate a definite preference for a helper of the same social class.

To assist learning-disordered disadvantaged students, Nadgrodsky (1977) urged educators to modify assessment tools and reading materials, employ a team approach, get parents involved, and use behavioral modification techniques.

Au and Mason (1981) tested the social-organizational hypothesis that poor school achievement by many minority children is related to the nature of the teacher-student classroom interaction. One group of teachers required minority students to wait to be called on, and then to speak one at a time. Another group of "high contact" teachers conducted lessons in a participation structure that allowed students to share in joint performance. The latter group of instructors tended to be more successful.

In one innovative program, described by Aronson and Osherow (1980), teachers placed students in learning groups of five or six. Each student in a group was responsible for teaching one part of the day's lesson to the other participants. Under this approach, students showed an increased liking for one another, an amplified and sustained interest in school, improved self-esteem, reduced competitiveness, and an increased belief that they could learn from one another. Students participating in the interdependent learning environment group were shown to achieve better than a control group.

Dansky (1980) advocated sociodramatic play for economically disadvantaged children as a way to enhance sociodramatic activity, imaginativeness, comprehension, and production of organized information. Exploration training helped the youngsters offer more accurate and detailed descriptions of concrete stimuli. Free play activity produced none of the above results.

Emotional development in the classroom. Rosenfield, Sheehan, Marcus, and Stehan (1981) recognized the resentments that can be engendered in a desegregated classroom and attempted to identify some of the social and emotional interactions occurring between majority white students and minority black students. They made the following observations:

1. The higher the percentage of black students in a class, the more white students tended to make friends with other white students.
2. The more the black students displayed hostility, the more the white students tended to have negative attitudes toward the black students.
3. The more alike the social class and achievement levels of white and black students, the more likely they were to have interracial friendships.
4. The higher the self-esteem of white students, the more positive their ethnic attitudes.

These findings suggest that desegregated classes, in order to function properly, should have a carefully considered balance of majority and minority students and a thorough assessment of their attitudes, achievement levels, and social backgrounds (Light, 2005).

Washington (1977) advocates programs that help disadvantaged adolescents gain a sense of control over their environment. One way to do this, according to Lewis and McAnulty (1980), is to teach individuals specific, useful techniques that will enhance their appearance and interviewing skills so they can gain work more successfully.

Many disadvantaged students seem emotionally inhibited and even depressed to teachers. Plante, Cote, Saint-Jean, and Pilic (1978) advocate free painting as therapy for these children. Using this approach with younger students, the authors found that inhibited students lost their depressed traits and appeared more alert and bright. Overtly depressed youngsters showed better school functioning, but improvement in emotional areas was difficult to demonstrate.

Fantasy-evoking techniques have proved useful in the education and emotional development of disadvantaged children. Saltz, Dixon, and Johnson (1977) trained 147 students in one of three types of fantasy activities: thematic fantasy play, fantasy discussion, and sociodramatic play. Over a period of one year, they investigated the effects of this training on various tasks designed to measure cognitive development and impulse control. Results indicate that physical enactment of fantasy experiences had a sizable effect on these variables, while simply listening and discussing were often no more effective than the control situation, in which the participants merely cut and pasted. Evidence suggests that fantasy play that was remote from reality facilitated development more than reality-oriented fantasy play (Burks, 1994, 1999, 2001).

The findings of Saltz et al. (1977) were replicated in another study (Burks, 1994). Using a fantasy-producing game, children from low-income families (in addition to emotionally disturbed, mentally retarded, and normal students) demonstrated a high level of interest and involvement in fairy tales and in the figures from these fables. When the youngsters could act out fantasy roles (i.e., use physical movement), excitement usually ran high.

Language handicaps. At the preschool level, educators can take the following steps to help young students overcome language difficulties:

- Emphasize perceptual discrimination.
- Supply opportunities for language acquisition.
- Read and talk to the children.
- Furnish the children with acceptable models of proper speech.
- Supply corrective grammar and pronunciation feedback.
- Develop listening skills.
- Develop memory skills.
- Develop attention-raising skills.
- Provide appropriate reading-readiness materials.

The language-deficient young child can present educators with challenging problems. Poor language skills impede the transition to abstract thinking. Many students need concrete learning props. The teacher may wish to use more audiovisual aids, laboratory materials, schematic models and diagrams, and role-playing activities than would ordinarily be employed.

Lower socioeconomic status (SES) children tend to have inadequate vocabularies. According to Pozner and Saltz (1972), lower SES youngsters also have trouble expressing thoughts, even though they comprehend instructions. Lower SES students, when asked to relay instructions, scrambled the messages, leaving both lower and middle SES listeners in a state of confusion. Conversely, lower and middle SES listeners had little difficulty understanding middle SES communicators. Pozner and Saltz postulated three reasons for the communications gap created by lower SES verbalizers. First, the lower SES students often were satisfied to present fragmentary information (despite the fact that they had previously demonstrated to the experimenters an ability to repeat the instructions in full). Second, the lower SES children apparently need to communicate visually with their listeners; and third, there was a strong tendency for lower SES students to manipulate experimental materials while talking to the listener, a habit notably lacking among middle SES students.

In short, Pozner and Saltz (1972) found that their results were markedly different from those of other studies that found lower SES listeners culturally deaf to middle SES communicators. They concluded that there was no indication that children of the same SES could understand each other better than they could children of a different SES.

Many implications arise from this study. Teachers cannot assume that lower SES children will adequately communicate thoughts to others even though they understand the messages given them. Further, educators must be aware that lower SES students often need to see the communicator (and to have concrete props) in order to comprehend the impact of sent messages. Finally, teachers must help lower SES students develop more sophisticated language patterns and abandon egocentric speech patterns (i.e., become more aware of listener needs).

According to Webster (1966), a verbally destitute student may be helped by

- protecting the child from derision and deprecation in the classroom;
- providing learning experiences that are concrete, specific, and meaningful;
- projecting a personality characterized by buoyancy, optimism, and energy;
- giving students every opportunity to hear and use standard English;
- making such children aware that a language problem exists;

- giving the students every opportunity to exercise and develop language arts (through discussions, plays, written work, etc.);
- restating messages to the students in as many ways as possible.

Techniques for Parents

Home environment. Parents can improve the home environment in the following ways.

1. Promote more organized conversation in the family. Some adults may need to be told how to do this. Instruct them to involve children in conversation as much as possible.
2. Encourage family members to eat meals as a group. Meals are important socialization events for children.
3. Urge children to maintain a sustained interaction with adults. In order to accomplish this, the parents must be told to eliminate or minimize home interruptions and distractions.
4. Organize television watching. Television can play an overly large part in the lives of lower SES and otherwise deprived children. Too much television watching can isolate the child from normal peer contacts.
5. Help children explore the wider world. The lives of many disadvantaged youngsters are too restricted (e.g., only watching television, going to church once a week, occasionally playing with one other child, or infrequent trips to the movies).
6. Provide suitable reading materials. Many parents need teacher assistance when picking out books and magazines.

Educators must not expect too much from parents of lower SES children. Many are not well educated, some are not trained in child-rearing tactics, and others do not have the time, energy, or financial resources to complete tasks urged on them by school personnel. In addition, many are distrustful of outsiders. Gaining the confidence of the parents is an essential first step that cannot be accomplished if the parents perceive school demands to be incomprehensible or unattainable.

The jargon used by educators can sometimes be an impediment to parental understanding. Many parents do not comprehend the meaning of phrases like "well-rounded development" and other noble-sounding terms that roll off the tongues of teachers and administrators. Simple, easily understood language must take the place of this kind of terminology.

If a child is not well fed, adequately clothed, or properly sheltered, attempts can be made to help the family acquire these necessities. Some of the following steps can be taken by educators:

1. Contact service clubs (Lions Club, Rotary Club, etc.), which often provide funds or materials for worthy student-assistance projects. The educator can offer to provide speakers for service club meetings to alert members to student needs. If any organization agrees to provide money or services, follow up with other meetings to report progress.
2. Get in touch with the Red Cross. It will sometimes assist families needing transportation to medical facilities.
3. Communicate with police departments. Juvenile division officers are often associated with boys' and girls' clubs. Most police departments will provide speakers for parent group meetings to discuss the role of the police in community matters; all will supply investigative personnel to study the problems of abused, mistreated, or neglected children. The attendance of a personnel worker at court hearings often influences the actions of a judge or referee regarding a juvenile offender.
4. Contact welfare centers. Some parents, particularly those who do not speak English well, do not know how to ask for assistance (food, clothing, housing) and may not comprehend written regulations.
5. Help nonworking adults get in touch with employment agencies and state and private training institutions that can prepare them for employment.

6. Direct families to aid offered by churches. Many churches will help members locate babysitters, arrange counseling sessions, and so on.

The preceding efforts may help educators gain credence with disadvantaged family members. Such direct and immediate assistance is often necessary to alleviate poverty-related difficulties. Merely discussing the problems with adults in the family (a method favored by some counselors) is generally useless.

Finally, many of these disadvantaged families need to learn how to negotiate the educational system. Middle-class parents, because they attended middle-class schools taught by middle-class teachers, tend to be well trained in these maneuvers. Lower SES and minority-group parents are not so skilled, and this makes them and their children less attractive to school authorities.

Therapeutic services. Insight therapy tends to be an inefficient approach when employed with most deprived families. Herrera and Sanchez (1980) advocate a prescriptive counseling model oriented toward group therapy using behavior-structured techniques. One such behavioral intervention program (Jason, 1977) focused on identifying and modifying mother-child interaction patterns. Using this technique, Jason reported a change for the better in child vocalizations and cognitive activities.

Guerney, Coufal, and Vogelsong (1981) assigned 108 mothers and daughters (mostly of low educational and socioeconomic status) to receive one of the following: no treatment, discussion-oriented traditional treatment, or relationship-enhancement treatment. There was no improvement with no treatment. Those participating in the traditional treatment showed improved communication skills and general relationships. Participants in relationship-enhancement treatment improved significantly and reached higher levels on each of the evaluation measures than did those in both other groups. Guerney et al. concluded that the relationship-enhancement method is superior to the traditional discussion-oriented treatment and stated that the significant portion of its effectiveness stems from the particular methods it employs.

The middle-class counselor who attempts to work with poverty-class and minority-group families may find himself or herself in an awkward situation: What looks like aberrant behavior to the therapist may simply be normal coping methods to handle stress and limited options. However, depression can be an outstanding personality feature of the disadvantaged person. Since struggle and adaptation to severe psychic and social stress is an everyday experience and a way of life for many deprived individuals, depression (an expression of helplessness) may be an expected symptom. Treatment of this environmentally caused depression is not easy. However, if the therapist remembers the close relationship between anxiety and depression (Toolan, 1981), he or she can assist by encouraging the individual to release repressed aggressive feelings that underlie the anxiety. Directing the individual to become more assertive (i.e., to fight back at forces causing worry) can also help.

How important is counseling for parents of disadvantaged children? A partial answer to this question was provided by Hayes, Cunningham, and Robinson (1977), who assessed the effects of direct versus indirect group counseling on student motivation and self-esteem. Some of the children were counseled directly, some were not counseled but their parents were, and some were given no treatment. An analysis of various measures revealed that there were no significant differences between the direct and indirect counseling groups, or between the direct counseling and the no-treatment groups. Participants whose parents were counseled, however, earned significantly higher positive scores on all measures than did those who received no treatment. The authors concluded that the results highlight the efficacy of counseling elementary school students indirectly through their parents. They also believe that the findings hold implications for change in counselor training and intervention strategies.

CHAPTER 25

Counseling the Parents

The usefulness of diagnostic counseling, described in chapter 1, depends on rapport between the counselor or teacher and the parents. The interviewer and the respondent can operate successfully only in an atmosphere of cordial understanding. This can be attained when participants

- respect the contributions each has to offer during counseling sessions;
- avoid a pose of intellectual superiority;
- exhibit a spirit of accommodation that ensures compromises likely to be in the best interests of the child in question.

None of these ideals is likely to be realized if parents are made to feel uncomfortable with poorly constructed interviews. This chapter is devoted to suggestions that may help counselors and/or teachers to enhance the quality of parent meetings. These include

- a questionnaire for parents that is designed to break the ice in initial individual or group interviews;
- a list of questions for counselors who want to ensure meetings will be conducted in comfortable surroundings;
- a list of interview pitfalls that should be avoided;
- suggestions for fostering parent cooperation during conferences;
- a discussion of group counseling techniques and goals.

BREAKING THE ICE

In an attempt to form a therapeutic alliance between counselor and parents, I constructed the What Should We Talk About? questionnaire (see figure 25.1), a diagnostic counseling device that I have used successfully in both individual and group conferences. It works best in early counseling sessions because it touches on topics related to the child's ability to function academically. Many parents are reluctant to bring up certain topics because they feel these subjects are not important to school personnel. This questionnaire gives the parents permission to voice anxieties they may feel about their child and his or her school experiences.

While concerns tend to center on troubled students, educators may also ask parents of normally behaved students to answer these questions at the beginning of the school year. Many so-called average children suffer unhappy episodes that can affect classroom achievement and parents of these youngsters should be given the opportunity to mention and discuss these events with school personnel. Upon being invited, most parents cooperate willingly.

For individual conferences, ask parents to arrive about 15 minutes early in order to complete the questionnaire. It is probably best to have them respond to the questions outside the teacher's presence. While other individuals answer queries, the teacher can be talking to the parents of another child. If the form is sent home to be filled out, many parents will forget to do it or forget to bring it to school. If it must be sent home, mail it—do not have the child take it to the parents.

WHAT SHOULD WE TALK ABOUT?

Harold F. Burks, Ph.D.

Put a check mark in the appropriate column after each of the following questions.

	Often	Sometimes	Seldom
1. Do you ever wish you were more informed about your child's course of study?	☐	☐	☐
2. Would you like to know what is most important for your child to learn?	☐	☐	☐

	Very detailed	Moderately detailed	Little detail
3. How detailed an explanation of your child's course of studies would you like?	☐	☐	☐

	Often	Sometimes	Seldom
4. Do you wish you knew more about how well your child is doing academically?	☐	☐	☐
5. Does your child talk about his or her schoolwork?	☐	☐	☐
6. Do you contact the school about your child's progress?	☐	☐	☐
7. Do you tend to be confused about your child's report card or grades?	☐	☐	☐

	Yes	No	Maybe
8. Do you know how your child is doing in the basic subjects (reading, arithmetic, etc.)?	☐	☐	☐

	Often	Sometimes	Seldom
9. Do you wish you knew more about your child's abilities and what to expect from him or her?	☐	☐	☐

	Yes	No	Maybe
10. Do you suspect that your child may have an academic handicap?	☐	☐	☐
11. Do you think your child might have abilities the school does not know about?	☐	☐	☐

	Often	Sometimes	Seldom
12. Do you wish you could talk to the teacher about some of your child's needs or problems?	☐	☐	☐

Figure 25.1a.

	Yes	No	Maybe
13. Would you welcome a home visit from the teacher?	☐	☐	☐
14. Would you welcome more opportunities for an individual conference?	☐	☐	☐
15. Do you suspect your child has an emotional or social difficulty?	☐	☐	☐

	Often	Sometimes	Seldom
16. Do you wish you had more specific, concrete ways to help your child academically?	☐	☐	☐

	Yes	No	Maybe
17. Does your child have one good friend?	☐	☐	☐
18. Does your child have trouble making friends in the neighborhood?	☐	☐	☐
19. Would you like your child to have more friends?	☐	☐	☐
20. Do you think that, in some respects, the way you see your child differs from the way others see him or her?	☐	☐	☐

	Often	Sometimes	Seldom
21. Does your child act very differently at home than at school?	☐	☐	☐

	At home	At school	No difference
22. Where does your child seem most productive and happy?	☐	☐	☐

	Often	Sometimes	Seldom
23. Do you think your child is depressed or unhappy about school?	☐	☐	☐
24. Do you feel confused about terms such as *grade level, intelligence, norms, expectancies,* and so on?	☐	☐	☐

Figure 25.1b.

These questions are also useful in initial group meetings. The format for this first session might be as follows:

1. Have the parents introduce themselves and give the names of their children (name tags are a good idea).
2. Discuss how often the group should meet (do not take too long on this; most groups meet once a month).
3. Discuss the location of meetings, who should chair the sessions, and whether refreshments should be scheduled (spend no more than a total of 20 minutes on these topics).
4. Have each parent take a few minutes to tell the group what he or she wants out of the meetings.
5. Distribute the questionnaire. After the parents have answered the questions, find out which areas are of most concern to the group by asking each person to list the three areas of greatest concern to them. The areas selected most frequently can be discussed first.
6. If time permits, open the meeting for a general discussion of the problems addressed by the questions. Do not ignore concerns of lesser interest to the group as a whole; for some, these may be of particular importance. The group may decide, however, that a parent could arrange to have a private conference with the teacher rather than to take the group's time on an issue of little general interest.
7. Close the meeting on time (even if all questions are not answered). Assure the participants that they will have other opportunities to cover the topics. Collect the parents' responses for the next meeting.

SETTING UP INDIVIDUAL CONFERENCES

When setting up individual conferences with parents, ask yourself the following questions.

Have you allowed enough time for the interview? Allow ample time, but do not let the session last longer than about 45 minutes. Participants tend to repeat themselves after that time period.

Have you ensured privacy and freedom from interruption for the participants? No other parents or children should be in the room while the conference takes place.

Have you secured a conference site that is comfortable and aesthetically pleasing? While it is not always possible to meet this ideal, certain standards can be met. For instance, adults should not be seated at children's desks.

Have you seated yourself in a nonthreatening position at the conference? Sit a comfortable distance from the parents but do not barricade yourself behind a large desk. Those interviewed tend to see the desk as a defense impeding free discussion.

Are you approachable? This may be a tough query to answer. Although an interviewer intends to be friendly, others may see that person as distant and aloof. Ask an acquaintance to rate your interview manners. Do you act in an easy, unhurried way? Do you give the participants time to respond? Does your body language belie your verbal message?

Are you well prepared for the conference? Have cumulative records on hand and review them carefully before the interview. Nothing is more irritating for a parent than to attend a school conference where the staff appears unready. The parents assume (rightfully so) that these educators are not interested in the student.

Have you arranged to have both parents present at the interview if possible? It is difficult for one parent to explain to the other what transpired at a conference. The one who was present may forget portions of the conversation (and feel defensive about doing so) and may find it hard to describe to the other parent the mood and feelings experienced during the conference. In addition, the parent who did not attend may find fault with the other's handling of the conference situation.

Have you arranged to write down conference conclusions? Toward the end of the interview, sum up the actions everyone present thinks should be taken with the child. Write them down. Present a copy to the parents and keep a copy for the child's educational records.

Have you arranged to follow up the interview by contacting the parents after a few days? A note sent to the home, an email, or a brief telephone conversation will suffice. This signals to the parents that you are really interested in the child and that you appreciate their help. It encourages them to contact you as new thoughts or problems come to light.

Have you acquainted the parents with school and community services? After they are informed, you are likely to hear that many parents are unaware of these educational resources.

Have you talked to the child about the parent conference? In most cases, the student is apprehensive about having his or her parents come to the school. Make some effort to calm the child's fears with a frank and open talk. This does not necessarily mean (in fact, rarely means) that you should tell the student everything that transpired in the meeting.

Interview Pitfalls

Certain counseling procedures can disrupt the formation of a constructive relationship with the parents. Consider the following suggestions.

1. Do not complain about the student. The parents will conclude (correctly) that you do not care for their child and that you feel powerless to do anything about his or her problem.
2. Do not dwell on difficulties that are not treatable. For instance, if a youngster is required to wear thick glasses, there is little point in referring to the teasing the child receives from other students. If such an issue is mentioned, casually discuss ways the parents might help the child respond to teasing. Do not overemphasize areas where the parents can do little to help.
3. In general, do not discuss the parents' religion, politics, or community activities. These matters are not the concern of the school, and to put them on the conference agenda will not help the student's educational career.
4. Do not gossip about other students or their parents.
5. Drop the discussion of a particular topic if the parents show unusual resistance. If it is important, come back to it later.
6. Do not confront the parents with more than they can handle at one interview. To do so will only confuse and irritate them.
7. Do not bring up a point unless you have a practical solution in mind or can get a useful suggestion from the parents. To leave them without direction can cause them needless worry.
8. Avoid using labels such as "emotionally disturbed," "socially maladjusted," or "neurotic." These designations convey no information about actual behavior and will be received negatively by the parents. Describe the student's misbehavior and actions in terms of specific incidents.
9. Do not hoard disturbing news until the end of the school year and then announce it. The parents will regard your conduct as unprofessional (and, of course, they are right).
10. Be cautious when asking parents to seek professional assistance. Take time to consider the following suggestions:

    * Do not refer parents to just one specialist (psychologist, physician, ophthalmologist, dentist, etc.); give them several names to choose from.
    * When in doubt, refer parents to the yellow pages of the phone directory.
    * Do not refer parents to specialists they cannot afford. In most instances, county health offices provide direct or indirect contract services for those who require professional assistance but do not have the financial resources to pay for them.
    * Do not refer parents to an agency without also making an effort to contact the agency for pertinent information.

11. Do not act like an infallible authority. If you do, the parents may become more dependent on you than is healthy. Sometimes, it may lead them to become distrustful of your advice when or if a recommendation does not work. Answer all questions frankly and openly. If you do not know something, say so. Remember, a crucial factor in any interview is the trust the parents have in you. Do not endanger this feeling of confidence by being evasive.

12. Do not do all the talking. The parents bring another point of view and may have as much to give to the interview as you do. Further, the parents' perception of the child may differ widely from the child's teacher. Honor that perception by listening to them. Dominating an interview by constant talking may be perceived by other participants as a way of covering up insecurities.

13. Do not raise problems in the interview that anger, confuse, or irritate parents. If these reactions surface, the parents probably are not yet ready to handle presented problems. Later, after they have had time to think about the difficulties, they may be more willing to discuss them with school authorities.

14. Do not assume that the problems you think the youngster faces are the ones his or her parents are concerned about. Listen to what they are saying and be willing to change the agenda to meet parental concerns.

15. Do not spend much time on discussions of the family's early home practices. Remember that you are not conducting long-term therapy. Concentrate on current behavior that can easily be changed.

16. Do not continue to conduct the meeting along prescribed lines if the parents are openly hostile. Lay aside the agenda and ask them if they wish to discuss their resentments (until this is done they will discount all of your suggestions anyway). If differences of opinion cannot be resolved to the parents' satisfaction, suggest that another person, perhaps an administrator or guidance counselor, be brought in to future conferences.

17. Do not assume that your recommendations will be effective if the parents disagree with each other. You may point out the apparent conflict by saying, "Apparently, we cannot agree on goals and methods for helping your child. What do you think we can do?" The resulting conversation may reveal some of the difficulties that hamper the youngster's progress in school. These problems can be pointed out to the parents, along with the suggestion that they must resolve some of their conflicts before the school can be fully effective.

18. Do not argue with the parents. If they wish to be contentious, simply state your point of view and then drop the topic. Arguments hardly ever change opinions.

19. Avoid topics that have little bearing on the child's educational program. For example, the question, "How can I get my child to show more respect to his elders?" is so vague that it defies an effective answer. Many questions are rhetorical and should be treated as such. Some parents who feel helpless to deal with their own children will express this helplessness in front of the interviewer. Do not get snagged into answering the same question over and over when the parents show no suitable response.

20. Do not assume that one interview will suffice. It often does not. Arrange for further follow-up contacts.

21. Do not offer recommendations the parents find offensive or threatening. Experience has shown that parents will not follow through on unwelcome suggestions.

22. Avoid the role of marital referee. In the midst of conflicts, parents may try to see which one can get the interviewer on his or her side in order to get back at the other. Point out to them that you are not in a position to judge the appropriateness of their circumstances and intentions.

23. Do not convey the idea that you expect the parents to change all aspects of their conduct immediately. An assumption like that will soon leave you and the parents feeling disappointed.

24. Do not assume that the parents see the school meeting as relevant to their child's needs. Ask them how meaningful they believe the conference is. If it is not significant to them, they will not change child-raising approaches.

25. Avoid nondirective counseling approaches. Most parents require direct and clear information about the student. However, do not preach—listen, but be prepared to give your insights and prescriptions when asked to do so. Subtle interview techniques are wasted on most parents. Neither they nor you have the time for such maneuvers. Most parents respect and follow clear-cut directions. A few need to be told, more or less bluntly, that their child-raising approaches are destructive. This is necessary when it is apparent that the child in question is being seriously affected by negative factors and when it is evident the parents are discounting school advice.

26. Do not attempt to treat issues that are beyond your competency. Simply tell the parents that you do not wish to become involved in a discussion of sensitive topics and suggest they seek help elsewhere.

27. Avoid weak questions. For example, "Do you think your child is doing better in school this year?" is an ineffective question that leaves the parents with few options except to answer yes or no. "Is he [she] doing the arithmetic homework?" also requires a negative or affirmative response, but it can lead to a more meaningful discussion of home factors about which the parents are knowledgeable.

Techniques to Foster Parental Cooperation

Parents often find themselves in situations where they cannot be assertive with the school. First, they are worried that their child will be affected negatively if they criticize educators. Second, they frequently feel put off by educators who stall, put blame on the parents, ignore the parents' presence, or conduct conferences that alienate them. The worst possible consequences can ensue from encounters of this nature. The enraged parents cannot vent their anger openly; they show resentment, however, by withholding support of the educational system and by being critical of school practices.

Parents must be encouraged to show more assertiveness in dealings with school personnel. I have developed two contrasting sets of techniques for handling conferences with parents (see table 25.1)—one guaranteed to enrage parents, the other guaranteed to win their cooperation.

GROUP CONFERENCES

Group meetings may be a more practical, convenient, and efficient way to provide parents with general information than individual conferences. In addition, group meetings are desirable when difficulties that pertain to more than one child can best be solved through discussion.

Extensive teacher involvement is a necessity for school-related group meetings. Teachers are the logical initial contact for parents. The teacher's commitment to the goals of the classroom and the teacher's belief in the relevance of parent meetings largely determines the success of the meetings. The teacher's participation is required even though others with special skills or experience are present. The teacher cannot hand the group meeting over to others in the hope that they can better interpret what the teacher is proposing to do in the classroom. Delegation of authority to others simply erodes the teacher's power base; it will not win the respect of parents.

Informational Group Meetings

The primary purpose of informational group meetings is to present specific information to parents. Such meetings should be carefully planned. A disorganized meeting can lead the parents to think that the teacher runs a disorderly classroom. The agenda should include topics of interest to the entire group. Keep the meetings relatively short; remember that a little information well understood is far better than a mass of hard-to-remember material. Allow time for discussion to clarify concerns.

Group turnout will be influenced by the type of invitation sent to parents. Written announcements should be sent as a personal invitation from the teacher or principal. In addition, telephone invitations might be extended to each parent on the meeting day.

Discussion Group Meetings

A number of years ago, I established a class for students with learning problems. The parents of these children were invited to attend monthly meetings in the children's classroom. Later, the parents decided to hold some of the sessions in their own homes. I remember with pleasure the friendships that were formed and the parents' and teacher's frequent remarks about how helpful the intense and often spirited discussions were. The meetings con-

Techniques for Parent Conferences

Techniques guaranteed to enrage parents	Techniques guaranteed to make parents more cooperative
Mumble; duck head; leave encounters quickly; be in a hurry.	Be open and relaxed; smile; take time to talk to the parents or gladly set a time in the future.
Stare over parents' heads; talk a lot; use lots of professional jargon; smile mysteriously.	Be attentive; look at the parents; answer questions openly; say "I don't know" if you don't know.
If parents won't come to you, adopt a "to hell with them" attitude. Don't go out of your way to contact them via home visits, telephone calls, or notes.	Recognize that many parents are afraid of schools. Follow through on contacts; present yourself as a person very concerned about their child.
Stall; neglect to return phone calls or written requests.	Show respect for parents by immediately returning all their calls. Do not show irritation.
Complain (in a whining voice) about the child (he or she is "somewhat lazy," "antagonistic," "aggressive," etc.).	Maintain a calm, relaxed tone. Be specific about what is happening (e.g., "He is not finishing his assignments lately").
Sit behind a big desk while parents are seated at children's desks (i.e., infantilize them); remind them that schools have not changed in 50 years.	Meet in homes or conference rooms; sit in a circle; make everyone as comfortable as possible.
Talk vaguely about goals and objectives; don't allow yourself to be cornered into being specific.	Have a specific plan for the meeting. Do not stress problems that cannot be solved.
At group meetings, bore parents with a long speech. Then act surprised that there is no time for questions.	At group meetings, give a very short speech; let the audience ask questions; incorporate questions into the agenda; be humorous; have a variety of things to do.
Imply that somehow the parents are to blame for all the child's misfortunes. Do not specify what the parents' delinquencies are, however.	Put the emphasis on what can be done now; place no blame, since that makes people defensive; encourage specific actions by particular people.
Condescendingly imply that "the teacher knows best"; be inflexible; never admit to being wrong.	Admit you need the parents' help; incorporate their suggestions into the program; stress flexibility.
Wait to break news about the student's slow progress until late in the school year.	Throughout the year, keep the parents informed of how their child is doing.
Insist that parents institute time-consuming programs that they do not understand and cannot afford.	Ask parents how well they understand the instructions, whether they can actually follow the program, and whether they have the financial means to implement it.
Hide behind records; peep over the top of them at parents occasionally; refuse to reveal the records' contents.	Do not use records unless you are willing to share their contents with parents; be aboveboard about test results and explain them thoroughly.
Do not follow through on agreements or implement proposed programs; if parents challenge you on these broken promises, say, "I'm really sorry."	Write all agreements down and review them at regular intervals; if you forget details, call the parents.

Table 25.1.

tinued for 4 years. During that time, the group learned that the following rules and conditions tended to make the sessions more rewarding and successful:

1. If possible, the meetings should be held in pleasant surroundings with comfortable chairs (a child's desk is *not* a comfortable place for an adult to sit).
2. The chairs should be placed in a circle (never in rows with a leader up front).
3. Refreshments (cookies, for example) are a pleasurable part of the meetings. Members can take turns bringing the refreshments. Coffee and tea should be available throughout the meeting, not served too late in the evening.
4. Meetings should last from one-and-a-half to two hours. Most parents like meetings to start about 7:30 or 8:00 p.m. When the stated closing time is reached, everyone should go home. Discourage group members from lingering longer.
5. A chairperson should be appointed (not necessarily the teacher). The chairperson's duties may include reminding others of the meeting time and place, arranging for others to bring refreshments, and contacting consultants or speakers for the group.
6. The role of the teacher in the group deserves special consideration:

   • The teacher is not and should not be expected to be an expert on all aspects of living. It is quite legitimate for the teacher to say "I don't know" when asked to give an opinion about something of which he or she is unsure. If the group wants to acquire the services of an expert (e.g., a pediatrician or psychotherapist), group members can be commissioned to approach a professional.
   • Although the teacher is responsible for the academic welfare of students in the classroom, he or she is not responsible for the students' basic personality development. That process largely occurs outside the influence of the school.
   • The teacher should not be the target for all irritations group members feel about school policies. No one person can defend all actions taken by large institutions. However, a discussion group can debate issues and attempt to change conditions while agreeing that it is usually futile to try to place blame for these practices.

7. No member of the group should expect (or be allowed) to take up most of the allotted time with his or her problems. Time limits may be set, but they should not be too rigid. The group as a whole may identify closely with a particular difficulty, in which case the discussion can be allowed to continue beyond time limits.
8. The determination of topics is a difficult task. All matters pertaining to school activities can be discussed freely. Home activities, if they affect the child's progress in school, are also legitimate subjects for discussion as well, unless they involve points of contention that are beyond the capacity of the group to handle. In short, if the main emphasis of a problem lies outside school-related functions, it probably should not be included on the agenda. For example, the group may suggest that television viewing in a particular home be reduced, but they should not be asked to judge whether a couple should, for instance, get a divorce.
9. The origins of problems are usually complex, and no member of the group should expect to receive an ideal answer for every problem presented.
10. In general, children should not be told the specifics of the group's discussions. Point out to the group that they have a responsibility not to use the group as a weapon over their youngsters. Also, all shared discussions are confidential and not to be gossiped about with people outside the group.
11. Do not continue group discussion meetings when the following conditions occur:

    • Many of the parents express resentment or anxiety about attending the meetings.
    • Many of the parents refuse to attend the meetings.
    • Many of the members, for one reason or another, refuse to participate in discussions.

- The appointed group leader finds it too difficult to manage or guide the group.
- The topics brought up by parents are too specific to be of general interest to other group participants. Private meetings with the parents concerned are more effective for this type of problem.
- It becomes evident that the problems shown by a child or children in the classroom are symptoms of large, unresolved family conflicts that cannot be handled in group meetings.

CONCLUSION

This brief overview of counseling techniques may clarify the importance of establishing a positive relationship between school figures and parents. The absence of sympathetic understanding can have unfortunate results. It may mean that the counseled person will discount messages received from the teacher or guidance expert. On the other hand, a good rapport tends to enhance the listener's receptiveness to messages (Dribben & Brabender, 1979).

The formation of a constructive relationship, by itself, does not guarantee that changes will occur in parent-child interactions. In fact, Caille (1982) argued that therapeutic intervention does not have the power to create durable, predetermined changes in living patterns. Even if improvements can be arranged, Caille asks this question: What has prevented the family from discovering such beneficial adaptations on its own? Caille suggests that the basic rules of the family prohibit it from changing, and even if members understand what caused a malfunction in the system, little benefit tends to result from such insights.

Caille's (1982) observations raise profound questions about the efficacy of counseling. It is tempting, for example, to tell parents that their academically failing child suffers from low self-esteem because of a dominating sibling. The counselor feels better—something has been done. In actuality, the insight may lead to an aggravation of the problem. Suppose the dominating sibling has been unconsciously chosen by the parents to be the "successful" child and the other, failing child to be the carrier of "bad" family symptoms (a common scapegoat syndrome). Subsequent to the school interview, the parents feel that they should stop the succeeding child from acting out his or her aggressions. However, that exacerbates the family difficulty because the favored child is thrown out of his or her formerly approved role, which can cause that youngster to react even more violently toward the failing brother or sister.

Caille (1982) believed, however, (and I concur) that the inherent healing capacities of the family can be facilitated in other ways. One method is to validate the present functioning of a family by helping its members understand each other's differing levels of self-perception. This, in turn, can lead to a reformulation of family beliefs and perceptions. When that happens, changes will occur—they must occur—regardless of the presence or absence of a stated willingness to change.

References

Achenbach, T. M. (1991). *Integrative guide for the 1991 CBCL/4–18, YSR and TRF profiles.* Burlington: University of Vermont, Department of Psychology.

Adams, M. J. (1990). *Beginning to read: Thinking and learning about print.* Cambridge, MA: MIT Press.

Ahlgren, A., & Johnson, D. W. (1979). Sex differences in cooperative and competitive attitudes from 2nd through the 12th grades. *Developmental Psychology, 15,* 45–49.

Aldrich, C. K. (1971, October). Thief! *Psychology Today, 4*(10), 66–69.

Alford, B. A., & Norcross, J. C. (1991). Cognitive therapy as integrative therapy. *Journal of Psychotherapy Integration, 1,* 175–190.

Allen, W. A., Nicholas, L., D'Amanda, P., & D'Amanda, C. (1992). *How drugs can affect your life.* Springfield, IL: Charles C. Thomas.

Alwon, F. J. (1979). An after school activity club program. *Child Care Quarterly, 8,* 266–278.

Ambert, A.-M. (1992). *The effect of children on parents.* New York: Haworth Press.

American Psychiatric Association. (1994). *Diagnostic and statistical manual of mental disorders* (4th ed.). Washington, DC: Author.

Anchor, K. N., Sandler, H. M., & Cherones, J. H. (1977). Maladaptive antisocial aggressive behavior and outlets for intimacy. *Journal of Clinical Psychology, 33,* 947–949.

Anderson, R. P., Halcomb, C. G., & Doyle, R. B. (1973). The measurement of attentional deficits. *Exceptional Children, 39,* 534–539.

Argulewicz, E. D., Elliot, S. N., & Spencer, D. (1982). Application of a cognitive-behavioral intervention for improving classroom attention. *School Psychology Review, 11,* 90–95.

Arlow, J. A., & Brenner, C. (1964). *Psychological concepts in the structural theory.* New York: International Press.

Arnott, W., & Gushin, J. (1976). Film making as a therapeutic tool. *American Journal of Art Therapy, 16,* 29–33.

Aronfreed, J. (1961). The nature, variety, and social patterning of moral responses to transgression. *Journal of Abnormal and Social Psychology, 63,* 233–240.

Aronson, E., & Osherow, N. (1980). Cooperation, prosocial behavior, and academic performance: Experiements in the desegregated classroom. *Applied Social Psychology Annual, 1,* 163–196.

Asher, S. R., & Cole, J. D. (1990). *Peer rejection in childhood.* Cambridge, England: Cambridge University Press.

Atkinson, J. W. (1965). Some general implications of conceptual developments in the study of achievement-oriented behavior. In M. R. Jones (Ed.), *Human motivation: A symposium* (pp. 45–63). Lincoln: University of Nebraska Press.

Attwell, A., Orpet, R. E., & Meyers, C. E. (1967). Kindergarten behavior ratings as a predictor of academic achievement. *Journal of School Psychology, 6,* 43–46.

Atwood, M. (2002, May 23). Cops and robbers. *New York Review of Books, 49*(9).

Au, K. H., & Mason, J. M. (1981). Social organizational factors in learning to read: The balance of rights hypothesis. *Reading Research Quarterly, 17,* 115–152.

Axelrod, S. (1971). Token reinforcement programs in special classes. *Exceptional Children, 37,* 371–379.

Azar, B. (1995a). Shy people have inaccurate self-concepts. *APA Monitor, 25*(11), 4–5.

Azar, B. (1995b). Timidity can develop in the first days of life. *APA Monitor, 25*(11), 5.

Azrin, N. H., & Foxx, R. M. (1974). *Toilet training in less than a day.* New York: Simon and Schuster.

Bakwin, H., & Bakwin, R. M. (1954). *Clinical management of behavior disorder in children.* Philadephia: W. B. Saunders.

Baldoni, J. (2004). *Great motivation secrets of great leaders.* New York: McGraw-Hill.

Bandura, A., & Huston, A. C. (1961). Indentification as a process of incidental learning. *Journal of Abnormal and Social Psychology, 63,* 311–318.

Bankart, C. P., & Anderson, C. C. (1979). Short term effects of prosocial television viewing on play of preschool boys and girls. *Psychological Reports, 44,* 935–941.

Barlow, D. H. (1988). *Anxiety and its disorders.* New York: Guilford.

Barnard, W. A., Loomis, R. J., & Cross, H. A. (1980). Assessment of visual recall and recognition learning in a museum environment. *Bulletin of the Psychonomic Society, 16,* 311–313.

Barnes, F. F. (1980). Travel and fatigue as causes of partial dissociative reactions. *Comprehensive Psychiatry, 21,* 55–61.

Barton, E. M., Baltes, M. M., & Orzech, M. J. (1980). Etiology of dependence in older nursing home residents during morning care: The role of staff behavior. *Journal of Personality and Social Psychology, 38,* 423–431.

Baugh, J. R. (Ed.). (1990). *Recovering from addiction: Guided steps through the healing process.* New York: Insight Books/Plenum Press.

Baumeister, R. F. (Ed.). (1993). *Self-esteem: The puzzle of low self-regard.* New York: Plenum Press.

Baumrind, D. (1968). Authoritarian versus authoritative parental control. *Adolescence, 3,* 255–272.

Bean, B., & Bennett, S. (1993). *The me that nobody knows: A book for teenage survivors.* New York: Lexington Books.

Beck, A. T., & Freeman, A. (1990). Cognitive therapy of personality disorders. New York: Guilford.

Beggs, D., & Buffie, E. (1967). *Nongraded schools in action.* Bloomington, IN: University Press.

Beiderman, J., Newcorn, J., & Sprich, S. (1991). Comorbidity of attention deficit disorder with conduct, depressive, anxiety, and other disorders. *American Journal of Psychiatry, 148,* 564–577.

Bender, L. (1946). *Bender Visual-Motor Gestalt Test.* New York: American Orthopsychiatric Association.

Bender, L. (1956). *Psychopathology of children with brain disorders.* Springfield, IL: Charles C. Thomas.

Bennett, N. (1976). *Teaching styles and pupil progress.* Berkeley, CA: Open Books.

Bentzen, F. (1963). Sex ratios in learning and behavior disorders. *American Journal of Orthopsychiatry, 33,* 92–98.

Berglas, S., & Baumeister, R. F. (1993). *Your own worst enemy: Understanding the paradox of self-defeating behavior.* New York: Basic Books.

Berkowitz, L. (1973). The case for bottling up rage. *Psychology Today, 7*(2), 24–31.

Berkowitz, L. (1993a). *Aggression: Its causes, consequences, and control.* New York: McGraw Hill.

Berkowitz, L. (1993b). *Aggression without (necessarily) anger.* New York: McGraw Hill.

Bernal, M. E., Klinnert, M. D., & Schultz, L. A. (1980). Outcome evaluation of behavioral parent training and client-centered parent counseling for children with conduct problems. *Journal of Applied Behavior Analysis, 13,* 677–691.

Bettelheim, B. (1950). *Love is not enough.* Glencoe, IL: Free Press.

Bettelheim, B. (1976). *The uses of enchantment.* New York: Knopf.

Blanco, F. (1972). *Prescriptions for children with learning and adjustment problems.* Springfield, IL: Charles C. Thomas.

Bland, J. (1982, January). The junk-food syndrome. *Psychology Today, 16*(1), 92.

Blatt, S. J. (1982). Dependency and self-criticism: Psychological dimensions of depression. *Journal of Consulting and Clinical Psychology, 50,* 113–124.

Blatt, S. J. (1995). The destructiveness of perfectionism: Implications for the treatment of depression. *American Psychologist, 50*(12), 1003–1020.

Blauner, S. R. (2002). *How I stayed alive when my brain was trying to kill me: One person's guide to suicide prevention.* New York: William Morrow.

Bloomingdale, L. M. (1984). Whither ADD (attention deficit disorder)? *Psychiatric Journal of the University of Ottawa, 9,* 175–186.

Blumberg, M. L. (1978). Depression in children on a general pediatric service. *American Journal of Psychotherapy, 32,* 20–32.

Bolvin, M., & Begin, G. (1989). Peer status and self-perception among elementary age children. *Child Development, 60,* 591–596.

Bongiovanni, A. F., & Hyman, I. (1978). Leviton is wrong on the use of corporal punishment. *Psychology in the Schools, 15,* 290–291.

Bornstein, R. F. (1993). *The dependent personality.* New York: Guilford Press.

Bottoms, G. (2001). *Angelhead: My brother's descent into madness.* University of Chicago Press.

Bower, E. (1960). The emotionally handicapped child and the school. *Exceptional Children, 26,* 232–242.

Brandt, L. J., & Hayden, M. E. (1974). Male and female teacher attitudes as a function of students' ascribed motivation and performance levels. *Journal of Educational Psychology, 66,* 309–314.

Brannigan, G. G., Barone, R. J., & Margolis, H. (1978). Bender gestalt signs as indicants of conceptual impulsivity. *Journal of Personality Assessment, 42,* 233–236.

Brenner, A. (1984). *Helping children cope with stress.* Lexington, MA: D.C. Heath.

Brent, D. E., & Routh, D. K. (1978). Response cost and impulsive word recognition errors in reading disabled children. *Journal of Abnormal Psychology, 6,* 211–219.

Brophy, J. E. (1983). Research on the self-fulfilling prophecy and teacher expectations. *Journal of Educational Psychology, 75,* 631–661.

Brophy, J. E., & Good, T. L. (1970). Teachers' communication of differential expectations for children's classroom performance. *Journal of Educational Psychology, 61,* 365–374.

Brown, N. W. (2001). *Children of the self-absorbed: A grown-up's guide to getting over narcissistic parents.* Oakland, CA: New Harbinger Publications.

Bruininks, V. L. (1978). Patterns and personality correlates of teacher's reactions with students. *Psychological Reports, 42,* 239–242.

Brumbach, R., & Weinberg, W. A. (1977). Childhood depression: An explanation of a behavior disorder of children. *Perceptual and Motor Skills, 44,* 911–916.

Bruno, F. J. (1993). *Psychological symptoms.* New York: John Wiley & Sons.

Bryan, C., & Dickie, R. F. (1976). The use of a changing criterion design in the elimination of talk-out behavior. *SALT: School Applications of Learning Theory, 8,* 32–37.

Bryan, T. H. (1978). Social relationships and verbal interactions of learning disabled children. *Journal of Learning Disabilities, 11,* 107–115.

Bryant, R. A., & Harvey, A. G. (2000). *Acute stress disorder.* Washington, DC: American Psychological Association Books.

Budd, L. S. (1990). *Living with the active alert child: Groundbreaking strategies for parents.* Englewood Cliffs, NJ: Prentice-Hall.

Bugental, D. B., Collins, S., Collins, L., & Chaney, L. A. (1978). Attributional and behavioral changes following two behavior management interventions with hyperactive boys: A follow-up study. Child Development, 49, 247–250.

Burns, D. D. (1999). *Feeling good: The new mood therapy.* New York: Avon Books.

Burks, H. F. (1955). *A study of the organic basis for behavioral deviations in school children.* Unpublished doctoral dissertation, University of Southern California, Los Angeles.

Burks, H. F. (1957a). The effect of brain pathology on learning. *Exceptional Children, 24,* 186–194.

Burks, H. F. (1957b). *A study of organic factors influencing reading success among fourth grade children.* Research report submitted to Elizabeth McCormick Memorial Fund.

Burks, H. F. (1960). The hyperkinetic child. *Journal of Exceptional Children, 27,* 18–26.

Burks, H. F. (1961, June). The hyperkinetic child. *Journal of Exceptional Children, 27,* 18–26.

Burks, H. F. (1962). *A special class for behavior problem children showing symptoms of brain impairment.* Unpublished manuscript, Office of Los Angeles County Superintendent of Schools.

Burks, H. F. (1964a). Effects of amphetamine therapy on hyperkinetic children. *Archives of General Psychiatry, 11,* 604–609.

Burks, H. F. (1964b). *Guiding the non-motivated, non-aggressive, underachieving child.* Unpublished manuscript, Office of Los Angeles County Superintendent of Schools.

Burks, H. F. (1965). *The incidence of a hyperkinetic syndrome among mentally retarded children and its relation to age, sex, and intelligence.* Unpublished manuscript, Office of Los Angeles County Superintendent of Schools.

Burks, H. F. (1968a). *Academic readiness scale.* Huntington Beach, CA: Arden Press.

Burks, H. F. (1968b). *Burks' behavior rating scale for organic brain dysfunction.* Huntington Beach, CA: Arden Press.

Burks, H. F. (1968c). Diagnostic implications of the electroencephalogram for behavior problem children. *Journal of School Psychology, 6,* 284–292.

Burks, H. F. (1968d). Discipline methods employed by some teachers of neurologically handicapped children. *Psychology in the Schools, 5*(2), 141–145.

Burks, H. F. (1968e). *The school attitude survey.* Huntington Beach, CA: Arden Press.

Burks, H. F. (1972). *Home and school work together.* Huntington Beach, CA: Arden Press.

Burks, H. F. (1973). *Chemotherapy for behavior problem children.* Huntington Beach, CA: Arden Press.

Burks, H. F. (1977a). *Burks' behavior rating scales.* Los Angeles: Western Psychological Services.

Burks, H. F. (1977b). *Burks' behavior rating scales: Preschool and kindergarten.* Los Angeles: Western Psychological Services.

Burks, H. F. (1985). *Diagnosis and remediation of learning and behavior problems in children: A handbook.* Los Angeles: Western Psychological Services.

Burks, H. F. (1994). *The imagine game.* Los Angeles: Western Psychological Services.

Burks, H. F. (1999). Revised Handbook. *Diagnosis and remediation of learning and behavior problems.* Los Angeles: Western Psychological Services.

Burks, H. F. (2001). Using the imagine game as a projective device. In R. Schaefer & E. R. Reid (Eds.), *Game play* (pp. 59–65). New York: John Wiley and Sons.

Burks, H. F. (2006a). *Burks' behavior rating scales II* (Rev. Ed.). Los Angeles: Western Psychological Services.

Burks, H. F. (2006b). *101 character profiles: A writer's reference guide.* Authorhouse.

Burns, D. D. (1999). *Feeling good: The new mood therapy.* New York: Avon Books.

Busch, B. (1993). Attention deficits: Current concepts, controversies, management, and approaches to classroom instruction. *Annals of Dyslexia, 43,* 5–25.

Caille, P. (1982). The evaluation phase of systematic family therapy. *Journal of Marital and Family Therapy, 8,* 29–39.

Camp, B. W. (1977). Verbal mediation in young aggressive boys. *Journal of Abnormal Psychology, 86,* 145–183.

Carpenter, C. (1972). *Thanks, doctor.* Whittier, CA: RDC Publishers.

Carter, E. N., & Reynolds, J. N. (1976). Imitation in the treatment of a hyperactive child. *Psychotherapy: Theory, Research and Practice, 13,* 160–161.

Cassidy, A. M., & Vukelich, C. (1977). The effects of group size on kindergarten children's listening comprehension performance. *Psychology in the Schools, 14,* 449–455.

Cattell, R. B., & Barton, K. (1971). Personality and IQ measures as predictors of school achievement. *Journal of Educational Psychology, 63,* 398–404.

Chansky, N. M. (1964). Progress of promoted and repeating grade 1 failures. *Journal of Experimental Education, 32,* 225–237.

Chapman, R. B. (1978). Academic and behavioral problems of boys in elementary school. *Counseling Psychologist, 7,* 37–40.

Chavez, E. L., & Gonzales-Singh, E. (1980). Hispanic assessment: A case study. *Professional Psychology, 11,* 163–168.

Chelinsky, R. (2005). *The perfectionist.* New York: Gotham Books.

Clarizio, H. F., & McCoy, G. F. (1976). *Behavior disorders in children.* New York: Thomas Crowell.

Clements, J. E. (1978). The yes-no graph: A parent involvement tool. *Academic Therapy, 13,* 323–328.

Coats, K. I. (1979). Cognitive self-instruction training approach for reducing disruptive behavior of young children. *Psychological Reports, 44,* 127–134.

Cobb, J. A. (1972). Relationship of discrete classroom behaviors to fourth-grade academic achievement. *Journal of Educational Psychology, 63,* 74–80.

Coleman, J. C. (1979). *Contemporary psychology and effective behavior.* Palo Alto, CA: Scott Foresman.

Collum, J. (1971). *Identity diffusion and the borderline maneuver.* Washington, DC: American Psychological Association.

Colter, S. (1995, July 12). Differences in male and female brains. *San Diego Union,* pp. 18, 42.

Conley, J. J. (1980). Family configuration as an etiological factor in alcoholism. *Journal of Abnormal Psychology, 89,* 670–673.

Conners, C. (1969). A teacher rating scale for use in drug studies with children. *American Journal of Psychiatry, 126,* 152–156.

Conners, C. (1970). Symptom patterns in hyperkinetic, neurotic, and normal children. *Child Development, 41,* 667–682.

Conners, C. (1971). Cortical visual-evoked response in children with learning disorders. *Psychophysiology, 7,* 418–428.

Cotter, K. C. (1967). First-grade failure: Diagnosis, treatment and prevention. *Childhood Education, 44,* 172–176.

Coulter, A., & Morrow, H. (1978). *The concept and measurement of adaptive behavior.* New York: Grune and Stratton.

Cowan, G., & Inskeep, R. (1978). Commitments to help among the disabled-advantaged. *Personality and Social Psychology Bulletin, 4,* 92–96.

Cronbach, L. J. (1954). *Educational psychology.* New York: Schocken Books.

Crow, G. A. (1978). *Children at risk.* New York: Schocken Books.

Csikszentmihalyi, M., & Larson, R. (1978). Intrinsic rewards in school crime. *Crime and Delinquency, 24,* 322–335.

Curtiss, G., Feczko, M. D., & Marohn, R. C. (1978). Rorschach differences in normal and delinquent white male adolescents: A discriminant function analysis. *Journal of Youth and Adolescence, 8,* 379–392.

Cutler, B. C. (1993). *You, your child, and "special education": A guide to making the system work.* Baltimore: Brookes.

Daley, D. C. (1991). *Kicking addictive habits once and for all.* New York: Lexington Books.

Dansky, J. L. (1980). Cognitive consequences of sociodramatic play and exploration training for economically disadvantaged preschools. *Journal of Child Psychology and Psychiatry, 21,* 47–58.

Davidson, H. H., & Lang, G. (1960). Children's perceptions of their teacher's feelings toward them related to self-perception, school achievement and behavior. *Journal of Experimental Education, 29,* 107–118.

Davis, J. M. (1976). Recent developments in the treatment of schizophrenia. *Psychiatric Annals, 6,* 71–111.

Day, R. D. (2002). *Introduction to family processes.* Matwah, NJ: Lawrence Erlbaum Associates, Inc.

De Silva, P., & Rachman, S. (1992). *Obsessive-compulsive disorder: The facts.* Springfield, IL: Charles C. Thomas.

Deffenbacher, J. L. (1978). Worry, emotionality, and task-generated interference in test anxiety: An empirical test of attentional theory. *Journal of Educational Psychology, 70,* 248–254.

DeFilippis, N. A., & Derby, R. (1980). Application of predictive measures of reading disability in a culturally disadvantaged sample. *Journal of Learning Disabilities, 13,* 456–458.

DeLoach, I. F. (1981). LD teachers' perceptions of severe learning disabled students. *Learning Disabled Quarterly, 4,* 343–358.

Dennison, S. J. (1993). *Diagnosing chemical dependence: A practical guide for the health care professional.* Springfield, IL: Charles C. Thomas.

Diaddigo, M., & Dickie, R. F. (1978). The use of contingency contracting in eliminating inappropriate classroom behaviors. *Education and Treatment of Children, 1,* 17–23.

Dickie, R. F., & Finegan, S. (1977). The long-term effects of self-recording on academic behavior rate in an emotionally disturbed boy. *SALT: School Application of Learning Theory, 9,* 38–48.

Didato, S. V. (1969). Recent trends in juvenile delinquency. *Mental Hygiene, 53*(4), 34–39.

Dirks, J. F., Schraa, J. C., Brown, E. L., & Kinsman, R. A. (1980). Psycho-maintenance in asthma: Hospitalization rates and financial impact. *British Journal of Medical Psychology, 53,* 349–354.

Doob, L. W. (1990). *Hesitation: Impulsivity and reflection.* New York: Greenwood Press.

Dougherty, E. H., & Dougherty, A. (1977). A daily report card: A simplified and flexible package for classroom behavior management. *Psychology in the Schools, 14,* 191–195.

Dowling, C. (1991). *You mean I don't have to feel this way?* New York: Scribner.

Doyal, G. T., & Forsyth, R. (1972). The effect of test anxiety, intelligence, and sex on children's problem solving ability. *Journal of Experimental Education, 41*(2), 23–26.

Drabman, R. S., & Creedon, D. L. (1979). Beat the buzzer. *Child Behavior Therapy, 1,* 295–296.

Dribben, E., & Brabender, V. (1979). The effect of mood inducement upon audience receptiveness. *Journal of Social Psychology, 107,* 135–136.

Duke, L. A., & Epstein, L. H. (1975). Oral overcorrection: Side effects and extended applications. *Journal of Experimental Child Psychology, 84,* 496–511.

Duncan, B. L., & Rock, J. W. (1991). *Overcoming relationship impasses: Ways to initiate change when your partner won't help.* New York: Plenum Press.

Dweck, C. S. (1986). Motivational processes affecting learning. *American Psychologist, 41,* 1040–1048.

Dyer, W. (2006). *The power of intention.* Carlsbad, CA: Hay House.

Eastman, B. G., & Rasbury, W. C. (1981). Cognitive self-instruction for the control of impulsive classroom behavior: Ensuring the treatment package. *Journal of Abnormal Child Psychology, 9,* 381–387.

Elliot, R., Barrish, H., Hale, T., & Wessman, K. (1977). A field study of a token classroom. *European Journal of Behavioural Analysis and Modification, 1,* 257–271.

Emerson, G. W., & Strauss, J. S. (1972). Acne and acne care. *Archives of Dermatology, 105,* 407–411.

Englander, E. K. (2001). *Understanding Violence.* Mahwah, NJ: Lawrence Erlbaum Associates, Inc.

Enson, D. (1995, August 24). Teacher mistreatment of pupils. *Los Angeles Times,* p. E6.

Epstein, M. H., Cullinan, D., & Sternberg, L. (1977). Impulsive cognitive tempo in severe and mild learning disabled children. *Psychology in the Schools, 14,* 290–294.

Erez, E. (1980). Planning of crime and the criminal career: Official and hidden offenses. *Journal of Criminal Law and Criminology, 71,* 73–76.

Eron, L. D. (1980). Prescription for reduction of aggression. *American Psychologist, 35*(3), 244–252.

Eysenck, H. J., & Eysenck, S. B. (1969). *Eysenck Personality Inventory.* San Diego, CA: Educational and Industrial Testing Service.

Eysenck, S. B., & Eysenck, H. J. (1977). The place of impulsiveness in a dimensional system of personality description. *British Journal of Social and Clinical Psychology, 16,* 57–68.

Fadely, J. L., & Hosler, V. N. (1992). *Attentional deficit disorder in children and adolescents.* Springfield, IL: Charles C. Thomas.

Farnham-Diggory, S. (1992). *The learning-disabled child.* Cambridge, MA: Harvard University Press.

Ferguson, G. (1999). *Shouting at the sky: Troubled teens and the promise of the wild.* New York: St. Martin's Press.

Feshbach, S. (1961). The stimulating versus cathartic effects of a vicarious aggressive activity. *Journal of Abnormal and Social Psychology, 63,* 381–385.

Fink, M. B. (1962). Self-concept as it relates to academic underachievement. *California Journal of Educational Research, 13,* 57–62.

Finkelstein, N. W., Gallagher, J. J., & Farran, D. C. (1980). Attentiveness and responsiveness to auditory stimuli of children at risk for mental retardation. *American Journal of Mental Deficiency, 85,* 135–144.

Flett, G. L., & Hewitt, P. L. (Eds.). (2002). *Perfectionism: Theory, research, and treatment.* Washington, DC: American Psychological Association.

Floyd, W. T., & Hughes, H. (1980). A systems intervention procedure for the management of aggressive behavior. *Exceptional Child, 27,* 99–105.

Fowles, D. C., Sutker, P. B., & Goodman, S. H. (1994). *Special focus on psychopathy and antisocial personality: A developmental perspective.* New York: Springer.

Frankel, S. (1977). The management aspect of psychotherapy with aggressive children. *Child Psychiatry and Human Development, 7,* 169–185.

Freund, J. H., Bradley, R. H., & Caldwell, B. M. (1979). The home environment in the assessment of learning disabilities. *Learning Disability Quarterly, 2,* 39–51.

Friedlander, K. (1947). *The psychoanalytic approach to juvenile delinquency.* New York: International Universities Press.

Friedman, R. (1973). *Family roots of school learning and behavior disorders.* Springfield, IL: Charles C. Thomas.

Frierson, E., & Barbe, W. (1967). *Educating children with learning disabilities.* New York: Appleton-Century-Crofts.

Frosch, J. (1977). The relation between acting out and disorders of impulse control. *Psychiatry, 40,* 295–314.

Fuqua, R. W., Bartsch, T. W., & Phye, G. D. (1975). An investigation of the relationship between cognitive tempo and creativity in preschool-age children. *Child Development, 46,* 779–782.

Garbarino, J. (1992). *Children and families in the social environment.* New York: Aldine de Gruyter.

Gellene, D. (2007, March 29). Antidepressants may not help fight bipolar disorder. *Los Angeles Times,* p. A10.

George, M. M. (1978). An introduction of borderline personality organization in the adolescent. *Forum, 13,* 1–8.

Getman, G. N. (1957). *How to develop your child's intelligence.* Luverne, MN: Author.

Getsinger, S. H., & Leon, R. (1979). Impulsivity, temporal perspective, and posthospital adjustment of neuropsychiatric patients. *Journal of Psychology, 103,* 221–225.

Gladwell, M. (1999, February 15). Running from Ritalin. *The New Yorker,* 80–84.

Glasbourg, R., & Aboud, F. E. (1981). A developmental perspective on the study of depression: Children's evaluative reactions to sadness. *Developmental Psychology, 17,* 195–202.

Glavin, J. P., Quay, H. C., Annesley, F. R., & Werry, J. S. (1971). An experimental resource room for behavior problem children. *Exceptional Children, 38,* 131–137.

Gleuck, S., & Gleuck, E. (1952). *Delinquents in the making.* New York: Harper and Row.

Goldberg, C. (1991). *On understanding shame.* Northvale, NJ: Jason Aronson.

Goldberg, J. C. (1993). *The dark side of love: The positive side of our negative feelings—anger, jealousy, and hate.* New York: Putnam.

Goldfarb, W., Braunstein, P., & Lorgo, I. A. (1956). A study of speech patterns in a group of schizophrenic children. *American Journal of Orthopsychiatry, 26,* 544–555.

Goldfarb, W., Goldfarb, N., & Scholl, H. (1966). The speech of mothers with schizophrenic children. *American Journal of Psychiatry, 122,* 1200–1227.

Goldfried, M. R., & Davison, G. C. (1976). *Clinical behavior therapy.* New York: Holt, Rinehart and Winston.

Goldstein, S., & Goldstein, M. (1992). *Hyperactivity: Why won't my child pay attention?* New York: Wiley & Sons.

Goodenough, F. (1926). *Measurement of intelligence by drawings*. Chicago: World Book.

Goodman, W. K., Rudorfer, M. V., & Maser, J. D. (2000). *Obsessive-compulsive disorder: Contemporary issues in treatment*. Mahwah, NJ: Lawrence Erlbaum Associates, Inc.

Goodyear, P., & Hynd, G. W. (1992). Attention-deficit disorder with (ADD/H) and without (ADD/WO) hyperactivity: Behavioral and neuropsychological differentiation. *Journal of Clinical Child Psychology, 21*, 273–305.

Gordon, M. (1991). *Jumpin' Johnny, get back to work: A child's guide to ADHD/hyperactivity*. DeWitt, NY: GSI Publications.

Gordon, M. (1992). *My brother's a world class pain: A sibling's guide to ADHD/hyperactivity*. DeWitt, NY: GSI Publications.

Gordon, M., & Grantham, R. J. (1979). Helper preference in disadvantaged students. *Journal of Counseling Psychology, 26*, 337–343.

Gottman, J. M. (1979). *Marital interaction: Experimental investigations*. New York: Academic Press.

Greene, R. W. (2001). *The explosive child*. New York: Harper Collins.

Greenhill, L. L., & Osman, B. B. (1991). *Ritalin: Theory and patient management*. New York: Mary Ann Liebert.

Grimes, J. W., & Allensmith, W. (1961). Compulsivity, anxiety, and school achievement. *Merill-Palmer Quarterly, 7*, 247–271.

Grunebaum, M. G. (1962). Fathers of sons with primary learning inhibition. *American Journal of Orthospychiatry, 32*, 462–473.

Gudjonsson, G. H. (1980). The relationship between the EPI extraversion score and impulsiveness on a perceptual-motor task. *Personality and Individual Differences, 1*, 177–180.

Guerney, B., Coufal, J., & Vogelsong, E. (1981). Relationship versus a traditional approach to therapeutic/preventative/enrichment parent-adolescent programs. *Journal of Consulting and Clinical Psychology, 49*, 927–939.

Gupta, B. S., & Nagpal, M. (1978). Impulsivity/sociability and reinforcement in verbal operant conditioning. *British Journal of Psychology, 69*, 203–206.

Hales, D., & Hales, R. E. (1996, January 7). Finally, I know what's wrong. *Parade Magazine*, 10–11.

Hall, R. V., Lund, D., & Jackson, D. (1968). Effects of teacher attention on study behavior. *Journal of Applied Behavior Analysis, 1*, 1–12.

Hallahan, D. P., Marshall, K. J., & Lloyd, J. W. (1981). Self-recording during group instruction: Effects on attention to task. *Learning Disability Quarterly, 4*, 407–414.

Hamache, D. E. (1973). *Motivation in teaching and learning*. Washington, DC: National Education Association.

Haney, W., & Gold, M. (1973, April). The juvenile delinquent nobody knows. *Psychology Today, 7*(4), 49–55.

Harper, J. M., & Hoopes, M. H. (1990). *Uncovering shame: An approach integrating individuals and their family system*. New York: Norton.

Harrell, W. A. (1979). Aggression against a remorseful wrongdoer: The effects of self-blame and concern for the victim. *Journal of Social Psychology, 107*, 267–275.

Harris, A. (1979). An empirical test of the situation specificity/consistency of aggressive behavior. *Child Behavior Therapy, 1*, 257–270.

Harris, J. R. (1999). *The nurture assumption: Why children turn out the way they do*. New York: Touchstone.

Harris, T. L. (1964). Summary of investigations relating to reading. *Journal of Educational Research, 57*, 283–327.

Hartup, W. W., & Smothergill, N. L. (Eds.). (1966). *The young child*. Washington, DC: Reviews of Research, National Association for the Education of Young Children.

Hayduk, A. W. (1978). Peer selecting modeling: A rapid treatment for aggressive-disruptive behavior. *Canadian Counsellor, 12*, 123–127.

Hayes, E. J., Cunningham, G. K., & Robinson, J. B. (1977). Counseling focus: Are parents necessary? *Elementary School Guidance and Counseling, 12*, 8–14.

Hayes, M. L. (1993). *You don't outgrow it: Living with learning disabilities*. Novato, CA: Academic Therapy.

Haywood, H. C., Meyers, C. E., & Switsky, H. N. (1982). Mental retardation. *Annual Review of Psychology, 33*, 309–342.

Hebben, N. A. (1981). Attentional dysfunction in poor readers. *Journal of Reading Disabilities, 14*, 287–290.

Hechtman, L. (1989). Attention-deficit hyperactivity disorder in adolescence and adulthood: An updated follow-up. *Psychiatric Annals, 19*, 597–603.

Heffernan, H. (1965). New opportunities for preschool children. *Childhood Education, 41*, 227–230.

Heil, J., Barclay, A., & Endres, J. M. (1978). A factor analytic study of the WPPSI scores of educationally deprived and normal children. *Psychological Reports, 42*, 727–730.

Hendlin, S. J. (1992). *When good enough is never enough: Escaping the perfection trap*. New York: Putnam.

Herbert, M. (1989). *Discipline: A positive guide for parents.* Oxford, England: Basil Blackwell.

Herrera, A. E., & Sanchez, V. C. (1980). Descriptive group psychotherapy: A successful application in the treatment of low-income Spanish-speaking clients. *Psychotherapy: Theory, Research and Practice, 17,* 169–174.

Hicks, E., & Hicks, J. (2005). *Ask and it is given.* Carlsbad, CA: Hay House.

Hill, E. L. (1978). Goal analysis for behavior problem learners. *Academic Therapy, 13,* 289–299.

Hintgen, J., Sanders, B., & DeMeyer, M. (1963, August). *Shaping cooperative responses in early childhood schizophrenics.* Paper presented at the meeting of the American Psychological Association, Philadelphia.

Hirschfeld, R. M. (1976). Dependency—self-esteem—chemical depression. *Journal of the American Academy of Psychoanalysis, 4,* 373–388.

Hirschfeld, R. M. (1977). A measure of interpersonal dependency. *Journal of Personality Assessment, 41,* 610–618.

Hobbs, N. (1982). *The troubled and troubling child.* San Francisco: Jossey-Bass.

Hobbs, S. A., & Forehand, R. (1977). Important parameters in the use of timeout with children: A re-examination. *Journal of Behavior Therapy and Experimental Psychiatry, 8,* 365–370.

Hobbs, S. A., & Lahey, B. B. (1977). The behavioral approach to learning disabled children. *Journal of Clinical Child Psychology, 6,* 10–14.

Hoffer, A., Goettsche, R., & Linden, F. (1980). A psychoanalytic approach to a therapeutic impasse with an impulsive adolescent: Permission to speak the unspeakable. *American Journal of Psychiatry, 137,* 1404–1409.

Hoffman, M. L. (1977). Moral internalization: Current theory and research. In L. Berkowitz (Ed.), *Advance in experimental social psychology* (Vol. 10). New York: Academic Press.

Hoggard, J. K. (1957). Readiness is the best prevention. *Education, 77,* 523–527.

Hollander, E., & Stein, D. J. (Eds). (2005). *Clinical manual of impulse-control disorders.* Washington, DC: American Psychological Association.

Holt, M. M., & Hobbes, T. R. (1979). The effects of token reinforcement, feedback and response on standardized test performance. *Behavior Research and Therapy, 17,* 81–83.

Hooper, S. R., Hynd, G. W., & Mattison, R. E. (Eds.). (1992). *Developmental disorders: Diagnostic criteria and clinical assessment.* Hillsdale, NJ: Erlbaum.

Hormuth, S. (1977). Impulse control and some personality dimensions of juvenile delinquents and non-delinquents. *Psychologische Beitrage, 19,* 350–354.

Horn, W. F., Wagner, A. E., & Ialongo, N. (1989). Sex differences in school-age children with pervasive attention deficit hyperactivity disorder. *Journal of Abnormal Child Psychology, 17*(1), 109–125.

Horney, K. (1939). *New ways in psycholanalysis.* New York: W. W. Norton.

Howard, M. P., & Anderson, R. J. (1978). Early identification of potential school dropouts: A literature review. *Child Welfare, 57,* 221–231.

Howe, M. J. A. (1990). *Sense and nonsense about hothouse children: A practical guide for parents and teachers.* Leicester, England: British Psychological Society.

Huffington, A. (2007). *On becoming fearless.* Boston: Little, Brown.

Humphries, T., Kinsbourne, M., & Swanson, J. (1978). Stimulant effects on cooperation and social interaction between children and their mothers. *Journal of Child Psychology and Psychiatry and Allied Disciplines, 19,* 13–26.

Iannotti, R. J. (1978). Effect of role-taking experiences on role taking, empathy, altruism, and aggression. *Developmental Psychology, 14,* 119–124.

Ikegami, T. (1979). Cognitive style in children: The relation between reflection-impulsivity and Rorschach scores. *Psychologia: An International Journal of Psychology in the Orient, 22,* 207–221.

Ilg, F. L., & Ames, L. D. (1965). *Child behavior: From birth to ten.* New York: Barnes & Noble.

Irwin, E. C. (1977). Play, fantasy, and symbols: Drama with emotionally disturbed children. *Americal Journal of Psychotherapy, 31,* 426–436.

Irwin, M., Belendiuk, K., McClosky, K., & Freedman, D. X. (1981). Tryptophan metabolism in children with attentional disorder. *American Journal of Psychotherapy, 31,* 426–436.

Janeksela, G. M., & Deming, R. R. (1976). Police-minority conflict and conflict resolution. *International Journal of Group Tensions, 6,* 45–56.

Jason, L. A. (1977). A behavioral approach in enhancing disadvantaged children's academic abilities. *American Journal of Community Psychology, 5,* 413–421.

Jaynes, J. H., & Rugg, C. A. (1988). *Adolescents, alcohol, and drugs: A practical guide for those who work with young people.* Springfield, IL: Charles C. Thomas.

Jenkins, R. L. (1973). *Behavior disorders of childhood and adolescence.* Springfield, IL: Charles C. Thomas.

Johnson, D. S. (1981). Naturally acquired learned helplessness: The relationship of school failure to achievement behavior, attributions, and self-concept. *Journal of Educational Psychology, 73,* 174–180.

Johnson, J., & O'Neill, C. (1999). *How do I feel about being angry.* Brookfield, CT: Millbrook Press.

Jones, C. (1991). *Sourcebook for children with attention deficit disorder in early childhood.* Tucson, AZ: Communication Skill Builder.

Jones, C. (1992). *Enhancing self-concepts and achievement of mildly handicapped students: Learning disabled, mild mentally retarded, and behavior disordered.* Springfield, IL: Charles C. Thomas.

Jordan, D., & Goldberg, P. (2001). *A guidebook for parents of children with emotional or behavioral disorders.* Minneapolis, MN: Pacer.

Jordan, M. D. (2005). *Blessing same-sex unions.* Chicago: University of Chicago Press.

Josselyn, I. M. (1950). Treatment of the emotionally immature child in an institution framework. *American Journal of Orthopsychiatry, 20,* 397–410.

Juliano, D. B. (1977). Reflection-impulsivity and concept learning in disadvantaged and middle class children. *Journal of Psychology, 96,* 103–110.

Kagan, J. D., & Moss, H. A. (1962). *Birth to maturity.* New York: Wiley.

Kagan, J. D., Sontag, L. W., Baker, C. T., & Nelson, V. L. (1958). Personality and IQ change. *Journal of Abnormal and Social Psychology, 56,* 251–266.

Kane, J. M., & Lieberman, J. A. (Eds.). (1992). *Adverse effects of psychotropic drugs.* New York: Guilford Press.

Kanner, L. (1944). Early infantile autism. *Journal of Pediatrics, 25,* 211–217.

Kaufman, I., Herrick, J., Willer, L, Frank, T., & Heims, L. (1959). Four types of defenses in mothers and fathers of schizophrenic children. *American Journal of Othropsychiatry, 29,* 460–472.

Kazdin, A. E. (1979). Advances in child behavior therapy: Applications and implications. *American Journal of Orthopsychiatry, 29,* 460–472.

Kazdin, A. E. (1986). *Treatment of antisocial behavior in children and adolescents.* Homewood, IL: Dorsey.

Keen, S. (1986). *Faces of the enemy: Reflections of the hostile imagination.* San Francisco: Harper & Row.

Keith, C. R. (1981). A paradoxical effect of guilt in the psychotherapy of children. *American Journal of Psychotherapy, 35,* 16–26.

Kelly, D. H. (1977). Labelling and the consequences of wearing a delinquent label in a school setting. *Education, 97,* 371–380.

Kelly, K. (1994). The elusive survey of sexuality. *Journal of Contemporary Psychology, 39*(9), 831–832.

Kendall, P. C., & Finch, A. J. (1979). Analysis of changes in verbal behavior following a cognitive-behavioral treatment for impulsivity. *Journal of Abnormal Child Psychology, 7,* 455–463.

Kennedy, L. D., & Halinsky, R. D. (1975). Measuring attitudes: An extra dimension. *Journal of Reading, 2,* 518–523.

Kephart, N. (1965). *The slow learner in the classroom.* Columbus, OH: C. E. Merrill Books.

Kermoian, S. B. (1962). Teacher appraisal of first grade readiness. *Elementary English, 39,* 196–200.

Kernberg, O. (1975). *Borderline conditions and pathological narcissism.* New York: Jason Aronson.

Kessler, J. (1966). *Psychopathology of childhood.* Englewood Cliffs, NJ: Prentice-Hall.

Kint, M. G. (1978). Schizophrenia is a family affair: Problems of families coping with schizophrenia. *Journal of Orthomolecular Psychiatry, 7,* 236–246.

Kirby, E. A., & Grimley, L. K. (1986). *Understanding and treating attention deficit disorder.* New York: Pergamon Press.

Kiyosaki, R. T. (2002). *Rich dad, poor dad.* London: Time Warner.

Klein, S. A., & Deffenbacher, J. L. (1977). Relaxation and exercise for hyperactive impulsive children. *Perceptual and Motor Skills, 45,* 1159–1162.

Kluger, J. (2006, July 10). The new science of siblings. *Time, 168*(2), 46–55.

Knapcyk, D. R. (1979). Diet control in the management of behavior disorders. *Behavioral Disorders, 5,* 2–9.

Kneedler, R. D., & Hallahan, D. P. (1981). Self-monitoring of an on-task behavior with learning-disabled children: Current studies and direction. *Exceptional Education Quarterly, 2,* 73–82.

Koenig, L.G., et al. (Eds.). (2004). *From child sexual abuse to adult Sexual risk: Trauma, revictimization and intervention.* Washington, DC: American Psychological Association.

Kohn, M., & Rosman, B. L. (1974). Social-emotional, cognitive, and demographic determinants of poor school achievement: Implications for a strategy of intervention. *Journal of Educational Psychology, 66*(2), 267–276.

Kozial, L. F., & Stout, C. E. (1994). *The neuropsychology of mental disorders: A practical guide.* Springfield, IL: Charles C. Thomas.

Krupski, A. (1979). Are retarded children more distractible? Observational analysis of retarded and nonretarded children's classroom behavior. *American Journal of Mental Deficiency, 84,* 1–10.

Krynicki, V. E. (1978). Cerebral dysfunction in repetitively assaultive adolescents. *Journal of Nervous and Mental Disease, 166,* 59–67.

Kuczen, B. (1982). *Don't let your child become a victim.* New York: Delacorte Press.

Kuhlberg, J. M. (1974). The school psychologist and the emotionally disturbed child. In B. Saunders (Ed.), *Approaches with emotionally disturbed children* (pp. 65–79). New York: Exposition Press.

Kumchy, C. I., & Sayer, L. A. (1980). Locus of control in a delinquent adolescent population. *Psychological Reports, 46,* 1307–1310.

Lahey, B. B., Green, K. D., & Forehand, R. (1980). On the independence of ratings of hyperactivity, conduct problems, and attention deficits in children: A multiple regression analysis. *Journal of Consulting and Clinical Psychology, 48,* 566–574.

Lahey, B., & Carlson, C. L. (1991). Validity of the diagnostic category of attention-deficit disorder without hyperactivity: A review of the literature. *Journal of Learning Disabilities, 24,* 110–120.

Landesman, S., & Ramey, C. (1989). Experimental psychology and mental retardation: Integrating scientific principles with treatment practices. *American Psychologist 44*(2), 152–161.

Langhorne, J. E., Paternite, C., & Loney, J. (1979). An alternative teacher consultation model: A case study. *School Psychology Digest, 8,* 235–239.

Lanning, F., & Robbins, R. (1966, August/September). Chart of development. *Instructor,* 130–132.

Lee, D. Y., & Cottreau, R. (1979). Training in conceptual tempo: Its effects on mentally retarded children's responding style to questionnaire items. *Psychological Reports, 44,* 198.

Lee, J. M., & Lee, D. M. (1958). *The child and his development.* New York: Appleton-Century-Crofts.

Leff, R. (1968). Behavior modification and the psychosis of childhood: A review. *Psychological Bulletin, 69,* 396–409.

Lesiak, J. (1978). *The reflection-impulsivity dimension and reading ability.* Reading World, 17, 333–339.

Levi, A. M., Buskila, M., & Gerzi, S. (1977). Benign neglect: Reducing fights among siblings. *Journal of Individual Psychology, 33,* 240–245.

Levy, D. (1943). *Maternal overprotection.* New York: Columbia University Press.

Lewis, L. A., & McAnulty, B. H. (1980). The three faces of interviewing: Hints for minority applicants seeking employment. *Journal of Non-White Concerns in Personality and Guidance, 8,* 91–98.

Licht, B. G., & Kistner, J. A. (1986). Motivational problems of learning-disabled children: Individual differences and their implications for treatment. In J. K. Torgesen & B. Y. L. Wong (Eds.), *Psychological and educational perspectives on learning disabilities* (pp. 93–108). New York: Academic Press.

Liddle, G. P., Rockwell, R. E., & Sacadet, E. (1967). *Education improvement for the disadvantaged in an elementary setting.* Springfield, IL: Charles C. Thomas.

Lifton, N., & Smolen, E. (1966). Group psychotherapy with schizophrenic children. *International Journal of Psychotherapy, 16,* 23–41.

Light, P. C. (2005). *The four pillars of high performance.* New York: McGraw-Hill.

Lilly, M. (1971). Improving social acceptance of low sociometric status, low achieving students. *Exceptional Children, 37,* 341–347.

Linehan, M. M. (1993). *Cognitive-behavioral treatment of borderline personality disorder.* New York: Guilford Press.

Lippitt, R., Fox, R., & Schmuck, R. (1967). Innovating classroom practices to support achievement motivation and ego-development. In E. M. Brower & W. G. Hollister (Eds.), *Behavioral science frontiers in education* (pp. 54–62). New York: Wiley.

Livingston, R. H., Kom, T. A., & McAlees, D. C. (1982). Alternative strategies in vocational rehabilitation. In C. R. Reynolds & T. B. Gutkin (Eds.), *The handbook of school psychology* (pp. 132–151). New York: John Wiley & Sons.

Locorto, C. (1991). *Sense and nonsense about IQ: The case for uniqueness.* New York: Praeger.

Loo, R. (1979). Role of primary personality factors in the perception of traffic signs and driver violations and accidents. *Accident Analysis and Prevention, 11,* 125–127.

Loos, F. M., Williams, K. P., & Bailey, J. S. (1977). A multi-element analysis of the effect of teacher aides in an "open-style" classroom. *Journal of Applied Behavior Analysis, 20,* 437–448.

Lothstein, L. M. (1980). The adolescent gender dysphoric patient: An approach to treatment and management. *Journal of Pediatric Psychology, 5,* 93–109.

Lovaas, O. I., Freitag, G., Gold, V., & Kassorla, I. (1963). Experimental studies in childhood schizophrenia. *Journal of Experimental Psychology, 66,* 67–73.

Lowy, C. (2007, June 3). Poll: 30 percent of families have problem children. *The Desert Sun.*

Lozoff, B. (1989). Nutrition and behavior. *American Psychologist, 44*(2), 98–108.

MacCrimmon, D. J., Cleghorn, J. M., Asarnow, R. F., & Steffy, R. A. (1980). Children at risk for schizophrenia: Clinical and attentional characteristics. *Archives of General Psychiatry, 37,* 671–674.

Madden, R., Gardner, E. F., Rudman, H. C., & Kelley, T. L. (1964). *Stanford Achievement Test: Reading tests.* New York: Harcourt Brace Jovanovich.

Mahler, M. S. (1975). *The psychological birth of the human infant: Symbiosis and individuation.* New York: Basic Books.

Mahler, M. S., Furer, M., & Settlage, C. F. (1959). Severe emotional disturbances in childhood psychosis. In S. Arieti (Ed.), *American handbook of psychiatry* (pp. 82–102). New York: Basic Books.

Main, G. C., & Munro, B. C. (1977). A token reinforcement program in the public junior-high school. *Journal of Applied Behavior Analysis, 10,* 93–94.

Mainville, F., & Friedman, R. J. (1976). Peer relations of hyperactive children. *Ontario Psychologist, 8,* 17–20.

Mallinger, A. E., & De Wyze, J. (1992). *Too perfect: When being in control gets out of control.* New York: Potter.

Mandel, P., & Marcus, S. I. (1988). *The Psychology of under-achievement.* New York: John Wiley & Sons.

Margolis, H., Brannigan, G. G., & Penner, W. J. (1978). Modification of impulsive visual discrimination performance. *Journal of Special Education, 12,* 29–35.

Margolis, H., Brannigan, G. G., & Poston, M. A. (1977). Modification of impulsivity: Implications for teaching. *Elementary School Journal, 77,* 231–237.

Marshall, J. R. (1994). *Social phobia: From shyness to stage fright.* New York: Basic Books.

Mash, E. J., & Barkley, R. A. (Eds.). (1989). *Treatment of childhood disorders.* New York: The Guilford Press.

Mason, R. L., Richmond, B. O., & Fleurant, L. B. (1976). *The emotionally troubled child.* Springfield, IL: Charles C. Thomas.

Masterson, J. (1972). *Treatment of the borderline adolescent.* New York: Wiley.

Maurer, R. G., & Stewart, M. A. (1980). Attention deficit without hyperactivity in a child psychiatry clinic. *Journal of Clinical Psychiatry, 41,* 232–233.

Maxym, C., & York, L. B. (2001). *Teens in turmoil.* New York: Penguin Books.

McClelland, D. C. (1961). *The achieving society.* Princeton, NJ: Van Nostrand.

McCombs, D., Filipczak, J., Friedman, R. M., & Wodarski, J. S. (1978). Long-term follow-up of behavior modification with high-risk adolescents. *Criminal Justice and Behavior, 5,* 21–34.

McCubbin, H. (1987). *Family assessment inventories for research and practice.* Madison: University of Wisconsin Family Stress, Coping and Health Project.

McElroy, M. A. (1981). A comparison of sport and nonsport occupational aspiration among disadvantaged youth. *Journal of Sport Psychology, 3,* 56–68.

McGraw, P. C. (2001). *Self matters: Creating your life from inside out.* New York: Simon & Schuster.

McGurk, B. J., Bolton, N., & Smith, M. (1978). Some psychological, educational and criminological variables related to recidivism in delinquent boys. *British Journal of Social and Clinical Psychology, 17,* 251–254.

Mednick, S. S., & Christiansen, K. O. (Eds.). (1977). *Biosocial bases of criminal behavior.* New York: Gardner Press.

Miller, G. R., & Stiff, J. B. (1993). *Deceptive communication.* Newberry Park, CA: Sage.

Miller, J. (1957). Academic achievement and social adjustment of children young for their grade placement. *Elementary School Journal, 57,* 32–38.

Miller, L. (1993). *What we call smart: A new narrative for intelligence and learning.* San Diego, CA: Singular Publishing Group.

Miller, S. M. (1979). Interrelationships between dependency, empathy, and sharing: A preliminary study. *Motivation and Emotion, 3,* 183–199.

Mills, B. C. (1972). *Understanding the young child and his curriculum: Selected readings.* New York: Macmillan.

Mitchell, S., & Rosa, P. (1981). Boyhood behavior problems as precursors of criminality: A fifteen-year follow-up study. *Journal of Child Psychology and Psychiatry and Allied Disciplines, 22,* 19–23.

Moore, D. R., Chamberlain, P., & Mukal, L. H. (1979). Children at risk for delinquency: A follow-up comparison of aggressive children and children who steal. *Journal of Abnormal Child Psychology, 7,* 345–355.

Mordock, J. B. (1979). The separation-individuation process and developmental disabilities. *Exceptional Children, 46,* 176–184.

Morrison, J. K. (1977). Relationship between psychiatric patients' attitude toward mental illness and attitudes of dependence. *Psychological Reports, 41,* 1194.

Moss, D. M. (1989). *Shelly the hyperactive turtle.* Kensington, MD: Woodbine House.

Mukherjee, S. C. (1972). A comparative study of the parents of low and high achieving students. *Dissertation Abstracts International, 32*(11-B), 6624-B.

Munday, M. (1999). *Mad isn't bad: A child's book about anger.* St. Meinrad, IN: One Caring Place/Abby Press.

Munro, A. (1999). *Delusional disorder: Paranoia and related disorders.* Cambridge: Cambridge University Press.

Musick, P. L. (1980). Creativity: Abreaction for the therapist. *Arts in Psychotherapy, 7,* 197–199.

Nadgrodsky, J. R. (1977). The LD/ED child: The practitioner's point of view from a Title I program perspective. *Behavioral Disorders, 2,* 152–156.

National Conference on Education of the Disadvantaged. (1966). *Title I, Elementary and Secondary Education Act.* Washington, DC.

Neki, J. S. (1976). An examination of the cultural relativism of dependence as a dynamic of social and therapeutic relationships: Socio-developmental. *British Journal of Medical Psychology, 49,* 1–10.

Neuland, C. (1995, October 11). No aggression without targets. *San Diego Union,* p. 31.

Neuville, M. B. (1991). *Sometimes I get all scribbly: Living with attention deficit/hyperactivity disorder.* La Crosse, WI: Crystal Press.

Nicholson, J. A. (2003). *Inventing personality.* Washington, DC: American Psychological Association.

O'Brien, C. P., & Jaffe, J. H. (1992). *Addictive states.* New York: Raven Press.

Ohbuchi, K., & Oku, Y. (1980). Aggressive behavior as a function of attack pattern and hostility. *Psychologia: An International Journal of Psychology in the Orient, 23,* 146–154.

Olin, J. (1996, May 2). Stressed kids. *San Diego Union,* pp. 8, 13.

Ollendick, T. H. (1974). Level of N achievement and persistence behavior in children. *Developmental Psychology, 10,* 457.

Ollendick, T. H., Finch, A. J., & Nelson, W. M. (1976). Correlates of question-asking by emotionally disturbed and normal children. *Psychological Reports, 38,* 923–929.

Olmeda, E. L. (1981). Testing linguistic minorities. *American Psychologist, 36,* 1078–1085.

Olweus, D. (1979). Stability of aggressive reaction in males: A review. *Psychological Bulletin, 86,* 852–875.

Osofsky, J. D. (1995). The effects of exposure to violence on young children. *American Psychologist, 50*(9), 782–788.

Parish, T. S., Ohlsen, R. L., & Parish, J. G. (1978). A look at mainstreaming in light of children's attitudes toward the handicapped. *Perceptual and Motor Skills, 46,* 1019–1021.

Parke, R. D., & Ladd, G. W. (1992). *Family-peer relationships: Modes of linkage.* Hillsdale, NJ: Erlbaum.

Parker, G., & Liscombe, P. (1980). The relevance of early parental experiences to adult dependency, hypochondriasis, and utilization of primary physicians. *British Journal of Medical Psychology, 53,* 355–363.

Parker, R. N. (1992). *Making the grade: An adolescent's struggle with ADD.* Plantation, FL: Impact Publications.

Parsons, G. E. (1957). Readiness for school. *Elementary School Journal, 57,* 272–275.

Paulsen, K. (1878). Reflection-impulsivity and level of maturity. *Journal of Psychology, 99,* 109–112.

Pearl, R. A., & Bryan, T. (1982). Mothers' attributions for their learning disabled child's success or failures. *Learning Disability Quarterly, 5,* 53–57.

Pelham, W. E. (1981). Attention deficits in hyperactive and learning-disabled children. *Exceptional Education Quarterly, 2,* 13–23.

Pelham, W. E. (1993). Pharmacotherapy for children with attention-deficit hyperactivity disorder. *School Psychology Review, 22,* 199–227.

Penifold, G. (1994, September 16). Genetics and temperament. *Desert Sun,* p. 16.

Pennington, B. F. (1991). *Reading disabilities: Genetic and neurological influences.* Norwell, MA: Kluwer Academic.

Peretti, F. (2000). *No more bullies: For those who wound or are wounded.* Nashville, TN: W. Publishing Group.

Peretti, F. (2001). *No more victims!* Nashville, TN: W. Publishing Group.

Perry, A. (2002). *Slaves of obsession.* New York: Ballantine Books.

Pevan, B. N. (1973). "Good news": Research on the nongraded elementary school. *Elementary School Journal, 73*(6), 333–341.

Phillips, K. S. (2001). *Purpose lies within: A motivational book for the heart and soul.* Decatur: Messenger Publishing.

Plante, G., Cote, H., Saint-Jean, M., & Pilic, I. (1978). Free painting as therapy for children from a disadvantaged urban area. *Canadian Psychiatric Association Journal, 23,* 567–571.

Plizka, S. R. (1990). Effect of anxiety on cognition, behavior, and stimulant response in ADHD. In Hertzig, M. E., & Chess, S. (Eds.), *Annual Progress in Child Psychiatry and Child Development* (pp. 454–456). New York: Brunner/Mazel.

Polson, B., & Newton, M. (1984). Not *my kid: A parent's guide to kids and drugs.* New York: Avon Books.

Porges, S. W., & Humphrey, M. M. (1977). Cardiac and respiratory responses during visual search in nonretarded children and retarded adolescents. *American Journal of Mental Deficiency, 82,* 162–169.

Porter, C. (1991, June 16). Parenting styles. *Los Angeles Times,* p. 42.

Pozner, J., & Saltz, E. (1972, December). Social class, conditioned communication, and egocentric speech. *Studies in Intellectual Development* (Report No. 2).

President's Committee on Mental Retardation. (1970). *The six hour retarded child.* Washington, DC: U.S. Government Printing Office.

Price, K., & Dequine, M. (1982). Peer tutoring: It builds skills and self-concept. *Academic Therapy, 17,* 365–371.

Quay, L. C., & Weld, G. L. (1980). Visual and auditory selective attention and reflection-impulsivity in normal and learning-disabled boys at two age levels. *Journal of Abnormal Child Psychology, 8,* 117–125.

Quinn, P. O., & Stern, J. M. (1991). *Putting on the brakes: Young people's guide to understanding attention deficit hyperactivity disorder.* New York: Imagination Press.

Rabinovitch, R. D. (1962). Dyslexia: Psychiatric considerations. In J. Mooney (Ed.), Reading disability: Progress and research needs in dyslexia (pp. 73–79). Baltimore: Johns Hopkins Press.

Raden, D. (1980). Authoritarianism and overt aggression. *Psychological Reports, 47,* 452–454.

Rakos, R. F. (1991). *Assertive behavior: Theory, research, and training.* New York: Routledge, Chapman & Hall.

Rapee, R. M., & Barlow, D. H. (1991). *Chronic anxiety: Generalized anxiety disorder and mixed-anxiety depression.* New York: Guilford Press.

Ray, J. J. (1980). Authoritarianism and hostility. *Journal of Social Psychology, 112,* 307–308.

Readence, J. E., & Bean, T. W. (1978). Impulsivity-reflectivity and learning: An individual difference that matters. *College Student Journal, 11,* 367–374.

Redfering, D. L., & Bowman, M. J. (1981). Effects of a meditative-relaxation exercise on non-attending behaviors of behaviorally disturbed children. *Journal of Clinical Child Psychology, 10,* 126–127.

Reid, J. B., Hinojosa Rivera, G., & Lorber, R. (1980). *A social learning approach to the outpatient treatment of children who steal.* Unpublished manuscript. Oregon Social Learning, Eugene.

Reidy, T. J. (1977). The aggressive characteristics of abused and neglected children. *Journal of Clinical Psychology, 33,* 1040–1045.

Rekers, G. A., Lovaas, O. I., & Low, B. (1974). The behavioral treatment of a transsexual preadolescent boy. *Journal of Abnormal Child Psychology, 2,* 99–116.

Remschmidt, H. (Ed.). (2001). *Schizophrenia in children and adolescents.* Cambridge: Cambridge University Press.

Reschly, D. J. (1981). Psychological testing in educational classification of placement. *American Psychologist, 36,* 1094–1102.

Reschly, D. J. (1982). Assessing mild mental retardation: The influence of adaptive behavior, sociocultural status, and prospects for nonbiased assessment. In C. R. Reynolds & T. B. Gulkin (Eds.), *Handbook of school psychology* (pp. 223–234). New York: Wiley.

Resnick, R. J., & McEvoy, K. (Eds.). (1994). *Attention-deficit/hyperactivity disorder: Abstracts of the psychological and behavioral literature, 1971–1994.* Bibliographies in Psychology, No. 14. Washington, DC: American Psychological Association.

Revenson, T. A., Kayser, K., and Bodenmann, G. (2005). *Couples coping with stress.* Washington, DC: American Psychological Association.

Reynolds, W. M., & Coats, K. I. (1986). A comparison of cognitive-behavioral therapy and relaxation training for the treatment of depression in adolescents. *Journal of Consulting and Clinical Psychology, 54,* 653–660.

Rhodes, W. C., & Paul, J. L. (1978). *Emotionally disturbed and deviant children*. Englewood Cliffs, NJ: Prentice-Hall.

Ribordy, S. C., Tracy, R. J., & Bernotas, T. D. (1981). The effects of an attentional training procedure on the performance of high and low test-anxious children. *Cognitive Therapy and Research, 5,* 19–28.

Rice, A. E. (1962). Rhythmic training and body balance prepare the child for formal learning. *Nations Schools, 69,* 232.

Risely, T., & Wolf, M. (1964, September). *Experimental manipulation of autistic behaviors and generalization into the home.* Paper presented at the meeting of the American Psychological Association, Los Angeles.

Roberts, T. (1979). Reflection-impulsivity and reading ability in seven-year-old children. *British Journal of Educational Psychology, 49,* 311–315.

Rosenfield, D., Sheehan, D. S., Marcus, M. M., & Stehan, W. G. (1981). Classroom structure and prejudice in desegregated schools. *Journal of Educational Psychology, 73,* 17–26.

Ross, A. O. (1981). *Child behavior therapy.* New York: Wiley.

Ross, E. T. (1963). Can potentially poor readers be detected during pre-school years? *Journal of Developmental Reading, 6,* 271–272.

Rotter, J. B. (1980). Interpersonal trust, trustworthiness, and gullibility. *American Psychologist, 35*(1), 1–7.

Rufus, K. (2003). *Party of one: The Loner's manifesto.* New York: Marlowe & Co.

Russell, A., & Low, G. L. (1977). Teacher attention and classroom behavior. *Exceptional Child, 24,* 148–155.

Sacco, W. P., & Hokanson, J. E. (1978). Performance satisfaction of depressives under high and low success conditions. *Journal of Clinical Psychology, 34,* 907–909.

Safer, D., & Krager, J. M. (1989). Hyperactivity and inattentiveness: School assessment of stimulant treatment. *Clinical Pediatrics, 28,* 216–221.

Saltz, E., Dixon, D., & Johnson, J. (1977). Training disadvantaged preschoolers on various fantasy activities: Effects on cognitive functioning and impulse control. *Child Development, 48,* 367–380.

Samalin, N. (1992a). *Love and anger, the parental dilemma.* New York: Penguin.

Samalin, N. (1992b). *Loving your child is not enough.* New York: Penguin.

Samuels, S. J., & Turnure, J. E. (1974). Attention and reading achievement in first-grade boys and girls. *Journal of Educational Psychology, 66,* 29–32.

Sarason, S. V. (1959). *Psychological problems of mental deficiency.* New York: Harper and Sons.

Saviola, M. E. (1981). Personal reflections on physically disabled women and dependency. *Professional Psychology, 12,* 112–117.

Schaefer, C. E. (1977). Motivation: A major cause of school underachievement. *Forum, 12*(1), 16–29.

Schewe, P. A. (2002). *Preventing violence in relationships: Interventions across the life span.* Washington, DC: American Psychological Association.

Schroeder, C. S., Schroeder, S., & Devine, M. (1977). Learning disabilities and reading problems. In B. Wolman, A. Ross, & J. Egan (Eds.), *Handbook and treatments of mental disorders in childhood and adolescence* (pp. 89–136). Englewood Cliffs, NJ: Prentice-Hall.

Schumacher, J. B., & Hazel, J. S. (1984). Social skills assessment and training for the learning disabled: Who's on first and what's on second? Part I. *Journal of Learning Disabilities, 17,* 422–431.

Schwartz, J. C. (1979). Childhood origins of psychopathology. *American Psychologist, 34,* 879–885.

Schwebel, A. I., & Cherlin, D. L. (1972). Physical and social distancing in teacher-pupil relationships. *Journal of Educational Psychology, 63,* 543–550.

Scott, B. (2002). *Relief for hurting parents.* Lake Jackson, TX: Allon Publishing.

Scott, R. (1981). FM: Clinically meaningful Rorschach index with minority children? *Psychology in the Schools, 18,* 429–433.

Sears, P. (1992, March 12). Is behavior inherited? *Los Angeles Times,* p. 32.

Sears, R. R., Maccoby, E. E., & Levin, H. (1957). The socialization of aggression. In R. R. Sears, E. E. Maccoby, & H. Levin (Eds.), *Patterns of child rearing* (pp. 48–62). New York: Harper and Row.

Segal, S. P., & Moyles, E. W. (1979). Management style and institutional dependency in sheltered care. *Social Psychiatry, 14,* 159–165.

Seligman, M. E. P. (1973, April). Fall into helplessness. *Psychology Today, 7,* 43–48.

Serbin, L. A., Geller, M. I., & Geller, S. E. (1977). Effects of social reinforcement for visual attention on classroom learning by disadvantaged preschoolers. *Perceptual and Motor Skills, 45,* 1339–1346.

Shamoo, T., & Patros, P. G. (1992). *Helping your child cope with depression and suicidal thoughts*. New York: Lexington Books.

Shapiro, E. S. (1989). *Academic skills problems: Direct assessment and intervention*. New York: Guilford Press.

Shapiro, J. E. (1976). The relationship of conceptual tempo to reading readiness test performance. *Journal of Reading Behavior, 8*, 83–87.

Shaw, C. R., & Lucas, A. (1970). *The psychiatric disorders of childhood* (2nd ed.). New York: Appleton-Century-Crofts.

Sherman, M. H. (1966). Resistance in family therapy. *American Journal of Orthopsychiatry, 36*(2), 226–227.

Shore, M. F., Brice, P. J., & Love, B. G. (1992). *When your child needs testing: What parents, teachers, and other helpers need to know about psychological testing*. New York: Crossroad.

Shumaker, J. B., Hovell, M. F., & Sherman, J. A. (1977). Analysis of daily report cards and parent-managed privileges in the improvement of adolescents' classroom performance. *Journal of Applied Behavior Analysis, 10*, 449–464.

Silver, L. B. (1992). *The misunderstood child*. Blue Ridge Summit, PA: Tab Books.

Sinha, J. B., & Pandey, J. (1975). Reinforcement and model's efficiency as factors in decision making of dependence prone persons. *Indian Journal of Psychology, 50*, 49–57.

Smith, B. D., Rypma, C. B., & Wilson, R. J. (1981). Dishabituation and spontaneous recovery of the electrodermal orienting response: Effects of extraversion, impulsivity, sociability, and caffeine. *Journal of Research in Personality, 15*, 233–240.

Smith, C. R. (1983). *Learning disabilities: The interaction of learning task and setting*. Boston: Little, Brown.

Smith, R. (Ed.). (1993). *Children with mental retardation: A parents' guide*. Rockville, MD: Woodbine House.

Snow, C. E., Barnes, W. S., Chandler, J., Goodman, I. F., & Hemphill, L. (1991). *Unfulfilled expectations: Home and school influences on literacy*. Cambridge, MA: Harvard University Press.

Snyder, J. J. (1977). Reinforcement analysis of interaction in problem and nonproblem families. *Journal of Abnormal Psychology, 86*, 528–535.

Snyder, M. (1984). *Incidence and characteristics of students meeting referral criteria for special education services for emotional/behavioral disorders* (research report). Marshall, MN: Southwest State University.

Solomon, A. (2001). *The noonday demon: An atlas of depression*. New York: Scribner.

Speers, R., & Lansing, C. (1964). Group psychotherapy with preschool children and collateral group therapy of their parents: A preliminary report of the first two years. *American Journal of Orthopsychiatry, 34*, 659–666.

Spivak, G., & Swift, M. (1977). "High risk" classroom behaviors in kindergarten and first grade. *American Journal of Community Psychology, 5*, 385–397.

Sprague, R. L., Barnes, K. R., & Werry, J. S. (1970). Methylphenidate and thiorozadine: Learning, reaction time, activity and classroom behavior in disturbed children. *American Journal of Orthopsychiatry, 40*, 615.

Spring, B., Nuechterlein, K. H., Sugarman, J., & Matthysse, S. (1977). The new look in studies of schizophrenic attention and information processing. *Schizophrenic Bulletin, 3*, 470–482.

Starr, W. (1965). *Early identification of reading problems* (Research Project 322). Bakersfield, CA: Bakersfield City Schools.

Staub, E. (1978). *Positive social behavior and morality: Social and personal influences* (Vol. 1). New York: Academic Press.

Sternberg, R. J., Werner, R. K., Williams, W. M., & Horvath, J. A. (1995). Testing common sense. *American Psychologist, 50*(11), 1214–1224.

Stimmel, B. (1993). *The facts about drug use: Coping with drugs and alcohol in your family, at work, in your community*. Dubuque, IA: Brown & Benchmark.

Stoneman, Z., & Berman, P. W. (1993). *The effects of mental retardation, disability, and illness on sibling relationships: Research and challenges*. Baltimore: Brookes.

Stores, G., & Piran, N. (1978). Dependency of different types in schoolchildren with epilepsy. *Psychological Medicine, 8*, 441–445.

Stouthamer-Loeber, M., & Loeber, R. (1986). Boys who lie. *Journal of Abnormal Child Psychology, 14*, 551–564.

Suh, M., & Carlson, R. (1977). Childhood behavior disorder: A family typology. *Psychiatric Journal of the University of Ottawa, 2*, 84–88.

Summers, F., & Walsh, F. (1977). The nature of the symbiotic bond between mother and schizophrenic. *American Journal of Orthopsychiatry, 47*, 487–494.

Susman, C. (2007, February 5). Portraits tell tales of mental illness. *Riverside Press Enterprise*.

Susman, E. J., Huston-Stein, A., & Friedrich-Cofer, L. (1980). Relation of conceptual tempo to social behaviors of Head Start children. *Journal of Genetic Psychology, 137*, 17–20.

Swallow, W. K. (2003). *The shy child: Helping children triumph over shyness.* New York: Warner Books.

Swire, M. R., & Kavaler, F. (1978). The health status of foster children. In S. Chess & A. Thomas (Eds.), *Annual progress in child psychiatry and child development* (pp. 124–146). New York: Brunner/Mazel.

Symor, N. K. (1977). The dependency cycle: Implications for theory, therapy, and social action. *Transactional Analysis Journal, 7,* 37–43.

Tate, D. C., Reppucci, N. D., & Mulvey, E. P. (1995). Violent juvenile delinquents. *American Psychologist, 50*(9), 777–791.

Taylor, H. G. (1989). Learning disabilities. In E. C. Marsh & R. A. Barkley (Eds.), *Treatment of childhood disorders* (pp. 231–268). New York: Guilford Press.

Taylor, W. F., & Hoedt, K. C. (1974, August). Counsel for parents. *Human Behavior, 3,* 35.

Thorndike, R. L., & Hagen, E. (1961). *Measurement and evaluation in psychology and education.* New York: Wiley.

Tiedens, L. Z., & Leach, C. W. (Eds.). (2005). *The social life of emotions.* Cambridge: Cambridge University Press.

Tieger, T. (1980). On the biological basis of sex differences in aggression. *Child Development, 51,* 943–963.

Tiegs, E. W., & Clark, W. W. (1972). *California Achievement Test.* Monterey, CA: CTB/McGraw-Hill.

Tjosvold, D., & Fabrey, L. (1980). Motivation for perspective taking: Effects of interdependence and dependence on interest in learning others' intentions. *Psychological Reports, 46,* 755–765.

Tomlinson, J. R., Acker, N., Canter, A., & Lindborg, S. (1977). Minority status, sex and school psychological services. *Psychology in the Schools, 14,* 456–460.

Tonn, M. (1974). The case for keeping mentally retarded children in your regular classroom. *American School Board Journal, 161,* 45.

Toolan, J. (1981). Depression and suicide in children: An overview. *American Journal of Psychotherapy, 35,* 311–322.

Torrey, E. (2001). *Surviving schizophrenia.* New York: Harper Collins.

Treegood, M., & Walker, K. P. (1976). The use of stimulant drugs in the treatment of hyperactivity. *School Psychology Digest, 5,* 5–10.

Uhlinger, C. A, & Stephens, M. W. (1960). Relation of achievement motivation to academic achievement in students of superior ability. *Journal of Educational Psychology, 51,* 259–266.

Veldman, D. J., & Brophy, J. E. (1974). Measuring teacher effects on pupil achievement. *Journal of Educational Psychology, 66,* 319–324.

Veldman, D. J., & Worchel, P. (1961). Defensiveness and self-acceptance in the management of hostility. *Journal of Abnormal and Social Psychology, 63,* 319–325.

Verdick, E. & Lisoviskis, M. (2003). *How to take the grrrr out of anger.* Minneapolis: Free Spirit Publications. Vicere, A. A., & Fulmer, R. B. (1996). *Crafting competitiveness.* Oxford: Capstone Ltd.

Wagner, G. (1962). Readiness for learning. *Education, 82,* 509–510.

Walsh, E. (1994, October 15). Male and female aggression. *Desert Sun,* p. 13.

Wang, M. C. (1987). Toward achieving educational excellence for all students: Program design and student outcomes. *Remedial and Special Education, 8,* 24–34.

Ward, R. R., & Trembley, P. W. (1972). Learning disability as a problem of motivation. *Academic Therapy, 7,* 453–460.

Washburn, W. C. (1963). The effects of sex differences on protective attitudes in delinquents and nondelinquents. *Exceptional Children, 30,* 111–117.

Washington, K. R. (1977). Success counseling: A model workshop approach to self-concept building. *Adolescence, 12,* 405–410.

Watzlawick, P. (1993). *The situation is hopeless, but not serious.* New York: Norton.

Webb, P. H. (1979). Consumer initial processing in a difficult media environment. *Journal of Consumer Research, 6,* 225–236.

Webb, P. H., & Ray, M. L. (1979). Effects of TV clutter. *Journal of Advertising Research, 19,* 7–12.

Webster, S. W. (Ed.). (1966). *Understanding the problems of the disadvantaged learner.* San Francisco: Chandler.

Webster-Stratton, C., & Herbert, M. (1994). *Troubled families—problem children: Working with parents: A collaborative process.* New York: John Wiley & Sons.

Wender, P. H. (1971). *Minimal brain dysfunction in children.* New York: Wiley-Interscience.

Werry, J. S., & Aman, M. G. (1993). *Practitioner's guide to psychoactive drugs for children and adolescents.* New York: Plenum Press.

Westlake, D. (2004). *Money for nothing.* New York: Warner Books.

Wetzell, J. W. (1978). Depression and dependence upon unsustaining environments. *Clinical Social Work Journal, 6,* 75–89.

Williams, D. G. (1973). So-called nervous habits. *Journal of Psychology, 83,* 103–109.

Williamson, P. (1990). *Good kids, bad behavior: Helping children learn self-discipline.* New York: Simon & Schuster.

Wilson, J. A., & Robeck, M. C. (1965). *Kindergarten evaluation of learning potential.* Charlotte, NC: Heritage Printers.

Wilson, K. E., & Shantz, C. V. (1977). Perceptual role-taking ability and dependency in preschool children. *Merrill-Palmer Quarterly, 23,* 207–211.

Wolman, B. B., & Stricker, G. (Eds.). (1994). *Anxiety and related disorders: A handbook.* New York: Wiley.

Wolpe, J. (1973). *The practice of behavior therapy.* Elmsford, NY: Pergamon Press.

Woods, D. (1986). The diagnosis and treatment of attention deficit disorder, residual type. *Psychiatric Annals, 16,* 23–28.

Woodworth, K. F., Siegel, M. G., & Eustin, M. J. (1958). Psychiatric study of mentally retarded children of preschool age: Report on the first and second years of a three-year project. *American Journal of Orthopsychiatry, 28,* 376.

Woollams, S. J., & Huige, K. A. (1977). Normal dependency and symbiosis. *Transactional Analysis Journal, 7,* 217–220.

Worchel, S., Arnold, S. E., & Harrison, W. (1978). Aggression and power restoration: The effects of identifiability and timing on aggressive behavior. *Journal of Experimental Social Psychology, 14,* 43–52.

Wyer, R. S., & Srull, T. K. (1993). *Perspectives on anger and emotion.* Hillsdale, NJ: Erlbaum.

Yando, R. M., & Kagan, J. (1968). The effect of teacher tempo on the child. *Child Development, 39,* 27–34.

Yellin, A. M., Spring, C., & Greenberg, L. M. (1978). Effects of impramine and methylphenidate on behavior of hyperactive children. *Research Communications in Psychology, Psychiatry, and Behavior, 3,* 15–26.

Yoemans, F. E., Selzer, M. A., & Clarkin, J. F. (1992). *Treating the borderline patient: A contract-based approach.* New York: Basic Books.

Younger, F. (1992). *Five hundred questions kids ask about sex and some of the answers: Sex education for parents, teachers, and young people.* Springfield, IL: Charles C. Thomas.

Zehavi, S., & Asher, S. R. (1978). The effect of verbal instructions on preschool children's aggressive behavior. *Journal of School Psychology, 16,* 146–153.

Zimbardo, P. G., Pilkonis, P. A., & Norwood, R. M. (1975, February). The social disease called shyness. *Psychology Today, 8*(2), 68–72.

ability and, 120; intervention strategies, 303–7; self-blame in, 21–22; withdrawal and, 63–64
disadvantaged students: emotional development, 304–5; language handicaps, 305–6; parents, techniques for, 306–7
discipline, social conformity and, 254–56
disengaged parents, 15
divorce, anxiety and, 58–60
documentation, 150
Doob, L. W., 167
Dweck, C. S., 97

eating disorders, 12
ego compensation, 35
ego strength, 91–92
electroencephalogram (EEG), 276–77
embarrassing topics, 132
emotional abuse, 58
emotional disorders, 1; academics and, 130–31; attention and, 161, 163; play activities and, 147
enabling, 266–67
environment, 1; ADHD and, 277–78; attention and, 161–62, 164–65; intellectual ability and, 122
Eron, L. D., 217
etiologic stimuli, 6
exclusive parent, 229
explosive parent, 220
expressive aggressiveness, 220, 221, 222, 226–27
eye contact, 283
Eysenck Personality Inventory, 168

family activities, 283
family counseling, 212
family group therapy, 156
family secrets, 133, 258
fantasy life, 4–5, 219
father, divorce and, 59–60
fearfulness: genetic factors, 9–10; in obsessive-compulsive disorder, 23; of slower-learning children, 167
flexibility, behavioral, 4
Friedlander, K., 248

Garbarino, J., 77
gender differences, 1, 3, 11–13; academics and, 136, 137, 143; aggressiveness, 217; anxiety, 32; attention and, 161; attention deficit disorder, 279; coordination, 10, 111; dependency, 80–81; impulse control, 169–70; self-blame and, 22
gender-inappropriate behavior, 185–86
genetic factors, 9–11; social conformity, 246; in withdrawal, 62–63

genetic routes, 7
Getman, G. N., 114–15
girls, tips for raising, 12. *See also* gender differences
goals, establishing, 150
Gold, M., 251
Goodenough, F., 112–13, 138
Goodenough Draw-A-Man test, 112–13
grade retention, 153
group conferences, 314–17
Grunebaum, M. G., 100
guidance games, 147
guilt: parental, 29–30; in self-blame, 20–21, 25–26

habit disturbance, 23
Hagen, E., 92
Halinsky, R. D., 144
Haney, W., 251
Harper, J. M., 21–22
Hazel, J. S., 98
helpless parent, 220, 228–29
Herbert, M., 18
hiding of negative emotions, 4
high valuing, 239
Hirschfeld, R. M., 79
home abuse, anxiety and, 57–58
Hoopes, M. H., 21–22
hospitalization, anxiety and, 52
hostile aggressiveness, 7, 220, 221, 222–23, 227–28
Howard, K., 96
Huige, K. A., 78
hysterical behavior, 23

identifying authentic childhood disorder, 2–4; criteria for judging, 2–3; factors to consider, 3–4
ignoring, 239
Ilg, F. L., 138
imagery, inward, 4
imagining exercises, 283
imperious children, 202–3
impoverished family life, 4
impulse control, 36, 167–72; behavior disorders and, 169; intervention strategies, 169–72; learning and, 168; theoretical background, 167–69
inconsistent parent, 77, 85, 88, 220, 226, 229
individual disparities, 4
indulgent parents, 15, 87
inferiority, feelings of, 40
insistent ordering, 241
instrumental aggressiveness, 220, 221, 222, 227
intellectual ability, 117–28; adaptive behaviors, 120, 121; environmental factors, 122; intervention strategies,

About the Author

Harold F. Burks is a clinical and research psychologist who has written seven books and numerous professional articles on the subject of child psychology. During his career, he received a number of research grants enabling him to uncover the characteristics of the attention-deficit (ADD) child. He then constructed instruments designed to detect the disorder. Under the auspices of the California State Department of Education, he set up treatment classes for ADD youngsters and acted as a consultant to schools and universities.

Dr. Burks has also written in the field of creativity and produced a popular game promoting imagination and innovation. But he is probably best known for creating the Burks Behavior Rating Scales, a psychological measuring device that has been employed internationally for many years to analyze the emotional and learning problems of many millions of kindergarten through high-school subjects.

As a clinical psychologist, trained on the field of psychoanalysis, he has also had extensive experience in the treatment of adult patients. This expertise combined with the knowledge acquired in child investigative efforts makes him uniquely qualified to write the present book.